Accession no.
36166969

KU-005-896

WITHDRAWN

WITHDRAWN

STRATEGIC MANAGEMENT

Students trying to navigate the strategy jungle may lose sight of the fact that strategic management is about creating value in an organization. Understanding strategic management is a core part of all business qualifications and this textbook brings a new and easy-to-follow understanding of this vital business function.

In addition to walking the student through the basics of the subject, the authors provide an array of analytical tools to help facilitate a comprehensive understanding of strategic management. The book addresses thoroughly the impact of financial markets on a firm's strategic capabilities, as well as looking at other challenging environmental factors.

Aided by an array of student-friendly features, such as learning objectives, 'strategic management in practice' case studies and review questions in each chapter, *Strategic Management* will help students to excel in their strategic management classes and better prepare them for the real business world.

Peter FitzRoy is Emeritus Professor at Monash University, Australia, where he has taught strategic management for several years. He has held appointments at a number of institutions worldwide and has extensive experience in lecturing on management development programmes in Asia, Australia, the UK and the USA. He is actively involved in the Strategic Management Society, and served for many years on the editorial board of the *Strategic Management Journal*.

James M. Hulbert is Visiting Professor at Peking University, China and RC Kopf Professor Emeritus at Columbia University, USA. He has taught or held visiting positions at numerous institutions and has also taught on executive development programmes worldwide. He has worked as a consultant with numerous global companies, including 3M, IBM, General Electric and Unilever. His research interests are strategy and planning, which have resulted in several published books and numerous articles in leading journals including the *Strategic Management Journal*.

Abby Ghobadian is Professor at the University of Reading, UK. He has taught or held visiting positions at a number of institutions in the UK, Europe and also at Monash University, Australia. His research interests are strategy and performance enhancement and he has published close to 100 journal articles, seven research monographs and two edited books. He is the Chairman of the British Academy of Management and co-editor of the *Journal of Strategy and Management*.

This textbook, competently written by world leading experts in the field of strategic management, provides an integrated theoretical and practical approach to strategic management for value creation. The logical development of the chapters draws on relevant theoretical frameworks, which integrate contemporary business issues into the model of strategy formulation, implementation, value creation and performance measurement. Such a comprehensive model provides todays' and future business leaders, managers and consultants with the relevant knowledge, in order to cope with the strategic challenge of formulating and executing sustainable value-creating strategies. The inclusion of the financial markets and performance measurement perspectives enriches the model by truly recognising the real challenges and dilemmas that managers face in today's global markets. The practical orientation of the textbook, also achieved with the use of contemporary examples and business cases, makes this textbook a valuable companion and easy reading for the wider community of students, academics, business leaders and managers.

Laura A. Costanzo, *University of Surrey*, UK

With the business world facing the worst crisis in generations, this book is a much needed reminder of the crucial importance of strategy in any organization. Dealing with a variety of contemporary issues, inter alia, managing innovation, cost structures, and social responsibility, it presents strategy from a whole new perspective. With a plethora of current examples, ranging from rock bands to multinational corporations from all sectors, it ties theory and international practice together exceptionally well. This is a must-read core text for students and academics involved in strategy formulation and strategic management.

Chris Liassides, Academic Director,
International Faculty of the University of Sheffield, UK

The authors present the complex topic of Strategic Management with a fine balance of latest thinking and references to traditional concepts. They "bring the concepts to life" in a practical and engaging way with their use of relevant examples. This text can truly help managers expand their understanding to make better business decisions. We will be using this book as an essential tool for the executive education programs we conduct throughout the world.

Mary Abbazia, Managing Director, *Impact Planning Group*

The authors use an accessible style in presenting key ideas of strategic management and bring a remarkable range of resources especially (through) updated (company/organizational) cases to enliven/enrich/illustrate their argument/discussion.

Highly original and insightful/resourceful, this book will be invaluable to postgraduates and advanced undergraduates in the fields of strategic management, international business/business studies and organization theory.

Andrew Chan, *City University of Hong Kong*, Hong Kong SAR

A well crafted strategic management teaching resource and a welcome update. The text has a nice balance between theory and practice, and connects in an accessible way to major issues, debates and trends in the subject area. I appreciated the attention to detail in use of the strategy vocabulary and the precision of explanations.

Tim O'Shannassy, *RMIT University*, Melbourne, Australia

FitzRoy, Hulbert, and Ghobadian have written a superbly comprehensive and up-to-date book, reflecting the latest scholarly insights and practical wisdom about strategy. The book, which is extremely readable and engaging, is loaded with examples from a wide array of industries and regions. If you want to become a more thoughtful and successful strategist, you should read this book.

Donald C. Hambrick, *The Pennsylvania State University*, USA

Writing a great strategy text is like cooking a five-star meal – and just as difficult. Many authors take similar ingredients and produce bland, insipid offerings: as the glazed look and mimetic thinking of legions of business students will attest. In contrast, FitzRoy, Hulbert and Ghobadian are master-chefs taking classic ingredients and adding new and unexpected ideas to produce an invigorating feast. *Strategic Management: The challenge of creating value* is more than food for thought, it offers a rare prize: differentiated thinking.

Pierre Berthon, *Bentley University*, USA

STRATEGIC MANAGEMENT

The Challenge of Creating Value

Second edition

PETER FITZROY,
JAMES M. HULBERT
and
ABBY GHOBADIAN

LIS LIBRARY

Date	Fund
10/12/12	bs-che

Order No

2358359

University of Chester

Routledge
Taylor & Francis Group

LONDON AND NEW YORK

First published 2012
by Routledge
2 Park Square, Milton Park, Abingdon, Oxon OX14 4RN

Simultaneously published in the USA and Canada
by Routledge
711 Third Avenue, New York, NY 10017

Routledge is an imprint of the Taylor & Francis Group, an informa business

© 2012 Peter FitzRoy, James M. Hulbert and Abby Ghobadian

The right of Peter FitzRoy, James M. Hulbert and Abby Ghobadian to be identified as authors of this work has been asserted by them in accordance with sections 77 and 78 of the Copyright, Designs and Patents Act 1988.

All rights reserved. No part of this book may be reprinted or reproduced or utilized in any form or by any electronic, mechanical, or other means, now known or hereafter invented, including photocopying and recording, or in any information storage or retrieval system, without permission in writing from the publishers.

Trademark notice: Product or corporate names may be trademarks or registered trademarks, and are used only for identification and explanation without intent to infringe.

British Library Cataloguing in Publication Data
A catalogue record for this book is available from the British Library

Library of Congress Cataloging in Publication Data
FitzRoy, Peter T.
    Strategic management : the challenge of creating value / Peter FitzRoy,
    James Hulbert, and Abby Ghobadian. — 2nd ed.
        p. cm.
    Includes bibliographical references and index.
    1. Strategic planning.   I. Hulbert, James M.   II. Ghobadian, Abby, 1951–
    III. Title.
    HD30.28.F573 2011
    658.4′012—dc22   2011009565

ISBN: 978-0-415-56763-3 (hbk)
ISBN: 978-0-415-56764-0 (pbk)
ISBN: 978-0-203-80440-7 (ebk)

Typeset in Minion Pro and Futura
by Florence Production Ltd, Stoodleigh, Devon
Printed by Bell & Bain Ltd., Glasgow

CONTENTS

TABLES AND FIGURES

FIGURES

TABLES

ABOUT THIS BOOK

DEVELOPMENTS IN STRATEGIC MANAGEMENT OVER YOUR CAREER

Whether you are nearing the end of your undergraduate course, or in the midst of an MBA, your career in business lies ahead of you. We have been mindful of this in writing this book and have therefore focused on how strategic management is likely to develop in future. Just as we believe that strategic management is about making decisions now to ensure the future success of a firm, so we believe that when studying strategic management, the focus should be on the future competitive environment in which you will work, not on the present.

So how do we think the practice of strategic management will develop in future? Markets are increasingly global, intensely competitive and characterized by rapid and turbulent changes. To create value for stakeholders in these circumstances is a complex task with no easy solutions. These challenges are reflected in each of the themes that run through our text.

Globalization

We live at an exciting time. Never before has our world been so globally interconnected. Electronic media have brought knowledge to billions, removing the literacy barrier. The fast-widening spread of the internet has revolutionized communications, which are no longer dominated by large companies and 'mass media'. Individuals communicate with each other and talk back to suppliers in unprecedented ways. Whether you work for a multinational, a regional, a national or a local firm, globalization will profoundly affect your life as a manager, and you will be living with very different and interconnected relationships with customers, suppliers and others. Reflecting these changes, we have drawn our examples from a wide range of countries, developed and developing, and included firms – both large and small – that are on the cutting edge of the changes created by the information revolution. Chapter 1, for example, has a mini-case on MTP Ltd, a small Irish technology firm facing possible opportunities in Europe. At the same time it must deal with the likely entry of global competitors into its domestic market, and develop a strategy in response, including identifying the new capabilities and skills that will be required.

Change

Not only is the world experiencing an increasing rate of change, it is also being battered by the increasing turbulence of that change. Pressures on business range from the blurring of industry and firm boundaries, driven by technology, de-regulation and globalization, to dealing with the demands of NGOs for more ethical behaviour and governments for reduced carbon emissions. Surely no strategy will last for long in tomorrow's world and you will be continually innovating in all the activities and elements of the firms for which you will work. Despite the pressures of managing for success today, however, you must prepare your firms for a changed and uncertain tomorrow. The UK-based firm HMV has experienced significant changes in its environment, with new technology such as internet downloading of music and books, as well as the expansion of supermarkets into both book and music categories. As we examine in Chapter 8, handling this turbulent environment has proved challenging for the firm's management. The need to manage both for today and for tomorrow is one of numerous dilemmas with which you will have to wrestle, and this book explores these issues in depth.

Intangible assets

Competitive advantage and value are more and more created through intangible rather than physical assets. The meteoric rise in the value of such firms as Google, Facebook and Groupon is embedded in their people, processes, technology and customer relationships. In a knowledge-based economy, the management of intangible assets and the firm's knowledge base take centre stage. In Chapter 12 we report on an interview with the chief technology officer of Dow Chemical, who discusses how that firm has addressed innovation and research and development. Our text spotlights the increased importance of knowledge and intangible assets as issues that will be central to your success as a strategic manager in the world of the future. Unfortunately, many traditional books on strategic management have failed to recognize this important transformation.

Firm performance

You will live in a world driven by tough competition, not just in product markets, but pressured also by the demands of financial markets. There is therefore in our view no alternative to the value-based approach to firm performance that we take: a firm is an economic entity!

As future strategic managers, it is critical that you understand the impact of financial markets on strategy – yet this topic is ignored by virtually every other book in the field, a staggering omission! Of course we recognize that firms have multiple stakeholders with varied interests in its performance. Environmental and social concerns will be important issues you will have to deal with. However, in a competitive world – whether in product markets or financial markets – the pre-eminent importance of customers and shareholders is self-evident. It is therefore vital that you understand that financial markets, besides pressuring a firm for performance, also facilitate and constrain the strategy it adopts. Focus

(DIY) is a UK-based retailer which has faced a challenging environment. The mini-case in Chapter 4 highlights the point that how the firm resolves its financial problems and high debt levels will be the key to its future.

Governance and ethics

Despite our concern that a firm generates value, the corporate scandals of the early twenty-first century underlined the importance of ethical behaviour on the part of senior executives. As you move into management roles, you must expect very stringent scrutiny of your behaviour and ethics. Nor is this an issue of morals alone. Governments in much of the world are slowly (too slowly!) recognizing that the ability of the state to provide ageing populations with adequate income is disappearing. The fact that countless millions have become dependent on private savings and pensions is already reflected in the increased activism of the institutions that manage these funds. The political pressures arising from these demographic and economic changes mean that senior managers' behaviour is now recognized as having a critical economic dimension. Our text contains dilemmas called 'The Challenge of Strategic Management' as well as many other examples. As you explore these, you will find that many of them have ethical dimensions, and you will find how difficult some of these issues – which may seem simple at first sight – can become. The Chapter 9 mini-case describes the disastrous results of the takeover of ABN Amro by the consortium led by the Royal Bank of Scotland. The case provides a graphic illustration of the need for an active board which is involved in the strategic management of the firm.

Synthesis

A key challenge in teaching strategic management is ensuring that students are able to think critically about problems which by their very nature are interdisciplinary. Developing and implementing strategy is a complex task, involving critical thinking, creativity and analytical rigour. Achieving this task requires a deep understanding of many academic disciplines. PerkinElmer is a US-based firm which has achieved success through superior strategic management. As Chapter 11 documents however, this has involved not only developing new strategies, but also successfully revising the organizational structure, installing a new culture and management systems, as well as innovating technologically.

We wrote this book for a capstone course on strategic management for advanced undergraduate and MBA students. You should therefore have had a basic foundation in marketing, economics, finance, accounting, information technology and organizational behaviour. Your challenge in mastering strategic management is to integrate these subjects, synthesizing them into an overall perspective on strategic management of the enterprise that can support you throughout your career. Our goal in writing this book has been to help you achieve this synthesis, and to help you do so in a way that is interesting, informative and enjoyable.

Action

Finally, strategic management is all about action, not plans. This is emphasized in the text using a plethora of real-world examples of 'Strategic Management in Practice'. Firms from all around the world are used to illustrating how managers have acted strategically, providing an invaluable link between concept and practice. These examples not only span the breadth of the globe, but also range from the smallest firms to the very largest organizations. Furthermore, in a unique, cutting-edge feature called 'View from the Top', we include interviews with top CEOs and senior executives, presenting students with an exclusive and illuminating insight into the working practices of such leaders as Howard Stringer, CEO of Sony, and Richard Lapthorne, Chairman of Cable and Wireless.

ORGANIZATION OF THE TEXT

To help you develop the understanding needed to handle these future challenges, our book contains five sections, each with several chapters. An overview is provided in Figure 0.

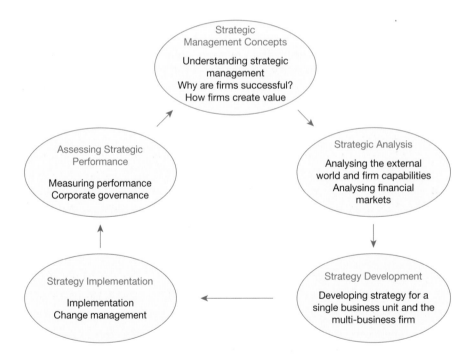

Figure 0 Structure of the book

HOW TO USE THIS BOOK

The book has many examples, features and tools to help you, the student, learn and put into practice relevant concepts in strategic management. The examples have been chosen to illustrate how strategic management concepts are applied in many different countries, industries and firms. This is designed to show you both the richness and the complexity involved in managing strategically in a global business context.

To help you learn, we use a common structure for each chapter.

Each chapter incorporates a set of **Learning objectives** – the capabilities you should develop from studying the chapter. These objectives cover a wide range from acquiring basic knowledge, through analysis, to the ability to synthesize and apply concepts from several disciplines.

Strategic management *in practice* opens each chapter by providing a short description of the situation faced by a real company, describing how the firm has utilized the material to be discussed in the chapter, and its level of success. The examples illustrate the relevance of the chapter's subject matter to the firm, providing an action link between concept and practice. By showing practical applications of strategic management by senior managers in successful – (and some unsuccessful) – firms we hope your understanding of the concepts will be enhanced.

'Concept' *in practice* examples are used to illustrate how a firm has applied or adopted a specific concept, such as outsourcing. These again link concept to practice, but are more narrowly focused.

The **Challenge of strategic management** questions are designed as discussion vehicles on the content and dilemmas of strategic management. Instructors will likely challenge you to think more deeply about these topics. We encourage you to engage in critical reflection on these challenges, grounding them in your own experience wherever possible.

Each chapter contains a **View from the Top**, highlighting the views of a senior executive, typically the CEO, indicating how a particular firm has used or implemented the concepts described in the chapter. These views demonstrate that the concepts we discuss are entrenched in practice – they are not just academic ideas. CEOs may not use the same words, but they use the same ideas! In some cases, the views they express may differ from ours, which permits a class discussion of why these different perspectives exist.

Key terms

Key terms are highlighted in blue when they first appear, and are defined in the margin at the most appropriate point in the text, as well as being a repeated in the glossary. Terms in orange are defined in the glossary at the end of the book.

Chapter

Extensive use is made of **Cross-references**, linking the material in different chapters. These indicate that strategic management, by its very nature, is interdisciplinary, requiring an understanding and synthesis of theories from many disciplines.

Each chapter includes a **Chapter overview** and **Summary**. These describe, respectively, the material to be covered and a summary of the main points of the chapter. These provide a useful aid for revision.

Mini-cases are used with each chapter to permit you to apply the material developed in the chapter to help you understand how strategic managers operate. In many of the mini-cases, chapter material will need to be integrated with material from other chapters. By its very nature, strategic management is integrative in nature, not compartmentalized. These short cases generally only provide limited information on the company and its situation. You may want to obtain more information from appropriate websites before making a recommendation on the case.

Each chapter contains a number of **Review questions**, designed to test your knowledge and understanding of the content of the chapter and how this content enhances the strategic management of a firm.

HOW TO USE THE ONLINE RESOURCES

The online resources accompanying the text provide the instructor and student with a range of teaching and learning resources, complementing text. Students can freely access this website. Instructors should contact their local Routledge representative to enable access.

Learning aids for students

- Flashcard glossary, to test your knowledge of essential terms
- An array of true/false questions for each chapter

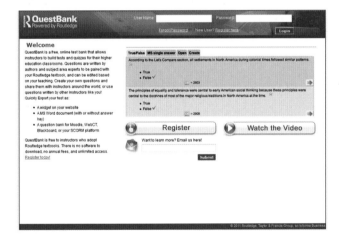

Teaching aids for instructors

- Comprehensive testbank including multiple choice, true/false and short answer questions for each chapter, with feedback
- PowerPoint lecture slides divided by chapter

- Case study library comprising a list, together with a short description, of additional cases for each chapter. These can be used either as exams or as part of continuous student assessment

- Pedagogy matrix, giving you a comprehensive overview of all the pedagogical features of the book

- Answers to end of chapter questions from within the book

- Additional case studies and related questions

- Regular updates on 'Strategy in the News'

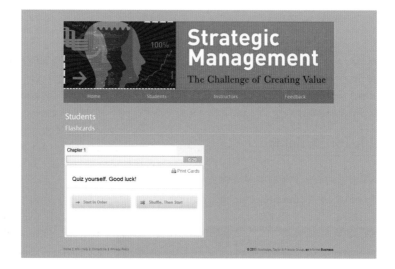

ABOUT THE AUTHORS

Peter Fitzroy is a Professor in the MBA programme at Monash University in Melbourne, Australia where he has taught Strategic Management for several years. He has held appointments at a number of institutions including Columbia University, the University of Illinois, the Manchester Business School, the Wharton School of the University of Pennsylvania, the University of Waterloo and Purdue University. He also has extensive experience in lecturing on management development programmes in Asia, Australia, the UK and the US. He is actively involved in the Strategic Management Society, and served for many years on the editorial board of the *Strategic Management Journal*.

James (Mac) Hulbert is Visiting Professor at the Guanghua School of Management of Peking University and R.C. Kopf Professor Emeritus at the Graduate School of Business, Columbia University. He has taught or held visiting positions at the Fundacao Joao Pinheiro (Brazil), Henley Management College, the London Business School, the University of Grenoble, Monash University and UCLA among others. He has also taught on executive development programmes in Europe, South America, North America, the Middle East, Africa and Asia. He has worked as a consultant with numerous global companies, including DuPont, 3M, IBM, General Electric, Chase Manhattan Bank, BASF, Philip Morris, Caterpillar, BHP Billiton, Unilever and Visa International. His research interests are strategy, planning and marketing. His many books have been translated into Spanish, Chinese and Russian, and he has written over 100 academic papers that have appeared in the *Strategic Management Journal, Sloan Management Review, California Management Review* and *European Management Journal* among others.

Abby Ghobadian is Professor at Henley Business School, University of Reading. He has taught or held visiting positions at Bristol Business School, Middlesex University Business School, Kingston Business School, Brunel Business School, Warwick Business School, Westminster Business School, Higher Commercial Management School of Moscow, Lodz University, Lubin Graduate School of Business at Pace University, Pecs University, ESCP-EAP, and Monash University. Abby has taught on executive programmes of companies such as Ford, Bechtel and Bovis Lend Lease, and in Russia, Hungary, Poland, Serbia and the

Middle East. He has consulted with a number of UK companies. His research interests are strategy and performance enhancement. He has published close to 100 articles in peer-reviewed journals, seven research monographs and two edited books as well as numerous book chapters and conference papers. He is Chairman of the British Academy of Management. He is co-editor of the *Journal of Strategy and Management* and serves on the editorial board of a number of journals in the UK, USA and Hungary. Abby was elected a Fellow of Academy Management in 2008, an Academician by the Academy of Social Sciences in 2010 and received an honorary doctorate from University of Pecs in 2004.

ACKNOWLEDGEMENTS

Many individuals and organizations have contributed towards this text. Although anonymous, we are very grateful to the large numbers of MBA students in the US, Australia, Europe and Asia who used some or all of the material as it was in preparation. We also owe a debt of gratitude to the anonymous reviewers who provided us with so much useful feedback on our earlier drafts. Finally, we wish to acknowledge the many colleagues who have influenced our thinking on strategy over the years.

We also express our appreciation to several organizations for the use of material from their web pages.

We also wish to acknowledge the help we received from the secretarial and library staff at Monash, Columbia and Henley, as well as the constant encouragement of our partners, Margaret, Madge and Anita.

We would also like to express our thanks to the staff at Routledge, including Terry Clague, Alex Krause, David Cox, Katy Hamilton, Faye Mousley and Emily Senior.

PHOTO ACKNOWLEDGEMENTS

'News Corporation' (p. 7) AFP/Getty Images; 'Restructured cartoon' (p. 35) ©Tim Cordell, reproduced with permission from www.cartoonstock.com; 'Electrolux' (p. 40) Bloomberg via Getty Images; 'Shell' (p. 47) for editorial use only © shutterstock.com/Robert Davies; 'Nestlé' (p. 47) © Showface |Dreamstime.com; 'MasterCard' (p. 82) editorial use only © istockphoto.com/DNY59; 'Intel' (p. 92) editorial use only © istockphoto.com/Nnehring; 'AMD' (p. 92) Getty Images; 'Vestas' (p. 121) istockphoto.com/rpaz; 'Linn' (p. 139) Linn Products Ltd; 'Lafarge' (p. 149) Bloomberg via Getty Images; 'Hostile takeover cartoon' (p. 163) © John Morris, reproduced with permission from www.cartoonstock.com; 'Superdry' (p. 167) for editorial use only © shutterstock.com/paul prescott; 'HSBC' (p. 189) © Digitalric | Dreamstime.com; 'ARM' (p. 200) Bloomberg via Getty Images; 'IBM' (p. 238) Getty Images; 'Canon' (p. 252) © Perolsson | Dreamstime.com; 'Haier' (p. 269) AFP/Getty Images; 'nVidia' (p. 285) AFP/Getty Images; 'Coca-Cola' (p. 286) © Lucian Milasan | Dreamstime.com; 'Tata' (p. 293) editorial use only © shutterstock.com/Max Earey; 'Unilever' (p. 296) AFP/Getty Images; 'Sandvik' (p. 337) Sandvik; 'Ryanair' (p. 338) editorial use only © istockphoto.com/ilbusca; 'HMV' (p. 343) editorial use only © istockphoto/jentakespictures; 'Premier Inn' (p. 388) Bloomberg via Getty Images; 'Philips' (p. 389) editorial use only © Bill Lunney | Dreamstime.com; 'Porsche' (p. 396) editorial use only © istockphoto/WendellandCarolyn; 'VW' (p. 397) editorial use only © istockphoto.com/gmalandra; 'Merger/Takeover cartoon' (p. 422) © John Morris, reproduced with permission from www.cartoonstock.com; 'Smirnoff' (p. 441) Bloomberg via Getty Images; 'ABN Amro' (p. 445) AFP/Getty Images; 'Costa' (p. 456) Bloomberg via Getty Images; 'Sea of pills' (p. 472) istockphoto.com/FotografiaBasica; 'British Airways' (p. 488) editorial use only © istockphoto.com/rypson; 'PerkinElmer' (p. 495) SSPL via Getty Images; 'Sony' (p. 536) editorial use only © istockphoto.com/ilbusca; 'Anglo American' (p. 538) Getty Images; 'Toyota' (p. 548) editorial use only © istockphoto.com/WendellandCarolyn; 'Air New Zealand' (p. 578) editorial use only © shutterstock.com/Robert Cumming; 'Siemens' (p. 593) © Viorel Dudau | Dreamstime.com; 'Marks & Spencer' (p. 611) © Naiyyer | Dreamstime.com; 'Flag of Germany' (p. 620) shutterstock.com/Route66; 'Flag of Japan' (p. 621) shutterstock.com/Route66; 'Flag of India' (p. 622) shutterstock.com/Andrew Chin; 'Flag of China' (p. 623) shutterstock.com/ekler; 'Palm Oil Plantation' (p. 624) © Kheng Guan Toh | Dreamstime.com; 'Cable and Wireless' (p. 626) AFP/Getty Images; 'Prudential' (p. 627) AFP/Getty Images.

Section 1

STRATEGIC MANAGEMENT CONCEPTS

CHAPTER 1

MANAGING STRATEGICALLY

LEARNING OBJECTIVES

Upon completing this chapter you should be able to:

1 Articulate the importance of strategic management to firm growth, innovation and performance.

2 Distinguish between strategic decisions, strategy and strategic management.

3 Contrast the major theories which endeavour to explain firm success.

4 Recognize why firms exist as economic entities and be able to describe alternate forms of economic exchanges.

5 Argue the need for continual innovation and change: nothing is fixed; all attributes of the firm are variable.

6 Apply the model of strategic management and be aware of the major changes driving the practice of strategic management.

STRATEGIC MANAGEMENT IN PRACTICE

NEWS CORPORATION

To illustrate many of the principles of strategic management, consider a brief history of News Corporation, a global news and entertainment firm.

In 2009, News Corporation reported revenues of $US30.4 billion, with cash and cash equivalents of $US6.5 billion and total assets of $US53.1 billion. This is a major achievement for a firm that started in the 1950s owning one newspaper, with assets of about $US1 million, in Adelaide, a small state capital in Australia. Its growth in becoming a global news and entertainment firm illustrates many of the principles of strategic management which will be covered in this and later chapters.

News Corporation started its growth in the 1950s through acquiring several small unprofitable newspapers in other geographic areas of Australia, including Sydney, Australia's largest city, where competition between newspapers was intense. Recognizing the opportunity presented by television, the company acquired a majority interest in an Adelaide TV station, demonstrating the ability to manage a technology completely new to the firm. These actions were followed by more aggressive growth during the 1960s, when News Corporation expanded internationally. The initial expansion was to New Zealand, a culturally similar country. This was soon followed by the acquisition of a magazine company in Hong Kong, characterized by both a new culture and a new industry. At the same time, News launched Australia's first national newspaper, which has become the leading quality newspaper in Australia. International expansion was further enhanced by the acquisition of *The Sun* and *The News of the World* in London – both of which were unprofitable at the time.

During the 1970s, the global expansion continued, with the purchase of newspapers in San Antonio and New York, again buying unprofitable papers. The UK presence was enhanced during the 1980s with the purchase of *The Times* and *The Sunday Times*, as well as other papers in Hong Kong, Chicago and Boston. In the UK, News Corporation was responsible for a massive restructuring of the newspaper industry when production was moved from Fleet Street to a technologically advanced plant, which resulted in major industrial action.

The level and nature of diversification increased during this period, with the launch of Fox, as the fourth TV network in the US and the acquisition of Twentieth Century-Fox, a major movie production company. European activities continued to expand in the 1990s. News Corporation's TV interests were merged with a competitor to form BSkyB and the firm acquired Telipiu from Vivendi, suffering substantial losses for several years.

In the 2000s, News Corporation divested several US TV stations and the *TV Guide* magazine. They also acquired Dow Jones at a cost of $US5.7 billion, representing a further diversification into information services. During this period the firm also moved its place of incorporation from Australia to the US to better reflect its geographic mix of businesses and to be closer to major financial institutions, customers and competitors.

Rupert Murdoch has been CEO and Chairman of News Corporation over this entire period and the Murdoch family maintains a significant shareholding in the firm. In terms of success, revenue has certainly increased over the duration, but over the last five years the share price has suffered a steady decline. This could possibly arise from shareholder concern with the challenges facing News Corporation in 2010. One of the most significant is the threat from online sources of news and a widespread view that the Internet is free. Gathering news stories is expensive, and the industry is faced with the challenge of how to get readers willing to pay for high-quality news stories (Shawcross, 1997; NewsCorp, 2009).

As of late 2011, News Corporation faces another major challenge. News International, the British part of News Corporation, was accused of phone hacking as long ago as 2005, and one of their reporters was jailed for four months in 2007. Allegations of further phone hackings took on a different dimension in 2011 when journalists from *The News of the World* were accused of hacking into the mobile phone of a missing girl who was later found murdered. Journalists were also accused of accessing personal data of politicians, and others, often with the acquiescence of the police. Following public outcry, the UK government initiated a judicial inquiry into the firm and its relationships with police, politicians and others. A few days later, the head of the metropolitan police, and a senior deputy, announced their resignations as did several senior *News of the World* executives. In the US, the FBI announced that it was investigating bribery allegations by the firm and its staff. As of late summer 2011, the crisis has had a significant impact on the strategy of News Corporation. The firm announced the closure of *The News of the World*, and the withdrawal of its £8 billion bid for the remaining 61 per cent of BSkyB that it did not own. What other impact this crisis will have is difficult to predict at the time of writing. News Corporation's share price has dropped, wiping more than $US10 billion from its market capitalization, possibly calling into question the future of the firm and of its chairman and founder, Rupert Murdoch. Mired in scandal and controversy, the situation not only raises major questions about the adequacy of governance procedures at News Corporation, but also illustrates dramatically the harm that can be caused to a major corporation by transgressions in one aspect of its business operations. The final resolution of these issues will occur after the publication of this book, but the crisis illustrates the turbulent and interconnected environment in which global firms operate and the challenge of consistently creating value.

LEARNING OBJECTIVE 1

Articulate the importance of strategic management to firm growth, innovation and performance.

The short example of News Corporation illustrates many important principles of strategic management. First, a firm exists in a turbulent and rapidly changing context, which includes both the external world and the firm's internal skills. As a firm in the media business, News Corporation has clearly been experiencing many changes in its external environment: the emergence of satellite TV; globalization; and more recently the digital revolution. Strategy is about understanding and capitalizing upon these changes. Context also includes the necessity for understanding the operations of financial markets. In early 1990 News Corporation had high debts and was almost brought down by a regional US bank but managed to survive. It has also weathered the 2008/2009 recession, albeit with reductions in sales volumes and significant losses. The firm has, however, been proactive in its environment, actively soliciting support from a broad range of interest groups such as politicians, governments, regulators, financial markets and allies in many countries. Context also includes development of new skills within the firm. Certainly News Corporation has had to develop new skills in TV, cable operations and international operations, among many others.

The case also illustrates that News Corporation's strategy displays both a constancy and an evolution over time. In the 2009 annual report, the CEO, Rupert Murdoch, described the firm as a creative media company that attracts and retains customers by giving them the news and entertainment that they value (NewsCorp, 2009). The firm's **vision** can clearly be characterized by aggressive growth with global aspirations. At the same time, the firm has sometimes shown opportunistic behaviour. Telipiu in Italy became an **acquisition** target due to cash flow problems experienced by its parent, Vivendi, and News Corporation was able to take advantage of this. In pursuit of its vision, it adopted both incremental and revolutionary strategies (▶Chapter 2). Geographic expansion by purchasing several regional papers in Texas was incremental. Setting up a new TV network in the US, or a new national newspaper in Australia was revolutionary.

Chapter 2

Strategy involves improving operating performance as well as the glamour of acquisitions. Acquisitions have been an important element in its strategy, but News Corporation has also improved the financial performance of many of its acquisitions, providing cash flow for further growth. It has also achieved ongoing improvement in existing operations, growing established markets as well as internally developing new businesses such as the fourth US TV network. These decisions have involved considerable risk. The acquisition of MySpace was initially hailed as a great success, but has since stumbled, with an exodus of key managers (Smith, 2009). Indeed, News Corporation has been close to collapse several times, so good understanding of financial markets has been essential.

In addition, News Corporation illustrates that strategic management is about making decisions (not plans), even when the outcome is uncertain. These decisions may involve 'betting' the company as with News Corporation's continued investment in Sky, which almost forced the firm into bankruptcy. Strategy is about change, both reacting to change (the emergence of satellite as a medium for TV broadcasting) and creating change (the launch of new newspapers). This has led News Corporation down a path of continuous change, with growth from geographic expansion, adoption of new technologies and entry into new industries. Indeed, News Corporation was an important part of the forces driving these industry changes. To support these strategic developments, the internal arrangements in

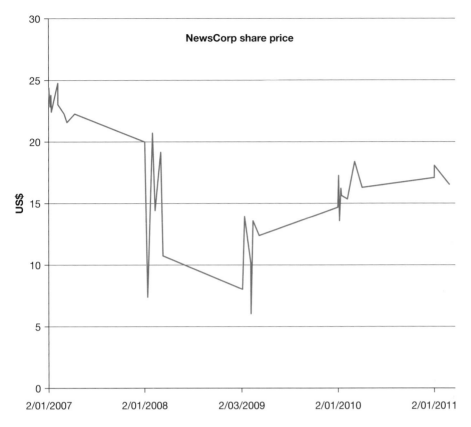

Figure 1.1 Five-year common stock performance of News Corporation (NewsCorp, 2010a)

News Corporation have also changed. Its organizational structure, processes, capabilities and people are different (➤Chapter 11). The incentives are different, the values and culture are different, and of course not all employees have accepted these changes.

    Finally, the financial performance of the firm has been variable. In fiscal 2009, for example, the firm reported assets of approximately $US53 billion and revenue of over $US30 billion. However, it also reported fiscal 2009 net losses of over $US3 billion, a huge swing from the 2008 net profits of over $US5 billion. Yet as an indication of how far the firm has moved from its Australian and newspaper roots, 55 per cent of revenue was generated in the US and 31 per cent in Europe, while newspapers and related information services were responsible for just 19 per cent of revenue (➤Chapter 12). At the time of writing, investors buying News Corporation shares in the last few years have been very disappointed, for the firm's shares have performed poorly, as indicated in Figure 1.1 (NewsCorp, 2010b).

    With its willingness to take risks and adopt a long time horizon, News Corporation has survived and prospered over the last 50 years. What the future will bring is hard to assess, but it is in a number of attractive industries, and seems to have the skills in its staff to make the best of the opportunities it both creates and is presented with.

Chapter 11

Chapter 12

CHAPTER OVERVIEW

Building on the News Corporation example, this chapter introduces our model of the strategic management process, which incorporates four interrelated elements: context – the internal and external environment in which the firm competes; strategy – what the firm decides to do in response to these changes; implementation – how the firm will put the strategy into practice; and performance – how well the firm is performing. We then introduce the differences between strategic decisions (decisions that affect the long-term well-being of the firm), strategy (the theme that underlies a set of strategic decisions) and strategic management (the managerial process of creating an organization which generates value).

This is followed by a discussion of the major theories about what determines firm success, and influences on the longevity of that success. Having established this understanding, we review the economic structure of the firm, and introduce some of the alternatives as they relate to economic exchange and firm boundaries, for example, which processes the firm should own directly and which can be outsourced. We briefly cover the importance of innovation and change, a major theme to which we return later. We then develop the strategic management model in more detail, indicating how the structure of the book relates to this model. This is followed by a discussion of some of the changes, such as corporate social responsibility, which are influencing the evolution of strategic management. To illustrate how the concepts discussed in this chapter are utilized in practice, we include a View from the Top, by the CEO of Electrolux, indicating how that firm has grappled with change. The chapter concludes with a mini-case – MTP Limited, a small Irish IT firm – providing an opportunity to put these concepts into practice.

1.1 INTRODUCTION

Globalization

The process which enables the free movement of goods, services, people, skills and ideas across political borders.

As the example of News Corporation illustrates, this is an exciting and challenging time for all organizations. The high rate of change, reflected in rapid **globalization**, rapid shifts in technology, major political and social upheavals, are all putting extreme pressure on governments, companies and not-for-profits, affecting their ability to survive.

In business, these changes pose both challenges and opportunities: some companies prosper while others atrophy and significant new firms arise while others die.

The last few decades have seen the emergence of major new organizations. The US witnessed the rise of Microsoft, Intel, Google and Facebook, Europe the success of IKEA, Airbus and SAP. From Asia come Haier of China, Tata of India, Acer of Taiwan and LG of Korea, now well known around the world. At the same time, existing firms such as Nestle and Unilever have demonstrated continued success, while others such as Woolworths UK, Arcandor, Northern Rock, Lehman Brothers, Sabena, Swiss Air and Fortis Bank have stumbled fatally. The FTSE 100 index was established on 3 January 1984, listing the largest 100 public companies by market capitalization. The constituents of FTSE 100 are reviewed each quarter and if necessary the membership is adjusted. A comparison between the original FTSE 100 in 1984 and those listed on 6 April 2009 reveals that only 29 firms have survived as FTSE 100 companies. Since its inception, 365 companies have entered and the same number have left the index, therefore movement in and out of the index is significant.

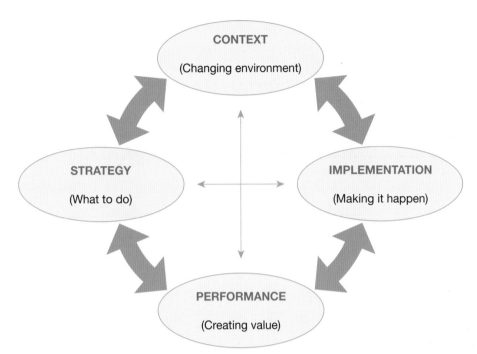

Figure 1.2
Simplified strategic
management process

These examples illustrate the difficulty that firms experience in developing and executing value-creating strategies over a long-term period. While the rewards from success are greater than ever, so are the penalties of failure. In such a dynamic world, any strategy must be modified as the world changes. Successful firms have both constancy of vision and flexibility in execution. In a turbulent and unpredictable world, innovation in all aspects of the firm is the only route to sustained success. This constitutes the strategic management challenge: how to create value in the present while building a platform for future value creation. Strategic management is an ongoing, continual process, not a single event or decision.

Figure 1.2 shows a simplified model of the strategic management process.

First, strategic managers must be aware of the changing **context** in which they compete (➤Chapters 3, 4). They need a deep understanding of environmental changes and their future impact. Coupled with this, they must understand what the firm is capable of, where it excels, what it is good at (➤Chapter 5). In other words, what **resources** and capabilities do the firm and its members possess? These must also be seen dynamically: firms must develop new skills and capabilities to survive over the long haul, as is vividly demonstrated by News Corporation.

Chapters 3, 4, 5

Strategy will be driven by a combination of external changes and the skills of the people in the firm. Management needs to decide how to respond to both challenges and opportunities. Since the world is changing rapidly, we can also expect the firm's strategy to do so (➤Chapters 6, 7). This may involve developing new bases of **competitive advantage** or completely new lines of business, either internally or via acquisition (➤Chapters 8, 9).

Chapters 6,7,8,9

**Chapters
10, 11, 12, 13**

But strategic management is not just about what to do; it is also about how to do it, how the strategy will be implemented. New skills and capabilities will likely be required to take advantage of opportunities created by a changing environment. In addition, the future may call for new leadership skills, changing the structure and/or culture of the firm (➤Chapters 10, 11). The firm must learn to operate in new environments with different competitors and possibly new technologies. Finally, the total strategic management process must result in organizations which create value over the long term (➤Chapters 12, 13).

As shown in Figure 1.2, these processes are interconnected. Strategic management and strategy development are not linear processes but are interactive and recursive.

LEARNING
OBJECTIVE 2

Distinguish between
strategic decisions,
strategy and strategic
management.

Definition of strategic management terms

Our text focuses on strategic management, the managerial aspect of strategy. We begin by distinguishing several concepts that are often confused; namely, strategic decisions, strategy and strategic management.

Strategic decisions

Strategic decisions
Those decisions that affect
the long-term well-being of
the organization.

Strategic decisions involve major resource commitments and are difficult to reverse, implying a long-term commitment. Decisions that can be regarded as strategic can occur at all levels of the firm. What is strategic depends on the entity we are considering. In this book we will concentrate on two levels of decisions – corporate and business. Corporate-level decisions are those that affect the entire firm, while business-level decisions affect a particular business or division. If there is only one business in the firm, then corporate and business levels are identical. What is regarded as long term will also depend on the firm and the industry in which it competes. For a firm developing software, long term may be as short as 2–3 years. For an oil company involved in all activities from exploration to retail, long term may be 15–20 years.

Strategic decisions *in practice* – ExxonMobil

In December 2009, ExxonMobil announced a $41 billion acquisition of XTO, a natural gas producer. This was seen by several commentators as confirmation that the future for energy companies was with natural gas, not petroleum. Natural gas is plentiful, and in countries which are politically secure. By contrast, under the leadership of John Brown, BP made significant investments in hydrogen technology. Each of these represents a strategic decision for the company involved, and each reflects different strategies.

Strategy

Strategy
The common theme
underlying a set of strategic
decisions.

In our view, an acquisition is a strategic decision, not a strategy. The strategy may be changing the business scope of the firm or changing the geographical scope to become

Strategy *in practice* – IKEA

IKEA has grown around the world with a strategy of organic expansion, exporting to many different countries a consistent store format and operating philosophy incorporating the use of long-term relationships with its network of suppliers (Baraldi, 2008).

IKEA's competitive advantage is built on a value-for-money proposition underpinned by:

- in-house design capability
- limited customer services
- self-selection by customers
- modular furniture design
- low manufacturing costs
- ample inventories
- logistic capabilities
- continuous evolutionary change.

global. The decision to acquire a particular firm is then a component of that strategy. Such a strategy may involve other significant decisions, such as increasing the level of debt to fund the acquisition. As a result of its 2010 acquisition of Cadbury, Kraft arranged £5.5 billion of debt financing to fund the acquisition (Crane, 2010). Strategy is about the firm's relationship with the environment and developing the resources and capabilities to enable it to prosper.

It is our view that all firms have a strategy and this strategy may be explicit or implicit. It may be developed with substantial analysis or not, pre-specified or allowed to develop in an evolutionary fashion. A firm's strategy can generally be expressed in relatively simple terms, although this may hide complexity within. When thinking about strategy, we must also recognize that in strategy nothing about the firm is fixed, it is all variable. The strategy may change a firm's scope, its culture, its structure, its vision or all of the above. When developing strategy, we must therefore think creatively about a wide range of possible changes.

Contrast the success of IKEA with the failure of MFI, a national British furniture retailer. MFI was one of the largest suppliers of kitchen and bedroom furniture in the UK, operating mainly in retail parks in out-of-town locations (just like IKEA). After success in its early decades, in more recent years it experienced recurring financial problems accompanied by several changes of ownership. On 26 November 2008 it was announced that the company had been placed into administration. The company ceased trading on 19 December 2008 after the administrators failed to find buyers. MFI failed not only because of the economic downturn and loss of consumer confidence in 2008 but also because it failed to deliver a consistent value proposition and the attendant poor publicity this generated.

Strategic management

Strategic management
Creating organizations that generate value in a turbulent world over an extended period of time.

Strategic management is a process that involves leadership, creativity, passion and analysis, building an organization that both generates and responds to change, developing compensation systems to reward staff, devising appropriate structures and systems, competing for funds in global financial markets and ensuring necessary resources are developed and allocated to worthwhile opportunities. Strategic management means both managing for the present as well as creating change so that the firm continues to prosper in a global, uncertain world.

Strategic Management *in practice* – News Corporation

News Corporation has grown from a small regional Australian newspaper to a global business with interests in many areas of communications. This has involved leadership, developing new skills, and balancing growth with financial and other constraints. Growth has not been an accident; instead, the management of the firm has driven it.

Chapter 2

The examples we have discussed underline the fact that organizational innovation is the key to strategy and wealth creation. The firm that finds an innovative approach is generally the one that shifts industry equilibrium in its favour. Further, the examples indicate that success is not pre-determined by the industry in which the firm operates; successful and unsuccessful firms may co-exist in the same industry. Indeed, two firms in the same industry can have different strategies, yet both can be successful, the so-called equifinality principle. Of course, success may be assessed in many ways. Different stakeholder groups, such as shareholders, customers and employees, may use very different criteria (►Chapter 2). Of one thing we are confident however: management makes a difference to organizational performance.

Only a few years ago a great deal of effort was expended to improve forecasting models and forecast accuracy. Indeed, forecasts of revenues, costs, investments and profit are central to much of the panoply of modern management. However, over time the business environment has become more turbulent, even chaotic, and too unpredictable for historical data to provide guaranteed guidance to the future, no matter how sophisticated the model. With turbulence, fixed investments and costs become more perilous, flexibility and variable costs more desirable (Economist, 2009). With these changes it is becoming more and more important for firms to experiment and to learn quickly from their experiences, and to incorporate different scenarios into their decision-making (Bryan & Farrell, 2009). Yet we must not throw the baby out with the bathwater. Forecasting has become more difficult, but at the same time the future is not completely unpredictable. Demand for many products and services such as petroleum, electricity, steel, education and banking is remarkably stable. Further, predictions of environmental trends such as population have little error associated with them in the short to medium term.

Developing strategy in today's environment is a challenging undertaking. When the world is turbulent and unpredictable, how should an organization respond? Should it respond purposefully or just drift? Some suggest that in such a world, strategy is obsolete before it can be developed. We reject this argument. We believe the firm must have a strategy for reacting and responding to developments. If it just drifts, it is unlikely to survive. A clear idea of where the firm is going is a necessary prerequisite to develop the resources, capabilities and, ultimately, the products and services required by targeted markets. Managers need to understand the way the world is evolving and what responses are likely to enhance the firm's survival and prosperity. Without some sense of direction, albeit imperfect, the firm cannot operate.

This discussion leads us to consider, and to clarify, what we mean by firm success.

1.2 WHAT DETERMINES FIRM SUCCESS?

LEARNING OBJECTIVE 3

Contrast the major theories which endeavour to explain firm success.

We define an organization as a set of individuals and other productive assets that voluntarily come together for a common purpose (Barney, 1991). In this text, we focus primarily on business organizations, organizations whose common purpose is primarily economic. The primary purpose of many organizations, such as UNICEF or the Metropolitan Opera in New York, is non-economic. While such organizations must pay some attention to their economic performance, this is not their primary focus.

The definition of success of a business firm depends on whose eyes we are looking through. Shareholders have a different view from employees, who in turn look at things very differently from customers. The firm has many stakeholders or constituencies, but these three are undoubtedly among the most important. In Chapter 2, we discuss success from each of these perspectives in more detail (➤Chapter 2). Here, we take the firm itself as the unit of analysis and explore three related questions:

Chapter 2

- What do we mean by the success of a firm?
- What determines firm success?
- What is the persistence of that success?

What do we mean by success?

At its simplest level, success may mean survival. If a firm only survives for a few years (or a few months, as with many start-up firms), then we would not consider it as a successful firm. By contrast, Akzo-Nobel can trace its origins back to 1646, with significant changes to its scope and, of course, management. Success has not depended on a single individual. Rather successful processes have been transferred to succeeding generations of managers. Continuity is certainly an element in defining success, but the challenge of strategic management is to create organizations capable of creating value over a sustained period.

We regard a firm as successful when it has the ability to create positive net economic profit as an entity; that is, the value created by the firm is greater than the costs incurred in creating that value. The objective of strategic management is to develop strategies, and to make strategic decisions so that this occurs. Let's look at what this implies in terms of value and costs.

The gross value created by the firm is the total revenue generated from the sale or lease of the goods and services it supplies to customers. This revenue must be larger than all the costs incurred in generating it. While there are many ways to classify costs, the most important ones are the costs of all inputs, material, labour and capital. The value created by the firm as an entity is then simply:

Value created by the firm = revenue less all costs

Economic profit
The revenue of a firm less all costs.

Economic profit is a different concept from the accounting profit, for in determining economic profit we also consider the amount and cost of capital employed in the business. A firm may make an accounting profit, but employ a huge capital base in order to do so. Since capital is not free, a capital charge must be included to measure economic profit. So we define economic profit as:

Economic profit = revenue minus all costs
including corporate taxes and capital costs (both equity and debt)

If a firm covers all other costs, but not capital costs, the firm is destroying value, and hurting its shareholders. Since they may easily move their funds from one investment to another, failure to generate economic profit will motivate them to invest elsewhere, rather than suffer opportunity losses.

Table 1.1 shows the economic profit earned by several US firms where economic profit is as defined above. The measurement of economic profit is discussed in greater depth in Chapter 12 (►Chapter 12).

Chapter 12

In Table 1.1, we have used economic value added (EVA®) developed by Stern Stewart, as a measure of economic profit (Uyemura *et al.*, 1996). Microsoft has consistently delivered a strong economic profit, even through the recession of 2008/9, as have Wal-Mart and Procter & Gamble. In 2009, Microsoft created an additional US$10.6 billion of wealth for its

Table 1.1 Economic profit of selected US firms (US$ millions) (Yang, 2009)

	EVA Nov 2009	EVA Nov 2008	EVA Nov 2004
Microsoft	10,680	14,170	8,313
Apple Inc.	4,876	4,246	−150
Wal-Mart Stores	7,910	7,267	5,407
Procter & Gamble Co.	3,225	3,305	3,708
Coca-Cola Co.	3,689	3,597	3,517
Motorola Inc.	−4,339	−3,370	−2,898
Time Warner Inc.	−12,824	−8,476	−7,249
Bank of America Corp.	−6,598	−1,609	5,655

shareholders than they would have received from other investments of equal risk. In contrast, Motorola and Time Warner have suffered large economic losses, indicating that they have actually destroyed shareholder value over the period 2004 to 2009. Bank of America has historically been a successful firm until it destroyed value during the financial crisis in 2008/09.

The purpose of strategic management is to ensure that the firm generates an economic profit that is available for distribution among its stakeholders, or which the firm can use for innovation to create additional value. How this surplus is distributed, however, will be a source of debate within the firm, reflecting the values of managers, available growth opportunities, and the political power of various stakeholders.

What determines success?

Although many concepts such as game theory and organization theory have influenced the development of strategic management, the literature generally suggests that there are two main models of successful performance. These are referred to as the 'structure–conduct–performance' model (SCP) and the 'resource-based view' (RBV), each of which have antecedents in earlier work, particularly by Chandler (Chandler, 1962) and Learned (Learned *et al.*, 1969).

The structure–conduct–performance (SCP) model postulates that the dominant influence on firm performance is the external environment in which it competes. By contrast, the resource-based model postulates that it is the unique resources, skills and capabilities of the firm that are the source of its success. We briefly discuss the contribution made by each model, subsequently developing our view that each is an incomplete framework for success.

Structure–conduct–performance model
The SCP model assumes that the structural characteristics of the industry determine business performance.

Structure–conduct–performance model

With the SCP model, the structural characteristics of the industry are seen as determining conduct (or what we would regard as strategy), which in turn determines the performance of the business (▶Chapter 3).

Chapter 3

Structural characteristics include such parameters as barriers to entry, customer concentration, the existence of substitutes and level of product differentiation between competitors, among others. These characteristics determine the conduct of the business that includes such elements as pricing, product strategy, R&D, advertising, levels of investment and so on. This conduct in turn is the primary influence on the performance of the business. This model was popularized for managers by Porter (Porter, 1980), but has a long history as documented by Caves (1998). The SCP model suggests that the industry in which the firm chooses to compete is more important than the choices managers make. Success occurs when the firm elects to compete in structurally attractive industries. Under this model, the emphasis in strategy is on optimal positioning: locate in an attractive industry and attempt to become market leader. The emphasis is on analysing the firm's environment to assess the overall economic profit of the industry since this is considered the major influence on firm profitability. We can see the importance of this approach in the airline industry, where average profitability is extremely low. This low profit arises from the structural characteristics of that industry – intense competition, high capital requirements, fluctuating demand and so on.

However, even in the airline industry, some competitors do significantly better than others. This situation also arises in commodity markets such as oil or iron ore. Some firms may be more skilled at reducing costs, or possess unique knowledge in processing, or be in possession of a high-grade ore body and are able to generate superior financial returns.

Under the SCP framework, strategy choices are seen as constrained by industry structure, with successful strategies being either producing at a lower cost than competitors, or producing a differentiated product for which customers are prepared to pay a premium. Which is to be preferred is determined by industry structure. All firms are assumed to possess similar resources, although there is some discretion for the firm – it may be able to implement strategy better than competitors.

While we agree that these structural characteristics influence the nature of the strategy that leads to success, successful firms must also be able to develop the skills required to implement the strategy. In management consulting, the ability to offer a global client a consulting project at the lowest possible price may not be an advantage. Instead, the successful firms are those with credibility, and the staff who can deliver on the proposal. Hence, while we regard industry structure as relevant, performance is linked to firm characteristics as well, which leads us to a consideration of the second approach – the resource-based view of strategy.

Resource-based view
Sees the firm as a collection of unique resources and capabilities that are the basis of its strategy and success.

The resource-based view of the firm

 Chapter 5

The **resource-based** perspective sees the firm as a collection of unique resources and capabilities that are the basis of its strategy and success (➤Chapter 5).

Resources are the more fundamental financial, physical and intangible attributes of the firm. Capabilities – which are largely intangibles – refer to the firm's ability to combine and integrate these resources. In this view, differences in firm success are explained by differences in resources available to each firm, not industry characteristics. Such a view of strategy also has a long history, with the early work on strengths and weaknesses (Learned *et al.*, 1969) and distinctive capabilities (Selznick, 1957).

Such resources and capabilities can only lead to superior returns if they are specific to the firm, so they must be valuable to customers and difficult to imitate by competitors (Rugman & Verbeke, 2002). To be valuable, the resource must increase revenue or reduce costs compared to what they would have been without the resource. If it is easy to transfer resources from one firm to another, any advantage would be quickly competed away. These resources then become the basis for competitive advantage, a necessary but not sufficient condition for success. Of course, over time, the firm will undoubtedly need to acquire new capabilities; thus we must think of them dynamically (Easterby-Smith *et al.*, 2009).

The resource-based view of the firm (RBV) focuses on the need to exploit differences between firms to establish unique positions of competitive advantage, a view aligned with Porter's later work. He notes that 'competitive strategy is about being different . . . choosing a different set of activities to deliver a unique mix of value' (Porter, 1996). Further, since the world changes, superior returns can only be sustained if new resources are generated (Markides, 1999). In our consulting example, a successful firm develops the intellectual ability and knowledge of its staff to ensure that these are superior to competitors.

Synthesis

We consider both of these frameworks to be incomplete, and now discuss some of their shortcomings.

The SCP model is concerned with the performance of a 'firm' which is assumed to compete in a single industry. Yet most global firms compete in many industries; consequently this model can only be relevant for a division, or what Chapter 2 describes as a business unit of the firm (▶Chapter 2). Most of the factors that the SCP model considers as affecting performance are actually industry factors. Their impact must therefore be on a business unit, not the overall firm, which may compete in many industries. As we have seen, News Corporation competes in newspapers, film and television and on the Internet, and the structures of these industries differ considerably. When we discuss 'firm success' we need to be clear whether we are discussing the success of the parent or the success of a business unit within that parent. If it is the former, then considerations such as the firm's degree and nature of diversification or level of debt may be relevant. If it is a business unit, industry factors have some relevance, but obviously they are not relevant for a diversified corporation; they can only be relevant for one of its businesses.

In addition, the focus on industry characteristics is also incomplete. If we consider a business unit, it exists in more than just an industry environment; it also exists in what in Chapter 3 we call the **remote environment** (▶Chapter 3).

This remote environment includes such things as anti-trust legislation, an overall economy, average income levels of the members of the economy, and other factors that will influence the profitability of the business. Possibly as a consequence of this remote environment, we see successful firms in unattractive industries and unsuccessful firms in attractive industries.

The RBV is also incomplete. A specific resource or capability has no value independent of the environment in which the firm competes (Priem & Butler, 2001). So a resource such as specialized knowledge may or may not be valuable. To return to our consulting example, the firm may have detailed and comprehensive knowledge of the auto industry. But if the firm has no clients in that industry, such knowledge has no value.

As shown in Figure 1.2, our model of strategic management is richer and more comprehensive than either of these two paradigms, but uses both as inputs. First, the firm exists in a changing external world and this world will have a bearing on its strategy. This external world has two elements, which we refer to as the product/market environment and the financial market environment (▶Chapters 3, 4). Both are relevant. The product/market environment includes such characteristics as the political context (say anti-trust law) which will influence many business units within the firm. It includes the industry environment, which can only affect the performance of a business in that industry. Financial markets –

Chapter 2

Chapter 3

Remote environment
The broad socio/technical/economic environment in which the firm competes.

Chapters 3, 4

the ability of the firm to raise debt and equity – also affect strategy and performance. We also need to clarify what unit we are talking about: the entire firm or a unit within that firm. For example, if we are talking about the performance of a unit within a diversified firm, then we may expect characteristics of the parent to influence the performance of the unit (Bowman & Helfat, 2001).

What the firm elects to do in the way of strategy will also be influenced by what the firm does well, what specialized resources and capabilities it possesses. However, strategic management is not only about a good idea; it is also about getting that idea to work. The strategy must be able to be implemented; if not, it must be changed. Finally, the firm estimates likely performance resulting from the chosen strategy. If this is not satisfactory, the strategy is likely to be revised. As will be discussed in Chapter 12 (➤Chapter 12), there are a number of performance measures which can be used for strategy assessment.

Chapter 12

Persistence of success

The challenge for strategic management is to build organizations capable of creating and delivering value over an extended period. This has proved to be extremely difficult. Typically, firms seem to have their day in the sun and then decline, either absolutely or relatively as new firms emerge in the growth sectors of the economy. Sustained success will only occur when strategic managers are able to both manage for today and manage for tomorrow (Abell, 1999).

Managing for today: exploitation of existing resources/capabilities

Managing for today typically involves fine-tuning current operations, introducing incremental changes with strategy staying reasonably fixed. These changes are smaller, more evolutionary; the managerial focus is on managing complexity. Ideally, vision and values are in place, deep in the firm, well understood and accepted by all. A key managerial concern is ensuring that the strategy is well understood and clear performance criteria are established and met. When managing for today, the firm's organizational structure is assumed to have been designed appropriately, as is the control system and performance management system.

Managing for tomorrow: exploration of new resources/capabilities

Chapter 6

Managing for tomorrow requires different skills. To have the foresight and knowledge to imagine how the firm will look in the future requires creating a vision of what the firm and its environment is likely to look like, a topic to which we return in Chapter 6 (➤Chapter 6). To move towards realizing such a vision demands not only good leadership skills, but also an understanding of what capabilities will be required and specific planning to acquire or develop them (Ambrosini *et al.*, 2009). This challenge will often require that we loosen up thinking in the firm. Managers and other employees must be open to change, willing to listen, keeping information systems open to external as well as internal inputs. Senior managers should not become overly dependent on formal systems or their immediate staff. Useful insights may come from suppliers, customers, universities and technical bodies, and other such sources. They must seek leading indicators of change in all dimensions – technological, socio-demographic, political, etc. The key is less trend identification than spotting turning points and points of inflection in growth curves. The company that is continually surprised by change is unlikely to deal with it well.

Given an uncertain future, a strategy cannot be set in concrete. It must evolve as the world evolves. At the same time, strategy must encourage a sense of common direction. Strategy making is an ongoing process, not something that is done periodically on a rigid planning cycle. The firm has to continually develop new ideas, a succession of initiatives over time. However, changes in strategy should be driven by change in circumstances, not the passage of time.

We can link today and tomorrow by recognizing that long-term sustainability of success depends upon to two factors:

- The extent to which the firm can exploit its existing capabilities in a given market or industry.
- The rate at which new industry sectors emerge and the ability of the firm to alter its scope and develop the capabilities required to compete in these new sectors.
- These two influences are depicted in Figure 1.3.

In a relatively free market, with no institutional barriers, any advantage will be competed away. Other firms will copy and/or enhance the initial competitive advantage and the rate at which this advantage is competed away is influenced by industry structure (Bou & Satorra, 2007). Strategic management has to ensure the invention and development of offerings that will create value in an uncertain future, as well as the creation of value through present offerings. If no value is created in the short term, the firm will lose the support of both customers and shareholders. However, if there is only a short-term focus, then the firm will have no future.

Thus strategic management involves creating and managing a process of ongoing change and improvement, adapting to a continuously changing world.

As we noted earlier, in strategy all characteristics of the firm are candidates for change. In the long term, nothing is fixed. Strategic management must create an organizational architecture that encourages continual re-invention alongside current operations. Strategic management therefore involves making either incremental and/or revolutionary changes to strategy to ensure sustained success for the firm.

When a firm is in difficulty, it is often because its strategy and its underlying assumptions no longer fit reality. Assumptions about the nature and form of competition, what values customers are

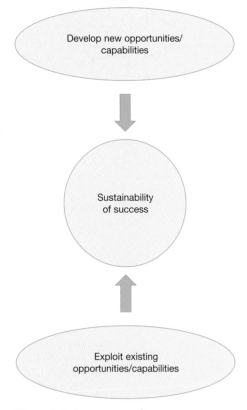

Figure 1.3 Persistence of success

Strategy *in practice* – Thomas Cook

Thomas Cook was the founder of the modern travel industry. His name lives on as '"Thomas Cook Plc", one of the world's leading leisure travel groups with sales of £8.8 billion, 22.3 million customers, 31,000 employees, a fleet of 93 aircraft and a network of over 3,400 owned and franchized travel stores and interests in 86 hotels and resort properties. It operates under five geographic segments in 21 countries' (ThomasCook, 2007). The company's recent history is a fascinating example of the ongoing change and adaptation necessary for survival in a rapidly changing world.

In common with other travel industry companies, Thomas Cook was in trouble in the early 2000s. However, a major turnaround initiative rapidly changed the outlook as shown in Figure 1.4.

Nor was the Thomas Cook saga yet finished. In 2001–02, the firm was acquired by German firm C&N Touristic AG, which then changed its name to Thomas Cook AG. In 2006, Thomas Cook AG became wholly owned by KarstadtQuelle, later renamed Arcandor. In 2007 Thomas Cook AG firm merged with the UK group MyTravel and was listed on the London Stock Exchange, when it became a FTSE 100 firm, with Arcandor holding a 51 per cent ownership share. In 2009, Arcandor declared bankruptcy, but the directors of Thomas Cook announced that the bankruptcy would have 'no impact on customers and is not expected to result in any adverse effect on any of the contractual arrangements of the Thomas Cook group' since it operated as a stand-alone entity (Finch, 2009).

Throughout its existence, Thomas Cook has demonstrated an ability to exploit existing capabilities, originally in rail travel, as well as develop new capabilities in air travel, computer reservation systems and global management.

Strategy *in practice* – Tesco

Tesco, currently the leading UK supermarket chain, could continue to seek new supermarket sites expand in the UK, using existing methods of operating. Or they could change the layout within their existing stores. Both of these would be incremental changes to the existing strategy. However, by introducing online shopping, Tesco significantly changed its historic strategy, as it did when it chose to expand outside the UK, where it now operates in 15 different countries. It has also added a bank, mobile, broadband and VOIP telecommunications services and acquired a major chain of garden centres. An even more radical change in strategy would be for them to become a global media company such as Time Warner!

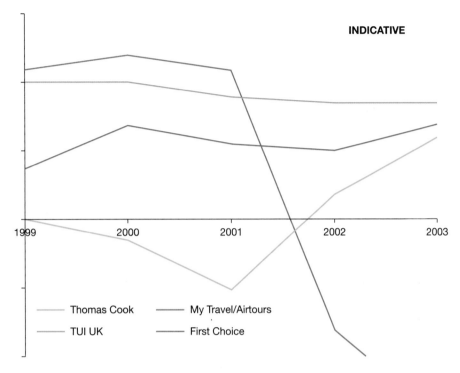

INDICATIVE

Thomas Cook ——— My Travel/Airtours
——— TUI UK ——— First Choice

Figure 1.4 Profit before tax – Thomas Cook turnaround (Ailles, 2004)

seeking, or the factors driving success become outdated. This is why the maintenance of an external perspective is a key element in strategic management. An early warning system is needed to see when the existing 'model' is in danger of becoming inadequate. We explore these issues in more depth in Chapter 2 (▶Chapter 2).

Chapter 2

Fundamental re-invention of strategy is much more difficult in practice than in theory. It requires innovation, creativity, and a deep understanding of the business, its customers and how the environment is changing. Further, implementation of a new strategy may outdate existing capabilities, requiring the firm to cannibalize existing products and threaten existing jobs. Previously successful firms often demonstrate an inability to change; they perceive the world though increasingly obsolete eyes. Indeed, some believe that most innovation in an industry comes from firms outside the industry, which are not constrained by the incumbents' implicit assumptions and mindsets.

Regardless, it is surely better that we cannibalize our business than allow others to do so. Yet many firms find this very difficult. They may re-invent themselves once, but then stop. For this reason, in many industries, relatively unknown companies that create and exploit new strategic positions have humbled once formidable companies with seemingly unassailable positions (Markides, 1999). Nor are these innovative approaches, witnessed by such innovators as Google and Facebook, limited to high-tech industries. Companies such as Aldi (the German discount retailer), Ryanair (the Irish low-cost airline) and Starbucks (the US coffee chain) have brought major innovations to traditional industries, enjoying strong commercial success. We have no doubt that there will be many more examples in the future.

In summary, to ensure sustainability of success, a firm needs a portfolio of strategy initiatives: some focused on the short term, others on the longer term (▶Chapters 8, 9). The firm has to compete in product markets, and in these markets competitive advantage is a necessary but not sufficient condition for success. We can be successful relative to competitors, but not create value as an entity. The challenge for strategic managers is to simultaneously create value in the present, while setting the stage for future value creation. This goal, in turn, poses a classic managerial dilemma: how much to invest in current businesses versus how much to invest in new businesses (Baghai *et al.*, 1999). We believe that in a changing world, successful firms will be those that both create and adapt to change. They will be firms that have, in fact, helped to change the world.

 **Chapters 8, 9**

LEARNING OBJECTIVE 4

Recognize why firms exist as economic entities and be able to describe alternate forms of economic exchanges.

 Chapter 7

Outsourcing
The transfer of a recurring, internal value-creating activity to an external provider, where the arrangement is specified in a formal contract.

Market-based exchange
A system in which exchanges of goods and services occur between two separate and independent entities.

1.3 THE CONCEPT OF THE FIRM

As was noted earlier, a business organization or firm is one whose primary purpose is economic. Since these firms are competing with other firms providing similar goods and services, they must organize themselves efficiently. An important determinant of firm efficiency is the selection of activities that it will undertake itself and those that will be bought in from others. Which activities are best grouped under common ownership and which are best handled by other arrangements? Should a firm employ its own accountants, or should this activity be **outsourced** (▶Chapter 7)?

These decisions constitute a fundamental issue in strategic management: what should be the scope of the firm, and where should firm boundaries be drawn?

The question of which activities should be retained within the firm and which should be pursued by other means is the content of organizational economics or the theory of the firm (Williamson, 1975). In this theory, it is generally considered that there are two archetypal forms of economic organization – the market and the hierarchy (or firm). With the market form of economic organization, the flow of goods and services occurs across separate legal entities. When transactions are handled within the firm, the economic activity is called a hierarchy. The fundamental proposition of organizational economics is that the firm will be more integrated (perform production activities using its own resources) when the combined costs of production and coordination are less than the price they would pay from a supplier together with all transaction costs (Safizadeh *et al.*, 2008).

With a **market-based** system, exchanges occur between two separate and independent entities.

When Ericsson purchases electronic components from a company such as Fujitsu, the transaction occurs in the market. In this arrangement, prices are used to coordinate the flow of goods across separate legal entities, each of which has its own objectives. These independent companies make their own decisions on what and how much to produce in response to price and demand signals. Incentives are relatively clear. Ericsson will continue to purchase from

Strategy *in practice* – airline industry outsourcing

Whereas in the earlier days of the airline industry most operators owned their aircraft and operated their own flight kitchens, today many lease their aircraft, which are actually owned by leasing companies, and buy in their meals from specialized suppliers. Some have even outsourced maintenance of their aircraft. The results of such outsourcing may well be questioned, as the chart for the US airline industry in Figure 1.5 suggests. We discuss outsourcing in depth later in the book.

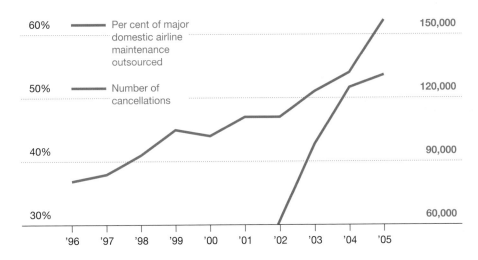

Figure 1.5 Airline industry outsourcing (ConsumerReports, 2007)

Copyright 2007 by Consumers Union of US, Inc. Yonkers, NY 10703-1057, a non-profit organization. Reprinted with permission for educational purposes only. No commercial use or reproduction permitted. www.consumerreports.org

Fujitsu provided it meets its requirements and there is therefore considerable pressure on Fujitsu to have a deep understanding of Ericsson's needs. In many cases these market-based systems involve long-term and stable relationships among firms, such that they constitute a network, as in the case of IKEA, mentioned earlier. Under a market-based system problems may arise if there is market failure – such as a monopoly, or when the two parties do not have access to the same information or when the transaction is one for which it is difficult to write a contract (Roberts, 2004)

With a **hierarchically based** system of exchange, goods are produced and exchanged between different units of the same firm, that is, transactions occur between entities under common ownership.

Such arrangements may be beneficial to the firm since all individuals are employed by the same firm and should possess similar objectives. There is a bargain between the obedience of the subordinate and the responsibility of the superior, resting on the capacity to form

Hierarchically based exchange

A system in which goods are produced and exchanged between different units of the same firm, sharing common ownership.

relationships of trust to reduce conflicts of interest, where individuals act in their own interests rather than those of the firm.

The question senior managers must resolve is when are hierarchies better than markets? The answer is determined by four considerations: production costs, governance costs, search costs and capabilities. Production costs can vary with each arrangement. Take an example of software. If it is produced within the firm, staff may be less skilled than outside specialists who have access to more sophisticated test and development equipment so that costs are higher. On the other hand, software produced within the firm may have superior functionality, since it has been developed specifically for an internal application.

Governance costs are the costs associated with managing transactions (Coase, 1937). With market-based transactions these include the costs of searching for, negotiating, monitoring and enforcing a contract with the external provider. Under conditions of high external uncertainty it is difficult to write a contract allowing for all future possibilities, thereby ensuring a fair return to both parties. Under these conditions we would expect transactions to take place within the firm. Governance costs also occur when transactions occur within the firm. These include coordination costs, costs of the bureaucracy, costs of complexity and slow decision-making.

A final consideration affecting firm boundaries is its capabilities. Distinctive capabilities, based on tangible and intangible firm assets, can be used to extend the firm's scope. They are also critical to developing a competitive advantage. The firm will want to ensure that current and future capabilities are kept within the firm, as they are the basis of future success. As firms become more knowledge-intensive, they must develop, protect and integrate this knowledge to enhance competitive position.

Managerial implications

These two forms of economic exchange represent extremes, as shown in Figure 1.6. Economic exchanges may be at one of the two extremes or they may occur through one of a wide range of other relational forms, such as networks or alliances, long-term supplier agreements, licensing, contract staff, franchising, equity spin-outs and so on. Managers should consider a variety of alternatives, since they may permit a better balance between individual initiative and structured cooperation (Day & Wendler, 1998).

The issues described above have implications for a number of strategic decisions, including mergers and acquisitions, networks, outsourcing, strategic alliances, joint ventures, vertical integration and relationships (Collis & Montgomery, 1998). At the same time, decisions on firm boundaries reflect mission, capabilities and innovation. Since these drivers are themselves in flux, decisions regarding boundaries are a dynamic process. Various

| Market | Network | Alliance | Franchise | Licensing | Hierarchy |

Figure 1.6 Alternative forms of economic exchanges

> **Challenge of strategic management**
>
> It is suggested above that developments in communications and information technology will make it easier for firms to form networks and alliances with partners from anywhere in the world. In your view, does this mean the end of the mammoth corporation, and that the future belongs to small, nimble and focused organizations who supplement their capabilities with the capabilities of others?

purchasing exchanges have been developed which allow the firm to reduce the costs of interacting with both customers and suppliers, permitting the firm to engage in more market-based transactions. The development of the World Wide Web has changed the economics of information, enabling a firm to effectively utilize a network of other firms, drawing on the talents of many people to create products using email, file transfers, Lotus Notes and other means to achieve real-time coordination. These firms can be geographically remote, even in different countries. One consequence of these developments is to encourage firms to concentrate on a small set of core capabilities, while making use of the core skills of other firms located anywhere in the world.

1.4 DYNAMICS OF CHANGE

LEARNING OBJECTIVE 5

Argue the need for continual innovation and change: nothing is fixed; all attributes of the firm are variable.

Change is not a new social or technological phenomenon, it has always occurred. What characterizes the new century is the rapid pace and unpredictability of change, and its global nature.

Figure 1.7 indicates the changes in the rate of penetration of new technologies in the twentieth-century US market. Notice that technologies introduced in the early part of the century, such as automobiles and electricity, not only had much slower rates of overall growth than more recent introductions but they also had longer latencies before 'take-off' occurred. Mid-century technologies such as radio and television also had long latencies, but then grew very quickly. But technologies introduced towards the end of the century, such as the Internet and mobile phones, had both minimal latencies and extremely rapid growth. Clearly, opportunities had to be realized quickly, or they might no longer be available. Developing strategy in these circumstances, which seem likely to prevail in the twenty-first century, cannot take place at the leisurely pace of earlier years.

Change is often considered as existing along a continuum, from incremental or evolutionary to radical or discontinuous. Looking at Figure 1.7, for example, the rate of growth of air travel looks like an incremental trend line. In contrast the growth of Internet access comes much closer to a discontinuity. Other examples of incremental change would be the ageing of the population, the addition of new product features to refrigerators and the move to smaller families. Perhaps the most striking example of discontinuous change was the collapse of financial markets and the consequent freezing of liquidity in 2008/09 when the survival of the world's financial system was in jeopardy, and many banks had to

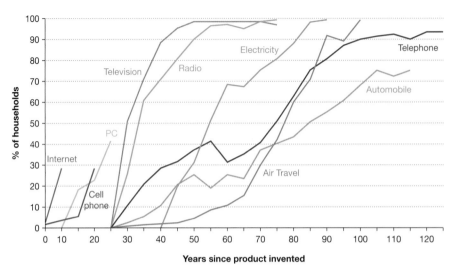

Figure 1.7 Rates of penetration of new technologies (Cox, 2002)

be rescued by governments. Another example would be the so-called 'Asian meltdown' in 1997, which was not predicted by most economic analysts. In general, economic systems, macro or micro, tend to cope well with incremental change but experience shock when major discontinuities occur!

The pattern that characterizes many markets is periods of incremental change coupled with radical change at various points. Such a pattern of change is referred to as a **punctuated equilibrium** model (►Chapter 2). Discontinuities are typically exogenous to the firm, in that it rarely creates them. The development of the Internet was not as a result of activities by any of the companies in such traditional industries as airlines, entertainment or retailing, but all have had to respond to maintain their competitive positions. Such radical changes are disruptive and are likely to fundamentally change competitive positions within the market as some firms adapt and others do not.

Chapter 2

LEARNING OBJECTIVE 6

Apply the model of strategic management and be aware of the major changes driving the practice of strategic management.

1.5 STRATEGIC MANAGEMENT PROCESS

Firms undertake the development of strategy in a variety of ways: the process can be formal or informal, intuitive or analytical. In this text we will emphasize more formal approaches. But we also have to remember that even when the firm has a formal strategy process, not all strategic decisions will flow from that process. The term 'Strategy as Action' is sometimes used to describe this more evolutionary and people-oriented view (Jarzabkowski, 2005). In addition, a company may supplement the formal processes with a 'project'-based process to decide upon strategy. Acquisition strategies are often conducted on a project basis, although pre-emptive candidate screening is increasingly common.

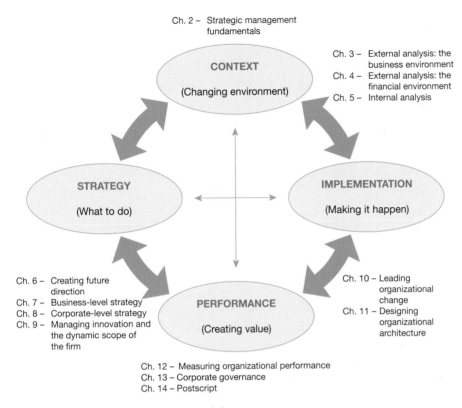

Figure 1.8 Strategic management model

Our model of the strategic management process is shown in Figure 1.8, which also indicates which chapters cover particular aspects.

As we have noted, strategic management is about creating organizations that can continue to generate value in a turbulent world over a sustained period of time. Such a challenge requires a holistic process, from understanding the external and internal environment, to developing strategy, to getting that strategy implemented, to understanding likely future performance and whether or not this is acceptable. In a changing, even turbulent environment, however, this process will itself need to be reviewed much more frequently, with much higher demands for innovation and strategic change than was traditionally the case.

We now review the four main elements of our model – context, strategy, implementation and performance.

Context

The firm exists within a changing external environment and managers have to understand these dynamics. This environment comprises two markets: the product markets within which the products of the firm compete for customers; and the financial markets, the markets within which the firm competes for capital. Managers must be able to identify prospective changes in these markets that are important for the firm, yet few predicted the meltdown of 2008/09. What is critical for one firm may not be for another. For banks, major changes have resulted from improvements in communications and information processing. These have resulted in the rise of 'non-branch' banking and a redefinition of banking. Which players will perform banking functions in the future? Will it be existing banks, new Internet-based entrants or other retailers such as supermarkets? For aluminium producers such as Hindalco Industries of India, the key environmental issues may be energy and raw material prices, inter-material substitution and access to financial resources. Almost all global firms are faced with significant concerns as governments attempt to develop emission trading and carbon pricing systems to combat human-induced climate change. Emission trading is an example of government regulation, and it is likely that regulation will increase in future as governments try to cope with the consequences of the global financial crisis. Managers have to ascertain the relative importance of changes that may occur, how significant they will be, when they may occur and their likely impact, topics that will be further developed in Chapter 3

 Chapters 3, 5 (▶Chapter 3).

At the same time, managers need to understand the firm's internal resources and capabilities. There is no point in developing a strategy that cannot be executed due to limited or non-existent resources. Chapter 5 explores the resource-based view of the firm (▶Chapter 5). Here we take a holistic view. Strategy will be based on a combination of the resources and capabilities of the firm and the changes occurring in the external environment, recognizing that resources and capabilities are dynamic. An important element of strategy, as we saw with Tesco and News Corporation, is the ability of the firm to generate new resources and capabilities.

Strategy

Senior managers must decide upon vision, strategy, and the firm's evolving business portfolio. Vision is a picture of an ideal future state. It should provide a purpose that will challenge and motivate staff and stretch the firm's capabilities. As will be developed in Chapter 6, firms also need to establish a set of values to guide the behaviour of the organization's members **Chapters 6, 7** (▶Chapter 6). These may be both implicit and explicit, and the former are typically more important, since they are the de facto guides of behaviour. Developing strategy also necessitates a mission, a statement that defines the scope of the firm, thereby delineating its boundaries.

Strategy describes the way in which the firm will accomplish the vision it has established and, as noted earlier, is the theme incorporated in a set of strategic decisions (▶Chapters 7, 8, 9). These decisions affect the long-term well-being of the organization but are made in the present. As the great business philosopher Peter Drucker put it:

> One cannot make decisions for the future. Decisions are commitments to action. And actions are always in the present, and in the present only. But actions in the present are also the one and only way to make the future.
>
> (Drucker, 1995)

Strategy *in practice* – RWE

RWE, a German company, is one of the largest European power generators. The pie chart in Figure 1.9 shows RWE's power plant capacity by type.

RWE is the biggest emitter of carbon dioxide in Europe. It is more heavily reliant on coal than its competitors. RWE's emissions per kilowatt hour of electricity are above the European average. In the third phase of the European Union's carbon emissions scheme, which starts in 2013, all generators will have to buy all the permits that they need at auction. The carbon-intense position of RWE threatens to put it at significant competitive disadvantage. RWE strategy is to reduce its dependency on coal. Therefore, unlike many other European generating companies, it has not curtailed its investment programme. It is planning to invest €7 billion annually, 40 per cent of which will go into lower carbon generation. In 2009, as a part of this strategy, RWE acquired Essent of the Netherlands for $US13.7 billion because of its significantly lower carbon intensity relative to RWE (Crooks, 2009).

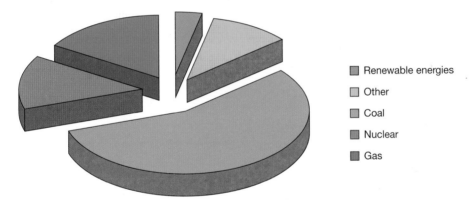

■ Renewable energies
□ Other
■ Coal
■ Nuclear
■ Gas

Figure 1.9 RWE pie chart

Strategy *in practice* – Napster and the recording industry

In deciding to attack Napster and the activity of downloading and file sharing, the recording industry unwittingly opened up opportunities for others. Some artists seized the opportunity to sever links with traditional recording companies, and the computer firm Apple became the leader in selling music over the Internet.

Thus, we must recognize that the future does not yet exist; it remains to be created by the actions of many, be they politicians, executives, consumers or sports stars. We should recognize that some of the decisions we make today will shape the future of the firm. These decisions may be taken at different levels in the firm, sometimes unwittingly or without understanding of their longer term impact.

Implementation

Strategic management is not just about generating strategy; it is also about getting strategy implemented. For many firms, the challenge is implementation rather than generation. In a strategic context, all company characteristics are considered variable. Managers can change structure, culture, products and services, regions of the world in which the firm competes; all are, at least in theory, under the control of management.

Chapters 10, 11

In Chapter 10 we explore the principles of how the firm can manage change (➤Chapter 10). Most global firms are undertaking a number of strategic decisions simultaneously, so strategic management includes an element of project management – managing several change programmes at the same time. Strategic managers need to decide who is involved in these programmes, what resources are available, what staff are used, will external consultants be utilized? Implementation also involves the design of what we call the 'organizational architecture' – the organizational structure, processes and human resource approach used by the firm. Many of these elements and their inter-relationships may constitute intangible assets, and are discussed at length in Chapter 11 (➤Chapter 11).

Performance

Strategic managers are responsible for the performance of the firm, in both financial and non-financial terms. Financial markets expect a satisfactory return, as do other stakeholders such as customers. Thus part of the strategic management challenge is to ensure that the firm has a performance culture. Chapter 12 explores the issues involved in measuring the performance of the firm (➤Chapter 12). We discuss a range of possible measures, financial and non-financial. The latter are often leading indicators of financial performance.

Chapters 12, 13

We must also appreciate that performance acts as a feedback element, reflecting the iterative nature of strategic management. The firm's performance will influence the vision, etc. that can be adopted. So strategic management is not a linear process; instead, it is an iterative, evolving and learning process.

In Chapter 13 we explore corporate governance, which has become a critical issue in recent years (➤Chapter 13). Corporate collapses, deceptive accounting, auditing failures and unethical behaviour by managers have all contributed to an intense public debate. Managerial salaries, 'perks' and share options have likewise caused concern, and strategic managers need a good understanding of governance, the role of the board, and how practices vary in different countries of the world.

> **Challenge of strategic management**
>
> Some business commentators have suggested that strategy development, while important, is subservient to strategy execution, actually getting change accomplished within the firm, getting the 'rubber to hit the road'. Does the relative importance of each of these depend on the industries in which the firm competes, such as the rate of change?

1.6 WHO 'DOES' STRATEGY?

There is no doubt that the primary responsibility for corporate strategy falls on the CEO, top management, and, ultimately, the board of directors (➤Chapters 11, 13). Nonetheless, in any successful firm many others are involved. Managers of major business units often have a role, while there may be a staff group supporting the strategic planning process. However, developing strategy is a line responsibility, and cannot be delegated to a staff group.

Chapters 11, 13

CEOs must both manage today and be the architect of change for tomorrow, requiring that they be both inductive and deductive, intuitive and analytical, incremental and revolutionary. However, it is naïve to believe that the fountain of all wisdom is the CEO, for new strategic ideas can come from anywhere within the firm. Hence, good CEOs recognize they can neither do all the strategy work nor implement strategy without the support of others. They actively encourage strategic thinking throughout the firm, leveraging their personal time and effort by working through people, structure and processes. Of course, the CEO carries primary responsibility for identifying where and how the company must change, but to transform a firm, the CEO needs committed and courageous entrepreneurs.

The task of the CEO is extremely difficult. Strategy is more than an idea, it is also about making that idea work. The CEO must perform in many roles – as change agent, communicator and public face of the company, decider, facilitator, teacher and mentor, as well as learner – requiring an almost holographic capability. Garten (Garten, 2001) suggests that the major factors complicating CEOs jobs are:

- Conflicting demands from financial markets and the need for long-term investments in developing new capabilities and a talented workforce.
- Inability to predict rapidly changing geopolitical and technological developments.
- Emergence of new competition and markets which do not yet exist, yet require huge investments if a sustainable position is to be attained.
- The fact that the CEO increasingly has to play many roles.

We describe our own views on the major factors affecting strategy development in the next section of this chapter.

1.7 CHANGES AFFECTING STRATEGIC MANAGEMENT

Figure 1.10 summarizes major influences affecting strategic management. Although the diagram suggests these influences are independent, they are all inter dependent. Many of the changes we briefly review in this section recur throughout the book, and will be explored in more detail later.

Globalization

Globalization and increased competition in product, capital and labour markets have been long-term trends since World War II. Most of us are personally familiar with product-market competition as we select from among domestically produced products and imports, between foreign and domestic brands. However, as businesses become more knowledge-intensive, it is also clear that competition for talent has erupted among countries as well as companies. Top talent managers and staff are now much more mobile, changing companies, industries and countries.

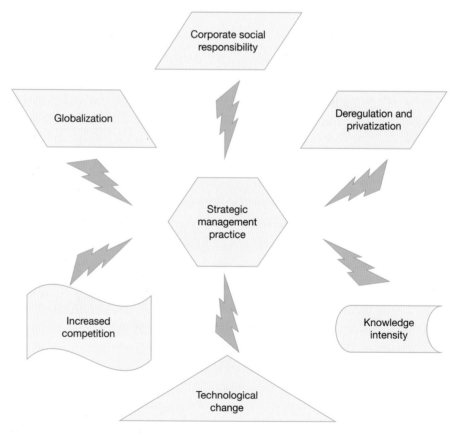

Figure 1.10 Changes affecting strategic management

> ## Globalization *in practice* – emerging markets
>
> Hindustan Lever developed a shampoo for the Indian market that was sold in single sachets at the rupee equivalent of 2 America cents (a large proportion of the Indian population cannot afford to buy larger sizes). Despite the low selling price, the shampoo was a profitable success for the company.
>
> GE is moving billions of dollars in research funds away from developing high-specification medical equipment towards lower cost technology. Over the next six years, GE Healthcare will devote half of its $1 billion R&D budget towards low-cost products designed for use in emerging markets and remote areas, up from only 15 per cent today, John Rice, GE's vice-president, said. The change in strategy comes after a sharp downturn in health spending in the US and a profound change in the political mood. Mr Rice said: 'We cannot continue to live in a world where healthcare costs go up 10 per cent per year. President Obama understands that.' GE revealed last month that profits from selling medical equipment had fallen by more than a fifth in the first quarter after a 9 per cent dip in revenue (Mortished, 2009).

Following the 2008 global banking crisis, many firms faced liquidity problems, finding it extremely difficult to raise new debt (►Chapter 4). As a result, firms were competing for funding globally. Large issues of government debt were swamping global credit markets, and most firms were seeking to de-leverage their financial structures by becoming less debt-dependent. At the same time, new financial instruments for managing interest and exchange rate risk (generally referred to as derivatives) have been developed, and there is therefore added complexity to financial decisions. National financial markets are now linked, and trading occurs 24 hours per day.

Chapter 4

There is also an international market for corporate control, with increasing numbers of cross-border mergers and acquisitions. Institutional investors own some 60 per cent of shares outstanding, with large pools of funds from insurance companies and pension funds. These investors have become more assertive in pressuring for performance, which in turn has driven the market for corporate control (Jensen, 1990).

The last part of the twentieth century also witnessed a coming of age for many emerging markets. The majority of the world's population, about six billion people, lives in such markets. In the past, many multinationals sold products designed for the highly industrialized and developed Western economies into these markets. Today, however, there is much more widespread recognition that their needs are different, and they are increasingly seen as prospective customers despite relatively low-income levels.

Increased competition

Most firms are facing increased competition in all markets, product, labour and capital. Rapidly escalating competition based on price, quality and innovation characterizes many markets, emphasizing the need for continual cost reductions to stay competitive. Squeezed net margins and shortened product life cycles underline the need to innovate. Firms must develop new competitive advantages and build required capabilities. They also have to cope with increasingly unpredictable discontinuities, meaning greater emphasis on flexibility, as well as developing a vision that balances short-term performance and longer term requirements. Increased competition means successful strategies will have shorter lives. New strategies must be invented, even if they destroy the validity of older strategies.

Industry
A group of firms producing essentially the same product using essentially the same production technology.

The blurring of traditional **industry** boundaries has also increased competition. As a result of deregulation and technological change industries such as telecommunications, media and computing are becoming hard to distinguish. Indicative of the change is talk of the TCM (Telecommunications/Computing/Media) industry. Other new words, such as cosmeceuticals, edutainment and nutraceuticals, indicate that such changes are by no means restricted to a few industries, but are more widespread. Such changes make it increasingly difficult to identify competitors, suggesting that many firms will face a turbulent and less predictable future.

The net result of many of the above changes is that industry structures have themselves become variable. Increased outsourcing has locked many companies into cooperating networks, while the growth of contract manufacturing cuts across traditional industry boundaries. Information technology has both disintermediated some industries (reduced the need for intermediaries such as travel agents), and also created new intermediaries such as Amazon and Yahoo! (➤Chapter 3).

 Chapter 3

Further, some companies are engineering their own dissolution through **spin-offs**, at the same time that others are merging and acquiring. The term 'structural competition' has been coined to alert executives to the fact that if they are not playing an active role in creating structural change in their industries, others are likely to do it for them!

Technological change

Technology has had the most important impact on the conduct of management of any change in the twentieth century. Though by no means restricted to information technology, from the mid-twentieth century onwards, the computer and associated telecommunications

---

New competition *in practice* – YouTube

On 19 May 2010, its fifth birthday, YouTube, the video site owned by Google, announced that more than two billion videos are being watched on its website every day (DNA, 2010). It is about ten times more popular than its nearest competitor. But Hunter Walk still thinks of it as an underdog.

For Mr Walk, director of product development at YouTube, the competition is not other websites: it is TV.

'Our average user spends 15 minutes a day on the site,' he said. 'They spend about five hours in front of the television. People say, "YouTube is so big," but I really see that we have a ways to go' (Helft, 2009).

Restructuring *in practice*

Typical of the many industries that have undergone enormous restructuring in recent years are banking, insurance, aluminium, steel, pharmaceuticals, defence and aerospace, airlines and automobiles.

"I've been restructured."

technologies began to have a profound impact. Companies implemented the automation of their accounts, and then began linking with suppliers using EDI. In industries as diverse as airlines (American Airlines Sabre reservations system, later divested), hospital supplies (American Hospital Supply/Baxter Healthcare's ASAP reorder terminals), drug distribution (McKesson Robbins Economost) and package shipping (Fedex's tracking system), mastering the application of information technology to solving customer problems led firms to strong, if not dominant positions in their industries. New brands proliferated: AOL, Yahoo!, Amazon, MySpace, Facebook, eBay, Twitter, YouTube, Google and more, almost without exception started by entrepreneurs, usually young, despite the presence of such media giants as News Corporation, Time-Warner, Viacom, Bertelsmann and others.

Today, of course, we are all familiar with the Web, a worldwide information utility that is revolutionizing the relationship between firms, their customers and their suppliers. The Internet permits customers to access company manufacturing operations to track order progress, and enables a two-way dialogue with customers. It increasingly allows co-design of products, as part of a move to what is now called mass customization. The Internet allows a person to 'work' in London while 'living' elsewhere. With its 24-hour access, virtually infinite capacity and open standards, the Internet has reduced the cost of search for buyers and sellers, with implications for firm boundaries. Transportation costs of such digital products as music and many financial products are dramatically reduced, creating potential for a major new distribution channel. Firms increasingly work together to build networks of suppliers, distributors and partners to create customer value, in turn leading to more outsourcing.

Dramatic reductions in the cost of computing power and storage, increasing bandwidth and lowered telecommunications costs combine to create enormously powerful forces for change. The scramble of media companies to position themselves for the age of high-speed real-time downloading of audio and video products is indicative of the change that awaits all who conduct business in products and services that can be digitized.

All industries have been affected by the information revolution to a greater or lesser extent. The widespread availability of information technology has had and will continue to have dramatic effects on which activities are performed inside and outside the firm, for transaction costs will be changed. Similarly, the ease with which price information can be obtained has already increased the competitiveness of product markets. Indeed, some commentators alleged that the low inflation experienced at the turn of the century was a direct result of these changes. One industry affected by these developments is publishing, with consumers from around the world being able to buy books from Amazon and from non-traditional sources such as India.

Knowledge intensity

Knowledge intensity
The extent to which a product or activity is based on knowledge.

Chapter 5

Increasing returns to scale
When the benefit of a product or service to an individual user increases as the total number of users of that product or service increases.

Corporate social responsibility
When the firm takes responsibility for the impact of its actions on the environment, consumers, employees and communities.

Chapter 13

Drucker and others describe advanced economies as 'knowledge' economies, since they are becoming less materials and energy intensive all the time (Drucker, 1992). Traditional factors of production – capital and skilled labour – are no longer the main determinants of the power of an economy. Now economic potential is increasingly linked to the ability to control and manipulate information.

Knowledge intensity is increasing for most products. Direct labour is now a small proportion of total costs for manufactured products, and the market value of more and more firms is becoming independent of the tangible assets on the balance sheet.

With increasing knowledge intensity, there is a commensurate shift in recognizing the relative importance of human capital versus traditional fixed capital (➤Chapter 5). The economics of knowledge products are different. Knowledge-based products generally show increasing returns to scale: the more widely they are used the more valuable they become to a user.

Social networking sites such as Facebook grow in value and importance with the number of users. The value of Windows is enhanced by the fact that it has many users, resulting in more people using it to write applications software programs, which again enhances its value. The iPad's enthusiastic acceptance was driven by the number of application programs available to its users.

With such products there can be substantial benefits to early market entry, establishing the product as an industry standard. It may also be beneficial to share the product with others, forming alliances early on. We may not want to 'hoard' the product but get wide application from others, including possible competitors. Note this is also a high-risk strategy, requiring major investment in R&D to develop and launch such innovations.

Corporate social responsibility and sustainability

There has also been a major change in corporate behaviour with respect to corporate social responsibility (CSR), the responsibility of business towards society (Pedersen, 2010), a topic we shall return to in Chapter 13 (➤Chapter 13).

Some firms, such as National Australia Bank, have published detailed reports on their CSR commitments and performance (NAB, 2009), obviously sharing Heal's view that such behaviour has a favourable impact on a variety of relevant audiences (Heal, 2008).

Concerns over global warming have led many companies to examine their energy usage, for example, and in turn to implement programmes to reduce carbon emissions. Some airlines now ask customers, when they book their tickets, whether they would like to pay extra for carbon offset schemes to ameliorate the carbon emissions associated with their flights. Energy companies are particularly sensitive on the emission issue. The French oil company Total, for example, has begun to make progress in reducing carbon emissions. Total has a broad range of CSR activities, and has committed itself to a code of ethics and integrity, employee health and safety, training and education, anti-discrimination, improving water quality, biomass and solar technologies and a wide range of other activities (Total, 2008).

Governments are also taking a variety of approaches to encourage better CSR performance. The British Upper House, for example, modified a climate change bill so as to mandate the inclusion of greenhouse gas emissions data in company annual reports (Dickson, 2008). Indeed, the general trend is to hold firms increasingly accountable for what were once regarded as 'externalities' (Pigou, 1962). These costs, traditionally borne by society as a whole, must now be covered by the firm. Recycling of containers is now encouraged by deposit legislation in some countries. In Europe, manufacturers of appliances and automobiles must now code components to facilitate recycling and carry at least some of the costs associated with this.

The sentiment of public opinion on these issues has become an important consideration for firms, for those failing in their CSR performance attract negative publicity, as the 'concept' in practice below indicates.

Social responsibility *in practice* – emissions reporting

The UK magazine *Marketing* recently reported that Google, Burger King and the AA were among 250 big name brands that failed to disclose carbon emissions performance data. This is one of the key findings from Brand Emissions, the first annual survey of the carbon performance of 600 of the UK's biggest brands, which was released today. Other brands that failed to report included Channel 4, Dyson and Facebook.

At the other end of the scale were 'Brand Emissions Leaders', such as T-Mobile, BMW, British Airways, Abbey and Dell.

The leaders, who also include all of the 'big four' supermarkets and Marks & Spencer, were awarded the status for delivering carbon emissions reductions or being top ranked on emissions intensity in their sector, having emissions targets above the UK government's climate change committee and reporting carbon emissions in compliance with accepted international standards.

In other findings McDonald's, Harvey Nichols and Porsche were revealed as having no public emission reduction targets. Of those that reported their emissions, 122 (54 per cent), including Barclays, Sky and Ebay, increased them in 2008 (Charles, 2009).

> ### Community responsibility *in practice* – Thomas Cook
>
> We firmly believe we should play an active part in the communities where most of our people live and work. Thomas Cook has a tradition of encouraging charitable donations, and of supporting voluntary activity and fundraising by employees.
>
> In May 2008, a pioneering new children's hospital opened in London, thanks to ongoing fundraising by Thomas Cook employees and customers. The £2.3m Thomas Cook Children's Critical Care Centre at Kings College Hospital is the first of its kind in the UK, housing both Paediatric Intensive Care and Paediatric High Dependency units.
>
> (ThomasCook, 2009)

Of course, initial government attempts to encourage firms to change behaviour have not always gone smoothly. Australia, for example, has had to retract its proposed carbon trading scheme for the time being, while steel giant Arcelor-Mittal has received an estimated £1 billion bonus from the EU for carbon credits that it will not be using (Leake & Pancevski, 2009).

Overall, however, most firms have changed behaviour in a positive direction with respect to their CSR activities. Many, for example, have increased their emphasis on charitable activities. Thomas Cook plc, mentioned earlier in the chapter, has a long-standing commitment to such endeavours, covering cancer care, child care and health.

Deregulation and privatization

Privatization
The transfer or selling off of state-owned firms and organizations to private ownership.

Deregulation and **privatization** has occurred in many industries around the world, as governments have concluded that they do not do a particularly good job of running a business, or that regulation has impeded consumer welfare.

Industries such as electricity, gas, water supply, banking and finance, telecommunications, airlines, railroads and trucking have all witnessed significant change in many different countries. In virtually every case there has been an increase in competition in these industries, together with increased rates of innovation not only in the core products and services, but also in such areas as pricing and customer service. Of course, after the global financial crisis of 2008/09, new constraints were placed on the financial industry, but no one has suggested re-regulating the many other industries that were freed from excessive regulation.

These changes have dramatically affected the pecking order in many industries, but have also introduced many new players, who do not use the same 'rules'. They have required commensurate changes in supervision, for few governments are prepared to privatize monopolies without safeguards for consumer welfare. Dealing with these arrangements has often created a new arena of competition, with some firms notably more adept in coping with the regulatory framework than others.

> **Challenge of strategic management**
>
> During the financial crisis of 2008/09 the role of governments in many countries expanded considerably as they attempted to rescue their financial system and prevent its collapse. Do you think that this means a much greater role for governments in future, with governments adopting a more interventionist approach?

 ## 1.8 SUMMARY

The foregoing discussion is replete with implications for the practice of strategic management. It is imperative that the firm adds value for shareholders and other stakeholders, but a new managerial mindset will be required. Good strategic management will require much more flexibility and creativity. As firms are becoming more knowledge-intensive, so the management of intellectual (human) capital becomes critical. Managers must be skilled at developing commitment – even passion – among their increasingly diverse workforce, for if human capital is the key to future success, then marshalling and managing these capabilities to their fullest potential will be essential.

New skills will be required to cope with the changing world. Creative strategic thinking and learning will be central to developing new business strategies in a world in which firm resources and capabilities are not fixed but must be continually developed.

Further, the very boundaries of firms and industries will be vague and changing. Questions such as how these boundaries should evolve, which activities should the firm engage in, which should be purchased from the market, what are the core activities of the firm, what it does better than its competitors, will be ongoing challenges to managers. New styles of organizations, emphasizing learning, anticipation and quick response, will predominate. Processes, teamwork and external networks will be constantly reviewed.

An uncertain environment makes forecasting more difficult, increasing the need for flexibility. The competitive landscape is complex and dynamic, and this too requires flexibility as well as speed and innovation. Managers need to manage both stability and change: to manage for the present and invest in the future at the same time.

Above all, we should recognize that strategic management is a process, and that this process must incorporate ideas on motivation, structure, processes, incentives and leadership. To neglect the human side of the enterprise and to focus solely on analytic tools is a crucial mistake, given the prospective scenarios of the twenty-first century.

VIEW FROM THE TOP

ELECTROLUX

Hit by the worldwide recession, Electrolux results for 2008 were very disappointing. In the words of Hans Stråberg, President and Chief Executive Officer, 'We had completed a very tough year and expected a continued challenging 2009. We had just taken comprehensive measures to adapt our costs to the weak market demand through decisions to decrease the number of employees. The difficult market was also the reason the AGM decided not to distribute any dividend for 2008 to our shareholders.'

Nonetheless, Stråberg was able to report that 2009 was 'one of the best ever for Electrolux . . . all our operations have improved their earnings and maintained their sales at the same time as demand has dramatically declined.' This improvement in earnings happened despite the fact that in 2009 the North American market for core appliances declined by 10 per cent and Europe by 7 per cent. Indeed, Stråberg pointed out that the North American market had lost a quarter of its size since its 2006 peak while Europe was down 15 per cent since 2007.

How could Electrolux do so well in an environment that can be described as very challenging, with increased competition at both the top end and the bottom end of the market (Knudsen, 2006)? Stråberg's answer was simple: 'Our results show we have the right strategy . . . the primary explanation for the strong development in 2009 is that we succeeded in areas that are strategically important for Electrolux: new products, strong brands and cost efficiencies.' He explained that a strong product offering of more advanced and expensive products improved the mix. These innovative products, combined with investments in the Electrolux brand and cost efficiencies, paid off. He added: 'after many years of continuously declining prices, we managed to increase prices in Europe at the beginning of 2009, at the same time as we maintained our price position in the American market. There are many factors, both coincidental and structural, that have contributed to this positive development, but it is fundamentally crucial to have a strong brand to successfully implement price increases.'

Stråberg concluded by saying, 'the result for 2009 is a proof that our strategy to increase the pace of new product offers, invest in marketing and implement efficiencies in our production is working even in an economic downturn. In 2010, we will further strengthen the Electrolux brand position, which will lead to increased marketing investments. We will continue to develop innovative products that consumers prefer and are willing to pay higher prices for.

'We still have more to do before we reach our target of an average operating margin of 6 per cent over one business cycle, and the very strong cash flow for 2009 has provided us with a balance sheet that gives us opportunities to utilize future business opportunities.'

The Electrolux example dramatically illustrates the power of strategy in determining superior company performance. Stråberg demonstrated an understanding that success depends not on one factor, but many. As CEO, he has demonstrated the ability to both manage for today and for tomorrow. Reducing the number of employees or not paying a dividend are not easy decisions. But decisions such as these are often essential to maintain current financial viability. At the same time he is managing for the future, continuing to invest in intangible assets such as brand equity and strengthening R&D and new product development. Due to his vision and leadership in strategy development and implementation, Electrolux seems well placed to succeed in the future.

Sources: Electrolux Annual Reports, 2008, 2009 (Electrolux, 2010)

MTP LIMITED

Ravi Shastri, the CEO of MTP Ltd, a small Irish firm, was contemplating the future of his firm and what strategy the firm should adopt. Ravi, together with two other partners, had founded MTP in Dublin in 2006, and revenue had grown to reach about €4 million in 2009. The future held promise, despite the financial turbulence of the past few years, but here were some difficult decisions to be made. Ravi had studied information technology at the Indian Institute of Technology in Bombay and then graduated with an MBA, majoring in marketing and information technology at the Smurfit Graduate Business School at University College Dublin. Following graduation, he then worked for ten years in the IT industry with Oracle and in logistics with TNT (Ireland). While with TNT he became aware of the need for accurate and timely temperature control in storage and transport to ensure chilled and frozen products did not suffer from deterioration.

Supermarkets were concerned that such chilled and frozen products arrived at their outlets in good condition, and this was an important element in the choice of a supermarket by consumers. Food regulators were also concerned. They wanted a complete history of the product, including transport, both to prevent any outbreak of disease and to provide a trail if disease did break out.

In conjunction with two friends from Dublin, Ravi developed an inexpensive system which enabled this to be done. When the system was installed in a transport vehicle, all data could be transmitted to a logistics centre, included data on the location of the vehicle via a GPS system, which aided in fleet management.

After developing and testing a prototype, partly with the assistance of TNT, Ravi and his two partners launched the firm in 2006. Initially they concentrated their efforts on food distributors, firms responsible for transporting fresh, chilled and frozen foods in Ireland, providing a temperature record which was valued by supermarkets and other retailers. With some funding from a local bank, in the form of a personal loan, MTP recruited several staff responsible for sales and marketing and for technical development. Their first staff member in sales and marketing, Sally Hill, had worked for a large Irish supermarket chain, and was very familiar with the industry. Part of the MTP's business strategy was to develop a 'pull' strategy, whereby supermarkets applied pressure on logistics firms to provide good data on temperature control, which the supermarket in turn could use in discussions with various food regulators.

MINI-CASE

As they continued to grow in Ireland, Ravi was aware that there were opportunities to expand in the wider EU, but thought that any decision on these could be delayed until they had reached saturation in the Irish market. The necessity to reach a decision on this was heightened when Sally showed Ravi an article in a major trade journal. The article reported that a major American firm, US Logistics, was developing a similar system and undertaking field tests in the US, and that they expected to launch globally within two years. Sally was very strong in her view that MTP had to enter the major EU countries prior to this; otherwise they would be struggling to catch up with US Logistics. While Ravi could see the logic in Sally's argument, he was concerned about the funding – where would this come from? While MTP was still not cash positive, it hoped to be so in two years' time, when it would be easier to raise additional capital.

As Ravi spent the next day thinking about the possibilities, fate intervened. He received a phone call from Loire Systems, a small French consulting company that specialized in logistics, but with no experience with temperature monitoring. Loire had become familiar with MTP, and was interested in exploring a joint venture with them in Europe. Taking advantage of some cheap airfares, Ravi decided to fly to Lyons to discuss a possible arrangement with Henri Vacroux, the CEO of Loire. They had a successful discussion, basically explaining to each other the details of their respective firms, how they could possibly cooperate in France, Germany and Italy, and what each would expect out of the joint venture. Essentially MTP would provide technical support, requiring two to three staff members to be located in Lyons, while Loire would be responsible for sales and marketing. However, there had not been any detailed discussions on finances.

Ravi was in a very positive mood for his flight back to Dublin. However, this did not last for very long. At a lay-over at De Gaulle airport, he ran into a classmate of his from UCD, Ned O'Reilly. After some polite chit-chat, Ravi told Ned what he had been discussing in Lyons. After listening for a while, Ned really took the floor. Ned wanted to know how much Ravi and his colleagues really knew about the continental European market, who were the major customers and retailers, where they were located, what were the regulations governing them? Did these vary from country to country? He then asked Ravi whether any of his team had any knowledge of Loire and what experience they had in managing joint ventures – to which Ravi had to reply in the negative. As his flight was being called, Ravi received a call on his mobile phone from Sally – US Logistics had put out a press release indicating that they had brought forward their plans to enter the EU market, including Ireland. They now expected to enter within the next six months.

QUESTIONS

1 If you were Ravi, what would be your vision for MTP?

2 Should MTP attempt a strategic alliance, or should they instead concentrate on the Irish market?

3 How would such a European venture be funded?

4 What new skills and capabilities would be required in the firm should they proceed with the joint venture?

5 Would Ravi be better off to approach US Logistics with an offer to sell the business to them?

REVIEW QUESTIONS

1 Identify the strategic decisions taken by a major firm with which you are familiar over the last five years.

2 Compare and contrast the strategies of two firms from the same sector that you are familiar with. What are the key differences? What was the impact of these differences on the performance of the firms?

3 Comment on the suggestion that management makes no difference to the economic performance of a firm.

4 Provide examples of 'strategies for today' and 'strategies for tomorrow' for a major firm with which you are familiar.

5 What are the trends that could influence a firm to adopt a more 'market-based' form of economic exchange?

6 Show how the strategic management concepts of context, strategy and firm characteristics have led to superior economic performance for a global firm with which you are familiar.

7 Anthony Habgood, former CEO and Executive Chairman of Bunzl, a UK FTSE 100 company, defined strategy as 'fundamentally I believe that strategy is about "beating" the competition. It means getting yourself into a position where you are fundamentally ahead. You know that you are winning if you are gaining market share from your competitors whilst achieving better returns. If you can succeed in doing that, you truly have some kind of competitive advantage. Strategy is also about getting into the right market segments – there are no long-term benefits in beating a competitor in a dying market!'

In the text, we defined strategy as 'the common theme underlying a set of strategic decisions'.

Which of these competing views do you find the most convincing? Why? What do you see as the limitations of each?

REFERENCES

Abell, D. F. (1999) Competing today while preparing for tomorrow. *Sloan Management Review, 40*(3), 73–82.

Ailles, I. (2004) *Revolutionising performance through co-sourcing and transformation.* Paper presented at the OutsourceWorld. www.outsource-world.com/london/conferenceprog_2004.htm.

Ambrosini, V., Bowman, C. & Collier, N. (2009) Dynamic capabilities: An exploration of how firms renew their resource base. *British Journal of Management, 20,* S9–S24.

Baghai, M., Coley, S. & White, D. (1999) *The Alchemy of Growth.* London: Orion.

Baraldi, E. (2008) Strategy in industrial networks: Experiences from IKEA. *California Management Review, 50*(4), 99–126.

Barney, J. B. (1991) Firm resources and sustained competitive advantage. *Journal of Management, Greenwich, 17*(1), 99–120.

Bou, J. C. & Satorra, A. (2007) The persistence of abnormal returns at industry and firm levels: Evidence from Spain. *Strategic Management Journal, 28*(7), 707–722.

Bowman, E. H. & Helfat, C. E. (2001) Does corporate strategy matter? *Strategic Management Journal,* *22*(1), 1–23.

Bryan, L. L. & Farrell, D. (2009) Leading through uncertainty. *Mckinsey Quarterly,* (1), 24–42.

Caves, R. E. (1998) Industrial organisation and new findings on the turnover and mobility of firms. *Journal of Economic Literature, 36*(4), 1947–1983.

Chandler, A. D. (1962) *Strategy and Structure: Chapters in the History of the American Industrial Enterprise.* Cambridge, MA: MIT Press.

Charles, G. (2009) Big brands fail to disclose carbon-emission data. *Marketing Magazine,* 25 November.

Coase, R. H. (1937) The nature of the firm. *Economica, 4,* 386–405.

Collis, D. J., & Montgomery, C. A. (1998) *Corporate Strategy: A Resource-Based Approach.* Boston: Irwin/McGraw-Hill.

ConsumerReports (2007, March) Airline maintenance. *Money_Airline Safety.* www.consumerreports. org/cro/money/travel/airline-safety-3-07/airline-maintenance/0307_air_flight.htm.

Cox, M. (2002) Rates of penetration of new technologies. *Federal Reserve Bank of Dallas.*

Crane, A. T. (2010) Reward for patience. Retrieved 13 May 2010, www.breakingviews.com/2010/ 01/19/kraftfinancing.aspx?sg=nytimes.

Crooks, E. (2009) RWE chief fired up over carbon. *The Financial Times,* 10 December, p. 16.

CSL CartoonStock (2010) Restructuring cartoon 1. *Restructuring cartoons.* www.cartoonstock. com/directory/r/restructuring.asp.

Day, J. D. & Wendler, J. C. (1998) The new economics of organisation. *McKinsey Quarterly,* (1), 4–18.

Dickson, P. (2008) Carbon emissions disclosure good for business. *The Daily Telegraph,* 28 April.

DNA (2010) YouTube marks fifth birthday by announcing two billion views per day. *Sci / Tech / Report,* 19 May. www.dnaindia.com/scitech/report_youtube-marks-fifth-birthday-by-announcing-two-billion-views-per-day_1384914.

Drucker, P. F. (1992) The new society of organisations. *Harvard Business Review* (September/October), 95–104.

Drucker, P. F. (1995) *Managing in a Time of Great Change.* New York: Truman Talley Books/Dutton.

Easterby-Smith, M., Lyles, M. A. & Peteraf, M. A. (2009) Dynamic capabilities: Current debates and future directions. *British Journal of Management, 20,* S1–S8.

Economist, T. (2009) Managing in the Fog. *The Economist,* 28 February, pp. 61–62.

Electrolux (2010) Annual report , 5 March 2009.

Finch, J. (2009) Thomas Cook's majority owner Arcandor files for bankruptcy. *Guardian,* 9 June. www.guardian.co.uk/business/2009/jun/09/thomas-cook-arcandor-bankruptcy.

Garten, J. (2001) *The Mind of the CEO.* London: Allen Lane.

Heal, G. (2008) *When Principles Pay: Corporate Social Responsibility and the Bottom Line.* New York: Columbia Business School Publishing.

Helft, M. (2009) YouTube in a quest to suggest more, so users search less. *The New York Times,* 31 December, p. B1.

Jarzabkowski, P. (2005) *Strategy as Practice, An Activity-Based Approach.* London: Sage.

Jensen, M. (1990) The market for corporate control. In C. W. Smith (ed.), *The Modern Theory of Corporate Finance.* New York: McGraw-Hill.

Knudsen, T. R. (2006) Escaping the middle-market trap: An interview with the CEO of Electrolux. *Mckinsey Quarterly,* (4), 72–70.

Leake, J. & Pancevski, B. (2009) Carbon credits bring Lakshmi Mittal £1 bn bonanza. *The Sunday Times,* 6 December. http://business.timesonline.co.uk/tol/business/industry_sectors/industrials/article 6945991.ece?%2522.

Learned, E. P., Christensen, C. R., Andrews, K. R. & Guth, W. (1969) *Business Policy*. Homewood, IL: Irwin.

Markides, C. C. (1999) A dynamic view of strategy. *Sloan Management Review, 40*(3), 55–63.

Mortished, C. (2009) Corporate giants forced to move downmarket in face of recession. *The Times,* 8 May, p. 46.

NAB (2009) Annual corporate responsibility review. Retrieved 13 May 2010, www.nabgroup.com/vgnmedia/downld/2009cr.pdf.

NewsCorp (2009) Annual report. Retrieved 13 May 2010, www.newscorp.com/investor_relations/annual_report_2009.

NewsCorp (2010a) Stock information. *Investor Relations*. Retrieved 13 May 2010.

NewsCorp (2010b) Stock prices. Retrieved 13 January 2010.

Pedersen, E. R. (2010) Modelling CSR: How managers understand the responsibilities of business toward society. *Journal of Business Ethics, 91*(2), 155–166.

Pigou, A. C. (1962) *The Economics of Welfare*. London: Macmillan.

Porter, M. E. (1980) *Competitive Strategy*. New York: Free Press.

Porter, M. E. (1996) What is strategy? *Harvard Business Review* (November–December 1996), 61–78.

Priem, R. L. & Butler, J. E. (2001) Is the resource-based 'view' a useful perspective for strategic management research? *Academy of Management Review, 26*(1), 22–40.

Roberts, J. (2004) *The Modern Firm: Organisational Design for Performance and Growth*. Oxford: Oxford University Press.

Rugman, A. M. & Verbeke, A. (2002) Edith Penrose's contribution to the resource-based view of strategic management. *Strategic Management Journal, 23*(8), 769–780.

Safizadeh, M. H., Field, J. M. & Ritzman, L. P. (2008) Sourcing practices and boundaries of the firm in the financial services industry. *Strategic Management Journal, 29*(1), 79–91.

Selznick, P. (1957) *Leadership in Administration*. New York: Harper & Row.

Shawcross, W. (1997) *Murdoch, The Making of a Media Empire*. New York: Touchstone.

Smith, D. (2009) MySpace shrinks as Facebook, Twitter and Bebo grab its users. *The Observer*, 29 March, www.guardian.co.uk/technology/2009/mar/29/myspace-facebook-bebo-twitter.

ThomasCook (2007) Home page. www.thomascookgroup.com.

ThomasCook (2009) Supporting charities and communities. Retrieved 12 January 2010, http://csr.thomascookgroup.co.uk/tcg/csr/home_communities.

Total (2008) Corporate social responsibility. Retrieved 12 January 2010, www.total.com/MEDIAS/MEDIAS_INFOS/1044/EN/Total-csr-en-2008.pdf.

Uyemura, D. G., Kantor, C. C. & Pettit, J. M. (1996) EVA for banks: Value creation, risk measurement and profitability measurement. *Journal of Applied Corporate Finance, 9*(2), 94–114.

Williamson, O. E. (1975) *Markets and Hierarchies: Analysis and Antitrust Implications*. New York: The Free Press.

Yang, L. (2009) America's best and worst wealth creators. Retrieved 13 January 2010, www.eva dimensions.com.

LIBRARY, UNIVERSITY OF CHESTER

For a range of further resources supporting this chapter, please visit the companion website for *Strategic Management* at www.routledge.com/cw/fitzroy.

CHAPTER 2

STRATEGIC MANAGEMENT FUNDAMENTALS

LEARNING OBJECTIVES

Upon completing this chapter you should be able to:

1 Provide examples of strategic decisions.

2 Illustrate what constitutes a strategy for a firm.

3 Describe the complexity of the strategic management task.

4 Design and/or modify a firm's business model.

5 Summarize the managerial process involved in strategy development and implementation, including major impediments.

6 Articulate the concept of value for different stakeholders of the firm.

SHELL, NESTLÉ

In January 2004 Shell astounded world markets by announcing that it had to re-categorize a staggering one-fifth of its proven oil reserves, approximately four billion barrels of oil, enough to supply the world for a total of 50 days (White, 2009).

In March 2005, newly appointed CEO Mr Jeroen Van der Veer made several changes. First, Van der Veer pushed through a major, simplifying reorganization to overcome the complexity of listing the separate components of the firm on different stock markets. He then set about trying to increase production and cut costs. While he did not cut costs as rapidly as desired by some commentators, Shell was in a better position when he left in June 2009. Second, he had to both find new sources of oil and invest in more unconventional sources – for example, the $18bn investment in Pearl Plant in Qatar, which converts natural gas to

liquids (GTL) such as diesel, and $14bn expansion of the Athabasca Oil Sands project in Canada. These projects, having devoured cash for nearly a decade, are now coming on stream and Shell is likely to be the fastest growing of all oil majors (Crooks, 2010).

Despite the apparent success of strategic and operational changes initiated by his predecessor, in July 2009 the incoming CEO Peter Voser also faced considerable challenges. Most of the known oil reserves are located in OPEC countries, Russia or in very deep water. The governments of easy-to-reach oil reserves in the Middle East, Russia and Venezuela are determined to maintain control over these important strategic assets so they are difficult for international oil companies to access. The remaining oil reserves lie deep under oceans and are challenging to explore. The BP Deepwater Horizon disaster is likely to make matters worse. It means far greater regulation, making exploration more expensive and a greater reluctance by countries to offer exploration licences. These changes are likely to result in a different business model with a patchwork quilt of activities in which smaller national and larger international oil companies must work together in new partnerships. Oil majors also need to reappraise the balance between the proven oil and gas reserves they hold. Shell is betting on gas because the known reserves are much larger than oil and technologies such as that used in the Pearl Plant enable conversion of natural gas to fuels. It is also possible to liquefy gas for transportation. Hence the acquisition of $4.7bn of assets from US gas producer East Resources in May 2010.

Of course Shell also has to effectively manage its current operations. The glut in oil-refining capacity and low margins produced by petrol stations has led Shell to sell two refineries and full- or part-stakes in as many as 9,000 petrol stations worldwide, part of a total of $8 billion of assets in non-core and low margin business areas. Voser also announced a major restructuring plan 'Transition 2009' in September 2009. In the first phase of the restructuring, Shell was able to reduce costs by $3.5 billion per year, partly due to the elimination of 150 of its 750 corporate executives and a total of 7,000 corporation wide (Anon, 2010).

Shell's strategy can be compared with that of Nestlé in the food and confectionary industry. Growth and margins in the confectionary industry are likely to come under increasing pressure because of health concerns and rising prices of raw materials, particularly cocoa. Some major confectionary companies have diversified within the overall confectionary market. Mars, for example, acquired chewing gum company Wrigley. In contrast, Nestlé has moved into the science-based nutritional food market, a global market growing at 6–8 per cent annually and worth $16bn in 2010. Demographic changes in Western countries mean a significant rise in the over-sixties, suggesting that this growth rate is likely to be sustained.

Nestlé entered this market through acquisition of Novartis's medical nutrition business, Jenny Craig, the Australian cereal business Uncle Toby's, and the iconic US baby food brand Gerber. In August 2010 it acquired Vitaflo, a small medical nutrition company in Liverpool, England. In September 2010 Nestlé announced plans to invest £320 million over the next decade to support the creation of stand-alone health science business to tackle obesity and chronic disease (Nestlé, 2010). This would be a pioneering industry sitting between food and pharmaceuticals that will develop products to combat such diseases as diabetes, heart problems and Alzheimer's. Some analysts are sceptical of Nestlé's ability to break into this area. They note the time it has taken arch rival Danone of France to see any payback from similar investments because of tougher regulatory standards. Nonetheless, Nestlé's transition to a nutrition, health and wellness company continues.

As this recent history of Shell and Nestlé illustrates, in today's fast-changing environment, firms cannot be complacent. Instead, strategy and many firm attributes must change to deal with the external changes they face. Firm success is increasingly transient, as is its basis. Shell was faced simultaneously with the need to become more flexible and fast-moving, to rebuild its reserves and production, while also cutting costs. Nestlé was faced with slow growth in its historic markets, forcing it to explore major diversification, which would require substantial investment, incurring both market risk and financial risk. These examples illustrate the complexity of the challenges facing CEOs of major firms, for these changes took place against a backdrop of great financial uncertainty and the greatest worldwide recession since the great depression of the 1930s.

CHAPTER OVERVIEW

This chapter explores in some detail the fundamentals underlying strategic management. In the preceding chapter we distinguished strategic decisions, strategy and strategic management, and we commence by exploring these in depth. We first examine the characteristics of strategic decisions – those decisions which have the feature of affecting the future of the business. Such decisions, for example, require a long-term focus and major resource commitments, which distinguishes them from more tactical, short-term decisions. This discussion leads us to an exploration of the distinguishing characteristics of strategy. Is the strategy incremental or revolutionary? Can major improvements in value creation be accomplished by incremental strategies or must they of necessity be revolutionary? One feature of strategy which is given emphasis is the need to build new capabilities within the firm. In a rapidly changing world, the basis of success in the future is likely to be different from what it was in the past, illustrating the complexity of the strategic management tasks.

We then discuss the features of strategic management. In the text we take a managerial perspective, with an emphasis on management as well as strategy. The critical task for strategic management is to create organizations which in turn create value for their numerous stakeholders. For this to occur, the ability to create and manage change is essential. These sections are followed by a brief discussion of **business models** – the method by which a business unit generates revenue, and creates and captures value for itself. For example, does Shell earn its profits from its upstream activities or from its downstream retail activities? We then examine some of the impediments in the strategy development process, paying particular attention to outdated **mental models** – the set of assumptions held by managers and/or employees about the firm, its industry and environment, and the nature of competition.

Reflecting the increasing number and diversity of constituencies with an interest in the firm and its activities, we examine the major stakeholders and the possible conflicting values held by each. Our View from the Top example explores the business model of MasterCard and whether this model is different from that of Visa. The mini-case which concludes the chapter, Argus Technology Ltd, provides an opportunity to apply the concepts developed in the chapter.

Business model
The method by which a business unit generates revenue, and creates and captures value for itself.

Mental model
The set of assumptions held by managers and/or employees about the firm, its industry and environment, and the nature of competition.

2.1 INTRODUCTION

Both firms in the previous example have demonstrated that the task of strategic management has become increasingly difficult, due to greater turbulence, complexity and competitiveness of the firm's environment. To cope with this change, the firm must continually innovate and re-invent itself if it is to survive and prosper. Consequently, the firm will be in a state of continuous change. But the firm is always under pressure for performance in both financial and product markets. Here, then, is a fundamental challenge of strategic management. Throughout the ongoing change process, managers must ensure that the firm delivers current value, earning a return greater than its cost of capital, as well as establishing the strategies and organizational architecture required to create future value. To achieve these outcomes in a fast-changing environment, managers must increase the capability of an organization to deal with change, an agenda requiring formal planning and analysis as well as intuition and judgement.

Environmental turbulence represents both an opportunity and a threat. Changes are threatening, since they will cause customers and competitors to behave differently. Firms must actively respond to the external changes over which they have no control. At the same time, firms can innovate, bringing change to the market to consolidate and/or improve their position. A significant amount of marketplace change results from the actions of firms in that market. When a firm invents new products or processes, adopts a new channel such as the Internet or expands globally, the effects reverberate through its industry, affecting the behaviour of both customers and competitors. Change in the firm will be both reactive and proactive, but only proactive change manifests managerial leadership.

<table>
<tr><td>

LEARNING OBJECTIVE 1

Provide examples of strategic decisions.

</td></tr>
</table>

2.2 CHARACTERISTICS OF STRATEGIC DECISIONS

> *Strategic decisions are those that affect the long-term well-being of the firm under consideration.*

There will be a relatively small number of decisions that shape the firm's future development. What makes these decisions and actions 'strategic' is their likely future impact on the entire organization and its ability to create and capture value, and the fact that these decisions are almost irrevocable: they are very difficult to reverse once implemented.

In our example of News Corporation from Chapter 1, we can identify several such strategic decisions – launching a fourth TV network in the US, purchasing Twentieth Century-Fox and acquiring Dow Jones. In the example above, Shell's recent strategic decisions have included selling off its onshore assets in Nigeria and increasing its focus on Qatar.

Figure 2.1 depicts four characteristics of strategic decisions, which we now review.

Create value

First, strategic decisions must be taken with the goal of creating value for the firm. Of course, some decisions may not create value, while value in any case may not accrue until sometime in the future. However, value creation involves more than the generation of sustainable competitive advantage. While creation of a competitive advantage is a necessary condition for creating value, it is not a sufficient condition. A competitive advantage is an attribute possessed by the firm and not by its competitors, such as a low-cost structure or offering customers a benefit not offered by other firms. Nonetheless, firms could have an advantage that does not translate into superior financial performance. Industry structure may be such that suppliers or customers capture the benefits of the firm's competitive advantage. In personal computers almost all industry profit goes to Intel and Microsoft, with relatively little for the computer manufacturers. For this reason it is essential that strategic decisions are

Chapter 12   seen as those that create value for the firm (➤Chapter 12).

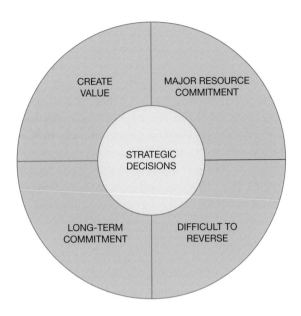

Figure 2.1 Characteristics of strategic decisions

Major resource commitment

A second characteristic of strategic decisions is that they involve major resource commitments by the firm, including acquisitions and **divestments**.

Acquisition *in practice* – Roche

In March 2009, the Swiss pharmaceutical firm Roche succeeded in its bid for the 44 per cent of shares it did not own in Genentech, a Californian biotechnology firm at a cost of $47 billion or $95 per share. Roche is hoping that Genentech's cancer treatment drug, Avastin, will become the world's best-selling drug over the next few years. Only a week prior, Genentech's independent directors had rejected an $86.5 per share bid from Roche. It has been estimated that the acquisition would result in annual cost savings of $800 million per year, and allow Genentech to compete globally. However, concerns were expressed as to whether Genentech's entrepreneurial culture would be maintained after the takeover, and whether a significant number of key staff would leave (Jack & Simonian, 2009).

The point we are making is that strategic decisions are about significant change to the composition of the firm, in terms of the products and services it provides, the markets it serves and/or the skills and capabilities required to accomplish the change. What is major obviously depends on the size of the firm: a strategic decision for Roche will usually involve more money than for a smaller pharmaceutical firm. A decision is clearly strategic when it has the potential to put the future of the company at risk.

Difficult to reverse

The third characteristic of strategic decisions is that they are difficult to reverse once made. The German firm Siemens is involved in a number of engineering businesses. It would be difficult for Siemens to drop its long-standing interests in engineering and start up as a fast food firm. History matters! At the same time, while strategic decisions may be difficult to reverse, firms need to maintain a degree of flexibility, since future developments in the world are increasingly unpredictable. This requirement is often manifest in a desire to delay commitment to enter new businesses. Yet if delay is excessive, others will seize the opportunity.

Long-term commitment

Strategic decisions reflect a long-term commitment by the firm. A firm such as Royal Dutch Shell has a long time horizon for its exploration processes, although firms in other industries may have much shorter horizons. But one of the essential features of strategic decisions is that they are concerned with the future, and must have a long-term focus and commitment. Such decisions are not simply a continuation of the present since, with strategy nothing is fixed: everything is variable. A strategic decision may require changing the culture of a firm, recognizing that this is a multi-year commitment.

What is considered 'strategic', and what time horizon is adopted will depend on the speed at which markets and technologies are evolving.

These long-term considerations are not just to do with the 'old' economy. Even in a fast-moving industry such as consumer electronics, developing an innovative product requires both persistence and substantial funding. It has been estimated that the development of the Kindle by Amazon took five years and cost in the order of $200 million ('Kindle 2 cost analysis', 2009).

The firm may try to make a strategic decision 'incremental', where only a portion of the plant is built on the understanding that capacity can be expanded later. But there are limits to this approach: the new plant cannot be of such a scale that efficiencies are non-existent.

Strategic decision *in practice* – Vale do Rio Doce

In industries such as resources, airlines, steel or plastics, strategic decisions on current and future capacity levels are necessary. In these industries a very long time horizon is required, for it may take 15 years to find, test and develop a new oilfield. For a company such as Vale, the Brazilian mineral resources firm, the decision to commit current resources to exploration activities must be based on assumptions about the likely demand and price of iron ore and steel, and the nature of competition and costs over the next 15 years.

Indeed, the ultimate success or failure of many biotechnology firms will not be known for many years. Strategic decisions often exhibit the characteristics of a large bet!

These examples highlight a difficulty with strategic decisions; namely, getting this long-term commitment from management. High managerial turnover and the subjective nature of valuing outcomes of strategic decisions exacerbate obtaining such commitment. Strategic decisions are generally very difficult to evaluate on strictly quantitative grounds. Despite valiant efforts to forecast and develop pro formas, the future is often too uncertain for reliable forecasts. If there is a senior management change just after a strategic decision, the new managers may well try to reverse it, reflecting their need to make a perceived mark on the firm. Furthermore, strategic decisions usually generate net cash outflows before net cash inflows. Do managers have the courage to continue implementing decisions when cash flow is negative and the financial markets are demanding greater short-term shareholder value?

2.3 CHARACTERISTICS OF STRATEGY

LEARNING OBJECTIVE 2

Illustrate what constitutes a strategy for a firm.

Strategy is the common theme underlying a set of strategic decisions.

This definition emphasizes the holistic nature of strategy; it is not a single decision such as an acquisition and is similar to the definition provided by Mintzberg of strategy as 'a pattern in a stream of actions' (Mintzberg, 1990).

As we noted earlier, strategy can be both deceptively simple and extremely complex. For example, the early success of Microsoft appears simple – it was able to get its operating system, MS DOS, installed on most IBM personal computers. However, this would not have guaranteed continued success since there were a number of other operating systems extant, including one developed by IBM itself. Microsoft strategy required a continual stream of decisions in a turbulent and dynamic environment. Of the many software firms contending for leadership in the so-called PC revolution, only Microsoft was successful in managing this stream of decisions; many others disappeared. Strategy requires both detailed understanding and the ability to develop a response that in retrospect is likely to be viewed as obvious.

As with a strategic decision, the purpose of strategy is to create value for the firm and its stakeholders, for which a competitive advantage is a necessary but not sufficient condition. Firm performance needs both a strategy and the means to put that strategy in place. In other words, the firm needs to excel at both strategy development and strategy execution. Strategy is not just a good idea; it is making that idea happen (➤Chapter 10). So strategy also implies that the organization should possess the capabilities appropriate for implementing the chosen strategy, as well as a strong performance culture, with clear accountability and incentives linked to performance.

Chapter 10

Firms that are regarded as winners adopt strategies that are different from those of their competitors. Yet in many industries we see strategy convergence. All firms seem to adopt the same strategy and differences between competitors are minuscule. Strategy differentiation is essential for success, but again it is a necessary but not sufficient condition. When companies

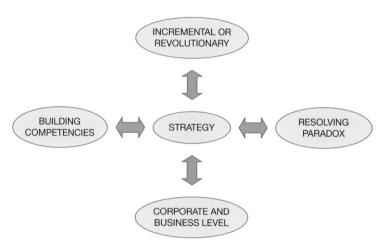

Figure 2.2 Characteristics of strategy

simply copy the leader, value is destroyed for all firms, including the leader. Lack of strategy differentiation in an industry leads to lower industry margins (Natterman, 2000). Thus strategy requires searching for new sources of advantage, inventing new rules and new games to become unique and create wealth.

We now review some characteristics of strategy, the common theme that links decisions together, as illustrated in Figure 2.2, above.

Incremental or revolutionary strategy

Incremental strategies
Strategies that manage current activities for high value.

Revolutionary strategies
Strategies that successfully create major change in the marketplace.

Legacy assets
The historic assets, both tangible and intangible, owned by the firm.

Two contrasting views of strategy are the incremental and the revolutionary. The difference is not merely a distinction between a short term and a long term. The two concepts are fundamentally different ways to create value. **Incremental strategies** involve managing current activities for high value. **Revolutionary** (radical) **strategies** are about successfully creating major change in the marketplace. Successful implementation of each of these strategies will involve innovation, which is the key determinant in establishing growth and performance in a rapidly changing world (Barsh *et al.*, 2008).

Financial analysts often divide incremental strategies into two components. First is the estimate of the net present value of cash flows from **legacy assets**, the historic assets, both tangible and intangible, owned by the firm, on the basis of no change in strategy.

Second is the estimated cash flow from growth opportunities realizable from these assets, such as market expansion (R. Gupta, 1998). We see both of these as incremental since they focus primarily on achieving competitive superiority through better management of current capabilities. Revolutionary strategies introduce major new products or services for which there was no pre-existing market. They necessitate developing significant new capabilities, but, if successful, generate significant increases in firm value. The three-way distinction is shown in Figure 2.3.

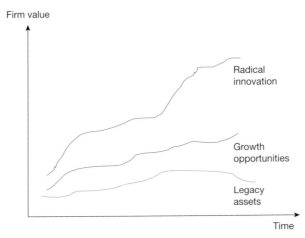

Figure 2.3 Value components for a firm

Radical innovation is more likely to create significant new wealth than continuous improvement, albeit with higher levels of risk. This risk may, however, be reduced through processes that facilitate rapid learning and adoption of low-cost, low-risk experiments. Incremental strategy also has a risk – the risk that the firm is made obsolete by successful innovators. Incremental and revolutionary approaches are not mutually exclusive. Successful firms undertake both types of innovation at the same time.

An alternative classification system is provided by the terms 'exploration' and 'exploitation' to describe alternative approaches to firm strategy (A. K. Gupta *et al.*, 2006). **Exploitation** is strategy which builds on the firm's existing capabilities, technologies and products. It typically involves themes such as efficiency and incremental development. **Exploration** as a strategy is the development of fundamentally new approaches and capabilities which may lead to the emergence of major new industries.

In our view, firms which are successful in the long term must do both, a synthesis which appears possible to achieve (Jansen *et al.*, 2008), although there is some evidence that firms engage in too little strategy of an exploratory nature (Uotila *et al.*, 2009).

We should not introduce these strategy distinctions without also considering the firm's external context and, in particular, its markets. Markets are complex systems, comprising

Exploitation
A strategy which builds on the firm's existing capabilities, technologies and products. It typically involves themes such as efficiency and incremental development.

Exploration
A strategy is the development of fundamentally new approaches and capabilities which may lead to the emergence of major new industries.

Challenge of strategic management

It is generally considered that major improvements in wealth creation can only occur when firms develop a revolutionary strategy, which involves 'exploring' or developing new capabilities which in turn lead to the emergence of major new industries. Yet few firms seem capable of achieving this. In your view, is this due to the short-term nature of most financial markets, the risk-averse nature of many managers, or the difficulty involved? Justify your answer through a discussion based on the literature.

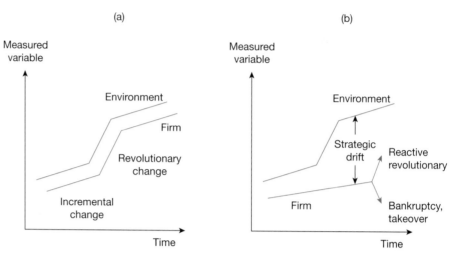

Figure 2.4 Types of strategic change

Path dependency

Occurs when future developments of a product or technology are conditional on an earlier state.

many dynamically interconnected parts. As Chapter 1 described, their behaviour can be described as punctuated equilibrium: periods of relatively slow change coupled with periods of dramatic change. The punctuated equilibrium model applies to both the environment faced by the firm and its response. Thus, external changes can be incremental or revolutionary and strategy can be incremental or revolutionary. Markets also demonstrate **path dependencies** where future developments are conditional on an earlier state (Beinhocker, 1999).

For example, compact discs were designed with a specific diameter, and this has influenced the physical configuration of a range of devices using CDs as well as the dimensions of the next generation of DVDs.

This dichotomy between incremental and revolutionary change is illustrated in Figure 2.4. In Figure 2.4 (a), firm change is aligned with the changing environment. Sometimes this change is fast, sometimes it is slow, but the firm keeps up with its changing environment throughout. In Figure 2.4 (b), the firm is also changing, but the rate of change is insufficient to maintain its alignment; instead the firm is drifting further and further away from where it should be, resulting in 'strategic drift' (G. Johnson *et al.*, 2008). At some point the firm faces a dilemma: either it undertakes revolutionary renewal, with all the risks that that involves (since it now has limited resources for change) or it falls victim to a takeover or bankruptcy.

Strategic drift

Occurs when the organization's strategy gradually moves away from relevance to the environment in which it competes.

The UK firm Psion Plc is an excellent example of a firm which suffered from strategic drift yet subsequently re-invented itself.

Incremental strategy

Running the business today requires a strategy – defining the business through focusing its resources, capital and people to meet current needs of customers. This necessitates targeting customer segments, positioning the business relative to competitors and deploying resources

> **Re-invention *in practice* – Psion Plc**
>
> Psion Plc can fairly lay claim to have been the first company in the world to offer what became known as personal digital assistant (PDA). Launched in 1984 as the 'Organizer', this was the world's first handheld computer (the acronym and product class PDA did not yet exist). A continuous series of improved and more powerful products followed, but Psion lacked the capabilities to crack the key US market, which preferred smaller, lighter and less expensive products. The Palm Pilot pioneered this change, seized US leadership and began to penetrate Psion's UK market. As market preferences evolved, Psion was left behind in a classic example of strategic drift. They stopped production and withdrew from the market in 2001 at the time of the dot.com crisis. The firm's capabilities in software remained, however, and it was a major contributor to the development of Symbian, the software that powers mobile phones by such wel-known names as Ericsson and Nokia. Psion's interest in Symbian was spun off, however, and the bulk of the firm's operations are now in Canada as a result of the 2000 $US 370 million takeover of Teklogix International. Psion retains a listing on the LSE, and describes its business as 'producing rugged mobile computer products and technology for industrial application' (Psion, 2010; answers.com, 2010).

in line with these decisions. The firm searches the customer and competitive landscape for opportunities, attempting to leverage existing resources that afford best fit with the environment. Managers must also align functional and supply-chain activities with the strategy, and harmonize organization structure, processes, culture, incentives and people. Change occurs, but it is of a 'tuning' type.

Incremental strategy usually focuses on cost reduction to create shareholder value by improving labour and capital productivity. Another common alternative is to increase revenues by targeting growth segments of the market, reducing customer defection and possibly making related acquisitions. Such a strategy can be successful, as is seen from the performance of Nestlé. It has been in business for over 140 years, with revenues in 2008 of CHF109.9 billion (€74 billion). The firm has continued to innovate over this period, expanding into new geographic markets and launching new products, demonstrating a remarkable consistency (Wetlaufer, 2001). Incremental strategy works reasonably well when environmental turbulence is low, but may be less valuable as turbulence rises (Berthon *et al.*, 2004).

Value from legacy assets

Any firm has a set of current activities. To support these, the firm must focus on asset and employee productivity, operating efficiently in all respects. The rising level of competitive intensity and increasing pressure on margins necessitate an inexorable drive for improved productivity and cost reduction in existing operations. In recent times, these pressures have been exacerbated by the recession and the global financial crisis, as Table 2.1 illustrates.

Table 2.1 Layoffs announced by European firms, 2009

Corporate layoffs by major European firms	Layoffs
ING	7,000
Corus	3,500
HP (Europe)	9,300
SAP	3,000
Philips	6,000

Source: EurActiv, 2010; Euronews, 2010

As Table 2.1 indicates, many firms are planning or have executed major reductions in employment. Such reductions are obviously traumatic for the firm and reflect the fact that senior management sees no short-term alternatives. Clearly, managers must be cost-focused, and the firm may need major cost reductions. But improving year-to-year productivity in existing operations is unlikely to be enough to generate long-term wealth. Due to the dynamic nature of the environment, value created by legacy assets generally declines, so managers must consider alternatives.

Growth opportunities

Firms can also create value through grasping growth opportunities in existing businesses. Line extensions, new product development and market expansion as well as related acquisitions may all contribute. A common strategy for many firms has been global expansion with existing products. Indeed, the very label 'multinational' reflects the historic strategy pursued by many large firms; namely, expansion into increasing numbers of national markets.

Incremental growth *in practice* – Unilever

The Anglo-Dutch firm Unilever has grown primarily through incremental means, staying close to its historic base of foods and detergents, while expanding globally to the point where its turnover in 2008 was €40.5 billion and it operated in over 150 countries (Unilever, Annual report 2008).

Nonetheless, organic growth may fail to meet managers' and shareholders' growth objectives, in which case more radical growth alternatives must be considered.

Revolutionary strategy

Major increases in wealth, for both firms and society, flow from innovation, not from optimizing the present. Some wealth is gained by perfecting the known, but venturing into and seizing the unknown, when successful, engenders large increases in wealth. This is the entrepreneurial challenge: to develop a deep understanding of our fast-changing world and to imagine the innovations that will create significant value. This requires managers to have foresight and creativity. It requires flexible thinking as well as the capacity to learn and adapt quickly since the future is increasingly unpredictable. Innovation is about agility, experimentation, imagination and diversity, while optimization is about scale, efficiency and hierarchy. Radical innovation generally requires managers who are radicals, if not heretics, who go beyond the established orthodoxy of the firm or the industry.

In a rapidly changing world, the firm must innovate as well as improve productivity. Unfortunately, some managers may not be learning as fast as the world is changing. They fail to recognize that strategies become obsolete very quickly. Meeting the entrepreneurial challenge requires a future focus, by both the CEO (who could be called the chief change officer) and other employees. The firm must focus on what the future is likely to be – not only where it is today – a difficult task in a rapidly changing environment. To take decisions now that will pay off in the future requires managers who are both thinkers and doers, endowed with imagination, creativity and passion.

Most firms find this combination of fundamentally different types of change – incremental and revolutionary – extremely challenging, part of the reason being that these processes require different skills and capabilities, a topic to which we return in Chapter 5 (➤Chapter 5). Further contributing to the difficulty of balancing short- and long-term considerations are financial market requirements that the firm continue to create value throughout this ongoing change process. Some, however, have excelled.

Chapter 5

Innovation *in practice* – Apple Inc

Apple has been successful in developing and introducing a number of radical innovations from the original personal computer to the iPod, iTunes, iPhone and their new iPad tablet computer, launched in early 2010 at a price of US$499, far below what analysts were expecting (Mintz & Metz, 2010).

Revolutionary strategy can be thought of as a high-stakes game, starting when management develops a vision of the company's future, then making major, hard-to-reverse decisions about where the company will focus its energies, capital and people, hoping their vision is correct. Since the future is difficult to predict, the risks of this approach are correspondingly high.

Of course, not all strategy is revolutionary. Major changes are fraught with danger and may be traumatic for staff. We may categorize such dramatic change by whether it is reactive or pro-active. It is generally much better to take a large number of small, fast steps than one large one to try to catch up. However, firms and their management are often subject to inertia. Instead of a series of smaller changes, they wait until only a large dramatic change will ensure survival. This often requires contraction of one or more of the firm's businesses, and a substantial number of employees to be laid off to quickly reduce costs.

Revolutionary strategies may also be pro-active, thereby becoming the force creating turbulence in the industry. Highly successful firms that either invented totally new industries or dramatically re-invented existing ones include IKEA, Aldi and SAP.

In environments that are characterized by discontinuous change, the firm may have to respond in a revolutionary way, such as a radical redefinition of the firm or the industry in order to survive. Such strategies are likely to challenge existing industry boundaries and norms and, if successful, re-invent the industry itself. In a discontinuous world, strategy re-invention is the key to wealth creation and survival.

The Internet afforded many firms an opportunity to pro-actively reconfigure their supply chain, with consequences for power relationships, number of suppliers, prices and so on. One may argue this is simply reacting to change, but the strategic innovation may well be novel in the originator's industry.

In other situations, the firm is beyond doubt creating change.

Creating change *in practice* – Intel

Intel revolutionized its industry with the invention of a standardized microprocessor, followed by continual development of faster and cheaper chips permitting new applications for personal computers and other digital devices. They were prepared to cast aside their past in memory chips in order to accomplish this. Philips and Sony invented the CD, and subsequently found many applications and developments that they had possibly never originally envisaged, including as a storage and recording media for personal computers, digital video discs and so on.

Leveraging
Creatively using current resources to engender future growth.

Such revolutionary strategies are about **leveraging** resources, about stretching the firm and developing new capabilities (Hamel & Prahalad, 1993).

They often involve innovations that affect the entire business system – the value chain, the target customer focus and the economic model may all be transformed (Buaron, 2000). They are more complex than product innovations, and therefore more difficult to emulate. As a result, more sustainable competitive advantage is likely to accrue to the successful transformational strategy.

A radical innovation normally changes the rules of competition in the industry, leads to major changes in industry leadership and strongly affects the previous incumbents. These revolutionary strategies generally deliver a major improvement to customers as their core (Lucier *et al.*, 2000). When these improvements are large enough, they can be shared with customers to drive rapid growth, with sufficient value retained to provide superior return to shareholders. In the commercial airline industry, the introduction of jet-powered aircraft provided such a major boost, lowering airfares in real terms and leading to a faster rate of growth in air travel. A similar boost took place when wide-bodied jets arrived.

Of course, these new models rarely emerge fully fledged. Learning and subsequent evolution occurs after the launch. However, when successful, these innovations produce major changes in industry structure, the change in rules spawning imitators, forcing incumbents to respond.

Corporate- and business unit-level strategy

In a global firm, strategic decisions occur at several levels. We distinguish between strategy and strategic decisions at two levels of the firm – corporate and business unit, as shown in Figure 2.5.

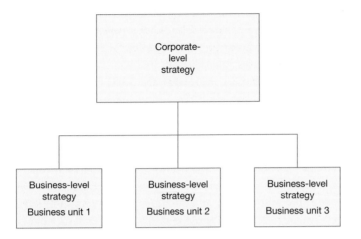

Figure 2.5 Corporate- and business-level strategy

Corporate-level strategy
Deciding the overall purpose and mix of businesses, partners, geographic markets, technologies and customers of the firm so that the total entity delivers value to stakeholders which is greater than the value delivered under any other organizational arrangement.

Business unit-level strategy
How a unit of the firm competes successfully to create value in its chosen markets.

Strategic business unit (SBU)
A unit of a firm which is relatively autonomous, responsible for developing its own strategy, with its own products, markets and competitors independent of other units within the same firm.

Corporate strategic decisions affect the future well-being of the entire organization, while business unit strategic decisions affect the future well-being of a unit of the total firm – a division, or what we will refer to as a strategic business unit. **Corporate-level strategy** includes developing a vision for the entire firm, decisions about the scope of the firm, the allocation of resources among business units, developing objectives and performance measures for each business unit, managing the culture of the firm, managing the synergies among different business units, designing organization structure, relations with financial markets and product markets, and forming relationships with other firms.

Strategy at the **business unit level** includes decisions on mission and objectives (normally negotiated with corporate staff), growth strategy (new products and new markets), outsourcing and developing a competitive strategy, among others. In any firm, most value is created at the business unit level; this is where most competition occurs.

Defining a strategic business unit (SBU)

A **strategic business unit** is a unit of the firm that is relatively autonomous, an entity responsible for developing its own strategy. A business unit is responsible for its own products and markets, with its own competitors. Most assets required to run the business are under its control and it has its own managerial resources (➤Chapter 7).

At the same time it is unlikely to be truly independent. There will be linkages with other units, either through markets served, technology, facilities and operations or R&D. From the business unit perspective, we have to ask what benefits the parent brings. If there were none, the business unit would be better off with another parent or as an independent entity.

Most value in a firm is realized in business units, through their ability to deliver goods and services at a profit. For the overall firm to create value it must contribute to the competitive advantage of the business units comprising its portfolio. A key aspect of corporate strategy is, therefore, to decide whether business units are better or worse off because they are part

Chapter 7

Chapter 8

of the firm. Managing the composition of the corporate portfolio (deciding which businesses should be part of the portfolio and how it should change over time) is the heart of corporate strategy (▶Chapter 8). Consequently, a central question for corporate-level management is whether or not the firm creates value through its multi-business activities. Ideally, the corporate centre should create value greater than the costs of its overheads and more than any other possible parent. In this way it can justify continued management of the firm's assets. The corporation would then, indeed, be the natural owner (manager) of these assets.

Business-level strategy is concerned with how to manage and develop strategy of the relatively autonomous unit in the context of the firm's corporate strategy. For example, the mission of a business unit should be subsumed within the corporate mission, and business objectives are developed after discussion with corporate. A key issue at this level is competitive strategy: how does the unit develop an advantage over its competitors? Note also that competition for customers occurs primarily at the business unit level, not at the corporate level. Competition is primarily a business unit concept. Further, business unit strategy includes decisions on growth strategy, what geographical focus to adopt and what capabilities to develop.

Business-level strategy may also represent part of the 'implementation' of corporate-level strategy. For example, a corporate strategy of international expansion is likely to have implications for all business units. A business also has to ensure that its strategies will deliver economic value, although this value may not be generated immediately. A growth business may sacrifice short-term profitability to create future shareholder value.

Decisions on a firm's business unit structure should not be taken lightly. The structure provides the basis for resource allocation decisions. If business units have been defined geographically, then resource allocation will occur on a geographic basis. If businesses have been defined on a product basis, then this will be the basis for resource allocation. In addition, decisions on the number of business units are corporate decisions, and should be reviewed periodically. In large global firms, rather than a two level structure of corporate and business, three or more levels may exist.

Challenge of strategic management

Imagine that you are the CEO of a business unit within a multi-business global firm. What tensions would you expect to be faced with in terms of your responsibility to manage the business unit to achieve high performance with the corporate pressure to consider the needs of other business units in the firm?

Strategy as building capabilities

Regardless of the degree of innovativeness of a strategy, it must be concerned with building firm capabilities. Capabilities are the skills and abilities of the firm, the things that a firm does better than its competitors. Capabilities are not static but must be built to support strategy. Due to the rapidly changing and turbulent world which firms face, new capabilities must be developed in order to survive and prosper. As Chapter 5 explains, a central element of strategy is building these capabilities faster and more effectively than competitors (▶Chapter 5). In many circumstances, these new capabilities will be developed through networks and alliances with other firms (Kodama, 2007). At the same time, the firm will have to forget old skills as new ones are learned.

Chapter 5

For example, the US retailer Wal-Mart has expanded into many other countries. We would expect them to transfer some of the skills, such as supply chain management, which made them a superior retailer in the US. But to succeed in their international expansion, Wal-Mart will need to build new skills, the most obvious one being an understanding of other cultures and languages. Indicative of the difficulties in transferring capabilities across borders, Wal-Mart has been successful in the UK with its ASDA subsidiary but decided to withdraw from Germany.

Strategy as resolving paradox

At the centre of every strategy is tension between two apparently opposing thoughts: a paradox. The challenge was succinctly described by F. Scott Fitzgerald: 'The test of a first rate intelligence is the ability to hold two opposed ideas in the mind at the same time and still retain the ability to function' (Hampden-Turner, 1990). The essence of paradox is that the firm must be at both ends of the spectrum simultaneously; it cannot operate solely at one end. The paradoxes include: short term versus long term; reflecting both creative and analytical approaches; demonstrating commitment to an idea and the flexibility to cope with unpredictable changes; being competitive as well as possibly cooperating with the same firms; showing some focus or centralization while permitting local autonomy; optimizing operations while allowing for innovation; and so on (Dodd & Favaro, 2006). Figure 2.6 indicates several of the relevant paradoxes to be addressed.

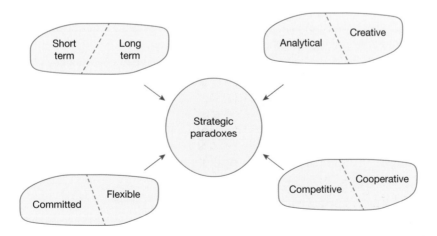

Figure 2.6 Strategy as resolving paradox

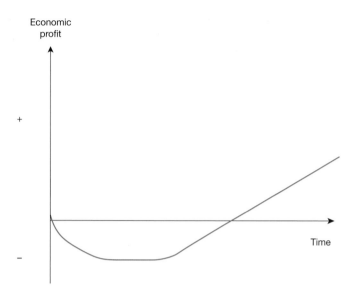

Figure 2.7 Economic profit profile of a new strategy

As we noted earlier, if the firm does not survive in the short term, then there will be no long term. During the recession of 2008/09, many firms cut employment dramatically to ensure financial viability as a response to major revenue reduction. If firms cease to meet short-term requirements of financial success, they may become insolvent. Yet over-emphasis on short-term results may put the long-term future of the company at risk. Short-term success can always be improved by starving the firm of long-term investment funds. The results of such actions may take several years (and a new generation of managers) to become apparent.

A new strategy often involves considerable investment in R&D, new facilities and market and product development, with negative cash flows and economic profit, as illustrated in Figure 2.7, above. The firm must be able to fund this negative cash flow with funds from other parts of the firm, together with new debt or new equity.

Firms with less access to funding will find their innovation opportunities limited. In periods of economic decline, weaker firms can get squeezed out while cash-rich firms have many more strategic options available.

Financial strength *in practice* – Apple Inc

As of the end of 2009, Apple reported that it was holding the equivalent of $US34 billion in cash, cash equivalents and marketable securities (Apple, 2010).

Long-term success is dependent on innovation, implying investments that will take time to come to fruition. At the same time, the firm needs to decide when to call it quits. When to exit from innovations which are unlikely to produce long-term success is not an easy question to answer. There may be temptation to withdraw at the bottom of the cycle, just before things pick up. This is not helped by the tendency of some managers to produce 'hockey-stick' forecasts for their superiors, where the major benefits are expected to accrue many years into the future.

Strategy must therefore reach an appropriate synthesis of the long term and the short term, addressing both the ongoing and innovation needs of the firm. If all management attention is directed at the ongoing business, innovation is stifled. Yet, too much attention to innovation and the core business may start to suffer.

Strategy also has to achieve a synthesis between the analytical and the creative. The former is characterized by detailed analysis of the environment, competitors and so on, from which the firm constructs a reliable, rational, unbiased view of the world. However, too much analysis can lead to indecision, so-called 'paralysis by analysis', conflicting with the need to speed up the pace of decision-making. More data is always required, more studies have to be undertaken, and more risk removed from the decision. But particularly for strategic decisions, we can never remove all risk. Strategic decisions always have a significant element of intuition and judgement, which is risky if the decision-maker lacks a valid mental model of the world and makes decisions based on prejudice and wishful thinking. The clever strategist learns to assess risk and take steps to mitigate the consequences wherever possible.

Another paradox is the tension between competition and cooperation. Strategy is not always a zero-sum game where if one firm wins another loses. There may be benefits from cooperation, even with major competitors, as we see in numerous alliances. So while one purpose of strategy is to be creative, get an advantage and outwit competitors, there are also times when a cooperative approach is called for. Nokia and Motorola compete in some markets and cooperate in others.

Strategy also involves a synthesis between commitment and flexibility (Ghemawat, 1998). The firm needs to be committed to the pursuit of its vision and objectives. There will always be obstacles making this difficult. These may arise from changes in the environment (including competitors), or perhaps from employees unconvinced by the firm's strategy. Yet when the world has changed irrevocably, in ways that make the strategy untenable, or when performance is far below objectives and is unlikely to improve, the firm must change. Recognizing when commitment descends into outright stubbornness is an essential, but difficult, aspect of strategic management.

Other characteristics of strategy

We address other strategy characteristics more briefly. First, by its very nature strategy is cross-functional, and different functional areas must be aligned. There is little value in attempting to become a global firm if the firm's human resources will not support this, or if financial resources are inadequate (▶Chapter 12). Different functional strategies must be aligned with the overall strategy. A corporate strategy focused on growth should lead to

Chapter 12

a discussion of how to fund this growth; should the firm fund it through debt or equity, should the dividend policy be altered? If the firm decides to raise additional debt, what currency and maturity should be used? Similarly a strategy to become more customer focused will need to be aligned with recruitment, training, development and reward practices. Just as a particular strategy requires aligned resources, so may constrained resources limit strategic possibilities. Two key resources in this regard are skilled personnel and financial resources. For example, if the firm is highly leveraged, then it may have to sell assets to ensure survival. On the other hand, if the firm is cash rich, or has access to cash in the form of debt or equity, it is much better equipped to exploit growth opportunities. There must also be alignment between strategy generation and implementation. There is little value in designing a strategy that firms are incapable of implementing.

Strategy is also an evolutionary process. Strategy cannot be an immutable timetable of what we will do in the future; the world is too turbulent and unpredictable for that to be successful. A strategy should incorporate a general direction and theme and, within that, sufficient flexibility to adapt as the world evolves. Strategy subsumes monitoring the changing environment, sensing changes and making required adjustments to the strategy. As a result, the actual realized strategy may not be the same as the intended strategy (Mintzberg & Waters, 1985). In a world characterized by punctuated equilibrium, strategies need to be evolutionary (Beinhocker, 1999), and the learning issue will be addressed in more detail in

Chapter 10 Chapter 10 (➤Chapter 10).

Finally, given the size and complexity of global firms, most will be engaged in multiple strategic initiatives. A firm may be acquiring a European competitor, developing new products for an emerging market in China, exploring opportunities in telecommunications, attempting to change its culture to become more entrepreneurial, and designing and implementing new systems such as CRM or ERP, all at the same time. Sound strategic management may, and generally will, have a 'project management' aspect, wherein senior managers are responsible for the design and successful execution of a number of initiatives. An important aspect of the CEO's job is to ensure that there are neither too few nor too many of these initiatives. Some firms suffer from 'initiative overload' whereas the lack of required initiatives in a fast-changing environment will mean competitors soon leave the firm behind. Management must thus ensure that priorities are set appropriately.

At the same time, a firm may need to bet on a number of developments when it is unclear which will eventuate, and it may use a different strategy for each. A combination of alliances, internal development projects and joint ventures can cover a number of possible developments. Here the firm is taking an options approach – placing small bets to see how a field develops, gaining information so as to act when appropriate. One reason is again the unpredictability of the future, so experimentation and trial is a good approach. At the same time, since resources are limited, trade-offs between these alternative futures will be necessary. No firm can cover all possibilities, particularly in capital-intensive businesses. The firm will need a mix of strategies in terms of time to fruition, risk and degree of innovativeness (Courtney et al., 1997).

2.4 CHARACTERISTICS OF STRATEGIC MANAGEMENT

LEARNING OBJECTIVE 3

Describe the complexity of the strategic management task.

> *Strategic management is the managerial process of creating organizations that generate value in a turbulent world over an extended period of time.*

Strategic management is first and foremost about creating organizations, although those organizations have one important feature – they must create value. Such value creation requires continual innovation. In a world characterized by uncertainty, complex interactions and ephemeral advantages, insight and foresight are essential managerial attributes. Certainly some industries are changing at slower rates than others, but disruptive change can arise from any number of sources, not just competitive or technological. So while foresight is always important, in some industries it will be essential (Barnett & Berland, 1999).

Creating value means that the firm must meet two demands: excellent execution with its current activities and developing the capabilities required to survive tomorrow. The ability to do both of these successfully is extremely difficult. Many firms can sustain a brief period of excellent performance, but not many are then able to sustain this superior performance. Firms tend to become set in their ways and are unable to respond to environmental changes (Beinhocker, 2006).

To repeat one of our themes, strategic management involves leadership skills and intuitive judgements as well as intellect, analysis and planning. It is about organizations, the people who comprise them, their motivation and power, as well as the environment within which the organization competes. It is most definitely not a purely analytical activity.

We now review several of the features of strategic management, reflecting on both its importance and the challenge.

Creating the organization

A fundamental role for strategic managers (including the CEO) is to create organizations that both respond to and introduce change. Change requires an entrepreneurial culture in the firm, encouraging creativity and innovation, experimentation and learning. CEOs cannot do everything themselves; they need to work with and through other members of the firm. Thus strategic management also involves such tasks as designing organization structure, systems and decision-making processes, culture and values, compensation and incentive methods, and selecting and developing people – what we term the architecture of the organization (►Chapter 11).

Chapter 11

Strategic management is deeply involved with such concepts as leadership, vision, integrity, empowerment, creativity and risk-taking. Despite the simplistic prescriptions of some gurus, there are rarely simple solutions to complex problems, and the strategic management agenda is therefore complex, requiring professional analytic skills (Hilmer & Donaldson, 1996). Strategic managers need strong vision and a sense of direction about where the firm should go. They must be prepared to go into new areas to create the future of their companies. They are often rule breakers, for to demonstrate industry leadership usually requires going outside traditional boundaries. They must also encourage such behaviour in their people, hiring and developing personnel who are skilled and entrepreneurial, who understand customers, competitors, industry trends, and who bring both information and interpersonal skills to the organization.

Lack of an innovative and creative culture is often due to the frame of thinking that managers in the firm, and others in the industry, have acquired. Based on a combination of education, experience, consultants and, often, the business press, this frame defines the company's understanding of itself and its industry. Managers have to continually challenge this 'dominant logic' which limits creative and lateral thinking.

In some industries, strategy convergence seems to occur, and all competitors follow a common industry recipe. Strategic management is about creativity, not following the herd. Winning companies have a strategy that is different from, and superior to, those of their competitors; a firm can never win if it has adopted a strategy identical to its competitors.

Successful firms such as Infosys, Honda, SAP, Aldi and Dell have developed innovative strategies that have delivered significant improvements to customers, thereby generating substantial increases in shareholder value. In a dynamic world, organizations must change and innovate if they are to be successful – of course there is a risk to this, but the risk of action is often lower than the risk of inaction.

Dominant logic
A frame of thinking common to managers in an industry based on their education and experience, which defines the firm and the industry, and may limit creativity.

Creating and managing change

To create value-generating organizations, strategic managers need an external perspective on the world and its developments. Given the turbulence and uncertainty we have discussed, it is becoming increasingly difficult for managers to develop strategies that sustain success. With a high rate of environmental change, firms must change as fast as or faster than their environment. Strategies themselves have a shorter and shorter life: they rapidly become obsolete in a changing world, particularly when discontinuous change occurs. Unparalleled changes call for unparalleled responses. Part of the explanation for the short life of strategies is that intense competition quickly reduces any competitive advantage. Technology is creating frictionless capitalism, with lowered transaction costs, whereby any efficiency gains accruing to a firm are quickly competed away. So firms must force change in their businesses, becoming pro-active and intellectual leaders of their industry. As noted by Rumelt (Lovallo & Mendonca, 2007) managers in successful firms spotted a window of opportunity and then grasped it. Such action requires entrepreneurial insight together with access to, or the ability to generate the required capabilities.

Strategic management needs this external perspective. One key requirement is to recognize what Andy Grove at Intel called 'inflection points', when major changes occur due to new technology, regulatory changes or changes in customer values and preferences (Puffer, 1999).

Inflection points
Occur when there is a substantial change in the rate of change of a phenomenon.

These require the firm to make fundamental strategic changes, yet senior management, often far removed from the 'coalface', is sometimes the last to notice the change. Rather than waiting until the performance of the firm has become degraded, strategic management must recognize when change is called for. It also needs the will to possibly cannibalize products and even businesses: to make a business obsolete before others do.

Strategic managers also need to recognize the possibility of new entrants, which often come from outside the industry but may not be new firms. These entrants could be established firms that are expanding their scope. In the UK, Tesco, a supermarket chain, is now a major petrol retailer. We also see markets reaching saturation very quickly. Global firms operate globally, no longer launching in their home market and then following this up with a measured global expansion strategy. Instead they launch globally on the same day.

Strategic managers should challenge the status quo, challenge the boundaries and positions within the firm, as well as consider how to invent new competitive spaces. They should challenge industry beliefs or norms, tap into the creative aspirations of all employees, and encourage ongoing questioning of traditional assumptions about the company and its businesses. Strategic managers must prevent cultural inertia, minimize resistance to change, encourage learning and experimentation, and develop new capabilities. This requires giving people the responsibility for engendering change, which involves both top-down and bottom-up processes. Management's job is to create an environment where people can share knowledge, understand industry trends as well as their own business, understand strategy and competitors, and talk about the future and the need for change. With the increasing importance of intellectual capital and high-performance employees, monolithic, centrally managed firms are a thing of the past.

Creating value

The organization created by senior managers, the activities with which it is involved and the way in which it undertakes those activities must create value. A firm is primarily an economic entity. It may have social/political features, but the reason for its existence is economic – it promises to deliver products and services to its chosen customers in such a way that its revenue is larger than its costs – including capital costs. If the firm does not generate value, it has no reason to exist. It must meet the expectations of financial markets (a topic to which we return in Chapter 4) (➤Chapter 4). This is a considerable challenge. It is easier to create firms that destroy value rather than generate value. As Schumpeter noted, 'creative destruction' is an ongoing process, and firms do not live forever (Schumpeter, 1976). Firms do not have any right to exist; instead this right to exist must be continually earned in the marketplace against fierce competitors (Foster & Kaplan, 2001).

Chapter 4

Research indicates how difficult it is for firms to generate value over sustained periods of time. A major study of US firms over the period 1917 to 1987 found that only Kodak and GE outperformed the overall share market (relative to the S&P 500), where performance was measured by growth in market capitalization (Foster & Kaplan, 2001). Yet this superior performance has been difficult to maintain; in more recent times both of these firms have experienced difficulties. A similar finding is apparent if we examine the FTSE 100. This index was established in January 1984 and comprises the top 100 firms, ranked by market capitalization on the London Stock Exchange. By July 2006, only 23 of the original 100 firms were still on the list. Forty-seven of the original members exited through takeover or merger; the other firms which exited were not able to continue to grow and were consequently replaced by different firms (King, 2006). One explanation for this finding is that firms cannot innovate and change as quickly as the economy, and it is the economy that is reflected in any broader share market index. As new industries grow and develop, the S&P, Nikkei, DAX and similar indices are updated to reflect this, whereas firms such as Corus are still basically in steel.

The difficulty of creating value over extended time periods is illustrated by other studies. In 2001 Collins identified a set of firms which he considered had made the move from 'good' to 'great' over the period up until 1995 (Collins, 2001). When the performances of these same firms were examined over the ten-year period to 2005, only one had outperformed the S&P 500 in terms of return to investors, with one, Kimberley Clark, being ranked 302 out of 500 (Niendorf & Beck, 2008). Since 2005, one of the original firms, Circuit City, has gone bankrupt and another, Fannie Mae, has had to be rescued by the US government.

These findings indicate that it is not easy for a firm to maintain superior performance over extended periods of time – although this should still be the goal. One explanation is that firms cannot innovate as quickly as the economy, and it is the economy that is reflected in any broad share market index such as the FTSE 100. Another possible explanation is that CEOs are able to add value in certain types of environments and not others. But certainly the finding lays down the challenge for strategic management.

Ethics

Strategic management must also include a commitment to a set of personal values, which includes factors such as integrity, trust and fairness. The recession of 2008/09 made it clear that there were far too many examples of firms around the globe, particularly in the financial sector, whose CEOs seem to have lost sight of this. Some CEOs seemed driven by a need for higher stock prices (possibly influenced by the options that they held), condoning loose accounting and ethical standards. Senior executive remuneration reached extreme heights, and was too often unrelated to firm performance. A commitment to transparency is also necessary, with greater communication and sharing of information within the firm.

In summary, strategic management is about capturing the full potential of the firm today, meeting shareholder expectations, and choosing tomorrow's game in the light of turbulence and discontinuity. This requires imagining the future and what the firm will have to do to get there, a task that mandates considerable intelligence, learning and feedback. By any measure, strategic management is not an easy task!

LEARNING OBJECTIVE 5	## 2.5 BUSINESS MODELS
Design and/or modify a firm's business model.	Business models are a relatively new concept in strategic management, though Drucker used a very similar term (business system) in the early 1990s (Drucker, 1994). A business model is the method by which the firm generates revenue and profit; it addresses the fundamental question of how the business makes money (Magretta, 2002).

A business model is a method of doing business by which a company generates revenue. Such a model spells out how a company makes money, by specifying what activities it

Business models *in practice* – aircraft engine makers

The airline industry provides an excellent example of different business models. Aircraft makers such as Boeing and Airbus earn money when they sell a plane, and are very sensitive to changes in the demand for air travel. Aircraft engine makers such as GE and Rolls Royce operate a fundamentally different model. Engine manufacturers make relatively small margins on engine sales. Instead, when the aircraft manufacturer (or, more correctly, the ultimate customer, the airline) buys an engine, they enter into a long-term service agreement with the engine maker. In this agreement, the original price normally represents about 20 per cent of the total cost of the engine over its 30-year life, so having engines in operation is a strong guarantee of future revenue – and to an extent isolated from the vagaries in new aircraft orders (Madslien, 2009).

undertakes, where it is positioned in the value chain and how it generates revenue. The business model idea is a very useful concept, but it is not the strategy of the firm, although some authors treat the two as synonymous.

In a given industry we may see two competing firms with fundamentally different business models. Dell and HP employ different models in the PC industry, Dell with direct distribution, HP using resellers. Thus, within an industry, there is competition between business models, and innovation can occur with the invention of a new business model that provides competitive advantage. In share trading, the traditional business model is the full service broker. One wave of innovation followed the elimination of fixed fees, producing discount brokers such as Charles Schwab. A more recent invention involves another business model – online trading. Sometimes a new model renders the old obsolete (disruptive innovation); sometimes it just captures an increasing proportion of customer demand. Perhaps one of the most dramatic examples is provided by Google, whose drastically different business model led to advertising revenues of $US21 billion by 2008, compared with two of the largest advertising agencies in the world, Omnicom at $US13 billion and WPP at £36 billion in 2008.

Business models *in practice* – Hilti

An example of an innovative business model is provided by Hilti, the Lichtenstein-based manufacturer of high-quality power tools for the construction industry. Hilti recognized that while contractors needed tools, they did not need to own them. The firm developed new capabilities in fleet management, distribution and service to deliver the right tool to the customer when it was needed on a leasing arrangement (M. W. Johnson *et al.*, 2008).

Innovation in business models is very important. Rather than being forced to re-invent business models by competitors, companies should be experimenting, on the alert for alternatives, whether precipitated by environmental change or by the firm itself.

A given business model has a life cycle – growth, maturity and decline (Slywotzky, 1996). Strategic managers should continually challenge and test their firm's business model. Innovation in business models requires first that we understand the current model, then de-construct it, understanding its underlying assumptions and analysing what could cause it to lack consistency with the environment or technology. We should also explore business models of other industries (part of so-called 'best-of-class' benchmarking) and consider constructing a new model. In some ways, the issues with business models parallel those in our discussion of strategy. The historic model for delivering shareholder returns was to reduce costs and explore revenue growth by targeting new growth segments, an incremental model. The new growth model instead places the emphasis on developing novel business models, which in turn requires a managerial model where innovation, change and uncertainty, rather than equilibrium, are the natural state: a revolutionary approach.

Components of a business model

A business model is the entire system for delivering value to customers and earning a profit on that activity (Slywotzky & Morrison, 1997). It incorporates a set of assumptions about customers and economics, giving insight into how the firm expects to compete. The model must fit external reality and be internally consistent. It can be broken down into two components – value creation and value capture, as shown in Figure 2.8.

Value creation

Value creation is how the firm creates value for the customer through providing an innovative solution to a fundamental problem. For some products we should recall that customer value is determined by the total life cycle cost of the product, not just the initial purchase price, and this may provide opportunities for innovation.

Value capture

Value capture is how the firm gets rewarded for the value it creates, and this value capture is itself dependent on competitive differentiation. The normal way to capture value is through product and service fees, but as we saw with electronic commerce, there can be other profit models. Automobile firms traditionally earned substantial profit not from the sale of cars but from the financing of car purchases. Retailers of consumer appliances may make more money from the sales of add-on warranties than from the sale of the appliances themselves, while manufacturers of ink-jet printers often sell their printers at very low prices to ensure a stream of revenues from the sale of replacement ink cartridges. Developing a financial model describing value capture by the firm requires a full understanding of all relevant costs, including inventory, key resources and key processes required to deliver the new business model.

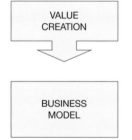

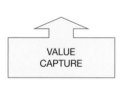

Figure 2.8
Components of a business model

Strategic managers need to think beyond new products to new business models that meet deep customer needs in unconventional ways. Sometimes a new model will destroy the old one; sometimes it captures an increasing proportion of the customers of the old model, reducing growth and profit for those companies that do not change. It introduces more strategic variety into a competitive domain, thus changing customer behaviour. It is not a means of positioning against competitors, but of going around them, and incumbents often find it difficult to emulate because they lack required skills, or are too slow to change. In many cases, incumbents are not prepared to cannibalize their existing model.

2.6 THE STRATEGY DEVELOPMENT PROCESS – A MANAGEMENT PERSPECTIVE

LEARNING OBJECTIVE 5

Summarize the managerial process involved in strategy development and implementation, including major impediments.

How do organizations, and managers within those organizations, actually develop strategy? In global organizations, senior line managers, often supported by a planning staff, typically develop strategy. Strategy is almost always the result of some type of collective decision-making process, with a number of managers involved. These processes are characterized by building diverse teams that challenge assumptions and increase the range of alternatives considered (Eisenhardt, 1999). Firms also attempt to minimize internal political activity, although there is almost always a political aspect to the strategy process.

Burgelman and Grove (2007) suggest that what distinguishes successful leaders is their ability to develop a strategy-making process capable of achieving a balance between exploitation and exploration. To ensure that value-creating strategies result, exploration may require involving a wider group, crossing organizational and industry boundaries, encouraging both new perspectives and experimentation.

Both managers and managerial researchers have debated the process of strategy development. The process appears to be a combination of the rational and the intuitive, of formal analysis and entrepreneurial activity. Unfortunately, in many firms the formal process often becomes rigid, with too much emphasis on data and financial forecasts at the expense of creativity. One survey suggests that only 25 per cent of strategic decisions were made through the formal strategy process (Dye & Sibony, 2007).

From one perspective, strategic thinking can be seen as a rational activity where managers gather facts, identify problems, develop alternatives and choose the best alternative against a clear objective. This process requires substantial analytical skills, to assess the importance of changes in the environment and the firm and the impact of these on the future.

Another view is that strategy is about intuition, judgement and feel. Such a process is often claimed to generate more creative and entrepreneurial solutions. Creative solutions generally go beyond existing data; they represent an inferential leap into an uncertain future, requiring deep understanding which may not be fully supported by any formal analysis. Intuition is often more holistic, looking at problems in a more inclusive way based on the decision-maker's prior experiences, knowledge and values (Burke & Miller, 1999).

We know the future is uncertain, and thus cannot be predicted with certainty, so strategic decisions have to be made without full information. The firm has a dilemma. Should it delay the decision until more and better information is available, or make a decision now without full information? If we delay, our competitors may decide to act and thus obtain a first-mover advantage. On the other hand, if a decision taken with less information is incorrect, the firm suffers accordingly.

In summary, some of the characteristics of the strategy process are:

- It requires analysis, but analysis will rarely remove the need for judgement.
- There is an increased need for speed in decision-making, as the costs of delay are rising.
- Good decision processes should focus on the problem, not on politics within the firm.
- There is a need for creativity and developing original solutions.

Impediments to the strategy process

Strategic decision-making may suffer from a variety of impediments as illustrated in Figure 2.9, the elements of which we now examine.

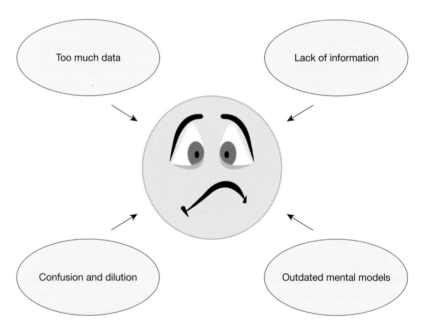

Figure 2.9 Impediments to developing strategy

Lack of information

With fundamentally new products or major new business developments that take time to come to fruition, lack of sufficient information is common. Many firms attempt detailed financial analysis, but the quality of such analysis is often poor. Where risk can be assessed, risk analysis tools can be utilized (Courtney *et al.*, 1997). In other situations, such analysis is virtually impossible, since the future is too uncertain and in fact unknowable. In these situations, strategic decisions rely mainly on judgement and intuition, supported with what analysis is possible, even if the latter has more of the characteristics of a ritual, rather than decision support (Bower, 1970).

Too much data

Sometimes strategic decision-making can suffer from too much data, but not enough information. We cannot determine what is important and what is not, and cannot put the data into a context. In the information age, this will be an increasing problem.

Confusion and dilution

We sometimes describe strategy and the process of developing strategy as the responsibility of the CEO, as if only the CEO is involved. This is far from the truth. Not only are there many individuals involved in collecting and analysing data, there is normally a group of senior managers who actually make the final decision. This group has some interesting properties. Its composition is generally variable as members join and members leave (either the group or the firm). It is sometimes unclear who made a decision or even if a decision has been made. Decisions sometimes result from creeping commitment; they are not clear until sometime after the event. Not only is responsibility for a decision thereby diffused, but also sometimes the very solution chosen is the result of compromise, lacking clarity or direction.

Outdated mental models

We have noted that firms exist in a world of complex adaptive systems, and that one characteristic of these systems is punctuated equilibrium, where periods of relatively slow change are interrupted by periods of radical and revolutionary change. As the world moves through these revolutionary periods, it becomes apparent that senior managers may be out of touch. Their experience and understanding was formed in a prior world; they have difficulty comprehending the new world. This discontinuity can be exacerbated by a tendency for senior executives to be insulated from reality, where staff does not report bad news.

The difficulty here can be understood through the concept of a cognitive map or mental model – a set of assumptions about the industry environment and the nature of competition. For example, is competition local or global, who are possible entrants, what are the changing political/social trends which determine how we understand the world, and so on? A mental model is a process of organizing reality, of determining what is important and what is not.

Mitroff suggests that in the 1980s the senior executives of GM had an outdated cognitive map. This led GM down a very expensive path of under-estimating the impact of overseas competitors, heavy spending on new plant and declining quality. Table 2.2 shows significant market share losses in the critical North American market, and highlight that GM failed to

Cognitive maps *in practice* – General Motors

In a study of General Motors in the 1980s, it was found that most senior executives of GM, and other US automobile firms, had a set of assumptions for success which included (Mitroff, 1988):

- Cars are status symbols, styling is more important than quality.
- The US market is isolated from the rest of the world.
- Workers do not have an important impact on productivity or quality.
- Managers need only a fragmented understanding of the business.

Table 2.2 Performance of General Motors

Year	Market share (%) Units, US cars and light truck	Share price ($) (Dec. 31)
1980	45	22.5
1982	44	31.2
1984	42	39.2
1986	38	33.0
1988	35	41.8
1990	35	34.3
1992	34	32.2
1994	33	42.1
1996	32	55.8
1998	31	71.5
1999	28	72.7
2000	28	50.9
2001	28	48.6
2002	28	36.9
2007	23.8	22.0
2008	22.3	4.0
2009	19.9	0.60

Source: Zesiger, 2000; MarketWatch, 2010

generate shareholder returns for a significant period. While we would not claim that an incorrect mental model alone determined this performance, it reflects the fact that many GM managers were out of touch with the environment in which they competed. The saga eventually ended in bankruptcy in 2009, with majority ownership ending up in the hands of the US and Canadian governments. As of late 2009, the new CEO Whitacre was reported as 'impatient to spur the plodding culture of GM, where decision by committee, an isolated upper management and fear of risk produced mediocre cars for years' (Krisher, 2009).

A mental model is a set of ingrained assumptions and generalizations that influence how we understand the world and take action. They tell us what is important, what will be noticed. Mental models can be very dangerous to good decision-making because they are typically implicit, not explicit. An auto executive may say, 'People are only interested in styling' whereas what is really meant is 'I have a mental model which says that people are only interested in styling'. These are actually very different statements. If the first, we believe it to be true. If the second, we could decide to test the model.

Mental models also develop over long periods of time and are therefore difficult to change. Further, a model becomes 'objective' if it is widely shared within the firm. This is one reason why firms have difficulty putting new strategies into practice. New strategies fail to get implemented because they conflict with strongly held internal beliefs of how the world works. Managers and employees do not believe that the world has actually changed; if they see a change, they rationalize it as temporary – in the near future 'sanity' (namely the past) will return. In this sense, management needs to undergo a paradigm shift, and this may require the injection of a complete new group of managers.

2.7 STAKEHOLDERS AND ORGANIZATIONAL VALUE

LEARNING OBJECTIVE 6

Articulate the concept of value for different stakeholders of the firm.

A firm creates value when the revenue generated is greater than all the costs involved in generating that revenue, including capital costs. Indeed, the purpose of strategy is to ensure that the firm generates an economic profit that is available for distribution among its stakeholders or utilized for innovation to create additional value. By providing jobs, it creates value for employees. By purchasing from suppliers, it creates value for them. If successful in the marketplace, it must of necessity be creating value for its customers. And, of course, by paying taxes it creates value for government.

The distribution of created value among these various constituencies is the subject of much dispute and profound disagreement. In a competitive world, companies will seek benign taxing environments. CEOs and senior executives whose compensation is not subject to appropriate board scrutiny all too often feather their own nests at the expense of shareholders. Strong unions that bargain unsympathetically can bring otherwise successful companies to their knees. Suppliers with monopoly power may extract so much value from their customers that they in turn can create little value for their own customers.

Achieving the right balance among these constituencies is a major challenge for managers, and, furthermore, takes place amid a welter of legislation and regulation nominally designed with the intent of ensuring that the firm's activities are ultimately in the interests

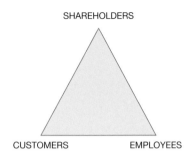

SHAREHOLDERS

CUSTOMERS   EMPLOYEES

Figure 2.10
Major organizational
stakeholders

of the broader society in which it operates. These constraints are themselves often in evolution, as they are subject to the onslaught of ingenuity, innovation and societal change. One of the most visible aspects of this process is the ongoing challenge to governance procedures.

While the firm has numerous stakeholders, and needs to create value for all, in this section of the chapter we will focus on three of the most critical stakeholders: shareholders, customers and employees, as illustrated in Figure 2.10. How economic profit is distributed among these stakeholders will be a source of debate within the firm, reflecting the values of managers, available growth opportunities and the political power of various stakeholders.

Shareholders

Shareholders have a financial investment from which they expect a return. Companies create *value for shareholders* when the return to equity is greater than the cost of that equity – or greater than what investors could earn from other investments with an appropriate adjustment for risk. Since investors have other investment choices, the firm must provide them with an acceptable return (generally financial). Shareholders can invest in government securities, which would generally be considered to have zero risk. So an investment in a higher risk class such as a firm must generate a return greater than what could be earned from this risk-free investment.

Some shareholders may also have non-financial expectations; for example, that the firm will invest ethically. They may be concerned with the firm's contribution to environmental issues, or that the firm only trade with acceptable countries – for example, not invest in countries that exploit child labour – or that the company pay employees in less developed countries at an acceptable level. While these issues may have to be considered, we will assume that the overwhelming reason for making and holding an investment is financial. Nonetheless, when assessing the magnitude of financial returns, an adjustment for risk must be made, and risk can be affected by the aforementioned ethical concerns.

Creating value for shareholders is different from shareholder returns. Returns to shareholders are generated through share price appreciation and dividend payments, and these returns are to some extent outside the control of management. Share prices are driven by factors apart from firm performance, as has been observed with the short-term volatility of share markets around the world. So while shareholder value, as defined above, is a useful criterion for decision-making, given its volatility, return to shareholders is less useful.

Should the firm not meet investors' expectations, shareholders may sell their shares, driving down the share price and increasing the possibility of a takeover by others who believe that they can manage the firm's assets better. This transferability of equity shares, and the rights associated with them, is referred to as the market for corporate control, a topic to which we will return in Chapter 4 (➤Chapter 4). The relevance of this market for the present discussion is that if managers do not produce acceptable returns for shareholders, it is likely that investors will cause management to be replaced.

Chapter 4

Customers

Customers also make claims on the firm. At a minimum, they want products and services that meet their requirements in terms of functionality, quality, safety, delivery and, of course, price. They also value innovation and the development of new products, and, in addition, often have much broader expectations, related to the psychological and socio-psychological satisfactions from owning and/or using a product or service, as well as non-product-related expectations similar to shareholders.

Just as investors have a wide variety of investment alternatives, so customers have numerous choices. Markets are more competitive, customers more knowledgeable, sophisticated and harder to satisfy. They have strong sanctions they can exert over the firm: they can take their custom elsewhere or, for many discretionary products and services, may choose the option of not purchasing at all, and saving or investing their funds.

A firm cannot survive without revenue, so a customer orientation will be one of the foundations for the firm's success. Many firms find this competition for customers increasingly difficult, and are wrestling with the challenge of acquiring a stronger customer focus.

Employees

The third vital stakeholder group is employees. Employees value both intrinsic and extrinsic rewards, and are motivated by more than salary. If expectations about job satisfaction, growth opportunities and the like are not met, they are likely to leave. Further, as competition becomes more knowledge-based, attracting and keeping high-calibre staff becomes critical. High-potential employees with valued skills have many choices in terms of where they work, for what firm and industry, and, increasingly, in what country. Strategic managers need to ensure that these individuals remain committed to the firm. If their expectations are not met, they will leave the firm, substantially reducing its capabilities. The increasing knowledge intensity of business is reflected in a global labour market, changing the policies used to recruit and retain high-calibre staff.

> ### High-talent employees *in practice* – Arthur Andersen
> Arthur Anderson was once one of the world's largest accounting firms. When its involvement in the Enron scandal became clear, the firm began to dissolve. Within a few weeks of the depths of the problems becoming evident, partners around the world initiated and secured arrangements that would protect their personal futures.

Achieving a synthesis

When we discuss the needs and requirements of these three groups of stakeholders, we have to ask whether or not the firm can deliver value to all three at the same time, or does it have to make choices among them? If choices have to be made, how should these choices be made? On the first question, there is a wide difference of opinion. Commentators such as Copeland suggest that firms should adopt shareholder value as their guiding principle (Copeland *et al.*, 2000). He suggests that companies that deliver to shareholders show better productivity and employment gains than low-performing companies. An alternative view, and one to which we subscribe, is that creating value for customers generates margins that permit value for employees and other stakeholders. Another view is that a firm could deliver superior value to one group of stakeholders and yet deliver low value to others; in other words that these three stakeholders are mutually exclusive: we can only satisfy one by not satisfying the others. If this view is adopted, one of the key tasks of the board is deciding what balance is to be achieved between these different stakeholders.

Other stakeholders

While we have focused above on three key stakeholder groups, there are others. With the growth in outsourcing and networks, suppliers have often become extremely important, and supply chain management is a major concern in many firms We would like suppliers to provide a secure source, good products, competitive prices and continual innovation. Suppliers typically have other customers, and they may be able to seek business elsewhere. Or they may not invest, reducing innovation that then has a flow-on effect to us. Individuals and organizations that supply debt finance often receive special consideration, since debt is a major source of funds. In the event of a cash flow crisis, their actions are often critical to the outcome. Likewise, government, a recipient of tax revenues from successful firms but sometimes the investor of last resort in the unsuccessful, is an important stakeholder, particularly in times of financial crisis such as 2008/09.

The firm must also attend to the needs of the social/political community in which it exists. Any firm is given some 'benefits' from the legal system of the country, such as limited liability or a defined tax rate. In return, it has to meet various social objectives and requirements. These include standards covering employment safety, occupational health, minimum salary, environmental protection, ethical behaviour and competition behaviour.

2.8 GETTING STRATEGY IMPLEMENTED

Strategy development and implementation are normally distinguished, since they require different skills and are often done by different individuals and groups within the firm. Strategy generation is often the responsibility of the senior management group, while implementation is the responsibility of middle management. However, development and generation are obviously interrelated since there is no benefit – and significant cost – to developing a strategy that cannot be implemented. There are good reasons to involve middle management in the development process since this encourages commitment that assists implementation. In addition, the quality of the strategy that is developed may well be improved by the active participation of middle managers. They usually have good knowledge of the here and now, although in other cases – such as acquisitions – security requires that strategy be developed with little middle management input.

A strategy needs to be broken down into smaller elements for implementation, necessitating a control system to ensure that the strategy is actually implemented. Strategy will be nested as it is implemented throughout the firm, and its numerous elements or components need to be aligned. CEOs cannot implement strategy on their own: others must do this. The role of the CEO and senior managers is to ensure that it is done, that resources for change are adequate, that personnel have the requisite skills. Senior managers must also recognize the difficulty of creating organizational change – there may be considerable resistance to change from other employees. The design of an incentive system which facilitates implementation is therefore another critical task for management.

Implementation of corporate strategy inevitably involves the use of teams which cross business functions. These teams require leadership at all levels of the firm. Since the firm will generally be implementing a number of strategies at the same time, there is also a requirement for project management skills (►Chapter 10). Given the complexity of the modern firm, it may have strategies to expand in Europe, develop and launch new business in the US, change the culture to be more entrepreneurial and customer-focused, undertake a major cost reduction, all at the same time. Keeping these strategies aligned and implemented in an ongoing and timely manner is not easy. While large, centrally managed corporations are typically a thing of the past, so too are central strategy departments. Firms have decentralized. Despite this, at the corporate level, there will generally be a few groups of people who spend 60–80 per cent of time on projects – planning and tracking – the balance of their time will be spent on traditional strategic planning – industry analysis and so on. High-potential individuals often rotate through these positions, not only getting good knowledge from the business units, but also ensuring that their mental models at a minimum reflect current marketplace realities.

Chapter 10

2.9 SUMMARY

Managing global firms is a difficult and complex task, for the world is changing rapidly and the future is very uncertain. Creating organizations which thrive and prosper in such an environment requires judgement and intuition as well as a deep understanding of the capabilities of the firm and its environment.

In a changing world, any strategy is likely to quickly become obsolete, so strategic management must be ongoing, continually developing new and different strategies. Value is typically created by innovation, not by mere replication of the present, but any change needs to be fully resourced, both financially and with human skills.

Strategy is not a single decision. It involves a stream of decisions, each significant in its own right. A strategy can only be successful when these decisions are aligned and integrated, and strategy therefore requires commitment of the entire firm.

Strategic management is about managing the entire process, including implementation and generating resources. A strategy for the future will generally involve capabilities not currently possessed by the firm, and only a holistic view will suffice.

VIEW FROM THE TOP

MASTERCARD

MasterCard, the global credit card group, describes its business model as consisting of three elements as follows.

Franchisor

Through the thousands of financial institutions that are MasterCard's customers, the company markets a strong portfolio of brands and products worldwide, including MasterCard, Maestro®, Cirrus® and MasterCard®. With these, MasterCard opens the door to commerce at an unsurpassed network of more than 28.5 million acceptance locations around the world and, in many cases, guarantees payment through its system.

Processor

MasterCard's streamlined and intelligent approach to processing enables efficient commerce on a global scale. It is based on an agile network, one of the largest VPNs in the world, which offers unparalleled speed, integration and reliability. MasterCard helps banks and merchants grow by enabling rapid adoption of new ways to pay and offering customized solutions that deliver value through technology.

Adviser

MasterCard provides industry-leading insight and solutions that advance commerce on a global scale. Using sophisticated processing and data-mining capabilities, for example, MasterCard tracks consumer behaviour and buying trends around the globe and provides that knowledge to its customers. Through MasterCard Advisors, the largest global professional services firm focused exclusively on the payments industry, the company provides strategic and operational solutions covering the payments process from end to end.

QUESTIONS

1   Is this description of a business model consistent with the definition used in the chapter?
2   Does this definition of their business model assist in distinguishing MasterCard from, say, Visa?

ARGUS TECHNOLOGY LTD

Phil De Puy, CEO of Argus Technology, was sitting in his office in Perth, Australia, contemplating the future of the company. Argus was a medium-sized firm specializing in servicing mining equipment. Australia is a major global supplier of resources, and BHP Billiton, Rio Tinto and Anglo American all have major operations in the country. These resources include iron ore, coal, bauxite, zinc and uranium, mainly from open cut operations, in several Australian states.

Perth is the state capital of Western Australia, a state with significant resource deposits. Equipment used in mining these resources includes trucks, trains, excavators, conveyors and other expensive capital equipment. Most of this equipment operates 24 hours a day, so breakdowns were critical and had to be avoided whenever possible.

Argus had been established in the 1990s by George Argus, who left his position at Rio Tinto to establish the firm. It had grown quickly, and now numbered 300 employees. While its head office was in Perth, most of the staff worked in the distant mines, generally about 1,000 km from Perth. Argus maintained staff and substantial inventories of parts and equipment in many remote sites. The firm had developed the ability to offer a relatively broad range of services and could handle physical problems, such as a broken conveyor belt, as well as electrical and electronic problems.

De Puy had been born in France, immigrating to Australia with his parents as a child. He studied engineering at the University of Western Australia in Perth and on graduating worked with several mining companies on the operations side. He then decided to take an MBA degree at the University of Queensland, where he was able to combine some limited study of resources with his MBA. Following graduation, he joined Argus as head of the mechanical services division. This was followed by time in a planning role for the company. Upon the retirement of George Argus, he had been appointed CEO in 2009. As a company, Argus had been characterized by rapid growth, taking advantage of two trends. First, the overall growth of the resources sector in Australia, which had seen high growth rates and substantial price rises on the back of growing demand for resources from developing countries such as China and India, as shown in Figure 2.11. Second, there had been a trend towards increased outsourcing of equipment servicing by mining companies.

As a result, Argus has grown at a compound rate of about 25 per cent per annum for the past ten years. This growth had been funded partly from operations, partly from increased debt and partly from an initial public offering in 2005 which had seen the firm become publicly listed, raising AU$200 million. After the listing, the founder, George Argus, was appointed as chairman and retained a 30 per cent holding in the firm.

De Puy was convinced that while there were still major opportunities for organic growth, he also had to explore acquisitions. The equipment services industry had been consolidating and he wanted to ensure that Argus was going to be part of that process. There were also opportunities for Argus to expand into several new areas. For example, most of its business was in Western Australia, but major gas and coal seam developments were occurring in Queensland, over 3,000 km away from Perth. Uranium mining also took place in Australia, although this area was susceptible to changes in government policy. Another opportunity was in the technology which facilitated remote sensing of equipment. A combination of sensors and telecommunications technology made it possible to report real-time information

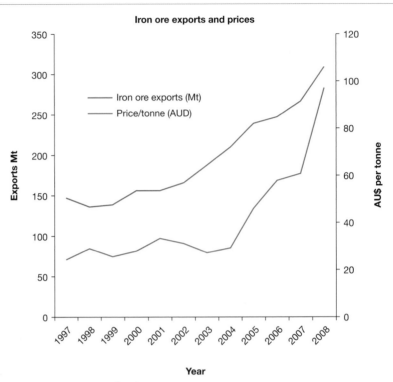

Figure 2.11 Australian iron ore exports and prices

Source: Australian Bureau of Agricultural and Resource Economics, 2010

on the operating performance of equipment. Such data could be analysed to understand when equipment needed service, and what kind of service was required. Service could be undertaken on a pro-active rather than a reactive basis, eliminating substantial downtime. While the firm had very little capability in this area, De Puy was convinced the opportunity was real. Moving into such an area would require a major change in the culture and capabilities of the firm, together with considerable ongoing investment. Such investment would depend on the strategy adopted to develop such a new area of business; would this be done through internal development, or should Argus actively search for possible acquisitions?

While thinking about the alternatives, De Puy attended a mining conference in Melbourne, and took the opportunity to visit Alto Limited, the investment bank which had assisted them in their IPO. When they were reviewing the prospects and opportunities facing Argus, one of the senior executives at Alto mentioned a firm which could be a possible acquisition candidate. This was Puerto del Rio, a medium-sized Brazilian firm which had recently developed technology to detect and report operating failures in deep water drilling rigs operating off Brazil. Staff at Alto had some detail on Puerto, and thought that the technology that had been developed could be adapted for use in mining and related areas, more in line with Argus's areas of expertise. Acquisition of Puerto by Argus would provide a platform into these markets, with first-mover advantages. It would take time to adapt the Puerto technology to the new applications but this would still be quicker than Argus developing the technology itself. De Puy estimated that Puerto's technology could be adapted to the mining sector in about 12 months, whereas it could take between three and four years to develop the technology internally. Further, the Puerto technology would allow Argus to enter completely new markets, namely the offshore drilling market in Australia and elsewhere, which could provide some protection against the substantial economic swings in iron ore export volumes and prices.

Argus was in a healthy financial position. It had seen substantial growth, but competition was expected to increase in its traditional markets. The Puerto acquisition would provide a significant competitive advantage in Argus's existing markets, as well as the possibility of expansion into adjacent markets.

De Puy had high expectations for the growth of the firm. The new technology would allow Argus to respond quickly if a machine was about to go down, and this technology had potential applications beyond mining and deep water drilling. For example, it might be possible to apply it to power stations and other major processing industries such as food manufacture.

If Argus was to diversify into this new technology, there could be major organizational implications. For example, would it be necessary to create a new division? How would Argus develop the required capabilities? There was also the question of should such a strategy be accomplished by acquisition or internal development? Acquisition of Puerto would probably cost about AU$200 million, and if it went ahead there would still be some expenses in adapting the technology to the new areas of application. On the other hand, acquisition of Puerto had several benefits. It would provide Argus with a strong position in what was seen as a fast-growing market – proactive diagnostic information on failure of mining equipment. It would also provide the firm with a position in another fast-growth market – applications in deep water drilling. Finally, the technology seemed to have applications in a wide array of other industries.

The question was whether Argus would be able to afford such an acquisition, and whether it could successfully manage the combined firm, with initial operations in both Australia and Brazil, as well as in two different industries, mining and deep water drilling. Further, the nature of the firm would change, becoming a combined technology and engineering services firm, with implications for continued R&D and recruiting.

QUESTIONS

1 What strategy would you advise for Argus?
2 Is the acquisition of Puerto part of your recommended strategy?
3 What are the strategic management implications if Argus proceeds with the acquisition?
4 What are the strategic management implications if Argus chooses not to bid for Puerto?

REVIEW QUESTIONS

1 Select a firm with which you are familiar. Describe the strategic decisions made by the firm, its strategy and the way that strategy has been managed over the last five years. Has the performance of the firm been satisfactory?

2 Describe the differences between an incremental strategy and a revolutionary strategy, and the circumstances when each may be used.

3 Select a firm with which you are familiar. Provide examples of incremental and revolutionary strategies adopted by the firm. Comment on the result achieved with each.

4 Select a firm with which you are familiar and describe its business model. Can you develop an alternative business model for this firm?

5 Specify what you would regard as the strategic time horizon for a national retail chain, a global resources firm and a management consulting firm. What causes the differences?

6 What is a stakeholder? Can a firm satisfy all stakeholders simultaneously or does it have to be selective?

REFERENCES

Anon (2010) 'Royal Dutch Shell', *Financial Times*, 30 July, p. 12.

answers.com (2010) Psion plc. www.answers.com/topic/psion-plc.

Apple (2010) Form 10-K – 2010. 3.

Barnett, F. W. J. & Berland, T. B. (1999) Strategic thinking on the front lines. *McKinsey Quarterly*, (2), 118–123.

Barsh, J., Capozzi, M. M. & Davidson, J. (2008) Leadership and innovation. *Mckinsey Quarterly*, (1), 37–47.

Beinhocker, E. D. (1999) On the origin of strategies. *McKinsey Quarterly*, (4), 47–57.

Beinhocker, E. D. (2006) The adaptable corporation. *Mckinsey Quarterly*, (2), 76–87.

Berthon, P., Hulbert, J. M. & Pitt, L. (2004) Innovation or customer orientation? *European Journal of Marketing*, 38(9/10), 1065–1090.

Bower, J. L. (1970) *Managing the Resource Allocation Process*. Boston, MA: Harvard Business School Press.

Buaron, R. (2000) New-Game strategies. *McKinsey Quarterly*, (3), 34–37.

Burgelman, R. A. & Grove, A. S. (2007) Let chaos reign, then rein in chaos – repeatedly: Managing strategic dynamics for corporate longevity. *Strategic Management Journal*, 28(10), 965–979.

Burke, L. A. & Miller, M. K. (1999) Taking the mystery out of intuitive decision making. *Academy of Management Executive*, 13(4), 91–99.

Collins, J. C. (2001) *Good to Great: Why Some Companies Make the Leap . . . And Others Don't*. New York: HarperBusiness.

Copeland, T. E., Koller, T. & Murrin, J. (2000) *Valuation: Measuring and Managing the Value of Companies*, 3rd edn. New York: Wiley.

Courtney, H., Kirkland, J. & Vigurie, P. (1997) Strategy under uncertainty. *Harvard Business Review*, (November–December), 66–79.

Crooks, E. (2010) Royal Dutch Shell's strategy finally seems poised to pay dividends. *Financial Times*, 17 March, p. 22.

Dodd, D. & Favaro, K. (2006) Managing the right tension. Harvard Business Review, (December), 62–74.

Drucker, P. F. (1994) The theory of the business. *Harvard Business Review*, (September–October), 95–104.

Dye, R. & Sibony, O. (2007) How to improve strategic planning. *Mckinsey Quarterly*, (3), 40–49.

Eisenhardt, K. M. (1999) Strategy as strategic decision making. *Sloan Management Review, 40*(3), 65–72.

EurActiv (2010) Europe hit by storm of mass layoffs. Retrieved 28 January 2010, www.euractiv. com/en/socialeurope/europe-hit-storm-mass-layoffs/article-178842.

Euronews (2010) Hewlett-Packard's European layoffs revealed. www.euronews.net/2005/09/12/hewlett-packard-confirms-european-job-cuts/.

Foster, R. N. & Kaplan, S. (2001) *Creative Destruction*. New York: Doubleday.

Ghemawat, P. (1998) Commitment versus flexibility. *California Management Review, 40*(4), 26–43.

Gupta, A. K., Smith, K. G. & Shalley, C. E. (2006) The interplay between exploration and exploitation. *Academy of Management Journal, 49*(4), 693–708.

Gupta, R. (1998) A case for corporate freedom. *McKinsey Quarterly*, (3), 154–162.

Hamel, G. & Prahalad, C. K. (1993) Strategy as stretch and leverage. *Harvard Business Review*, (March–April), 75–84.

Hampden-Turner, C. (1990) *Charting the Corporate Mind*. London: Basil Blackwell.

Hilmer, F. & Donaldson, L. (1996) *Management Redeemed*. New York: Free Press.

Jack, A. & Simonian, H. (2009) Roche crosses line in Genentech takeover saga. *Financial Times,* 13 March, p. 25.

Jansen, J. J. P., George, G., Van den Bosch, F. A. J. & Volberda, H. W. (2008) Senior team attributes and organizational ambidexterity: The moderating role of transformational leadership. *Journal of Management Studies, 45*(5), 982–1007.

Johnson, G., Scholes, K. & Whittington, R. (2008) *Exploring Corporate Strategy*, 8th edn. Harlow: Prentice-Hall.

Johnson, M. W., Christensen, C. M. & Kagermann, H. (2008) Reinventing your business model. *Harvard Business Review*, (December), 51–59.

Kindle 2 cost analysis (2009) Retrieved 15 January 2010, http://ireaderview.com/2009/04/26/kindle-cost-analysis.

King, M. (2006) Two reasons to avoid Footsie trackers. *MoneyWeek Investments*, 5 July. www.money week.com/investments/stock-markets/two-reasons-to-avoid-footsie-trackers.aspx?'

Kodama, M. (2007) *Knowledge Practice: Strategic Management as Practice*. Cheltenham: Edward Elgar.

Krisher, T. (2009) GM's Whitacre wants automaker to move faster, pledges quick repayment of government loans, 15 December. Retrieved 15 January 2010, http://ca.news.finance.yahoo. com/s/15122009/2/biz-finance.

Lovallo, D. P. & Mendonca, L. T. (2007) Strategy's strategist: An interview with Richard Rummelt. *McKinsey Quarterly*, (4), 56–67.

Lucier, C., Moeller, L. & Torsilieri, J. (2000) *Breaking Out: A Strategy Process That Works*. Paper presented at the Strategic Management Society, Vancouver, September.

Madslien, J. (2009) Aerospace investors eye engines for growth. *BBC News*, 18 June. http://newsvote. bbc.co.uk/mpapps/pagetools/print/news.bbc.co.uk/2/hi/business/8109391.stm?ad=1.

Magretta, J. (2002) Why business models matter. *Harvard Business Review*, (May), 86–92.

MarketWatch (2010) GM 5 year share price. *Big Charts*. http://bigcharts.marketwatch.com/quickchart/ quickchart.asp?symb=gm&sid=0&o_symb=gm&freq=2&time=12.

Mintz, J. & Metz, R. (2010) Apple's Jobs unveils 'intimate' $499 iPad tablet.

Mintzberg, H. (1990) The design school: Reconsidering the basic premises of strategic management. *Strategic Management Journal, 11*, 171–195.

Mintzberg, H. & Waters, J. A. (1985) Of strategies, deliberate and emergent. *Strategic Management Journal, 6*(3), 257–272.

Mitroff, I. (1988) *Break-Away Thinking*. New York: John Wiley.

Natterman, P. M. (2000) Best practice = best strategy. *McKinsey Quarterly*, (2), 22–31.

Nestlé (2010) Nestlé Health Science S.A. and Nestlé Institute of Health Sciences established to target new opportunity between food and pharma, 27 September. .www.nestle.com/MediaCenter/PressReleases/AllPressReleases/Nestle-Health-Science-SA-and-Nestle-Institute-of-Health-Sciences-established.htm.

Niendorf, B. & Beck, K. (2008) Good to great, or just good? *Academy of Management Perspectives, 22*(4), 13–20.

Psion (2010) Company profile. www.psionteklogix.com/about/company-profile.htm.

Puffer, S. M. (1999) Interview with Andrew Grove. *Academy of Management Executive, 13*(1), 15–24.

Schumpeter, J. A. (1976) *Capitalism, Socialism and Democracy*. New York: Harper & Row.

Slywotzky, A. J. (1996) *Value Migration*. Boston, MA: Harvard Business School Press.

Slywotzky, A. J. & Morrison, D. J. (1997) *The Profit Zone*. St Leonards, NSW, Australia: Allen & Unwin.

Unilever (2008) Annual report. www.unilever.com/investor-centre/annual-report-2008.

Uotila, J., Maula, M., Keil, T. & Zahra, S. A. (2009) Exploration, exploitation, and financial performance: Analysis of S&P 500 corporations. *Strategic Management Journal, 30*(2), 221–231.

Wetlaufer, S. (2001) The business case against revolution. *Harvard Business Review*, (February), 113–119.

White, G. (2009) New Shell boss must dig deep on costs and production. *The Daily Telegraph*, 8 June, p. B3.

Zesiger, S. (2000) GM's Big Decision: Status quo. *Fortune*, (21 February), 71–74.

For a range of further resources supporting this chapter, please visit the companion website for *Strategic Management* at www.routledge.com/cw/fitzroy.

Section 2

STRATEGIC ANALYSIS

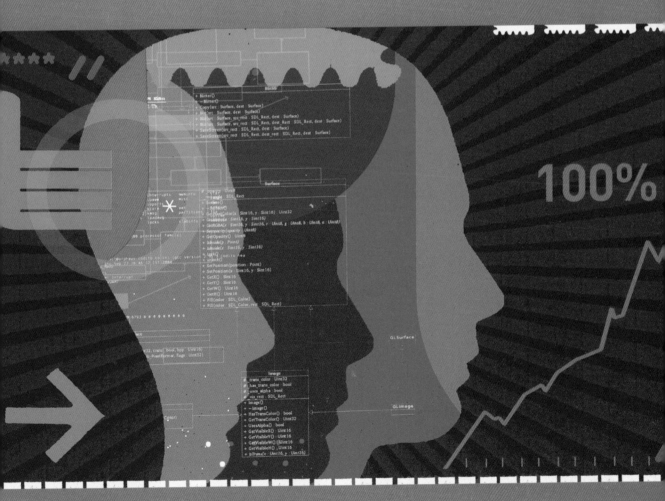

CHAPTER 3

EXTERNAL ANALYSIS

The business environment

LEARNING OBJECTIVES

Upon completing this chapter you should be able to:

1 Recognize that strategy is realized in the future: decisions are made now but their realization occurs in the future.

2 Apply the appropriate level of environmental analysis, depending on the locus of the decision-making group, corporate or business unit.

3 Identify the major changes in the remote environment and consequences for strategy generation and implementation.

4 Evaluate how changes in the industry environment influence strategy development and implementation.

5 Be able to incorporate an understanding of the major trends influencing the firm when developing strategy.

STRATEGIC MANAGEMENT IN PRACTICE

CHIP MAKERS

In November 2009, Intel announced that it was going to pay $US1.25 billion to AMD to settle a private anti-trust action. Intel agreed to drop its counter-suit, and further agreed that a patent-sharing agreement with AMD could be extended to the new joint venture chip manufacturing company, GlobalFoundries, into which AMD had spun off its manufacturing operations (Hesseldahl, 2009). GlobalFoundries Inc. is majority owned by Abu Dhabi's Advanced Technology Investment Company. In September 2009 it acquired Chartered Semiconductor Manufacturing Co Ltd at a cost of $US3.9 billion. This bid had been supported by Temasek Holdings, the Singapore government-controlled investment outfit, which had held 62 per cent of Chartered (Globalfoundries, 2009).

Despite the large payment to AMD, Intel is not yet clear of trouble. The Federal Trade Commission and New York State Attorney

General Andrew Cuomo are both investigating the company's practices for possible anti-trust violations (Patrizio, 2009). Some observers believe that Intel's chances of escaping these prosecutions have improved as a result of their out-of-court settlement with AMD. However, the company has also been ordered to pay $US1.45 billion, the largest fine in EU history, for anti-trust violations. Intel is appealing the ruling and the fine.

In their joint statement announcing agreement, Intel and AMD stated: 'While the relationship between the two companies has been difficult in the past, this agreement ends the legal disputes and enables the companies to focus all of our efforts on product innovation and development.' However, John Spooner, senior analyst for Technology Research Bureau, believes that 'The big win AMD expects to gain is in market share by eliminating the fear factor among OEMs of them spending too much time with AMD over Intel' (Patrizio, 2009).

This example emphasizes the complexity of the issues faced by managers of firms that compete globally. Intel and AMD compete all over the world, yet they also collaborate via an exchange of intellectual property to enable their customers to build computers that will work with either firm's chips. The anti-trust action above has been brought by AMD in the US, where Intel is still under investigation. At the same time, Intel is facing a fine levied by the European Union.

Ironically, although AMD is Intel's fiercest competitor, Intel really needs to ensure the survival of AMD, as Bradley points out (Bradley, 2009). Were AMD to fail, Intel would become a monopoly and face much more stringent anti-trust action. Thus Intel, known as a particularly aggressive competitor for many years, will have to moderate some of its more aggressive practices if it wishes to avoid future anti-trust difficulties, whether in Europe or the US.

Global firms must recognize that when they operate in multiple countries their strategy will be influenced by global as well as domestic considerations. Globalization adds a further degree of complexity to decision-making, and managers responsible for strategy development and implementation must understand this complexity. The chip makers example also illustrates how rapidly the business environment might change, shortening the life of a given strategy. Strategy must be reconfigured more frequently to reflect these changes.

CHAPTER OVERVIEW

As is clear from the above, developing strategy requires that managers have a detailed understanding of the external environment in which they compete so that a strategy can be developed to take advantage of any attractive opportunities or ameliorate emergent problems. This process of understanding the external environment is the subject of this chapter. Recognizing that strategy is realized in the future, we begin by reviewing the need for scanning the environment, paying attention to the need to be open to so-called 'weak' signals, trends for which the data are incomplete and even contradictory. We then review the broader or remote environment such as the major economic and political forces which will influence strategy development. However, firm strategy and success is also influenced by industry-specific factors; for example, are substitutes a major threat? This is followed by an analysis of the specific competitors of the business, addressing detailed questions such as 'Are customer requirements changing?' or 'Is the basis of market segmentation changing in ways which present an opportunity for the business?' We then briefly consider some additional considerations for firms engaged in networks. This is followed with a View from the Top by Rod Aldridge of the Capita Group where he discusses competitor analysis. The chapter concludes with a mini-case, Linn Products Limited, a small Scottish manufacturer of music systems which must develop a strategy while competing in a turbulent environment.

3.1 INTRODUCTION

The rapidly changing external environment faced by firms has placed heightened demands on strategic managers. Not only must they identify the changes, but they also have to develop a strategic management response – how the firm's strategy and architecture will be altered to adapt to and exploit these changes. At the same time, the value of any strategy and thus the firm's performance is also affected by these changes. Some of the changes make traditional business models obsolete – witness the growth of downloading of music and entertainment. Others change the rules for existing competitors, and challenge the assumptions of others, both new and old. Environmental analysis is therefore not a passive exercise, but rather an active and essential input to strategy development, helping the firm and its business units identify attractive opportunities and make decisions on where, and how, to compete.

The drivers of change are for the most part external to the firm. There is little that managers can do to influence a major demographic or socio-cultural trend. But they can react to such changes, or preferably anticipate these changes and utilize them in strategy development and implementation. There are numerous examples of firms that ignored major trends, as there are examples of other successful firms which identified and acted on emerging trends to help them establish strong positions in growth markets. In the twenty-first century, changes in the global economy are taking place on multiple fronts at an ever-increasing pace. The economic crises of 2008 and 2009 resulted in the demise of several major banks around the world, the nationalization of others, a huge increase in debt levels for government, and a recession in several major economies such as the US and the UK. Earlier crises such as the

> **LEARNING OBJECTIVE 1**
>
> Recognize that strategy is realized in the future: decisions are made now but their realization occurs in the future.

SARS epidemic and the eruption of an Iceland volcano severely disrupted global travel. These illustrate the turbulence of the environment in which firms operate, and the speed with which turbulence in one region or economy can be transmitted throughout the global economy.

Environmental scanning

Despite the fact that the logic above is irrefutable, it is often the case that firms do not do a very good job of environmental scanning. Instead it appears to be quite common for senior managers to ignore some environmental signals which, if they occur, will threaten the very survival of the firm. At the individual level, this reflects a tendency to filter information which conflicts with prior beliefs. At the organizational level, 'group think' can occur, where all managers seem to 'see' the world in the same way. This is another example of the risk when outdated mental models are held by senior managers, as was discussed in Chapter 2

 Chapter 2 (▶Chapter 2). To illustrate, almost all financial institutions ignored the signs of a collapse in the US sub-prime mortgage market, despite the fact that Warren Buffett warned of its strong possibility in 2003. Yet there were several danger signals about the impending bubble and the unrealistic expansion of derivatives, particularly the mortgage-backed securities. Senior managers at firms such as Northern Rock, Royal Bank of Scotland and Lehman Brothers all ignored these early signs of collapse. Instead, they acted as if they believed that the good times would last forever. Possibly the outsized bonuses they were receiving restricted their ability to interpret environmental changes.

For this reason, Schoemaker and Day suggest that firms should actively seek out weak signals, to try to find data which would invalidate the current strategy (Schoemaker & Day, 2009). Senior executives need to prevent group think; they need to challenge the mental models adopted by managers. They also need to encourage multiple perspectives and get constructive discussion about possible futures. Senior managers always need to be aware of the improbable, the environmental change or technological development that can put the future of the firm at risk. Yet Schoemaker and Day indicate that less than 20 per cent of global companies have the capacity to surface and interpret weak signals.

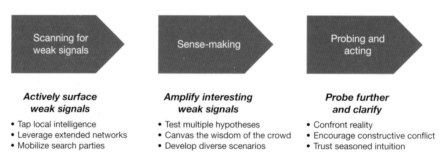

Figure 3.1 A process for making sense of weak signals

© 2009 from MIT Sloan Management Review/Massachusetts Institute of Technology. All rights reserved. Distributed by Tribune Media Services

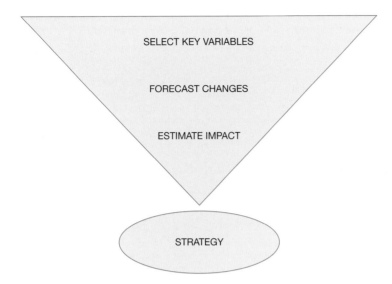

Figure 3.2 Process of environmental analysis

Schoemaker and Day go on to elaborate a process for building such capacity, as summarized in Figure 3.1 (Schoemaker & Day, 2009).

Strategy development requires the firm to understand what critical variables are changing, the pace at which these changes are occurring and their likely impact on the firm, as illustrated in Figure 3.2, above.

Select key variables

First, managers need to select the key variables that can affect their firm or business. These will depend on the firm, and the judgement, knowledge and intuition of the senior managers to identify what is relevant. Consider, for example, forecasting the demand for automobiles. Such variables as household income, interest rates and consumer confidence would probably be very helpful. On the other hand, in forecasting the demand for baby food, the birth rate would be a key explanatory variable. So what is relevant and important depends on the business concerned.

A framework for deciding which variables should be considered is shown in Figure 3.3. Possible variables are classified on two dimensions: their probability of occurrence and their impact if they do occur. While some attention needs to be given to all four cells, most attention will be devoted to the high-probability/high-impact set of variables with little attention to the low-probability/low-impact possibilities. Of particular concern are those events which have low probability but high impact – all too often senior managers pay too little attention to these, as was illustrated with the global financial crisis.

Another example of the danger of ignoring these low-probability/high-impact events is provided by the blow-out of the Deepwater Horizon oil rig in the Gulf of Mexico in 2010.

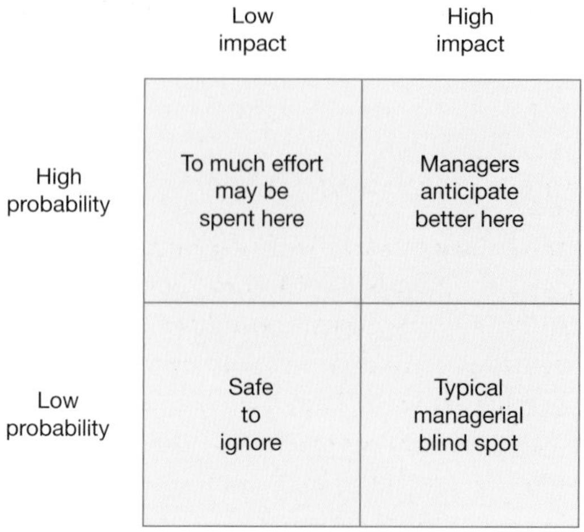

	Low impact	High impact
High probability	To much effort may be spent here	Managers anticipate better here
Low probability	Safe to ignore	Typical managerial blind spot

Figure 3.3 Environmental changes impact vs. probability

There had not been a major leak from an offshore oil well for 40 years – so it was a low-probability event. Yet the operator of the rig, Transocean, had been issued with a safety warning in 2005 on a key safety device, the blow-out preventer, which failed in the Gulf of Mexico rig (Mason, 2010). The question faced by managers is how much to spend on these infrequent events, particularly when consequences when they occur are huge. It has been estimated that the oil leak will cost BP $12 billion to clean up, while its market capitalization has been reduced by $30 billion since the event (*The Economist*, 2010a). One tool that can be used to loosen up thinking here is scenario analysis (Ralston, 2006).

Selecting key variables is a process characterized by both intuition and analysis. Good managers have insight into the most important drivers of strategy. At the same time, detailed analysis can assist in developing cause-and-effect chains.

Forecast changes

Second, we need to estimate, or forecast, the nature and pace of these changes. If forecast changes are likely to occur in the distant future, we may just keep a watching brief. Continuing the baby food example, birth rates in much of the world are declining. This is a relatively slow process, occurring over many years, so while its impact in any year is relatively minor, its long-term impact is substantial. Other changes, such as those in data storage and communications, are occurring very rapidly and the firm's response must be more immediate. In some industries the problem is to identify points of discontinuity, times when change is occurring very rapidly. Innovations such as the Internet, electronic books or developments in mobile phones and their applications, are examples of developments which generate entire new industries and place established firms under considerable pressure (Downes & Mui, 1998). In addition, some of these changes, such as population growth, will be relatively easy to forecast and a variety of forecasting techniques may assist in this process. For example, times series and regression models can prove very helpful (Hanke & Wichern, 2009) for these kinds of changes. Other changes, such as the future of the Russian legal system, are much less predictable.

Estimate the impact of the changes

Finally, we need to estimate the potential impact of these changes on the firm. Some changes will have a major impact, some very minor. The firm should clearly allocate the majority of its environmental scanning resources towards those changes that have both a high probability of occurring within the relevant time horizon and a major impact on strategy. However, we must always beware of the tendency to dismiss low-probability, high-impact events. Today, we take for granted technologies that our grandparents would have found almost impossible to conceive, and they have had an enormous impact on our way of life.

The reason for trying to understand the changing world is that strategy and strategic decisions are realized in the future, not the present. Strategic decisions are made now, but their implications are not realized until the future.

> The success or otherwise of a strategy depends not on the state of the world today but on the state of the world in the future.

Challenges of strategic management

We have emphasized previously that the world is changing rapidly, and often in unpredictable ways. For some people, this implies that there is no value in attempting to undertake detailed analysis of the environment, since any forecast will be wrong.

■ How would you respond to this statement?

Levels of environmental analysis

In analysing the external environment faced by a firm or a business unit, we distinguish three levels, designated as the remote, industry and competitive environment as shown in Figure 3.4, and use this framework to enable strategy to be developed at the corporate and business unit levels.

> Successful strategy development requires an understanding of changes at all three levels.

- **Remote environment**: the broad socio/technical/economic environment in which the firm competes. This environment is global in nature, exerts a powerful influence on strategy, and in many instances is slow acting. Due to the breadth of these changes they can be expected to affect a number of industries.

LEARNING OBJECTIVE 2

Apply the appropriate level of environmental analysis, depending on the locus of the decision-making group, corporate or business unit.

Remote environment
The broad socio/technical/economic environment in which the firm competes.

Remote environment

Remote environment

Figure 3.4 Levels of environmental analysis

Industry environment

Environmental changes that affect all competitors in a specific industry.

Competitive environment

Changes in customers, direct and indirect competitors that influence the competitive strategy of a particular business unit.

- **Industry environment**: changes that affect all competitors in a specific industry. Examples are changes in entry barriers from altered government regulation, new technology or the development of substitutes. Such changes influence all firms in the industry, possibly in different ways.

- **Competitive environment**: changes in customers and direct competitors that influence the competitive strategy of the business unit such as the development of new products by competitors, the emergence of new channels of distribution and the emergence of new customer values.

Which level of analysis is required depends on the level of strategy that we are considering – corporate or business unit – as shown in Figure 3.5.

When developing corporate level strategy, key decisions are which businesses should the corporation be in, what should be its geographic scope and how should resources be allocated among the business units? At the corporate level, analysis will generally be undertaken at two levels: the broad remote level and an analysis of developments in each industry in which the firm competes. Flowing from the remote analysis is a better understanding of major threats to the firm or opportunities that it may wish to pursue.

Strategy level	Analysis level	What analysed	Strategic decisions
Corporate	Remote	Broad environmental trends affecting all business units	New opportunities, resource allocation among SBUs
	Industry	Structural changes in the industry	Resource allocation
Business unit	Remote	Environmental trends influencing the specific SBU	Competitive strategy
	Industry	Suppliers, entrants, substitutes	Competitive strategy
	Product/ market	Customers, competitors	Competitive advantage

Figure 3.5 Corporate and business unit level of environmental analysis

For example, the firm may decide to move a substantial element of its manufacturing off shore to China, as many others have done (►Chapter 7). Since it is likely that such an investment may take several years to become profitable, the decision must incorporate a view on a number of broad socio-economic variables such as anticipated political stability in China and future exchange rates. Industry analysis is undertaken at the corporate level to ensure that the corporate level has a sound understanding of the attractiveness of the industries in which its various business units compete, enabling corporate executives to form a view on prospective profit levels of its businesses. Such decisions, whether to enter new businesses or to commit major resources to an existing industry, must be based on anticipated future results, possibly as far ahead as five to ten years. The firm must have a view on the future before it can commit resources, even if there is considerable uncertainty.

Chapter 7

Business unit managers need to undertake analysis at all three levels. Strategy for a given business unit will be influenced by certain developments in the remote environment, although which elements are critical will depend on the specific business unit. They must also understand changes specific to their industry. As we noted, a business unit must create value, with revenue greater than its costs. But it is possible for the industry structure to be such that while the firm creates value, it cannot capture that value for itself. If the business is in an extremely competitive industry, buyers or suppliers may capture all the value created.

Industry structure *in practice* – UK food company

The founder and former CEO of a successful British food company told one of the authors that he had sold his business because the demands of major supermarket chains such as Tesco and Sainsbury's had made it impossible for him to earn what he regarded as a fair profit. He remarked that he wished the new owners the best of luck if they believed they could!

Source: private communication

As this example demonstrates, in a fragmented industry powerful buyers can force industry prices down to unsustainable levels for their suppliers. Should this happen, we may see suppliers merging, to achieve not only economies of scale but also countervailing power. Alternatively, it may be that a firm in another industry has developed a substitute product with price/performance characteristics that will have a major impact on the revenue, and thus the profitability, of the business. Thus an understanding of the nature of the industry, and how this is changing, is essential in developing business level strategy.

Strategy at the business unit level is interlinked with the concept of competitive advantage, and should focus on developing such an advantage. This requires a detailed understanding of customer needs and how these differ across customer segments, how these needs are changing and likely future strategies of competitors.

In considering the subject matter in this chapter, there are two key ideas you should bear in mind. First, do not assume that the future will be a mere extrapolation of the past. Many alternative futures are possible, for the future does not yet exist. Where we are uncertain about the future, it may be very beneficial to consider alternative scenarios, opening our minds to the idea that change is inevitable and the need to be flexible when changes cannot be accurately forecast (Ringland, 1998). Second, you should recognize that since the future does not yet exist, we might be able to influence it through our decisions. Do not assume that the remote or industry environments are not subject to influence. Some of the most successful competitive strategies have involved doing that very thing!

LEARNING OBJECTIVE 3

Identify the major changes in the remote environment and the consequences for strategy generation and implementation.

PESTLE

Acronym for Political, Economic, Socio-cultural, Technological, Legal and Environmental aspects of the overall business environment.

3.2 THE REMOTE ENVIRONMENT

There are obviously many different aspects of the remote environment that can have a significant impact on the operation of the firm, its competitors and its customers. Some likely trends include resource scarcity, a slowing in the rate of globalization, a larger role for government, the continuing rise of China and India as economic players, and increased competition (Beinhocker *et al.*, 2009).

A simple acronym that can assist us in overviewing these aspects is the **PESTLE** model, so called because it covers the Political, Economic, Socio-cultural, Technological, Legal and Environmental aspects of the overall business environment, as shown in Figure 3.6.

Figure 3.6 depicts the firm as comprising a number of strategic business units to reinforce our emphasis that the analysis of the remote environment will be undertaken at both the

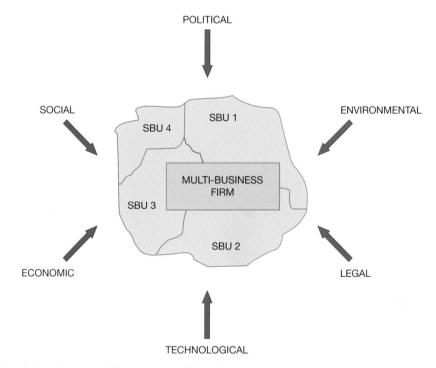

Figure 3.6 Framework for analysis of the remote environment

corporate and the business unit level. Since the firm's SBUs operate in different product/markets, they each need to undertake their own analysis of the remote environment, analysing the variables and changes appropriate to them. At the same time, corporate level staff will also be analysing the environment, possibly to identify merger and acquisition candidates or other growth opportunities. For example, both corporate and business unit managers at Unilever may be monitoring economic developments in Malaysia. When this occurs, the firm needs to ensure these two entities coordinate their activities. Firms often utilize corporate support staff to develop a view on relevant future variables, and all business units adopt that view. For example, corporate economic staff may forecast future exchange rates which are then adopted throughout the firm.

Economic

For most products, market attractiveness is strongly influenced by the size and growth of demand, which in turn is influenced by the country's economic well-being. There are a number of economic variables which may be relevant in determining opportunities, as shown in Table 3.1.

Many related measures of economic well-being are available but critical metrics include total GDP as well as per capita measures such as GDP per capita and disposable income per capita. In addition, since we are interested in the future, the growth rates of these economic variables would also be relevant. China is an attractive market for many firms, not because its GDP per capita is high, but because its growth rate is high and it is expected to become an even bigger market in the future.

Increasing globalization implies that an economic downturn in one country or region is quickly transferred to the entire global economy, and enhanced communications means that this is done quickly. The Asian crisis of 1997 originated in Thailand which had incurred unsustainable levels of foreign debt, mainly denominated in $US. In response, the government decided to float their currency, the baht, instead of having it pegged to the US dollar, resulting in a collapse of the currency. In Thailand, the currency fell from 26 baht to the $US in February 1997 to 54 baht to the $US in January 1998 before settling down to 36 in February 1999. As of 2010 it is about 32 to the $ (x-rates.com, 2010). This in turn resulted in a crisis of confidence in the currencies of other countries of the region, leading to currency collapses in Indonesia and South Korea. Other Asian countries such as Hong Kong, Malaysia and Japan were also affected to some extent, with a drop in the currencies, stock markets and asset prices.

The financial crisis of 2008/09 was deeper and moved around the world faster. While its effect was experienced most strongly in the US and Europe, other countries in Asia and South America were also caught up. A major contributor to the crisis was the huge increase in sub-prime mortgage lending in the US. Mortgages were

Table 3.1 Selected economic variables

Selected economic variables
GDP, GDP per capita
Disposable income
Interest rates
Exchange rates
Inflation
Unemployment
Balance of payments
Savings rate
Capital productivity
Labour cost and productivity

offered to people with quite limited credit-worthiness, individuals with no income, no jobs and no assets, often with low interest rates for the first two years. There was little scrutiny of mortgage applicants and their financial position. Other contributing factors to the crisis were cheap credit, poor risk management in the financial sector, weak financial regulation and a culture of greed in banking.

The assumption that house prices would increase forever was widespread. One other contributor was that in many US states, mortgages are on a non-recourse basis; that is, if the borrower defaults on payments, they can walk away from the loan; the lender can take possession of the house but no other assets. Consequently, this action was an attractive proposition when house prices collapsed and many borrowers had negative equity. Some of the same features occurred in the UK; for example, some mortgages were for 120 per cent of the purchase price of the house.

A further issue was how these mortgages were repackaged. Normally the mortgage originators did not keep the mortgages; instead, they were packaged together and sold as asset-backed securities, referred to as collaterized debt obligations, to other investors. This meant that the lender was not concerned with whether the loan was credit-worthy; they were more interested in whether they could sell it on to somebody else.

Typically, a portfolio of these sub-prime mortgages was separated into three tranches (or groups): a senior tranche, a mezzanine tranche and an equity tranche, with the senior tranche promised a return of 6 per cent, the mezzanine 10 per cent and the equity tranche 30 per cent. The senior group was generally rated AAA, the mezzanine rated BBB and the equity group unrated. The senior tranche had first call on repayments, and the levels below only received payments when the level above had been satisfied in terms of its guaranteed return. The three groups were also treated differently if there was any drop in the value of the assets behind the loan. The first 5 per cent of loan losses were borne by the equity group. If losses exceeded 5 per cent, the equity group lost its entire principal, with the balance passing to the mezzanine group. If losses exceed 25 per cent, both the equity group and the mezzanine group lose their entire principal and some losses are borne by the senior tranche. So the equity group was the last to receive payment and the first to bear any losses in value. It was typically held by the mortgage originator, since it was difficult to find buyers for these securities (Hull, 2008).

Added complexity occurred when groups of mezzanine tranches were combined, again split up into three groups, and sold as a collaterized debt obligation, with a proportion again sold as a senior tranche and rated AAA. However, this second tranche is only paid if the original mezzanine tranche does not suffer losses. And indeed this occurred. In this way, losses were transmitted throughout the system, and since investors seemed to undertake little in the way of due diligence, risks were unknown or ignored. In July 2008, Merrill Lynch sold senior tranches of those CDOs that had a principal value of $30 billion for 22 cents in the dollar (Hull, 2008). The problem was also influenced by the accounting principle of 'mark to market'; any decline in the market value of an asset was reflected in the income statement, leading to large announced losses for banks and others.

These mortgage-backed securities were insured against default, with only two firms offering this service – Lehman and AIG – with a product denoted as a credit default swap or CDS. These products were not seen as insurance, and in the US were not subject to any regulation.

As a consequence of the collapse, Lehman Brothers declared bankruptcy, AIG was taken over by the US government, Bear Stearns was rescued by a forced sale to J. P. Morgan, Northern Rock was nationalized, Fortis was split up and partly nationalized, the Royal Bank of Scotland was taken over by the UK government, and several Icelandic banks went bankrupt. Liquidity in the financial sector was frozen as firms attempted to restore balance sheets, and credit creation went into reverse.

How this will work out in the future is still uncertain. Many banks have a high proportion of toxic assets (loans) on their books, which will take some time to work out. The US government developed a $700 billion rescue package for the finance industry, an initiative replicated in many other countries such as Germany, the UK, Japan, Korea and China. Concern has been expressed that this will severely inhibit the ability of governments around the world to use fiscal measures in economic policy in the short and medium term.

What started as a financial crisis was quickly transferred to the real economy, with many countries entering into recession. For example, GDP in the UK fell significantly from late 2008 to late 2009, dropping a total of about 6 per cent before beginning to recover in early 2010. While the impact of this crisis was felt globally, not all countries were affected equally. For example, Australia, Brazil and China were less affected.

While the world was grappling with the longer term implications of this banking and liquidity crisis, in 2010 two new concerns emerged. First was the possibility of a 'double-dip' recession in 2010 and 2011 (Monaghan, 2010). Second was concern at the level of sovereign debt in several European countries such as Portugal, Ireland, Italy, Greece and Spain. In 2010 German banks had an exposure of $33 billion to the Spanish public sector and $23 billion

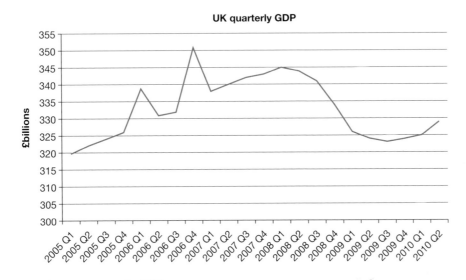

Figure 3.7 UK quarterly GDP

Source: Office of National Statistics

to the Greek public sector (Avdjiev *et al.*, 2010). In April 2010 S&P downgraded Greece's debt to BB+ and in May 2010 the EU announced an assistance package of €110 billion to try to stabilize the situation. While there is possibility of Greece defaulting on its debt, the more likely result would be a rescheduling with short- and medium-term debt converted into long-term debt. Any decision by Greece to default or to withdraw from the Euro zone is seen as having extremely severe consequences for Europe and the rest of the world (Evans-Pritchard, 2010). How this situation will develop is still very uncertain at the time of writing.

Of equal importance to strategists is not just gross domestic product on either a national or a per capita basis; strategy is also influenced by its distribution across the population. In India, although average incomes are still quite low, there is a large middle class, estimated at over 200 million people, representing a significant market opportunity for quite sophisticated products. Major PRC conurbations such as Shenzhen, Guangzhou, Shanghai and Beijing provide similar opportunities. One of the major global forces identified by McKinsey in 2010 was the contribution to global growth from emerging economies (Bisson *et al.*, 2010). They suggest that for the first time in 200 years, emerging economies will contribute more to global growth than developed economies, creating new middle-class consumers, with consequent impacts on innovation and product design.

The economic development of China exerted significant pressure on the rest of the world, particularly while China had such low labour costs of US 60c per hour. Along with European and US companies, Asian firms also established production facilities in China. Half the information technology products of Taiwanese firms are currently made in China. This movement resulted in many firms changing their value chains. When their manufacturing is outsourced to China, firms typically focus on marketing, design and innovation, developing differentiation and brand image, concentrating on intangibles. In recent years, however, Chinese labour costs have been rising. Chinese garment and toy manufacturers have felt increased competitive pressures from countries such as Vietnam, whose labour costs are lower. At the same time, foreign firms have been establishing technology and design centres in China itself, as General Motors has done with Buick.

Globalization *in practice* – Buick

The 2010 Buick LaCrosse was created in General Motors' Shanghai design centre – the Pan Asia Technical Automotive Center. This decision was made for a compelling commercial reason. In 2009 GM sold over four times as many Buicks in China as it did in the US (Ghetti, 2009). In the same year it was announced that China's passenger vehicle production and sales had become the largest in the world (Li, 2009).

For global firms, exchange rate movements can have a major effect on profitability and costs. A resources company may find that its revenues are in $US, but its costs are in South African Rand. Changes in the exchange rate can have a major impact on profitability unless the firm takes some hedging action. Firms use a range of derivatives, such as currency swaps, to attempt to reduce risk, as we discuss later in Chapter 4 (➤Chapter 4). The US dollar is the major currency used for international trade and is an international reserve currency. Due to the devaluation of the dollar after the financial crisis, China has proposed that it be replaced by Special Drawing Rights offered by the International Monetary Fund and is attempting to get the Yuan used more in international trade (*The Economist*, 2009d).

Chapter 4

The European Union, the most advanced grouping of nations, introduced a single currency, the 'Euro', in 12 member countries on 1 January 2001. For the first time, European consumers are able to directly compare prices in different countries without having to worry about exchange rates. At the same time, firms can more easily assess the performance of subsidiaries operating in different countries since they now all use the same currency. For example, a Dutch business such as Philips can more easily assess the financial performance of its Italian subsidiary, which now reports in Euros. This common currency places restrictions on the member states, since if a member country faces economic difficulties it is limited in the extent to which it can use exchange rates or interest rates in monetary policy. This was the problem faced by Greece in late 2009.

These economic variables have to be treated holistically. For example, we have already commented on the size of budget deficits in a number of countries, including the US, Greece, Spain, the UK and Ireland. During 2009 the US trade deficit had improved as the dollar weakened and the domestic economy slowed, but worries remained. The dollar was strengthening again, but the US economy had been kept afloat by the willingness of foreign institutions to buy US government debt. Given the uncertainty about the future performance of the US economy, however, it was feared that foreigners would no longer be prepared to support this trade deficit with inward investment.

As mentioned above, in late 2010 a major economic concern was the likelihood of a so-called 'double-dip' recession – that the world will slide back to negative GDP growth after a quarter or two of positive growth – with pundits divided on the issue. There was concern at the slowdown in the US, the UK and Japan, although China and India have maintained their historically high economic growth rates. This concern with the US was based on poor employment growth, a fall in house sales, more stringent consumer credit conditions and a widening trade deficit. Characteristic of the concern was the announcement from Intel that consumer demand for computers appeared to be slackening, resulting in the firm reducing its gross margin forecast (Menn & Nuttall, 2010). Offsetting this, the chairman of the US Federal Reserve Board announced that the US would do whatever was needed to avoid a double-dip recession (Hosking, 2010). At the time of writing, data from several sources appears contradictory and has created considerable uncertainty about future economic growth in the major Western economies. Goldman Sachs estimated in August 2010 that the probability of a double-dip recession was perhaps 25–30 per cent, still high for many people (*The Economist*, 2010b). This heightened economic uncertainty, with the medium-term future likely to be between moderate economic growth and a recession, makes any strategic decision exceedingly difficult.

Table 3.2 Selected political variables

Selected political variables
Competition policy
Taxation policy
Privatization
Regulation of financial markets
Employment law
Government stability
Multinational agreements
Government spending

Political

Governments set the rules for business in areas such as competition policy, taxation policy, multinational agreements and others, as shown in Table 3.2. Historically, governments intervened in national economies both to pursue political ends and to redress the perceived failure of market mechanisms to fulfil consumer welfare goals. In some countries, such as the US, this intervention has involved government regulation while in others such as the UK and France state ownership of business corporations was at one time vigorously pursued. In other countries such as India and China, state-driven mercantilism to increase exports and reduce imports has been the pattern.

For much of the twentieth century increased government involvement was the norm around the world. However, from the early 1980s until the late 1990s there was a marked shift in competition policy with an increasing reliance on free markets. Regulatory barriers around the world in such industries as airlines, banking, railroads, insurance, telecommunications and trucking were reduced. Governments seemed to have concluded that regulations designed to protect consumers or competitors in an earlier era were no longer beneficial. It was certainly true that far too often regulation had locked-in inefficient competitive structures, restricted entry and innovation, denying consumers the benefits of competition. In Europe, the EU is taking a more pro-active stand towards cartels, including higher fines, in order to enhance competition (Morgan, 2009).

Government involvement *in practice* – European banks

In early 2008, following a run on deposits that had jeopardized the bank's liquidity, the British government nationalized Northern Rock. This was the first of a series of actions that greatly increased the involvement of the British government in the ownership and control of various British banks (Croft, 2008). In August 2008, the UK government injected an additional £3.4 billion into the bank, which was in addition to the £30 billion injected earlier (Croft & Eaglesham, 2008).

In May 2009, the Allied Irish Bank announced it needed an additional €1.5 billion, in addition to the €3.5 billion already committed, to bolster its balance sheet by increasing its tier 1 capital (Brown, 2009).

In January 2009, Commerzbank received a capital injection of €8.2 billion from the German government, lifting its total support to €18 billion. In return the government took a 25 per cent stake (Atkins *et al.*, 2009). There were other conditions – the bank had to divest some businesses and was prevented from making acquisitions of related businesses for three years.

> ## Government involvement *in practice* – European discounters
>
> For many years French law inhibited the growth of such 'hard discounters' as German retailers Aldi and Lidl by restricting the size of inner-city stores. As one of many changes introduced by President Sarkozy and Christine Lagarde, Economy Minister, with the goal of lowering prices to spur economic growth, France will now permit larger stores in city centres. This is likely to assist the expansion of the hard discounters in French retailing (*The Economist*, 2008b).

Beginning in 2008, however, there was a dramatic increase in government involvement in the financial industry, described above, as the full scope of the global financial crisis became apparent. Governments in Eastern Europe, Germany, Iceland, Ireland, the UK, the US and other countries took drastic measures to ensure the ongoing viability of their respective financial sectors, including nationalization.

On the other hand, as global competition has increased, some legislation has come to be viewed as limiting the ability of corporations to compete on a global scale. While enforcement policy has changed somewhat, there may still be some way to go. Thus US regulations have sometimes constrained overseas firms attempting to operate in the US, and similar patterns exist in Europe. One such country is France, which has attempted to inhibit price competition in retailing through regulation.

Another major area where government action affects firm strategy is the country's taxation regime. Corporate tax levels vary around the world and as a consequence some firms have relocated their tax head office to low-tax countries such as Liechtenstein or Monaco. Location decisions are also affected by decisions on income tax rates for individuals. Following the British government's announcement of an increase in the maximum income tax rate to 50 per cent, and a special tax on bankers' bonuses, Bob Diamond, the American head of Barclays Bank, the largest British bank, and one which survived the global financial crisis (GFC) without taking government funds, said:

> If different countries regulate and tax the financial sector in different ways, banks in some centres will be put at a disadvantage, regulatory arbitrage will ensue, talent will flee and, in this case, the UK will suffer.
>
> (Ahmed, 2009)

Another issue to consider is which income will be taxed in which country. US firms and individuals are liable for US tax on their worldwide income. Some countries have reached a negotiated joint tax agreement with the US so that the taxation on their US subsidiaries is reduced.

Germany changed its tax system by removing any capital gains tax when companies sell their investments in other firms (*The Economist*, 2002). The impact of this has been small due to the decline in share markets, but it is expected to have greater impact in the future, when there could be a major reshaping of the German industrial landscape as shares in several of that nation's companies change hands.

In many countries, however, previously government-owned organizations such as airlines and utilities are being privatized and joining the private sector as governments adopt the view that private enterprise is more effective than government in promoting consumer welfare. The trend started in Europe in the 1980s and is now occurring even in such previously unlikely countries as the People's Republic of China (PRC). This trend has been aided by political change such as the collapse of Communism in the USSR and Eastern Europe (Yergin & Stanislaw, 1998). This change may even be accentuated by the GFC, as governments seek to reduce their debt burden by selling off assets.

Overall, the net result of the GFC is likely to be new regulation, particularly of the financial sector. Some have even mooted a fundamental change in the basic underlying economic philosophy, away from market economics to a more interventionist philosophy by government. This movement, however, is unlikely given the fact that countries are increasingly entering into multinational agreements through bodies such as the World Trade Organization (WTO), the International Monetary Fund and the United Nations. After many years, China has finally been admitted to the WTO despite the fact that this opens up many of its inefficient state-owned enterprises to global competition. In Europe, the European Union is taking on increasing importance as individual nation-state members are subject to its regulations, while many other countries have joined together to form economic and political unions, as illustrated in Table 3.3.

The ability of individual national governments to pursue independent economic policies has undoubtedly been limited by increased economic interdependency and emerging international institutions. Indeed, one of the major pressures resulting from such arrangements is to seek a so-called 'level playing field'. Such pressures mean that whenever privately owned and financed firms face competitive threats from government-subsidized or -owned firms, there is likely to be political uproar, as well as the prospect of action from such bodies as competition authorities or the US International Trade Commission. The likelihood of future

Table 3.3 Regional trading blocks

Regional trading blocks	
ASEAN (Association of Southeast Asian Nations)	Brunei Darussalam, Cambodia, Indonesia, Laos PDR, Malaysia, Myanmar, The Philippines, Singapore, Thailand, Vietnam
European Union	Austria*, Belgium*, Bulgaria, Cyprus*, Czech Republic, Denmark, Estonia, Finland*, France*, Germany*, Greece*, Hungary, Ireland*, Italy*, Latvia, Lithuania, Luxembourg*, Malta*, Netherlands*, Poland, Portugal*, Romania, Slovakia*, Slovenia*, Spain*, Sweden, United Kingdom

* = Euro currency (EU, 2010a)
EU candidates: Croatia, The Former Yugoslav Republic of Macedonia, Turkey

problems is magnified by the growth of so-called 'hybrid' companies that 'blur the line between the public and private sectors' (*The Economist*, 2009c). These partially state-owned firms are most common in developing countries, but are almost always politicized and are particularly prevalent in Russia and China (➤Chapter 13). Such firms are likely to pose difficult problems for both privately owned companies and regulators alike as they expand internationally (Guillén & García-Canal, 2009).

Chapter 13

Looking forward in the political arena, we expect further attempts to increase economic cooperation as the world economy becomes ever more tightly integrated. On 1 January 2010, China and the Association of Southeast Asian Nations (ASEAN) started operating the world's largest free trade area, reducing tariffs between the two parties to about 0.6 per cent (ChinaDaily, 2010).

Given the stresses created by the GFC, there is even a risk that the world may be moving towards a structure of regional trading blocs, and that economic 'warfare' might break out between the blocs. The opinions of most analysts suggest this is unlikely, but it is a scenario that prudent global managers should consider, particularly as they expand global sourcing.

The political stability of a country is an important issue when considering investment decisions. In the recent past there has been considerable instability in such countries as Zimbabwe, Pakistan, Fiji, Iran, Sri Lanka, China (Tibet) and the Middle East. In addition, Greece in 2010 was facing possible problems with high government debt and a consequent possibility of default. In Europe, concern at their dependence on Russian oil and gas has resulted in firms adopting some interesting approaches.

Political lobbying *in practice* – RWE

European governments are growing increasingly nervous about their dependence on Russian oil and gas. The dispute between Russia and Ukraine over gas supplies served as an alert mechanism. Two alternate supply lines are now under construction, even though some commentators point out that Russia never failed to supply any customer who paid them, including Georgia throughout the Georgia/South Ossetia/Russia conflict (*The Economist,* 2008a). This development also provides an illustration of the need for strategic managers to be pro-active politically. RWE, part of the consortium behind one of the pipelines, has hired the former German foreign minister to act as a 'political communications adviser' to assist in their endeavours (Lawton, 2009).

Finally, in many countries with federal forms of government, such as China, Germany or India, state or provincial governments or local considerations often have a major impact, as is shown by the illustration below involving Tata of India.

> ### Politics *in practice* – Tata
>
> Tata Motors has developed a new very small car, the Nano, selling for 100,000 rupees or $US2,100. It was to be built in West Bengal, but after protests, manufacture has been moved to the state of Gujarat, and this despite the fact that Tata is Indian, and well regarded. The move is indicative of the types of the problems foreign firms may have with provincial governments (*The Economist*, 2008c).

Socio-cultural

Strategy will also be influenced by changes in a number of socio-cultural variables, as indicated in Table 3.4.

Culture can be defined as 'the distinctive customs, achievements, products, outlook etc. of a society or group; the way of life of a society or group' (*The New Shorter Oxford English Dictionary*, 1993).

The society or group may be the inhabitants of a nation-state such as Chile, a geographic region within a nation-state such as the South or the Mid-West in the US, a geographic region encompassing multiple nation-states (for example, Hispanic) or a people without regard to geographic location such as the Armenian, Jewish and Chinese Diaspora. Furthermore, a single individual may 'belong' to multiple groups each having different cultures such as Turkish immigrants domiciled in Germany who adhere to Islam.

Cultures differ one from another on many bases; for example, language, religion, values and attitudes, education, social organization, technical and material culture, politics, law and aesthetics. They also change over time. Furthermore, within any individual cultural group, subcultures develop that may reflect both the broad group culture and the specific subcultural elements; for example, baby-boomers and Generations X, Y (Neuborne, 1999) and Z (those born between the mid-1990s and late 2000s). The buying behaviour of these different cultural groups varies significantly. In Western families, for many products and services, the female head of household traditionally did the shopping, whereas in rural Bangladesh, men do the shopping.

Population size, growth and distribution must also be analysed. Significant strains may result from such demographic shifts. One of the best known is the impact on social security systems as birth rates drop, longevity rises, and the number of older beneficiaries rises relative to the number of contributors. Not only does this change raise possibly divisive strains, it has significant economic and political ramifications. As shown in Table 3.5, the median age in countries such as Japan, Germany and Italy is forecast to increase dramatically, raising the possibility of a crisis in aged pensions and an unsustainable expansion of government expenditure. In response, several countries have raised their immigration rate to reduce the

Culture
The distinctive customs, achievements, products, outlook, etc. of a society or group; the way of life of a society or group.

Table 3.4 Selected socio-cultural variables

Selected socio-cultural variables
Cultural
Population size and growth
Population age and ethnic mix
Lifestyle changes
Social mobility
Educational levels
Labour market participation rates
Religion
Attitudes towards technology

median age. In other countries, a growing proportion of the older population has private pension arrangements, which will ameliorate the state-funded pension problem. In turn, these demographic changes create new opportunities and relationships for insurance and mutual funds.

Other socio-economic changes that may need to be analysed are lifestyle changes such as the increasing sophistication of customers, higher levels of education, better access to information and a greater acceptance of and familiarity with technology. The advance of automation and information-based industries typically leads to (relatively) decreased demand for unskilled labour and increases in demand for highly skilled technical and professional labour. The net result is bigger income differentials within societies, differentials that create a number of social implications, such as permanent unemployment of those individuals who cannot cope with the modern knowledge-based society. Another component of these changes is the shifting attitude towards globalization and the tension between localism and globalism. On the one hand, individual groups both seek their own identities and act out their group membership in various ways. Important bases for group membership include religion and nationalism. Thus, the growth of Muslim and Hindu fundamentalism is an important factor in the Middle-East/North African region and India respectively, but also has wider implications. In such diverse geographies as Turkey, Wales, the Basque country of Spain, Northern Italy, Brittany in France, Texas in the US and others, local and regional pressures are evident.

Concern has been raised about American, and general Western influence in many countries. The French government is fighting what some regard as a rearguard action against what it views as an American cultural invasion in general and an anglicizing of the French language in particular. However, concern is not limited to language. In late 1999, protests in many European countries against genetically modified foods led to rejections and/or bans on Monsanto's Roundup Ready™ soybean seeds. Protesters angry at the impact of globalization have disrupted several WTO meetings. Malaysia and other Asian countries have also expressed concern at the 'Westernization' of their societies and have issued calls for a return to Asian values.

To a large extent people do not notice culture on a day-by-day basis, but it becomes very evident when they encounter different cultures as firms move from domestic into foreign markets. Here, the issue is less one of cultural change than it is of attempting to understand a culture that is different. Companies acting in an ethnocentric manner may ruin an otherwise promising strategy implementation.

Table 3.5 Median age by country

Country	Median age, 2009	Median age, 2050
Japan	44.4	55.1
Germany	43.9	51.7
Italy	43.0	50.5
Slovakia	36.8	49.5
Indonesia	27.9	41.1
Mexico	27.2	43.9
Uganda	15.5	24.2
World	28.9	38.4

Source: UN, 2008

Technological

Virtually all observers of the business scene agree that not only is the pace of technological change extremely fast, it is also accelerating. If we were to arbitrarily select the end of World

Table 3.6 Selected technological variables

Selected technological variables
Information technology
R&D spending
New products
New technology
Global technology transfer
Technological advantages of a country
Networking and the organization
Incremental and disruptive technologies
Bio-technology

Moore's Law

The number of transistors on a computer chip will double every 18 to 24 months, and consequently the speed of microprocessors will double every 18 to 24 months.

 Chapter 5

War II as a start date, we would find that so many of the products and services we take for granted today have been developed since that time. A partial list includes colour televisions, dry copier machines, synthetic fibres and almost all plastics, cellular telephones, computers, integrated circuits, microwave ovens, passenger jet aircraft, communication satellites, virtually all antibiotics and numerous other life-saving drugs, ATMs, space travel, video and audio tape-recorders, CDs, DVDs, PDAs, the World Wide Web and innumerable other innovations. In many countries, an increasing number of households have given up their landline phones and rely solely on mobile phones. In the US, 25 per cent of households only have a mobile phone (*The Economist*, 2009a). Many of these innovations have fundamentally restructured industries and changed the lives of many of the world's citizens. Some of these technological changes are shown in Table 3.6.

Information technology is having a pervasive impact on firms and their strategy, driven by the rapid and continuing reductions in the price of these products. This rapid decline in costs is well expressed by 'Moore's Law' that the number of transistors on a computer chip doubles every 18 to 24 months and thus that the speed of microprocessors, at constant cost, also doubles every 18 to 24 months. Moore's Law means that computing power will become ever faster and cheaper.

Although some observers anticipate that exponential gains in chip performance will slow eventually, most experts agree that Moore's Law will govern the industry for at least another ten years. Other technological developments have resulted in faster processing speeds, as well as reduced heat and power consumption (Markoff, 2002).

In response to such developments, broadband penetration is rising rapidly across the globe, as Figure 3.8 indicates, with up to 500 million subscribers around the world.

As a consequence of these changes, significant developments can be expected in electronic books, putting traditional publishers under pressure. Newspapers are also under challenge, as people download news and information from the Internet. In addition, Internet advertising is growing faster than print advertising, adding to the pressure. A question for senior newspaper managers is whether they can develop a business model which allows them to charge for content to support their news-gathering activity.

Not only will increasing numbers of people around the world have access to powerful computing, computer power can be built into devices other than computers themselves. Already, computers allow such diverse products as vehicles, aircraft, surgical equipment, fruit harvesting equipment and elevators to operate more efficiently, predictably and safely. In the future we may even see computer chips in packaging as costs continue to decline (Ferguson, 2002). These applications reflect the effects of the convergence of computing, communications and media technologies, and the growth of the knowledge economy, topics to which we will return in Chapter 5 (➤Chapter 5).

The changes above are illustrative of the impact that information technology is having on business practices. This impact is also manifest in the changing mix of capital investment.

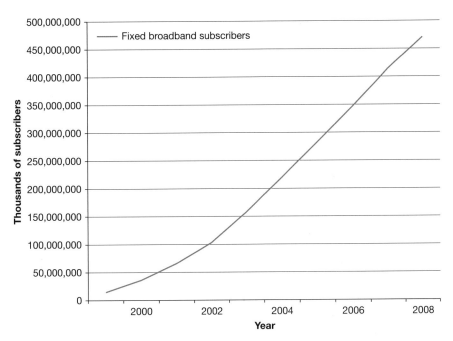

Fixed broadband subscribers

Figure 3.8 Global broadband penetration

Source: Selected data taken from the report, data extracted manually from a graph at www.itu.int/osg/
blog/2008/11/29/GlobalBroadbandSubscribersExceeded400MillionInNovember2008.aspx

As shown in Figure 3.9, US firms have been allocating an increasing proportion of their
capital expenditure to information technology, computer hardware and software, and communications equipment. This chart shows the ratio of investment in information processing
equipment and software to investment in all other fixed assets by US businesses over the
period 1970 to 2007. As can be seen, this ratio has increased dramatically, from 40 per cent
in 1976 to 90 per cent in 2008. There was a slight reduction following the overspending on
the millennium change (Y2K) during 2000 but the ratio appears to again be increasing. In
dollar terms, IT investment has increased from $US20 billion in 1976 to $US1,000 billion in
2008.

The Internet is a major new technology affecting the business landscape. The Internet
is, or can be, many things. It is a distribution channel, a communications tool, a marketplace
and an information system. For example, it can alter the way in which the firm communicates
with its customers and suppliers, the way in which it collects customer data and the amount
of information available to customers. We have already noted that firms are created because
the costs of organizing and maintaining them are lower than transaction costs in the market.
One of the implications of developments in computers, networks, communications and data
storage is that they have changed transactions costs and hence are opening up the possibility

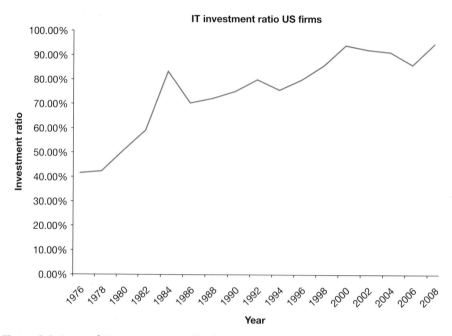

Figure 3.9 Ratio of IT investment to all other investment by US firms

Source: Bureau of Economic Analysis (US), National Economic Accounts, Fixed Asset Table 2.7 (BEA, 2009)

Disintermediation
The process whereby the function of an intermediary can be eliminated.

of significant industry restructuring. These developments may also create **disintermediation**, where the function of an intermediary can be dispensed with.

When buyers and sellers of, say, insurance can find each other easily over the Internet, who needs intermediaries such as brokers? Extending this example, in a recent study, McKinsey and Co identified a number of technological trends which they considered had the potential to reshape organizations and their strategy. One such trend is technology which allows the development of web-based communities that develop, market and support products and services. For example, many companies support and encourage bloggers who post their comments and reviews about products and services (Bughin *et al.*, 2010).

These changes are most likely to occur in industries where 'products' can be digitized. A good example is personal financial services. Table 3.7 shows the average cost per transaction in retail banking for five different modes.

As the data above indicate, there is a substantial incentive for retail banks to move to other channels of distribution, but they are constrained by their legacy assets of a branch network. A new entrant without this high-cost structure may find barriers to entry have been reduced, the new barrier being technology, customer acceptance of technology and data security. Similar

Table 3.7 Average cost per transaction in retail banking

Mode	Cost/transaction ($AU)
In-branch teller	$5.40
Telephone: CSO	$5.20
ATM (excluding deposits)	$0.60
Telephone; voice response	$0.16
Internet	$0.06

Source: Internal Costing Data, Major Australian Bank

developments have occurred in industries such as hotels, car hire and share trading, where online trading now accounts for about 20 per cent or more of all trades.

The Internet is an example of so-called **Metcalfe's Law**, namely that the value of a network to an individual user is proportional to the square of the number of users. Hence the interest in interconnection, open standards and the development of new protocols such as XML that carries information on what data is being transmitted as well as the format of that data. At the same time, the Internet increased firms' concern with data security from external hackers or internal staff abusing the system. In early 2010 Google created a major stir by announcing that it and other major multinational firms had been subject to a cyber attack from China, and that it was considering withdrawing from the Chinese market. Certainly, data security is one of the major obstacles to the widespread adoption of e-commerce, and developments in sophisticated encryption systems will be critical.

Many technological innovations are characterized by non-linear growth patterns, and often follow a logistics adoption curve. Managers who project initially low growth rates into the future may be surprised as inflection points are passed and rapid growth occurs (Foster, 1986). As Christensen has noted, technological change can be categorized as sustaining or disruptive (Christensen, 1997). **Sustaining technologies** improve the performance of established products along the dimensions that mainstream customers in major markets have historically valued. This type of technological change rarely precipitates the failure of established firms – it represents a continuation of the present. Such changes are seen as more controllable by management.

Disruptive technologies are those that bring a new and very different value proposition to the customer. Such innovations have features that are highly valued (initially) by a limited number of customers, often customers new to the market. These new products are often seen as inferior by existing customers, initially under-performing established products. They are often simpler, smaller, cheaper and easier to use than existing products. In new applications, these attributes may have significant value. Such disruptive technology may precipitate the failure of leading firms, since they pay too much attention to the issue of cannibalization of their existing products. The real problem often arises from their lack of awareness of the rate of technological change, and consequent functional improvement, of the new technology. Since it is difficult to analyse such markets, established and bureaucratic firms are unlikely to give them the attention they require.

Business history is also replete with examples of major companies that turned down inventions which were ultimately extremely successful. Chester Carlson, inventor of xerography, was turned down by IBM, RCA, A. B. Dick and many other companies before Joe Wilson, CEO of a relatively small Rochester company, Haloid Corporation, had the courage to bet the future of his company on Carlson's invention (Dessauer, 1971). One inventor who overcame numerous obstacles was James Dyson in the UK. After being rejected by several major companies, Dyson went on to found his own company and become a major competitor to those firms that had earlier rejected him.

Metcalfe's Law
The value of a network to an individual user is proportional to the square of the number of users.

Sustaining technology
Improves the performance of established products and services along the dimensions of performance that mainstream customers in major markets have historically valued.

Disruptive technology
A new technology which brings a new and different value proposition to the market, thereby disrupting and possibly destroying the market for the older technology.

> ### Innovation *in practice* – Dyson
>
> All major appliance manufacturers turned down James Dyson, inventor of the bagless vacuum cleaner, when he approached them with his invention. He eventually started his own company which by 2001 was the market leader in the UK (Rohrlich, 2002). Hoover, a brand once so dominant that its name was a generic for vacuum cleaners in many countries, had turned down the technology but subsequently were found guilty of copying it (Uhlig, 2000). By 2005 the Dyson company had rocketed to number one position in Japan, the USA, Ireland, Spain, Belgium, Switzerland and Australia. Trevor Baylis, inventor of the clockwork radio, had similar disappointments before a new South African company started producing his design (Bayliss, 2010). Because of his experiences, he set up a company to advise other would-be inventors on how to overcome these difficulties (Stone, 2005).

Legal

As we saw with the opening strategic management in practice example, global firms must pay considerable attention to legal considerations and ensure that their strategies comply with legal requirements, as illustrated in Table 3.8.

The legal framework of a country influences firm strategy through its laws on mergers and acquisitions, capital movements, industry regulation and employment conditions among others. Legal frameworks differ across countries. The US and the UK have a well-developed legal system based on precedence and case law. In most of Europe the basis of the legal system is the Napoleonic Code. Other countries are still trying to establish a strong and independent legal system. For example, economist Andrei Markov, now with the World Bank, but previously associate dean at Moscow State University, explains the growth of gang warfare in Russia as a consequence of a poorly developed system of commercial law, and the absence of an effective police force (personal communication).

Many industries, particularly high-technology industries, are prone to patent disputes, where one firm claims that a competitor has infringed its technology. So Nokia and Apple have been in conflict for some years, with each claiming the other has used its technology. Nokia has claimed that Apple infringed its patents on antenna innovations for compact devices, while Apple has claimed that Nokia infringed its patents in smart phones (BBC, 2010). Resolution of these claims can be lengthy and expensive for both firms.

Similarly, the PRC has been struggling to develop a commercial code, and the law governing business activities is still in evolution, adding an element of risk to all business decisions affecting one of the world's largest and fastest-growing economies.

Most developed countries have an active and politically independent regulatory framework. In the EU, there are several

Table 3.8 Selected legal variables

Selected legal variables
Legal framework
Status of the rule of law
Regulatory framework
Trade practices
Consumer protection
Patents

The Competition Commission

The Competition Commission (CC) is one of the independent public bodies which help ensure healthy competition between companies in the UK for the benefit of companies, customers and the economy.

We investigate and address issues of concern in three areas:

- In mergers – when larger companies will gain more than 25 per cent market share and where a merger appears likely to lead to a substantial lessening of competition in one or more markets in the UK.
- In markets – when it appears that competition may be being prevented, distorted or restricted in a particular market.
- In regulated sectors where aspects of the regulatory system may not be operating effectively or to address certain categories of dispute between regulators and regulated companies.

Directorate-Generals responsible for defined areas of regulation. There is a D-G Competition, a D-G Environment and a D-G Health and Consumer Protection. The latter body is responsible for food labelling in general, and with labelling of genetically modified foods in particular ('Activities of the European Union', 2003). In addition, individual countries have their own regulators, such as the UK's Competition Commission, responsible for ensuring healthy competition between firms in the UK.

In the US, bodies such as the Environmental Protection Agency (EPA), Securities and Exchange Commission (SEC) and the Federal Trade Commission (FTC) are powerful actors which have to be considered when establishing strategy. In a global world, it is imperative to recognize that the reach of such agencies often goes beyond their immediate geographies.

Banking, accounting and securities rating industries are also under considerable pressure from governments around the world to change their practices. One concern is about conflict of interest: can a rating agency perform with integrity when it is to be paid by the issuer

Mergers *in practice* – Linde

The US FTC prevented the takeover of a British firm, BOC, by a combination of L'Air Liquide (French) and Air Products (US). Following the failure, the two firms had to pay BOC a breakup fee of $US100 million for failing to secure the deal (BBC, 2000). BOC was eventually taken over by the German company Linde and approved by EU regulators (Cadwell, 2006).

In similar manner, European competition authorities were successful in blocking GE's attempted takeover of Honeywell. They also vehemently opposed the merger of Boeing and McDonnell-Douglas, but were unable to prevent it.

of the security? Can an audit firm provide an unbiased and independent audit when it also engages in consulting work for the same client? Should banks be shorting the very same securities that they are also selling to their investor clients? Can a bank provide unbiased investment reports on a firm when it is also touting for consulting work, mergers and acquisitions or IPOs with that same firm? These practices have always been of concern, but they came into worldwide focus as a result of the global financial crisis of 2008/09. New and different regulatory regimes, particularly of the financial services sector, seem certain to be introduced in future.

Chapter 13

Different countries have different views on the social responsibility of the firm. Germany has always been on the forefront of employee consultation and board participation (see Chapter 13) (▶Chapter 13) but now the EU is strengthening the obligation of European firms to 'inform and consult' workers' representatives about company strategy. The EU employment commissioner has suggested that employees are the main stakeholders in a firm. This may affect the ability of a firm to close a plant or reduce employment in the EU, as experienced by Marks and Spencer when it attempted to close several stores in continental Europe. Some managers regard these requirements as an infringement on the right to manage, since it will make labour markets less flexible. However, the Collective Redundancy Consultation (under an EU Directive) requires that any employer contemplating collective redundancies must hold consultations in good time with the workers' representatives, with a view to reaching an agreement. The specific conditions are quite complex, and are designed to protect workers affected by lay-off decisions (EU, 2010b). Almost all countries offer some kind of protection against arbitrary lay-offs ('Statutory or voluntary redundancy and lay-off rights', 2007).

Some professional bodies also have a major impact on firm behaviour. International accounting bodies now require firms to record all financial assets and liabilities at their current market value rather than at their historic cost (IASB, 2010). The goal is to provide more realistic information since financial markets are now more volatile. This change has had major implications for banks. The value of their loans now fluctuates with changes in interest rates and property values. This forced banks to write down loans and played a part in creating the conditions that led to the GFC. These changes have to be incorporated into banks' income statements, producing large accounting losses for some firms.

International Financial Reporting Standards (IFRS)
A set of understandable, enforceable and globally accepted financial reporting standards, developed by the IASB, an independent not-for-profit organization.

All listed EU companies have been required to use the International Financial Reporting Standards (IFRS) since 2005, and around the world, companies and firms have agreed to converge on these standards. Most will be in compliance by late 2011, although US companies may take a little longer to convert exclusively to IFRS from their statements prepared according to the Generally Accepted Accounting Principles (GAAP), the prior US requirement.

Looking at likely future trends, we believe that countries are likely to maintain policies which lead to competition in product markets. On the other hand, in such areas as health and safety, the environment, rights of various minorities and so on, it seems likely that firms will face more stringent standards in the future. Further, globalization is beginning to have significant repercussions for the legal environment.

Environmental

Senior managers can expect to have to deal with a variety of environmental issues that will have significant impact on their companies' future prospects, as shown in Table 3.9. In many cases, firms have made voluntary changes, but there is an increasing volume of legal and regulatory requirements with respect to the environment. For example, EU Article 6 EC embraces the concept of sustainable development which is expected to result in its incorporation into EU company law (Sjafjell, 2008).

Table 3.9 Selected environmental variables
Selected environmental variables
Environmental legislation
Carbon emissions
Role of non-government organizations
Social responsibility
Sustainability

Executives in the automobile industry, for example, have been subject to increased pressure from governments, environmental groups, various single-issue advocacy groups and the public at large. The EU has established targets for the disposal of automobiles that have reached the end of their life. Member states are required to ensure the reuse of components which are suitable for reuse, the recovery of components which cannot be reused and to give preference to recycling when environmentally viable. By 1 January 2015, the reuse and recovery is to be increased to a minimum of 95 per cent of the weight of the vehicle (Kanari *et al.*, 2003).

Changes in the physical environment, roughly viewed as comprising the natural and man-made environment, affect our daily lives and the functioning of our organizations. Natural and man-made forces coexist in an uneasy equilibrium but whereas some natural forces seem independent of human action, other changes in the natural environment result from it. More fundamental changes may have a variety of consequences. For example, heightened awareness of the damage to the natural environment caused by pollution has given rise to new industries such as pollution control and renewable energy. In countries such as France, Germany and Australia pollution has become an important political issue and legislators are elected as members of 'green' parties. Indeed, in many countries, the strength of the environmental movement has led to strong legislation affecting firms' production systems, products and packaging.

If for no other reason than shortage of landfill sites and increasing property prices, recycling has become a major issue that affects many firm decisions. Packaging waste is the focus of many consumer groups, but there has been great progress in recycling some materials. The EU has long had aggressive targets in this area, having set the goal of having at least 60 per cent by weight of packaging waste to be recovered or incinerated at waste incineration plants with energy recovery by the end of 2008. Specific goals by material type were established: 60 per cent by weight for glass, paper and board; 50 per cent by weight for metals; 22.5 per cent by weight for plastics and 15 per cent by weight for wood. We have been unable to determine whether or not these targets were achieved, but in almost every developed country there has been a significant increase in the extent of recycling. Indeed, within the EU, new waste management requirements came into place on 12 December 2010.

Even when recycling, however, quite sophisticated analysis of the total system may be required, since almost all recycling activities themselves create carbon emissions. In some cases they may actually increase net carbon emissions if significant transportation is involved.

Chapter 2

The example below indicates some of the issues that managers need to consider when developing an environmentally sustainable strategy.

Even broader in its implications are the pressures for managing and reporting of carbon emissions. As we noted in Chapter 2 (➤Chapter 2), many large firms are now reporting on their carbon footprint and making commitments to reduce them. Most countries in the EU

Challenge of strategic management

As concerned consumers, should we be purchasing beverages in cans or plastic bottles, assuming initially that both are made from virgin materials, neglecting any benefit from recycling?

Aluminium cans take a great deal of energy and natural resources to process and transport. Aluminium begins as bauxite ore, is refined into aluminium oxide, and ends up as blocks of aluminium, a supply chain that can take it halfway around the planet. Next the blocks are heated and turned into large rolls of aluminium before being transported yet again. The sheets are stamped and manufactured into cans, which are then filled and distributed to stores.

Plastic bottles are made from PET (polyethylene terephthalate) and have a less complicated supply chain, which involves making pellets from petroleum derivatives and then blow-moulding the bottles. Plastic contains more petroleum, but aluminium requires more energy because of its higher melting point and complex processing.

The amount of petroleum used in making the 2-litre bottle is around 325 g, and the resulting greenhouse gas emissions from its manufacture are around 825 g. An aluminium can made from virgin materials results in the emissions of 280 g of carbon dioxide. Does this mean that the can is better? Well, keep in mind that the bottle holds more beverage, so we need to take that into account. You would need to buy 5.6 cans, almost a full six-pack, to equal the volume of the bottle. The 5.6 cans would be responsible for 1,568 g of carbon dioxide emissions. So it looks like the 2-litre bottle results in about half of the greenhouse gas emissions of the equivalent amount of cans. Is this the end of the story? What about transportation emissions?

Let's assume that both beverage containers are filled in the same facility and shipped to the store with the same truck. The bottle weighs 2.05 kg when full (2 litres plus 50 g) and the 5.6 cans weigh 2.084 kg (2 litres plus 84 g). This means that the cans require slightly more fuel to transport than the bottles. This suggests that plastic bottles produce less greenhouse gas emissions. A more complete analysis would consider the impact of recycling. The US recycles about 56 billion aluminium cans per year, reducing the need to use virgin aluminium. On the other hand, plastic bottles can be melted and extruded into fine fabrics used to make winter fleeces.

As this example demonstrates, answering what seems to be a simple question of aluminium can versus plastic bottle requires detailed analysis of emissions over the entire life cycle of the alternative.

(Paster, 2008)

---

participate in its Emission Trading Scheme, aimed at reducing carbon dioxide emissions. Australia and the United States have announced their intentions to introduce similar plans. However, an all-party committee of UK Members of Parliament has reported that the permits are priced far too low to be effective. They suggest that the price needs to rise from €15 to €100 per ton to be effective (Wilson, 2010). Such a price increase would have a major impact on all energy-intensive industries. The failure of the Copenhagen global warming conference to reach any agreement has undoubtedly set back the effort to reduce global emissions, but individual countries and regions will be continuing their efforts to tackle the problem.

Lest we sound too gloomy, it is important to emphasize that changes such as restrictions on carbon emissions also favour the development of whole new industries. Technologies such as solar, nuclear, wind, methane, hydro and wave all stand to gain from these changes.

Innovation *in practice* – Vestas

The Danish firm Vestas is the world's leading producer of wind turbines, with a 20 per cent share of the world market. Denmark has led the way in installing wind farms, which account for about 20 per cent of the country's electricity generation. Vestas' vision and strategy are shown below:

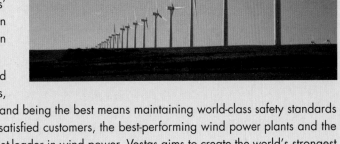

- **Vision**: Wind, Oil and Gas is Vestas' vision, which expresses the ambition of making wind an energy source on a par with fossil fuels.
- **Strategy**: Vestas's strategy is called No. 1 in Modern Energy. To Vestas, being No. 1 means being the best, and being the best means maintaining world-class safety standards at all Vestas' sites, having the most satisfied customers, the best-performing wind power plants and the greenest production. Being the market-leader in wind power, Vestas aims to create the world's strongest energy brand.

Being the industry's leading player and a pure-play spokesperson, Vestas aims to ensure that wind power remains at the top of the political agenda. This is achieved through dialogue with politicians, public servants, interest groups and NGOs the world over and through advice and information to the public about the potential of wind power, both in individual markets and worldwide.

(Vestas, 2010)

Vestas is clearly very committed in its focus, and has benefited from a favourable national sentiment in Denmark, and the movement towards limiting carbon emissions. It is interesting to note how perceptive they are in understanding the political context of their operations, since they intend to have dialogues not just with customers, but also with politicians, public servants, interest groups and NGOs the world over.

Of course, wind power is not the only route to sounder environmental practices. A small whisky producer in Scotland has developed its own approach.

Innovation *in practice* – Bruichladdich

Bruichladdich, the 1881 malt whisky distillery, has bought two anaerobic digesters. Using the waste malt from the distillery the digesters will produce biomethane that will be used to generate electricity. The firm estimates that the digesters will save them over £50K a year in transport and energy costs, paying for themselves in three to five years. Bruichladdich will become the greenest Islay malt of all in an industry with one of the highest carbon footprints of all food and drink producers.

(FurlongPR, 2010)

Chapter 2

In response to the many environmental pressures now impinging on firms' operations, some individuals have proposed that business firms should adopt the concept of the triple bottom line, suggesting that the firm must pursue social, environmental and economic objectives (Elkington, 1997). As we saw in Chapter 2 (►Chapter 2), many firms are now reporting in great detail on their fulfilment of their social responsibility agendas.

Although the PESTLE approach makes the elements of a remote environment scan easy to remember, there is a potential danger. Many of the changes we have discussed are in fact interrelated. Such technological innovations as the computer or the World Wide Web have enormous socio-cultural and political implications. Legal-regulatory decisions may have vital economic, environmental and political dimensions, and so on. There is therefore a danger of over-compartmentalizing, when the important changes in our time typically have multiple and interrelated effects. When planning strategy, you should never allow debates over 'which box?' to impede an understanding of the potential impacts of expected changes; after all, that's what's important!

Global firms, by their very nature, need to be aware of these changes in the remote environment in every region of the world. In addition, a diversified firm will need to undertake such an analysis at several levels. It will need to understand the changes occurring which are important for the firm as a total entity, such as the admission of China and Taiwan to the WTO. At the same time, we reiterate that each of the individual business units will need to undertake a thorough analysis of its own remote environment. We have used a general approach to analysis, but the specific dimensions and tools used to understand changes will depend on the specific firm and business unit for which strategy is being developed.

3.3 THE INDUSTRY ENVIRONMENT

LEARNING OBJECTIVE 4

Evaluate how changes in the industry environment influence strategy development and implementation.

While the remote environment will have a major impact on the firm's strategy, our next level of analysis goes deeper, exploring the characteristics of the industry in which a business competes, and the effect of these on strategy. Since global firms are likely to operate in a number of different industries, this level of analysis is more appropriate at the business unit level. Corporate level staff would be expected to undertake this analysis when exploring mergers and acquisitions, or when setting performance standards for a business unit.

Figure 3.10 depicts our model of **industry structure**, where industry structure incorporates suppliers, buyers, entrants, substitutes as well as **direct competitors**. The depiction is based on the work of Michael Porter, and is sometimes referred to as 'the five forces model' with the structural factors being grouped into five categories (Porter, 2008).

Industry structure
The major factors which affect, possibly differentially, all firms in the industry. They are generally grouped into five categories – suppliers, buyers, entrants, substitutes and rivalry.

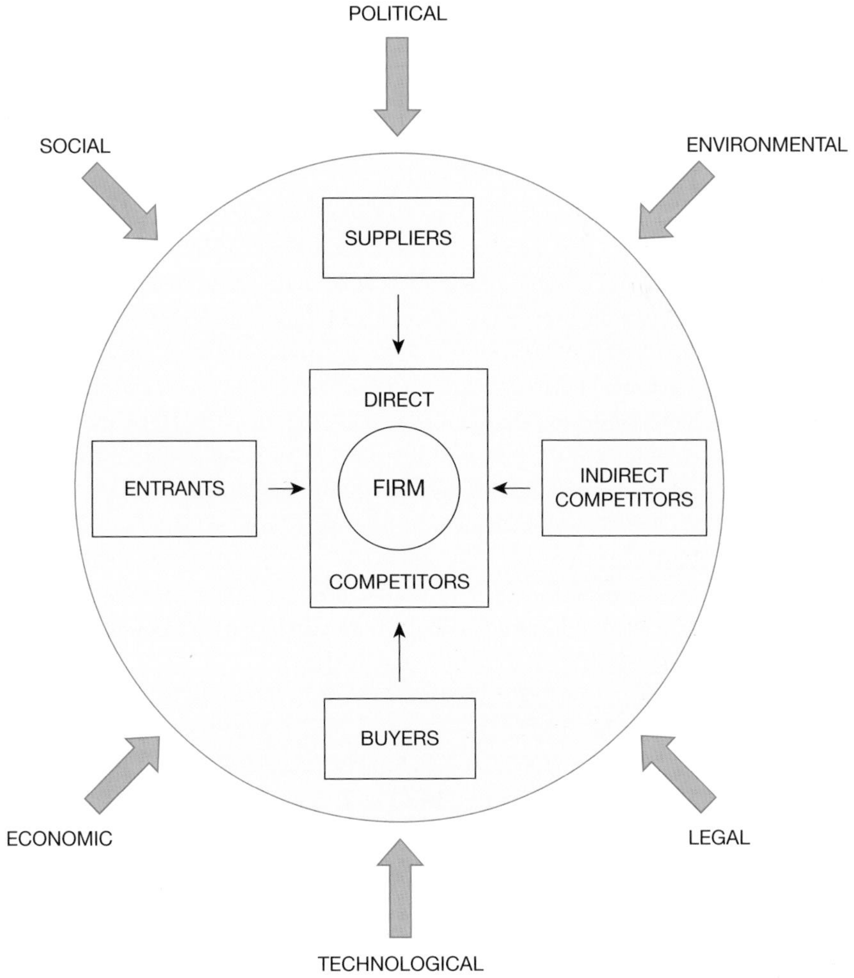

Figure 3.10
The industry environment. Adapted with permission Impact Planning Group.

Source: Porter, 2008

The structural variables identified in the model affect all the firms in the industry, but not all firms will be affected equally. An industry analysis helps us to understand the power relationships among the players in the industry, which in turn influence current and future levels of prices, investment in the industry and firm profitability. Such an analysis may also assist the firm in choosing a basis for competitive advantage that capitalizes on opportunities or mitigates problems. We now review each of these five categories.

First is the level of competitive intensity within the industry, the competition from direct competitors. If intensity or competitive rivalry is high, the profitability of firms in the industry is likely to be low as margins are competed away. One factor influencing rivalry is the number and size distribution of competitors. A small number of equal-sized competitors are likely to result in intense price competition as the different firms vie for a leadership position. This effect will generally be exacerbated when the industry growth rate is slow.

The second structural characteristic are barriers to entry to the industry: the level and nature of the barrier that must be overcome by firms desiring to enter the industry. Barriers to entry include the capital required to enter as well as non-financial barriers such as access to distribution channels, knowledge and economies of scale, as we discuss in later chapters. We expect that industry profitability will be low when entry barriers are low, since the entrants are likely to compete aggressively on price to gain business. On the other hand, high current levels of industry profitability will encourage entry, as will high rates of market growth.

Entry barriers
Characteristics which make it difficult for an organization to enter a specific industry.

Profitable markets, however, do not just attract potential direct competitors; they also attract substitutes, or indirect competitors. These are competitors capable of meeting the same customer needs as our own business but which do so in a very different manner. Thus cotton fabrics compete with man-made fibres in clothing while books will increasingly compete with e-books such as Kindle.

Substitutes often feature new technology that has basic quality and high cost early in its life cycle. This may cause incumbent firms to dismiss the threat posed by the substitute. Too often incumbents ignore the potential for rapid technology advancement with the substitute. Digital cameras have killed off the silver-halide equivalents, but few people seem to realize the scale of the dramatic changes in price/performance relationships that have occurred.

This is an increase in performance of greater than one order of magnitude, and a reduction in price of well over one order of magnitude. Clearly, product development has to

---

Innovation *in practice* – Canon

- In July 1995 a Canon digital SLR, the EOS DC3 sold for $US22,449, had 1.3 megapixels of resolution, and weighed 1,800 grams ('Canon camera museum', 2003).
- In February 2010 the Canon EOS 50D had 15.1 megapixels, weighed 730 grams and sold for $US1,129 complete with lens!

('Digital cameras', 2010)

be an ongoing task at Canon; such is the pace of innovation and change! Illustrating the dynamics of industry evolution, Nokia today is the largest camera manufacturer in the world, and the impact of the camera phone has been so great that Minolta and Konica, who had merged, withdrew from the photography market in 2006. Just as many young people own only a camera phone, not a camera, so do more and more rely solely on a mobile phone, with no landline. Landline revenues are collapsing fast for many telecoms companies, driven not only by the ubiquity of mobiles (cell phones) but also by the growth of **voiceover internet protocol (VOIP)** from competitors such as Skype.

The rate of technological development of film-based cameras was negligible by the mid-1990s. In complete contrast, technology drove down prices for digital cameras at the same time as the physical size and weight of these were reduced while picture resolution increased. Since these are salient characteristics influencing purchase, the value of the product to customers increased significantly over the time period. This is a classic example of the well-known **S-curve** of technological change: improvements occur slowly at first, accelerate and then slow down as the technology reaches its limit (Foster, 1986).

It may be difficult for executives in firms using traditional technology, for which technological improvements are gradual, to recognize the threat posed by a disruptive technology.

Without doubt, technological advance and deregulation have combined to vastly increase the threats posed by indirect competition. The probability that new indirect entrants will be successful is typically viewed as lower than that for parallel competitors, but the effects of their infrequent successes may be devastating. They provide examples of the low-probability, high-impact event against which it so difficult to defend.

The other forces bearing on the firm act vertically. The pressure from suppliers is very much dependent on their importance to the firm. Sometimes this can be assessed in terms of the importance of the input product as a percentage of the firm's total costs. In other cases a supplier can be critical for different reasons. They may add appeal for the firm's subsequent customers, or their product or service may be critical to the continuity of the customer firm's production processes. Whenever dependency is high, however, the supplier's bargaining power is enhanced, and this tends to be reflected in their margins vis-à-vis those of their customer, as well as in other dimensions such as delivery time and flexibility.

Of course, as the power of suppliers rises, so does the threat of their forward integration down the channel of distribution into direct competition with the firm. This may occur via direct entry or acquisition. In other cases the supplier may engage in promoting its brand directly to the firm's customers. This increases the firm's switching costs as their customers' preferences move towards products incorporating the promoting supplier's products. Intel provides one of the best-known examples. Many of their customers that manufacture PCs have co-branded 'intel inside'™ on their own products, recognizing that their customers' brand associations should be favourable and lead to improved sales of their products, compared with those using other manufacturers' chips. Intel's advertising budget in 2008 was $US1.86 billion, and it was these monies and the way they were used to influence computer manufacturers' choice of chip supplier that led to the anti-trust actions against Intel that were mentioned earlier in this chapter.

Voiceover internet protocol (VOIP)
The delivery of voice communications and other multimedia over the Internet.

S-curve
A common pattern for technological change whereby improvements occur slowly at first, accelerate and then slow down as the technology reaches its limit.

Very similar forces operate with respect to the relationship with the firm's immediate customers. If the firm becomes dependent on a few large customers, its bargaining power is significantly diminished. These large customers will pressure for discounts, and their margins will usually benefit at the expense of those of the seller. In the early twenty-first century, these battles were being actively fought between the suppliers to the major automobile firms and their customers – the auto firms. US automobile firms, faced with over-capacity and declining market shares, were able to pressure suppliers for price reductions of up to 15 per cent.

Structural characteristics may significantly affect firm and industry profitability. For some industries, structural characteristics are such that almost no firm in the industry is able to make an adequate return, yet firms refuse to exit. For example, profitability in the paper industry worldwide is poor, and has been for many years. The international airline industry has also been a poor profit performer, and since 2001 many airlines have been reorganized or have disappeared through bankruptcy or merger (AIU, 2010). Some of the better-known examples include Sabena, Swissair and JAL, the last entering bankruptcy in January 2010 (Tabuchi, 2010).

Industry value chain

Industry value chain

The linked set of firms in an industry and the activities undertaken by those firms.

Industry analysis of the type discussed above is incomplete since it neglects the dynamics of what we will call the industry value chain – the linked set of firms and the activities undertaken by those firms. Indeed, sometimes a significant part of a firm's competitive advantage is based on its superiority in managing its supply chain. Both Dell and Wal-Mart owe a large part of their success to such superiority.

Inter-industry competition is also increasingly common in today's world, as we noted earlier. In such cases competition can be seen as occurring between two complete industry value chains. Consider the beverage packaging market, with the two competing packaging systems: aluminium cans and plastic bottles. Figure 3.11 compares the industry value chain for each type of container.

Changes at any level of the value chain for aluminium cans influence the competitiveness of cans versus bottles. For example, aluminium smelting is a very energy-intensive process, using huge amounts of electricity. Any increase in electricity costs will obviously increase the cost of cans made from virgin aluminium. On the other hand, a large proportion of aluminium used in can-making is now recycled. In comparison, feedstock for the plastic bottles is dependent on petrochemical prices, which will undoubtedly be influenced by the actions of the OPEC cartel. Currently, bottles made from PET have high levels of permeability, making them unsuitable for beverages such as beer. Should technological developments overcome this characteristic, the impact on the aluminium can industry is likely to be severe. Whether a firm is in the aluminium, plastics or packaging industry, its managers should be monitoring changes at every level of the chain, not only for their own industry but also for those with which it competes in end-use markets and applications.

Profitability may also vary dramatically at each stage in this chain, depending on power relationships. This, in turn, may influence decisions on where to compete. Consider the

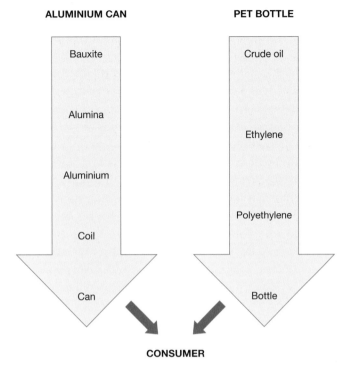

Figure 3.11 Industry value chain, aluminium and plastic packaging

case of Microsoft and Intel, which were the main beneficiaries of IBM's decision to out-source the operating system and microprocessor in its personal computers. The margins of Microsoft and Intel were significantly higher than those of IBM, an issue to which we return in Chapter 7 (►Chapter 7).

Chapter 7

Industry value chains also allow us to examine disintermediation, where one level in the value chain is eliminated. The vast improvements in information technology and the advent of the Web have shifted the economics of direct marketing. As we have already noted, for information products such as airline tickets disintermediation is quite widespread, as any ex-travel agent can attest.

Challenge of strategic management

An industry analysis is seen as a necessary initial step in developing a strategy for a business unit. Given that industry boundaries are increasingly becoming blurred, and many firms are involved in alliances and networks, do you think that industry analysis is still relevant?

Limitations of the industry model

Before moving on, we should take note of important limitations of the popular 'five forces' model. First, it is predicated on the assumption that firms are single-business, single-industry entities. Consequently, in a multi-business firm the model is only relevant for an individual business unit. A firm such as Siemens has many business units, each of which competes in its own industry. But the corporation as an entity does not compete in an industry. The model of industry analysis can only be applied at the business unit level, so its use is limited. Further, competition occurs increasingly among more or less formal alliances of firms or networks and again the five forces model, with its concept of a clearly defined entity, is of little assistance in analysing these cooperative/competitive conditions. Indeed, Sir Martin Sorrell, CEO of WPP, one of the world's largest advertising agencies, coined the term 'frenemy' to describe his firm's relationship with Google, but has since modified it to 'froe' (Sorrell, 2008).

A second assumption is that we can define 'an industry' with little difficulty. The mere fact that 'substitutes' (indirect competitors) appear in the economic model suggests that the problem of defining 'an industry' may be a little more difficult in reality. In the last part of the twentieth century some curious new words began to creep into the English language, terms such as 'cosmeceuticals', 'edutainment' and the like referred to in our first chapter. Each of these words symbolizes the observation that the boundaries of an 'industry' are indistinct, fuzzy, and often permeable. Where is the boundary between communications, entertainment, publishing and computing? Is Nokia in competition with News Corporation? Anyone who has actually tried to define where one industry (or market) stops and another begins will testify that the problem is by no means as simple as it may at first sight appear. We are convinced that much innovation in fact occurs at the boundaries of what traditional players refer to as 'the industry', with results that may be devastating for incumbents. Indeed, some specific innovations result from the juxtaposition and cross-fertilization of what were previously regarded as different industries.

Third, the model assumes that the structure of an industry has a major impact on the profitability of a business unit within that industry; in other words, that there are significant differences in profitability of business units across industries, resulting from structural differences between the industries. One study by Rumelt found that industry effects were actually quite small (Rumelt, 1991). Other studies by Porter found more significant industry effects, although they did not use business unit profitability as the dependent measure (McGahan & Porter, 1997). A more recent study found that firm-specific factors were more important than industry effects for industry leaders and laggards. For firms in the middle, neither dominant nor laggard, industry effects were important (Hawawini *et al.*, 2003). These researchers conclude that superior management works, irrespective of industry, while average management needs an attractive industry structure to be profitable. Perhaps we can conclude by saying that industry structure will have an impact – the presence of powerful customers, for example, may depress profitability – but it is only one of the many factors affecting business profitability.

Fourth, the model fails to convey the dynamic nature of most industries. Some industries are characterized by rapid changes in product innovation, rapidly escalating competition based on price-performance characteristics, with competitors attempting to establish first-mover advantages in both products and markets – a form of competition which has been referred to as 'hyper-competition' (D'Aveni, 1994). Other industries such as petroleum, steel and cement are characterized by relatively slow structural change, a characteristic noted by Porter (Porter, 2008).

The automobile industry is going through a transition at the moment. Historically, firms such as Ford and General Motors built huge, vertically integrated systems that offered advantages through common ownership. New strategic patterns have now developed. Ford and GM (prior to its bankruptcy) sold off their captive component suppliers, Delphi and Visteon respectively, moving from hierarchy- to market-based transactions hoping to achieve the cost and flexibility advantages that firms such as Toyota and Honda enjoyed. However, a rejuvenated VW group, festooned with multiple brands for different market segments, and the merged Korean firm Hyundai-Kia represent increasing threats to Toyota's market leadership.

Clearly, it is vitally important that managers treat the structure of their industry as variable rather than fixed. The term 'structural competition' was coined to capture the idea that today's senior manager must learn to think as much like an investment banker as an operating executive. Unless this game is played well, our firm may end up out in the cold, isolated by the structural moves of its competitors. Thus, to assist in developing strategy, we must concentrate on the dynamics: how will the industry look in the future? Will it remain attractive or should we consider exiting? As managers, it is essential to keep this future focus, and not to regard the industry, its boundaries or its structure, as fixed.

Managers should also realize that industry structure is influenced by the firm's actions, and that some strategic decisions are taken to influence this structure. In the face of powerful buyers, suppliers may undertake horizontal mergers, increasing their power relative to buyers. Such mergers may also reduce competitive rivalry, and move competition from a price to a non-price basis, affecting average industry profitability. Faced with a powerful supplier possessing specialized assets, the firm may integrate backward to reduce their power.

Finally, the players that affect industry structure in the real world constitute a much more complex set than is portrayed in the simple five forces model. While some of these may legitimately be viewed as among the external forces depicted in Figure 3.12, others belong inside the 'magic circle'. The issue of defining the scope of the players we should consider, and defining the boundaries of the industry, is the subject of the rest of this section.

Figure 3.12 portrays the complexity of the players involved in determining industry structure by showing examples of the entities that may influence the same. We label as 'Allies' entities that may favourably influence structure. We view allies as a broader class than those often named as complementors (Brandenburger & Nalebuff, 1997). Thus, allies might include government agencies or regulators that could be viewed as influences in the remote environment; they also include those who benefit from our firm's activities even though they are not directly involved in its value chain. Inhabitants of local communities, businesses such as hotels and restaurants that benefit from their proximity to the firm's facilities, as well

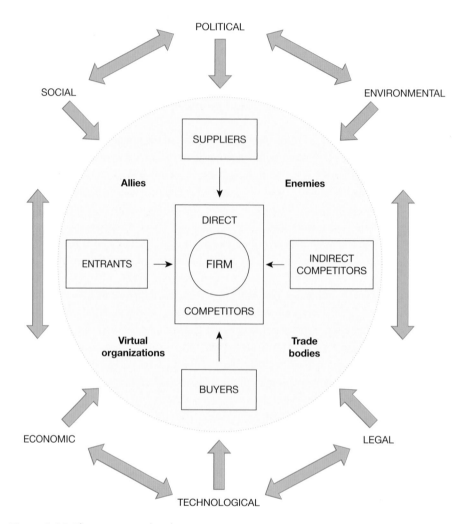

Figure 3.12 The augmented industry environment

as special interest groups or non-government organizations (NGOs) might all conceivably constitute allied constituencies. Clearly, suppliers and customers may also be allies, although they do not always behave as such!

Just as some entities may support the firm's strategies, others oppose it. Union opposition is frequent when major changes of strategy threaten to disrupt the lives of union members, while those allied with the firm's competitors may have comparable influence. Further, trade bodies such as trade associations, professional associations or technical groups may exert favourable or unfavourable influence. Finally the growth of Internet access has made all firms vulnerable to the negative website phenomenon, where disgruntled employees, customers and others may use 'virtual organizations' to exert influence over large organizations (Tescopoly, 2010).

Figure 3.12 also indicates the importance of regarding 'industry' boundaries as permeable by showing a dotted line rather than a solid line. Technology and deregulation are both powerful forces affecting the permeability of these boundaries. In many countries it was not so long ago that we had commercial banks, building societies (savings and loans) and insurance companies, but today the 'financial services' nomenclature has become common as mutual funds de-mutualize, building societies metamorphose into banks, and all scramble to develop an Internet presence.

Further, firms are moving away from a model of an independent entity with arm's-length transactional relationships with other firms. Instead we now see the rise of network structures where firms work together to create a network of suppliers, distributors, other service providers and customers. Value is created by the entire network, which also makes the concept of a rigid and well-defined industry somewhat questionable.

The moral that astute managers should draw from these examples is to keep their antennae tuned to the happenings at the periphery of what others regard as 'the industry', for it is there that some of the most interesting and innovative competitive developments will occur.

3.4 THE BUSINESS UNIT ENVIRONMENT

The final level of external environmental analysis is undertaken to assess changes that could influence the position of the business unit relative to its competitors and the nature of its competitive advantage. The major focus is upon identifying opportunities or problems resulting from changes in the competitive milieu and/or in customer requirements. This process should be seen as dynamic, creative and opportunity-focused, based on sound analysis.

Customer analysis

Customer analysis involves developing a detailed understanding of customers, their needs and values, how these needs may vary within a market (market segmentation), how they are changing, and what the firm can do to introduce change to the marketplace.

Growth comes not from doing the same as competitors, but from being creative, with insight about how to respond to or create marketplace change. Such skills are an important intangible asset.

Customer analysis
A detailed understanding of customers, their needs and values, and how these needs may vary within a given market.

Customer value

Understanding the sources of customer value is a large and complex subject, better explored in a marketing course. However, as we noted in Chapter 2 (➤Chapter 2), understanding customer value is essential to designing a business model, so we will examine some of the issues involved in determining sources of value. One of the most important is understanding who the customer is. Any person whose actions can influence the decision to purchase the

Chapter 2

firm's products and services, not just those who pay, should be viewed as a customer. We should also recognize that customers are always individuals inasmuch as organizations do not make decisions: people do. We need to clearly understand the needs and dissatisfactions of customers and how these are changing. Such changes may open up an opportunity for the astute firm. For example, following the economic difficulties of 2009/10, there seemed to be a significant shift in consumer expenditure towards store brands, which are often about 75 per cent of the cost of manufacturers' brands. In Germany these store brands account for about 40 per cent of supermarket sales. In response to these changes, Proctor and Gamble has introduced a line of low-priced basic products – which can open up problems of cannibalization with existing products (*The Economist*, 2009b). In Chapter 7 we discuss measures of customer value in more depth (➤Chapter 7).

Chapter 7

Market segmentation

Markets are characterized as comprising buyers, either individual or institutional, with different needs and requirements. Meeting the needs of customers requires developing different types of offers, each focused on the needs of a defined segment. Market segmentation is the process of grouping together actual and potential customers whose needs are similar so that target segments can be selected and appropriate marketing programmes designed.

Market segmentation

The process of grouping together actual and potential customers whose needs are similar so that target segments can be selected and the appropriate marketing programme designed.

For industrial products, such segmentation typically requires a thorough understanding of customer economics, since these are likely to constitute one of the purchase criteria. Segmentation permits the firm to focus on those segments in which it has a competitive advantage, permitting greater differentiation of the offer and, consequently, better margins.

Since customer needs are constantly changing, the business will need to monitor and update its segmentation approach and the number and description of its chosen segments. For many firms, their growth strategy (discussed in detail in Chapter 7) (➤Chapter 7) is achieved through the identification of new market segments that have strong growth opportunities. Rapidly growing segments typically exhibit increased turbulence, making share gain more feasible. Growing share in a very stable market is usually difficult, but in a growing market there are new customers, new values, new needs and benefits required. The possibility of designing products with different features may lead to rapid share gain if managers have the foresight to create the opportunity and build capabilities to exploit it.

In some markets there is minimal variation in either the price charged, or characteristics of the product or service offering. Customer choice will be based primarily on price, with consequent implications for the business's competitive strategy. Other markets exhibit substantial price variation and clear differences among competitors' offerings, reflecting strong differences in customer preferences. In such markets, price plays a lesser role; the firm must develop a strategy based upon well-understood dimensions of customer value.

Customers often play different roles – gatekeeper, influencer, decision-maker, buyer and user – in a purchase process. Failure to understand these roles may preclude sufficient understanding of sources of value. Different customers also have differing needs and wants depending upon socio-cultural and situational factors, as well as role in the purchasing process. There are clearly many ways to think about these needs and wants. However, considering three types of needs and wants – functional, psychological and economic – provides a useful framework for understanding the benefits delivered by a product or service. First, however, we must distinguish between features and benefits.

Features versus benefits

In marketing a product or service it is useful to distinguish between features/attributes and benefits. Firms produce and deliver products and services but customers only perceive value in the benefits that these products and services provide. In its factories, Bosch manufactures electric drills whose features include colour, drill speed and weight, hardness and size of bit, presence/absence of battery and battery life, ability to embrace other tools (e.g. sander) and so forth. For the most part, customers have little interest in these features per se; what concern customers are the benefits offered by the drill: the holes it can make and the ease of making them. Similarly, retailers and wholesalers may care little for the specific products they sell; they are more interested in such benefits as net profit, sales per linear foot and return on investment.

Focus on benefits versus features has the additional virtue of broadening the view of competition. To return to Bosch, when the focus is on features, key competitors are other electric drill manufacturers. When the focus of attention is on benefits, the firm necessarily considers other methods of making holes. The substitutes or indirect competitors may include nails, adhesives, water drills and lasers, an important broadening of the competitive scope that prepares the firm for new forms of competition.

When considering the benefits offered by a product or service it is useful to categorize these as functional, psychological and economic. Functional benefits serve a particular purpose, typically by allowing an individual or family or organization to do something that needs to be done. Psychological benefits usually make people feel good about themselves. With economic benefits, the focus is on price, cost savings or credit terms. In many cases purchase decisions involve a combination of motives, but failure to appreciate these, and the priorities placed upon them by different customers, leads to poor decisions. Chapter 7 presents frameworks for integrating consideration of value and cost in designing the competitive strategy of the business unit (➤Chapter 7).

Chapter 7

Analysing competitors

Most competitor analysis is undertaken at the business unit level. In undertaking to analyse specific competitors we are making an implicit assumption that the unit in question is engaged in oligopolistic competition since under perfect competition there would be no purpose in the exercise. There is a defined process that we should follow in conducting a competitor analysis, the stages in which are shown in Figure 3.13.

Since the best competitive strategies are typically pre-emptive, identification is a very important stage that should encompass not only today's competitors, but also those that could represent a threat tomorrow. Further, we define a competitor as any entity capable of meeting the same set of customer requirements we intend to meet. Whereas in day-to-day

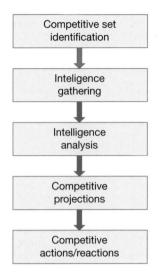

Figure 3.13
Process for competitor analysis

Modified with permission of Professor Michel Pham

Chapters 4, 5, 7, 8

decision-making actual direct competitors are likely to dominate in our thinking, the key to longer term ownership of market positions is to anticipate potential competitors, which may be indirect competitors. Micro-economics tells us that economic profits will inevitably attract competitors, so that good profit performance is a leading indicator of increased competition. The old saying that an ounce of prevention is worth a ton of cure has much merit when developing competitive strategy!

Once competitors have been identified, we must target those that are most likely to prevent us from achieving our goals. Key to making this decision well is the ability to understand the world from the perspective of the competitor, since, seen through their eyes it will look very different. If we are unable to do this, we are unlikely to be very successful in plotting competitive strategies, yet this a major problem for many managers.

Profiling competitors involves gathering intelligence that will help us understand them better. As we noted, the prime focus of competitor analysis is typically at the business unit level, but in Figure 3.14 we have illustrated the types of information about a competitor that might be collected at different levels.

Analysing competitive intelligence may employ a variety of techniques such as analysis of resources and capabilities (see Chapter 5) (►Chapter 5), assessment of financial capabilities (as discussed in Chapter 4) (►Chapter 4), portfolio analysis (see Chapter 8) (►Chapter 8), and close examination of the competitors' value chains (see Chapter 7) (►Chapter 7). Yet, without the ability to integrate the information and recognize underlying patterns, little that is useful will result. Skill in pattern recognition is one of the key requirements for a good analyst, whether they work for the CIA or a global company.

The difficulty of divining competitors' strategies was long ago acknowledged by Sun Tzu, the ancient Chinese strategist and author of *The Art of War*, who explained it thus:

> All men see the tactics whereby I conquer, but none see the strategy out of which victory evolved.

Sun Tzu (500 BC)

Level of analysis	Financial performance	Portfolio	Resources and competences	Management capabilities, proclivities	Degree of vertical integration	Value chain	Market performance	Positioning	Marketing mix
Corporate	✓	✓	✓	✓					
Business unit	✓	✓	✓	✓	✓	✓	✓		
Product-market	✓	✓	✓	✓	✓	✓	✓	✓	✓

Figure 3.14 Types of competitive information at different levels

The final stage in the process involves an interactive game, which means exploring alternative projections of competitors' strategies and subsequent testing of alternatives on our part. Game theory may help in this process, as will an in-depth understanding of competitors, but as the above discussion suggests, there is no absolute certainty in competitor analysis. Nonetheless, our potential strategies should be tested against these scenarios, seeking options likely to prove robust regardless of competitive actions. One of the most unimaginative, and often dangerous, competitive moves is simply to ape the actions (anticipated or otherwise) of a competitor. As global competition intensifies, attrition will ensure that, on average, the survivors are smarter and more adaptable than their failed predecessors. Survivors will be building strategies that capitalize upon their own distinctive capabilities. To imitate is tantamount to letting the competitor choose the weapons and the battlefield, a violation of a most basic principle of strategy.

> ## Challenge of strategic management
> Assume that you are the CEO of a significant strategic business unit of a diversified firm. How would you decide the budget allocation for environmental analysis between the three levels discussed in the text: the remote environment; the industry environment; and the competitive environment? What factors would influence this allocation?

3.5 MULTI-INDUSTRY COMPETITION

Much of our recent discussion has implicitly assumed that competition takes place among single-industry firms. Indeed, much of Chapter 7 (▶Chapter 7) on business level strategy will assume this context. Yet, as noted, in many industries, understanding competitive strategy is a much more complex task than is implied by the industry model. We distinguish a minimum of four levels of competition: network-to-network, company-to-company, business-to-business and product-to-product. The last is a market level of competition with which we shall not concern ourselves in this book, while business-to-business competition will be dealt with in Chapter 7 (▶Chapter 7). In this chapter we conclude by briefly examining the issues raised by network-to-network and company-to-company competition.

 Chapter 7

Network competition

In response to rapid change and the increasing cost of business and product development, more and more firms are moving to organize themselves as network competitors. Other factors have contributed to this change. One is the aforementioned desire to variate fixed costs by outsourcing. As markets become more competitive globally, the ability to sustain internally less-than-world-class activities deteriorates. Outsourcing typically results in networked relationships with suppliers. The quality movement has also contributed to a drop

> ### Networks *in practice* – WiMax
>
> The WiMAX Forum is an industry-led, not-for-profit organization formed to certify and promote the compatibility and interoperability of broadband wireless products based upon the harmonized IEEE 802.16/ETSI HiperMAN standard. One of the WiMAX Forum's goals is to accelerate the introduction of these systems into the marketplace. WiMAX Forum Certified™ products are fully interoperable and support broadband fixed, portable and mobile services. Along these lines, the WiMAX Forum works closely with service providers and regulators to ensure that WiMAX Forum Certified systems meet customer and government requirements.
>
> (WiMax, 2010)

in supplier numbers. As buying firms become more demanding in seeking reliable quality, a relationship model supersedes the traditional bid-based transaction model. As firms globalize they also tend to seek global support. Suppliers that are not world-scale must enter into alliances and networks to maintain their business position. Finally, attempts to improve supply chain efficiency and minimize working capital, again fostered by ever-more competitive markets, result in closer, networked relationships among firms, which must cooperate in sharing information to derive benefit from the arrangement.

Rather than depict the firm's organization structure in the normal fashion, we might consider thinking about the network organization as a member of a web of interrelationships as depicted in Figure 3.15. The WiMAX Forum consists of almost 500 companies, united by a common purpose.

The vision of the Forum is to 'Promote global adoption of WiMAX™ as the broadband wireless Internet technology of choice anytime, anywhere'. This technology is beyond the

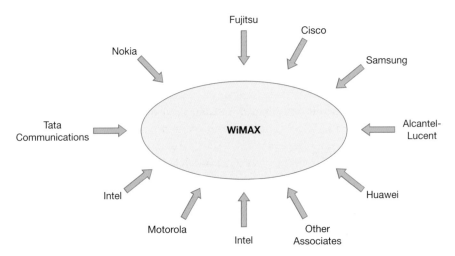

Figure 3.15 WiMAX network firms (selected firms only)

capabilities of any single firm; hence the establishment of the forum, consisting of a huge variety of network operators, hardware and software manufacturers and consultants. There are obviously large stakes involved in establishing such a standard, so **first-mover advantages** and standards will be critical.

As Figure 3.15 indicates, the network model is by no means restricted to the firm and the suppliers with which it interacts in its now deconstructed business system. Increasingly, erstwhile competitors are allying where they believe their joint interests are best served by such arrangements. Although Japan has long witnessed rivalry between major keiretsu, network vs. network competition is fast growing elsewhere in the world. One of the most visible illustrations is provided by the major alliances in the airline industry, Star, Oneworld and SkyTeam.

Corporate-level competition

Corporate-level competitors are perhaps best identified by means of assessing the overlap in their business portfolios (▶Chapter 8). Shell and Exxon, Siemens and GE, Airbus and Boeing, VW and Toyota are obviously corporate-level competitors because each pairing of companies competes in multiple businesses. Rolls Royce Aero Engines is an important business-level competitor for GE in its gas turbine business, but is not a key corporate-level competitor. The responsibility for competitor analysis and strategizing with respect to Rolls Royce would therefore lie at the business level within GE, although major strategic decisions with respect to its GE's aero engine business would rise to the corporate level.

Typically, targeting efforts in competitor analysis depend not only on the extent of the portfolio overlap, but also upon judgements about the intent of a particular competitor's management. This demands insight into the competitor's capabilities, but also the intentions of its managers. Thus, while a typical corporate profile would involve gathering information about the competitor's financial performance, business portfolios, physical facilities, knowledge assets, functional strengths and the like, it should also embrace gathering information and insight about the management of the targeted competitor.

Chapter 8

 ## 3.6 SUMMARY

Sensing of the environment is key to strategic thinking. Broad environmental trends affect many industries and firms, including our own suppliers and our customers. Yet exposure to this external environment does not come of its own accord. Indeed many of the admonitions to management, such as concentrating on core capabilities, create the danger of insulating senior managers from the very forces that should be their preoccupation in strategy development. A prerequisite for senior managers is the adoption of this external perspective, to identify and perhaps anticipate the external changes which will require fundamental changes to the firm's strategy.

Such an analysis requires an understanding at several levels of aggregation, which we have denoted as the remote, industry and firm levels. Understanding the factors which make

LEARNING OBJECTIVE 5

Be able to incorporate an understanding of the major external trends influencing the firm when developing strategy an industry more or less attractive are important corporate inputs to any diversification decision. Business level strategy will be influenced by changes at all three levels. Changing socio-cultural characteristics, such as the ageing of the population, may require significant changes in strategy. So too may the emergence of powerful customers, with their resulting pressure on prices. Business units also need to undertake detailed analysis of their immediate competitors, to ensure that any competitive advantage is not being eroded.

We also need to recognize that some change is difficult to predict, and thus there needs to be a balance between focus and commitment with flexibility and responsiveness. However, major trends seldom arise overnight. Instead, there are generally some signals, albeit weak, suggesting that change is likely to occur. The managerial challenge is to be open to these developing trends, ensuring that detailed analysis is undertaken, and developing strategy which takes advantage of the opportunities inherent in the changes. The overarching need is to develop strategies that will be successful in the world of the future, not the world of the present.

VIEW FROM THE TOP

CAPITA GROUP PLC

Capita Group plc describes itself as the UK's leading business process outsourcing and professional services company. The firm delivers back office administration and front office customer contact services to private and public sector organizations across the UK and Ireland (Capita, 2008). Rod Aldridge, OBE, founded the company, retiring from the position of executive chairman in 2006. When interviewed by the *Journal of Strategy and Management*, he described the circumstances that led to the basic strategy as follows.

Rod Aldridge: We did not want to be a consultancy company. We took the view that if organizations have problems, it is better to take the problems away than advise them about the problems, particularly if you take responsibility for improving it and are accountable in doing so. That was the new territory, because you had to transfer staff from the public sector and put long-term contracts in place.

I think what was great about us was that we created our own culture and ultimately Capita has created a new industry with staff wanting to be in the industry and committed to it. Culturally, the large consultancy firms found it difficult to move from being advisers to being providers. Similarly, it was difficult for the major IT companies to move away from just providing the hardware and software to actually providing everything. Starting with a blank canvas meant that we were able to create this type of culture nationally. The lack of attention paid to us by the consultancies meant that we moved so fast and they were left behind.

We knew that it would be very difficult to compete with the large consultancy firms that were well ensconced in local government . . . We derived a different model where we focused on contracted revenue over a five-year period, for which we delivered certain outputs . . . In effect we created a new product in the market . . . the momentum has been moved away from buying consultancy to buying solutions . . . we . . . could use any one of a number of suppliers such as ICL, IBM or Honeywell. Customers bought the solution rather than the hardware. This meant that we could take a different stance say to hardware suppliers. They need to think about working with Capita as opposed to Capita working with them.

Source: Abstracted with permission from
O'Regan & Ghobadian (2009)

QUESTIONS

1 What does this interview suggest about the adequacy of the competitor analysis performed by a) consultancies and b) IT hardware manufacturers?
2 What ideas discussed in the text for Chapter 3 might have proved helpful to the managers of Capita's competitors?

MINI-CASE

LINN PRODUCTS LIMITED

Early years

Linn is a medium-sized family-owned precision engineering company based in Glasgow. It designs, manufactures and markets complete music and theatre systems for discerning customers worldwide. The company was established in 1972 by a Scottish-born engineer Ivor Tiefenbrun. Music and engineering led him to establish Linn. Ivor firmly believes that music

brings pleasure to life. According to him, music can pick you up, calm you down, move your feet and stimulate your mind. Ivor was frustrated that he could not buy hi-fi good enough to satisfy his needs, so he decided to make one himself. The conventional wisdom in the early 1970s was that the hi-fi chain started with the speakers and worked down to the source of music – at that time, a turntable. This mindset dominated the way industry designed new systems. Ivor believed in the complete opposite. Common sense told him that the source of music was the most important element.

His interest in music taught Ivor that the sound reproduction process was only as strong as its weakest link. He was determined to develop a system that reproduced sound as faithfully as possible to the original recording. To this end Ivor developed the Sondek LP12 turntable in 1972, the longest-lived hi-fi product still in production anywhere in the world, and still the benchmark by which all the turntables are judged.

Ivor's values and beliefs have shaped Linn's future. He firmly believes that the exceptional sound quality of Linn systems would encourage owners to invest in and maintain their systems. Therefore Linn, unlike many other hi-fi manufacturers, uses modular design. Its systems are readily expandable and upgradable. Hence customers can develop their system over a lifetime, gradually improving its perform-ance in line with changes in their circumstances and keeping up with changes in technology without having to invest in a completely new system. This product philosophy in the hi-fi industry offers a win–win to both customers and Linn.

Linn uses an integrated process – from product design to after-sales service – predicated on the belief that close integration is fundamental to delivering 'true to music' systems. Unlike most medium-sized companies Linn undertakes its own research and development, designs its own equipment and writes its own software. It employs 40 development engineers, designers and software specialists. Linn, unusually and against the prevailing trend in the industry, makes its own circuit boards, castings and precision-machined components. According to Ivor, 'by doing as much as we can in-house, we bring designers into contact with manufacturing which makes for better products, and means we can react quickly to changes in demand'.

Ivor believes that everything can be improved by human interest and attention to detail. This is why Linn, unlike the rest of the industry, does not use production lines for the assembly of its products. At Linn, the same person builds, tests and packs a complete product from start to finish. The employee responsible for building the product personally signs his/her name on the back of the product before packing it for dispatch. Every product can be tracked all the way from that individual to the customer, anywhere in the world.

The unyielding belief in the importance of human interest and its link with the working environment led Ivor to build a new factory in the countryside outside Glasgow in 1986, at the considerable cost of £4.5 million. He had to fight hard with the local authority to obtain planning permission and, unusually, the factory was designed by the leading architect Lord Rogers. He also equipped the facility with state-of-the-art equipment, including high-tech machine tools, robotic carts to ferry the components around, and an automated stockroom.

Linn is unusual in other ways too. All the management and administration team including Ivor work in open offices. Love for music is an essential prerequisite for working at Linn. The organization is flat and non-hierarchical. The canteen serves excellent food and Ivor, like any other employee, has to wait for a seat to become vacant. Customers are encouraged to visit the factory and there are a number of demonstration rooms. Linn owns its own record label – Linn Records – with a roster of mainly jazz and classical artists.

The changing face of the music industry

The earliest commercial medium for recording and reproducing sound, phonograph cylinders, were produced in 1888, following the invention of the first consumer sound- or music-playing gadget, a tin-foil phonograph, by Thomas Edison in 1877. The tin-foil phonograph played recorded sound from round tin-foil cylinders, but the sound quality was poor and each recording lasted for a few plays only. Over the next few years Edison improved his invention, eventually replacing tin-foil with wax cylinders. Wax cylinders could be played many times; however, each cylinder had to be recorded separately, making the mass production of the same music or sounds impossible.

On 8 November 1887, Emile Berliner, a German immigrant working in Washington DC, patented a successful system of sound recording using flat disks or records. The first records were made of glass, later zinc, and eventually polyvinyl chloride, commonly referred to as vinyl. A spiral groove with sound information was etched into the flat record. The record was rotated on the gramophone. The 'arm' of the gramophone held a needle that read the grooves in the record by vibration and transmitting the information to the gramophone speaker. Berliner's disks (records) were the first sound recordings that could be mass-produced by creating master recordings from which moulds were made. From each mould, hundreds of disks were pressed. Small-scale production of records began in 1890 with mass production following in 1894 after the establishment of the Gramophone Company in the same year.

Records and cylinders existed side by side until the 1910s when the gramophone record system triumphed in the marketplace to become the dominant commercial audio medium. The commercial mass production of phonograph cylinders ended in 1929.

The gramophone system improved over the years but the basics remained the same until the late 1980s. A new storage device compact disc (CD) was first publicly demonstrated by Sony in September 1976 and became commercially available in 1982. By the late 1980s, digital media had gained a larger market share, and the mass production of the vinyl record ended in 1991. Vinyl records regained some popularity in the new millennium and 2.9 million vinyls were sold in 2008. The new-found popularity of vinyl resulted in the resumption of limited commercial production. Vinyl records are predominantly used by young adults, as well as DJs and audiophiles for many types of music. They are also used by independent and alternative music artists.

In 1991 the Fraunhofber Institute invented the MP3 file compression format and MP3.com was launched in 1997. The first handheld MP3 player hit the market in 1998 and Napster – the online peer-to-peer file-sharing service – was launched in 1999. Other notable developments were the launch of iPod in 2002, iTunes music stores in 2003, and the MySpace music social networking site in 2005. By 2005 Apple had sold 500 million tracks through iTunes and 20 million iPads globally. By 2008 digital made up 78 per cent of all single tracks sold. As shown in Table 3.10, there has been a steady decline in music CD sales in the UK since 2004. A similar trend occurred in the US. In the first quarter of 2007, the music industry sold 89 million CDs to US consumers, compared to 112 million CDs sold during the same period in 2006. Another trend is the decline in sales of albums and the rise in the sale of singles, as shown in Table 3.11. This is indicative of the popularity of à la carte music selection made possible by the new distribution system. Again, the trend is similar in the US. In fact whenever a legitimate market for online music downloads is established in a country, the sales of physical music formats fall significantly followed by downward pressure on prices for recorded music in all outlets. In 2007 for the first time songwriters and publishers earned more from broadcasts and legal downloads of their music than from the copyright on sales of CDs.

2004 to 2008

From a start-up company Linn grew into one of the world's leading producers of top-quality audio equipment. Ivor explains the difference between Linn's music systems and the high end of the mass-production system using a food metaphor. Linn systems are gourmet food and high-end mass-produced systems are beef burgers. In 2004, Linn achieved sales revenues of £32 million with a pre-tax profit of £500,000. In 2003, Ivor asked his son, Gilad, to join Linn. Gilad left his job at Symbian, a company making operating systems for mobile phones, and joined Linn as engineering director.

Ivor became ill in 2004 and was absent for long periods of time. Consequently, he was unable to devote enough time to the business. He gave control to a trusted lieutenant who had worked with him for many years as the finance director. In pursuit of revenue, the new management entered into an agency agreement with Loewe, the German-based maker of high-quality domestic equipment. It also had started making hi-fi equipment for Aston Martin.

On his return to work and resuming the position of CEO in 2007, Ivor faced a number of major challenges. The Lowe TV businesses and the Aston Martin hi-fi business were effectively lost by the previous managing director. The loss of these two lines of business resulted in a 50 per cent reduction in turnover from circa £30m to circa £15m over the period 2006/07, a significant turndown, since Linn employed 300 people as at January 2007. To further compound the difficulty faced by the CEO, Linn lost £2.2m in the financial year 2006/07. The bank had made it clear that losses would not be funded any further. Profit was a must in 2007/08, as was cash generation. Net debt was already circa £5m, and the bank was looking for the business to return to profit and repay debt in order to continue to support the company.

Ivor had to make a number of decisions quickly. These included:

- How to stem the losses and restructure in light of the loss of Loewe TV business and Aston Martin car hi-fi business.
- Succession – how to restructure the top management team? Should he build a professional board of directors including independent non-executives to support the management team? Should he relinquish day-to-day involvement with the business and become its chairman? Should he move his son, Gilad Tiefenbrun, from his current role as engineering director and ask him to step up to managing director or appoint someone externally?
- Should they stop making CD players?
- How to unlock the full potential of digital streaming (DS) technology that Gilad had nurtured since 2004 against some opposition? With digital streaming, music was stored on a computer or a specialist storage device, controlled via one of several alternatives and streamed for listening over a home network. The new technology offered a better fit with Ivor's philosophy of 'true to sound' but the development costs were considerable.
- If a digital streaming strategy was adopted, what did this mean for people and capital investments and divestments of assets required to achieve financial targets in the shortest time?

Table 3.10 UK retail sales of albums by format (thousands of units)

Format	2004	2005	2006	2007	2008	2009
CD	162,357	158,310	151,415	131,419	122,973	112,485
LP	453	351	251	205	209	219
Digital	—	—	2,799	6,249	10,309	16,096
Other formats*	596	328	277	194	153	146
Total	**163,406**	**158,989**	**154,742**	**138,067**	**133,644**	**128,946**

*Other album formats include cassettes, mini discs, DVD audio, DVD video and DMD

Table 3.11 UK retail sales of singles by format (thousands of units)

Format	2004	2005	2006	2007	2008	2009
7" and 12"	3,229	3,149	2,298	1,843	740	332
CD	22,713	17,523	11,312	6,633	4,075	2,470
Single-track downloads	5,771	26,392	52,505	77,545	109,769	148,792
Other	554	818	809	539	554	1,154
Total	**32,267**	**47,882**	**66,924**	**86,560**	**115,138**	**152,748**

Table 3.12 Trade income (£ million) by format, 2004 to 2009

	2004	2005	2006	2007	2008	2009
Physical						
Singles	52.8	43.1	31.8	19.0	10.2	7.6
Albums	1,102	1,057	983	816	749	699
Other	63	64	49	37	29	33
Subtotal	*1,218*	*1,164*	*1,064*	*872*	*788*	*740*
Online						
Tracks	2.7	12.4	25.2	40.9	54.9	83.7
Albums				30.7	43.7	67.3
Other					2.9	3.0
Subtotal	*2.7*	*12.4*	*25.2*	*71.6*	*101.5*	*154.0*
Other formats					26	35
Total	**1,220**	**1,176**	**1,089**	**943**	**916**	**929**

Source: British Recorded Music Industry (BPI) Statistical Handbook 2010

REVIEW QUESTIONS

1 Why should a firm undertake a detailed, systematic analysis of their environment? What are the consequences if this understanding is left to management intuition?

2 Select a firm with several business units. Which remote environmental variables, in your view, are important for the firm and each business unit?

3 Give an example of a firm that appears to have failed to understand its changing environment. Can you provide reasons why this occurred?

4 Select an industry and review the structural factors affecting its profitability. Are the boundaries of this industry changing? If so, what is driving these changes? What is the likely structure of this industry in five years' time?

5 For a firm of your choice, carry out a full external analysis and suggest how the firm has developed a strategy to take advantage of these changes.

REFERENCES

Activities of the European Union (2003) http://europa.eu.int/comm/index.

Ahmed, K. (2009) Barclays president Bob Diamond: Why no bank is too large to fail. *Daily Telegraph*, 12 December. www.telegraph.co.uk/finance/newsbysector/banksandfinance/6796088/Barclays-president-Bob-Diamond-why-no-bank-is-too-big-to-fail.html.

AIU (2010) Defunct airlines. www.airlineupdate.com/airlines/airline_extra/defunctairlines/defunct airlines_index.htm.

Atkins, R., Benoit, B. & Wilson, J. (2009) Berlin steps in to rescue Dresdner takeover. *Financial Times*, 9 January, p. 15.

Avdjiev, S., Upper, C. & von Kliest, K. (2010) *Highlights of International Banking and Financial Market Activity*. Basle: Bank for International Settlements.

Bayliss, T. (2010) About us, 2010. www.trevorbaylisbrands.com/tbb/aboutus/trevorbaylis/trevor.asp.

BBC (2000) BOC merger collapses. Retrieved 10 May 2000, http://news.bbc.co.uk/2/hi/business/743841.stm.

BBC (2010) Nokia sues Apple for 'patent infringement'. *BBC News*, 8 May.

BEA (2009) *Fixed Asset Tables. Table 2.7*. www.bea.gov/national/FA2004/TableView.asp?SelectedTable= 51&FirstYear=2003&LastYear=2008&Freq=Year.

Beinhocker, E. D., Davis, I. & Mendonca, L. T. (2009) The 10 trends you have to watch. *Harvard Business Review*, (July–August), 55–60.

Bisson, P., Stephenson, E. & Viguerie, P. (2010) Global forces: An introduction. *McKinsey Quarterly*, (June).

Bradley, T. (2009) Intel's legal woes don't end with AMD settlement. *PC World*, 12 November.

Brandenburger, A. M. & Nalebuff, B. J. (1997) *Co-Option*. Broadway Business.

Brown, J. M. (2009) AIB chiefs resign to head off showdown. *Financial Times*, 1 May, p. 16.

Bughin, J., Chui, M. & Manyika, J. (2010) Clouds, big data, and smart assets. *McKinsey Quarterly*, (August).

Cadwell, K. (2006) Linde / BOC merger complete. *Gas World*, 7 September.

Canon camera museum (2003) Canon website. www.canon.com.

Capita (2008) About us. www.capita.co.uk/about-us/Pages/Our-company.aspx.

China Daily (2010) China-Asean free trade area starts operation. *China Daily*, 1 January.

Christensen, C. M. (1997) *The Innovator's Dilemma*. Boston, MA: Harvard Business School Press.

Croft, J. (2008) London to nationalise troubled mortgage lender. *Finanial Times,* 18 February, p. 1.

Croft, J. & Eaglesham, J. (2008) New row over GBP3 billion Northern Rock debt swap. *Financial Times*, 6 August, p. 1.

D'Aveni, R. A. (1994) *Hyper-Competition*. New York: Free Press.

Dessauer, J. H. M. (1971) *My Years with Xerox: The Billions Nobody Wanted*. Garden City, NJ: Doubleday.

Digital cameras (2010) Retrieved 15 February 2010, www.jr.com.

Downes, L. & Mui, C. (1998) *Unleashing the Killer App: Digital Strategies for Market Dominance*. Boston, MA: Harvard Business School Press.

Elkington, J. (1997) *Cannibals with Forks: The Triple Bottom of 21st Century Business*. Oxford: Capstone.

EU (2010a) About the EU. Retrieved 15 February 2010, http://europa.eu/about-eu/27-member-countries/index_en.htm.

EU (2010b) Employee involvement. Retrieved 14 February 2010, http://ec.europa.eu/social/main.jsp?catId=707&langId=en&intPageId=215.

Evans-Pritchard, A. (2010) Break-up of EMU 'would dwarf failure of Lehman'. *The Daily Telegraph*, 8 July, p. 4.

Ferguson, G. T. (2002) Have your objects call my objects. *Harvard Business Review*, (June), 138–144.

Foster, R. N. (1986) *Innovation: The Attacker's Advantage*. New York: Summit.

FurlongPR (2010) Small whisky brand trumps rivals with methane story. Retrieved 18 January 2010, www.furlongpr.com/small-whisky-brand-trumps-rivals-with-methane-story.

Ghetti, C. (2009) How new Buicks took shape in China. *New York Times*, 1 November, p. AU 7.

Globalfoundries (2009) About us. Retrieved 22 January 2010, www.globalfoundries.com/about/.

Guillén, M. F. & García -Canal, E. (2009) The American model of the multinational firm and the 'new' multinationals from emerging economies. *Academy of Management Perspectives, 23*(2), 23–35.

Hanke, J. E. & Wichern, D. W. (2009) *Business Forecasting*, 9th edn. Upper Saddle River, NJ: Prentice Hall.

Hawawini, G., Subramanian, V. & Verdin, P. (2003) Is performance driven by industry or firm specific factors? A new look at the evidence. *Strategic Management Journal, 24*(1), 1–16.

Hesseldahl, A. (2009) The Intel-AMD settlement: A play-by-play. *Business Week*, 13 January.

Hosking, P. (2010) Not so gloomy. *The Times*, 28 August, p. 51.

Hull, J. (2008) Derivatives and risk management. In R. Martin (ed.), *The Financial Crisis and Rescue* (pp. 19–31). Toronto: University of Toronto Press.

IASB (2010) Fair value measurement. Retrieved 21 April 2010, www.iasb.org/News/Press+Releases/IASB+FASB+quarterly+report.htm.

International Telecommunications Union (2010) ICT indicators database: Broadband. 2010. www.itu.int/ITU-D/ict/statistics/.

Kanari, N., Pineau, J.-L. & Shallari, S. (2003) End of life recycling in the European Union. *Journal of the Minerals, Metals and Materials Society*, (August).

Lawton, M. (2009) German lobbyists work for gas pipelines. Retrieved 7 July 2009, www.dw-world.de/dw/article/0,,4461363,00.html.

Li, F. (2009) China leads the world in auto sales, production. *China Daily*, 8 December, p. 13.

Markoff, J. (2002) The increase in chip speeds is accelerating, not slowing. *New York Times*, 4 February C1.

Mason, R. (2010) Transocean-BP rig had safety valve problem in UK. *Daily Telegraph*, 6 May, p. 1.

McGahan, A. M., & Porter, M. E. (1997) How much does industry matter, really? *Strategic Management Journal, 18* (Special Issue), 15–30.

Menn, J. & Nuttall, C. (2010) Intel alert adss to double-dip recession fears. *Financial Times*, 28 August, p. 15.

Monaghan, A. (2010) We'll avoid double-dip recession, says Buiter. *The Daily Telegraph*, 8 July, p. 3.

Morgan, E. J. (2009) Controlling cartels – Implications of the EU policy reforms. *European Management Journal, 27*(1), 1–12.

Neuborne, E. (1999) Generation Y: Today's teens – The biggest bulge since the boomers-may force marketeers to toss their old tricks. *Business Week*, 15 February, 80.

The New Shorter Oxford English Dictionary (1993) Oxford: Claredon Press.

O'Regan, N. & Ghobadian, A. (2009) Building a FTSE 100 company by hitting the sweet spot of strategy: An interview with Rod Aldridge OBE. *Journal of Strategy and Management, 2*(2), 188–185.

Paster, P. (2008) Should I buy soda in plastic bottles or aluminium cans, *Salon Environment*, 28 January. Retrieved 22 February 2010, www.salon.com/mwt/feature/2008/01/28/ask_pablo_plastic/index.html.

Patrizio, A. (2009) Winners and losers in the Intel-AMD settlement. Retrieved 12 November 2009, www.internetnews.com/bus-news/article.php/3848326/Winners+and+Losers+in+the+IntelAMD+Settlement.htm.

Porter, M. E. (2008) The five competitive forces that shape strategy. *Harvard Business Review*, (January), 86–104.

Ralston, B. (2006) *The Scenario Planning Handbook*. Mason, OH: Thompson South Western.

Ringland, G. (1998) *Scenario Planning: Managing for the Future*. New York: John Wiley.

Rohrlich, M. (2002) Science of suction hits the dirt. *The New York Times*, 29 August, F 1.

Rumelt, R. P. (1991) How much does industry matter? *Strategic Management Journal, 12*(3), 167–186.

Schoemaker, P. J. H. & Day, G. S. (2009) How to make sense of weak signals. *MIT Sloan Management Review, 50*(3), 81–89.

Sjafjell, B. (2008) Internalising externalities in EU Law: Why neither corporate governance nor corporate social responsibility provides the answers. *George Washington International Law Review, 40*(4), 977–1024.

Sorrell, M. (2008) Google going from 'frenemy' to 'froe', 20 June http://paidcontent.org/article/419-sorrell-google-going-from-frenemy-to-enemy-wpp-ceo-grills-goog-yhoo-msf/.

Statutory or voluntary redundancy and lay-off rights (2007) Retrieved 21 May 2007, http://www.articlesbase.com/law-articles/statutory-or-voluntary-redundancy-layoff-rights-150883.html.

Stone, A. (2005) How I made it: Trevor Baylis, inventor of the clockwork radio. *Sunday Times*, 22 May. http://business.timesonline.co.uk/tol/business/entrepreneur/article524972.ece

Tabuchi, H. (2010) JAL bankruptcy filing sets off re-organization and State-led bailout. *New York Times*, 20 January.

Tescopoly (2010) About us. www.tescopoly.org.

The Economist (2002) Loosen up or lose out. *The Economist*, 7 December, p. 8.

The Economist (2008a) Dependent territory. *The Economist*, 23 August, pp. 42–43.

The Economist (2008b) The Germans are coming. *The Economist*, 16 August, pp. 55–56.

The Economist (2008c) A new home for the Nano. *The Economist*, 11 October, p. 77.

The Economist (2009a) Cutting the cord. *The Economist*, 15 August, pp. 45–46.

The Economist (2009b) The game has changed. *The Economist*, 22 August, pp. 49–50.

The Economist (2009c) The rise of the hybrid company. *The Economist*, 5 December, p. 69.

The Economist (2009d) Yuan small step. *The Economist*, 11 July, pp. 67–69.

The Economist (2010a) Black storm rising. *The Economist*, 8 May, pp. 68–70.

The Economist (2010b) A turn for the worse. *The Economist*, 21 August, p. 29.

Uhlig, R. (2000) Dyson cleans up in patent battle with rival Hoover. *Daily Telegraph*. www.telegraph.co.uk/news/uknews/1368860/Dyson-cleans-up-in-patent-battle-with-rival-Hoover.html.

UN (2008) World population prospects: The 2008 revision, 2008.www.un.org/esa/population/publications/wpp2008/wpp2008_highlights.pdf.

Vestas (2010) About us. Retrieved 22 February 2010, www.vestas.com/en/about-vestas.aspx.

Wilson, P. (2010) Carbon price too low argue British MP's. *Australian,* 13–14 February, p. 18.

WiMax (2010) About the WiMax forum. www.wimaxforum.org.

x-rates.com (2010) Historic exchange rates. hwww.x-rates.com/cgi-bin/hlookup.cgi.

Yergin, D. & Stanislaw, J. (1998) *The Commanding Heights: The Battle Between Government and the Marketplace That is Remaking the Modern World*. New York: Simon & Schuster.

For a range of further resources supporting this chapter, please visit the companion website for *Strategic Management* at www.routledge.com/cw/fitzroy.

CHAPTER 4

EXTERNAL ANALYSIS

The financial environment

LEARNING OBJECTIVES

Upon completing this chapter you should be able to:

1 Discuss the importance of financial markets in strategy development.

2 Manage external funds appropriately to support the firm's strategy.

3 Calculate the cost of equity for the firm.

4 Describe the risks and benefits of debt financing.

5 Develop a strategy for the firm which gives consideration to the requirements of financial markets.

6 Employ derivatives as a means of controlling risk.

LAFARGE

In January 2008, Lafarge SA, the world's largest cement maker, acquired Orascom, the Middle East's largest cement producer. The cost of this acquisition was €10 billion with the purchase financed by an increase in debt by Lafarge. Following the financial crisis of 2008/09, in February 2009 Lafarge announced a range of initiatives aimed at reducing its debt levels. These initiatives included major asset sales, a rights issue of new shares and a halving of its dividend. The CEO, Bruno Lafont, announced that due to the unprecedented financial and economic environment, their objective was to reduce debt during 2009 ('Lafarge to sell shares, assets to reduce debt', 2009).

Lafarge's net debt had risen from €8.7 billion at the end of 2007 to €16.9 billion at the end of 2008 as a result of the Orascom purchase. The firm had increased its gearing to enable it to make several acquisitions during the construction boom of 2007/08. Over this period, its net debt-to-equity ratio had risen from 72 per cent in 2007 to 115 per cent in 2008, and by the end of 2009 it was still 87 per cent. The firm had an S&P rating of BBB minus, just above junk level (Lafarge, 2009).

Economic conditions were also difficult for the firm. With a recession in several of its major markets having a major impact on the construction industry, cement volumes had dropped and margins were depressed. In 2008 the firm suffered a loss in its US businesses. Reflecting these trends, the share price dropped 65 per cent during 2008.

The company then took a series of actions designed to reduce debt. As mentioned, 2008 dividends were cut by half to €2 per share, to try to conserve cash. In addition, Lafarge decided to sell off a series of assets. These assets included businesses in Canada, Chile, Switzerland, Turkey, the UK and Venezuela. Funds from these divestments allowed debt to be reduced by approximately €1 billion (Lafarge, 2009).

Lafarge also announced a rights issue for €1.5 billion in April 2009. This rights issue was offered at a 46 per cent discount on the closing share price on 30 March 2009 and the full sum raised was used to pay down debt (Daneshkhu, 2009).

The example above indicates the close relationship between Lafarge's global strategy and the dynamics of financial markets. Had there not been a financial crisis, which meant that banks and other financial institutions were not prepared to offer debt to major companies such as Lafarge, it is likely that the firm's global expansion would have gone ahead as expected. Instead, management had to make a fundamental change in strategy: from growth to survival. This involved reducing dividends, conserving cash, selling major assets and offering new shares at a substantial discount to prevent the firm from collapsing.

STRATEGIC MANAGEMENT IN PRACTICE

CHAPTER OVERVIEW

In this chapter we examine the interaction between the firm and financial markets – the external debt and equity markets which are an important source of funds for companies. The behaviour of financial markets can have a major impact on the firm's strategy, such as when the firm finds it difficult to raise external funds at an acceptable cost. In some situations, financial markets will force a firm to drastically alter its strategy, selling assets to reduce debt and strengthen its balance sheet. We begin by reviewing the nature of the two markets in which the firm competes – product markets and financial markets – and the need to understand these two markets together with issues of the market for corporate control and risk types. We then examine in more detail the major participants in financial markets, with a focus on their global nature. This is followed by a discussion of equity markets, the role of institutional investors and a consideration of the firm's cost of equity. As we discussed in Chapter 3 (▶Chapter 3), firms can get into major difficulties when debt markets freeze up, and this forms the basis of our discussion of the risks, benefits and types of debt, the role of rating agencies, with a brief description of Islamic banking. Given these inputs, we are then able to determine the weighted average cost of capital for the firm, a major consideration in firm valuation. Recognizing the increasing turbulence within which firms compete, we examine risk management concerns with a brief discussion of the role of derivatives. This is followed by a View from the Top, observations of the chairman of HSBC on the future of the global financial system. The chapter concludes with the mini-case Focus (DIY) Limited, a UK company, which illustrates the linkage between financial markets and the firm's strategy.

4.1 INTRODUCTION

LEARNING OBJECTIVE 1

Discuss the importance of financial markets in strategy development.

The Lafarge example above underlines the importance of integrating all aspects of strategy, and, in particular, ensuring there is alignment between the financial position of the firm and its strategy. Financial markets, reflecting the interests of shareholders and debt holders, exert a strong influence on firm strategy. Many firms have had to divest business units in order to reduce corporate debt levels, regardless of the apparent attractiveness of the unit. No firm is isolated from financial markets, and consequently it is critical that strategic managers have a deep understanding of these markets and of the relationship between financial markets and the strategic management of the firm.

To finance its operations, a firm can use either internally generated funds or external capital. Data on sources of funds indicate that global firms generate between 50 per cent and 80 per cent of the funds required for growth and innovation from internal sources (free cash flow from existing operations) (Grinblatt & Titman, 2002). Most companies must therefore supplement internally generated funds with external funds. In approaching financial markets for new debt or equity, managers must be aware of the demands and requirements of these markets. For example, if a company's debt has just been downgraded, new debt may be difficult to arrange. Or if there is turbulence in equity markets, raising new capital may be impossible, negating a variety of strategic options including, for example, a proposed takeover.

Managers must also pay attention to the firm's **liquidity** – its ability to meet short-term financial responsibilities such as paying staff, suppliers and debt holders. If the firm is unable to meet such requirements, or if its liabilities exceed its assets, the directors must legally declare the firm insolvent. The basic procedures for declaring a firm insolvent are either that the firm itself files for bankruptcy, or its creditors bring action to declare the firm bankrupt. The procedures on who can file for bankruptcy show some variation across countries in Europe. For example, in Germany, when a company cannot repay its debts, the company alone can file for bankruptcy, while creditors are also entitled to file when liabilities exceed assets. In Spain, if the company files for bankruptcy, the managers remain in their current positions, subject to the intervention of an external insolvency administrator. If, however, proceedings are initiated by the creditors, management of the company is transferred to the insolvency administration (Coughtrie *et al.*, 2009). Following bankruptcy, the task of either the incumbent managers or administrators is to try to keep the firm operating, possibly by finding a buyer, or by restructuring debt, subject to agreement of the creditors. If this is not possible, the firm will be liquidated and proceeds distributed among the creditors. This means that other stakeholders such as customers, employees and shareholders may receive little or nothing.

The risk of insolvency is influenced by the firm's financial decisions, in particular the level of debt. If the firm is highly leveraged, interest payments as a proportion of cash flow will be high. Should product markets turn down and margins fall, cash flow and the ability to service debt deteriorate. Exchange rate movements can similarly alter revenues and expenses quite dramatically, jeopardizing financial viability. These trends need to be understood and integrated with the firm's product market or business level strategy.

At the same time, several factors are driving an increasingly competitive market for investment funds, which provides managers with additional alternatives. Financial markets have become global and firms can raise funds in any market as the providers of funds see opportunities on a global basis. At the same time, these providers of funds assess investment opportunities globally, increasing the pressure on firms for performance. Given the increased regulation of financial markets following the financial crisis of 2008/09, there may be some restrictions on the free flow of funds globally in the future.

Due to technological developments, information about financial markets is available in real time, while innovative new financial products such as derivatives provide firms with many more choices for managing risk. At the same time, increased levels of complexity, particularly with some of the derivative products such as collaterized debt obligations (CDOs) and credit default swaps (CDSs) (➤Chapter 3), meant that assessing the risk associated with these new products became significantly more difficult. Indeed, some industry experts seem to feel that the rate of innovation and change has outstripped the industry's ability to deal with it.

As is apparent from this discussion, financial markets determine the availability and cost of finance for the firm, and these in turn influence the firm's strategic options. The CEO and the board must be familiar with the operations of financial markets, the participants and how they behave. Such knowledge can constitute an important intangible asset.

Liquidity
The ability of the firm to meet its financial responsibilities such as paying employees, suppliers and debt holders.

Chapter 3

4.2 THE TWO MARKETS IN WHICH FIRMS COMPETE

Any large global firm can be considered as competing in two fundamentally different markets: financial markets for debt and equity and product markets for customers. Strategic management involves decisions about how to compete in both markets. This duality is represented in Figure 4.1. The ways of competing in these two markets are dramatically different, but in this chapter we focus on financial markets. Thus strategic management must address such questions as:

- How will the strategy be financed?
- What financial performance do these financial markets require?
- How will financial risk be managed?

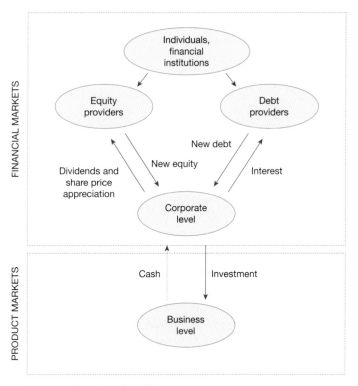

Figure 4.1 The two markets in which firms compete

To succeed in this interconnected world, senior managers required an understanding of the following issues.

Competition in financial markets

Financial markets are where firms requiring funds for future investment come together with individuals, institutions and corporations with money to invest.

At the corporate level, the firm competes for investment funds with other firms – and indeed governments – in these global markets. If financial markets do not regard the firm as an attractive investment, any new debt will incur a cost premium.

Financial markets have grown in both complexity and importance over the last 25 years. In addition to debt, equity and hybrid instruments such as convertible preference shares, a wide range of new financial products generally referred to as derivatives has emerged. These are investments whose value today, or at a future date, is derived from the value of an underlying asset. Managers now have many more choices regarding the nature, cost and risk of an almost bewildering array of financial instruments. Strategic managers should be aware of the range and risks of these instruments. The global financial crisis (GFC) of 2008/09 demonstrated quite clearly that many managers and investors did not understand the risk associated with their choices and the implications for non-financial firms following the collapse of financial markets (▶Chapter 3).

Financial markets
The markets where firms requiring investment funds come together with individuals and institutions with funds to invest.

Chapter 3

Competition in product markets

The corporate level of the firm manages the collection of businesses that comprise its portfolio. Each business competes for customers in its respective product market, against other firms in the same or related industries. Through its parenting role, or through developing synergies and shared resources, the corporate level can influence results at the business level.

Relationship between the two markets

The funds raised by corporate are used to support the operations of the firm which take place primarily at the business unit level. Corporate management invests in a selection of business units depending broadly on the opportunities and costs of the business unit. The business units then may return net cash to the corporate level, with the magnitude of this cash flow being dependent on the margins, growth rate, investment intensity and so on of the business unit. Corporate management uses these returns to pay external capital providers as well as to support innovation and growth.

Market for corporate control

Another form of competition at the corporate level is the **market for corporate control**, where different management groups vie for the right to manage the firm's assets (Jensen, 1990).

The market for corporate control is the market for the buying and selling of companies, or their components, as opposed to the market for products and services. This market is also referred to as the takeover market, both friendly and hostile – the latter being when the

Market for corporate control
The market in which different management groups vie for the right to manage the firm's assets.

Chapter 13

target firm's management resists the takeover. This competition among management teams (and/or owners) for the right to manage the firm's resources is assumed to eliminate any tendency for managers to act in their own interests rather than in the interests of shareholders (➤Chapter 13).

Challenge of strategic management

In several countries hostile takeovers of domestic firms, particularly from overseas countries, are severely limited by government regulation.

▇ As a manager, what controls, if any, do you believe governments should place on hostile takeovers?

▇ As a shareholder, what controls, if any, do you believe governments should place on hostile takeovers?

The managerial challenge

Managing the relationship with financial markets is the responsibility of the CEO and the board, usually relying heavily on the advice of the CFO. As the opening example illustrates, financial markets put pressure on the firm for performance. Shareholders expect a return commensurate with the level of risk of their investment, while debt holders expect periodic interest payments.

Chapter 2

We take it as a fundamental principle that a firm must create value, but what is meant by value depends on the perspective adopted. As we saw in Chapter 2 (➤Chapter 2), the firm has a variety of stakeholders and each defines value in different ways. Here, we extend that discussion and examine the concept of value from two perspectives: that of the firm and that of the shareholder.

Firm value

We consider a firm to be primarily an economic entity. That entity only creates value when the revenue generated by the firm is greater than the costs incurred in producing it. In determining value all costs must be considered, including the cost of the capital required to produce that revenue. Value defined in this manner is also called economic profit and is different from accounting profit. Economic profit includes explicit consideration of the cost of capital. On an ongoing basis we expect the firm to deliver a positive economic profit after all expenses, including tax and the cost of capital, have been included. When calculating accounting profit a charge for depreciation is deducted, but this is not a capital charge per se, it is a period charge reflecting the run down in the value of the fixed assets. We return

Chapter 12

to this topic, including how to measure economic profit, in Chapter 12 (➤Chapter 12).

Shareholder value

From a shareholder perspective, the best measure of value is the **total return to shareholders**: share price appreciation plus dividends over a time period.

Since the current share price reflects expectations about the future, an individual shareholder may fail to get a return if market expectations change. As Figure 4.2 shows, many shareholders would have lost heavily on UBS if they bought shares at 80 Swiss francs in September 2007 only to see the price collapse to less than 20 Swiss francs by early 2009.

Share prices are influenced by market sentiment about the future of the economy as a whole, as well as developments in the industry sector in which the firm is located, and therefore show substantial volatility. Consequently, while managers must be aware of and understand the importance of delivering value to shareholders, their ability to achieve this may, at least in the short term, be limited. First, other factors apart from firm performance drive share prices. Second, share prices exhibit considerable volatility, and are difficult to use as an immediate criterion for management decision-making. Nonetheless, it would be a brave manager who completely ignored market signals contained in share price movements.

Total return to shareholders

The annualized return to shareholders from maintaining their investment in a stock over a period of time. It is calculated as the total of dividends received and share price appreciation over the time period.

Risk types

Risk is a central theme in strategic management. As we saw in Chapter 1, strategic decisions are made in the present but the consequences are realized in the future (➤Chapter 1). This

Chapter 1

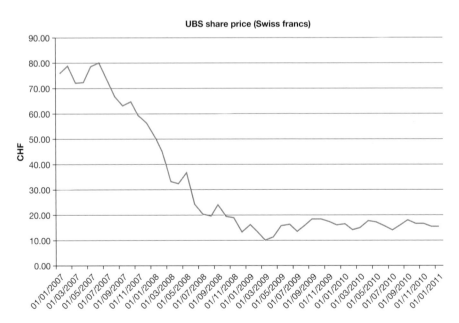

Figure 4.2 UBS share price, 2007–11

Source: UBS website, 2011

future is unknown and in some instances unknowable, and strategic management must include an understanding of risk management – what risk is and what actions can be taken to control the level of risk. We classify risk into two broad categories: business risk and financial risk (Pike & Neale, 1996).

Business risk

Business risk

The year-to-year (or quarter-to-quarter) variability in operating cash flow of the firm.

Business risk is the year-to-year (or quarter-to-quarter) variability in operating cash flow of the firm.

Firm, industry and competitive characteristics will influence the level of this risk. A firm with a high ratio of fixed costs to variable costs would have greater business risk, since cash flow is extremely sensitive to relatively small changes in demand. Firms competing in markets in the early stages of a product life cycle would have high business risk due to the effects of competitor actions or substitutes. A high-technology start-up would generally have a high business risk since the growth rate of the market, future market share, future competitive behaviour, level of innovation and the nature of innovation are all difficult to predict. On the other hand, a product in the mature stage of the life cycle would generally be considered to have lower levels of risk, since such characteristics as market growth, competition and innovation are generally easier to predict. Debt holders, who receive a fixed interest payment, bear no business risk unless the firm goes into receivership, an example of insolvency risk for them.

Financial risk

Financial risk

The ability of a firm to service its debt.

Financial risk is the ability of the firm to service its debt.

Debt is a fixed charge that must be paid, regardless of the firm's financial performance. When a firm utilizes high debt levels there will be a high fixed cost of repayments and consequently higher financial risk. Hence financial risk is also described as leverage or gearing, since financial risk magnifies business risk. If debt is not paid in full and on time the firm becomes insolvent and new managers (administrators) are appointed to run the firm. These receivers are legally required to run the firm in the interests of debt holders, not equity holders. Common measures of financial risk are the firm's debt/equity ratio and its interest cover, the ratio of net income to interest expenses. The firm's capital structure therefore provides one means to assess financial risk, and this structure must be managed accordingly. As we will see, there had been a long-term trend by most companies to increase the amount of debt in their capital structure, thus leveraging returns to their shareholders. While this had assisted shareholders in the short term, it had had major implications following the financial crisis of 2008 – debt markets froze and many firms found it almost impossible to roll over their debt. As a result, they had to adopt measures to increase cash flow, including asset sales and reducing dividends.

Total risk for the firm is the sum of these two components: business risk and financial risk. We would expect firms with high levels of business risk to have low levels of financial leverage (low debt/equity ratios). Such firms are financed almost solely by equity and not by debt, as we see with start-ups financed by venture capital firms. In contrast, firms in mature industries with stable cash flows can sustain higher debt/equity ratios (higher levels of financial risk) due to the low level of business risk.

Should a firm become insolvent there is generally a legally mandated order of payment, with secured creditors being paid first, unsecured creditors such as suppliers next and, finally, shareholders. This is part of the reason why shareholders are considered to have higher risk and expect a premium for assuming this risk. Consequently, the required return to debt holders will be lower than the required return to shareholders. Or, to put it another way, the cost of equity to the firm will always be above the cost of debt.

4.3 FINANCIAL MARKETS

Financial markets comprise debt markets and equity markets and each market is made up of a number of actors, as shown in Figure 4.3. One group of actors in equity markets is individual shareholders who buy and sell shares. Other important institutions are financial intermediaries: mutual funds, insurance companies and pension funds that typically collect the savings of individuals and corporations and channel them to firms to finance new investment. Other participants include banks, stockbrokers, financial advisers, security analysts, and exchanges such as the London Stock Exchange together with various regulatory bodies – for instance, the UK's Financial Services Authority (FSA) or the US Securities and Exchange Commission (SEC). Debt markets comprise some of the same actors as well as

LEARNING OBJECTIVE 2
Manage external funds appropriately to support the firm's strategy.

Individual shareholders   Security analysts
Institutional shareholders   Stock exchanges
Stockbrokers   Regulatory authorities

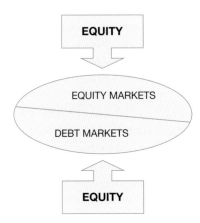

Institutional bondholders   Security analysts
Rating agencies   Banks
Brokers   Government

Figure 4.3 Financial market participants

new ones: rating agencies and banks. Government has a major role in both markets through legislation, taxation, the regulatory framework, and, sometimes, direct investment.

Prior to the financial crisis of 2008, it was generally believed that financial markets were becoming more efficient, with participants receiving and acting on all the relevant information. Certainly the availability of information concerning a security's future prospects had increased, since publications such as *The Financial Times*, the *Wall Street Journal* and *The Economist* are now available globally on the Web, while Reuters and Bloomberg provide real-time data on financial markets. As a result, it was widely thought that investors, institutions and banks had become more sophisticated and more knowledgeable. The crisis demonstrated beyond any doubt that these assumptions were faulty. Many securities purchasers had an almost naive faith in the ability of ratings agencies, paid by security issuers, to accurately appraise risk. That there might be **moral hazard** in such a system appears never to have crossed their minds. Ultimately, events were to prove that their faith was wildly misplaced, and their judgement faulty.

The world's leading financial centres are New York and London with others in Frankfurt, Hong Kong, Paris, Singapore, Sydney and Tokyo. These financial centres differ in terms of liquidity and regulation. Liquidity is the ease with which financial assets may be traded. When there are limited numbers of buyers or sellers the market would be considered illiquid. The New York and London markets are seen as having an advantage with their liquidity. Maintaining these advantages is seen as critically important by both US and UK governments, since the financial industry is very important to both economies.

US financial markets, with their stringent rules on disclosure and insider trading, were thought for many years to be among the most efficient. However, the Enron and other scandals raised significant doubts. The independence of auditors, security analysts and rating agencies has subsequently been questioned in the US and elsewhere. As a consequence, several major accounting firms have separated their consulting and auditing practices. The US Sarbanes-Oxley Act of 2002 was the first wave of legislation that is expected to significantly change the ground rules for participants in financial markets. Sadly, the Satyam scandal in India indicates that problems still remain and that people will be less willing to invest in Indian technology companies and possibly in other global financial markets (Balachandran, 2009a).

All governments regulate the financial markets that fall under their jurisdiction, but the nature of the regulation varies widely, particularly with regard to the amount and accuracy of information available to investors. Regulations include rules on insider trading, capitalization ratios for financial institutions and what activities institutions can engage in. The New York and London markets provide considerable information, and are seen as more transparent. In Germany, banks can own equities, but this is not permitted in the US.

As a result of the financial crisis in 2008/09, firms around the world found themselves in great financial difficulty. Among the well-known companies that either failed or were wholly or partially taken over by government were Fannie Mae, Freddie Mac, Washington Mutual, AIG, Lehman Bros, General Motors, Chrysler, Bear Stearns and Citicorp (US), Northern Rock, RBS and HBOS (UK), Dubai World (Gulf States), Fortis (Belgium) and Hypo Real Estate in Germany. In response, governments around the world have strengthened

Moral hazard
Arises when an individual or organization does not assume the full consequences of their actions; another party is then forced to assume some or all of the consequences.

the regulatory framework for the finance industry to reduce the possibility of future financial meltdowns.

Despite the trend towards globalization in financial markets, there are still significant differences among different countries' regulatory frameworks. One notable example of these differences is so-called bearer instruments. In several European countries, shares and bonds may be issued as bearer instruments where the ownership of the security is unknown (Samuels *et al.*, 1999). Indeed, historically markets such as the Eurobond market have essentially been unregulated.

In Japan, banks are generally large holders of company shares and during the past decade they have seen the value of these shares decline. Under new accounting rules, Japanese banks must now incorporate these book losses into their income statements, imperilling their capital adequacy ratios and threatening the entire Japanese banking system. In 2009 Sumitomo Mitsui Financial Group, one of Japan's biggest banks, was reported as taking total write-downs of $US2.2 billion on its equity investments, including over $US530 million on its investment in Barclays Bank alone. The problem was so bad that Japan's central bank offered to buy back up to $US10.0 billion-worth of shares that the country's banks were holding, even though this was reported to be a small proportion of the total equity holdings by all banks (Wang, 2009).

Elsewhere, non-performing loans continue to be a major problem. In 2009, non-performing loans in Italy increased by €59 billion over their 2008 levels and are expected to increase further in the future (PricewaterhouseCoopers, 2010). In Spain, non-performing loans were reported as 5.39 per cent in February 2010, up by 25 per cent over the year (Euro Intelligence, 2010). These data suggest that the lending market is likely to contract significantly for some time in the future. China has reported a drop in non-performing loans but some observers were not convinced, with ratings agency Fitch reporting that falling non-performing loans do not indicate that banks' asset quality is improving (Wall Street Pit, 2010). Indeed, the People's Bank of China recently ordered China's large banks to raise their reserve requirement ratios to 17 per cent, partly because authorities want to allay fears that a credit binge last year could have created too many non-performing loans, even though this may reduce the capacity for Chinese banks to offer loans in future (Tett, 2010).

Major participants in financial markets

We now review some of the key actors and characteristics of global financial markets.

Shareholders

Shareholders are the firm's owners, and their holding of shares in the firm represents this ownership – the equity of the firm. A distinguishing characteristic of the modern firm is that the liability of shareholders is limited to the amount they paid for the shares. The firm is a separate legal entity and the debts of the firm cannot normally be transferred to its shareholders. This may not be the case with other kinds of legal structures such as partnerships. While shareholders are the owners, they do not exercise direct control as a result of ownership; instead, they have the right to attend the firm's annual general meeting, to appoint directors and to vote on major changes to the firm, such as whether or not to accept an acquisition bid.

Shareholders receive a financial return on their investment from two main sources – dividends and any appreciation in the price of the shares since the time of purchase (capital gain). In most countries dividends are regarded as income to the shareholder and taxed accordingly. Share price appreciation, however, is generally treated as a capital gain when shares are sold and is usually taxed at a lower rate.

Debt holders

Lenders to the firm have a contract specifying their claims – generally fixed, periodic payments regardless of the firm's financial performance. They are also first to be paid in the event of bankruptcy, although in some countries there is ongoing political debate on whether secured creditors or employees should be paid first. Debt can be short term or long term, arranged through financial intermediaries such as banks, or arranged directly by the firm. The cost of debt is affected by the financial strength of the firm, in turn influenced by ratings from agencies such as Standard & Poors or Moodys. Interest payments on debt are generally tax-deductible, reducing the true cost of debt to the firm. When a firm faces liquidity problems or breaches covenants on its debt, as so many did during the recent financial crisis, the debt holders are the most powerful players in determining the outcome. Their willingness to reschedule debt payments or to trade debt for equity will determine whether or not the firm survives as an independent entity, as the following example with the Japanese airline, JAL, makes clear.

Decisions regarding investment choices and the source of funds for new investments are central to strategic management. Strategies and associated new investments can be funded from three sources – retained earnings, new debt or new equity. Firms generally demonstrate a clear preference order among these three sources of funds. Most firms prefer to fund investments from retained earnings, and to maintain a steady dividend stream over time. If additional funds are required, the second preference is for more debt. Traditionally, additional equity has only been issued as a last resort. This is generally described as the 'pecking order' theory in corporate finance.

If there is excess cash the firm is likely to pay off debt, or exercise a share buyback scheme rather than increase dividends to shareholders (Grinblatt & Titman, 2002). However, in the face of reduced debt availability, attitudes towards additional equity issuance may well be changing. For example, to pay for its proposed acquisition of AIG's Asian business, Prudential had planned to engage in a substantial rights issue to raise more equity from existing shareholders.

Since the cost of neither debt nor equity is the same for all firms, the cost of funds can be a source of competitive advantage, especially in capital-intensive industries. Among other things, this cost of funds may be affected by how astute the company is in managing its finances, an important intangible asset.

Pecking order

The order in which firms generally use their three sources of funds – internal development, new debt and new equity.

Bankruptcy *in practice* – JAL

In January 2010 Japan's Minister of Land, Infrastructure, Transport and Tourism met with Japan Airline Corporation's major creditor banks to seek approval for a court-led rehabilitation plan for Asia's largest carrier that will involve filing for bankruptcy protection.

The government is expected to issue a statement to confirm its stance on the matter and to allay public concerns about the carrier's operating potential. This stance by the Japanese government is opposed by JAL's president and CEO who believes that it will impact negatively on customer sentiment towards Japan's oldest and largest carrier, sources said.

JAL's biggest lender, the Development Bank of Japan, has already approved bankruptcy measures as being the most prudent step forward for the cash-strapped carrier, while the government has asked two other major creditor banks, Mitsubishi UFJ Financial Group and Sumitomo Mitsui Banking Corp., to continue their financial support for the carrier, ahead of the state-backed Enterprise Turnaround Initiative Corp. of Japan pursuing a court-led restructuring process (China View, 2010). Shortly after these events, Japan Airlines' main lenders were reportedly unwilling to provide the bankrupt carrier with further relief unless they see evidence that it is making strides in slashing costs, in particular by cutting back on international services.

To ensure the carrier is able to continue operating during the bankruptcy process, it has been able to access ¥900 billion ($9.9 billion) from the Enterprise Turnaround Initiative Corp. of Japan and the Development Bank of Japan, both of which are government-backed institutions. The ETIC is overseeing the bankruptcy process and in this capacity it has asked JAL's major creditors to forgive more than ¥700 billion in liabilities. However, all the banks are hesitant in providing aid because they have not yet seen sufficient progress in cutting costs by JAL (Air Transport World, 2010).

In January 2010 the firm filed for bankruptcy, and in May asked that the date for this submission be changed to August 2010. To support this extension the firm claimed that it planned to reduce its workforce of 47,000 by 19,100 by the end of 2015, as well as selling two subsidiaries and other assets (Thomas, 2010).

Global nature of financial markets

The global nature of financial markets is manifest in the choices that investors have as to where to invest, a phenomenon illustrated in Figure 4.4.

As seen in Figure 4.4, potential investors can choose from among many different regions of the world. Investors who decide to invest in Europe can choose from among cash, equities, debt or real assets such as property. Should investors invest in equities, they can select any business sector, such as retailing, banking or manufacturing. Within the broad manufacturing

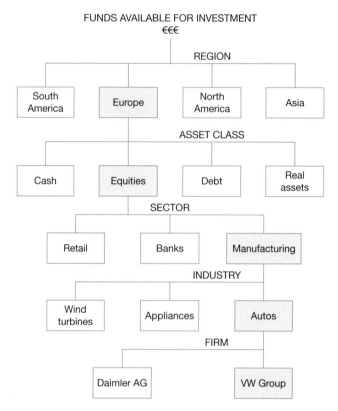

Figure 4.4 Global choices for investors

Source: Adapted from a chart prepared by G. Addison

sector, they can invest in firms focusing on home appliances (e.g. Electrolux), wind turbines (e.g. Vestas), automobiles, etc. If they invest in the automobile sector, they can choose from among Daimler-Benz, VW or others. In addition, individual investors can invest directly in a company, or via a fund such as Vanguard or Fidelity.

This wide choice is available to both individual and institutional investors, and both groups are becoming more sophisticated. Capital flows are now less controlled, with few restrictions in most countries for investing in other countries (although there are still some exceptions, such as India, China and Malaysia). Over the last decade, however, many countries, especially in the developing world, have engaged in strenuous efforts to improve liquidity and transparency of their financial markets. This reflects the increasing role of financial markets in economic development, a role likely to grow in the future. As a consequence of these changes, firms must be internationally competitive in terms of returns to shareholders. They cannot hide behind protective barriers, and must generate appropriate shareholder returns or suffer the consequences of declining share prices.

There are some differences between capital markets in different countries. In a number of countries, for example, the role of banks in the provision of debt financing has decreased:

an example of disintermediation. In contrast, Japanese banks are still the primary source of a firm's debt and can own up to 5 per cent of a company's stock. European and Japanese shareholders are generally seen as more passive than American investors. This may reflect the composition of the share register of companies where banks have significant equity holdings, as do other companies with whom the firm does business. While the pace has been affected by the recent liquidity crisis, Europe is seeing a longer term trend towards an increasing number of hostile takeovers, driven by shareholder pressure for better returns. This trend is expected to continue, despite the fact that Germany has successfully reduced opportunities for hostile takeovers. European and Japanese capital is often considered more patient: investors in these countries are more interested in long-term results than short-term results. This observation should be treated with caution, since US research suggests that up to 80 per cent of the price of many shares is represented by expectations of future performance (Bruckner *et al.*, 2000). One feature of US financial markets that is of interest to non-US firms is **American depository receipts** or ADRs (Grinblatt & Titman, 2002).

With an ADR, a non-US firm deposits some of its shares with a local (non-US) custodian appointed by a US depository bank. The US bank then issues ADRs to the US investor. Thus the ADR is a negotiable certificate backed by the underlying company shares. The holder of the ADR is able to trade these securities on the US equities markets and receive

American depository receipts (ADRs)
Negotiable securities issued by a US bank which are backed by the ordinary shares of a non-US firm.

Hostile takeover *in practice*

In Europe, hostile and unsolicited takeover bids appear to be increasing. Possible reasons for this development are the increase in the number of publicly listed firms following the privatizations of the 1990s. Another is the increase in the number of European business leaders with experience outside Europe, particularly in the US. A further factor is the rise of companies from emerging economies such as ArcelorMittal, originally from India and now registered in Luxembourg, which has been an aggressive acquirer (Boston, 2006).

"Wipe that silly grin off your face, Benson - this is a hostile takeover."

any dividend, in US dollars, from the underlying non-US firm – minus a fee to the bank. For example, Burberry, the UK retailer, offers these ADRs through Deutsche Bank Trust Company Americas (Burberry, 2010). Through these ADRs US investors can purchase foreign shares as easily as shares in firms listed on the US exchanges. Similar instruments exist in other financial markets apart from the US.

Another major trend in financial markets has been a dramatic increase in the proportion of equity held by institutional investors such as mutual funds and pension schemes. Since they acquire stock on behalf of other investors, fund managers in these institutions pressure firms for superior financial performance, reflecting the pressure on them from their own senior management and investors. In these institutions, a small number of professionals make the buy/sell decisions on investments and although they are agents for their own investors, they represent a powerful set of shareholders with whose goals their incentives are not necessarily aligned. The total value of financial assets held globally by pension funds alone was £13 trillion in 2006, 11 per cent of which were held by UK firms and 61 per cent by US firms (Bollen, 2008). Managers of these pension funds compare investment opportunities on a worldwide basis in the search for superior performance that can be passed on to their individual holders.

Chapter 13

Large institutional investors are also getting more active in corporate governance (►Chapter 13). Historically institutions sold shares when firm performance was poor. Increasingly they now pressure management for improvements, which may involve major changes to senior management personnel (Rubach & Sebora, 2009). They also want more information on strategy and boards with strong independent directors. This can produce a conflict between senior management and the board, since firms are prohibited from treating any shareholders differently. If they provide additional information to large institutional shareholders, there can be a problem with insider trading.

Another major development in financial markets has been changes in technology and communications. This is manifest in the faster, smarter information systems, such as Bloomberg, Reuters and Datastream that provide real-time data on share prices and financial analysis globally. These developments have seen financial markets operate on a 24/7 basis, with online trading by individuals. It has become easy to monitor and execute orders from any country in many other countries, and with the increasing number of institutional buyers this trend is expected to continue. The information deluge also makes it difficult for managers to hide inferior performance.

Current concerns with financial markets

Over the past decade, there has been considerable concern over the accuracy of financial reports prepared for investors, which we now discuss.

Accuracy of financial data

In the recent past, there have been problems with the financial reports prepared by firms such as Enron, Parmalat and Satyam, among others. US regulatory and accounting procedures – once seen as a model for other countries – have been shown to be lacking and a variety of remedial measures are being implemented.

Objectivity of auditors

There has been deep concern at the objectivity of auditors. Auditors are appointed by and should report to the board. But auditors may get too close to management and lose their objectivity. Historically, the major accounting firms, which undertake audits, also had

---

Financial data *in practice* – Satyam

Satyam, India's fourth largest outsourcing IT firm, counted among its clients such blue chip firms as BP, GE, State Farm and Nestlé. Yet in January 2009 its name was added to a list of companies involved in fraudulent financial activities when its CEO, Ramalingam Raju, took responsibility for broad accounting improprieties that overstated the company's revenues and profits and reported a cash holding of approximately $1.04 billion that simply did not exist. Having studied several of these cases, Columbia Business School Professor Sudhakar V. Balachandran concluded that executives 'start by fudging the number a little – and then it grows. It is usually a response to competitive pressures. Companies have targets that they need to reach every month, quarter and year. These targets can come from their internal budgets or from the expectations of their shareholders and stock market analysts.

'The fiddle is easy to rationalize at first. Managers typically have confidence in their skills and believe that their company is fundamentally sound. Given that, it's easy to rationalize that while we're just a little short on the numbers *now*, we will make it up in the future, and nobody will know. When the company is unable to make up the gap, a larger distortion is needed to cover it up. This in turn creates pressure to deliver even better results – which leads to bigger cover-ups, and so on' (Balachandran, 2009b).

The Satyam case led to the resignation of PricewaterhouseCooper's head of audit and two other partners in India, while Satyam's chairman, CEO and CFO were in prison awaiting trial at the time of writing (Judge, 2009).

---

consulting arms. The audit part of their business was less profitable than consulting, so the accounting firm might use a 'soft' audit as a way to get consulting business from the client. Accounting firms such as Ernst & Young, KPMG and PricewaterhouseCoopers have all separated their accounting and consulting businesses, or indicated that the accounting firms would no longer serve as consultant and external auditor for the same client. In making these changes, the accounting firms were probably acting just ahead of the regulators (Glater, 2002).

Objectivity of analysts

Concern has been expressed in the US at the objectivity of financial analysts, particularly those employed within banks, and stockbrokers. One study indicated that brokerage firms reward analysts who provide optimistic reports, including a 'buy' recommendation, on stocks the brokerage firm is promoting (Taylor, 2002). Such optimistic forecasts are still common, as indicated in a recent McKinsey report (Goedhart *et al.*, 2010). Such reports can have a significant impact on a firm's share price, particularly in the short term. The market capitalization of Nokia, for example, fell over $bn 60, or 26 per cent, in one day due to downgrades by analysts after the firm indicated lower projected earnings.

Senior executives should clearly be very careful about what information they report to the financial press. For example, speculation about possible future acquisitions must be handled carefully, not only to counter a major fall or rise in share prices but also to ensure that no insider trading occurs.

Objectivity of ratings agencies

Billions of dollars, Euros and yen are invested based on the ratings produced by companies such as S&P and Moody's. As a result of the financial crisis and the disastrous investment decisions made as a result of these agencies' judgements of credit quality, governments are currently reviewing the merits of a system in which such agencies are paid by the issuers of the very securities they are rating. It is to be hoped that one outcome of the current reviews of financial regulation that are taking place in many parts of the world will be removal of the moral hazard inherent in such a system.

<table>
<tr><td>**LEARNING OBJECTIVE 3**

Calculate the cost of equity for the firm.</td></tr>
</table>

4.4 EQUITY MARKETS

To raise funds on equity markets firms have numerous alternatives, some of which are discussed below (Grinblatt & Titman, 2002). The most common form of equity is ordinary shares, others being preferred and non-voting shares. An ongoing firm may make a rights offer – an offer of new shares restricted to existing shareholders, generally at a discounted price. Such an offer has the feature of not affecting the distribution of shares – assuming all shareholders take them up. In contrast, a new offer may result in quite different shareholders and possibly the dilution of the power of existing shareholders.

Initial public offering (IPO)

Occurs when a firm offers a tranche of equity to investors for the first time.

An **initial public offering** (IPO) occurs when a firm issues a tranche of equity for the first time. It is generally difficult to set a price for these issues, as has been seen in the last few years with new technology stocks. Some dropped in price well below the listing price, others increased dramatically. An IPO can be expensive; the cost can be from 10 to 15 per cent of the sum to be raised, depending on the sum (Brigham & Houston, 2001). Sometimes the price of the IPO is fixed; in other countries such as Australia the price can be flexible with a price band dependent on demand for the issue or the type of investor. Yet as the Superdry example below demonstrates, companies with a successful record and a good strategy for the future can raise funds even when equity markets are subdued.

Types of investors

As noted, shareholders can be split into two broad groups: individual and institutional. Institutional investors include financial institutions such as pension funds, investment companies and insurance companies, as well as other non-financial companies investing surplus cash.

Over the last few decades institutional investors have become more important. Recent data on institutional investors in the US is shown in Figure 4.5.

IPO *in practice* – Superdry

Despite the doom and gloom that dampened investor enthusiasm around the globe, Cheltenham-based UK fashion retailer Superdry had a very successful London Stock Exchange IPO in March 2010, raising £120 million (Tyldesley, 2010). The company's mixing of Japanese and American retro seems to appeal broadly to the youth market, and the fact that Superdry gear has been worn by football superstar David Beckham hasn't hurt them either!

The company's founders have announced further expansion plans. Superdry already has outlets in nearly all House of Frazer's 60 UK department stores, opened 18 of its own stores in the UK and Ireland in 2009, and plans to open another 20 in 2010. Superdry is already established in Benelux, France, Venezuela, Panama, Australia and the US, and is planning further overseas expansion (Luu, 2010) .

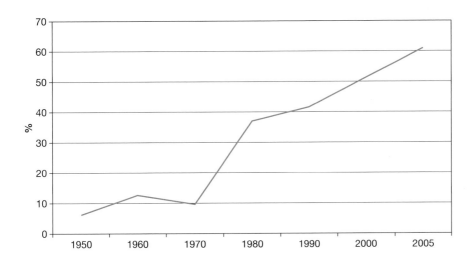

Figure 4.5 Percentage of shares ($ value) of major US companies held by institutional investors

Source: Aghion *et al.*, 2009

Chapter 13

In the UK, the proportion of shares held directly by individuals has fallen from 55 per cent in 1963 (Useem, 1998) to 10.2 per cent in 2008 (Office for National Statistics, 2010). Such a decline has been offset by an increase in indirect equity ownership through mutual and pension funds. This growth in institutional investors has several implications for managers and boards of directors (►Chapter 13). Senior managers need to understand the needs of shareholders, and how these vary among different types of shareholders. Some shareholders may prefer dividends; others may prefer capital gains due to a more favourable personal tax treatment. The preference between dividends and price appreciation will be influenced by the tax regime faced by the investor. If the shareholder is a tax-exempt investor, such as a pension fund in the US, they pay no tax and therefore may prefer dividends.

Imputation credits

A tax system in which the firm pays tax (at the corporate tax rate) on dividend and this payment is a tax credit for the shareholder.

In countries with a system of **imputation credits**, the company pays tax (at the corporate tax rate) on any dividend and this payment is a tax credit for the shareholder (Samuels *et al.*, 1999). The tax paid by the company can be offset against the tax due by the shareholder. The value of such a scheme depends on the tax rate of the investor. Investors who pay no or little tax would see no benefit, nor would foreign shareholders, since tax credits only apply in the country of origin of the dividend.

Shareholders may also differ in how they regard share ownership. Some institutional investors are more short term; they see the investment as just that, an investment. They are not interested in exercising ownership and if the firm is not performing, they sell. Such investors seldom attempt to challenge management to achieve better performance. On the other hand, many believe small shareholders to be more patient investors; they are there for the long term.

There is interesting evidence, however, that ownership structure has a number of impacts on firm performance. Grant and Kirchmaier have shown that for a number of major European economies the dominant form of ownership is not the most efficient one. Across Continental Europe, legal control by a large shareholder, or coalition of shareholders who control the board, is the dominant ownership category, but in Germany and Spain widely held firms significantly outperformed those under legal control (Grant & Kirchmaier, 2004). Research at the same centre of the London School of Economics has also found that the type of ownership can affect innovation, a subject we investigate directly in Chapter 9 (Aghion *et al.*, 2009) (►Chapter 9).

Chapters 9, 13

The contrasting needs and requirements of different investors suggest that there is an important role for investor relations. It may be necessary to apply marketing concepts such as segmentation to the share register to understand the needs of different investors, and their possibly different risk profiles. It also highlights the need to communicate with investors, informing them about the firm and its strategy. Such investor relations are an important role for the CEO and the board, as discussed in Chapter 13 (►Chapter 13).

The cost of equity capital

The fundamental assumption underlying shareholder value is that investors have numerous investment alternatives, as illustrated in Figure 4.4, and that the alternatives have different risk levels. Consequently, investors require a level of return on an investment commensurate

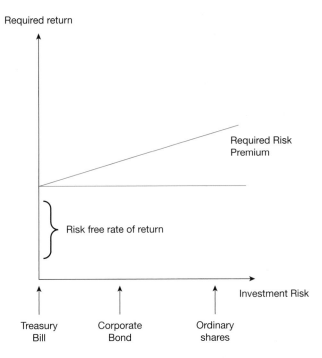

Figure 4.6 Required rate of return by an investor

with its level of risk. As the level of risk of an investment increases, so does the required return, as shown in Figure 4.6.

The risk/return relationship may not be a linear relationship, as shown in the figure, but it is certainly monotonic. That is, investors require higher returns from risky investments to compensate for the possibility of losing their investment.

The lowest level of risk is generally reckoned to be a government security, in the UK a Gilt, in Germany a Bund or in the US a Treasury bill. These investments were traditionally assumed to be risk free, since any national government is unlikely to default on the redemption or the payment of interest on any security issued in its name. However, in the aftermath of the financial crisis, this assumption must be questioned. Figure 4.7 shows how the risk premiums associated with government bonds from various European countries rose as the extent of the budget problems of the so-called PIGS (Portugal, Ireland, Greece and Spain) became evident in late 2009. As we write, these risk premiums have reached historic highs, with Irish bonds attracting a premium of 950 **basis points**, which may put the Euro as a unified currency at risk of collapse (BBC News, 2010).

Despite these problems, however, the risk of default on sovereign debt is generally low. Since any investor can invest in these government securities, if the firm is to attract equity investment, it must promise shareholders a return greater than this 'risk-free' rate, the so-called risk premium.

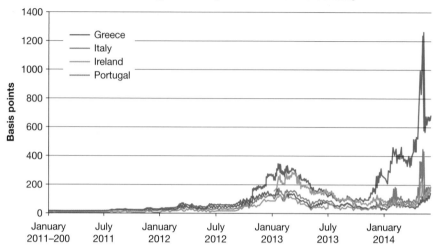

Figure 4.7 Spreads of 10-year government benchmark bonds to German bunds
Source: Gyntelberg *et al.*, 2010

We can express the rate of return required by an investor, for a particular investment, as:

Required return = Risk-free rate + Risk premium

Capital asset pricing model (CAPM)
A method for calculating the rate of return required by an investor for a particular investment.

The risk premium is specific to the investment under consideration. To calculate this premium, modern financial theory suggests the use of the **capital asset pricing model** (CAPM) (Pratt & Grabowski, 2008), whereby the rate of return required by the shareholder is given by:

Required return = Risk-free rate + beta*(expected return on the market – risk-free rate)

In this formulation, the risk-free rate is the return on government securities, the expected return on the market is the average return from a portfolio of shares based on the share market as a total entity and beta is a measure of risk for the security or firm in question. Values of beta are widely published (Brealey & Myers, 2000).

Cost of equity capital
The minimum return required by shareholders to compensate them for the level of risk involved in investing in the firm.

This required rate of return is the **cost of equity capital** for the firm. It is the return required by a shareholder to compensate for the level of risk of that investment. The cost of equity depends on such factors as the nature of the industry (high technology needs a high return) and stage of development (higher cost if the product or technology is in the early stages of the life cycle). Typically, young, entrepreneurial, high-technology firms have a very high cost of equity capital, reflecting the risk involved.

While the capital asset pricing model is commonly used to calculate the cost of equity capital, it does have some problems (Grinblatt & Titman, 2002). For example, the model is historical in nature. Values for the risk premiums are deduced from past data and may not be valid in the future. This poses a particular problem for new high-technology firms which have no track record. The model also assumes that shareholders are interested only in risk and return, whereas non-economic considerations such as religious or ethical criteria may influence investment choices. At least for the UK, the results suggest that returns for ethical investing are no worse, and possibly better than average, so that choosing to invest in this manner may not be 'non-economic' (Investment Management Association, 2009).

Trends in equity markets

In the past decade many firms have engaged in share repurchase schemes, using surplus funds to buy back shares on the open market, as illustrated in the following example.

Share repurchase
Occurs when a firm uses excess cash to buy its own shares in financial markets.

> ### Share repurchase *in practice* – AstraZeneca
>
> In July 2010 the UK pharmaceutical firm AstraZeneca, with their share price at a four-year high, offered a $2.0 billion (£1.3 billion) share buyback to be completed in 2010. This offer was an increase on its initial target of $1 billion made earlier in the year and followed a 10 per cent increase in pre-tax profits (King, 2010). Future expectations were raised when it was revealed that a major new product had received regulatory approval in the US, and that a US court had upheld AstraZeneca's patent on a second new drug. In announcing the offer, the board stated that the decision had been made after providing for business investment and meeting their debt obligations (AstraZeneca, 2010).

Share repurchases increase share prices (thus possibly benefiting managers with share options) by reducing the number of shares outstanding, thereby increasing earnings per share, which is often used as a basis for valuing shares (➤Chapter 8). It is also usually tax-efficient compared with increasing dividends, since capital gains taxes are generally lower than income taxes.

Another trend is for firms to be listed on more than one exchange, with some of these cross-listings being quite complicated.

Chapter 8

> ### Dual structure *in practice* – Unilever
>
> Unilever has two parent companies, Unilever NV and Unilever plc. Despite these two companies being separate legal entities, with separate stock exchange listings, the firm operates as a single entity. Unilever NV is listed on the Amsterdam, German and Luxembourg exchanges, among others, while Unilever plc is listed on the London exchange and as ADRs in New York. In 2005 the firm considered changing this structure, but eventually concluded that a unified structure would create additional costs and disrupt the business ('Unilever says it will keep its dual structure intact', 2005).

LEARNING OBJECTIVE 4

Describe the risks and benefits of debt financing.

Debt

A promise by the firm to pay a specified return for a specified time period.

Covenants

A restriction on a borrower that attempts to limit risk for the lender.

4.5 DEBT MARKETS

Debt is a promise by the firm to pay a specified return for a specified time period. From the provider's perspective debt has low risk and the holder will accept a lower return than an equity holder. From the firm's perspective, debt is cheaper than equity.

There is some risk to the debt provider, since the firm can default on paying a debt due to insolvency. Consequently, firm debt carries higher interest rates than government securities. Yet holders of corporate debt are in a preferred position relative to shareholders, since they generally have some legal protection and are paid first in the event of insolvency. In addition, interest payments are a legal liability of the firm and are paid before any dividends. Creditors are often the trigger for instituting restructuring or formal bankruptcy proceedings, since, if they have not been paid as required, they can establish a legal claim on the firm's assets.

Many debt holders attach restrictive **covenants** to debt. These covenants provide more protection for the lenders, since violations permit debt holders to call in their loans, which could cause insolvency and subsequent bankruptcy filing. Covenants might include limits on additional debt and capital expenditure or specify minimum levels of profit and maximum levels of leverage. Covenants inevitably reduce management's decision-making discretion.

Types of debt

Firms employ a wide range of debt instruments in their search for funds. They typically utilize a mixture of short- and long-term debt, where short term is defined as debt that must be repaid within a year (Samuels *et al.*, 1999). In debt markets, a bond is a generic name for tradable, long-term debt raised by a borrower who agrees to make specific payments, usually regular payments of interest and repayment of principal on maturity. Debt with a floating interest rate is generally priced with respect to a benchmark interest rate such as the London Inter-Bank Offered Rate (LIBOR) or Treasury bills in the US. A zero-coupon bond pays no interest, but is issued at a discount below par or redemption value, so the holder gets capital appreciation through deferred interest, which normally means preferential tax treatment.

Debt also differs in terms of security. Senior debt that is paid first in the event of a default (before any subordinated debt is paid) has the lowest level of risk for the investor. The US Federal Reserve Board publishes a more complete description of debt types and interest payment characteristics (*Trading and Capital-Markets Activities Manual*, 2001).

A global firm will have a range of debt instruments, generally in different currencies and with different maturity dates. The cost will be influenced by several factors, including the general level of interest rates and the maturity of the debt, with the relationship between interest rates and maturity being expressed by a yield curve. As a debt becomes due, the firm may roll it over, and here debt holders can exert substantial pressure on the firm to lower its risk profile and improve its ability to service the debt by divesting some of its current assets or businesses.

As debt markets have become more volatile, some firms have replaced short-term debt with long-term debt, despite the higher interest rates. Firms were also worried that short-term debt markets might lose liquidity and that market sentiment might close the bond market to the firm, or that banks would restrict lending. In the aftermath of the liquidity crisis these problems were particularly acute for firms in the property industry, as the following example demonstrates.

Debt levels *in practice* – Dubai World

Dubai World is an investment company owned by the government of Dubai that manages a number of businesses including DP World and Nakheel. DP World acquired P&O Ports in 2006 and is the third largest port operator in the world. Nakheel Properties is the world's largest privately held real estate firm and was responsible for the development of the Palm Jumeirah, a man-made island off the coast of Dubai. One consequence of the global financial crisis was that the Palm Island development suffered a major collapse. The building boom rapidly turned into a property slump, leaving many buildings unfinished and empty, with asset prices collapsing by up to 50 per cent.

In November 2009, Dubai World announced that it was unable to meet the repayments on a $3.5 billion loan due in December. It proposed to delay repayment on a debt of $23 billion for up to six months. Most of the debt was associated with Nakheel; other businesses such as DP World appeared to have sufficient cash flow to service their debts.

In late 2009, the Dubai government established the Dubai Financial Support Fund to manage this restructuring process and the associated negotiations with lenders which included the Royal Bank of Scotland. In another response to its debt crisis, Dubai World laid off 10,500 employees, about 15 per cent of its workforce. Any attempt to raise cash through asset sales was hampered by the collapse of asset prices following the economic downturn.

In May 2010, Dubai World announced that it had reached agreement in principle with several of its banks to restructure debt of $23 billion; this was to take the form of delaying payment on all debt for at least six months. The restructure also involved converting $9 billion of debt into equity. However, this agreement had to be ratified by other banks not involved in the negotiations. At the same time, Dubai World announced that DP World, the port operator and its debt, were not part of the restructuring process. This was an attempt to reassure ocean carriers and shippers that the position of DP World was secure.

Since Dubai World is owned by the government, there was concern that the Dubai government would default on its debt. This concern was partly alleviated when in February 2010 the Dubai government announced that it had secured loans from several Abu-Dhabi banks. However, the government has not disclosed how it plans to pay back substantial sovereign debt as it comes due in the immediate future, leading to further concern in financial markets (Sharif & Cochrane, 2009).

This example illustrates how high debt levels can quickly lead to liquidity problems which can then threaten the viability of other areas of the firm, and even a country's financial system.

Traditionally, the banking sector is a major source of debt funds, and this is still the case in many parts of the world. The financial crisis of 2008/09 had a major impact on the ability of banks to lend, since they had built up excessive leverage through both on- and off-balance sheet loans. Banks were forced to improve their capital adequacy ratios and had to reduce the level of loans on their books. One consequence of this was a massive contraction of liquidity and credit availability to the real economy. So firms had extreme difficulty in obtaining loans. This problem was exacerbated by the fact that firms could not roll over loans as they became due. As a consequence, rather than banks lending to the non-financial sector, this sector actually paid back loans to the banks. As shown in Figure 4.8, in October 2007 private UK non-financial firms received loans totalling £16.8 billion from UK resident banks and building societies. By July 2009, the flow of cash was the other way, with the non-financial firms paying back a total of £15.4 billion to the banking sector.

This repayment of debt had a significant negative effect on the cash flow of firms. Since firms did not want to default on their loans, which would have resulted in bankruptcy, cash had to be generated by whatever means possible. Some firms attempted to offset this flow to the banks by raising new equity to strengthen balance sheets, and offering bonds directly to investors, bypassing the banking sector. But the funds raised by these means were insufficient to offset the loan repayments to banks. Firms were forced to adopt other draconian means to raise the cash required. These means included reducing the number of employees, cutting back on investment spending, and selling assets where possible, even at very low prices. Consequently, as was noted in Chapter 3, many economies in the world were forced into a recession with negative economic growth (▶Chapter 3).

Chapter 3

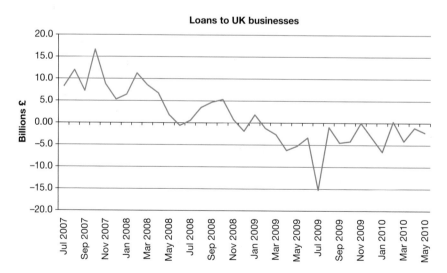

Figure 4.8 Loans to UK private non-financial corporations (Bank of England, 2010)
Reprinted with permission of the Bank of England

Firms have the option of issuing their own debt rather than using banks as an intermediary. These firms have the financial strength to issue high-grade debt without the use of a bank. In fact, some firms have a higher credit rating than banks! These firms often use a bank as an adviser, which has been reflected in the changing mix of business in banks, with fee income replacing interest income. The introduction of the Euro nullified national requirements for pension and insurance assets to be invested in the same currencies as their liabilities. So European stock and bond markets have become larger and more liquid, with debt being easier to raise from numerous providers. Over the longer term these financing options should lower European firms' cost of capital and put competitive pressure on their banks.

There is potential for a conflict of interest between managers and debt holders. Managers may be tempted to undertake risky investments, since if these succeed the managers achieve large gains, as do the equity holders who can get a return many times their investment. But debt holders get a fixed return, independent of the success of the firm. If the investment fails, debt holders may lose their investment. While the same is true for equity holders, the relation is not symmetrical. Equity holders can get huge returns; normally debt holders can never get more than the interest and/or the principal back.

Ratings agencies

Agencies such as Standard & Poors (S&P) and Moody's, which rate the debt of companies and other organizations, play a critical role in debt markets, since their ratings influence the cost of debt.

A credit rating represents the opinion of the agency, S&P or Moody's, on either the general credit-worthiness of a firm, or the credit-worthiness of a specific debt security. We will concentrate on the former. The credit rating for a firm is based on a number of factors such as financial measures of the firm together with a review of the industry, including its growth prospects, threat of technological change and possible government regulatory actions. Such a rating is done independently of the firm, although the firm may be consulted prior to public release of such a rating.

Standard & Poors rates industrial firms on a scale from AAA to D, where AAA is the strongest and D is used where the firm is in default. Ratings from AA to CCC may be modified by the addition of a plus or a minus. Definitions of the S&P ratings, in summary form, are given below (Standard and Poors, 2010):

- **AAA** – capacity to meet its financial commitments is very strong
- **AA** – differs from AA in a small degree, capacity to meet financial commitments is very strong
- **A** – strong capacity to meet financial commitments, but somewhat susceptible to adverse economic conditions and changes in circumstance
- **BBB** – adequate capacity to meet commitments but adverse economic conditions could lead to a weakened capacity to meet financial commitments.

Firms rated as BB or lower are regarded as possessing significant speculative characteristics. Their bonds are referred to as 'junk bonds':

- **BB** – faces major ongoing uncertainty or adverse conditions that could lead to inadequate capacity to meet financial commitments
- **B** – more vulnerable to adverse business or economic conditions but currently has the capacity to meet financial commitments
- **CCC** – currently vulnerable to non-payment and dependent on favourable economic conditions to meet financial commitments.

Junk bond

A bond issued by a firm which has a quality rating by one of the rating agencies of less than investment grade.

So-called **junk bonds** have a quality (rating by an agency) at less than investment grade. This is defined as a Moody's rating at or below BA, or a Standard & Poors rating of BB and below. Such a rating is critical, since the articles of some large institutions prohibit them from holding junk bonds (Grinblatt & Titman, 2002). Nonetheless, there has been a significant expansion in this junk bond market, and S&P is forecasting that 2010 will be a record year for junk bonds in Europe.

Junk bond market *in practice* – Europe

High yield is poised for a record year in Europe, Standard & Poors said in a report in April 2010. The $21.7 billion (€16.2 billion) of high-yield debt issued in Europe is the highest in the last ten years, according to Dealogic data.

The scale of high-yield debt issued in Europe this year has led S&P to predict that it could surpass the record value of bonds issued in 2009. Last year, companies issued €36.7 billion, including European bonds issued in the US, S&P said.

For many years the European lending market has been dominated by loans from banks rather than bonds, and many think this is an opportunity for bonds, which are far more popular in the US, to strengthen their position in Europe.

For example, two of the largest buyouts sealed in Europe, EMI Group and Alliance Boots, were structured using loans. Some transactions such as the buyout of Dutch semiconductor company NXP have involved bonds rather than loans, but for buyouts these are the exception rather than the rule.

(Lewis, 2010)

While firms do pay attention to their credit rating, and react negatively if the firm is downgraded, it is unclear just how important this is. In October 2009, Pfizer had its credit rating reduced by S&P following a long-term debt increase from $7.1 billion to $31.8 billion to finance its takeover of Wyeth (Steverman, 2009). This increased Pfizer's debt/equity ratio to 34 per cent, which is considered high for an AAA rating. This downgrading left just four US firms with an AAA rating: Exxon Mobil, Johnson and Johnson, Automatic Data Processing

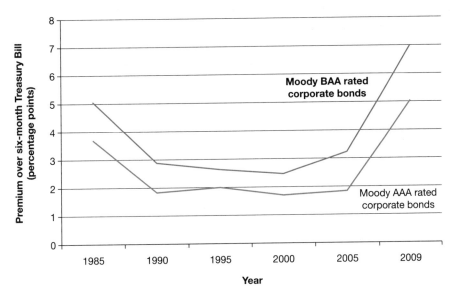

Figure 4.9 Interest rates for treasury and corporate bonds

Federal Reserve Board, 2010

and Microsoft. By contrast, in 1979 there were 58 US firms with an AAA rating (Wiggins, 2002). In the US it appears that firms have increased debt levels to improve ROE, leading to concern at the state of financial health. In recent times US firms have been forced to strengthen their balance sheets by repaying debt. This reduces free cash flow and will ultimately result in lower growth and innovation.

The financial strength of a firm can be a significant competitive advantage: a credit-worthy firm is able to raise debt more cheaply than less credit-worthy firms, as is evident from Figure 4.9 which shows the premium for different Moody bond ratings.

Over the 24-year time period, AAA bonds have averaged 2.7 per cent (or 270 basis points) above treasury bonds while BAA bonds have averaged 3.8 per cent above. Credit-worthy firms have been able to raise debt considerably more cheaply, saving an average of 90 basis points, which represents a considerable competitive advantage.

Rating agencies can put pressure on firms through their ability to downgrade their debt. Such a downgrade sends a negative signal to the market that the firm is now more of a credit risk with a resultant rise in the cost of debt.

Islamic banking

What we have described above is the situation in a typical Western banking system. However, we need to be aware that there are other banking systems, the main one being the Islamic banking system – in wide use throughout the Middle East as well as in countries such as Pakistan and Indonesia (Qorchi, 2005).

Impact of a debt downgrade *in practice* – Drax

Drax is the owner of Europe's largest coal-fired power station in the UK. In 2009 the company suffered a severe downturn in demand and a consequent fall of 77 per cent in pre-tax profits for the six months to June 2009. In May 2009 their debt rating was downgraded by S&P to BBB minus, a rating just above junk status. This negative outlook reflected concern over the firm's future prospects and the strength of its balance sheet. It was important for Drax to retain the investment grade debt rating, since such a rating underpinned their trading contract arrangements. Retaining an investment grade rating meant that their customers would be unable to force Drax to post collateral to cover potential losses.

To strengthen its balance sheet, Drax undertook two actions. First, it undertook a share placement in June 2009 which raised £107 million, issuing 25.5 million new shares at a price of 425p per share. These shares were offered at a substantial discount, since the share price was 480p on 4 June 2009. Funds raised from this issue were used to pay down debt. Second, the firm reached agreement to refinance its debt. Debt which had been due in December 2010 was extended until December 2012. These new facilities were charged at 350 basis points above the LIBOR, a significant premium. The firm believes that its capital structure is now secure (Crooks, 2009).

The basic principle underlying Islamic banking is that interest is considered to be usury and is prohibited on religious grounds. Instead, under this system the investor or lender takes a share of any profits of the venture for which the money has been lent. Banks thus attempt to convert an interest payment to a capital gain. This generally involves some form of pre-determination of profit and what percentage of this will be returned to the investor.

Challenge of strategic management

In their pursuit of creating value, firms are encouraged by financial analysts to operate an 'efficient' balance sheet, reducing to a minimum any cash holdings which could be earning just the government bond rate. In their view, strategic management involves taking decisions which involve risk, with the firm earning a premium above the cost of capital for taking this risk. At the same time, turbulent environments often raise the prospect of a tightening of liquidity with firms facing difficulty in raising funds externally, and even possibly having to pay back lenders. This means that the firm needs an adequate cash balance to enable it to survive any downturn and to be able to innovate and take advantage of opportunities.

■ If you were the CEO of a global firm, how would you resolve this dilemma?

In addition, some Islamic investors are precluded from investing in some 'undesirable' sectors such as alcohol and gaming (Edwardes, 2000).

4.6 COST OF CAPITAL AND FIRM VALUATION

LEARNING OBJECTIVE 5

Develop a strategy for the firm which gives consideration to the requirements of financial markets.

The firm exists to create value, which it does when the revenues it generates are greater than all of its costs, including the cost of capital. To determine whether or not value is created we must understand how to calculate the firm's cost of capital. Indeed, comprehending how value is created and measured is critical to understanding the task facing strategic managers.

Cost of capital reflects the firm's capital structure, captured by the extent to which its operations are financed by debt and equity. These two sources of funds have different costs to the firm, reflecting their different risk levels. The firm's cost of capital is the weighted average cost of these two sources:

So if we let

D = level of debt of the firm

and

E = equity financing of the firm,

then the total capital of the firm is

D + E

and the weighted average cost of capital (WACC) is:

$$\text{WACC} = (E/(D+E)) * \text{cost of equity} + (D/(D+E)) * \text{cost of debt} * (1.0 - \text{tax rate})$$

This weighted average cost of capital is the value used to calculate economic profit and to discount future cash flows of the firm.

Firm valuation

Investment analysts and shareholders use a number of measures to assess the value of the firm. These measures are not only critical for senior management in understanding the value of their own firm, but they also play a major role in corporate strategy when the firm is manipulating its portfolio of businesses through M&A or restructuring activities of various kinds. We now discuss valuation models.

Market capitalization

Market capitalization is the value of the firm as measured by the share market and is calculated as the number of shares outstanding multiplied by the share price. Share prices are composed of two components: value from current operations (including incremental improvements) and value from expectations of future growth through innovation. Investors

Market capitalization
A measure of the value of the firm, calculated as the number of shares outstanding multiplied by the current share price.

and analysts make explicit and/or implicit forecasts of the short- and long-term performance of the firm and its industry, and the expectations based on these forecasts are reflected in the share price. Share prices can thus be considered to represent the stock market's assessment of the net present value of all the firm's present and future strategies and capital investments at a given time.

Volatility data indicate that share prices, and thus the market capitalization of firms, is influenced by a number of transitory events outside of management control, such as government policy on interest rates, the performance of the economy and the likely future performance of the sector in which the firm competes. At the time of writing, the Euro zone crisis is raising investor concerns about the recovery of European economies from the global crisis and consequent recession. Should the recession be a protracted double dip, the future profit prospects of many firms will be affected, yet the factors responsible are not subject to management control. Thus, many variables influence expectations about a firm's future performance and the level of risk involved. Further, stock markets often seem to display a 'herd' mentality, chasing stock as prices are rising and selling stock as prices are falling.

Share prices are also influenced in the short term by the difference between actual performance and the expectations of investors and investment analysts. If these expectations are high, and the company performs well, but below these expectations, share prices will decline. Consequently, some firms seem to be on an expectations treadmill – the better they do, the better the stock markets expects them to do (Dobbs & Koller, 1998). It is also not uncommon for a major shift in share price to occur with the departure of a current CEO or the announcement of a new CEO, suggesting that new expectations have been developed. Senior managers in global firms take an active interest in 'managing' shareholder expectations through such actions as briefings to brokers and fund managers, ensuring that financial markets are aware of the strategy which the firm is pursuing.

Although it is difficult to use the share price as a basis for managerial decisions, senior managers favour high share prices for several reasons. First, share appreciation is often an important component in shareholder returns. Managers holding shares or options also benefit from such appreciation. In addition, high share prices discourage takeover attempts and put the firm in a strong position to take over other firms, particularly when shares are used to finance the takeover. Use of the company's shares was very important in the early growth of Autogrill, although later it was able to use cash to support its growth (see below).

Market value added

Market value added

A measure of the value of the firm, calculated as the current market capitalization of the firm minus the book value of capital employed by the firm.

Market value added (MVA), developed by Stern Stewart, is the difference between the market capitalization of a firm and the accountants' measure of all capital in the firm, both debt and equity (Stern *et al.*, 2001).

It is expressed in monetary units and is a measure of how well the firm has created value over what has been invested in it.

From the balance sheet, capital employed is calculated as:

$$\text{Capital employed} = \text{Total assets} - \text{current liabilities}$$
$$= \text{Fixed assets} + \text{working capital}$$

Leverage *in practice* – Autogrill

In 1995 Autogrill was an Italian food and beverage company that operated a number of motorway sites, with sales of approximately €800 million. Since then the firm has undertaken a number of acquisitions, expanding its business and geographic scope. In 2009, the firm operated in 42 countries with revenue of €5.7 billion. Autogrill provides food and beverage and retail services for travellers, operating at airports, motorways and other venues.

In 2007 it acquired Carastel, a Belgium airport firm, allowing Autogrill entry into several European airports, including Brussels and Hamburg. It also acquired the Alpha Group, which ran airport shops and provided in-flight meals in the UK, and was Autogrill's initial entry into this market (Hawkes, 2007). In 2008 it acquired World Duty Free from BAA, the UK airport operator, in a cash deal worth £545 million (Jameson, 2008). This deal resulted in Autogrill becoming the world's largest food and drink provider at service stations, airports and rail stations. Ferrovial, BAA's owner, was keen to sell to enable it to reduce its debt. Autogrill also acquired an additional 49.95 per cent of Aldeasa in Spain from Imperial Tobacco for €275 million, bringing its ownership to 99.9 per cent.

Since 2005, Autogrill has raised some €2.2 billion in debt to finance these acquisitions. Over the period 2007 to 2009 its debt/equity ratio increased from 1.38 to 2.38 while its share price dropped from €11.65 at the end of 2007 to €5.41 at the end of 2008, increasing to €8.8 at the end of 2009 (Autogrill, 2009).

which is equivalent to:

Capital employed = long-term debt + equity.

Market value added is then calculated by:

Market value added = market capitalization – capital employed.

MVA relates the current market derived value of the firm to the amount of capital invested over the life of the firm.

Market-to-book ratio (M/B)

Since MVA is in monetary terms, it is sensitive to firm size, complicating inter-firm comparisons. This is overcome by using the dimensionless ratio called the **market-to-book** ratio:

M/B = market capitalization/book value of capital employed.

Market capitalization is the share market's view of the total value of the future strategies of the firm. This can be expressed as the value which can be generated from the total asset base of the firm. As we will discuss in more detail in Chapter 5 (▶Chapter 5), the total assets of **Chapter 5**

the firm can be categorized into two groups: tangible and intangible assets. Thus the market capitalization of the firm can be interpreted as the current value of both intangible and tangible assets, whereas book value of capital employed is the value of all tangible assets on the balance sheet. Consequently the M/B ratio can be seen as a measure of the relative importance of intangible and tangible assets in the value of the firm. M/B ratios are high for firms whose capital is primarily intangible, representing the skills of staff, brand names, patents and so on.

Across all firms in the Fortune 500, the average M/B was about 3.5 in 1998, suggesting that accounting systems drastically undervalue the firm's assets when these are primarily intangible (Srivastava *et al.*, 1998). Such undervaluation could lead senior managers spending too little time managing the intangible assets and too much time managing the tangible assets, a topic to which we return in Chapter 5 (➤Chapter 5).

Chapter 5

Total return to shareholders

Total return to shareholders (TRS) is the total return to shareholders from maintaining their investment in a stock over a period. It is the sum of dividends and price appreciation of the shares of the company over the time period expressed as a percentage of the initial value. Total return to shareholders is by its nature a corporate, not a business unit measure, and cannot be calculated for private companies. It can, however, be used to compare the performance of different companies since it is not affected by the size of the company.

As is apparent from Table 4.1, Apple has been an outstandingly successful company, due to its innovations with the iPhone and the iPad. But firms can generate superior returns to shareholders even when they operate in several mature markets, as seen by the success of Monsanto. The lack of success of *The New York Times* reflects the increasing substitution of print media by electronic media.

Like market capitalization and MVA, managers may find it difficult to use TRS as their main decision-making tool. TRS focuses solely on the market value of a firm and its dividend

Table 4.1 Total return to shareholders for selected US firms, 2008
(*Wall Street Journal*, 2008)

Company	Industry	Shareholder returns over five years
Apple	Computers/telecommunications	94%
BE Aerospace	Aircraft components	71
Monsanto	Agriculture	66
Cummins Inc	Engines	58
New York Times	Newspapers	−16%
Eastman Kodak	Imaging	−7
Pfizer	Pharmaceuticals	−3

stream. If the market is an efficient judge of business, then TRS will demonstrate the value added by management, although the impact of other factors on share prices must be recognized. Nonetheless, TRS overcomes difficulties that occur with accounting measures, such as book values bearing little relationship to current values or a high ratio of intangible to tangible assets.

Challenge of strategic management

We have discussed several methods of valuing a business enterprise. As a CEO, would you adopt any of these as a single measure of value? Does this value measure provide you with insights on how to improve the performance of the firm? If you were to adopt more than one measure of value, are the different measures consistent with each other or do they each provide different insights?

Accounting measures of profitability

The firm's accounting system is the primary source of information for assessing a firm's financial performance. Accounting standards have been developed in the US by the Financial Accounting Standards Board (the Generally Accepted Accounting Principles or GAAP) and the International Accounting Standards Board in London (the International Financial Reporting Standards or IFRS). While there are some minor differences between the two systems, most global firms report under the IFRS basis. The financial reporting systems have been developed to indicate the state of the business as a going concern, and are used by financial markets in valuation. Several of these measures are discussed below, although, as we will see, they are not always the most appropriate measures for assessing performance.

The measure most closely followed by analysts, stockbrokers and investors is **net income** or earnings, both current and projected. This value is reported in the income statement and is broadly measured as revenue minus certain expenses.

Both are reported on an accrual basis, meaning that net income is not a measure of cash flow. Net income is calculated after a combination of cash and non-cash expenses, the most important non-cash expense being depreciation. This presents some difficulties, since depreciation is a partly subjective number, based as it is on historic costs, and assumptions about the economic life of an asset. Net income may also be reported as pre- or post-tax, and before or after interest expenses. Given this lack of uniformity, other common measures are earnings before interest and tax (EBIT), and **earnings before interest, tax, depreciation and amortization (EBITDA).**

While the latter is more closely related to cash flow, it is not a true measure, since changes in fixed and working capital are excluded. Such a measure favours firms with high capital expenditures, since these do not appear on the income statement.

Although net income measures the firm's earnings, it does not include the capital necessary to generate that income. Consequently, there is a need for measures which explicitly consider the level of capital used to generate net income. In the ratios below we use net

Net income
A performance measure of the firm which is generally reported on the statement of profit and loss and measures revenue less certain expenses.

Earnings before interest, tax, depreciation and amortization (EBITDA)
Revenue less operating costs.

income as the numerator but it is also common to use EBIT, particularly at the SBU level. Efficiency measures include:

- Return on equity (ROE): net income/shareholders' equity
- Return on assets (ROA): net income/total assets
- Return on capital employed (ROCE): net income/capital employed
- Return on sales (ROS): net income/total operating revenue

Values for shareholders' equity, total assets and capital employed are obtained from the balance sheet.

LEARNING OBJECTIVE 6

Employ derivatives as a means of controlling risk.

4.7 RISK MANAGEMENT AND DERIVATIVES

Strategic management involves making decisions now, knowing the consequences will occur in the future. How the world develops during this time is uncertain, hence uncertainty and risk are central themes of strategic management. As discussed earlier in the chapter, a firm faces risks from two primary sources. Business risk is related to the underlying nature of the business and industry in which it competes. Financial risk is related to interest rates, exchange rates, changes in equity markets and commodity prices. For example, many firms have cash streams from different countries and currencies which expose the firm to exchange rate risk. Alternatively, the firm may be considering raising additional debt in the future, and so it may face an interest rate risk – the risk of a rise in interest rates. Should the firm need to raise additional equity in the future, changes in the levels of equity markets may present it with an equity market risk. Finally, some firms operate in commodity markets, purchasing or selling a commodity such as iron ore or oil, and these commodity markets are characterized by major price fluctuations, exposing firms to price risk.

Managers of non-financial firms generally accept and are responsible for the business risk of the firm. The question we pose here is: should managers accept the financial risk inherent in the firm? For example, if the firm is an exporter, does it bundle in an exchange rate risk with the business risk of the firm? We believe the firm should quantify its risk exposures and select appropriate instruments to offset the risk. One important class of instruments is derivatives – a range of financial instruments whose value depends on the value of an underlying asset or index (Chance, 2001).

Derivatives

A broad range of financial instruments whose returns are derived from the returns of other financial instruments.

Chapter 8

Although these instruments carry risk themselves, they may also be used to limit risk for a firm, or allow it to seek higher profits at higher risk, and form a part of the risk management operations of the firm. When such instruments are used, risk is transferred, at a price, to another party prepared to assume it. While risk management operations are the responsibility of specialist staff, it is important for the CEO to understand the role, uses, limitations and the possible implications of risk management techniques (►Chapter 8). Such firms as Barings, P&G, Sumitomo, Allied Irish Bank, Northern Rock, Lehman Bros and many others have all got into difficulties due to poor risk management.

Risk management *in practice* – Computer Components

With increasing globalization and turbulence in financial markets, firms are exposed to much more risk, and need to take action to limit their exposure. As an example, suppose that Alcatel, the French telecommunications firm, sells a component to Compal, the Taiwanese laptop computer manufacturer. Assume this contract calls for the supply of the component from Alcatel over some time period at a fixed price. Since the component is globally traded it is priced in $US.

Alcatel faces a business risk with this component, which it is likely to sell to other manufacturers. What is the demand for the component? What are competitors doing? What is the likely future behaviour of prices and margins? What substitutes exist? And so on. At the same time, its contract with Compal creates exchange rate risk – it sells in $US yet most of its costs are in €. Should Alcatel decide to accept the risk of changes in the €/$ exchange rate, engaging in currency speculation? If it does, it is bundling foreign exchange rate risk with the product it is selling. Alternatively, should Alcatel hedge to reduce or eliminate exchange rate risk arising from this contract?

Compal has even more difficult choices. Its value chain comprises a set of costs, some of which are in $US (purchases), some in Taiwanese $ (its R&D and possibly marketing expenses) and some costs in Chinese Renminbi, since the computer is made in its Chinese plant and sold to Compaq in $US. Compal is exposed to three currencies and their exchange rates.

This simple example illustrates one impact of globalization: firms have the potential to be exposed to a high degree of currency risk, with a major potential impact on profitability. Responsible strategic managers will attempt to limit the exposure of the firm to such sources of risk by establishing a risk management programme. The CEO does not manage all the details, but should ensure that processes designed to adjust risk exposure are in place and that the appropriate risk management instruments are selected. Much of this activity involves the use of derivatives and so managers need some understanding of their features and use. Yet, since hedging has a cost, a firm cannot hedge all risks: managers have to decide which risks to hedge against. Given the devastating impact that poor decisions can have, many firms avoid leveraging positions which magnify risk and could be interpreted as speculation. Risk management processes will be discussed in more detail in Chapter 8 (►Chapter 8).

Chapter 8

The use of derivatives has increased so much that they are now the dominant activity in the world's financial system. This is a huge market. Turnover in the last three months of 2009 was reported as $US 444 trillion, although this was well below the peak of $690 trillion reported in early 2008 (Avdjiev *et al.*, 2010). We briefly discuss two types of derivatives below.

Options

Option

A contract in which the writer of the option grants the buyer of the option the right, but not the obligation, to purchase from or sell to the writer something at a specified price within a specified time.

An **option** is a contract in which the writer of the contract grants the buyer of the contract the right, but not the obligation, to purchase from or sell to the writer something at a specified price within a specified time (Crawford & Sen, 1996). For this right the option writer charges the buyer a price called the option price. An option to sell is referred to as a put option, while the option to buy is referred to as a call option.

Unlike futures, the option contract involves a choice for the purchaser. On the date the option expires the purchaser can decide whether or not to exercise the option. If the purchaser decides not to exercise the option, all that is lost is the cost of purchasing the option. Options may be issued over-the-counter or traded on several of the futures exchanges.

With an option, risk is not symmetrical. The option buyer can lose no more than the option price if they decide not to take up the option, while the option writer has substantial risk.

In general, whether such an option is attractive to the buyer will depend on a number of factors including the current price, the exercise price, the time to expire, the volatility in prices of the asset, interest rates and the option price. Detailed formulae on how to value options, based on the models derived by Black and Scholes, is given in many texts on capital markets such as Chance (Chance, 2001).

Swaps

Swap

A contract in which two parties agree to exchange the cash flows from an asset or liability.

A **swap** is a contract in which two parties agree to exchange the cash flows from an asset or liability. The most common form of derivative is an interest rate swap, where one party swaps its liabilities on a fixed interest loan with another firm which has borrowed at a floating interest rate. A simple example of another common swap, a currency swap, follows.

Currency rate swap

Consider an Australian wine and beer firm, called Aussie, which wants to expand its wine processing plant in France. Since the firm is domiciled in Australia, Aussie has good bank contacts in Australia, but none in France. A French bank would view the Australian firm as risky, and Aussie would have to pay a high interest rate for any funds borrowed from a French bank. Suppose at the same time a French hotel chain, Eiffel, is considering building a new hotel in Melbourne. Eiffel faces a similar problem; it has excellent relationships with French banks but not with Australian banks. So the two firms trade.

Situation:

- **Aussie** want to expand wine processing in France.
- **Eiffel** wants to build a new hotel in Melbourne.

Resolution:

- **Aussie** – borrows $A in Australia, gives the funds to Eiffel to build the hotel.
- **Eiffel** – borrows Euros in Europe, gives the funds to Aussie to extend the processing plant.
- **Aussie** – receives Euros from their plant in France, gives these to Eiffel to pay interest on the Euro loan.
- **Eiffel** – receives $A from the new hotel, gives these to Aussie to pay interest on the $A loan.

Note that this arrangement is cheaper for both firms than if each had borrowed in their respective foreign financial market. However, there is now a counter-party risk: either Aussie or Eiffel could default on their respective loans. To overcome this there is generally an intermediary between the two parties, normally a commercial bank, which absorbs some of the risk for a fee. It is not necessary to have counter-parties with equal and opposite needs. A bank may decide to commit to one side of the transaction and then look for parties for the other, perhaps aggregating a number of these.

In summary, derivatives markets provide a firm with opportunities to manage risk. They enable firms who wish to reduce their risk to transfer it to other firms for a fee. They are an element in the overall risk management system of the firm, and are generally utilized as a hedge – an action taken to reduce risk. Managers need to understand how they can be used and recognize that if leverage is involved, small price changes can lead to large profits or losses. Speculation is not one of the tasks of the managers – they should be hedging, not speculating!

 ## 4.8 SUMMARY

This chapter has highlighted the importance of financial markets to strategic management. Financial markets impose their own conditions and performance measures on the firm, and managers must recognize that demands from financial markets can result in significant changes in strategy.

A firm has two primary external sources of funds, debt and equity, and one of the tasks of management is to manage these two sources with due regard for the cost, type and availability of these funds. The cost of debt will be influenced by factors outside the control of the firm, such as general economic conditions and the actions of rating agencies. Equity is not free for the firm but has a cost which will always be above the cost of debt. This cost of equity is largely determined by the level of risk of the firm, and it is typically measured with the capital asset pricing model. The cost of capital for the firm is then simply the weighted average cost of capital, reflecting the firm's financial structure.

Strategic managers need to understand that financial markets have a set of performance measures, which influence their attitude towards the firm. These measures include market capitalization, market value added and the market-to-book ratio. Such measures supplement the traditional managerial measures such as return on equity and return on capital employed. Failure to recognize the importance of these financial market measures may result in the firm experiencing difficulty raising the capital required to support its chosen strategy.

Over the past several decades there had been pressure on companies to have 'efficient' balance sheets, characterized by relatively high leverage and returning cash to shareholders if it is not needed for investment in the business. Companies were discouraged from hoarding cash to cope with downturns – it was assumed that debt would be freely available at a reasonable cost (*The Economist*, 2009). The financial crisis of 2008/09 changed this completely. After September 2008, credit markets dried up almost completely, forcing companies to adopt radical measures to conserve cash. Among the actions taken by companies to free up cash was reduced discretionary spending, reduced investment, reduced dividends and cutting employment (Bryan & Farrell, 2009). Through these means, companies attempted to reduce their dependence on banks for finance. At the same time, companies attempted to raise funds directly, bypassing the banks, through issuing their own bonds and commercial paper.

These developments highlight that developing strategy requires the firm be able to assess and incorporate the demands of financial markets as well as product markets. The firm competes for funds in these increasingly global financial markets, which occasionally demonstrate a high degree of turbulence. Lack of success in obtaining these external funds severely limits the strategic choices open to the firm.

Risk is an essential component in strategic management since the future is uncertain; however, the firm can, to some extent, manage this risk through the use of derivatives. The firm does this by shifting risk, at a cost, from itself to other individuals and organizations that are prepared to accept that risk. This is a complex area of corporate finance, fraught with difficulties, but managers must understand when such instruments are useful, and the consequences of both using and not using these instruments.

The chapter has also highlighted concerns with the accuracy of financial reports prepared by firms. There have been numerous examples of firms reporting financial results that are quite irregular. Since investors rely on these reports and the objectivity of auditors to make investment decisions, such a lack of credibility is likely to lead to major regulatory changes to strengthen the objectivity of financial reports.

VIEW FROM THE TOP

HSBC HOLDINGS PLC

During the crisis of 2008/09, HSBC's performance was excellent, reporting pre-tax profits in 2007, 2008 and 2009. The excerpt below is taken from the Chairman's letter to shareholders in the firm's 2009 annual report (Green, 2009).

Building a sustainable financial system for the future

S. K. Green, Group Chairman, HSBC Holdings plc

As policymakers and industry participants take the necessary steps to improve the way our markets work, there are also some important over-arching challenges which we must address.

It is imperative to strike the right balance between strengthening the financial system and supporting economic growth. 'De-risking' the banking system, if taken too far, will throttle recovery and drive risk into other, unregulated parts of the capital markets. It is in the collective public interest to get this balance right. We must not rush to implement hastily conceived responses and policy must be co-ordinated internationally if we are to manage risk better in a truly global industry.

Policymakers also need to evolve new macroeconomic tools which will assist them to manage the supply of credit, as well as the cost of credit, in the economy. I believe a key element of this involves managing bank capital on a countercyclical basis which strikes the right balance between financial system stability and the prospects for economic growth. We cannot deliver a sustainable financial system without improving the wider framework for macroeconomic management too.

Finally, in the context of a wide-ranging discussion on the appropriate size and shape of banks, we must recognize that corporate structure and liquidity management are at least as important as size per se. This debate has sometimes been given the unhelpful shorthand 'too big to fail', but the reality is more complex than the headlines suggest. We believe that the financial system needs banks which are 'big enough to cope' by having a diversified business portfolio, helping to reduce risk and to generate consistent returns. There has likewise not been enough consideration given to the need for banks to be 'broad enough to serve' those global customers who have increasingly diverse financial needs. In short, it is undesirable and impractical to prescribe some ideal model for a bank. The crisis clearly demonstrated that systemic importance is not a function of size or business focus.

HSBC has always believed in having a transparent structure based on separately capitalized subsidiaries, takes a conservative approach to liquidity management, and has built a business with the scale to provide broad, diversified services to its global customers. While the detail and timing of regulatory change remain uncertain, we are confident that our focus on these fundamental positions us strongly and competitively to respond to the challenges ahead.

QUESTIONS

1 Do you that the banking system should be more tightly regulated?
2 What do you think would be the impact of non-financial firms of any increased regulation?

FOCUS (DIY) LIMITED

Focus (DIY) Limited markets a range of do-it-yourself (DIY) products primarily to individual consumers engaged in light home improvement or gardening projects. The merchandise includes: power tools, appliances, hardware, decking and flooring, contemporary home and patio furniture, garden buildings, and plants and seeds. Focus sells its product through approximately 180 stores in the UK and Ireland, as well as its website. The website offers guides, price list and a calculator for DIY projects.

Focus (DIY) had been founded by Bill Archer and Greg Stanley in 1987. They had substantial experience in the DIY market, having previously built up and sold a small chain of stores called Fads. Archer and Stanley, using their homes as collateral, first acquired a small chain called Choice DIY (Ltd), which had six stores in the Midlands and the north of England. In 1988, with financial backing of £4.5 million from Duke Street Capital, the two founders acquired the Focus chain of DIY stores, consisting of six stores. All stores were then rebranded as Focus (DIY).

From 1988 to 1998 the business grew organically from 12 stores to 72 stores. In 1998 the Focus growth strategy was broadened to include acquisitions, with the purchase of the 'Do It All DIY chain' from Boots in 1998. These stores were then rebranded as 'Focus Do It All'.

In September 2000 the group was successful in acquiring Wickes, a DIY chain focused on building supplies, on their third attempt. In March and May of that year offers of 375p and 430p per share had been rejected by Wickes shareholders. Their final successful offer was for 485p per share, a premium of 19 per cent over the previous day's close. This offer valued Wickes at £289m. The group name was changed to Focus Wickes but the two distinct retail formats and identities were retained. In December 2000, Focus acquired the Great Mills chain from RMC Group in December 2000 for £285m. Most of these stores were rebranded as Focus, and a smaller number as Wickes. By 2002 the Focus Wickes group was the second largest DIY retailer in the UK by turnover and had 430 stores (Focus 291 and Wickes 139).

In 2000, there was also a change in their shareholders. Apex Partners acquired a 28.9 per cent stake from Duke Street Capital, GE Capital, Standard Life and the company Chairman and CEO Bill Archer for £120m in cash. The purchase was part of recapitalization of Focus Wickes. ING Bank, Bank of Scotland and Goldman Sachs provided debt facilities of £180m to the newly incorporated company, where the equity of the target firm was transferred. As a part of the transaction, Focus Wickes repaid its £125m of 11 per cent senior notes due in 2010, together with its £45m 13 per cent redeemable senior notes again due in 2010, via a cash tender offer and solicitation of consent.

In 2005, Focus Wickes divested the Wickes business to Travis Perkins (TPK), builder's merchant, in 2005 for £950m. This acquisition enabled TPK to move into what was seen as the attractive DIY market. Part of TPK's rationale, apart from a move into an adjacent market, was Wickes's customer base. TPK believed that 65 per cent of Wickes customers were tradesmen or serious DIY enthusiasts, the same sorts of people who use TPK for building supplies, permitting a degree of cross-selling by TPK. Focus's rationale for selling Wickes was to create a better focus on its core market, the individual DIY consumer.

In 2009, market estimates put the size of UK's DIY market at £7.5bn. The needs of the market are served by two distinct types of providers: nationwide multiples and the much smaller regional multiples and single retailers. The largest national multiple is B&Q with approximately 15 per cent market share, followed by Homebase with 12.5 per cent market share and Focus (DIY) with 9 per cent market share. Independents have around 50 per cent of the market. For the multiples the value drivers are scale (economies of scale in purchasing), merchandising mix (type of product and range of products) and customer service. Smaller companies compete by catering to contractors, offering speciality products, a high level of service and expert advice, and by serving areas unattractive to national multiples because of limited customer concentration.

DIY demand is driven mainly by residential real estate construction and renovation. The busiest time for DIY stores is the Easter bank holiday and the two public holidays at the beginning and the end of May. The timing of and weather at Easter has a significant influence on multiples sales and profitability. The DIY market experienced good growth over the period 2000–05, stoked by the property market and numerous television programmes extolling the virtues of home renovation. The growth petered out in 2006 not least because of the arrival of tradesmen from Eastern Europe who tended to prefer builders' merchants to retail stores. The demand further declined in 2007 and subsequent years because of the falling housing market, weaker consumer confidence, and wet Easters and summers in 2008 and 2009. The DIY market was showing signs of recovery in 2010.

This decline in demand had an impact on Focus who saw their turnover (excluding Wickes) decline from £522.4m in 2004 to £470.9m in 2005 before increasing marginally to £472.6m in 2006. Over the same period, gross profit fell from £140.9m in 2004 to £119.5m in 2006 and profit before tax declined from £20m in 2004 to a loss of £40m in 2006.

Following the failure of talks between Duke Street Capital and Apex Partners on the future of Focus, the two major shareholders of Focus (DIY) and its bondholders agreed to restructure its £280m (nearly 16 times its operating profit in 2006) of debt. NM Rothschild was called in to conduct a strategic review of the business. Their advice was to sell the business as a going concern. Financial information was sent to potential buyers at the end of February 2007.

Focus (DIY) was sold to the US private equity firm and specialist in distressed debt, Cerberus, in June 2007 for £1. As part of the arrangement, Cerberus agreed to pay off an estimated £225m of debt amassed by Focus (DIY). This was less than the total net debt of the company, which stood at more than £330m. Banks got all their money but holders of bonds with the face value of £100m, including Goldman Sachs, collected 40p in a pound or £40m. Focus (DIY) owners, the founding Chair Bill Archer with 11.5 per cent, Apex with 30 per cent, and Duke Street Capital with 43 per cent collected nothing for their shares. But as analysts noted, Duke Street as well as Apex and Archer had profited from their involvement by taking money out of the business in 2005 in a leveraged recapitalization that added further debt to the company at a time when the DIY sector took a turn for the worse. Focus had become a byword for asset stripping. Peter Taylor, a Duke Street Partner, admitted to the Treasury Select Committee that with hindsight Focus may have been carrying too much debt. Another analyst noted that Focus had traded well in a difficult market but it needed more working capital and trading capital to flourish. These were denied to Focus because of its weak balance sheet.

Cerberus appointed Bill Grimsey as CEO and Bill Hoskins as finance director. The two executives had substantial experience in the overall DIY industry. They had both joined Wickes in 1996 after a financial scandal took the company to the verge of bankruptcy, where they executed a major turnaround, aimed at meeting the needs of small builders and serious DIY enthusiasts. As mentioned, they sold the company to Focus (DIY) in 2000 for 495p per share. The two are also credited with turning around another ailing retailer, Iceland, after leaving Wickes.

In June 2007, while the deal with Cerberus was being finalized, Bill Grimsey visited many Focus (DIY) stores incognito. He concluded that the group was operationally in a shambles, staff morale was at an extremely low ebb, and suppliers had not been delivering for months because of lack of credit insurance cover for deliveries to Focus and consequent concern with the ability of Focus to pay its bills. So their first act was to communicate with staff to assure them that the business was in a turnaround mode, not a crisis, and that it had a future. To address the issue of store performance they brought in Hilco, the retail and restructuring specialist, to indentify the loss-making and poor-performing stores. As a result, Focus hived off 52 stores and placed them in a separate, financially ring-fenced vehicle, co-owned with Hilco. Hilco set about either selling these stores or negotiating its way out of leases with landlords in order to close them down. By the end of 2007 Hilco had sold 41 stores to DIY competitors and supermarkets for £68m. The money was used by Focus (DIY) to pay down its debt mountain. Another 39 stores were earmarked for sales. Another problem was that in many locations store sizes were too large, so they started working with landlords to identify complementary retailers.

The biggest challenge, however, was to find a niche in the market and upgrade Focus's dilapidated stores. To find the right proposition, Grimsey hired Richard Bird, a former Wickes colleague. They piloted different formats and merchandise range and mix in search of a winning mix with the aim of rolling out the most promising. Their experience told them that women had a key role in decisions, particularly when it came to decorating and garden centre products. They also noted that B&Q was not particularly female friendly and Homebase was moving much more towards the home enhancement and soft furnishing end of the market; therefore, they identified 'female friendliness' as an opportunity. As a part of this process, Focus piloted 11 stores with a new format. These stores were refitted with pet supplies, household goods (cleaning materials, etc.), housewares, and additional cut-price items under the revival of the Payless brand. Sales in these stores were promising and ahead of expectation. The upgrading of all stores required significant capital expenditure which was unfeasible to undertake given Focus's balance sheet.

In September 2009, Focus secured the agreement of 93 per cent of its creditors to enter into a corporate voluntary agreement (CVA) on how to deal with the debt which they were unable to pay as it became due. Under the terms of the CVA arrangements Focus was able to save £8.6m annually by cancelling the leases of its 38 closed stores trading mainly under the Payless brand. In return Focus offered these landlords a share of a £3.7m compensation fund. Moreover, they secured the landlords' agreement to pay rent monthly rather than quarterly which assisted their cash flow. The success of the CVA was crucial to Focus's plans for a wider debt restructuring. HBOS and GMAC, Focus's lenders, had agreed that if CVA was approved they would grant the company a two-year extension to its £50m revolving credit facility, which was due to expire at the end of 2009.

Despite these improvements Focus remained under pressure, with high debts and a reduction in credit insurance cover to its suppliers. The accounts of the company (see Appendix) show that Focus made an operating profit of £1.7m in the year to 28 February 2010, a considerable improvement compared to 2009, 2008 and 2007 when it made operating losses of £12.2m, £19.9m and £46.3m.

Focus's loans and overdrafts stood at £382.6m at the end of February 2010, comprising about £38m in bank overdrafts and £344.6m in short-term loans. Some £190 of the total debt is with the parent company Cerberus, with the balance owned to GMCA and Lloyds Banking Group. Due to its weak financial position, this debt was very costly. One finance agreement, relating to a £60m loan, carries an onerous interest rate at 7 per cent over LIBOR – the rate that banks lend to each other. Due to their inability to repay this loan, at the end of January 2010 some £19m interest had accrued on top of the £60m debt. With a second loan of £100m, the interest was postponed until March 2011. The cost of the £50m bank overdraft held by Focus is 4.75 per cent over LIBOR.

Despite substantial improvements in both strategic positioning and operations, Focus is still suffering from a weak balance sheet. You are part of a team of investment bankers called in by Focus's parent company to look for radical ways to revive the fortunes of the heavily indebted business.

■ What actions do you suggest?

Source: Focus (DIY), 2010

Appendix: Focus financial statements

Table 4.2 Profit and loss account

	28/02/2010 12 months	28/02/2009 12 months	29/02/2008 10 months	30/4/2007 6 months
	£, 000	£,000	£,000	£,000
Turnover	365158	371335	374286	237797
Cost of sales	–261468	–270365	–271752	–177418
Gross profit	103690	100970	102534	60379
Administration expenses	–101939	–113241	–122463	–106650
Operating profit	1751	–12271	–19929	–46271
Other income	71	680	247	140
Exceptional Items	–12176			
Profit (loss) before interest	–10354	–11591	–19682	–46131
Interest received				
Net interest	–1352	–2644	–1149	–611
Profit (loss) before tax	–11706	–14235	–20831	–46742
Taxation	31	–29	–69	–58
Profit (loss) after tax	–11675	–14264	–20900	–46800
Number of employees	3250	3463	4983	5091

Table 4.3 Balance sheet

	28/02/2010 12 months	28/02/2009 12 months	29/02/2008 10 months	30/04/2007 6 months
	£,000	£,000	£,000	£,000
Fixed assets				
Tangible assets	38537	41377	43704	46355
Intangible assets	47359	59535	71710	81857
Investments	320	320	320	320
Fixed assets	86216	101232	115734	128532
Current assets				
Stock & W.I.P.	59880	68599	84335	97108
Trade debtors	2313	2272	1670	1517
Bank & deposits	970	873	13082	1598
Group loans (asset)	427481	425627	419353	411945
Other assets	5976	7099	7407	7185
Current assets	496620	504470	525847	519353
Current liabilities				
Trade creditors	–37587	–43577	–58755	–71259
Bank overdrafts	–37935	–33648	0	–15687
Group loans (short term)	–344684	–345894	–361888	–342985
Total other current liabilities	–24815	–28023	–44188	–34400
Current liabilities	–445021	–451142	–464831	–464331
Long-term liabilities				
Hire purchase leases		–32	–448	–907
Provisions for other liabilities	–10899	–14581	–22121	–8236
Long-term liabilities	–10899	–14613	–22569	–9143
Shareholders' funds				
Issued capital	287425	287425	287425	287425
Total reserves	–160509	–147478	–133244	–113014
Shareholders' funds	126916	139947	154181	174411

REVIEW QUESTIONS

1 Explain the linkages between competition in product markets and competition in financial markets.

2 For a firm of your choice, analyse how the firm has used external funds to support its strategy.

3 How do leverage (gearing) and the contextual environment interact to affect prospects for bankruptcy?

4 The return on government securities is generally assumed to be risk free. Do you agree with this assumption? What evidence can you present to support your point of view?

5 What are the limitations of the capital asset pricing model for developing the cost of equity of a firm?

6 Identify a firm which has had to dramatically modify its strategy due to pressure from financial markets and explain how they handled the situation.

7 Explain the value of derivatives in risk management.

REFERENCES

Aghion, P., van Reenen, J. & Zingales, L. (2009) *Discussion Paper 911: Innovation and institutional ownership*. Centre for Economic Performance.

Air Transport World (2010) JAL's creditors not satisfied with bankrupt carrier's cost-cutting, 5 April. http://atwonline.com/airline-finance-data/news/report-jals-creditors-not-satisfied-bankrupt-carriers-cost-cutting-0427.

AstraZeneca (2010) Second quarter and half year results, 29 July 2010. www.astrazeneca.com/mshost 3690701/content/resources/media/investors/10809118/AZN-Q2–2010-Narrative.pdf.

Autogrill (2009) Annual Report, 30 July. www.autogrill.com/investor-relations/bilancirelazioni/bilanci annuali.aspx?iis=1.

Avdjiev, S., Upper, C. & von Kleist, K. (2010) *Highlights of International Banking and Financial Market Activity*. Basle: Bank for International Settlements Quarterly Review June 2010, 15–28.

Balachandran, S. V. (2009a) Satyam failure hurts all investors, 8 January. www4.gsb.columbia.edu/ publicoffering/post/53556/Satyam+Failure+Hurts+All+Investors.

Balachandran, S. V. (2009b) The Satyam scandal, 1 July. www.forbes.com/2009/01/07/satyam-raju-governance-oped-cx sb 0107balachandran.html.

Bank of England (2010) *Trends in Lending: July, Series LPMB93K*. www.bankofengland.co.uk/ publications/other/monetary/TrendsJuly10.pdf.

BBC News (2010) Euro bonds come under new attack. *Business*, 30 November. Retrieved 2 December 2010, www.bbc.co.uk/news/business-11877552.

Bollen, J. (2008) UK pension fund returns at a five-year low. *ifa online*, 28 January. www.ifaonline. co.uk/ifaonline/news/1344201/uk-pension-fund-returns-low.

Boston, W. (2006) Hostile takeovers, Euro-style. *Business Week*, 21 April.

Brealey, R. A. & Myers, S. C. (2000) *Principles of Corporate Finance*, 6th edn. Boston, MA: Irwin/ McGraw-Hill.

Brigham, E. F. & Houston, J. F. (2001) *Fundamentals of Financial Management*, 9th edn. Orlando, FL: Harcourt Brace.

Bruckner, K., Leithner, S., McLean, R., Taylor, C. & Welch, J. (2000) What is the market telling you about your strategy? *McKinsey Quarterly*, (3).

Bryan, L. L. & Farrell, D. (2009) Leading through uncertainty. *McKinsey Quarterly*, (1), 24–42.

Burberry (2010) ADR. *Shareholder Information*. www.burberryplc.com/bbry/shareinfo/adr/.

Chance, D. M. (2001) *An Introduction to Derivatives and Risk Management*, 5th edn. Fort Worth, TX: Dryden.

China View (2010) Japanese gov't seeks bank approval for JAL bankruptcy China View, 12 January. http://news.xinhuanet.com/english/2010–01/12/content 12796110.htm.

Coughtrie, D., Morley, J. & Ward, T. (2009) Restructuring in bankruptcy: Recent national case studies, 12 December. www.eurofound.europa.eu/emcc/erm/studies/tn0908026s/tn0908026s 3.htm

Crawford, G. & Sen, B. (1996) *Derivatives for Decision Makers*. New York: Wiley.

Crooks, E. (2009) Drax suffers plunge in demand. *Financial Times*, 5 August, p. 14.

Daneshkhu, S. (2009) Lafarge and Saint Gobain both seek cash through rights issue. *Financial Times*, 21 February, p. 17.

Dobbs, R. F. C. & Koller, T. M. (1998) The expectations treadmill. *McKinsey Quarterly*, (3), 33–43.

Edwardes, W. (2000) *Key Financial Instruments*. London: Pearson.

Euro Intelligence (2010) Spain's non-performing loans, 21 April. www.eurointelligence.com/article. 581+M534796784e7.0.html.

Federal Reserve Board (2010) Selected interest rates: Table H15, 26 July. www.federalreserve.gov/releases/h15/.

Focus(DIY) (2010) History. www.focusdiy.co.uk/history.

Glater, J. D. (2002) Ernst & Young latest auditor moving to alter some practices. *New York Times*, 5 February, C1.

Goedhart, M., Raj, R. & Saxana, A. (2010) Equity analysts still too bullish. *McKinsey Quarterly*, (April).

Grant, J. & Kirchmaier, T. (2004) *Corporate Ownership Structure and Performance in Europe*. Centre for Economic Performance Discussion Paper 631.

Green, S. K. (2009) Group Chairman's Statement. *Annual Report*, 1 March. www.hsbc.com/1/content/assets/investor relations/hsbc2009ara0.pdf.

Grinblatt, M. & Titman, S. (2002) *Financial Markets and Corporate Strategy*, 2nd edn. Boston, MA: Irwin/McGraw-Hill.

Gyntelberg, J., Hördahl, P. & King, M. R. (2010) Overview: Fiscal concerns shatter confidence. *BIS Quarterly Review*, (June), 1–14.

Hawkes, S. (2007) Autogrill Alpha bid. *The Times*, 5 June, p. 51.

Investment Management Association (2009) A guide to ethical investing, 23 October. www.investmentuk.org/factsheets/ei/performance.asp.

Jameson, A. (2008) BAA raises GBP545 as duty-free chain is sold to Autogrill. *The Times*, 10 March, p. 42.

Jensen, M. (1990) The market for corporate control. In C. W. Smith (ed.), *The Modern Theory of Corporate Finance*. New York: McGraw-Hill.

Judge, E. (2009) PwC India audit head resigns amid Satyam scandal. *The Sunday Times*, 27 January. http://business.timesonline.co.uk/tol/business/industry sectors/technology/article5599165.ece.

King, I. (2010) AstraZeneca shares receive a booster as profits leap. *The Times*, 30 July, p. 41.

Lafarge (2009) Annual Report. www.lafarge.com/06112009-press publication-2009 annual report-uk.pdf.

Lafarge to sell shares, assets to reduce debt (2009) *The Boston Globe*, 20 February. www.boston.com/news/world/europe/articles/2009/02/20/lafarge to sell shares assets to reduce debt/.

Lewis, T. (2010) S&P says European junk bonds set for record year. *Dow-Jones, Financial News*, 21 April. www.efinancialnews.com/story/2010–04–21/junk-bonds-europe.

Luu, P. (2010) Brand profile: Street-wear label Superdry. *Daily Telegraph*, 10 February. www.telegraph. co.uk/fashion/7199150/Brand-profile-street-wear-label-Superdry.html.

Morris, T. (2010) Business cartoons. *Business Cartoons*. www.businesscartoons.co.uk/shop/index. php?act=viewProd&productId=816.

Office for National Statistics (2010) Share ownership survey 2008. *Statistical Bulletin*, 27 January. www.statistics.gov.uk/pdfdir/share0110.pdf.

Pike, R. & Neale, B. (1996) *Corporate Finance and Investment*, 2nd edn. Hemel Hempstead: Prentice Hall.

Pratt, S. P. & Grabowski, R. J. (2008) *Cost of Capital*, 3rd edn. Hoboken: Wiley.

PricewaterhouseCoopers (2010) NPL Europe, Issue 2, June. www.scribd.com/doc/33695195/Non-Performing-Loans-Europe-June-2010-PricewaterhouseCoopers.

Qorchi, M. E. (2005) Islamic finance gears up. *Finance and Development, 42*(4).

Rubach, M. J. & Sebora, T. C. (2009) Determinants of institutional investor activism: A test of the Ryan-Schneider Model. *Journal of Managerial Issues, 21*(2), 245–264.

Samuels, J. M., Wilkes, F. M. & Brayshaw, R. E. (1999) *Financial Management and Decision Making*. London: International Thomson Business Press.

Sharif, A. & Cochrane, L. (2009) Dubai World seeks to delay debt payments as default risk soars. *Bloomberg*, 25 November. www.bloomberg.com/apps/news?pid=newsarchive&sid=a.LazCgxcywM.

Srivastava, R. K., Shervani, T. A. & Fahey, L. (1998) Market-based assets and shareholder value: A framework for analysis. *Journal of Marketing, 62*(1), 2–28.

Standard & Poors (2010) Credit rating definitions. www.standardandpoors.com/ratings/definitions-and-faqs/en/us#def 1.

Stern, J. M., Shiely, J. S. & Ross, I. (2001) *The EVA Challenge*. New York: John Wiley & Sons.

Steverman, B. (2009) Pfizer loses its triple-A credit rating. *Bloomberg Business Week*, 16 October. www.businessweek.com/investing/insights/blog/archives/2009/10/pfizerlosesitstriple-acredit rating.html.

Taylor, P. (2002) Bullish analysts more likely to be promoted. *Financial Times*, 1 February, p. 27.

Tett, G. (2010) Grey areas in Chinese loans give pause for thought. *Financial Times*, 21 May, p. 30.

The Economist (2009) Debtor's prison. *The Economist*, 19 February.

Thomas, G. (2010) JAL to slash more than 19,000 jobs by March 2015. http://atwonline.com/atw-china/news/report-jal-slash-more-19000-jobs-march-2015–0809.

Trading and Capital-Markets Activities Manual (2001) Washington DC: Federal Reserve Board.

Tyldesley, H. (2010) Investors snap up Superdry owner's shares. *SkyNews*, 23 March. http://news.sky. com/skynews/Home/Business/Supergroup-IPO-Complete-Superdry-Cult-SurfCo-California-Owner-Prepares-To-Trade-On-Stock-Market/Article/201003415580126?f=rss.

UBS (2010) Share Price. www.ubs.com/1/e/investors/share information/charts.html.

Unilever says it will keep its dual structure intact (2005) *The New York Times*, 19 December. www.nytimes.com/2005/12/19/business/worldbusiness/19iht-hot.html.

Useem, M. (1998) Corporate leadership in a globalizing equity market. *Academy of Management Executive, 12*(4), 43–59.

Wall Street Journal (2008) Yearly Scorecard. *Wall Street Journal*, 24 February. http://online.wsj.com/ mdc/public/page/2 3025-scoreboard2008 bestperformers.html#5year.

Wall Street Pit (2010) China's non-performing loans down in 2009. Wall Street Pit, 15 January. http://wallstreetpit.com/14073-chinas-non-performing-loans-down-in-2009.

Wang, T. (2009) Worries rise over Japanese banks, 10 April. www.forbes.com/2009/04/10/sumitomo-mitsui-loss-markets-equity-megabank.html.

Wiggins, J. (2002) AAA-rated club loses yet another member. *Financial Times*, 24 April, p. 20.

For a range of further resources supporting this chapter, please visit the companion website for *Strategic Management* at www.routledge.com/cw/fitzroy.

CHAPTER 5

INTERNAL ANALYSIS

Managing capabilities, costs and knowledge

LEARNING OBJECTIVES

Upon completing this chapter you should be able to:

1 Explain the nature of resources and capabilities and their importance in strategic management.

2 Be able to identify and appraise the resources of the firm.

3 Demonstrate how capabilities are linked to competitive advantage.

4 Argue that in a turbulent world an integral role for strategic management is building new capabilities.

5 Analyse the major cost drivers of a business and its likely future costs.

6 Summarize why strategic management will include an understanding of knowledge-based competition.

ARM HOLDINGS

ARM Holdings was founded in 1990 as a joint venture between Acorn Computers, Apple Computer and VLSI Technology. It was then called Advanced RISC Machines, and its purpose was to further develop the RISC chip, originally used in the Acorn Archimedes. The name was changed to ARM Holdings in 1998, when its shares were listed on the LSE and NASDAQ. By 2008, ARM had revenues of £280 million. ARM develops microprocessor designs which are used in a number of electronic devices, including mobile phones. Their design is used in more than 95 per cent of the world's mobile phones, including the Apple iPhone, despite competition from Intel with their recently launched 'Atom' microprocessor. The company has no manufacturing. Instead its business model is one where partner companies pay an up-front licensing fee to gain access to a design, and a royalty for every chip that uses the licensed design. An essential component in their strategic management model has been the development of new capabilities. As a design company, R&D is essential, and here they have developed capabilities in the design of new processors for applications beyond mobile phones. These new applications areas include digital TV, hard disk drives and washing machines. In 2008, R&D expenses were £84 million, representing 32 per cent of revenue. To leverage this expenditure, ARM has also developed capabilities in developing and managing collaborative research with several universities. Supporting this has been the development of detailed customer knowledge as they expand into new application areas. Third, they have developed capabilities in managing a global business – they have operations in Europe, Asia, India and the US. Another significant capability is their ability to engage in joint development with a wide range of leading semiconductor and OEM manufacturers. At the end of 2008, more than 200 leading companies had licensed more than 580 of their designs. Given the technical sophistication of their designs, ARM offer training for customers in software and hardware. To support this initiative, they have developed a global network of 14 training centres with other providers, located in Europe, the US and Asia. Recently, ARM announced that they were moving into processor design for low-end laptop computers, facilitating a move into tablet computers and e-books (ARM Holdings, 2010).

From its beginning as a joint venture, ARM Holdings has successfully managed the transition from a small British firm with a narrow focus into a global firm, with a much wider range of products and services, and is recognized as a technological leader in its field. In this transition, ARM has utilized existing skills and capabilities, but the firm has also developed and built new ones. This example illustrates a major theme of our approach: strategic management is not just about exploiting current capabilities, the current skills of the firm. Rather, an essential strategic management task is to identify and develop the capabilities that will be required in the future. For ARM, this future may be up to ten years away as they move into major new application areas (ARM Holdings, 2009).

Examples of these skills are new design skills, the ability to manage collaborative research structures and developing customer information systems. These new skills have permitted the firm to capture a strong position in the high-growth markets for mobile devices, thereby expanding its scope and financial performance. ARM is a classic example of an information-era company, for it manufactures nothing but is able to market its intellectual property and intellectual assets to many of the world's leading electronics companies.

STRATEGIC MANAGEMENT IN PRACTICE

CHAPTER OVERVIEW

In Chapter 1 we discussed two major theories regarding the determinants of firm success, the structure–conduct–performance theory and the resource-based theory. In this chapter we explore the latter, the resource-based theory, in more detail. As the ARM Holdings example illustrates, successful firms which enjoy substantial growth possess unique skills and capabilities, and these skills must be continually developed to be able to take advantage of new opportunities. So firm success depends on the strategic management of the firm, ensuring that current capabilities are exploited and new capabilities are developed to take advantage of new opportunities. We commence this chapter by reviewing the role of resources – the tangible and intangible assets owned by the firm which are combined to form these skills. Resources by themselves are a necessary but not sufficient condition for a capability; for example, a firm may have highly qualified R&D personnel and still be poor at new product development. So we explore how the firm develops these capabilities, which almost always requires integrating the resources available to deliver a competitive advantage. Given the high rate of change in the firm's external environment, we then move on to examine how management must ensure that new capabilities are developed over time, introducing the concept of dynamic capabilities.

We then examine tools for assessing the cost position of the firm, relative to its major competitors, using a value chain approach. This involves an analysis of the activities of the firm, what costs are incurred at each and what are the major drivers of costs for each activity. For example, in many manufacturing activities economies of scale are the major driver of costs. When this is the case, small competitors operate with a severe cost penalty which affects their competitive position. Reflecting the growing importance of the knowledge economy, we then discuss different types of knowledge, the characteristics of knowledge products and the impact these characteristics have in terms of strategy. For example, with knowledge products such as computer software there is often a substantial first-mover advantage; early market leaders generally maintain their leadership.

The chapter concludes with a View from the Top by IBM, where they describe future capabilities required by organizations, based on a comprehensive global survey of CEOs.

5.1 INTRODUCTION

As we highlighted earlier, the fundamental question in strategic management is how firms achieve and sustain superior financial performance. Successful firms must achieve this performance in a world characterized by intense global competition, with strong rivalry in terms of the price/performance characteristics of competing products, where all firms are attempting to innovate with new products and business models. The ARM Holdings example demonstrates that success is strongly influenced by the unique skills and capabilities of the firm – what is referred to as the resource-based view (often abbreviated to RBV) (Mauri & Michaels, 1998). Strategy must be concerned with the development and deployment of firm-specific factors that will contribute to competitive advantage. This view contrasts with the structural view of success discussed in Chapter 1 (►Chapter 1), which suggests that strategy involves the firm finding an attractive industry and taking actions to achieve a strong position

LEARNING OBJECTIVE 1

Explain the nature of resources and capabilities and their importance in strategic management.

Chapter 1

within that industry. With this view, success depends upon industry characteristics such as barriers to entry, weak customers or the non-existence of substitute products or services.

While structural characteristics of an industry are important, they are not the sole determinants of success. This can be seen from data on the variability of firm profitability within an industry, as shown in Table 5.1 for three European-based supermarkets. No matter which measure is adopted, profitability varies significantly. In 2008, before the worst of the global financial crisis, Tesco was significantly more profitable than Carrefour or Ahold, regardless of the measures used.

Strategy *in practice* – European supermarkets

Table 5.1 Variability of firm profitability within the supermarket industry – 2008

Firm	Operating profit/ sales (%)	Operating profit/total assets (%)	Net income/ shareholders equity (%)
Tesco	6.2	13.1	39.6
Carrefour	3.8	6.3	20.2
Ahold	4.9	8.8	21.0

Source: Annual Reports, tesco.com; carrefour.com; ahold.com

Of course, the firms shown in Table 5.1 have different business portfolios. All three firms have significant operations outside their country of origin, although Tesco has the smallest percentage of 'overseas' sales. Ahold is very dependent on the US market, an extremely competitive and lower margin market, while Carrefour is more Europe-focused, albeit with significant operations in Latin America and Asia. Tesco also employs a higher ratio of debt capital, which leverages the firm's returns on shareholder equity.

Broader research than our illustration above confirms that industry factors account for only a small proportion of the observed variation in firm performance (McGahan & Porter, 1997). Even in structurally unattractive industries (such as airline travel), some firms such as Ryanair and SouthWest are able to achieve superior financial performance. To explain success we must clearly look at characteristics of individual firms, as well as those of the industry in which they compete, that is, the resource-based view of the firm. RBV emphasizes that the essence of firm profitability lies not in doing what other firms do, but in exploiting the unique characteristics possessed by the firm (Hawawini *et al.*, 2003). We now address this topic.

Resources
Stocks of important factors that the firm owns or controls. They are frequently grouped into tangible and intangible resources.

The resource-based view suggests that firms succeed financially because they have unique and hard-to-imitate resources that permit them to develop a competitive advantage, thus generating superior financial performance. RBV conceptualizes firms as bundles of **resources**, stocks of important factors that a firm owns or controls in order to function.

The approach assumes these resources vary across firms (resource heterogeneity) and that they are difficult for competitors to imitate (resource immobility), so that differences may persist over time. Superior performance arises from the deployment of these resources, while sustainability requires the development of the new resources required to compete in a new and different world.

The resources developed by the firm must, of course, be aligned with the competitive circumstances it faces. The resources needed by a successful clothing firm are different from those required to be a successful biotechnology firm. Resources may be deployed across all the businesses in the firm's portfolio, or they may only be used within one or a limited number of business units. A powerful corporate brand name such as Sony, for example, will typically add value to all products to which the name is applied, whereas Dassault's expertise in military aircraft does not help its art auction house or its newspaper – *Le Figaro* (Groupe Dassualt, 2010).

In a dynamic world all sources of competitive advantage will have a limited life. Since competitors will eventually imitate the resources possessed by a successful firm, sustainability can only be achieved as a consequence of innovation. In addition, since the world is continually changing, what succeeds today may not succeed tomorrow. Resources may depreciate in value as the environment changes and therefore companies must manage their transition from dependence on one set of resources to another. In other words, continual renewal and/or extension of the resources of the firm are required for sustained success in a changing environment.

Nonetheless, resources in and of themselves do not lead to competitive advantage. For example, during the 1980s, General Motors possessed significant resources – substantial cash, large plants, good brand names and an extensive distribution network – yet Japanese competitors gained significant market share from them in the critical US market. Resources per se are a necessary but not sufficient condition for superior financial performance. It is the way in which the firm combines these resources that is critical to success.

These combinations of resources are what we will call **capabilities** and it is the possession of capabilities that creates the value for an outside party that is crucial to financial success.

Generally this outside party is the customer. However, capabilities could equally well create value for a supplier. We may have capability in supply chain management that allows us to create value in the supply chain and share this with the supplier. This capability in supply chain management may draw on resources such as information technology and human resources, and may ultimately lead to additional customer value through lower prices. Thus a capability does not have to be restricted to something that directly adds value to customers; it could add value in other ways. In many parts of the world the relationship with government is critical for success, and this could be one of our capabilities.

Summarizing, the resource-based view of the firm adopts the perspective that firm resources are central in formulating strategy. They are primary constructs upon which firms build their strategies for profitably developing market opportunities. Capabilities are combinations of these resources, reflecting the ability of the firm to deploy resources. The key to the resource-based approach to strategy formulation lies in understanding the relationship between resources, capabilities, competitive advantage and performance.

Capabilities
Combinations of resources, typically embedded in the firm's processes, which the firm is able to perform better than its competitors. A core capability is one which provides the firm with an advantage over competitors.

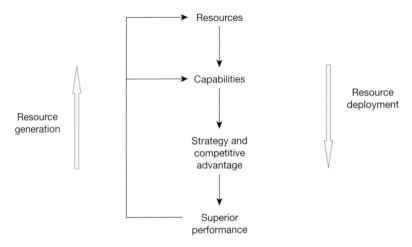

Figure 5.1 Resources and performance

A competitive advantage is a necessary but not sufficient condition for superior performance. Superior resources will only contribute to superior performance when the firm is able to capture the economic value these resources create (Crook *et al.*, 2008).

This requires the development of strategies that exploit each firm's unique characteristics at the same time as ensuring that the resources and capabilities required for the future are being developed, so that sustained profitability is achieved. This resource-based view of the firm is illustrated in Figure 5.1. The basic elements are the resources of the firm. The linkages between these, the strategy of the firm including its competitive advantage, and financial performance are illustrated in Figure 5.1.

As Figure 5.1 shows, the resource-based view emphasizes both **resource deployment** (how well the firm utilizes current resources) and **resource generation** (how well the firm creates new resources or new combinations of existing resources).

Figure 5.1 also distinguishes between superior performance and competitive advantage. A firm may possess a competitive advantage and yet not earn an economic profit. A **competitive advantage** is measured relative to competitors, while economic profit is relative to the capital employed in the firm.

We begin by examining the concept of resources, both tangible and intangible, and their contribution to strategic management. Next, we expand the discussion to introduce the idea of capabilities, combinations of resources that help us beat our competitors. The deployment of capabilities to obtain competitive advantage is the next topic, and from there we consider the dynamic or temporal dimension of capabilities, recognizing that old capabilities may no longer suffice, and new ones must often be developed. We then examine the issues of value and cost, using the value chain or business system as a starting point. The understanding of costs and cost behaviour is critical to the changes taking place in the world's economy, and it is therefore appropriate that we next cover the increasing role of intellectual capital in distinguishing successful firms from the crowd. We look at knowledge as a strategic resource,

Resource deployment
How well the firm utilizes current resources.

Resource generation
How well the firm creates new resources or new combinations of existing resources.

Competitive advantage
The way in which the firm utilizes its resources and capabilities to generate a value-creating strategy which other firms find difficult to imitate.

and the management of knowledge as a crucial capability in the years that lie ahead, concluding with a brief discussion of the implications for managers.

5.2 RESOURCES

Resources are firm-specific assets that the firm owns or controls. They have the potential, when used in combination, to allow the firm to perform activities in a manner superior to competitors. In the short term, strategies are constrained by the firm's current resources and the speed with which it can acquire or develop new ones. Examples of resources are patents, trademarks, financial strength, plant and equipment, and knowledgeable employees. Some of these may be difficult to transfer to other firms; that is, they are difficult to imitate. However, as we will see, resources may be more easily imitated than capabilities, since capabilities are integrated sets of resources.

Identifying resources is difficult, but a good place to start is to examine the major types of each. The purpose of this analysis is not simply to describe the resource, although that is a necessary starting point. Instead, it is to try to understand whether the particular resource should be extended or modified, whether it can be used differently or whether it can be used more efficiently. Such an analysis must also include an understanding of the changing environment, so that judgements can be made on what new resources are likely to be required and how these are to be developed.

To understand resources, we divide them into two broad categories: tangible resources – many of which appear on the balance sheet; and intangible resources – almost all of which do not.

> **LEARNING OBJECTIVE 2**
>
> Be able to identify and appraise the resources of the firm.

Tangible resources

The tangible resources of a firm can be broken down into two main subgroups: financial and physical.

Financial resources

Financial resources relate to the firm's capacity for future investment, whether this is in plant, people, processes, acquisitions or innovation. If the firm has limited levels of financial resources, then its strategic flexibility is correspondingly reduced. Financial resources include the firm's borrowing capacity, its capacity to raise capital in the form of debt or equity, and its ability to generate funds internally as measured by free cash flow. The total of these resources determines the firm's capacity for investment expenditures in future products and facilities, as well as its ability to innovate and handle fluctuations in demand and profits.

On 26 September 2009, Apple had some $US34 billion in cash, cash equivalents and marketable securities, sufficient liquidity to support a large number of innovative ventures (Apple, 2009). These financial resources include the firm's credit rating, since this influences its ability to raise debt, the cost of that debt and the ability to raise equity. But while financial resources are a necessary condition for innovation, they are not sufficient. Without financial resources innovation is very difficult to achieve. If the firm has financial resources, these can be used wisely or they can be wasted.

Physical resources

Physical resources include the firm's buildings and plant, the technical sophistication of operations, the flexibility of operations, and its reserves of raw materials.

British Airways, with its fleet of 245 owned and leased aircraft, has larger resources than EasyJet with its fleet of 79 aircraft. Of course, in this industry the value of such a resource depends on other factors such as the age of the aircraft and the number of different types in the fleet. Other physical resources include the size of the firm, its geographical location, its information systems and databases, distribution networks and customer information systems. For some firms a major tangible resource is an automated warehouse system, which permits lower inventory costs.

Tangible resources may be standard across an industry and thus not a source of competitive advantage. Many firms in an industry use very similar physical plant so there is rarely competitive advantage in the plant itself. A Boeing 777 operated by Singapore Airlines is almost identical to the 777 operated by another airline.

Intangible resources

Intangible resources
Resources that are non-physical in nature, such as patents, business processes, trademarks and brand equity. Such intangible resources are generally not included on the firm's balance sheet.

Intangible resources are typically not represented on the balance sheet and thus are more difficult to capture and to describe. They are less visible and consequently more difficult for competitors to understand, to purchase and to imitate. These intangible resources will generally include the leadership of the firm, its culture and structure. As we will see later, these intangible resources are generally knowledge-based and may provide a relatively secure basis for competitive advantage. In the knowledge economy, the importance of these assets is rising in comparison with the tangible assets recorded on the balance sheet.

Classically, the resources necessary for an industrial firm were considered to be the tangible resources of land, labour and capital, where capital includes the financial and economic resources required. But in modern firms the new resources derive from the skills, knowledge, brainpower and creativity of the firm and its members. These resources are what we call **intellectual assets** or **capital** and these are increasingly important to many organizations. In management consulting or advertising, the factors critical for success are employees, not buildings or location.

Intellectual assets/capital
Knowledge, information, skills and experience used by the firm to create value. They are generally partitioned into three categories: human, structural and customer.

This trend is occurring in most industries where intellectual assets are displacing physical and financial capital as key factors of production. Intellectual assets and knowledge play a key role in determining competitive advantage, while the relative importance of intellectual capital continues to grow. Such assets were clearly critical to the success of ARM Holdings, yet whether we are talking about plumbers or doctors, the knowledge content of most jobs is increasing and the jobs themselves are being redefined. The number of knowledge workers is increasing and products are becoming more knowledge intensive.

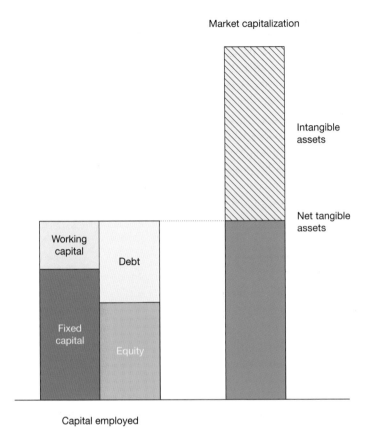

Figure 5.2 Tangible and intangible assets

It is not easy to quantify the increasing knowledge intensity of a firm due to the lack of accepted measures of intellectual assets; however, one surrogate for them is the M/B ratio of the firm. As will be discussed at more length in Chapter 12 (▶Chapter 12), this ratio is the market capitalization of the firm (share price multiplied by the number of shares outstanding) divided by the book value of the assets of the firm, as reported in its balance sheet. This relationship is depicted in Figure 5.2.

Chapter 12

Market capitalization reflects the views of financial markets on the firm's prospects of producing future cash flows. These cash flows can be interpreted as the expected return from all the assets of the firm, both tangible and intangible. Capital employed is based on historic accounting principles and primarily reflects the value of the tangible assets of the business.

Thus the M/B ratio is a measure, possibly imperfect, of the relative importance of intangible and tangible assets in the valuation of the firm by financial markets. The intangible or intellectual assets include brand name or **brand equity**, the skills and knowledge of employees, customer loyalty and patents as well as the knowledge base of the company in systems and processes, technology, R&D and so on. Few if any of these assets appear on

Brand equity

The value the organization receives from its branded product or service compared with the value from an identical unbranded product or service.

Table 5.2 Market-to-book ratios, UK firms

Year	GlaxoSmithKline	Sainsbury
2003	13.5	0.9
2004	10.7	1.2
2005	9.7	1.3
2006	9.3	1.3
2007	8.3	1.9
2008	7.3	1.4
2009	7.1	1.2

Source: ThomsonReuters, 2009

the balance sheet of the firm. The value of GlaxoSmithKline or Coca-Cola is not based on bricks and mortar; the share market valuation is based on expectations of the value of the intellectual capital of the firms. In the case of GSK, this is primarily the value of its patents and R&D, the ability to develop new drugs in the future. In the case of Coca-Cola, these intangible assets are mainly accounted for by the equity of the Coca-Cola brand, the value of which was estimated to be $US68.7 billion in 2009 (Interbrand, 2009).

Table 5.2 shows the market-to-book ratios for two major UK firms, GlaxoSmithKline and Sainsbury, over the past seven years. As is clear from Table 5.2, the market-to-book ratio for GlaxoSmithKline is consistently high, much higher than for Sainsbury. Among other things, this reflects shareholder expectations on the future value of the firm's R&D expenditure, which is likely to result in major new businesses. For GSK, only a very small proportion of its total value is actually captured on its balance sheet in the form of tangible assets. Nonetheless, the trend decline in their ratio indicates that investors are increasingly sceptical about GSK's ability to innovate in the future. This is a characteristic of many traditional pharmaceutical companies. Sainsbury has far lower levels of market to book, indicating that it possesses little in the way of intangible assets, although there is some suggestion that it is actually increasing.

Challenge of strategic management

As Table 5.2 indicates, Sainsbury has a relatively low M/B. Which of Sainsbury's intangible assets do you believe could be enhanced so that shareholders would place a higher value on the firm? How would you suggest doing this?

As a consequence of these developments in intangible assets, it is clear that the real value of many companies, as expressed by share markets, is not given by traditional accounting measures recorded on the balance sheet. When a firm invests in a tangible asset, the asset is booked on the balance sheet, with no cost on the income statement. The cost on the income statement occurs as the tangible asset is depreciated. Investment in an intangible asset such as R&D is shown on the income statement as a cost but not on the balance sheet. Yet the value of intangible assets is becoming more important, as reflected in the increase in the M/B ratios of firms over time.

Figure 5.3 indicates the importance of intangible assets for a balanced sample of publicly listed European firms in both the low-technology and the high-technology sectors. As can be seen, the ratio of intangible assets to total assets has risen from about 7 per cent in 1991 to about 30 per cent in 2004. As Hall notes, this figure understates the true share of intangible

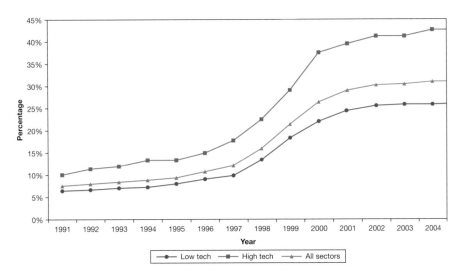

Figure 5.3 Intangible assets as a percentage of total assets – European firms
Source: Hall, 2007, © voxEU.org

assets, since accounting standards do not allow capitalization of R&D and because only intangible assets which are actually on the balance sheet are included. Other intangible assets such as human capital are excluded. However, the data clearly highlights the growing importance of intangible assets for firms, and the need for managers to actively manage these assets.

Classifying resources

Resources may also be classified in a manner which reflects their ownership. The categories which result are normally called human capital, structural capital and customer capital (Edvinsson & Malone, 1997).

Human capital

Human capital is in the minds of individuals; it is the knowledge, skills, ability, experience, intelligence, creativity, enthusiasm and motivation of individuals. The firm can use the human capital of its employees, but the firm does not own it.

Employees with a high degree of human capital should be considered as volunteers, not as employees – or, expressing this same idea a little differently, such employees can be rented but not owned. This human capital can be traded by the individual in the form of better salary, better employment conditions, or even a job with a new employer. Individuals with high levels of human capital are generally very mobile and can move to other firms if current employment conditions are not meeting their requirements. The firm itself cannot trade

Human capital
The skills, knowledge, ability, experience, intelligence, creativity and motivation of the individuals who comprise the firm's workforce.

human capital unless it sells the entire group or division and the employees elect to stay with the divested entity.

The firm uses this human capital in its current operations. The relevant employee knowledge may be about processes within the firm, but could also be about relationships with customers, suppliers and alliance partners. At the same time, the firm must facilitate the generation of new human capital, where employees develop new skills and more creativity. An issue for many firms is what knowledge is owned by the individual and what knowledge is owned by the firm, which brings us to a discussion of structural capital.

Structural capital

Structural capital
Capital that is owned by the firm, not by a specific individual.

Structural capital is capital that is owned by the firm, not by a specific individual. Structural capital is that which does not go home at night! It may be contained in the firm's processes, hardware, software, databases and structure, and includes the company's values, culture and philosophy. In a study of Spanish firms from a number of industries, 62 per cent of firms indicated that 'systems and procedures' were an important component of their structural capital (Gallego & Rodriguez, 2005). Tesco, the UK supermarket chain, has a customer Clubcard, which permits the firm to maintain a complete record of customer purchases. This sophisticated database and data analysis system is a valuable resource for the firm, not currently possessed by its competitors.

If an individual leaves the firm, such capital stays with the firm, its value and use is not confined to an individual; rather it is a collective concept. Since the firm owns structural capital it can be reproduced, shared and traded. A patent owned by the firm can be sold; a process that has been developed by the firm can be licensed, as Amazon has done with its information systems ('Internet pioneers', 2001). Unique market positions, technological knowledge and accumulated experience may also create advantages difficult for competitors to copy.

Since one of the tasks of management is to build corporate assets, managers need to develop structural capital from the human capital of its members. Whereas the individual owns human capital, the firm owns the structural capital. Clearly, then, it is possible to get into a conflict between the individual and the firm regarding what knowledge to share and what rewards will be offered to the individual to share this personal knowledge. What are the intellectual property rights of individual employees? What incentives will be offered to translate human knowledge into structural knowledge, which in turn is the basis for a competitive advantage for the firm? Human rights activists are increasingly concerned about these attempts. They argue that efforts to extract this knowledge from individuals and share it throughout the organization strike at the very heart of an individual's personal value in the labour market, and see the whole area as the new frontier in a battle for individual freedom. Knowledge workers may also be more loyal to their profession than their employer. This is another reason for the increased popularity of gain-sharing rewards such as stock options, for there is a real need to improve the loyalty of knowledge workers as the role of intellectual capital expands. We are convinced that structural capital is likely to be a basis for competitive advantage for the firm, but it is difficult to manage and accumulate.

When structural capital can be legally protected it is called **intellectual property**, and is owned by the firm. Examples of intellectual property are trademarks, patents and copyrights. Patents are one measure used to evaluate the success of R&D, and this has been an active area of academic research. However, the most recent studies confirm that firms able to generate significant innovations experience above-average profitability and growth, particularly when the innovations are built on internally generated knowledge rather than acquired externally (Bogner & Bansal, 2007).

The firm can extract the value of its intellectual property in other ways. For example, it could sell the intellectual capital to another firm, as when a firm sells a patent it owns (➤Chapter 9). Or it could license it and obtain royalties, as Bell Labs did when it licensed the transistor to a small entrepreneurial Japanese company that later changed its name to Sony. There is a growing market for trading intellectual assets, where the firm is both a buyer and a seller. Companies may buy knowledge to leverage their complementary assets – for example, many large companies are better at commercializing products than at developing them, and consequently they buy in new ideas rather than develop them themselves. In 1997 pharmaceutical companies derived 34 per cent of revenue from products licensed from other companies, a significant increase from 29 per cent in 1992 (Torres, 1999). ARM, the microprocessor designer, obtains 43 per cent of its revenue from licence fees and 40 per cent from royalties (ARM, 2008).

When the firm wants to trade this intellectual property it needs to be aware of the level of legal protection afforded or the intellectual property regime that applies. A problem for many firms is the ease with which intellectual property can be copied in several countries of the world. As a consequence, there is ongoing debate within the World Trade Organization (WTO) around the protection of the intellectual property rights of firms, whether these involve software, patents or copyright. In some Asian countries in particular, laws protecting intellectual property are relatively weak, and it is easy to buy fake luxury goods such as watches, pirate CDs or DVDs and software.

As a condition of its membership to the WTO, China agreed to respect intellectual property rights in trademarks and copyright, reflecting a strengthening of the legal regime. Indeed, more intellectual property cases are now entering Chinese courts, including situations where Chinese firms are accused of appropriating the intellectual property of other Chinese firms.

> **Intellectual property**
> Structural capital which is owned by the firm and which can be legally protected.

Chapter 9

Intellectual property *in practice* – Microsoft

In 2010 a Chinese court ordered Microsoft to stop selling versions of its Windows operating system that included fonts designed by a Chinese firm, Zhongyi Electronics. Microsoft announced its intention to appeal, but an analyst commented, 'The majority of operating systems on the (*Chinese*) market today are illegal copies', arguing that the ruling would have little impact on Microsoft's business (Yu, 2009).

We expect to see increased trade in intellectual property in the coming years, with firms taking a more aggressive stance towards its development. Other forms of knowledge may have limited legal protection. The US-initiated trend to the patenting of business processes has caused considerable controversy. Indeed, some firms prefer not to patent new ideas, since they reveal what is being patented and hence make it easier for other firms to copy or enhance.

Customer capital

Customer capital
The value of the firm's relationship with its customers, including an understanding of customers' demands and preferences.

Customer capital is the value of the firm's relationship with its customers, including an understanding of customers' demands and preferences. Indicators of customer capital are brand equity, customer perceptions, customer retention rates, satisfaction measures, profitability and market share.

Firms are increasingly interested in customer retention rates, since small increases in brand loyalty can have a substantial impact on profit. It is generally more profitable to retain an existing customer than to acquire a new one. Indeed, there is a movement to co-designing and even co-producing with customers, since these investments in joint innovation will usually build customer capital (Berthon *et al.*, 1999). Not only do we want to be able to charge a premium to customers, we want to enable them to charge a premium to their customers. A resource may be one that the firm has access to, even though it does not own it. For example, for many firms a major resource is its network of customers, but the firm does not 'own' such a network.

For many firms a major intangible asset, and a major component of customer capital, is the value of brand equity. The value of a brand name such as 'Samsung' is owned by the entire firm and exists independently of the individuals who comprise the firm. A survey conducted in 2009 on the value of 100 global brands shows that Coca-Cola headed the list, with an estimated brand value of $US69 billion, as shown in Table 5.3.

A number of leading fast-moving consumer goods companies have installed a system of brand health indicators to assess the direction of change, if any, in brand equity and to identify key issues that might otherwise pass unnoticed. These systems, further discussed in

 Chapter 12

Chapter 12 (▶Chapter 12), also help remedy a major defect in measuring of brand manager performance inasmuch as a focus solely on such results as profit, volume or market share is rather like asking a corporation to show only an income statement. Brand equity can be seen as the balance sheet for the brand, and provides assurance that good short-term results have not been achieved at the expense of the brand's future (Berthon *et al.*, 1999).

Intangible resources are a significant source of competitive advantage, since they are difficult for competitors to imitate and are often characterized by path dependency and causal ambiguity. For example, a competitor may be able to purchase modern equipment but this does not imply that they can get that plant to operate efficiently and effectively. To do so requires an infrastructure, including other intangible resources such as trained, knowledgeable and committed employees. This leads us to a discussion of capabilities, the ability of the firm to integrate a number of resources, a process requiring time, money, leadership and skill.

Table 5.3 Value of selected global brands (Interbrand, 2009)

Brand	Country	Rank	Value (2009, US$ billions)
Coca-Cola	United States	1	68.7
Nokia	Finland	5	34.8
Toyota	Japan	8	31.3
H & M	Sweden	21	15.4
HSBC	United Kingdom	32	10.5
Philips	The Netherlands	42	8.1
Zara	Spain	50	6.8
Nestlé	Switzerland	58	6.3
Hyundai	Republic of Korea	69	4.6
Burberry	United Kingdom	98	3.1

5.3 RESOURCES AND CAPABILITIES

LEARNING OBJECTIVE 3

Demonstrate how capabilities are linked to competitive advantage.

An individual resource typically has no value in isolation; its value is realized when it is combined with other resources. We designate these combinations of resources as the capabilities of the firm. For example, strong finances are by themselves not a competitive advantage. They only have value when they are combined with other resources to constitute what we denote as a capability. This resource deployment and integration allows the firm to excel in the delivery of a process critical to an outside party. Such a process may be one that delivers quality to customers, or it could be a process that delivers benefits through the supply chain, but the essential point is that the capability ultimately contributes to the competitive advantage of the firm or its business units.

Capabilities are embedded in the firm's processes and organizational routines such as new product development, order generation and fulfilment, brand management or integrated logistics and supply chain management.

This is illustrated in Figure 5.4, where we have taken new product development and customer service as examples of capabilities possessed by the firm. For a pharmaceutical firm, its capability may be the ability to integrate the different scientific disciplines which is required to develop a new drug (Barney & Clark, 2007). Capability in new product development requires technical R&D skills, the ability to operate in teams, an excellent database system and skills in understanding consumers. The firm will excel in this process – in other words, possess a capability in new product development – if it can integrate these disparate functional groups (among which there may well be interdepartment conflict) and their knowledge. The new product development process must be managed on an end-to-end

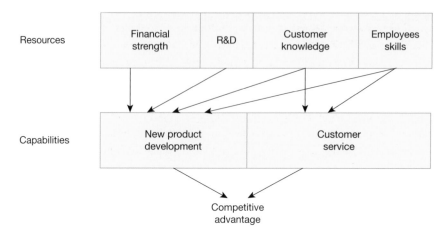

Figure 5.4 Resources and capabilities

basis, with all departments working together as a team towards a common objective. The new product development process has performance criteria such as speed, time to launch, new product success rate and the resources consumed which can be benchmarked relative to competitors to assess the magnitude of the capability possessed by the firm.

Capabilities include discrete business-level organizational processes fundamental to running the business (order entry, customer service, quality control) as well as generalized organizational skills such as 'managing the acquisition process' or 'managing outsourcing'. For example, a major textile firm was identified as having capabilities in international

---

Capabilities *in practice* – Bang & Olufsen

Bang and Olufsen, the Danish consumer electronics firm, reports that it has eight capabilities which constitute its competitive advantage. These include picture, sound, user interaction among others. Its capability in picture reproduction is described as follows:

> Bang & Olufsen strives to ensure that the consumer has a picture reproduction that is as faithful to the real-life experience as possible. Towards this aim, we have identified and worked with a number of parameters, which affect the picture quality. We have built a special facility, which is unique within the trade, where we can test picture reproduction under a variety of viewing conditions to be able to continuously improve the experience we offer the customer. The whole idea is to dynamically adapt and make the best performance at all times with as little disturbance to the viewer as possible.
>
> (Bang-Olfusen, 2010)

transportation logistics, linking operational goals to compensation plans and managing costs (King *et al.*, 2001). As another example, many multinationals from emerging economies such as Korea, India and Turkey are seen as having a 'political capability', dealing with possibly unstable governments (Guillén & García-Canal, 2009). Thus capabilities can exist at both the business and the corporate level. Firms that are successful acquirers have developed capabilities in pre- and post-merger activities: they are able to assess the worth of a target firm and successfully integrate it into the existing firm. Capabilities are hard to develop and therefore any firm will possess only a limited number. By their nature, capabilities are 'global' in character and, since they contribute to competitive success, should only be assessed relative to other firms.

Among the firm's relatively small number of capabilities, some will be more important than others. These we will call core capabilities – they are fundamental to performance and have the following properties:

- They have a disproportionate impact on ultimate customer satisfaction or the efficiency with which that value is delivered, or
- They provide a basis for entering new markets (Prahalad & Hamel, 1990).

Obviously the firm should excel at these core capabilities, while less critical capabilities may be considered as outsourcing candidates. If the firm possesses a core capability, it performs this activity in a manner superior to competitors. A core capability will generally focus on a user need (so that there is a source of revenue), be unique (so that prices can be set to some extent independent of competition) and difficult to replicate (so profits will not be competed away). A core capability should not be very general, like 'marketing', but rather constitute 'a combination of complementary skills and knowledge bases embedded in a group or team that results in the ability to execute one or more critical processes to a world-class standard' (Coyne, 1997).

Hamel and Prahalad observed that Canon has four core capabilities in precision mechanics, fine optics, microelectronics and electronic imaging, and describe how these have been deployed across its product line (Hamel & Prahalad, 1994). In a study of a number of multinationals, core capabilities included superior technical know-how, reliable processes and relationships with external parties (Mascarenhas *et al.*, 1998).

Core capabilities are seen as drivers of strategy, but they are difficult to identify and define, and it is not always easy to separate out core and non-core capabilities. As we will explore shortly, what is regarded as a core capability will change over time. For example, in the global automobile market, core capabilities have purportedly evolved from the possession of a global distribution network and quality production processes to niche marketing and flexibility (Johnson *et al.*, 2008).

We now discuss the properties of capabilities that enhance their propensity to contribute to competitive advantage. Note that these would also be desirable properties of resources.

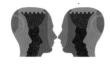

Challenge of strategic management

Bain and Company

Companies are outsourcing more and enjoying it less these days. According to a Bain survey, 82 per cent of large firms in Europe, Asia and North America use outsourcers, and 51 per cent are using offshore outsourcers. But nearly half say their outsourcing programmes do not meet expectations, even when measured purely on cost improvements. A mere 6 per cent say they are 'extremely satisfied' with their outsourcing arrangements.

The problem is that few companies have developed comprehensive sourcing strategies. For years, 'sourcing' has meant procurement. And procurement, while financially material, has been strategically peripheral. Today, many companies make their outsourcing decisions on a piecemeal basis, guided by the traditional, narrow goal of minimizing costs.

We need to reframe the issue. For best practice, companies outsourcing has become so sophisticated that even engineering, R&D, manufacturing and marketing can – and often should – be moved outside. It is no longer a company's ownership of capabilities that matters but rather its ability to control and make the most of critical capabilities, whether or not they reside on a company's balance sheet. We call this new discipline capability sourcing. Done well, it creates a new operating blueprint for the organization – the right capability at the right cost from the right source and the right shore (Calthrop *et al.*, 2010).

Question

■ The authors of the above views are consultants at Bain and Company. Given our discussion of core capabilities, and the general history of outsourcing, do you agree with their argument that the ability to control and make the most of critical abilities matters more than ownership of a capability?

5.4 CAPABILITIES AND COMPETITIVE ADVANTAGE

To evaluate the profit-earning potential of a capability, we need to assess it in terms of a number of properties, as shown in Figure 5.5.

Valuable

The essential feature of a capability is that it makes a significant contribution to the fulfilment of customer needs. A capability is valuable to the extent that it allows the firm to reduce costs or increase revenue over what it would have been without the capability. Federal Express provides its customers with software, called Powership, free of charge, which allows them to

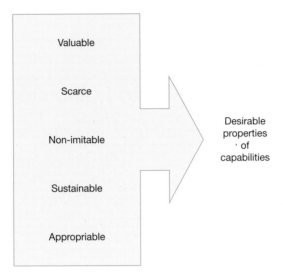

Figure 5.5 Properties of capabilities

schedule shipments, manage accounts, track packages and order supplies electronically. To some extent using this system locks in customers, but it also provides them with additional value. Sony has a capability in miniaturization of electronic products, which has been utilized in CD players, computers and video cameras, since for such products smallness is a major consumer benefit. Wal-Mart, the company with the greatest sales volume in the world, possesses a set of resources and capabilities, which include store location (reduced rental), brand reputation (reduced advertising) and supply chain management (reduced logistics costs), which combine to provide a major cost advantage for Wal-Mart relative to the industry (Collis & Montgonery, 1998).

Since customer needs change over time, the firm must continually reassess the extent to which its capabilities are contributing and whether or not new ones are required. Many of Microsoft's competitive successes have been tied to the personal computer. With the advent of so-called 'cloud computing' and the explosion of non-PC digital devices such as PDAs, mobile phones, netbooks, iPads and the like, these historic strengths and capabilities may well become rigidities that slow its growth.

Scarce

A capability is valuable if it is not widely shared by other firms. If many firms develop the same capability, none will earn a substantial return on that investment. We can also distinguish capabilities required to maintain competitive parity from those that add to competitive advantage. In many markets firms need the capability to deliver high-quality products, but quality itself often fails to create competitive advantage: it has become a prerequisite for survival.

Non-imitable

Capabilities and resources differ in the extent to which competitors can imitate them. A resource such as location for a retail store is difficult to imitate. Similarly with a brand name. A competitor cannot easily duplicate the advantage that flows to Coca-Cola from its brand name. However, capabilities which involve complex interactions may be even more difficult to duplicate, partly because the capability demonstrates causal ambiguity; that is, it is not clear what it involves. The success of SouthWest Airlines or Ryanair is a complex mixture of culture, recruitment, schedule, routes, focus, planes and so on.

A new factory provides little advantage when competitors can purchase the same plant from the supplier. However, if the resource is traded, the competitor may have to pay such a high price for it that all future benefits are capitalized in the price. The benefits a firm expects to accrue from possession of resources should not be dissipated in the competitive struggle to acquire them. The ease with which competitors can create a capability cannot easily be generalized. Sometimes the follower can create a capability at lower cost than the pioneer: the imitator learns from the pioneer's mistakes. In other cases the pioneer has a significant advantage that is hard to dislodge.

Sustainable

Related to the above, it should be evident that the more difficult it is to imitate a capability, the longer it is likely to last. Other things being equal, the firm should obviously seek capabilities that are likely to prove durable. Since developing and sustaining capabilities is necessarily a cost-incurring activity, we should always prefer one that promises a return over a longer period of time. As we see later in the chapter, such capabilities are more and more dependent on the possession of privileged knowledge not available to other firms. Sustainability of a capability will also be influenced by the rate of environmental change, which could result in the capability becoming obsolete, as well as the availability of substitutes.

Appropriable

Finally, there is the issue of whether or not the firm can appropriate the returns that the capability delivers. This is determined by property rights and the relative bargaining power of the actors. Ideally, the firm wants to capture the benefits of the capability but profits may flow not to the firm that 'owns' the resource but to employees, suppliers or customers. In financial services, the capability may be the network of relationships with clients, but these often go with the employees, not the firm. This may also be the case with an advertising agency.

The firm needs to exploit the full competitive potential of its resources by managing its structure, reporting system and management processes, including incentives. As firms move towards more of a knowledge base, with a greater proportion of high-calibre professional employees, so the need to capture the knowledge of individual employees who work in systems and software increases.

Capabilities *in practice* – Medicare Australia

Medicare is an Australian government agency delivering a range of payments and services to the Australian community – with a focus on health and family assistance.

Catherine Argall is the CEO of Medicare Australia. In 2008 she sent the following message to her employees:

> Over the next three to five years, Medicare Australia will deliver a range of new programs and services. The change will include new services, offered for the first time through our branches and contact centres, and changes to the way we deliver existing services. This will require our people to focus more on providing advice, information and other services to Australians and will lead to improvements to our systems and infrastructure.
>
> As we take on a broader range of programs, we need to identify the skills and attributes that are required in this emerging business environment. The capability framework is a first step towards realigning the capabilities of our people. The framework identifies nationally consistent broad capabilities needed to continue our reputation for excellence in service delivery.
>
> The framework will assist us to determine what learning and development strategies we need to implement in order to ensure our current people can acquire the capabilities we need now and in the future. As it is integrated into all HR functions, the framework will guide the attraction, selection, learning and development, performance support and workforce planning at an organisational and job specific levels.
>
> The capability framework defines the six broad capability clusters that identify the focus of our capability requirements. These include:
>
> - Exemplifies great service
> - Shapes strategic thinking
> - Achieves results
> - Cultivates productive working relationships
> - Exemplifies personal drive and integrity
> - Communicates with influence
>
> The first capability cluster has been drawn from our service charter and the work identifying the behaviours that demonstrate 'Our Promises' to our customers. It is important that the framework reinforces our service culture and that great service be recognized as a key capability for all our people. This also means that those providing service to internal customers are expected to deliver on these promises as much as our front line Customer Service Officers. The other five capability clusters are based around those developed by the Australian Public Service Commission (APSC) and reflect the capabilities required of all APS employees in a career based service.
>
> (Argall, 2010)

Questions

1 Do you believe that a CEO message like this is an effective way to communicate the need for new capabilities?

2 If you were called in as a consultant to Medicare and asked to help them assess their progress in developing and implementing these capabilities what advice would you give them?

LEARNING OBJECTIVE 4

Argue that in a turbulent world an integral role for strategic management is building new capabilities.

5.5 DYNAMIC CAPABILITIES

As we have emphasized throughout this book, organizations exist, and have to prosper, in a rapidly changing and unpredictable world. The capabilities and skills that lead to success today may not be those required for future success (Schreyögg & Kliesch-Eberl, 2007). There is also evidence that the sustainability of firm-specific advantages is becoming more temporary, due to the fast-changing environment faced by the firm (D'Aveni *et al.*, 2010). Yet generally the fact that a firm has developed a current capability implies that a particular process has been standardized and become routine. When change occurs, whether caused by customers, competitors, technology or substitutes, this standardization becomes a source of inertia (Newey & Zahra, 2009). The firm cannot rely on its historic capabilities which brought it success in a world which has gone. Instead, the firm must have the capacity to develop new capabilities, either by new combinations of pre-existing resources or by developing resources new to the firm. The processes involved must be an integral component of strategic management. The need to both deploy resources for current competitive success and generate the resources and capabilities required for future success is another of the dilemmas facing strategic management, yet another choice between stability and change. These resources 'can include human capital . . . technological capital, knowledge-based capital and tangible-asset-base capital, among others' (Easterby-Smith *et al.*, 2009).

We will refer to these mechanisms for building and reconfiguring existing resources and capabilities as **dynamic capabilities** (Teece *et al.*, 1997). How good is the firm at renewing its capabilities and resource base? How good is the firm at renewing itself, at creating and handling change? Long-term competitive advantage lies in the ability of the firm to develop the resources and capabilities required to address its changing environment faster, more astutely and at lower cost than competitors (Eisenhardt & Jeffrey, 2000).

Dynamic capabilities
Mechanisms for building new resources and capabilities or reconfiguring existing ones.

> With dynamic capabilities, sustained competitive advantage comes from the firm's ability to leverage and reconfigure its existing capabilities and assets in ways that are valuable to the customer but difficult for competitors to imitate. Dynamic capabilities help a firm sense opportunities and then seize them by successfully reallocating resources, often by adjusting capabilities or developing new ones.
>
> (Harreld *et al.*, 2007)

This process is like double-loop learning. The firm needs a set of capabilities to be successful today, but it also needs to be able to forget or terminate those which are no longer required, enhance some that have become more important and build fundamentally new ones. In turbulent environments, sustaining a competitive advantage requires the ability to continuously create new capabilities as well as utilize the firm's current capabilities (Teece, 2007).

Managing the transition from one set of capabilities to another is a considerable challenge and takes time to accomplish. In many situations it can be argued that firms either fail to see the threat early enough and/or are unable to change quickly enough (Harreld *et al.*, 2007).

When we examine successful firms it becomes apparent that they have developed a range of new capabilities, expanding out from their initial capabilities in a combination of incremental and revolutionary steps. Sony began as a firm repairing radios and making kits to convert AM radios into short-wave receivers. They then aggressively developed the capabilities which enabled them to develop miniature transistor radios, audio tape decks, TV, colour TV, VCRs, PSPs, Blu-ray™ disks and many other products, through a combination of internal development, alliances and licensing of technology. Despite this commendable record, however (Helfat & Raubitschek, 2000), Sony have had considerable difficulty in recent years, and in 2005 appointed British CEO Sir Howard Stringer to try to turn the firm around.

The need to create new capabilities is illustrated by the dilemma confronting firms that face obsolescence in their core products. Do they focus their strategy on the changed needs of their current customers, or do they attempt to develop new markets for their current skills?

Consider Nokia and the challenge it has faced from Apple's iPhone. Hampered by its software, Nokia, the world's largest mobile phone company, has seen its US market share fall from 35 per cent in 2002 to 7 per cent in 2009. However, the firm is fighting back, appointing a new CEO for US operations, who is also a main board member. Nokia is also cooperating more closely with network operators, and has made its Symbian software open source in attempts to attract developers. The firm has also extended its capabilities, developing a sophisticated market segmentation scheme for phone users and launching a netbook computer under the Nokia brand name. At the time of writing it is too early to know whether these changes will help Nokia to rebuild share in its important US market (O'Brien, 2009).

We can visualize a firm as a portfolio of capabilities and that the composition and emphasis of each element in this portfolio will change over time in response to the changing environment, as shown in Figure 5.6. Some capabilities possessed by the firm in, say, 2011 will become less relevant in 2016. Others will become more important, and will need to be developed through a combination of means. The processes by which these capabilities are altered are the dynamic capabilities of the firm. Some firms have found it difficult to manage this transition (Tripsas & Gavetti, 2000), while others such as Nissan have been more successful (Witcher *et al.*, 2008).

As noted above, these dynamic capabilities are critical for long-term survival in fast-changing markets and industries. So what do they look like? Examples would be skills in:

- Experimentation
- Improvisation
- Developing employee skills through training
- Selective recruitment
- Multi-functional task teams.

Alternatively they may result from licensing, acquisitions, joint ventures and alliances. Sony originally licensed the transistor from Bell Laboratories, but was then able to leverage

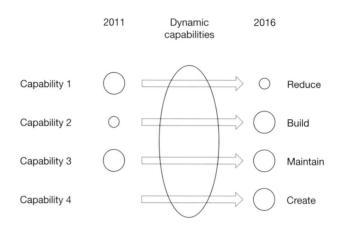

Figure 5.6 Dynamic capabilities

Chapter 3

Dynamic capabilities *in practice* – DuPont

In a recent address, the Chairman and CEO of DuPont suggested that firms must become adept at anticipating and recovering from major external shocks, such as terrorist attacks, category five hurricanes and other potential business disruptions. Firms must build robust systems to cope with any turbulent situation. It is difficult, or even impossible, for a business to plan for every threat, especially low-probability events, as discussed in Chapter 3 (►Chapter 3). The suggested solution is to build a robust capability, not about identifying each individual risk. One of the most important capabilities is the robustness of the firm's computer systems. It was reported that 93 per cent of companies that lost their data centre for ten days or more (for any reason) went bankrupt within a year (Bryner, 2007).

the underlying technology, allowing it to develop major new markets, such as portable radios. In contrast Virgin generated new resources by leveraging its brand into such new domains as airlines, mobile phones, cosmetics, soft drinks, bridal wear and rail transportation (Ambrosini *et al.*, 2009).

To identify a firm's capabilities, two approaches are generally used: functional and value chain. Using the functional approach, capabilities are assessed relative to competition in each of the major functional areas of the business unit or firm. With the value chain approach, the focus is on the specific activities undertaken by the firm and their competitive assessment.

We now go on to explore the concept of a value chain in some more detail.

Challenge of strategic management

Resource deployment and resource generation is another example of the need for strategic managers to both manage for today and manage for tomorrow, and the need for the firm to adapt to a changing environment. Yet we saw in Chapter 2 (►Chapter 2) that there were several impediments to developing strategy.

Chapter 2

■ Why do some firms have difficulty generating new capabilities? What do you think are the major impediments to developing new capabilities? What style of management would facilitate the development of new capabilities?

5.6 THE VALUE CHAIN

A useful tool for assessing capabilities and analysing a business unit is the value chain, popularized by Michael Porter (Porter, 1985). The **value chain** for a business describes that business in terms of the activities that the firm has chosen to undertake in order to be able to compete. These activities are the basis for examining the opportunities for reducing costs or adding value (improving differentiation) at each stage of this value chain.

We will organize our discussion of the value chain by first examining **cost drivers**, then looking at value added. However, ultimately cost and value must be integrated into an understanding of the complete chain. When they are not, we run the risk of attempting to reduce cost by eliminating or sub-optimizing activities critical to adding value for customers.

Table 5.4 (overleaf) shows the value chains for two directly competitive firms: one from Australia, the other from New Zealand. Each produces a timber product that is exported to Singapore. The data in the figure are the unit costs per tonne of the six major value-adding activities, from purchasing to service. Since this product is a commodity, they each sell it in Singapore for the same price: $600 per tonne.

Such information is essential to fully understand a business's competitive position. When developing a value chain we have to decide what level of detail to use. For example, in Table 5.4 we used one activity, 'outbound logistics,' but this could have been broken down into more detailed elements, such as local freight, port handling, ocean freight and Singapore distribution. Such a chain would be more complex but provide more complete information. We also have to decide which costs are relevant. Here costs were fixed and variable, including capital costs via depreciation, measured in terms of annual costs divided by annual volume in metric tonnes. The ideas behind the value chain can also be applied at the level of the entire industry, where costs for each of the industry participants are analysed to ascertain how profitability is distributed within the industry. For example, in the automobile industry how is profitability split between component suppliers, car manufacturers, dealers and providers of finance. We return to this topic in Chapter 7 (►Chapter 7).

Firms in other industries have their own value chain, different from the above. For example, in retail banking one critical activity is transaction processing. Transaction costs

LEARNING OBJECTIVE 5

Analyse the major cost drivers of a business and its likely future costs.

Value chain

The activities within a firm which it has chosen to undertake in order to be able to compete. It is also used to describe the linked set of firms which together create a product or service.

Cost driver

Any factor or event that has a direct or indirect effect on the cost of an activity.

Chapter 7

Value chain *in practice* – forestry industry

Examining the data in Table 5.4 it is apparent that the two competing forest products firms have quite dissimilar cost structures. The value chain provides a framework for highlighting the magnitude of these differences in costs, what determines the magnitude of these differences and what actions management can take to overcome them. The most significant cost for each firm is purchasing – the unit cost of raw materials. As can be seen, the New Zealand firm enjoys a cost advantage of $50 per tonne, a substantial benefit. When this is examined in detail, it transpires that

Table 5.4 Competitive value chains

	Australian competitor	New Zealand competitor
	Unit costs, AU$	
Purchasing	150	100
In-bound logistics	20	30
Operations	160	180
Out-bound logistics	50	30
Marketing	50	60
Service	20	20
Margin	*150*	*180*
Price	600	600

the difference is due to exogenous factors – trees in New Zealand grow faster due to better climate and rainfall, a feature outside the control of management. The next largest cost component is operations, the cost of actually making the finished product. Here the Australian firm has a cost benefit of $20 per tonne. Analysing this cost further, it turns out that there are significant economies of scale in manufacturing, and Australian plants are on average larger. Managers of Australian firms may want to seriously consider mergers, to enhance their cost position. Similarly, New Zealand managers may want to consider the same strategy to increase their average plant size and gain the economies of scale possessed by the Australian firms.

The consequence of benchmarking these different cost structures is to reveal that the New Zealand firm enjoys a margin of $180 per tonne while the Australian firm has a margin of only $150 per tonne. Overcoming this differential will be difficult, since several of the costs are outside the control of management. However, the Australian firm may be able to reduce their outbound logistics costs – possibly by outsourcing.

are generally considered a back office function in the bank, with the total cost being a combination of processing and transmission costs, each of which has been influenced by technology. As transmission costs have fallen, banks and other financial institutions have been able to decouple the back office from the front office. Many call centres and transaction-processing centres are in locations such as India or Ghana. As with the forest products firms, the magnitude of the different cost elements varies from bank to bank. The management task is to understand their relative importance and what actions can be taken to reduce them – the concept of cost drivers.

5.7 COST DRIVERS

In a competitive environment, businesses have unrelenting pressures to reduce costs. The value chain provides a useful framework for understanding costs and their relative magnitude. Here we will focus on the drivers of long-term cost behaviour and how costs might be reduced. Ideally, we benchmark ourselves against competitors at each stage in the value chain. We first discuss two major drivers of cost: economies of scale and experience effects.

Economies of scale

Economies of scale are a major driver of strategy. They are the rationale behind many mergers and acquisitions based on the assumption that the merged entity will have lower costs through economies of scale, often with consequent job losses.

> **Economies of scale** *in practice* – Kraft
>
> Kraft CEO Rosenfeldt announced a target of $675 million cost savings over the three years following Kraft's successful bid for British confectioner Cadbury. Some sources fear large layoffs will be a consequence (Jones & Dorfman, 2010).

Economies of scale
Occur when the unit costs of a product, service or activity decline as the size of firm, or plant, increases.

Figure 5.7 shows a typical relationship between long-run average costs per unit and a measure of firm size – the number of units produced per year. When economies of scale are present, unit costs decline as the size of plant increases. As shown in Figure 5.7, the plant producing 200 units per year has lower unit costs than the plant producing 100 units per year. This difference is not due to capacity utilization, it is inherent in the production technology used by the two firms.

Consider the firm producing 100 units per year. At this production level its costs are at a minimum. If it produces 95 units per year or 105 units per year, its costs will rise, since these costs are given by the firm's short-run cost curve, where technology is assumed to be fixed. Graphs of economies of scale assume that the firm is operating optimally, given the technology available for a particular size of plant. Economies of scale are determined by the industry long-run cost curve which assumes different production technologies for different levels of output.

Relevant questions then become:

- How significant are economies of scale? Economies of scale will be significant when the firm is capital intensive. There are no economies of scale if all costs are variable. Consequently there are major economies of scale in industries such as commodity

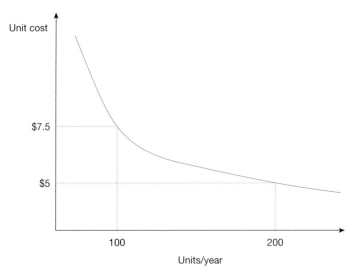

Figure 5.7 Economies of scale

chemicals, computer chips and aircraft manufacture. In these industries there are major benefits for being large – small competitors are cost uncompetitive.

- In which activities do economies of scale occur? Scale economies are often thought to be confined to manufacturing operations, but they can occur in other activities such as R&D and marketing. It may cost $M500 to develop a new ethical drug – so the firm has to be large. On the other hand, capital requirements for production are often low, permitting the entry of relatively small generic manufacturers when the innovator's patents expire.

- To what extent do scale effects act as a barrier to entry? If large scale effects characterize the industry, entrants have a dilemma. Do they enter on a smaller scale, requiring less capital investment and lower volumes to fill their facility, with the consequence that their costs will be uncompetitive? Or do they elect to construct a large plant so as to achieve economies of scale? This represents a significant investment and the firm needs to gain a substantial market share to break even.

- To what extent is optimal scale in the industry changing? Are there increasing benefits from scale or is the industry heading towards smaller scale, as shown in the two diagrams in Figure 5.8?

If there are increasing benefits of scale (Figure 5.8 (A)), then the optimal size of plant is increasing and we would expect to see increasing industry consolidation, with mergers and acquisitions. Firms that recognize the change can proactively acquire others and have a better chance of surviving the consolidation while retaining their autonomy. In the car industry, just such a process of consolidation built General Motors. More recently, Volkswagen A.G. has pursued just such a policy, grouping Audi, Seat, Skoda, Bentley, Bugatti and

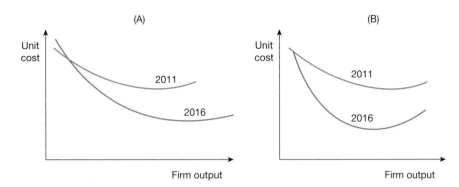

Figure 5.8 Changes in economies of scale

Lamborghini under their corporate Volkswagen umbrella. Similar consolidation has occurred in the pharmaceutical, banking, chemical, supermarket, food and insurance industries, as well as among such service companies as advertising agencies, law and accounting firms. When such consolidation occurs, firms not engaging in acquisition may well become targets for others.

Alternatively, the graph of economies of scale could be moving to the left, with smaller plants or firms developing advantages over larger firms, as shown in Figure 5.8 (B). This occurred in steel, where mini-mills had a significant cost advantage over large, integrated mills, so much so that many large firms such as Bethlehem Steel went out of business (Harreld *et al.*, 2007). This example highlights the need for continual innovation if a firm is to remain successful. The firm which is successful in innovating and altering the fundamental shape of the economies of scale curve will enjoy a possibly significant first-mover advantage.

Scale economics rest upon the ratio of fixed to variable cost, the volume sold and the impact of technology on long-run average cost. Each of these assumptions needs to be examined carefully in the light of already existing knowledge, as well as in the light of prospective future developments. Changes in economies of scale create substantial turbulence and change in an industry. Whether increasing scale leads to consolidation, or decreasing scale produces new entrants and lower prices, changes in economies of scale are one of the drivers of industry restructuring. Firms that recognize that scale economics are changing, and act in a timely manner, will usually enjoy a competitive advantage. Competitive advantage cannot be based on what was successful in yesterday's world; managers need to understand the economic characteristics of the world of the future (Christensen, 2001).

Challenge of strategic management

Economies of scale imply that larger firms enjoy lower unit costs than smaller firms. Is this always the case? What can cause larger firms to have higher unit costs than smaller firms?

Experience effect

Experience effect

Occurs when the unit cost of a product or service declines with cumulative output – the total number of units that the firm has ever produced.

Another major driver of costs is **experience effect** or learning. As a firm does a specific activity more often, it learns to do that activity better and more efficiently; in other words, its costs decrease.

As shown in Figure 5.9, the experience effect postulates that there is a relationship between unit cost and cumulative output, the total number of units of the product that the firm has ever produced, when the relationship is plotted on logarithmic scales. This cost decline has been observed in many industries, but is particularly noticeable in electronics. There have been dramatic reductions in the price (and, of course, the cost) of disk drives in terms of price per megabyte of memory, measured in constant dollars, dropping from about $400 in 1977 to about $0.10 by the mid-1990s and to $.001 by the late 1990s.

This dramatic drop in price has created many new market opportunities for such devices. One cause of this cost reduction is learning, a different concept to scale. Learning means we do things better, faster, with less wastage. We also modify the product to make it easier to manufacture, employing better inventory systems to reduce investment and adopt new technology. These cost reductions do not occur automatically; they are made to happen by aggressive managerial action.

In a competitive market, a firm needs to reduce costs along the characteristic industry cost curve. If not, its costs become uncompetitive and it may not survive. If a firm can expand faster than its competitors, it may be able to slide down the experience curve faster

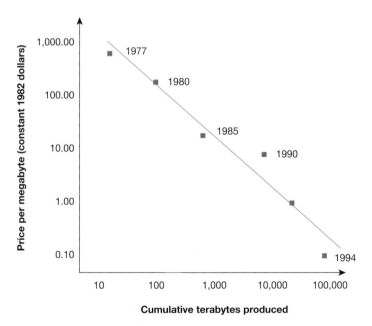

Figure 5.9 Disk drive experience curve

Source: C. M. Christensen, *The Innovator's Dilemma*, Boston, MA, 1997, p. 8, Copyright © 1997 by the Harvard Business School Publishing Corporation: all rights reserved. Reprinted by permission of Harvard Business School Press.

than these competitors, reducing costs more rapidly. So growth may be the overriding objective for the business, particularly if the overall market itself is growing rapidly.

These ideas lead to a possible strategy imperative: find a growth market, have a strategy which focuses on growth, drive costs down with this growth, reduce prices to get faster growth and end up with a dominant position in the market at maturity. At this time it may be impossible for the small share producer to achieve the same cost structure as the market leader. So the strategy imperative is 'dominate or divest', epitomized by Jack Welch's admonition to GE's businesses to be first or second in every market in which they competed.

An important qualifier of this argument occurs when a major innovation takes place. New technology may change the design of the product or the production process, perhaps enabling a competitor with less cumulative experience to leapfrog the existing cost leader. In economists' terms, we have to distinguish between the long-run and short-term cost curves.

Value drivers

As we noted earlier, any consideration of value chains that focuses exclusively on costs is potentially dangerous, for we should simultaneously consider how and where value is added for customers. Outsourcing or drastically reducing activities that are key to adding value for customers can create enormous problems.

5.8 KNOWLEDGE AND INTELLECTUAL CAPITAL

LEARNING OBJECTIVE 6

Summarize why strategic management will include an understanding of knowledge-based competition.

The national and international economy is being transformed by the increasing knowledge intensity of economic activity and by the growing importance of trade in knowledge products such as interest rate swaps. As several commentators have noted, we are moving to a knowledge-based society with firms becoming more knowledge intensive (Dumay, 2009). As indicative of this trend, the OECD has developed a knowledge index for products, based on products' R&D intensity. When this measure was used to assess the knowledge intensity of manufactured exports for the world economy as a whole, it was found that the index was stable during the 1970s at a level of about 0.70. However, by 1997 the index had risen to about 1.04, indicating the growth in knowledge intensity of products (Sheehan & Tegart, 1998).

Many of the successful companies of the last decade have been knowledge intensive. Firms such as ARM Holdings, Google, SAP and Apple have each blazed new pathways. Other companies are using technology to develop products and services in which an increasing amount of knowledge is embedded. The economic value of a drug, or a computer or a film is well beyond the materials of which it is composed. We can now purchase cars fitted with GPS systems, which provide a significant customer benefit in terms of locating lost or stolen cars. When digital city or regional maps supplement such systems, drivers can determine, in real time, better routes to their destinations that avoid heavy traffic or other impediments. Other knowledge-based innovations in cars include features such as fuel management systems, active suspension systems, electronic stability control, tyres that detect punctures and even diagnostics. Massey-Ferguson has developed a satellite system to record agricultural yield per square metre, so that the company is now in the business of yield management as well as tractors.

The increasing knowledge content of products and jobs arises from developments in information technology, which have allowed 'old' economy firms to develop smart systems containing substantial intellectual property rights. For example, in the early days of EFTS, Citibank developed sophisticated hardware and software to operate its retail banking system, including ATMs, but the value of the software never appeared on its balance sheet. Toyota, Wal-Mart, Aldi and many other firms have developed or purchased enhanced information systems to reduce inventory levels and the need for warehouses, reducing their capital intensity and enhancing their financial performance.

In other sectors of the economy, there has been major growth in what are generally called symbolic goods; that is, goods that can be compressed for transmission over lines. There has been, and continues to be, growth in the ability to digitally store, locate and transmit information (Blumentritt & Johnston, 1999). Financial advice, X-ray pictures, music and movies can all be transmitted over networks, the reach of which is not limited geographically. Innovation continues to increase the range of goods thus traded. For example, in the finance sector there has been an increase in what can be traded, with currency and interest rate swaps, index futures and so on. Increasing electronic connectivity arising from user-friendly interfaces, common standards and protocols and the ability to digitize data have facilitated these developments, which have been accompanied by explosive growth of the Internet and the World Wide Web. We are witnessing the emergence of a global knowledge economy, with the ability to deliver codified knowledge quickly and cheaply on a global basis.

These developments are being driven by the rapidly falling costs of information storage and transmission. Financial advisers distribute information electronically; consumers can buy and sell stock electronically, banks are allowing (or forcing) customers to perform their transactions electronically, either via ATMs or the Internet; the phenomenon is ubiquitous and pervasive. Indeed, in December 2009, the UK announced that cheques will be phased out as a medium of exchange by 2018 (Collinson, 2009).

An understanding of knowledge and its importance to strategy development is considered essential for strategic management. As Peter Drucker has noted, 'knowledge has become the key economic resource and the dominant, perhaps the only, source of competitive advantage' (Drucker, 1995). Before discussing knowledge and knowledge management, it is necessary to distinguish the difference between data, information and knowledge (Leonard, 2007).

Data consist of discrete objective facts about events, which are generally unstructured, without any meaning in themselves. Meaning comes from some analysis we perform on the data. For any firm there is generally a structured record of a transaction, which is the source of the data. For example, in buying groceries, we can describe the transaction in terms such as what products were purchased, at what price, who did the purchasing, what time of day, who was with the shopper, in which outlet did the purchase take place. Other data would be historical share prices or the profit levels of an acquisition target. Non-financial data might include employees' qualifications, or their attitudes as revealed on some scale. Such data are generally stored in a system, which can be evaluated in terms of cost, speed, capacity, as well as relevance and access.

Information is processed data that are intelligible to the recipient and are meant to change the way the recipient perceives something. Using the above example, information could be an analysis of the number of customers who bought, at the same shopping occasion, both products A and B. Information is data endowed with relevance and purpose and moves around a company in hard and soft networks. Hard networks include databases, reports and email while soft networks would comprise presentations and conversations. Information gives us an analysis of the data; it can be formalized in databases, manuals and documents and can be easily transmitted.

Knowledge is richer, broader and deeper than information. It is a combination of information together with experiences, values, context and insight. It reflects cognition and thinking by the recipient. In the case of a potential acquisition, knowledge would be reflected in the answers to such questions as, 'Is the price acceptable?' 'Can we integrate it with our current business?' Knowledge is fluid, aware of what is not known and contains judgement. Knowledge is thinking and comes from experience tested against others, informed by theory, facts and understanding. It is fuzzy, hard to communicate, difficult to express in words and depends on the owner. Knowledge is normally communicated by informal means and evolves with experience.

Knowledge can be considered to be a construction of reality rather than something that is true in an abstract or universal way. To the extent that knowledge represents 'truth' it offers a reliable basis for making predictions and developing causal associations. In the context of an economic entity such as a firm, knowledge should be close to action and should be evaluated by the decisions and actions to which it leads. It is knowledge that makes data relevant and meaningful. Many firms have too much data and have difficulty turning this into knowledge that can be used for decision-making. The firm is likely to get transaction data from such sources as an enterprise resource planning system, a customer relationship management system, a retail point-of-sale scanner or from e-commerce transactions, but they often have difficulty making use of these data. For example, in one study few firms indicated specific examples of decisions affected by ERP (Enterprise Resource Planning) data (Davenport, 2001).

Insight comes from the ability to combine knowledge in new ways to 'see' something that others have not. The history of invention is replete with examples of such insight. Dyson observed that the action of using a vacuum cleaner results in progressive blocking of the filter that in turn reduces its efficiency. Based on this insight, he persevered for years until he was able to perfect the bagless cleaner that has disrupted the vacuum cleaner market. Trevor Baylis observed that in the poorer countries of the world, large numbers of people were deprived of access to media because they had no mains power and could not afford batteries. He determined that he would design a clockwork radio to remove dependence on either. Some observers believe that Apple's iPad has a reasonable chance of disrupting the existing e-book market, since Apple plans a generous fee-sharing arrangement with publishers that has already resulted in a severing of the relationship between Amazon, and Macmillan, one of the world's largest English-language publishers (Allen, 2010).

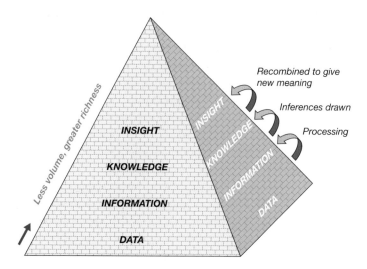

Figure 5.10 The relationship between data and insight
Reprinted and modified by permission of Robert Christian and Impact Planning Group

This relationship between data and insight is shown in Figure 5.10, emphasizing that data are raw and voluminous, while insight is rich and parsimonious, creatively drawing on many inputs.

Following Sullivan we believe it is sensible to discuss knowledge from both an individual and a collective perspective (Sullivan, 2000). Certainly individuals possess knowledge, but we also argue that organizations, as entities, also possess knowledge, such as values, group skills and unwritten rules and procedures. Organizational knowledge may be concentrated in particular individuals, with problems for the firm if they leave. A firm can lose knowledge through downsizing, so managers need to understand the knowledge base of the company and how to develop it.

Types of knowledge

Knowledge is difficult to come to grips with, but we need to be able to classify it to be able to discuss it in a meaningful manner, and to be able to manage its generation, transmission, storage and use. Possibly the most useful way to categorize knowledge is whether it is explicit or tacit. This relates to how easily knowledge can be codified in terms that enable it to be understood by a wider audience. If knowledge can be codified it can be made explicit and easily transferred.

Explicit knowledge

Explicit knowledge can be put on paper. It can be codified in sentences or articulated in books, scientific formulae, specifications, manuals and reports. It can be transmitted using formal language. Since explicit knowledge can be codified it is readily and cheaply transferable.

Explicit knowledge exists at both the organizational and the personal level. Organizational explicit knowledge should be easily accessible by any member of the firm, have a life beyond the tenure of an individual employee and be continually updated and improved. It is typically codified in the firm's systems and databases. For example, the firm may have a formal process for the evaluation of acquisition candidates, with information on market characteristics, competitors and so on (►Chapter 9). Under these conditions an explicit document exists, which can be examined, changed, improved and modified. Documentation of processes enables them to be communicated, learned by new employees and transferred from one set of employees to another, providing opportunities for both individual and organizational learning. Management consulting firms, for example, try to document their experience on a given project, explicating what lessons were learned and what can be used on other assignments. Information technology, with its rapidly reducing costs, has been a major enabler and facilitator in the transfer of explicit knowledge both within and between organizations. As we will see later, there are a number of technological platforms, such as data warehouses, which have been adopted to facilitate knowledge transfer.

Chapter 9

Tacit knowledge

Tacit knowledge is knowledge that is difficult to articulate in a meaningful and complete way, it is hard to see and to explain. It is tied to the senses, skills and perceptions of individuals and is not easily transferred to others. Tacit knowledge is unarticulated and includes intuition, perspectives, beliefs, values, know-how and skills. Tacit knowledge exists in people's heads, and is augmented and shared through interpersonal interaction and social relationships. Often oral, it can be spread when people tell stories around the water cooler. However, it is deeply rooted in individuals' actions and experiences as well as their values and emotions. It is therefore usually highly personal, hard to formalize and difficult to communicate or share with others. Tacit knowledge is automatic, and is accessed and used with little thought. But it can also be wrong, but hard to change, which can pose formidable management difficulties.

Examples of tacit knowledge include the advertising executive who 'knows' what a good advertisement looks like, an R&D scientist who 'knows' that a particular technological solution will work, a CEO who 'knows' that the organizational culture of a takeover target is compatible. In each case the individual finds it impossible to clearly enunciate the basis for the view that they hold.

We suggest that tacit knowledge also exists at the organizational level. Organizational tacit knowledge subsumes culture, values and principles as well as ways of doing things. When we discuss knowledge transfer in Chapter 11 (►Chapter 11), we will see that a major challenge for strategic managers is to find ways to transform individuals' tacit knowledge into organizationally explicit knowledge, so that the firm as a whole may capitalize upon it. Some firms have developed expert systems and artificial intelligence systems to assist in this process.

Chapter 11

Knowledge can also be categorized depending on whether it is firm-specific or not. The most general level of knowledge would be scientific, knowledge that is widely known and understood by all professionals in a field. Examples would be knowledge of the statistical tools in market research, or the scientific knowledge behind encryption for e-commerce security systems. Such knowledge is easily obtainable and equally valuable to many businesses.

Industry knowledge is widely known to all competitors within an industry, for example, how to operate a blast furnace or the principles behind electronic fuel management systems for cars. In some circumstances firms can leverage such industry knowledge, as when a consultant or a lawyer specializes by industry and is used by many clients in the same industry.

These two levels of knowledge are essential to operate within an industry, but generally do not provide any measure of a competitive advantage. They may provide a barrier to entry, since it may be more difficult for firms outside the car industry to acquire detailed knowledge of technology currently used within that industry, whether it is satellite navigation systems or the fluid mechanics of automatic transmissions.

In contrast, firm-specific knowledge is unique knowledge that exists in one firm but not in others. Since it is unique, such knowledge is difficult to duplicate by competitors. To do so would take considerable time and resources. Knowledge of this latter type is the only real basis of a competitive advantage for a firm.

Characteristics of knowledge products

Knowledge is different from other resources such as labour and capital. Its unique properties influence how it can and should be managed, as well as what kinds of strategies are appropriate. We now review some of its relevant characteristics.

Network effects and increasing returns

Knowledge products often show **network externalities** (Teece, 1998). Under these conditions, the value of the product or service to a given user increases with the number of users of the product or service. This phenomenon is referred to as Metcalfe's Law. Examples of such network effects are the Windows operating systems or the Internet. Since Windows is widely used, other firms apart from Microsoft write compatible application programs, so it becomes more valuable to users and thus even more widely used. In markets with strong network effects, when one brand gets a significant market share, the value to users rises, creating a strong incentive for people to use the product or service more.

In the production of physical goods, economists worked on the basis of diminishing returns, with the assumption that all industry participants were using the same production technology and that at some volume marginal costs increase, limiting scale advantages of a firm (i.e. the long-run average cost curve eventually begins to rise because of so-called diseconomies of scale). Such is not the situation with many knowledge-based products. In knowledge-based industries with increasing returns, the firm that is ahead tends to stay there. No matter how a firm gets ahead in the early stages of a market, whether by luck or good strategy, increasing returns amplify the advantage. In technology markets, these increasing returns may also be driven by standards, particularly when these are 'owned' by a single firm. The more a protocol gains acceptance, the greater the consumer benefits and the better chance the standard has of becoming dominant. A major goal for the firm in knowledge-intensive markets is therefore to ensure that the product or service that it has developed becomes the standard in the industry, actual or de facto. The innovating firm may even give away technology to help it become a standard. Alternatively, it may enter into alliances with competitors and customers to get the product adopted as a standard. As we saw in Chapter 4 (▶Chapter 4), the WiMAX Forum is developing alliances with customers, suppliers and competitors to ensure an industry standard that it has developed. Indeed, Linux has achieved great success in the server market based on giving away its operating system, a success that Nokia obviously hopes to emulate with Symbian. Customers typically favour so-called 'open systems' approaches because of the freedom of choice they engender.

Chapter 4

Since increasing returns tend to create 'winner-take-all' markets, different corporate strategies emerge. In these markets, rewards go to the firms that excel at sensing and seizing opportunities. Seizing opportunities involves identifying and combining the relevant complementary assets needed to support the business. Winners are those with the cognitive and managerial skills to discern the shape of the play. Consequently, firms need to be highly entrepreneurial, with a flat hierarchy, powerful success incentives, high autonomy and the ability to navigate quick turns; in short, companies able to rapidly transform and change themselves. Once these leader firms are established they become very difficult to dislodge. A classic example of the difficulty in replacing an incumbent is provided by the QWERTY keyboard, which was invented in the late 1880s for mechanical typewriters. The layout of the keyboard was established to minimize the possibility of the strikers hitting one another. Once this keyboard layout was established, it proved very difficult to replace, even though technology removed the original basis for its design.

High leverage

The bulk of the costs of knowledge products lies in the fixed costs of their creation, not in their manufacture or distribution. Information technology has large up-front costs in research, development and design engineering, so the first copy of a piece of software may cost millions of dollars. The second has a direct manufacturing cost of almost zero. Hence, winners in knowledge-intensive industries have to make huge bets early. Forming partnerships early is therefore not only helpful in establishing a standard, but is also a method of risk reduction. Another alternative (if affordable) strategy is to operate with very low margins to build the business at the expense of short-term profit. This appears to be the strategy with Amazon.com, which has incurred substantial development costs.

Other properties of knowledge products

Knowledge has some characteristics of a public good, in that it can be used without being consumed. One individual can use a piece of knowledge and this does not diminish another person's ability to also use it. Knowledge can be in more than one place at the same time and we can sell knowledge to more than one person. This is not the case for tangible products. We cannot (or, at least, should not!) sell the same car to more than one person. An airplane can only be assigned to one route, but an airline reservation system can be used simultaneously in multiple tasks with multiple customers. As is common with knowledge products, such a system is scalable. Systems can be designed to handle huge increases in use with little additional expense.

It is also difficult to judge the value of knowledge before you purchase. Knowledge has uncertain value; it is difficult to predict who will get the value from knowledge. The firm may bear the cost of development only to find that others reap the benefits, as would be the case with pirated software. These characteristics may result in the firm under-investing in knowledge products. Further, the value of knowledge can depreciate very quickly. Knowledge of future share prices would have considerable value; knowledge of historical share prices has very limited value. So knowledge is often very time sensitive. Finally, knowledge also becomes increasingly fragmented over time; it gets deeper and more complex and has to be continually renewed and extended.

 ## 5.9 SUMMARY

In this chapter we have emphasized the importance of the resource-based view of the firm as a determinant of success. Firm performance is strongly influenced by the resources of the firm, and how well these resources are integrated into capabilities. In addition, future success requires that the firm continue to develop and expand its resources and capabilities.

Strategy development also requires an understanding of where the firm creates value, the costs incurred in creating this value and the drivers of these costs, such as economies of scale and learning. The value chain is a useful tool to use to disaggregate total costs into the relevant activities so that a better understanding of costs and their behaviour can be developed. We would emphasize that such analyses should not be static. Managerial foresight in understanding how the firm's value chain is evolving can provide the basis for an innovative firm strategy. A firm, which recognizes the increasing importance of economies of scale, can develop strategies to exploit this understanding, such as a merger, to achieve a competitive advantage.

Managers are responsible for managing the assets under their control, both tangible and intangible, and for many firms the value of intangible assets outweighs the value of their tangible assets. Yet accounting systems focus almost entirely on tangible assets, which are represented on the balance sheet at cost less accumulated depreciation. These intangible assets complement the tangible assets of the firm and managers need to reorient their attention towards them. When intangible assets are ignored in the financial statements of the firm, managers may be inclined to under-invest in these assets and over-invest in tangible assets, resulting in a misallocation of resources. At the same time, managers may not develop the skills required to develop and manage intellectual capital. Management of intellectual assets requires capturing and disseminating what the firm has learned over time, sharing ideas and experiences across functional and organizational boundaries. In a rapidly changing global world, these intangible assets, including knowledge, have become the key economic resource and the dominant – and perhaps the only – source of competitive advantage (Drucker, 1995). This makes it imperative that the firm develops systems to measure, and manage, these intangible assets (Stewart, 1999).

Measures such as return on equity or return on assets will overstate performance, since intellectual capital is not included in the denominator. Leveraging intellectual capital means that managers should promote, not restrict its use and ensure it is disseminated and used throughout the organization. The firm must develop an infrastructure that facilitates the development, sharing and use of knowledge. Connecting the relevant parties, capturing know-how in context and delivering it when and where it is needed requires the existence of a culture that values intellectual capital and provides incentives for knowledge generation, sharing and use. This was a major motivation behind the concept of the 'boundary-less' corporation articulated under Welch's leadership at GE, but in many firms the obstacles to sharing across internal organizational lines are still considerable.

Finally, developments in knowledge and information technology are affecting firm boundaries by altering the mix between those activities undertaken by the firm and those provided by outsiders. Knowledge-based theory suggests that activities with a high degree of non-firm-specific knowledge and which are also explicit will move to the market and be provided by outsiders. Already there is major growth in contracted employees and other forms of non-regular employment (Burton-Jones, 1999). Only activities that involve high levels of tacit and firm-specific specialized knowledge will remain in the firm, and become the core activities through which the firm generates a competitive advantage. Since information technology is likely to continue to reduce the uncertainty and complexity of market contracting we expect to see more outsourcing, inter-firm cooperation, franchising, disintermediation and electronic markets.

Managing intellectual capital requires new organizational forms and new managerial skills. Firms will have to change in the way they behave with respect to people, incentives, technology and culture. The focus will be on attracting and retaining high-calibre employees, which requires a different culture and style in the firm, in particular, a move away from a command-and-control culture. In addition, the form of the relationship with employees will change and full-time employees will increasingly be viewed as volunteers active in managing their own careers rather than employees per se. The firm does not own people, and individuals who possess valuable intellectual capital can walk out of the door at any time if they consider that the firm is treating them poorly. If knowledge workers have loyalty to their profession, rather than the company, an autocratic style of management is unlikely to be successful. Firms of the future will have to pay considerable attention to attracting and retaining high-calibre employees and need to develop rewards that align their personal interests with those of the firm. For some employees this may mean stock options and retention bonuses; for others it may mean a sense of professional challenge and allowing the individual free time to create new knowledge.

But while managers may intuitively believe that strategic advantage comes from superior knowledge assets, they still find it difficult to make the linkage explicit. Such an alignment is difficult when knowledge is primarily tacit and in the minds of individual employees. The link between knowledge and culture is vital. Managers must facilitate a culture that values the creation, sharing and use of knowledge, one that includes incentives for sharing.

VIEW FROM THE TOP

IBM

In 2008 IBM conducted a worldwide study of over a thousand CEOs, asking them what capabilities would be required for the enterprise of the future (IBM, 2009). The findings are summarized below:

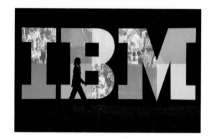

- **Hungry for change**. The enterprise of the future will be capable of changing quickly and easily. Rather than responding to changes it will shape and lead them, seeing market and industry shifts as a chance to move ahead of the competition.
- **Innovative beyond customer imagination**. Such a firm will surpass the expectations of customers. Deep, collaborative relationships will enable it to surprise customers with innovations that will make both them and its own business more successful.
- **Globally integrated**. The enterprise of the future will be strategically designed to access the best capabilities, knowledge and assets from wherever they reside in the world and apply them wherever they are required in the world.
- **Disruptive by nature**. Such a company will radically challenge its business model, disrupting the basis of competition. It will shift the value proposition, overturning delivery approaches, and, as opportunities arise, will re-invent itself and its entire industry.
- **Genuine, not just generous**. The enterprise of the future will go beyond philanthropy and compliance, and will reflect genuine concern for society in all its actions and decisions.

QUESTIONS

1 What do you think of this list of capabilities? Would you add or subtract anything?
2 Do you know of firms that already exhibit any or all of these characteristics?
3 What would be some of the problems you would anticipate in working in an organization of the type described above?

OATS

OATS (Oil Advisory Technical Services) was established in 1984 by two entrepreneurs, one with marketing expertise and the other with technical expertise, one of whom had an order for a lubricant recommendation book. By 1994, the company offered two services reflecting the two owners' areas of expertise: a lubricants recommendation book for the UK market and an advertising agency servicing a range of industries.

Today OATS offers lubricant data solutions. In its basic form this simply means providing a speedy and accurate answer to the question 'which oil?' Lubricant manufacturers' technical people need to understand the changes taking place among products offered by OEMs to ensure that they develop the appropriate lubricants, their marketing managers need information regarding the application of lubricants to market them, sales people need the information to advise clients, and IT people need the information to provide accurate data to internal and external stakeholders.

OATS is effectively an intermediary between OEMs and lubricant companies, collecting information continuously from each so as to provide a comprehensive and versatile lubricant solution service enabling lubricant manufacturers and re-sellers to solve their specific lubrication problems, and offering a service to match the oil company's products to the specifications. Figure 5.11 shows OATS's position in relation to its two key stakeholders – OEMs and lubricant manufacturers.

Figure 5.11 highlights the complexity of the problem. On one side there are tens of thousands of pieces of equipment, each requiring specific types of lubricant and on the other side a large number of lubricants with different properties (such as viscosity, volatility, flash and fire points) from many lubricant manufacturers. Matching the equipment with the right lubricant is not simple, as the number of potential possibilities is large and the right selection is dependent not only on the technical specification of equipment but also on the specific operating condition and the marketing decisions of a the specific oil company. So where does the information come from? The technical information comes from

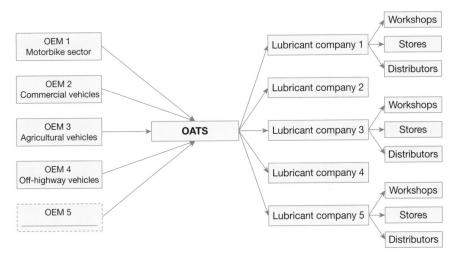

Figure 5.11 OATS's position in the lubricant value chain

MINI-CASE

OEMs and lubricant information from the oil companies. This is a classic 'make or buy' decision. An oil company can collect the information from OEMs and develop an in-house database or it can license a service, from OATS.

From its inception in 1984 to 1993 OATS had never made a proper profit, and in 1993 the firm was heavily in debt for over £140k, and with no realizable assets. It housed two incongruous businesses – an advertising agency and a lubricant recommendation guide business. Turnover was £640k; revenue split between the advertising agency and the lubricant recommendation guide was 66 per cent and 34 per cent, respectively. All the sales revenue was generated from activities in the UK. Nonetheless, OATS possessed valuable knowledge in the shape of a lubricant recommendation database and UK-based customers with strong brand names. Almost all the leading lubricants marketers in the country, including Shell, BP, Castrol, Esso, Total, Elf and Fina, were on the database.

Sebastian Crawshaw, OATS's current chairman and chief executive, acquired the company in late 1993. While he had no prior knowledge of running an advertising/marketing business, he considered that his MBA experience would enable him to manage it with the assistance of the leading account director.

The advertising agency business operated in a crowded marketplace (143 competitors advertising in the local Yellow Pages), lacked scale and margins were low. The lubricants database business offered more promise, with a small renewable revenue stream.

The foundation of the data business was scarce knowledge, difficult to assemble, and relied on lubricants expertise. Being UK-centric, it was produced only in English, on paper, and its breadth of OEM equipment coverage was limited (only three industrial sectors). A competitor was already offering several languages and more sectors. Globally, however, the market space contained only a handful of competitors.

Crawshaw wanted to focus his resources on developing a database business with a growing renewable revenue stream, but he kept the marketing services business going, providing essential working capital. Eventually, however, it shrank to virtually nothing in 2002 and was given away to the original account director.

The key strategic decisions both before and following the divestment of the advertising business were how best to deploy the firm's scarce financial and human resources. To be competitive the lubricant data business required significant financial resources and know-how. To avoid diluting his scarce resources (limited capital, development capability and marketing capability), Crawshaw decided to focus his efforts on a single industry, the lubricants sector of the oil industry, not least because of its scale (over S30bn market p.a.).

Confidence in OATS's capability to maintain confidentiality of commercially sensitive material entrusted to it by competing lubricant manufacturers was of paramount importance. Maintaining a close relationship with OEM manufacturers and good lines of communication in order to update information was also critical. Abilities to partner and liaise upstream and downstream, gather and provide accurate information in a timely manner, customize services, and retain partner confidence and trust were among the key success factors.

It was the view of the CEO that to succeed the service had to be offered internationally because of domestic market size constraints and the international nature of the oil business. The successful implementation of this strategy was predicated on: (a) development of close partnerships with the key customers, the leading home-based oil companies; (b) to leverage the credibility developed in the base country to expand overseas; and (c) continued focus on value-added elements.

The essential challenge was to develop a close fit between value propositions of OATS's lubricant solution service and the market needs. This revolved around four key issues: understanding the target customers within lubricant businesses; depth and breadth of information – horizontal (sectors covered) and vertical (extent of OEM coverage within the chosen sectors); format; and the functionality of the offerings.

Market evolution

Lubricant specifications had been mainly driven by fuel economy and extended drainage intervals up to the 1990s. As a result, the cycle of specification change was reduced from every ten years to every five years. The rate of cycle specification changes gathered further speed in the late 1990s. The key was the change in attitudes towards climate change. The Kyoto agreement in 1997 was followed by emission control legislation in the EU, US and Asia. The primary aim of legislation was to reduce the emission of greenhouse gases. To meet the requirements of legislation, OEMs had to speed up their drive for fuel economy, and further extend intervals between lubricant drainage. As a result, OEMs are producing more demanding engineering solutions, and lubricant manufacturers need to respond with new products to keep pace with changes made by the OEM and legislation/regulation governing emission. This produced another significant reduction in the time interval between lubricant specification changes. Furthermore, as the result of these changes new standards emerged. The universal standard until the turn of the century was US API (American Petroleum Institute) but in the late 1990s the European Automotive industry launched its own standards, ACEA, adding further to the complexity of lubricant specifications.

In 1997 OATS won a contract with BP-Mobil to provide a floppy disk service for around 500 distributors. OATS leveraged this opportunity and took advantage of the emerging technology to initially replace the paper lubricant recommendation guide with floppies and then CDs. This reduced costs and enabled OATS to create added-value features.

Later on OATS took advantage of widespread diffusion of the Web and started offering web-based solutions, using it as a distribution medium for the OATS database – renamed EARL (Electronic Automotive Recommended Lubricants).

The move to different formats required careful project management and relied on in-house lubricant, programming and IT development capabilities. The volume of data – number of OEMs' equipment and sectors where equipment is used – is an important competitive factor. OATS progressively increased the coverage of database from three to five sectors. In 2007 EARL, the basic OATS database, covered 65,000 pieces of equipment and lubricant recommendations relating to over 350,000 possibile applications.

The lubricant solution business was traditionally aimed at technical specialists in companies producing lubricants. Visiting hundreds of lubricant producers across a large number of countries provided Cranshaw and his team with unrivalled insight in terms of structure, roles, requirements, etc. This customer intimacy and insight was critical in identifying other users such as marketing specialists, sales specialists, IT specialists and lubricant general managers. OATS used its basic database and expertise to develop applications with functionality targeted specifically for use by these different stakeholders.

Expanding the business overseas raised the need to translate the database into other languages. This was another major and costly project. The other issue was customization to meet specific needs of particular markets or regions. Figure 5.12 shows OATS's transformation from 1984 to 2007.

Over the years, OATS has redefined its vision. Its current vision is:

> to be the preferred provider of information and productivity solutions for the lubricant sector, worldwide.

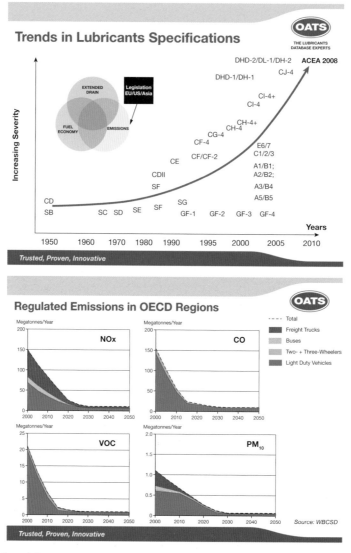

Figure 5.12 Trends in lubrication specification and permitted emissions in OECD region

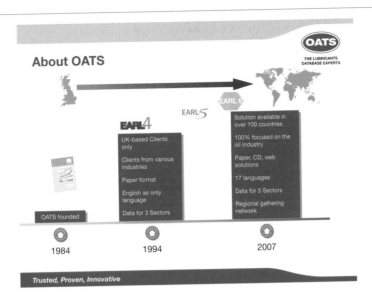

Figure 5.13 Transformation since 1984

The competition

OATS's main European competitor is Olyslager. Founded 60 years ago, it has undergone a series of major ownership changes. In 2007 the firm was part of a Swiss-based automotive information service, Eurotax-Glass, owned by a private equity firm. The Olyslager database contained more information, some of which was very old. While they had not invested in the value-added tools in the same way as OATS had, they have benefited from a data restructuring to meet the needs of the emerging automotive catalogue market. Previously another competitor, Emergie, based in France, failed to invest to create the scale needed and ultimately OATS acquired the remains of the bankrupt business.

The cost of entry to the market is high because of the high cost of customer acquisition and path dependency of some KSF factors such partnering with user groups (oil companies), effective lines of communication with a large number of OEMs, trust, deep customer insight, and brand recognition.

The future

OATS is now a successful company that has been growing steadily with a focus on 'which oil?' In 2007 its turnover was approximately £1.7 million, with an operating margin of 45 per cent, and ROA of 14 per cent and is generating cash. The company employs close to 20 people who come from a range of different countries. These employees are roughly evenly split between lubricant technical function, sales/marketing and administration with some software development capabilities.

OATS has identified that oil company documentation could be an interesting area for complementary expansion. Oil companies (as part of the wider Chemicals sector) have to provide extensive technical documentation. Every product needs to have Technical Data Sheets, Product Data Sheets and Material Safety Data sheets (in the appropriate language for the market) some of which are linked via the EARLWEB sites. This will require deep software development skills.

■ Where should the emphasis of OATS's development be placed?

■ While the US is the world's largest lubricants market, it is expected that the world's manufacturing base will move to lower cost countries in the East. What should OATS do about this? Should they expand in Europe? Seek to buy their main rival, Olyslager? Expand in the US? Develop in Asia? Should they expand into the documentation business? What about the automotive cataloguing business? Should Cranshaw use the hard-saved cash to build or to buy?

QUESTIONS

You are an intern at OATS and you have been asked to prepare a short report addressing the following points:

1 Identify the capabilities and competencies essential to OATS's transformation thus far.
2 OATS faces a number of strategic choices. Taking into account OATS's vision and capabilities/ competences, suggest an appropriate course of action.
3 In the light of the strategies you propose, make recommendations regarding capabilities and competences that should be retained in their present form, those that should be further developed, and those that would not serve a useful purpose going forward.

REVIEW QUESTIONS

1 Why is it important for a firm to understand its internal resources and capabilities? Is an understanding of the internal environment more important than an understanding of the external environment?
2 What are the differences between tangible and intangible resources? Are intangible resources a superior basis to tangible resources for developing and sustaining a competitive advantage?
3 For a firm with which you are familiar, identify one or more capabilities and discuss these capabilities in terms of the five properties discussed in this chapter.
4 For the firm selected above, can you identify any new capabilities developed by the firm over the last five years? How were these developed?
5 Select a retail firm such as a supermarket. Develop the value chain for this firm and discuss the changes occurring at each level of the chain. What new strategies could the firm adopt to take advantage of these changes?
6 Provide examples of firms which have restructured their value chain. How was this achieved?
7 Knowledge will become the dominant means of achieving competitive advantage in the future. Discuss.

REFERENCES

Allen, K. (2010) Amazon shelves Macmillan titles in ebook row. Retrieved 31 January. www.guardian. co.uk/business/2010/jan/31/amazon-shelves-macmillan-titles.

Ambrosini, V., Bowman, C. & Collier, N. (2009) Dynamic capabilities: An exploration of how firms renew their resource base. *British Journal of Management, 20*, S9–S24.

Apple (2009) Form 10–K, 2009. Retrieved 20 January 2010. www.apple.com/sitemap/about-apple/ investors/form-10-k-2009.

Argall, C. (2010) CEO message on capabilities. *About Medicare*, 18 May. www.medicareaustralia. gov.au/about/careers/capability/ceo-message.jsp.

ARM Holdings (2009) *Annual Report*. http://ir.arm.com/phoenix.zhtml?c=197211&p=irol-reports annual.

ARM Holdings (2010) ARM Holdings Plc Results, 26 October, from http://ir.arm.com/phoenix. zhtml?c=197211&p=irol-irhome.

ARM (2008) Annual report.

Bang-Olufsen (2010) Competences. *Company*. www.bang-olufsen.com/picture-sound-competences.

Barney, J. B. & Clark, D. N. (2007) *Resource-Based Theory: Creating and Sustaining Competitive Advantage*. New York: Oxford University Press.

Berthon, P., Hulbert, J. M. & Pitt, L. F. (1999) To serve or to create? Strategic orientations towards customers and innovation. *California Management Review, 42*(1), 37–58.

Blumentritt, R. & Johnston, R. (1999) Towards a strategy for knowledge management. *Technology Analysis and Strategic Management, 11*(3), 287–300.

Bogner, W. C. & Bansal, P. (2007) Knowledge management as the basis of sustained high performance. *Journal of Management Studies, 44*(1), 165–188.

Bryner, M. (2007) DuPont CEO: Improve business capability continuity capability. *Chemical Week*, 7 August.

Burton-Jones, A. (1999) *Knowledge Capitalism*. Oxford: Oxford University Press.

Calthrop, P., Gottfredson, M. & Puryear, R. (2010) Capability sourcing: From the periphery to the core. *CEO Forum Group: Strategy and Growth*. www.ceoforum.com.au/article-detail.cfm?cid=6108&t=/ Mark-Gottfredson—Bain—Company/Capability-sourcing-From-the-periphery-to-the-core/.

Christensen, C. M. (2001) The past and future of competitive advantage. *Sloan Management Review, 42*(2), 105–109.

Collinson, P. (2009) Cheques to be bounced into history. *The Guardian*, 15 December. www.guardian. co.uk/business/2009/dec/15/cheques-bounced-out-history.

Collis, D. J. & Montgomery, C. A. (1998) *Corporate Strategy: A Resource-Based Approach*. Boston, MA: Irwin/McGraw-Hill.

Coyne, K. P. (1997) Is your core competence a mirage. *McKinsey Quarterly*, (1), 40–54.

Crook, T. R., Ketchen, D. J. J., Combs, J. G. & Todd, S. Y. (2008) Strategic resources and performance: A meta analysis. *Strategic Management Journal, 29*(11), 1141–1154.

D'Aveni, R. A., Dagnino, G. B. & Smith, K. G. (2010) The age of temporary advantage. *Strategic Management Journal, 31*(13), 1371–1385.

Davenport, T. H. *et al.* (2001) Data to knowledge to results: Building an analyical capability. *California Management Review, 43*(2), 117–138.

Drucker, P. F. (1995) *Managing in a Time of Great Change*. New York: Truman Talley Books/Dutton.

Dumay, J. C. (2009) Intellectual capital measurement: A critical approach. *Journal of Intellectual Capital, 10*(2), 190–202.

Easterby-Smith, M., Lyles, M. A. & Peteraf, M. A. (2009) Dynamic capabilities: Current debates and future directions. *British Journal of Management, 20*, S1–S8.

Edvinsson, L. & Malone, M. S. (1997) *Intellectual Capital.* New York: HarperCollins.

Eisenhardt, K. M. & Jeffrey, M. (2000) Dynamic capabilities: What are they? *Strategic Management Journal, 21*(Special Issue), 1105–1121.

Gallego, I. & Rodriguez, L. (2005) Situation of intangible assets in Spanish firms: An empirical analysis. *Journal of Intellectual Capital, 6*(1), 105–126.

Groupe Dassult (2010) History and people. www.dassault.fr/en/portail1.php?docid=4.

Guillén, M. F. & García-Canal, E. (2009) The American model of the multinational firm and the 'new' multinationals from emerging economies. *Academy of Management Perspectives, 23*(2), 23–35.

Hall, B. H. (2007) The value of R&D and patents in European firms. www.voxeu.org/index.php?q=node/727.

Hamel, G. & Prahalad, C. K. (1994) Competing for the future. *Harvard Business Review,* (July–August), 122–128.

Harreld, J. B., O'Reilly, C. A. & Tushman, M. L. (2007) Dynamic capabilities at IBM: Driving strategy into action. *California Management Review, 49*(4), 21–43.

Hawawini, G., Subramanian, V. & Verdin, P. (2003) Is performance driven by industry or firm-specific factors? A new look at the evidence. *Strategic Management Journal, 24*(1), 1–16.

Helfat, C. E. & Raubitschek, R. S. (2000) Product sequencing: Co-evolution of knowledge, capabilities and products. *Strategic Management Journal, 21*(Special Issue), 961–979.

IBM (2009) The enterprise of the future. *IBM Global CEO Study.* www-935.ibm.com/services/us/gbs/bus/pdf/ceo-study-executive-summary.pdf.

Interbrand (2009) Best global brands, 2009. www.interbrand.com/best_global_brands.aspx

Internet pioneers (2001) *The Economist,* 3 February, pp. 73–75.

Johnson, G., Scholes, K. & Whittington, R. (2008) *Exploring Corporate Strategy,* 8th edn. Harlow: Prentice-Hall.

Jones, D. & Dorfman, B. (2010) Kraft snares Cadbury for $19.6 billion, 19 January. www.reuters.com/article/idUSTRE60H1N020100119?type=globalMarketsNews.

King, A. W., Fowler, S. W. & Zeithaml, C. P. (2001) Managing organizational competencies for competitive advantage: The middle management edge. *Academy of Management Executive, 15*(2), 95–106.

Leonard, D. (2007) Knowledge transfer within organizations. In K. Ichijo & I. Nonaka (eds), *Knowledge Creation and Management.* Oxford: Oxford University Press.

Mascarenhas, B., Baveja, A. & Jamil, M. (1998) Dynamics of core competencies in leading multinational companies. *California Management Review, 40*(4), 117–132.

Mauri, A. J. & Michaels, M. P. (1998) Firm and industry effects with strategic management: An empirical examination. *Strategic Management Journal, 19*(3), 211–219.

McGahan, A. M. & Porter, M. E. (1997) How much does industry matter, really? *Strategic Management Journal, 18*(Special Issue), 15–30.

Newey, L. R. & Zahra, S. A. (2009) The evolving firm: How dynamic and operating capabilities interact to enable entrepreneurship. *British Journal of Management, 20*(Special Issue), S81–S100.

O'Brien, K. J. (2009) Nokia tries to undo blunders in US. *The New York Times,* 18 October. www.nytimes.com/2009/10/19/technology/companies/19nokia.html?_r=2.

Porter, M. E. (1985) *Competitive Advantage.* New York: Free Press.

Prahalad, C. K. & Hamel, G. (1990) The core competence of the corporation. *Harvard Business Review,* (May–June), 79–93.

Schreyögg, G. & Kliesch-Eberl, M. (2007) How dynamic can organizational capabilities be? Towards a dual-process model of capability dynamization. *Strategic Management Journal, 38*(9), 913–933.

Sheehan, P. & Tegart, G. (eds) (1998) *Working For the Future*. Melbourne: Victoria University Press.

Stewart, T. A. (1999) *Intellectual Capital*. New York: Doubleday.

Sullivan, P. H. (2000) *Value-Driven Intellectual Capital*. New York: Wiley.

Teece, D. J. (1998) Capturing value from knowledge assets: The new economy, markets for know-how and intangible assets. *California Management Review, 40*(3), 55–79.

Teece, D. J. (2007) Explicating dynamic capabilities: The nature and microfoundations of (sustainable) enterprise performance. *Strategic Management Journal, 28*(13), 1319–1350.

Teece, D. J., Pisano, G. & Shuen, A. (1997) Dynamic capabilities and strategic management. *Strategic Management Journal, 18*(7), 509–533.

ThomsonReuters (2009) M/B values. *Data Stream*. http://thomsonreuters.com/.

Torres, A. (1999) Unlocking the value of intellectual assets. *McKinsey Quarterly*, (4), 28–37.

Tripsas, M. & Gavetti, G. (2000) Capabilities, cognition and inertia: Evidence from digital imaging. *Strategic Management Journal, 21*(Special Issue), 1147–1161.

Witcher, B. J., Chau, V. S. & Harding, P. (2008) Dynamic capabilities: Top executive audits and hoshin kanri at Nissan South Africa. *International Journal of Operations and Production Management, 28*(6), 540–561.

Yu, E. (2009) Microsoft. *China Business Weekly*, 7 December.

For a range of further resources supporting this chapter, please visit the companion website for *Strategic Management* at www.routledge.com/cw/fitzroy.

Section 3

STRATEGY DEVELOPMENT

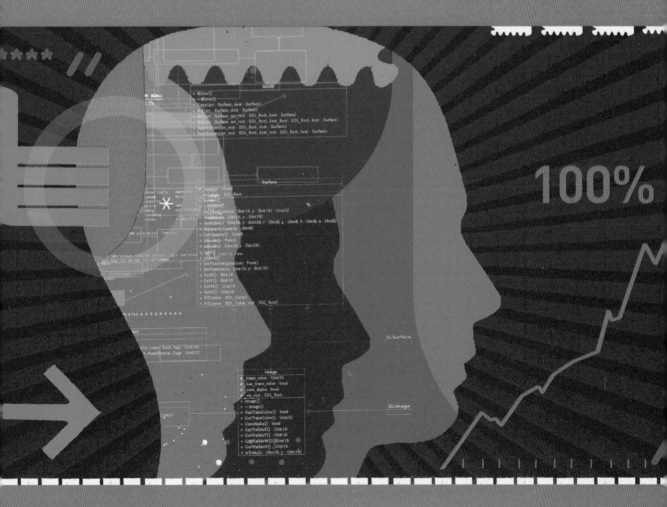

CHAPTER 6

CREATING FUTURE DIRECTION

LEARNING OBJECTIVES

Upon completing this chapter you should be able to:

1 Formulate a strategy which includes an understanding of what that strategy is designed to achieve.

2 Utilize the key concepts of effective vision, values, mission and objectives.

3 Apply the concepts of vision, values, mission and objectives at both the corporate and the business unit level.

4 Give examples of non-financial as well as financial objectives.

5 Integrate the concepts of vision, values, mission and objectives in a consistent manner.

CANON

In common with many companies around the world, Canon was severely affected by the 2008/09 recession. Nonetheless, the company remained constant in its vision, aiming 'To make the company admired and respected the world over by contributing to society through technological innovation' (Mitarai, 2009). This vision was part of the 'Excellent Global Corporation Plan' introduced in 1996. In early 2010, five strategies were seen as key to realizing the vision:

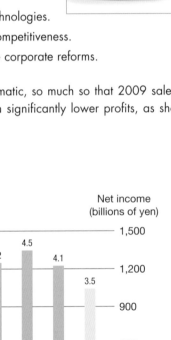

- Achieve the overwhelming no.1 position worldwide in all current core businesses.
- Expand business operations through diversification.
- Identify new business domains and accumulate required technologies.
- Establish new production systems to sustain international competitiveness.
- Nurture truly autonomous individuals and promote effective corporate reforms.

The effects of the recession on Canon performance were dramatic, so much so that 2009 sales were expected to be no greater than those achieved in 2004, with significantly lower profits, as shown in Figure 6.1.

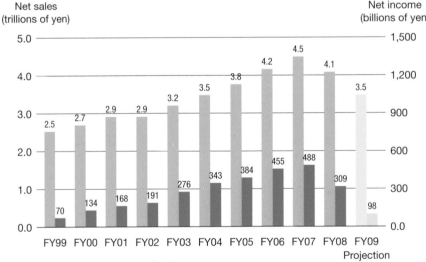

Figure 6.1 Overview of 2008

STRATEGIC MANAGEMENT IN PRACTICE

Due to the severe market environment which Canon expected to face in the future, the firm revised its 2010 targets and introduced a major shift in emphasis towards improved management quality.

To accomplish the next 'leap forward' would entail changes in the management of the supply chain and inventory management, a more selective capital expenditure programme, reduced costs in production and the ratio of SG&A to sales, while maintaining R&D expenditure with a focus towards new domains.

Even though it was severely affected by the global recession of 2008/09, Canon decided not to change its vision of technological innovation. However, it did make other changes to its desired future direction. For example, Canon decided to become more diversified in the future – changing what we will refer to as the mission of the firm – the business areas in which it decides to compete. Canon also changed the level of individual autonomy of its managers, an example of what we will refer to as the values of the firm. They also made changes to the quantitative financial targets to be achieved in future – what we will refer to as the objectives of the firm. All these changes must then be reflected in new strategies for the firm, with major implications for all of its business units. As this example demonstrates, strategies cannot be developed without a sense of purpose, without a sense of what the strategy is expected to achieve. We regard the development of a sense of the future of the firm as the starting point for strategy and one of the most important tasks for strategic managers.

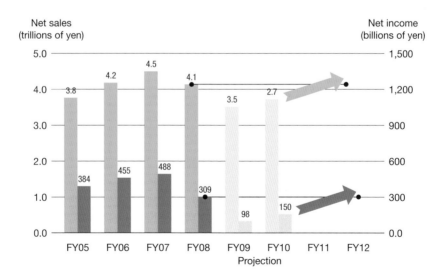

Performance outlook

Figure 6.2 Outlook for 2010 and beyond

STRATEGIC MANAGEMENT IN PRACTICE

CHAPTER OVERVIEW

The chapter opens by stating the view that all members of the firm appreciate it when senior managers have developed a sense of purpose for the firm, what the firm will look like in the future and what people are expected to achieve. We follow this general discussion with a simple model expressing the relationship between the four major concepts discussed in the chapter: vision, values, mission and objectives. Vision refers to the desired future state of the firm. For example, the BBC's vision is to be the most creative organization in the world, clearly an ambitious vision yet one with far-reaching implications. We then discuss the values of the firm: what set of beliefs should members of the firm possess? For example, what are the values of organizational members regarding honesty in our treatment of customers and the general community? A third element in establishing future direction is establishing the domain or scope of the firm, what we call the firm's mission. In what kinds of markets should it compete, how diversified should it attempt to be? Finally we expand on objectives, the measurable targets, financial and non-financial, that the firm is expected to achieve over the defined time period. Here we emphasize the need for these objectives to be achievable and integrated. Our View from the Top is a statement on the importance of a vision statement from the founder and CEO of nVIDIA, a semiconductor company. The chapter concludes with a case study examining the vision, values and mission of Coca-Cola.

<table>
<tr><td>

LEARNING OBJECTIVE 1

Formulate a strategy which includes an understanding of what that strategy is designed to achieve.

</td><td>

6.1 INTRODUCTION

The above example illustrates that Canon's senior managers see developing a sense of the future of the firm as an important component in the strategic management process. Managers and all employees in an organization have an interest in the future of the firm and we believe that senior managers should be able to give reasonable answers to such questions as:

</td></tr>
</table>

- What do you think the firm will look like ten years into the future?
- What organizational values can we be committed to?
- What changes can we expect in the next year or two?
- What are we expected to achieve over the next few time periods?

Answers to these questions mandate a sense of purpose, a sense of where the firm is going and what it aspires to be. This is a confusing area within strategic management, since firms use different terms to try to convey these ideas to external and internal stakeholders. Terms such as *mission, vision, purpose, intent, philosophy* and *credo* all attempt to capture the need for the firm to be able to express, in some form, its aspirations for the future. The major reason for some kind of statement about future direction is the need to motivate and guide the efforts of employees.

Despite the evident importance of such a statement, Peter Drucker noted some time ago (and it is still true today) that business purpose and mission are major sources of business frustration and failure because they are seldom given adequate attention by senior managers (Drucker, 1973). We regard such a sense of the future as essential to generate employee passion and commitment. Employees seem to demonstrate commitment and enthusiasm when they have a strong personal attachment to the aspirations of the firm, and what the firm stands for (Campbell *et al.*, 1993). In recent years, the need for such a sense of common purpose has increased rather than diminished. As organizations have decentralized and become flatter, decision-making occurs deep down in the firm. To empower employees to make decisions without ensuring a shared organizational vision is downright dangerous for ensuring alignment, and coordination across the firm may become impossible. In our opinion, companies that continue to enjoy success have aspirations and values that are relatively enduring, while their strategies are continually adapting to a changing world.

Generating such a view of the firm's future requires original thinking and imagination. Strategic management is not a purely analytical, left-brain activity, but involves creativity, passion and commitment. Contrary to the views that have permeated much of the literature on strategic planning, we recognize that creativity and imagination are absolutely central to good strategic management. We do not suggest that these are the only qualities required in a CEO, nor would we wish to suggest that CEOs are the only persons in the organization in whom these qualities are desirable. Indeed, vision setting is not simply a task for the CEO, as each unit or group within the firm can benefit from a shared vision to which people in that unit can aspire. However, the firm as a whole does need a sense of future direction, and developing this is one of the major responsibilities of the CEO and the board.

We also believe that a manager who is incapable of imagining the future is incapable of creating it. Of course creating is typically harder than imagining, but imagining is an essential first step. In this chapter, we begin with the concept of a vision statement, a critical and motivating feature. Next, we discuss values and their role in shaping behaviour, before moving to the issues involved in mission definition. We conclude with the often difficult but nonetheless vital task of setting objectives. Each of these concepts is applicable at both the corporate and the business unit level of the firm. We defer the discussion of business and of corporate strategy per se to Chapters 7, 8 and 9.

In discussing the future direction of the firm we distinguish four concepts, as shown in Figure 6.3.

Internally, vision, values, mission and objectives:

- guide management's thinking on strategic issues, particularly during periods of turbulence;
- guide employee decision-making;
- inspire employees to work more effectively by creating a focus and common goals;
- define expected performance standards.

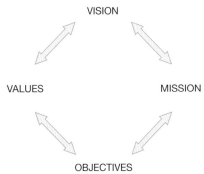

Figure 6.3 Elements of aspirations

Externally, vision, values, mission and objectives:

- create links and better communication with key external stakeholders, customers, suppliers, media and so on;
- serve as a public relations tool;
- help in enlisting external support.

We briefly describe each of these concepts, examining them in more detail later in the chapter. While we deal with these concepts sequentially, they are very much interrelated, as the Figure 6.3 indicates.

Vision

Vision without action is a daydream; Action without vision is a nightmare.

Japanese proverb

Vision

The ideal future state of the total entity, a mental image of a possible and desirable state of the firm.

A **vision** statement describes the desired future state of the total entity. It is a mental image of a possible and desirable state of the firm. A vision needs to be realistic, credible and attractive, and should provide a bridge from the present to the future. Such a vision is essential for strategy formulation, since what the firm decides to do must be subservient to what it wants to achieve.

The development of a vision is a major responsibility of senior management as it is the logical antecedent to strategy development as well as a major motivator for employees. To function as a motivator, however, the vision must be communicated to and embraced by all employees. The box below shows the BBC's vision statement.

BBC vision

- To be the most creative organization in the world (BBC, 2010).

This statement is simple and thus easily communicated, yet it is clearly ambitious, suggesting that it might serve as motivator for some time. Engendering aspiration is a major goal of a good vision statement.

Values

Organizational values

A common set of beliefs designed to guide the behaviour of organizational members.

Values (or organizational values) refer to the beliefs designed to guide the behaviour of employees. Explicit values statements will usually include guidance on integrity and honesty, how employees will be treated, how customers and suppliers will be treated, and so on.

Values may be quite general, but should provide guidelines for employee behaviour. The box below shows the BBC's values statement.

BBC values

Trust is the foundation of the BBC: we are independent, impartial and honest.

- Audiences are at the heart of everything we do.
- We take pride in delivering quality and value for money.
- Creativity is the lifeblood of our organization.
- We respect each other and celebrate our diversity so that everyone can give their best.
- We are one BBC: great things happen when we work together.

This is a relatively brief and concise statement which is always desirable. Statements that try to say too much are obviously difficult to remember and are less likely to guide behaviour. The engineering company Balfour Beatty Civil Engineering Limited clearly understands the importance of remembering values, since it presents them in the form of an *Inspire* acronym.

Values *in practice* – Balfour Beatty

Our values provide the identity by which Balfour Beatty Ireland is recognized, demonstrated through our actions and behaviour which consistently match our words.

Integrity

We are open, honest and trustworthy and deliver on our promises.

Safety

Health and safety is central to everything we do.

Passion

We believe in providing an exciting, enjoyable and stimulating work environment that encourages creativity.

Innovation

We encourage and reward initiative and flair to develop new ideas.

Respect

We value our customers, partners and staff and are socially and environmentally responsible.

Excellence

We are committed to delivering superior value and quality and developing the full potential of our staff.

Source: BalfourBeatty, 2009

Mission

Mission

A generalized statement specifying the domain of the firm, where and how it elects to compete, and its activities and operations.

Mission

The **mission** specifies the domain of the firm: where and how it elects to compete. It defines in fairly general terms the activities and operations of the firm. Such a mission statement should be specific to the firm and permit a person who reads such a statement to understand what the firm is, what it does and, just as important, what it does not do. Mission statements should clarify firm vision, and provide a tangible direction that helps establish congruence among the actions of employees. Often such mission statements reflect the firm's priorities among its key stakeholders and embrace a commitment to these stakeholders.

BBC mission

- To enrich people's lives with programmes and services that inform, educate and entertain.

While we might argue that this statement is very broad, in fact, over the years, the BBC has greatly expanded its scope. As a result it has come in for considerable criticism, since, as a publicly funded institution, it does not compete on an equitable basis with private providers (Porter, 2009).

Objectives

Objectives

Quantitative targets to be achieved by the firm or one of its units.

Objectives

Objectives are targets to be achieved by the firm and its units. These objectives typically specify in quantitative terms what the firm expects to achieve in both the short and the longer term. Most firms have a hierarchy of such objectives, which cascade down from the corporate level to business units and beyond. They include both financial and non-financial objectives, and represent the accomplishments which management believes must be attained in order to fulfil the mission and achieve the vision that has been established.

LEARNING OBJECTIVE 2

Utilize the key features of effective vision, values, mission and objectives.

6.2 VISION

As our model of the strategic management process in Figure 6.3 indicates, strategic management is not a linear step-by-step process. Rather, it is a recursive, interactive, circular process, with analysis leading to some ideas on strategy leading to questions of how to implement, with a forecast of potential results, all possibly leading back to a revised strategy. One element in this circular process is the generation of a vision for the firm. A firm consists of a voluntary collection of individuals for a common purpose, and an important task for strategic managers is to generate a sense of the future for the entity that is widely shared and understood within and outside the firm. This is what we will refer to as the vision of the firm, a sense of what the firm is, where it is going, what it is trying to achieve. Of course, not all firms use the term *vision* per se, but many talk about the same concept, using words such as *purpose*, *intent* or *goal*. A vision of the firm's future can be expected to have a high degree of stability. But the world does change, and consequently the firm's view of its future may also change – in strategic management, nothing is fixed. We regard changing the vision to be one of the most challenging tasks for strategic managers.

A vision may be created at the corporate level, for the firm as a whole, or at a lower level, such as a business unit. Regardless, a vision should possess several characteristics. First, it must provide a general sense of direction, and thus will focus on strategy development and decision-making. The other important property of a vision is that it must serve to motivate employees. A well-designed vision statement provides the inspiration around which all members of the firm or unit can focus their energy and creativity. Finally, it must clearly convey to other stakeholders the forward direction of the organization.

The vision statement

Our definition of vision follows Bennis, who described it as follows:

> To choose a direction, a leader must first have developed a mental image of a possible and desirable future state of the organization. This image, which we call a vision, may be as vague as a dream or as precise as a goal or mission statement. The critical point is that a vision articulates a view of a realistic, credible, attractive future for the organiza-tion, a condition that is better in some important ways than what now exists.
>
> (Bennis & Nanus, 1985)

A corporate vision describes some ideal future state of the organization as a whole, but the concept is equally applicable at the business unit or even functional level. Good vision statements should not be excessively restrictive, for employees must find in the vision something to inspire them personally (Collins & Porras, 1996). Neither should visions be too specific nor easily achievable, for their focus is the long run. A vision should be compelling, ambitious and ask a lot of employees – although possibly its most important characteristic is the extent to which all employees are fully committed to it. GlaxoSmithKline, the global pharmaceuticals firm, provides an example of such a vision statement (GlaxoSmithKline, 2009).

Vision *in practice* – GlaxoSmithKline

Our global quest is to improve the quality of human life by enabling people to do more, feel better and live longer.

A vision statement in which nobody believes will not serve its intended purpose. Indeed, it is generally counter-productive, producing cynicism among the firm's employees.

As we mentioned earlier, despite the desirability of some stability, in a changing world, visions must also evolve – a good example of the paradoxes that often underlie strategic management. Consider the Microsoft example below.

Changing vision *in practice* – Microsoft

In 1999, Microsoft changed its vision from 'A computer on every desk and in every home' to 'Giving people the power to do what they want, where and when they want, on any device' (Moeller *et al.*, 1999). As a consequence of this change in vision, Microsoft has expanded its lines of business well beyond computers; it is now a major player in a number of new business areas such as PDAs, mobile phones and video games. By 2009 Microsoft was no longer using the concept of vision per se, but described its mission as helping people and businesses throughout the world to realize their own potential (Microsoft, 2009).

Some firms use the term strategic intent to describe a concept similar to what we call vision. Hamel and Prahalad (1994) claim that successful firms often have intents that embrace bold ambitions, an obsession with winning and the commitment to build the resources required for this.

As we have noted, many successful firms establish ambitious aspirations, which are audacious and not easy to achieve. We consider that the terms *vision* and *intent* express a similar idea, an aspiration for the firm which is challenging, requiring new capabilities, with strong commitment from all employees and yet is seen as credible and realistic. Aspirations are based on current capabilities, but also embrace evolving opportunities that will require generation of new capabilities. As such, they therefore reflect both an internal and an external focus.

A vision statement should appear desirable and feasible to all stakeholders, providing guidance in decision-making, flexibility to allow for individual initiative and the ability to communicate to all stakeholders. It must be rooted in the reality of markets, competition and technology. Strictly financial visions are unlikely to provide much in the way of motivation

---

Vision *in practice* – BASF

We are 'The Chemical Company' successfully operating in all major markets.

- Our customers view BASF as their partner of choice.
- Our innovative products, intelligent solutions and services make us the most competent worldwide supplier in the chemical industry.
- We generate a high return on assets.
- We strive for sustainable development.
- We welcome change as an opportunity.
- We, the employees of BASF, together ensure our success.

(BASF, 2010)

---

for employees. More legitimate and inspiring aspirations are captured in statements such as the GlaxoSmithKline vision described earlier. At the same time, the vision statement should not be so broad and grandiose that it loses any meaning (Langeler, 1992). We should point out, however, that firms often use very differently terms such as *vision*, that we and other academics (Bennis & Nanus, 1985) define in a particular way. BASF, for example, defines its 'vision' much more specifically, as the above example indicates.

This BASF statement implies a number of objectives, and also communicates some desired organizational values, but stands in quite a contrast to a statement such as Glaxo's, shown earlier.

Having described what a vision statement is and its purpose, we now address the characteristics of vision statements and develop an understanding of the process used to create such a vision.

Characteristics of vision statements

The first and most important feature of a vision statement is its description of the desirable future for the organization. This serves as an essential input to the strategy development process. In a turbulent world, one might question whether this is possible or even desirable. We believe, however, that all successful firms need a vision (or its equivalent) to provide a focus for its endeavours over the longer term; otherwise there will be distracting differences about what the firm is expected to achieve. However, since visions are generally fairly broad, this benefit should not be overstated.

At the same time, the vision statement must motivate and inspire all employees. The envisioned future should be ambitious, real and visible but will also involve dreams, hopes and a sense of passion (Collins & Porras, 1996). Motivating people to implement plan-driven actions was never part of the lexicon of traditional strategic planning. Indeed, it was implicitly and blithely assumed that where the plan pointed, the people would follow. Not so! Hence the rationale for, and potential contribution of, the vision statement.

Effective vision statements result from activating the right side of the brain, that which deals with affect and emotion. As Peter Senge puts it:

> A shared vision is not an idea. It is not even an important idea such as freedom. It is, rather, a force in people's hearts, a force of impressive power . . . [it] is the answer to the question 'What do we want to create?' Just as personal visions are pictures or images that people carry in their heads *and hearts,* [emphasis added] so too are shared visions that people throughout an organization carry. They create a sense of commonality that permeates the organization and gives coherence to diverse activities.
>
> (Senge, 1990)

As Senge also elaborates, however, too many visions are imposed on organizations, and at best create compliance rather than commitment. To evaluate the effectiveness of a vision statement, we must ask such questions as:

- Are we sure the vision is shared?
- Is the vision compelling and inspiring?
- Does it ask something of us?
- Does it create a sense of direction for the organization?
- Does it facilitate personal meaning and involvement?
- Is it difficult to achieve, will it stretch the firm?
- Is it unique and differentiating?
- Do all employees embrace ownership?

The final point is perhaps the most critical of all. To be effective a vision must be shared, it must be owned by all organizational personnel. If you ask most executives about visions, by far the majority will respond with a statement such as 'Well, the company has one . . .', implying that the executives have not internalized it. It is distressingly common for senior executives to agonize over developing such a statement, to pronounce it to various assemblies of subordinates, and to then be surprised that it is not enthusiastically internalized and acted upon. A moment's reflection will reveal the naiveté embedded in such an approach. Visions that are not shared cannot be effective, and the only way we know of to ensure such sharing is to ensure the maximum possible participation in the visioning exercise. As with so many exercises involving the development of commitment, this may at first sight appear to be time-consuming and inefficient; yet, over the long haul, there is probably no greater inefficiency than having the current members of the firm acting without a sense of common purpose.

Challenge of strategic management

Paula Phelan is a consultant who has worked closely with CEOs of companies, both large and small for over 15 years. She points out that while each CEO brings a unique set of characteristics to the table, there are some commonalities between those that are able to steer their companies to success and those that fall short of their potential.

She believes that the most important attribute possessed by a successful leader is the ability to focus on a vision and to communicate that vision to stakeholders:

> 'Being at the top of the pyramid, a great CEO must be able to clearly communicate the vision of the company in order to inspire staff, investors and customers. As the company flag-bearer, all eyes turn to the CEO for direction and example' (Phelan, 2010).

■ Do you agree with this statement? Why or why not?

Creating a vision statement

Developing a good vision statement is fundamentally a creative act. Indeed, we must begin with an understanding that we are attempting to affect human emotions.

- Ask yourself what are the phenomena that stir your emotions?
- Unless such stirring occurs, the vision will not achieve its intended ends.

> ### Challenge of strategic management
> It is common for the senior managers of a firm to have a similar view of the world, a common mental model. Does this imply that a new vision can only be generated by a CEO new to the firm?

Clearly, then, developing a vision statement is different from developing a cash flow statement. Visions require intuition, a sense of passion and creativity, together with an understanding of what drives human feelings. Creating the vision also requires foresight among the senior managers – who are the organizational personnel primarily responsible for its creation (Hamel & Prahalad, 1994). Industry foresight is about becoming the intellectual leader in the industry, the firm which has a superior understanding of the industry and its structure, the customers and competitors, the current technology and that of substitutes as well as a deep knowledge of how these are changing and what the impact is likely to be.

Industry foresight
The ability of managers to have superior understanding of the changes in the industry, customers, competitors and technology and their likely future impact.

Managers should understand how the benefits which current and potential customers seek are altering, and what capabilities will be needed in the future to deliver these benefits, as well as the emergent technological possibilities that may create new needs and wants. Some managers have excellent backsight and poor foresight. They can easily identify the changes over the last ten years but have considerable difficulty even contemplating likely changes in industry structure and the nature of competition over the next ten years.

- Consider the attitude of the recording industry to the early adopters of downloading: they persecuted them! (Backsight).
- The world leader in downloaded music became a computer company, Apple with iTunes (Foresight).

Creating good visions also requires some diversity of views to facilitate creativity. If all managers think alike it will be difficult to envision new ideas, since new ideas are often on the boundary of the present. Again a balance is needed. Too much diversity can be detrimental to progress; too much uniformity will inhibit creativity. There may also be diversity in process and subject matter, with a search for images and metaphors, with a focus on the future state of the firm, not how to get there.

This process may take considerable time. Developing a new vision is one of the most challenging tasks for strategic managers. It is not easy to create a vision which is practical, specific to the individual firm and reflects its history, yet one which represents a stretch for the firm. It must be contemporary, while not needing to be altered on an annual basis. Nonetheless, there will be times when the firm will have to alter its vision. As we will discuss in

Chapter 10 more detail in Chapter 10 (➤Chapter 10), one of the tasks of leaders is to create the vision for the future of the firm, and the ability to accomplish this is one of the distinguishing character-istics of a great leader. Thus, vision and leadership have a number of elements in common.

Rather than asking current senior managers to develop a vision, some companies ask the people who will actually be managing the company in the future. A promising team of younger managers will also usually provide challenges to current thinking at the top of the company. This can also be the route to a fascinating and productive dialogue. Another projective technique that can be very effective is the organizational personality comparison, wherein executives are asked to describe an organization as a personality, comparing what they see now with what they believe they will have to be in the future. We also find that it is sometimes easier to ask executives to draw a picture of how the company will be rather than what it is today; again this approach tends to activate the right side of the brain.

6.3 VALUES

The second element in creating a future direction is creating and reinforcing organizational values – a common set of beliefs that guide the behaviour of organizational members. Values indicate how managers and employees intend to conduct themselves, the principles that under-lie how they go about their day-to-day activities. Values can be described as 'the way we do business around here'; they are guidelines that govern the behaviour of employees as they strive to achieve the vision of the firm. Such values may be implicit or explicit. Explicit values could include how colleagues will be treated (as trustworthy and respected?), concern for employee development, integrity and honesty in all dealings both inside and outside the firm, values towards customers and the community, the risk of failure, organizational change and so on.

Values include consideration of what is regarded as ethical behaviour within the firm, a topic that has grown in importance following the accounting scandals and disgraceful senior management behaviour at such firms as Parmalat, Northern Rock, Satyam and Enron. The cavalier way in which many financial institutions dealt with derivatives and collaterized debt obligations (CDOs) during the financial collapses of 2008/09 has further heightened concerns over the morals and ethics of the financial industry as a whole.

As with vision, the task of infusing a set of values into the organization typically falls to the CEO and other organizational leaders. It is considered axiomatic that an individual feels a personal sense of mission, or finds meaning in their work, when the organization's values match those of the individual. Such values can act as both a motivating factor with individuals and a control mechanism – individual behaviour is consistent with their own value system and, if these are in harmony with organizational values, a control system to ensure alignment is less necessary (Deal & Kennedy, 1982). Clear understanding of these organizational values is also important when recruiting new staff – we want individuals who are committed, and who will act in accordance with the values of the organization.

We regard organizational values as integral to company success but, with some notable exceptions, they have tended to be implicit rather than explicit. More recently, environmental pressures, as well as pressure from shareholders have led executives to rethink corporate values and to make them explicit rather than implicit. Values can be thought of as 'hard' (profitability, economic profit, market share) and 'soft' (integrity, respect for others, trust and pre-eminence of customers). Indeed, these 'soft' values are becoming intangible assets that pay dividends for shareholders, as the following example demonstrates.

A study undertaken by Heal gives quantitative and qualitative evidence for the argument that principles do pay (Heal, 2008). As noted in a review of the book, one area was in human resources. Starbucks saves millions of dollars a year by retaining their employees longer (50 per cent turnover) than the industry average. Another point was that an analysis of the EPA's Toxics Release Inventory and stock prices shows that the more a business pollutes, the more its stock price tends to fall. Finally, Goldman Sachs has indicated that social and environmental impact data are valuable for stock picking (Stewart, 2008).

As with vision, values statements are only worthwhile if they are embraced throughout the organization. Organizational members' 'buy-in' is typically influenced by the extent of participation in their development. Values can provide the 'cultural glue' that enables some firms to thrive in times of rapid change, whereas others struggle to survive.

Unfortunately, it is quite common to find that senior management behaviour is inconsistent with the values promoted by the firm. This was seen with firms such as the Icelandic banks, which misled investors, shareholders and financial markets on their creditworthiness and betrayed their trust. When such hypocrisy is evident, there is likely to be a strong negative impact on the morale of employees, since employees pay more attention to actions than they do to words.

As an example of a statement of corporate values, in the box below we reprint the values for Tata, the Indian conglomerate (Tata, 2010).

Corporate values *in practice* – Tata

Tata has always been values-driven. These values continue to direct the growth and business of Tata companies. The five core values underpinning the way we do business are:

- **Integrity**: we must conduct our business fairly, with honesty and transparency. Everything we do must stand the test of public scrutiny.
- **Understanding**: we must be caring, show respect, compassion and humanity for our colleagues and customers around the world, and always work for the benefit of the communities we serve.
- **Excellence**: we must constantly strive to achieve the highest possible standards in our day-to-day work and in the quality of the goods and services we provide.
- **Unity**: we must work cohesively with our colleagues across the group and with our customers and partners around the world, building strong relationships based on tolerance, understanding and mutual cooperation.
- **Responsibility**: we must continue to be responsible, sensitive to the countries, communities and environments in which we work, always ensuring that what comes from the people goes back to the people many times over.

Producing written statements of values may not be for everyone – some British executives, for example, are reluctant to develop such statements. But for many it provides another tool in the armoury for creating and guiding organizational change.

For young entrepreneurial firms, organizational values are often strongly linked to the values of the founder. The return of founder Steven Jobs to Apple rejuvenated the company, and the values of innovation, which had seemed to wither in his absence, rapidly returned. Sometimes, the values of a founder can persist for many generations of managers. The so-called 'HP Way' at Hewlett-Packard is still considered a value and is attributed to Bill Packard, one of the founders.

Some of the most important organizational values are the (often implicit) values towards risk innovation, growth and the future. In some firms, corporate values favour steady, incremental growth. In others, the values are at the other end of the spectrum. News Corporation, as we have seen, has values that drive its growth and risk-taking, values shared with firms such as Oracle, SAP and Sony. Other firms, such as Exxon-Mobil and Nestlé, have values, perhaps implicit, which seem to espouse steady, long-term and incremental growth, rather than explosive growth with the risks that entails.

Values as a source of problems

Values can also present problems. There may be significant variation in values across units within the same firm. This phenomenon is called organizational differentiation, and one of the commonest manifestations within most companies is the difference in values across the various functional specialties within the company (Lawrence & Lorsch, 1967) (▶Chapter 11). Such differentiation may also exist between the different business units of a multi-business company, and the more diversified the firm, the greater this variation is likely to be. Both kinds of differentiation can result in difficulty in achieving coordinated strategies, as well as implementation. Indeed, in many companies the values that actually guide behaviour are implicit rather than explicit, and we must remember that when we talk of values in the context of strategic management, there is usually the assumption that these values are something that management is (or should be) actively managing. Clearly it is easier to 'manage' explicit values statements than to deal with implicit values. Further, the de facto values of the organization, while they may be implicit, are typically reflected in a variety of its systems and procedures ('standard operating procedures') such that the very infrastructure of the organization serves as a major impediment to management attempts at change, a topic we explore in greater depth in Chapter 10 (▶Chapter 10).

Values can also impede the integration of acquisitions. The values of the acquiring firm and the acquired firm are often different, and as we will see in Chapter 10, these value differences are a significant cause of post-merger difficulties.

Values also create difficulties in hiring. The values of an individual are often quite well formed by the time they take a job. Influenced by a prolonged process of acculturation, they

Chapters 10, 11

are therefore quite difficult to change. Further, as companies become global, these individual values are likely to become increasingly diverse, and are less likely to reflect the values of the home country of the global firm and its cadre of senior managers.

A successful Australian resources company moved rapidly into international trading of commodities. They found that a number of their new overseas recruits did not share the prevailing Australian values with respect to honesty and integrity, and were forced to release a number of employees and rethink their hiring and training practices.

As most managements would undoubtedly prefer that their employees do 'the right thing', it is instructive to consider where problems are likely to arise. Ignoring blatant dishonesty, which is outside the scope of this book, it is clear that, as the ethicists point out, the most difficult decisions are typically a result of a conflict between two 'rights'. A classic example arises when dealing with an unhappy customer, when the goal of profitability may appear in conflict with satisfying the customer. Companies that have put in place systems to enable customer service representatives to adjudge the longer term as opposed to the immediate costs and benefits of alternative courses of action greatly assist employees in making an appropriate economic decision, since in these cases a conflict between the goal of short-term firm profitability and customer satisfaction is a frequent and uncomfortable occurrence. Similar conflicts arise between the oft-avowed goal of developing a more entrepreneurial set of behaviours within the company and the strict budgetary limits that are imposed in order to ensure fiscal discipline. Systems may have to be significantly changed to facilitate changing the necessary behaviours.

Challenge of strategic management

What might cause a firm to attempt to change its values? What mechanisms can be adopted to change the values of a firm?

Values can also create major impediments to organizational change (►Chapter 10). At times of significant change in the competitive environment, significant adjustment of firm values may be required. Imaginative use of the tools of human resource management – selection, development, appraisal and reward – assist the change process. Without advance planning, however, wholesale employee turnover is likely to result if rapid change is required. This can create widespread dislocation of company operations, which can worsen what may already be a crisis situation. Figure 6.4 illustrates some of the values changes that a number of companies are trying to accomplish over the longer term.

Chapter 10

From	To
Accounting prodfit	Economic profit
Stand-alone	Networked
Rigidity	Flexibility
Budget-driven	Strategically driven
Transactional	Relational
Tradition-bound	Open to innovation
Inwardly focused	Socially responsible

Figure 6.4 Commonly sought values transitions

6.4 MISSION

The third element in creating a future direction is establishing a mission statement, an expression of the domain in which the firm and/or its businesses elect to compete. A mission statement describes the business the firm is in, or the business in which it desires to be. Such a mission statement should be externally focused and contain a general description of the scope of the activities of the firm, often in terms of the products it intends to produce and the markets it will serve. Such a statement on the boundaries and scope of the firm and/or its businesses is ideally in line with the firm's vision and values and the expectations of major stakeholders. For a summary of the mission statements of 301 top American firms, see Abrahams (Abrahams, 1999).

A mission statement therefore defines the areas in which the company wishes to do business. It should simultaneously recognize areas of opportunity while capitalizing upon the firm's capabilities. It should neither be so general as to admit too broad a variety of possibilities, nor so narrow that it impedes all attempts at growth. Of course, multi-business firms need to develop mission statements at the business level, as well as the corporate level. The missions of the individual business units should be subsumed by, and consistent with, the corporate mission. Mission statements not only codify opportunities where the firm does well or aspires to do well, however, for in doing so they typically demarcate the competitive set as well. While there is no strong evidence that the quality of a mission statement has a demonstrable effect on firm performance, it appears that mission statements that emphasize such concerns as being responsible to employees and society as a whole may have a beneficial effect (Bartkus et al., 2006).

Examples of mission statements for several firms are presented below. Haier America, the US subsidiary, has its own mission statement, and goes on to elaborate some of its future strategy, as do a number of companies (HaierUS, 2009). Unfortunately some companies do not seem to grasp the purpose of a mission statement. Consider what Intel describes as its mission on its website. This is a motherhood statement that could well be used about any company in any business. It may embrace some sound goals, but it is useless in defining the domain of Intel. To be fair to the company, however, this is taken from the Intel website, a promotional vehicle for the company. Intel may well use a different mission statement internally.

Unilever, the Anglo-Dutch consumer goods firm, has a much lengthier mission statement, which they call 'Our Purpose' as below (Unilever, 2010). While lengthy, this statement reveals a great deal about the values that senior management believes should be guiding the behaviour of company employees.

Haier America mission statement

Our mission is to combine quality, innovation and style for the comfort and convenience of your home

At Haier America, we are committed to paving a new path. We are at the forefront of the next wave of home appliances and consumer electronics and have made a conscious effort to design and develop high-end and high-quality products. As our growth continues, we will surpass the challenges presented by new markets while maintaining the quality and dependability that our customers have come to associate with Haier America. Our offerings are constantly expanding and evolving as we strive to create products that allow consumers to lead better and healthier lifestyles.

Intel's mission statement

Intel's mission is to meet and exceed the expectations of our customers, employees and shareholders.

Unilever's mission statement

Our purpose

At the heart of the corporate purpose, which guides us in our approach to doing business, is the drive to serve consumers in a unique and effective way. This purpose has been communicated to all employees worldwide.

A vitality mentality

Unilever's mission is to add vitality to life. We meet everyday needs for nutrition, hygiene and personal care with brands that help people feel good, look good and get more out of life.

Our deep roots in local cultures and markets around the world give us our strong relationship with consumers and are the foundation for our future growth. We will bring our wealth of knowledge and international expertise to the service of local consumers – a truly multi-local multinational.

Our long-term success requires a total commitment to exceptional standards of performance and productivity, to working together effectively, and to a willingness to embrace new ideas and learn continuously.

To succeed also requires, we believe, the highest standards of corporate behaviour towards everyone we work with, the communities we touch, and the environment on which we have an impact.

This is our road to sustainable, profitable growth, creating long-term value for our shareholders, our people and our business partners.

Decisions about mission are among the most important of strategic decisions, and should not be taken lightly. Managing the evolution of mission statements is a responsibility of senior management, who may decide to broaden or narrow the mission.

- *Broaden the mission statement due to*:
  - Lack of sufficient growth opportunities
  - A target of opportunity has been identified.

- *Narrow the mission statement due to*:
  - Resources are stretched too thinly
  - Poor financial performance
  - To defend against a takeover.

In addition, new leadership often sets new directions via a revised mission, and capital market pressure may play an important role, even for relatively focused firms, if financial analysts believe that company breakup will 'release value'.

Underlying the concept of a mission is the idea of leveraging company capabilities by focusing on a limited number of opportunity areas rather than spreading their resources, perhaps too thinly, over many different markets. Academic research and general opinion suggest that in general companies succeed when they build on their core capabilities (Prahalad & Hamel, 1990), focusing only on what the firm does well (▶Chapter 5).

Chapter 5

Corporate versus business unit mission statements

Mission statements are useful strategic concepts for business units, as well as for the firm as a whole. Consider the case of United Technologies Corporation (UTC), a diversified company whose products include Carrier heating and air conditioning, Hamilton Sundstrand aerospace systems and industrial products, Otis elevators and escalators, Pratt & Whitney aircraft engines, Sikorsky helicopters, UTC Fire & Security systems and UTC Power fuel cells.

George David (David, 2006), UTC CEO, described the company's 'product mission' as:

> To convert energy into useful work. Our products overcome two essential forces in our world: gravity and weather. The first for flight and for vertical transportation in buildings, and the second to make our buildings comfortable and clean in all seasons.

Within the company, however, the Otis business unit has a much more focused description of its business, as follows (Otis, 2009):

> Otis elevator is the world's leading manufacturer, installer and maintainer of elevators, escalators and moving walkways – a constant, reliable name for more than 150 years.

In ideal terms, we would like the business unit missions for a corporation to be encompassed by the corporate mission, but to be mutually exclusive such that the domain of each business unit is clearly specified, and non-overlapping with other business units. This ideal, however, may be shattered by innovation, which often seems to occur at the boundaries of what might have traditionally been considered as a 'market' or an industry.

Consider such new terms as *cosmeceuticals* (cosmetic products with functional 'pharmaceutical' properties), *functional foods* (foods with demonstrable health benefits, such as cholesterol-lowering margarines), *chilled foods* (neither preserved by freezing or canning, nor 'fresh' produce) or even the strategy of Mars in transforming its candy bars into ice-cream desserts. In every case, these innovations have wrought new patterns of competition and have caused strategic managers to rethink their strategies, and even their entire conceptualization of the business.

Characteristics of mission statements

Vision and values statements usually suggest ideals about how employees of the company will behave, and what the firm hopes to become. In contrast, corporate and business mission statements have a more pragmatic and more immediate purpose. They exist to *guide* and to constrain the firm's future growth. They guide in the sense that they suggest where managers should be looking for future opportunity. They constrain by deterring selection of other kinds of opportunities.

As the examples above indicate, mission statements can be as short as a sentence or as long as a page. To be useful, as with vision and values, they must also be communicated to, and understood and embraced by all the members of the organization. Indeed, in the era of networked and outsourced organizations, this understanding can be usefully extended to other stakeholders, notably including suppliers.

A mission statement:

- encourages unanimity of purpose, specifies what the organization does, and, just as important, what it does not do;
- directs the search for new activities;
- highlights points of differentiation and basis of competitive advantage;
- atracts and deters potential staff;
- does not change too frequently.

Creating and changing a mission statement

Although we do not believe that mission statements should change too frequently, obviously they cannot stay unaltered forever, and the faster the environment is changing, the more frequently they should be reviewed. New opportunities will arise even as older ones disappear, and a successful firm must inevitably outgrow its earlier missions. Most firms begin with a fairly simple and narrow mission statement, chosen from one of the types to be outlined below. As the successful firm grows, however, its mission statement will broaden, reflecting its growing capabilities and view of opportunities, and its mission statement may well include several dimensions.

Bases for mission definition

Mission statements can be developed on several 'pure forms' bases: three supply-side – natural resources, technology and product/service; and two demand-side – market/market segment and customer needs. We look at each in turn, illustrating how the mission definition can affect choices among opportunities:

Natural resources. These businesses maximize value from a natural resource. For example, the mission 'We are a forest products company' could lead the firm to consider making any product, using any technology, sold in any market, so long as it is made from wood.

Technology. These businesses focus on a core technology, for example, 'We are a glass company', or 'We are an electronics company'. An 'electronics' firm's search for opportunity would be based solely on electronics, its products could be sold to any market and use any raw material, so long as they were based on electronics.

Product/service. These businesses focus on particular product(s)/service(s); for example, 'We are an automobile firm'. Although this mission implies a sole focus on automobiles, they may be powered by various fuels (gasoline, diesel, ethanol, LPG, natural gas) and use various technologies (steam, electric, internal combustion, gas turbine), and could be sold into many different markets around the world.

Market/market segment. These businesses offer selected markets/market segments/a variety of products/services (made from various raw materials using various technologies). For example, consumer packaged goods firms target families and offer various household and personal care products. Market-based definitions, often based on geographic or socio-economic segments, are most common among retail and distribution businesses.

Customer needs. This mission focuses solely on customer needs. For example, a mission to serve transportation needs might lead a firm to offer bicycles, automobiles, trucks, helicopters and airplanes.

Individual pure forms missions may be used separately or combined with other bases to develop narrower mission statements. For example, Courtyard by Marriott combines product/service and market segment: 'To provide economy and quality-minded frequent business travellers with a premium lodging facility, which is consistently perceived as clean, comfortable, well maintained and attractive, staffed by friendly, attentive and efficient people.'

Mission not only influences choice of market opportunity but, via outsourcing, may lead firms to rid themselves of responsibility for activities that consume management talent and investment capital, but do not provide significant competitive advantage. The commonest everyday parlance for these kinds of changes is for managers to talk of 're-focusing on the core business'. Unfortunately, these statements are often made in response to an earlier period of management excess. When firms are profitable, the principal/agent divergence often seems to provoke unwise diversification. The resulting expensive acquisitions are often rationalized in later, usually more difficult times by refocusing on the core business. This activity is many times undertaken by managers other than those who overpaid for the acquisition!

Our research also suggests that rather than pro-actively managing mission statements and taking them seriously, most companies tend to forget about them when times are good, and worry about them when they get into difficulty (Capon *et al.*, 1988). Even more common are those cases where executives appear to ignore their businesses' missions. When decisions are made that are in obvious disregard of a mission statement, managers destroy their own credibility. We are convinced of the importance of mission statements, but must reluctantly admit that when middle managers in an organization dismiss the whole exercise as mere 'wordsmithing', they may well be giving an accurate description of what has occurred, but it constitutes an unfortunate commentary on the strategic management of their companies.

Some firms have been very successful in changing their mission statement in response to environmental changes or where analysis suggests that continuing with the current mission would not create desired levels of value. Others indicate that this is one of the most difficult strategic decisions to accomplish successfully.

Changing mission *in practice* – Nestlé

In 2009/2010 the Swiss company Nestlé made major changes in its portfolio. It agreed to sell its holding in eye-care company Alcon to Novartis for a reported $28.1 billion (Sargent, 2010) and purchased Kraft's frozen pizza business for $3.7 billion (Matlack, 2010). The net result of these changes was to leave Nestlé less diversified, with a food-focused portfolio.

One of the more successful examples of evolution in mission is provided by the case of the Finnish company Nokia, with its transformation to a telecommunications company. Nokia Corporation was formed in 1967 with the merger of three firms: a paper-making business, a rubber works and a cable business. Over time it evolved into completely new areas of business, from radio telephones, to TV and computers. In 1992 a new CEO divested what were by then regarded as 'non-core' businesses and focused on telecommunications and the digital age. The firm's evolution is described very well on its website (Nokia, 2009).

6.5 OBJECTIVES

Organizations must specify what they hope to achieve in the future by formulating a set of objectives – measurable targets to be achieved. Objectives are clear, quantifiable and measurable targets to be achieved by the firm, or a unit of the firm, within a defined time scale. All objectives should contain:

- An attribute which can be measured, such as revenue growth.

- A scale on which that attribute can be measured, such as $.

- A level to be achieved, such as $100m.

- A time scale for the achievement of the target, such as the year 2015.

LEARNING OBJECTIVE 3

Apply the concepts of vision, values, mission and objectives at both the corporate and the business unit level.

Corporate and business unit objectives

Objectives are generally established in many areas of the firm, and there is typically a cascading down the firm: corporate objectives are established, then business unit objectives and then more detailed product/market objectives within these. The ideal is for all of these to be consistent and aligned. In practice, there is often a quite protracted negotiation process that involves consultation throughout the entire firm. The top management team, in consultation with the board, will establish corporate objectives as well as review corporate strategies and corporate performance. Business unit objectives will be established by business unit managers in consultation with the top management team, while there may be a secondary level of interaction with the board, depending on the importance of the business unit. Strategy development at the business unit level involves primarily business unit managers and corporate managers, although the board may be involved with major businesses. Business unit performance is again primarily a matter between corporate managers and business unit managers, with the board playing a secondary role in some circumstances. As is shown in Figure 6.5, objective setting, strategy development, strategy implementation and performance measurement are not linear processes but involve a series of iterations.

As would be expected, establishing objectives is frequently a political process, characterized by bargaining and conflict, coupled with rational analysis. Choosing appropriate objectives requires a deep understanding of the external environment and the opportunities it presents, together with an analysis of the capabilities of the firm, the vision and values of the firm and the demands of financial markets.

Of course, the types of objectives that are set at the corporate level and the business unit level can differ quite significantly. At the corporate level, the CEO has to focus considerable attention on capital markets, whereas the concern of the business unit manager is much

Chapter 12

more with product markets (▶Chapter 12). However, the two perspectives cannot and should not be viewed as separate. Performance in the business units' product markets will affect growth in volumes and margins, which are the prime operating drivers of cash flow, and therefore of economic profit and, ultimately, return to shareholders of the corporation.

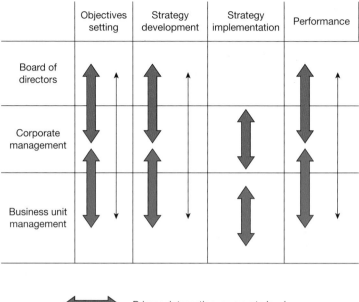

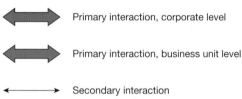

Primary interaction, corporate level

Primary interaction, business unit level

Secondary interaction

Figure 6.5 Iterative loops in the strategy process (illustrative only)

2009

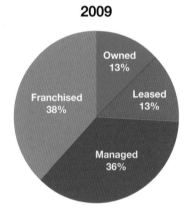

2015

Objectives *in practice* – Accor

The French hotel group, Accor, has recently announced a significant change in its objectives. Historically, the firm has owned a high proportion of its hotel sites – in 2004 it owned 60 per cent of its hotels. With a stagnating share price, and pressure from two major shareholders, Accor has decided to increase the number of hotels operated by a management contract. Figure 6.6 shows the proportion of hotel openings for 2009, and their objectives for 2015, by operating type. As can be seen, in 2009, 36 per cent of new hotel openings were managed, and by 2015 this is expected to increase to 50 per cent (Accor, 2010).

Figure 6.6 Accor Group hotel openings

Adapted from data taken from their website

Table 6.1 Corporate and business unit objectives

Corporate objectives	Business unit objectives
Shareholder return	Growth
Economic profit	Operational excellence
Growth	Quality
Portfolio balance	Market share gain
Innovation	Employee development
Staff excellence	Capital productivity
Corporate social responsibility	Competence development

> ### Objectives *in practice* – Siemens
>
> At the same time as establishing these divisional objectives (see Table 6.2), Siemens established a set of corporate objectives including:
>
> - Return on capital employed of 14–16%
> - Organic revenue growth at two times GDP
> - Capital structure, net debt/EBITDA of 0.8–1.0
> - Reduction in selling, general and administrative costs of 10%.

Table 6.2 Siemens' objectives

Division	Margin range (%)
Healthcare diagnostics	16–19
Oil and gas	10–14
Building technologies	7–10

As can be seen from Figure 6.6, Accor has changed its objectives – reflecting a change in its strategy. With the increased turbulence in its external environment, Accor is attempting to reduce its level of fixed assets employed in the firm and is moving towards a higher proportion of hotels which will be managed by the group, but not owned by the group.

Table 6.1 contrasts the kinds of objectives that might be set at the corporate versus the business unit level.

It is common in a diversified firm for these objectives to vary across the different businesses in the corporate portfolio. Siemens, the German power and technology firm, established specific objectives for the year 2010 for each of its three divisions, as shown in Table 6.2 (Siemens, 2009), with these objectives reflecting the competitive circumstance of each division.

Chapter 13

These objectives provide a basis for evaluating managers and units, and are an essential input to a control system, as we will discuss in more detail in Chapter 13 (➤Chapter 13). Thus, although ideally we would prefer that, as with other elements of this direction-setting process, we obtain acceptance and buy-in from all employees, there are times when objectives will be imposed from the top.

Such an edict may follow from concern at the current and likely future profit levels of the firm, and senior managers see no alternative but to adopt drastic and dramatic steps to improve profitability. During the recent global financial crisis, many firms experienced substantial decline in revenues, which in turn forced the adoption of draconian measures to ensure financial viability. In July 2008 Siemens, one of many firms affected by the financial crisis, announced that it was reducing its staff by 4 per cent, or 16,750 jobs (*The Economist*, 2008).

Financial and non-financial objectives

LEARNING OBJECTIVE 4

Give examples of non-financial as well as financial objectives.

It is vitally important to recognize that business is not just about achieving good financial performance. The way in which financial performance is achieved is also important. Society recognizes this by imposing legal constraints upon the way in which firms may choose to go about generating profit. These include regulations on such issues as competitive behaviour (e.g. anti-trust laws), pollution, employment, minimum wages, child labour laws and the like. Nor are concerns with means restricted to governmental regulations, since, if company values statements are to be meaningful, there must be some kind of mechanism for ensuring compliance, which may well be reflected in performance objectives (e.g. days lost to workplace injuries), and even reward systems.

Sandvik, the Swedish industrial firm, believes that stakeholders of major global firms require a holistic approach to setting objectives to include financial, environmental and social objectives. Reflecting their customer orientation, a major objective for Sandvik is the development and marketing of products and services which facilitate higher customer productivity and profitability. Their corporate financial goals emphasize measures such as revenue and market share growth, and, as we saw with Siemens, Sandvik recognizes that these will vary according to the business unit, reflecting the different industry structure and level of competition for each business unit (Sandvik, 2008). However, the firm also has corporate social responsibility objectives (►Chapter 13), as indicated below.

Chapter 13

Social objectives *in practice* – Sandvik

Sandvik social objectives include such measures as the following:

- Reduced air and water emissions
- Reduced environmental impact from hazardous chemicals
- Reduced frequency of occupational injuries
- Long-term sustainable development.

As these examples demonstrate, global firms develop corporate objectives of both a financial and a non-financial nature, and that the corporate centre also develops objectives for the various business units. For most firms there is a strong emphasis on financial measures, but these are supplemented by a set of non-financial and social responsibility measures.

Setting objectives

Responsibility for setting objectives lies with the top management team of the organizational entity under consideration. Objectives need to be kept up to date and to reflect the current competitive position and opportunities of the organization. They are generally set with some consultation and input from members of the entity, but in some circumstances will be imposed. As we saw, the global financial crisis resulted in many firms adjusting their short-term objectives to place more emphasis on survival and cash flow as demand dropped and financial markets froze up.

Categories of financial objectives

Chapter 2

We have classified objectives into two categories: financial and non-financial measures. But as was noted in Chapter 2, we regard a business firm as a group of productive assets brought together primarily for economic purposes (►Chapter 2). Thus financial objectives can be expected to play a dominant role. In extreme circumstances the only relevant objective may be survival, with all others being secondary. But generally the different values of the stakeholders of the firm ensure that it will pursue a more balanced approach. The nature of this balance will be very dependent on the characteristics of the top management team, and the economic conditions faced by the firm.

Two major operating drivers for improving shareholder value are revenue growth and operating margin. It follows, therefore, that if we accept the maxim that we should be increasing economic profit, then growth and margin targets must be foremost in establishing the operational objectives of the corporation and its constituent businesses.

Revenue growth

Almost all firms establish some objectives for future revenue growth which can be broken down into three components:

- Organic growth from existing businesses.
- Growth from developments of these existing businesses.
- Growth from new businesses/acquisitions.

The specific levels to be set here reflect a trade-off decision between the major alternatives open to the firm and a trade-off between growth and margins. Growth generally comes at the expense of current margins, and the decision on the balance between these two is one that must be made by senior management. Investor expectations, and thus the share price, are strongly influenced by perceived growth opportunities of the firm. Significant growth opportunities generally come from major innovations or acquisitions, but these are typically much riskier than organic growth from existing businesses. This balance between mature

Chapter 9

and growth businesses will be discussed in more detail in Chapter 9 (►Chapter 9).

Margin

In our view, an essential managerial task is ongoing cost reduction and productivity improvement of both labour and capital. Firms need to focus on continuous improvement, ensuring that all existing processes are operating efficiently. For many firms, this has led to increased adoption of information technology and increased attention to supply chain management. Increased prices are difficult to achieve in markets experiencing higher levels of competitive intensity, so most margin improvements will come from cost reductions.

The competitiveness of today's markets means that merely to maintain a position firms must improve their operations at the same rate as their competitors. To improve their position relative to competitors demands that managers reconsider many of their basic assumptions about the business, including considering the outsourcing of any non-core activity that is performed at less than world-class levels of excellence. Margin improvement therefore demands ongoing benchmarking of performance versus best-of-class competitors, and a willingness to innovate in seeking structural solutions that go significantly beyond traditional boundaries.

The goal of improving margins has different implications at the corporate and business unit level. At the corporate level, all group or corporate level activities should ideally incur very low levels of overheads. Unless corporate activities are demanded by the operating businesses such that significant shared economies can be created by retaining them at corporate, they should instead be placed within the businesses where allocation is no longer an issue, and they can be prudently managed within a normal single-business framework. There is substantial justification for this philosophy in economic theory, since investors are capable of diversifying their own investment portfolio at very low cost.

Within a business unit the value chain provides a very useful framework for understanding and generating opportunities for raising margins. In our experience, active management of the value chain is a fairly recent phenomenon, and there are still many companies in which managers restrict their actions to incremental changes and improvements in the existing business system, but do not consider structural changes therein, as was discussed in Chapter 2 (➤Chapter 2).

Chapter 2

Financial structure

As we have seen, firms need to consider their financial structure, in particular their leverage, and ensure that it is kept within reasonable limits. High leverage increases the financial risk for the firm, which could well result in liquidity problems should there be changes in financial markets such as occurred in 2008. While we are not suggesting that Accor's leverage is currently too high, their objectives for 2015 will certainly have the effect of reducing their financial risk.

Level of objectives

Chapters
7, 8, 9

In addition to the pressures from the capital market perspective, there are very real pressures driven from the markets of individual business units. Decomposing corporate objectives to the business unit level is in part a portfolio issue (▶Chapters 8, 9), in part a competitive strategy issue within the firm's businesses, but also a behavioural issue. We address the setting of business-level objectives in Chapter 7 (▶Chapter 7) but suffice here to say that in general the level at which objectives are set demands finding an appropriate behavioural compromise. Objectives that are set at a level that lower levels of management regard as unfeasible motivate withdrawal behaviour rather than higher levels of effort. On the other hand, some degree of 'stretch' is necessary to motivate reconsideration of basic assumptions that might otherwise never be explored.

In our view an appropriate level of objectives can only be established by a participative exercise, with an open-minded attitude towards addressing the difficult trade-offs that must typically occur to resolve the tension between the 'top-down' capital market pressures and the 'bottom-up' pressures of competitive business markets. Time spent on these issues is usually time well spent from the shareholders' perspective.

Further, there are some important principles that should guide the setting of objectives. First, an overwhelming number of companies establish objectives and measure performance benchmarked not against competitors but against a previous period, often last year. When we see improvement over the previous year, this is often encouraging and motivating, but nonetheless can also be delusionary. We must never forget that business is a competitive game, and wherever possible, more appropriate benchmarks are external. Whether we are looking at sales gains, ROEs, margins, or any other measure, we are well advised to compare these against competitors rather than the previous year. Wherever possible, we should be looking forward and outward, offsetting what seems to be a frequently prevailing tendency to look backwards and inwards!

Problems in setting objectives

We now explore three major problems in setting objectives: determining priorities, excessive stretch and the issue of unintended consequences.

Determining priorities

Since the firm and its units must establish a nested set of objectives, cascading down the firm, we need to ensure that these are consistent with each other. For example, an objective of cost reduction may not be compatible with an objective of innovation. In other words, in setting objectives we must recognize that there are often trade-off decisions to be made, and it is essential that these decisions be made explicitly and clearly communicated. While in an ideal world we might wish to have everything at once, in the real world this will not occur. Consider as an example the potential problems posed by growth objectives.

As we saw in Chapter 4, the typical large company cannot fund its own growth solely from internally generated funds, but must have recourse to financial markets (►Chapter 4). The reasons are quite straightforward: to grow requires investment funds, whether these go into new facilities, equipment, hiring and training new employees, or advertising. Whereas in some instances we may be able to generate sufficient funds internally, the faster we wish to grow (the more ambitious the growth targets), the less likely this is to occur, particularly for a single business corporation that cannot internally cross-fund. In other words, there is a trade-off between targeted growth rates and cash flow. Unfortunately, there is a very human tendency to want to have everything at once, and unless the trade-off issue is addressed explicitly, disappointment is certain. Portfolio analysis techniques, and the building of appropriate financial models can help avoid this problem, and we address these issues at more length in Chapters 8 and 9 (►Chapters 8, 9).

Chapters 4, 8, 9

Excessive stretch

In the last part of the twentieth century, some consultants were advocating the concept of BHAG, 'Big, Hairy, Aggressive Goals' to their clients (Collins & Porras, 1994). In some companies this advocacy resulted in a meaningless numbers game. Allow us to explain.

The idea behind BHAG was that very ambitious goals could motivate people to achieve at much higher levels. We don't doubt that under appropriate conditions this may occur. Human beings have shown that they can sometimes achieve the extraordinary against considerable odds. However, to believe that the extraordinary can become routine is almost certainly a triumph of optimism over reality, while the constraints – implicit or otherwise – created by the organization too often guaranteed the impossibility of achieving the BHAGs. To achieve the exceptional may be possible, but will usually require the availability of appropriate resources and/or the relaxation of constraints, such that the problem can be approached differently. In addition, objectives that are essentially unattainable will generally have a negative impact on performance – managers realize that they cannot be met and hence do not even try. Marchionne, the CEO who revitalized Fiat, set very ambitious objectives, but, with a challenging yet supportive management approach, showed that they were indeed achievable, contrary to the assumptions of many pundits (Marchionne, 2008).

Unintended consequences

This problem is usually obvious in retrospect, but is rarely seen at the time. Quite simply, human beings verge on genius when asked to perform against any particular standard. We find a way to do it! For many years US airlines competed, among other bases, by promoting the shortest scheduled times between airports. When, however, the US Department of Transportation decided that passenger choice would be facilitated by publishing the airlines' arrival time performance, the almost immediate response was to lengthen the scheduled times for their flights so that the on-time record immediately improved! When researching the management of multinational subsidiaries, we found that the response of subsidiary CEOs to what they regarded as unfair budget limitations from head office (e.g. all expenditures over €50,000 must receive prior approval from HQ) was to ensure that invoices were paid with a series of smaller payments, none of which exceeded the budget limit (Hulbert & Brandt, 1980).

The only advice we can offer here is to avoid emphasis on any single measure by (a) achieving the balance of priorities we discussed, earlier and (b) ensuring some measurement redundancy (i.e. measure the same construct by alternative means and methods wherever possible). In fact, deviant behaviour is much less likely when objectives are negotiated and agreed upon, following the approaches we have advocated in this chapter. Wherever targets are externally imposed and perceived as unfair or arbitrary, and where reward and punishment is linked to performance against these objectives, however, problems become more likely.

Synthesizing the concepts

So far we have talked about the concepts of vision, values, mission and objectives, but have spent little time talking about their interrelationships. We have discussed the idea that a vision cannot possibly become a reality if the values (and therefore the behaviour) of the organization are not consistent with its realization. Similarly, along a chronological dimension, it would seem highly desirable that the evolution of a firm's business mission progresses over time towards the realization of its vision, even though we would expect a mission statement to be subject to much more frequent revision, and to encompass considerably more detail. Similarly, we would hope that the corporate and business level objectives that are established will help the firm fulfil its mission.

LEARNING OBJECTIVE 5

Integrate the concepts of vision, values, mission and objectives in a consistent manner.

6.6 AN INTEGRATIVE EXAMPLE

We have covered a number of very important concepts in this chapter and have stressed how they should be integrated in a consistent manner. We illustrate this principle by using the example of Petrobras, the large Brazilian oil and energy company at both the corporate and business unit levels (de Azevedo, 2008). We chose the bio fuels business unit for our example. Due to its large sugar production Brazil is a major producer of ethanol, which has been available as a fuel in that country for many years. Vision, mission and objectives are shown for the Petrobras Company, and mission and objectives for the bio fuels business unit.

The Petrobras website contains much more information on the details of company and business unit strategies, but the excerpts above illustrate very well many of the concepts we have discussed in this chapter. A future sense of direction is clear from the 2020 vision statement, while both company and business unit missions are described. The statement of corporate objectives contains both financial and non-financial objectives, and serves to emphasize how important the latter are for a very high-profile company such as Petrobras.

Future direction *in practice* – Petrobras

Petrobras corporate level

Vision 2020

We will be one of the five largest integrated energy companies in the world and the preferred choice among our stakeholders.

Mission

Operate on a safe and profitable manner in Brazil and abroad, with social and environmental responsibility, providing products and services that meet client's needs and that contribute to the development of Brazil and the countries in which it operates.

Corporate objectives

Production

Total production from Brazil and international operations in 2020 (000s b/day)

Oil production – Brazil	3,920
Gas production – Brazil	1,177
Oil production – international	409
Gas production – international	223

Costs

Lifting costs – Brazil	6.13	$US per barrel

Investment

Invest $US174 billion over the period 2009–2013, of which $US88 billion is to be in production and $US17 billion in exploration.

Finance

Leverage (D/D+E) (2012)	20%
Return on capital employed (2012)	14%

Human resources

Lost time percentage employees (2012)	2.18

Social responsibility

Social responsibility image (2012)	81%
Employees commitment to social responsibility (2012)	98%

Petrobras business unit level

Bio fuels business segments

Mission

Operate on a global basis in bio fuels commercialization and logistics, leading to the domestic production of bio diesel and expanding participation in the ethanol segment.

Objectives

Ethanol exports in 2012	4,750,000 cubic metres

6.7 SUMMARY

In this chapter we covered some of the most important concepts in strategic management. They cover the gamut, from the 'soft' side of visioning and values to the 'hard' side of missions and objectives, all of which play an important role in creating the future direction of the firm.

As Figure 6.7 illustrates, each concept plays a distinct yet related role in establishing the future direction of the enterprise.

You should recognize that the strategic management of an organization requires that you master both 'sides'; for one without the other will ensure that you fail in your managerial duties. As we have seen from the company examples we have examined, senior managers of virtually all large companies are very much aware that while achieving good financial results for shareholders is important, the firm has multiple stakeholders that can affect its future prospects. As the operations of large companies become more transparent, it is very clear that how results are achieved is as important as the results themselves, and good strategic managers will be aware that they cannot serve the longer term interests of shareholders without regard for this important principle.

Corporate objectives	Business unit objectives
Shareholder return	Growth
Economic profit	Operational excellence
Growth	Quality
Portfolio balance	Market share gain
Innovation	Employee developent
Staff excellence	Capital productivity
Corporate social responsibility	Competence development

Figure 6.7 Role of different concepts

Reprinted by permission of Impact Planning Group and Robert Christian

VIEW FROM THE TOP

NVIDIA

Jen-Hsun Huang co-founded nVIDIA Corporation in April 1993 and has served as president and CEO since its inception. Under his leadership, nVIDIA became one of the largest fabless semiconductor companies in the world. nVIDIA has received numerous business and technology awards, including Fortune's Fastest Growing Companies, *Wired Magazine*'s Top 40, and Stanford Business School's Entrepreneurial Company of the Year. Mr Huang has been a trustee of the RAND Corporation since 1999 and often speaks on technology and business trends.

Mr Huang, in discussing the importance of having a big vision when starting a new venture, said: 'you should not be daunted when others, including early customers, don't share your vision because they don't share your world view'. Huang's vision for nVIDIA involved building a culture of innovation, with the conviction that if you aren't re-inventing yourself, you are slowly dying.

Every successful thing about a technology company has to eventually be torn down and rebuilt, says Huang, and this is one of the most gut-wrenching challenges behind effective leadership. This task is both gratifying and destructive, but is an axiomatic demand of the marketplace in this sector.

He continues: 'If you have a great idea, many other people probably have that idea too. When you start a company, you must assume that similar companies will form to compete with you. Be prepared to fend them off. Every company looks for a fundamental advantage, but in reality there are none. Most large markets are designed to foster competition. The question that must be addressed is not how to create one single fundamental advantage for the company but rather ongoing advantages.'

Edited and abstracted from Huang, 2009

QUESTIONS

1 Mr Huang clearly has a firm grasp of the competitive realities of the high-tech world, but how realistic is it to believe that you can create a vision that can be sufficiently lasting in such a dynamic environment?

2 Mr Huang also claims that 'everyone has a perspective but to call it a "vision" implies elitism and exclusion'. In 1993, he says, his company's perspective was 'the first of its kind, and the results have proved . . . disruptive to the status quo. This perspective – not vision – allowed them to create new technology, new markets, new customers, and widespread success.' Do you agree that visions are necessarily elitist and exclusionary?

COCA-COLA

Shown below are the vision, values and mission statement for Coca-Cola, the global beverage company (CocaCola, 2009).

Coca-Cola's vision

Our vision serves as the framework for our Roadmap and guides every aspect of our business by describing what we need to accomplish in order to continue achieving sustainable, quality growth.

- **People**: be a great place to work where people are inspired to be the best they can be.
- **Portfolio**: bring to the world a portfolio of quality beverage brands that anticipate and satisfy people's desires and needs.
- **Partners**: nurture a winning network of customers and suppliers; together we create mutual, enduring value.
- **Planet**: be a responsible citizen that makes a difference by helping to build and support sustainable communities.
- **Profit**: maximize long-term return to shareholders while being mindful of our overall responsibilities.
- **Productivity**: be a highly effective, lean and fast-moving organization.

Coca-Cola's values

Our values serve as a compass for our actions and describe how we behave in the world.

- **Leadership**: the courage to shape a better future.
- **Collaboration**: leverage collective genius.
- **Integrity**: be real.
- **Accountability**: if it is to be, it's up to me.
- **Passion**: committed in heart and mind.
- **Diversity**: as inclusive as our brands.
- **Quality**: what we do, we do well.

Focus on the market

- Focus on the needs of our consumers, customers and franchise partners.
- Get out into the market and listen, observe and learn.
- Possess a world view.
- Focus on execution in the marketplace every day.
- Be insatiably curious.

MINI-CASE

Work smart

- Act with urgency.
- Remain responsive to change.
- Have the courage to change course when needed.
- Remain constructively discontented.
- Work efficiently.

Act like owners

- Be accountable for all our actions and inactions.
- Steward system assets and focus on building value.
- Reward our people for taking risks and finding better ways to solve problems.
- Learn from our outcomes – what worked and what didn't.

Be the brand

- Inspire creativity, passion, optimism and fun.

Coca-Cola's mission

Our roadmap starts with our mission, which is enduring. It declares our purpose as a company and serves as the standard against which we weigh our actions and decisions.

- To refresh the world.
- To inspire moments of optimism and happiness.
- To create value and make a difference.

QUESTIONS

Comment on these statements addressing the following questions:

1 Are the statements clear, concise and actionable?
2 How do these statements compare to the definitions of vision, values and mission developed in the text?
3 Do these statements provide a sense of direction for managers?
4 Do these statements motivate managers?

REVIEW QUESTIONS

1 Choose a firm with which you are familiar. What is the vision statement for that firm? Do you think that this vision statement is correct?

2 Indicate, for the firm chosen in question 1, how the vision selected by the firm has influenced the strategies developed by the firm.

3 Table 6.3 shows the vision statements of a number of well-known firms. Identify the key features of each vision. What are their strengths and weaknesses?

4 Discuss the comment: 'all staff in a firm must have a good understanding of what the firm will look like in ten years' time'.

5 It has been suggested that too many vision statements are bland and do not generate staff commitment. Why does this occur?

6 What values do you think will become more important for global firms over the next ten years?

7 Table 6.4 shows the mission statements of a number of well-known firms. Identify the key features of each mission. What are their strengths and weaknesses?

Table 6.3 Review question 3

Company	Vision	Source
Honda	The Power of Dreams	http://corporate.honda.com/search/index.aspx
GE	We bring good things to life	http://www.1000ventures.com/business_guide/crosscuttings/vision_mission_strategy.html
Ford Motor Company	To become the world's leading consumer company for automotive products and services	http://www.1000ventures.com/business_guide/crosscuttings/vision_mission_strategy.html
Pepsi Cola	PepsiCo's responsibility is to continually improve all aspects of the world in which we operate – environment, social, economic – creating a better tomorrow than today	http://www.pepsico.com/Company/Our-Mission-and-Vision.html
Vivendi	Promoting cultural diversity	http://www.vivendi.com/vivendi/Cultural-diversity?var_recherche=Vision
Ericson	Transforming Telecom Management	http://www.ericsson.com/technology/whitepapers/telecom_services/transforming_telecom_management.shtml
Sony Ericsson	Our vision is to become THE communication entertainment brand. We inspire people to do more than just communicate. We enable everyone to create and participate in entertainment experiences. Experiences that blur the lines between communication and entertainment	http://www.sonyericsson.com/cws/corporate/company/aboutus/mission
Siemens In Brazil	A world of proven talent, delivering breakthrough innovations, giving our customers a unique competitive edge, enabling societies to master their most vital challenges and creating sustainable value	http://www.siemens.com.br/templates/v2/templates/TemplateC.Aspx?channel=9006#index01

Table 6.4 Review question 7

Company	Mission statement	Source
Shimano	To promote health and happiness through the enjoyment of nature and the world around us	http://www.shimano.com/publish/content/global_corp/en/us/index/about_shimano/mission_statement.html
Sony Ericsson	To establish Sony Ericsson as the most attractive and innovative brand in the mobile handset industry. We want to make things happen, to create the spark between people, and to make Sony Ericsson open to everyone. Our brand, and what it stands for, makes great things happen in people's lives	http://www.sonyericsson.com/cws/corporate/common/searchresult
CEMEX	To serve the global building needs of our customers and build value for our stakeholders by becoming the world's most efficient and profitable building materials company	http://www.cemex.com/home/this-is-cemex
Danone	To bring health through food and beverages to a maximum number of people	http://www.danone.co.uk/
Indesit	To be the European leader, producing technological solutions compatible with the environment, to create quality of time for people day after day	http://www.indesitcompany.com

REFERENCES

Abrahams, J. (1999) The mission statement book: 301 corporate mission statements from America's top companies. Retrieved 5 January 2010. www.cadbury.com/investors/our-vision-and-strategy.

Accor (2010) Network today and objectives. *Hotel Development*. www.accor.com/en/hotels/hotel-development/network-today-and-objectives.pdf.

BalfourBeatty (2009) Vision and values. Retrieved 31 May 2010. www.bbireland.ie/visions.php?%22.

Bartkus, B., Glassman, M. & McAfee, B. (2006) Mission statement quality and financial performance. *European Management Journal, 24*(1), 86–94.

BASF (2010) Strategy. *About BASF*. Retrieved 15 February 2011. www.basf.com/group/corporate/en/about-basf/strategy/index.

BBC (2010) About the BBC. www.bbc.co.uk/info/purpose/.

Bennis, W. & Nanus, B. (1985) *Leaders: The Strategies for Taking Charge*. New York: Harper & Row.

Campbell, A., Devine, M. & Young, D. (1993) *A Sense of Mission*. London: Pitman.

Capon, N., Farley, J. U. & Hulbert, J. M. (1988) *Corporate Strategic Planning*. New York: Columbia University Press.

CocaCola (2009) Mission, vision, values. Retrieved 18 January 2010. www.thecocacolacompany.com/ourcompany/mission-vision-values.

Collins, J. C. & Porras, J. I. (1994) *Built to Last*. New York: HarperBusiness.

Collins, J. C. & Porras, J. I. (1996) Building your company's vision. *Harvard Business Review*, (September–October), 65–78.

David, G. (2006) *Leadership remarks*. Paper presented at the international conference on intelligent green and energy-efficient building and technologies. www.utc.com/utc/home/news.

de Azevedo, J. S. G. (2008) 2008–2012 Business plan. Retrieved 8 January 2010. www2.petrobras.com.br/about petrobras/strategicplanfor2020,2008–2012Businessplan.

Deal, T. E. & Kennedy, A. A. (1982) *Corporate Cultures*. Reading, MA: Addison-Wesley.

Drucker, P. (1973) *Management: Tasks, Responsibilities, Practices*. New York: Harper & Row.

GlaxoSmithKline (2009) Our mission and strategy. Retrieved 8 January 2010. www.gsk.com/ourmissionandstrategy.

HaierUS (2009) Mission. Retrieved 8 January 2010. www.haieramerica.com/about.

Hamel, G. & Prahalad, C. K. (1994) Competing for the future. *Harvard Business Review*, (July–August), 122–128.

Heal, G. (2008) *When Principles Pay: Corporate Social Responsibility and the Bottom Line*. New York: Columbia Business School Publishing.

Huang, J. (2009) Vision matters. *Podcast*. Retrieved 31 May 2010. http://ecorner.stanford.edu/search.html?keywords=nvidia%20%20vision%20matters.

Hulbert, J. M. & Brandt, W. K. (1980) *Managing the Multinational Subsidiary*. New York: Holt Rinehart and Winston.

Langeler, G. H. (1992) The vision trap. *Harvard Business Review*, (March–April), 46–55.

Lawrence, P. & Lorsch, J. W. (1967) *Organizations and Environment*. Boston, MA: Harvard University Press.

Marchionne, S. (2008) Fiat's extreme makeover. *Harvard Business Review*, (December), 45–48.

Matlack, C. (2010) New year brings two sweet deals for Nestlé. *Business Week*, 13 January.

Microsoft (2009) About Microsoft. Retrieved 8 January 2010.

Mitarai, F. (2009) Corporate strategy conference. Retrieved 6 January 2010. www.canon.com/investor relations/IRevents/corporatestrategyconference.

Moeller, M., Hamm, S. & Mullaney, T. J. (1999) Remaking Microsoft: Why America's most successful company needed an overhaul. *Business Week*, 106.

Nokia (2009) About Nokia. Retrieved 8 January 2010. www.nokia.com/about-nokia/story-of-nokia.

Otis (2009) Otis mission. Retrieved 8 January 2010. www.otisworldwide.com/.

Phelan, P. (2010) 5 Essential attributes of successful CEO's. *Online business/hosting*. Retrieved 31 May 2010. http://onlinebusiness.about.com/od/dailyoperations/a/5-ceo-traits.htm.

Porter, A. (2009) BBC expansion should stop, says minister. *The Daily Telegraph*, 17 September.

Prahalad, C. K. & Hamel, G. (1990) The core competence of the corporation. *Harvard Business Review*, (May-June), 79–93.

Sandvik, A. (2008) Sandvik business concept, goals and strategies. Retrieved 5 January 2010. www.sandvik.com/businessconcepts,goalsandstrategies.

Sargent, C. (2010) Novartis may raise public Alcon bid. *Business Week*.

Senge, P. M. (1990) *The Fifth Discipline*. New York: Doubleday.

Siemens, A. (2009) Siemens Fit42010. Retrieved 5 January 2010. www.siemens.com/aboutus/strategy/fit42010.

Stewart, D. (2008) Principles do pay: Wanted: A Thomas Aquinas of the business world, 22 May. http://fairerglobalization.blogspot.com/2008/05/principles-do-pay-wanted-thomas-aquinas.html.

Tata (2010) Values and purpose. Retrieved 8 January 2010. www.tata.com/aboutus/articles/inside.aspx?artid=CKdRrD5ZDV4=.

The Economist (2008) The world this week business, Siemens. *The Economist*, 12 July.

Unilever (2010) Purpose and principles. *About Us*. www.unilever.com/aboutus/purposeandprinciples/
ourpurpose/?WT.LHNAV=Our_purpose.

For a range of further resources supporting this chapter, please visit the companion website
for *Strategic Management* at www.routledge.com/cw/fitzroy.

CHAPTER 7

BUSINESS-LEVEL STRATEGY

LEARNING OBJECTIVES

Upon completing this chapter you should be able to:

1   Understand the inter-relationship between corporate-level and business-level strategy.

2   Analyse the changing environment in which the business unit is competing.

3   Develop a strategy for a business that recognizes the three key decisions – where to compete, how to compete and how to grow.

4   Apply the concept of a competitive advantage and appreciate the need for ongoing enhancement of this advantage.

5   Formulate a growth strategy for the firm.

TATA GROUP

Tata Group is India's largest company, with operations in 85 countries. It operates in a wide variety of industries and geographies, generating 64.7 per cent of its $US70.8 billion revenues outside its Indian base. It has grown both organically and via acquisitions, but acquisitions have become increasingly important. In the last eight years, the company has made overseas acquisitions totalling $US18 billion, adding such major brands as Tetley, Brunner Mond, Corus, Jaguar and Land Rover in the UK, Daewoo Commercial Vehicles in South Korea, NatSteel in Singapore, and Tyco Global Network and General Chemical in the US under the Tata umbrella.

The Tata Group is organized into seven business sectors:

- Information technology and communications
- Engineering products and services
- Materials
- Services
- Energy
- Consumer products
- Chemicals.

The corporate task to manage the total mix of sectors and companies, and how that portfolio evolves over time, is the topic of Chapters 8 and 9.

Each of the seven sectors comprises a number of businesses, which we refer to as strategic business units. The Engineering Products and Services sector comprises eight strategic business units:

- Tata Motors
- Tata Motors European Technical Centre
- Jaguar Land Rover
- Hispano Carrocera
- Tata AutoComp Systems
- Tata Daewoo Commercial Vehicle Company
- Tata Cummins
- Telco Construction Equipment.

The focus of this chapter is the strategic management of one of these business units, such as Tata Motors.

STRATEGIC MANAGEMENT IN PRACTICE

Tata Motors is India's largest automobile company. Established in 1945, it is also among the world's top five manufacturers of medium and heavy trucks and the world's second largest manufacturer of medium and heavy buses. It entered the passenger vehicle market in 1991 and now ranks second in India in this market. Formerly known as Tata Engineering and Locomotive Company, it began manufacturing commercial vehicles in 1954 with a collaboration agreement with Daimler Benz of Germany. Today, Tata Motors has over 1,400 engineers and scientists in six R&D centres in India, South Korea, Spain and the UK. Its vehicles are exported to Europe, Africa, the Middle East, South and Southeast Asia, and South America. The product range includes:

- Passenger cars: Tata Motors launched the compact Tata Indica in 1998, the sedan Indigo in 2002, the station wagon Indigo Marina in 2004, and the low-cost Nano in 2008. Tata Motors also distributes Fiat's cars in India.
- Utility vehicles: the Tata Sumo was launched in 1994 and the Tata Safari in 1998.
- Commercial vehicles: the commercial vehicle range extends from the light 2-tonne truck to heavy dumpers and multi-axle vehicles in the above 40-tonne segment.
- Passenger buses: Tata Motors also manufactures and sells passenger buses, 12-seaters to 60-seaters, in the light, medium and heavy segments.

In addition, Tata Motors has formed a number of subsidiaries, such as a finance group, as well as joint ventures with partners such as Hitachi and Fiat (Tata Group, 2010).

The Tata example highlights the complex structure of the modern global firm, with a corporate level, a sector level and finally a business unit level. As Tata Motors illustrates, even the business units are complex, with the business unit having operations in many countries and operating with a wide product line that includes trucks, buses and cars. Strategy development within Tata Motors will be influenced by strategy adopted by Tata as a corporate entity, as well as strategy adopted at the sector level. At the same time, Tata Motors is able to utilize the resources and capabilities of the entire Tata Group. For example, a significant corporate intangible asset is the global franchise inherent in the name Tata which is of value to all business units with their customers. The Tata brand has gained international recognition. Brand Finance, a UK-based consultancy firm, valued the Tata brand at $11.2 billion in 2010, ranking it sixty-fourth among the world's Top 100 brands (BrandDirectory, 2010). Tata Motors should also benefit from being able to share such capabilities as technological expertise with other businesses in the Engineering Products and Services sector that are also automotive businesses (Tata, 2010).

CHAPTER OVERVIEW

We begin by considering the relationship between the firm and its business units, and the necessity to develop a vision, mission and objectives for the business in cooperation with the corporate centre. Developing business-level strategy necessitates understanding the changing product/market environment of the business, which we briefly review. We then examine tools for internal analysis of the business, paying particular attention to the value chain of the business and the implications of this analysis for strategy development. The essence of business unit strategy is how the business should compete in the industry in which it is located. This involves creating and maintaining a competitive advantage, exploiting and enhancing its core capabilities and responding to changes in its product/market environment. Our model of the strategy development process for the business is introduced, indicating that business unit strategy requires decisions in three interrelated areas – where to compete, how to compete, and how to grow – that are then examined in depth. Where to compete is concerned with where the business should position itself, vertically in the value chain and horizontally with respect to market segments. We then evaluate the alternative ways in which the business can develop a competitive advantage in its industry. The third element is possible growth alternatives for the business.

This is followed by a View from the Top, a discussion of the strategy of a business unit within Sandvik, the Swedish engineering firm. The chapter concludes with a mini-case, Ryanair, where you are asked to evaluate the reasons for the success of their strategy.

7.1 INTRODUCTION

Corporate and business unit relationships

LEARNING OBJECTIVE 1

Understand the inter-relationship between corporate-level and business-level strategy.

Different business units must develop their own individual strategy and be managed in ways that reflect their distinctive competitive context, while also drawing on resources provided by the corporate level of the firm. The challenges facing any particular business unit in the firm are likely to be different from the challenges facing the firm's other businesses, as would be the situation with the two Tata businesses: Tata Motors and Tata Consulting.

Nonetheless, while business units have a degree of autonomy and are managed relatively independently of other business units, they are all part of a larger enterprise, which can add value and/or create problems for the business unit (➤Chapter 2). The existence of **synergy** among various business units, such as sharing of knowledge, skills, technology and information, may compromise the independence of a specific business. On the other hand, if the corporate centre is to add value to justify owning the business, then there should be benefits from leveraging corporate capabilities such as R&D, or such intangible corporate assets as brand name or shared corporate values. As was discussed in Chapter 5 (➤Chapter 5), these constitute structural intangible assets.

The strategy and performance of the corporate parent as well as the performance of other business units within the company also influence the strategy of a business. Sometimes,

Chapters 2, 5

Synergy
Occurs when two or more activities or processes complement each other so that the value created by the two units working together exceeds the value created when the two units operate independently.

Sharing values *in practice* – Unilever

Four Acres, Unilever's International Training Centre in Kingston-on-Thames, plays an important role as a vehicle for sharing concepts and strategies, spreading success stories and acculturating managers into the Unilever way, sometimes called 'Unileverization' (Jones, 2005).

from a corporate perspective, a business unit is part of the implementation process for corporate-level strategies. A corporate strategy of 'corporate social responsibility' has implications for all business units; it is not something that a given business unit can opt out of. This illustrates that some elements of business-level strategy follow directly from corporate-level strategy, suggesting low levels of independence. In truth, no business unit can be truly independent of either other business units or the corporate parent. Since one of the major tasks of a diversified firm is to enhance the synergy among business units to maximize corporate value, such cooperation should be viewed positively.

The corporate level is the source of funds and other resources for all businesses in its portfolio; no business unit would make an approach to financial markets for funds without corporate involvement. The business unit is a recipient in the capital allocation process within the firm. It makes proposals for strategies and their associated funds, but the corporate level makes the final decision. In this allocation process, the corporate level must balance the competing demands for cash from its various business units. We also have to recognize that there are different styles of corporate centres, which will be addressed in Chapter 8 **Chapter 8** (▶Chapter 8) (Goold *et al.*, 1994). In some firms the corporate centre is deeply involved in strategy at the business unit level so as to achieve synergy across the entire firm. In other firms, the corporate centre acts essentially as an internal capital market, leaving strategy development to the unit. Which style is adopted by the corporate level will affect strategy at the business level, in particular the degree and nature of the interaction with other business units and the corporate head office. Since a business unit is part of a larger whole, consideration needs to be given to strategy at the corporate level when we are developing business strategy.

Challenge of strategic management

If you were the CEO of a business unit within a diversified firm, how independent would you want the business unit to be? Would you want to be responsible for revenue; for profitability; for deciding the mission of the business? What benefits would the business enjoy by being part of a larger corporate entity?

Strategic management of the business

Strategic management at the business unit involves not only developing strategy but also the following:

- Negotiating objectives, mission and scope with the corporate level.
- Providing leadership and leading change within the business.
- Ensuring that distinctive capabilities are exploited and enhanced.
- Developing and implementing the organizational architecture to support the strategy, including structure, decision processes, human resources and culture.
- Understanding technology requirements, including information technology.
- Accepting responsibility for the performance of the business.

Figure 7.1 reproduces the simplified model of strategic management (Figure 1.2 from Chapter 1 (➤Chapter 1), which can be applied at the business unit level. In this chapter, we focus on analysing the changing external and internal context of the business and on developing business unit strategy. Discussion of implementation and performance will be deferred until Chapters 10, 11 and 12 (➤Chapters 10, 11, 12).

Chapters
1, 10, 11, 12

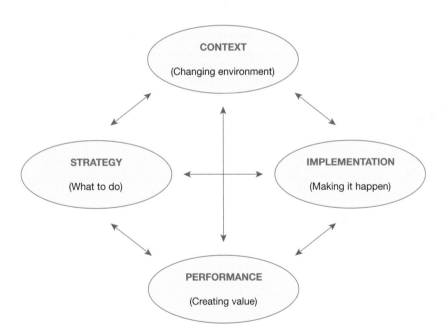

Figure 7.1 Simplified strategic management model

Business vision and objectives

Chapter 6

The concepts of vision, values and mission discussed in Chapter 6 (►Chapter 6) are, as we noted there, highly relevant for business units. Unless these are understood, widely shared and endorsed, alignment will be difficult, if not impossible, and resources will be wasted. Research suggests that in far too many businesses, managers have an incomplete understanding of the strategy which they are supposed to be implementing (Collis & Rukstad, 2008).

Establishing a future direction for the business is a crucial task. A business unit's vision, values and mission, while important to define, are qualitative and directional. Beyond these, the business unit must also have a set of quantitative targets, to be met by the strategy over some defined time period. These targets are the objectives for the unit. Objectives are a statement of what the unit expects to accomplish over a particular planning horizon. Strategy must be tested against these targets. If the strategy does not meet the objectives, then another strategy must be developed or the objectives revised. Of course, in a turbulent world, objectives may need to be revised as a result of unexpected developments. Nonetheless, successful businesses are characterized by a performance culture, part of which is the existence of defined quantitative targets, so that it is clear whether or not they have been reached.

As with vision, values and mission, the corporate centre plays a major role in establishing business unit objectives. The centre may unilaterally impose objectives for a given business or develop them more collaboratively, linking business-level and corporate-level strategy. If, for example, the corporate level were to dictate objectives to 'become number one or number two in every industry', or to 'achieve 20 per cent ROA', these would have major ramifications for all the firm's businesses.

Objectives are quantifiable, measurable, time-specific milestones of what the business wants to achieve. A business should have only a limited number of objectives, and they should be consistent with one another. Many firms set such objectives at levels that represent a 'stretch' for the business, but they must be achievable if employees are to be held accountable for results.

Chapter 12

Business objectives may be solely financial, but we recommend a broader approach. One framework for establishing a broader set of objectives, which we will discuss in more detail in Chapter 12 (►Chapter 12), is the balanced scorecard (Kaplan & Norton, 2001). This framework uses four major performance dimensions: financial (profit and growth), customer (satisfaction and retention), innovation (new products and processes) and internal measures (efficiency and costs). If we limit our focus for the moment to financial measures, however, common financial objectives are the following:

- *Growth* – what growth in revenue, net profit or assets is expected?
- *Net profit* – measured as earnings before interest and tax (EBIT) or earnings before interest, tax, depreciation and amortization (EBITDA) – what dollar value of profit is expected, and is this to be measured before interest and depreciation or not?
- *Cash generation* – will the business be a net cash generator or user over the period?

- *Return on assets* – what return on the assets is expected? This is a superior measure to margins, since it shows how well we are using the assets of the business whereas margins ignore any element of asset productivity.

- *Economic profit* – what economic profit is the business expected to earn? We should not expect all businesses to earn a positive economic profit, since growth businesses in their early development typically will not do so.

Considering only financial objectives, most companies attempt to achieve both profitability and revenue growth. Achieving these simultaneously is difficult, a result achieved by very few firms (Chakravarthy & Lorange, 2008), although the ability to achieve both will be influenced by industry structure, particularly the long-term industry growth rate.

Growth *in practice* – Raiffeisen

Raiffeisen International is a subsidiary of Raiffeisen Zentralbank Österreich AG (RZB), the third largest bank in Austria, and is an example of a firm which has been successful at achieving profitability and growth. It has generally grown via acquisitions in Central and Eastern Europe. In 2005, RZB acquired Aval Bank of the Ukraine for $US1.03 billion. In 2006, this was followed up by two further acquisitions: Russian Impexbank and the Czech Republic's eBanka (RZB, 2009). Raiffeisen has achieved significant growth in assets, currently approximately €80 billion, while bank earnings have increased by an average of 55 per cent over the last five years (iStockAnalyst, 2008).

While some firms are able to achieve both growth and profitability, and this should be the goal, for many firms the choice reflects a classical dilemma, and firms seem to choose one for a period of time and then the other. This suggests that most firms need to make choices in terms of objectives, and that the strategy developed will depend on these choices. If the objectives emphasize growth, immediate profit and/or cash flow may be poor or negative since the strategy to meet these growth objectives must be aggressive. If objectives focus on short-term profit, the strategy might emphasize cost reduction or price improvement.

Cost reduction *in practice* – pharmaceutical industry

Amid the fallout from the 2008/09 downturn, pharmaceutical company AstraZeneca announced that there would be 13,000 layoffs by 2013, while rival GSK was expected to shed 10,000 jobs. These drastic employment cuts were intended to reduce costs significantly, indicating the importance of these context-specific factors in strategic decisions (Jobvacanciesinlondon, 2009).

Objectives also need to achieve a synthesis between innovation and change on the one hand and efficiency on the other. Innovation is key to long-term performance, while efficiency may be vital for short-term survival. In competitive markets, pressures for cost reduction are always present and are exacerbated in a downturn.

LEARNING OBJECTIVE 2

Analyse the changing environment in which the business unit is competing.

7.2 THE CHANGING PRODUCT/MARKET ENVIRONMENT OF THE BUSINESS

Business level strategy rests upon detailed understanding of the unit's product/market environment and we adopt the framework of Chapter 3 (▶Chapter 3) to analyse the external changes in the environment in which the business competes.

Remote environment

Chapter 3

All business units face a changing remote environment, and the PESTLE model, introduced in Chapter 3 (▶Chapter 3), is a useful framework for understanding these changes. This model is an aid to thinking, not a rigid template to be applied mechanistically to all businesses. Strategic management is a combination of the analytical and the intuitive, and gaining insight into what external factors will be relevant for a specific business is at least partly intuitive. As highlighted previously, the principles of environmental assessment must be applied to individual businesses, since changes, their timing and their impact will be different for different business units.

> ### Environmental analysis *in practice* – Jaguar
>
> Tata Group owns Jaguar, a UK luxury car manufacturer. A number of external factors influence the demand for Jaguars, including, among others: exchange rates; disposable income; interest rates; economic conditions; technological developments in car electronics such as GPS systems; and exhaust emission regulations. Another business unit of Tata, such as Tata Daewoo Commercial Vehicle Company, will also be influenced by changes in its remote environment, but these influences will be different, since the customers and competitors are different. Commercial vehicle demand may be influenced by parameters such as business investment, legislation on road and rail use, economic growth and so on.

Industry environment

A business unit can be viewed as a member of a vertical network of firms that transforms inputs to deliver value to final customers. We have referred to this as the industry system or value chain. Such systems have both vertical and horizontal members. Vertical members are suppliers and customers, while horizontal members are entities providing inputs at the same level, such as accountants, market research firms and law firms.

Industry analysis is most relevant at the business unit level. The principles of competitive rivalry, substitutes, entrants, buyer power and supplier power discussed in Chapter 3 (▶Chapter 3) are important to understand not just in the present but also dynamically, to reveal what changes are likely to occur (Bensoussan, 2008). For example, are entry barriers for the industry falling, suggesting the likelihood of future entrants and lower margins? Changes influencing an industry affect some firms more than others; we need to understand possible impacts on specific business units.

Chapter 3

Competition between industry systems

In many cases, competition is broader than that between two independent firms; instead, there is generally competition occurring between two complete industry systems. There is competition between copper wire and optical fibres in telecommunications. Steel, aluminium and composites compete in automobile manufacture, while in-store and electronic shopping compete for retail custom.

A vital initial step in developing business strategy is therefore to understand the extent, degree and nature of competition between such industry systems. Whenever products from different technology platforms satisfy the same customer needs, each system must be thoroughly understood through an analysis of the respective industry value chains (▶Chapter 5). Changes in costs, technology or product characteristics at any level in either chain will influence relative competitiveness and the strategy required to ameliorate or take advantage of such developments. For example, multinational environmental agreements, such as a global emissions trading scheme, alter the basis of competition among coal, oil, natural gas, nuclear and renewable sources in electricity generation.

Chapter 5

Value creation and capture in the value chain

We must also understand how much value is created in the complete system and which firms capture the value generated. Figure 7.2 shows the value chain for the US personal computer industry, with the various stages shown along the horizontal axis, comprising microprocessors, components, the PC assemblers, software and so on. For each stage, the length on the horizontal axis is equal to that stage's share of the total industry revenue. So microprocessors account for only 3 per cent of total industry revenue, while personal computers, the firms which actually assemble the PCs, account for 40 per cent of industry revenue. From a revenue perspective, personal computer assemblers and other component manufacturers dominate the industry. But examination of the vertical axis reveals a very different result. This vertical axis shows the average margin of the firms at each stage in the value chain. For firms in the microprocessor stage, the average margin on sales is 35 per cent while for PC assemblers the average margin is 3 per cent. As is clear from Figure 7.2, in the personal computer industry in the US, profitability is concentrated in two stages of the value chain, microprocessors and software, and the two dominant firms in these stages are Intel and Microsoft, respectively.

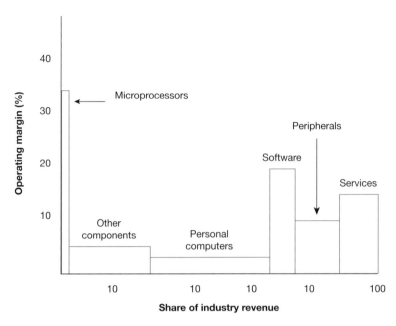

Figure 7.2 The US PC industry's value chain

Reprinted by permission of Harvard Business Review. Exhibit from Gadiesh & Gilbert, 1998. Copyright © 1998 by the Harvard Business School Publishing Corporation; all rights reserved.

This distribution of value among firms involved in different stages of a chain is influenced by such structural characteristics as relative power, the competitive intensity at different levels, entry barriers and costs, brand name and product differentiation.

All businesses in an industry system must decide where to position themselves, which activities they should perform, which activities should be done by other firms, and which organizational arrangements should exist among the firms. In the example above, personal computer manufacturers could attempt to diversify into 'other components' or into 'services' searching for higher margins. Whether they can develop the required capabilities, and develop a competitive advantage against the incumbents is certainly open to question. At the same time, Microsoft and Intel should be concerned at the low margins at other stages. A business is less likely to invest if the other players in the industry capture all the value which is created, and personal computer manufacturers may decide to exit or reduce innovation. This, in turn, might encourage customers to switch to a different industry system, jeopardizing the prospects of the entire industry, including the profitable microprocessor manufacturing stage. High margins at one stage may also encourage more regulatory attention.

Within an industry system, value capture is often adversarial – a zero-sum game in which 'if I get it, you do not'. But value creation can also be cooperative. Wal-Mart works cooperatively with suppliers to increase efficiency in the supply chain, by giving them access to Wal-Mart sales and inventory data. However, it also bargains very hard to extract for itself as much of the jointly created value as possible.

Industry system changes and disintermediation

Another consideration is whether or not the industry system is being reconfigured: are stages being eliminated, is the system undergoing a process of deconstruction and reconstruction? Such changes are disruptive and might allow new leaders to emerge.

Historically, the electricity industry comprised vertically integrated firms involved in all three stages of generation, transmission and retail. More recently, this industry has begun to fragment, with the development of new businesses at these three levels as well as in the business of meter reading which is a new element in the value chain (Crawford *et al.*, 1999). The value chain has been reconfigured in many other industries such as share trading (with Internet brokers such as E-TRADE or Charles Schwab), music (with intermediaries such as iTunes) and book selling, with e-book sellers such as Amazon and Apple competing with different models.

Major drivers of disintermediation are developments in information technology and communications, enabling the creation of new value chains. Managers must be aware of the nature of competition between different industry chains, the drivers of costs at each stage, and whether or not technology is causing stages to be eliminated or reconfigured. Value chains are a useful concept, but they should not be viewed statically, as they provide a framework for understanding the industry dynamics. To benefit from these changes, many firms will have to develop new capabilities (see ➤Chapter 5), as Tesco did when it plunged head-first – but successfully – into internet shopping.

Chapter 5

Customer value

The value chain can also provide a framework for considering where and how to add value for customers. These values are often in flux, but customers buy on the basis of the difference between price and the perceived value of the product or service, as illustrated in Figure 7.3. Buyers place a value of V on the product, which we assume to be greater than C, the cost to supply the product to the customer.

The value created by the business is then V–C. It creates value by converting inputs at a cost of C to generate a product on which customers place a value of V. The business charges a price, P, which can be interpreted as splitting the surplus value, V–C, between producer and customer. The business may capture more value by either reducing costs while holding prices constant or by increasing perceived value so that customers willingly pay higher prices (even though costs may rise). The level of P determines how the value the business has created is shared between producer and buyer.

Assessing customer value

Customer value is measured by the benefits that customers perceive they are receiving from a product or service compared with the perceived benefits offered by competitive products or services. Of course, as indicated in Figure 7.3, these benefits have to be weighed against the costs incurred by the customer, which include not only their perceptions of the price of

Customer value
The benefits customers receive from a product compared to the benefits they receive from competitive product. This value is perceptual.

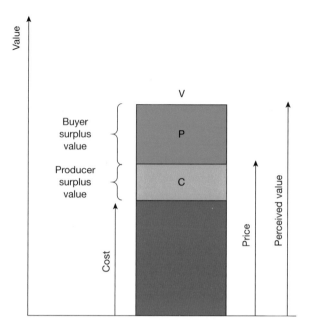

Figure 7.3 Price and value creation

the product or service, but also other 'costs', such as time to search, effort in searching and risk in the purchase.

There are a number of ways to measure customer value, including perceived value, conjoint analysis and value-in-use analyses (Capon & Hulbert, 2007). It is clearly critical that business managers understand **value drivers**, the factors that create the perception of value in the minds of customers, since the perception of value is the most important determinant of the upper bound on price.

Value driver

Any factor or event that has a direct or indirect effect on the perceived value of a good or service in the minds of customers.

Competitor analysis

A broad view of competition is essential to developing competitive strategy. We should be quite circumspect about any definition of competition that revolves around industry or products, since, as we have just seen, inter-material and inter-industry competition is a very real phenomenon. Ultimately, the customer decides which alternatives compete to fulfil a particular need or application. Business unit managers should therefore consider the following:

- Current direct competitors that want to improve their market position.
- Possible new entrants that are expanding, or perhaps because the segments are converging.
- Firms with substitutes; that is, different products targeting the same customers or the same needs.
- Suppliers and customers that could integrate forwards or backwards into the business.

The end result of competitive analysis is to enable managers to construct better strategies. This requires projecting possible competitor moves and developing strategies that deal with this variety of projected scenarios. To accomplish this will typically require analysing strategies competitors have employed in the past and how successful these strategies have been. We must also consider changes in competitors' circumstances (e.g. changes of ownership or management) before we can project what strategies they are likely to adopt and how we can address these. This analysis includes an understanding of what they are doing differently, how they compete in which segments, and their resources and capabilities. The results must influence our own business strategy, or we will have wasted our time constructing it.

7.3 INTERNAL ANALYSIS FOR DEVELOPING STRATEGY

Many different analyses can create the insight required for developing business strategy. We focus primarily on the use of the value chain or business system, an analytical framework that allows the business unit to develop a strategy that will achieve competitive advantage. This framework was developed by McKinsey and Co (Gluck, 1980), and extended by Michael Porter, who referred to it as the value chain (Porter, 1985).

The business value chain

A value chain for a business describes the activities the business has chosen to undertake in order to deliver its product or service. These activities provide a basis for examining the opportunities for reducing costs or adding value (improving differentiation) at each stage. As Figure 7.4 indicates, to apply the value chain concept we must first identify the activities involved in the value chain. To understand their relative importance, we must next identify their relative costs and value added for customers, as well as isolating the drivers of cost and the drivers of value added. For each step in the value chain, we need to ask such questions as: How does the business perform this step? What do competitors do? Are competitors' costs different to ours and if so why? Can costs or value be improved for this stage? However, to establish improvement priorities, we must integrate cost and value.

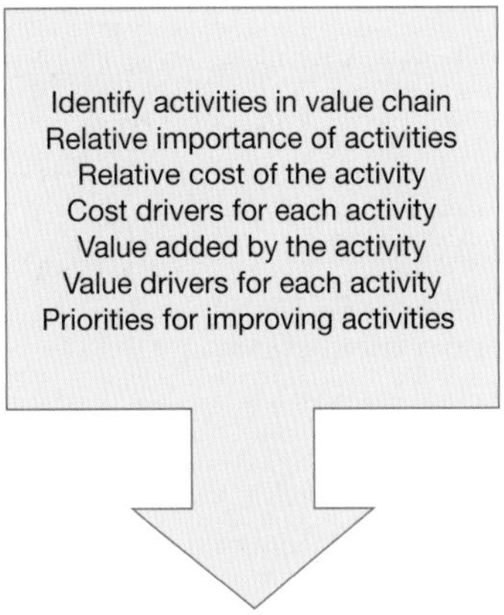

The first stage in this process is to describe the activities a firm has chosen to undertake in order to compete. Figure 7.5 describes typical value chains for the lending operation of a branch-based retail bank (Figure 7.5(a)) and a manufacturer (Figure 7.5 (b)).

In Figure 7.5, the activities of the retail bank have been collapsed into three broad stages: raising funds, processing transactions and marketing of loans together with a profit margin. This value chain provides a framework for ascertaining cost and investment drivers at each stage. The first stage is raising funds from depositors. The cost to the bank of these funds (the depositor's interest rate) depends on the general level of interest rates in the economy and the perceived risk of the individual bank. The former is

Identify activities in value chain
Relative importance of activities
Relative cost of the activity
Cost drivers for each activity
Value added by the activity
Value drivers for each activity
Priorities for improving activities

Figure 7.4 Using the value chain

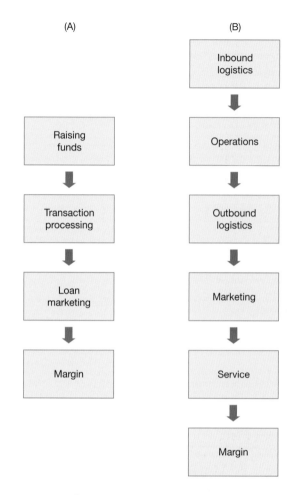

Figure 7.5 Illustrative value chains

dictated primarily by macro-economic conditions and government policy, but management can influence the latter through its risk management policies.

Transaction costs are a back office function, comprising a combination of processing and transmission costs. As data transmission costs have fallen, banks and other financial institutions have decoupled the back office from the front office. Many call centres and transaction-processing centres are in remote locations, even international ones. This offshore outsourcing (or offshoring as it is sometimes called) allows the bank to capitalize on lower wage rates.

The cost of loan marketing depends on factors such as the bank's distribution channels, its branch network efficiency and its use of technology to support these marketing activities. No company value chain is static, as businesses should constantly be seeking improvement opportunities.

The value chain can be employed to ascertain the nature and extent of our competitive advantage at any stage. This is illustrated in Figure 7.6, which describes a business unit with just two activities: manufacturing and logistics. The firm has analysed its costs for these two activities, relative to industry best practice. Its manufacturing activity is operating at industry best practice with regard to cost. However, its logistics costs are well above best practice.

One interpretation of the situation in Figure 7.6 is that logistics is being subsidized by manufacturing. In highly competitive markets, such cross-subsidization is unsustainable. No firm can afford to engage in activities in which it suffers a competitive disadvantage relative to competitors. The business must either improve its logistics performance or outsource it to achieve lower cost.

Cost driver

Any factor or event that has a direct or indirect effect on the cost of an activity.

Chapter 5

Cost drivers

In highly competitive markets there is constant, unrelenting pressure for cost reductions, as well as innovation, if a business is to remain competitive. These pressures dictate that business unit managers must understand the **drivers of cost** and value enhancement, and the value chain provides a framework for this understanding.

As discussed in detail in Chapter 5 (➤Chapter 5), two of the major drivers of long-term costs are economies of scale and learning. Both need to be understood dynamically. As an illustration, economies of scale are a major rationale behind many horizontal mergers and acquisitions, where it is assumed that the merged entity will have lower costs.

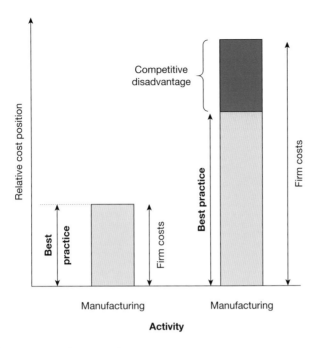

Figure 7.6 Competitive advantage by activity

Economies of scale *in practice* – Allianz

In 2008, the insurance giant Allianz announced it was selling Dresdner, its loss-making bank subsidiary, to Commerzbank for €9.8 billion, having acquired it for €24 billion in 2001 (Montia, 2008). Cost savings of €1.9 billion were expected from rationalizing the IT and branch networks. Overall, 9,000 job losses were forecast, with 1,200 of these coming from Dresdner Kleinwort, the London-based investment bank (Wachman, 2008).

Economies of scale are influenced by technological change and the relative importance of fixed and variable costs. If all costs are variable, then economies of scale are absent. However, management must be pro-active in understanding the dynamics of scale, since changes create turbulence and consequent opportunities. If scale is becoming more important, the industry is likely to face restructuring through acquisitions as firms attempt to achieve lower costs. Firms unaware of this will end up as acquisition targets. Should scale become less important, the business can expect new entrants, with subsequent pressure on margins. Firms that act in a timely manner usually enjoy a competitive advantage as a result of such changes. Competitive advantage cannot be based on what was successful in yesterday's world; managers need to understand the economic characteristics of their world in the future (Christensen, 2001).

Learning

Chapter 5

Learning effects can be particularly dramatic in high-growth markets, with significant cost reductions occurring as cumulative volume increases. This was illustrated in Figure 5.9, where the costs of disk drives declined from about $US400 per megabyte in 1977 to $US0.10 per megabyte in the mid-2000s (➤Chapter 5). Businesses unable to reduce costs in line with the average industry cost curve were forced to exit.

One possible strategy for a business is to identify a growth market and develop a strategy focusing on high growth to ensure a long-term dominant position at the expense of short-term profit. One risk with this strategy is that a competitor might introduce a major innovation, revolutionizing industry cost structures and thus nullifying the leader's advantage.

Business unit analysis

As well as understanding the external context of business strategy development, we must also be intimately familiar with the business unit's strengths and weaknesses, and those of the corporation of which it is a part. These are not part of the external context of strategic management, but the same disciplined and objective analysis is required. The resources and capabilities discussed in Chapter 5 (➤Chapter 5) must be subject to rigorous and objective analysis, benchmarked against competitors, and reviewed in the light of the requirements of customers not only in the current markets, but also in those that the business unit expects to serve in the future. We may therefore want to develop a list of current sources of advantage and the unit's position on them, assessing them relative to the life cycles of the business's products and markets. We should also compare our financial and market performance with that of our competitors. We explore these analyses in more detail in Chapter 12.

Chapter 12

(➤Chapter 12)

The overall objective of the external and internal analysis we have just discussed is to get an understanding of who is winning and why, what the requirements of the market are (price or other forms of advantage), and whether or not we are using our competitive advantage well. This in turn requires an understanding of the economics of the business, its cost structure, and its value chain. A very useful template which can be used to diagnose the performance of the business unit in greater depth is described in Gottfredson (Gottfredson & Schaubert, 2008).

LEARNING OBJECTIVE 3

Develop a strategy for a business that recognizes the three key decisions – where to compete, how to compete and how to grow.

7.4 DEVELOPING BUSINESS-LEVEL STRATEGY

We defined strategy as the common theme underlying a set of strategic decisions, which in turn require significant resources and commitment and will affect the future direction of the business unit. Its purpose is to generate value through creating competitive advantage in selected markets. Strategy is also about doing different things or doing the same things differently from and better than competitors. This requires a balance between creativity and realism. Creativity is important in strategy development. Strategy is not formula driven, and innovation is often a critical component. Creative analysis can lead to major improvements in customer value, so-called value innovation (Kim & Mauborgne, 1997). Yet strategy must also be based on a sound understanding of the market, competitors and our own capabilities. A strategy that cannot be implemented is unrealistic. By its very nature strategy is concerned with the future. The results of decisions made now are not realized until sometime in the future. This indicates that a strategy will need a degree of flexibility to take advantage of unpredicted external changes.

Having developed a strategy, we need to estimate its expected returns and relate these to the returns from the current strategy. This involves posing questions: What is the current strategy? Will the current strategy meet expectations? What risks are there with the current strategy? What are its cost structure, profitability, and profitability by segment, channel of distribution, customer type or size? How does profitability vary by product line or geographic region, where in the value chain are profits generated? When developing strategy we should also try to test assumptions. For example, the assumption of no new entrants into a profitable high-growth market is unrealistic unless there are significant barriers to entry. If uncertainty is high, we should consider using scenario planning or performing a probability distribution of returns with a simulation exercise (Vose, 2000). Alternatively, a real options approach, to be discussed in Chapter 8 (▶Chapter 8), may be adopted.

Chapter 8

A strategic decision framework

Developing business unit strategy usually requires a number of strategic decisions, summarized in the framework in Figure 7.7.

We can expand on the key questions of Figure 7.7 as follows:

- **Where to compete**

    - *Vertical positioning of the business*
      Where in the vertical value chain should we position the business? What is the activity scope of the business? Which activities should be undertaken by the business and which should be outsourced?

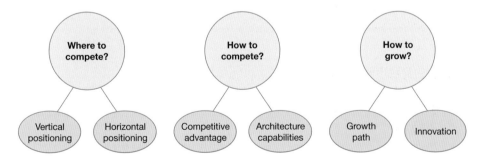

Figure 7.7 Critical business strategy questions

– *Horizontal positioning of the business*

In which segments should the business compete – how many segments, how many products? What is its width of market and product coverage? The vision and mission of the business, which should determine its scope, will obviously affect these decisions.

- **How to compete**

  – *Competitive advantage and strategy*

  Which combination of difficult-to-replicate factors does the business possess that will allow it to either produce at a lower cost or better meet customer needs than its competitors? How sustainable are these advantages, and how will the business develop new bases of advantage? How will these be deployed against competitors?

  – *Architecture and capabilities*

  What capabilities are required to enable the business to implement its strategy and improve its competitive position? How competitive is its current knowledge base? Are its processes, systems and structure supportive of the strategy? Does it possess the flexibility required to compete in a turbulent environment?

- **Business growth strategy**

  – *Growth and innovation strategy*

  What options does the business have for growth? Should it grow through new product development or by expanding into new market segments? Should these be executed by internal development, acquisition or alliance? What are the alternatives and the risks associated with each?

We will discuss each of these decisions. Although we discuss them independently, they are nevertheless all interrelated.

7.5 WHERE TO COMPETE

Decisions about where to compete are obviously dependent on how the business's mission statement defines its scope, but managers must usually make more specific decisions about the vertical and horizontal positioning of the business. We now examine such decisions.

Vertical positioning

Managers must decide which activities the business will undertake and which will be undertaken by others. Strategic managers must decide which activities are best done under common ownership and which are best done via market-based transactions. A valuable framework for clarifying these issues is the value chain discussed earlier.

The CEO of a major textile and garment business once described his job to one of the authors as follows: 'There are five stages of value added in our business. My job is to decide where in the world each of them will be performed.'

Airline companies once believed that they had to own aircraft to be in the business, but today most lease their aircraft (and often other equipment), and many have outsourced such activities as maintenance and catering.

Outsourcing *in practice* – Qantas

The Australian airline Qantas uses mainly internal employees for maintenance. Qantas has never had a fatal accident in over 70 years of operation and sees its safety record as a major source of competitive advantage. (We could note that not all their customers may share this perception.) If we accept that this is indeed the situation, then a decision to outsource maintenance would be critical for Qantas, which has to balance possibly lower costs from external providers against the loss of direct control. If this activity is outsourced, will the firm lose a core capability? Can the maintenance and safety record continue to be superior if it uses the same external providers as its competitors?

The emergence of the Internet has provided an opportunity for disintermediation and re-intermediation in the airline industry. Historically, airlines used a network of independent agents to make reservations. Agents were able to make worldwide reservations on a common system. With the emergence of the Internet, consumers are now able to directly access airline websites and make reservations. The cost of such direct booking is low, but it places traditional airlines in direct competition with travel agents. In the pursuit of lower costs, newer airlines, such as Ryanair or EasyJet, dictate that all bookings have to be made on the Internet (or by phone). In the airline industry, different firms have decided to undertake different sets of activities, and this choice has been a relevant component of their strategy.

When considering this vertical industry system, the firm must decide whether or not to expand its scope into immediately adjoining stages. This is normally referred to as vertical integration, and we now turn our attention to these decisions.

Vertical integration

Vertical integration occurs when a firm acquires or develops a business that is the current concern of either its customers (forward) or its suppliers (backward), with the objective of getting higher profitability through the elimination of the customer/supplier, bringing their margins under the firm's control. Backward integration requires new operational skills; forward integration requires new marketing skills, at the same time creating competition with existing customers (Harrigan, 1983).

Vertical integration is motivated by the idea that the business can create additional value when more activities share common ownership. So where do these advantages come from? One source may be joint production economies – there are efficiency gains from linking two activities together.

Integration may also provide protection against asset specificity, where the business can be held to ransom by a monopoly supplier or customer. In these cases of market failure, the

Vertical integration
Occurs when a firm acquires or develops a business which is the current concern of either their customers (forward) or their suppliers (backward).

> ### Vertical integration *in practice* – Radiohead
>
> In 2007 Radiohead, the British rock band, sent shock waves through the music industry when it announced that it would release its latest album online, without a record label. This is an example of forward vertical integration, disintermediating the record company and its distributors. Radiohead also announced that fans could pay whatever they wanted to for it – including nothing at all. For Radiohead, this means that the group gets to keep the entire price of each album sold, not just a small fraction of it, although some observers speculated that this would be a one-time experimental release by a well-known band (Wharton School Publishing, 2007).

firm probably has no choice but to vertically integrate, as has occurred in some resource-based industries such as aluminium. In many food products however, the market for raw materials is more competitive, and few food processors have vertically integrated backwards into agriculture.

There are several issues with vertical integration as a business strategy. Vertical integration inevitably results in an increasing proportion of a firm's or business's assets being in one industry, thus increasing dependency on it. In the car industry, for example, if we currently make cars and acquire a tyre producer, we have not diversified in terms of industry; we have even more assets in the car industry, increasing exposure to changes in industry demand. Such actions may be taken defensively, to protect our original investment, although this may be dangerous, throwing good money after bad.

It may also be difficult to balance scale and capacity (Díez-Vial, 2007). We can see this by using a hypothetical but realistic example from the car industry. Suppose the efficient size of plant for cars is 400,000 units per year, requiring two million tyres per year. Let us further assume that the car firm builds an efficient-sized tyre plant that produces three million tyres per year. The question then is: What do we do with the extra one million tyres per year? Do we attempt to sell them to our competitors and will they purchase from a competitor? Or will we sell the extra product to the aftermarket for replacement tyres? If so, we will need a strong retail marketing group. If neither of these alternatives seems feasible, the tyre plant will produce only two million tyres per year. If there are strong economies of scale, the plant will be a high-cost facility, making the cost of tyres to the car company uncompetitive. This example reinforces that an integration decision must be well thought out before choosing it as a course of action.

Vertical integration also opens up a transfer price problem. If we are the upstream unit, selling to a sister business downstream, what should be our selling price? How are conflicts resolved? Is the downstream unit given the right to purchase the product on the open market? How do we ensure that the upstream unit is efficient? Is there a service agreement between the two units?

There is often very vigorous debate over these matters, particularly if the intermediate product has no external market, making it impossible to determine a 'fair' market price.

There are also quasi-integration strategies, such as long-term contracts, joint ventures, alliances, technology licenses, asset ownership (we own the asset but contract out manufacture) and franchising. These are various forms of cooperation between the firm and competitors, suppliers, and customers. These are looser forms of organization than is normally implied by integration, which has an assumption of ownership.

There appears to be a movement towards less vertical integration (Stuckey & White, 1993). The risk of market failure in many industries is reducing as deregulation permits new entrants. Faster and better communications have facilitated the emergence of global markets, increasing the number of potential suppliers and/or customers. In addition, low levels of vertical integration lead to greater flexibility, a source of competitive advantage in turbulent times. Indeed, Díez-Vial found that vertical integration is inversely related to uncertainty, supporting the idea that a turbulent world is less conducive to this strategy (Díez-Vial, 2007). Finally, increased competition has resulted in firms reassessing the value of vertical integration, often leading to vertical 'dis-integration' or outsourcing, as we next explore (Hutzschenreuter & Grone, 2009).

Outsourcing

Outsourcing occurs when the firm transfers some of its recurring internal activities to outside providers, with the arrangement specified in a formal contract (Greaver, 1999). The resources for undertaking these activities are provided by the outside firm, which is also responsible for making decisions regarding those resources and meeting certain outcomes as specified by the contract.

Outsourcing
The transfer of a recurring, internal value-creating activity to an external provider, where the arrangement is specified in a formal contract.

In many industries, economies of scope are changing – firms and their suppliers are becoming increasingly specialized and outsourcing activities that are not regarded as core. The outsourcing movement is also driven by the increasing competitiveness of business. No firm can afford to undertake activities internally unless these activities are being performed at a world-class level, thereby contributing to competitive advantage. Yet for most businesses, a significant number of internal activities are likely to be performed well below best practice.

Outsourcing *in practice* – pharmaceutical industry

Contract (or toll) manufacturing has long been a feature of industries such as chemicals, electronics and garments. Driven by cost and margin pressures, stringent regulatory requirements and patent expiries, large pharmaceutical companies are increasingly outsourcing manufacturing to low-cost destinations. India and China offer skilled manpower and a robust manufacturing infrastructure. Firms in these key outsourcing destinations have been improving their manufacturing infrastructure to increasing their global competitiveness. The global pharmaceutical contract manufacturing market is expected to grow at a CAGR of 11.4 per cent to reach $US40 billion by 2011. In India and China, however, contract manufacturing is forecast to expand at a CAGR of 20 per cent to 2011 (FierceBiotech, 2010).

Increasing pressure for performance and the need to deliver economic value lead managers to search for new approaches, and outsourcing is one.

These developments have been greatly assisted by improved communication systems. As search costs fall, firms seek outsourcing partners from a wider, often global, pool. Improvements in information technology permit outsourcing contracts to be better managed than before. The central reason behind outsourcing is that the business must focus its resources on activities essential to its survival and leverage peripheral activities (Insinga & Werle, 2000). In markets such as the United States and Europe, service firms have become large and sophisticated relative to the scale and expertise of service groups within integrated companies – so they may provide better and less costly services. These outside suppliers can often develop better depth of knowledge, invest in software and training, be more efficient, and even offer employees better wages (Quinn, 1999).

Outsourcing *in practice* – Daimler

In 2008, Daimler Financial Services announced a five-year contract with CGI, a global provider of IT services (CGI, 2008). As CGI notes, 'your back office becomes our front office' as firms convert a fixed cost in-house system to a more flexible managed service, allowing the firm to reduce capital expenditure while acquiring a high-performance system from the provider. Daimler Financial Services believes that it will obtain a system allowing it to streamline its processes for international vehicle financing. At the same time, CGI acquired an IT platform, Phoenix, developed by Daimler, which it plans to expand to the global asset finance market.

If supplier markets were totally reliable and efficient, business managers might outsource everything except core capabilities, although there are risks and some unique transaction costs for searching, contacting and controlling these suppliers. In the longer term, the firm may become dependent on outside suppliers and may be held to ransom, since outside firms now have specialized assets. With outsourcing, firms need more personnel involved in procurement and contract management. Lack of these skills is a major cause of outsourcing failure. However, there are often hidden costs of activities performed within the firm, since lack of innovation, delay and internal bureaucracy too often go unrecognized. Possible reasons for outsourcing are summarized in Table 7.1.

McIvor suggests that there are three key factors in the decision to outsource (McIvor, 2008). First is the relative capability of a firm in a given process. If the firm can perform an activity uniquely well, then this process should continue to be carried out internally. The second consideration is the contribution of the process to the firm's competitive advantage – those most critical should clearly remain internal. Finally, he argues that potential outsourcers should beware of the opportunity for opportunism. Foolproof contracts may be difficult to write under conditions of uncertainty, while there may be difficulties in process transfer and ensuring contract compliance.

Table 7.1 Reasons for outsourcing

Reason	Explanation
Strategic	The outside firm has a specific expertise, such as tax accounting, allowing the business to obtain specialized expertise in the area. Outsourcing may also provide increased flexibility in responding to changes in demand or technology.
Financial	Outsourcing normally reduces the need for capital employed by the business. The supplier may be able to obtain higher levels of capital productivity, and since we do not provide the capital ourselves, our business is essentially variating its fixed costs and increasing its flexibility, which may help it respond to unanticipated changes in demand. In a turbulent world, this may be particularly advantageous.
Cost	A major reason for outsourcing is lower costs. For example, suppliers may achieve scale economies since they deal with multiple customers, and competition forces these cost savings to be passed on. But outsourcing involves transaction costs, which may make outsourcing cost more than performing the activities ourselves.
Organizational	The business decides to focus on what it does best so as to increase customer value, outsourcing activities it performs relatively poorly. Here the business needs to take a long-term perspective. The US electronics industry may have outsourced the foundations of future capabilities when it outsourced elements of its TV business, in particular screens. US competitors lost the skill to develop and produce screens, which reduced their later participation in products with display screens, such as calculators and computer monitors.

Through outsourcing, business managers often expect to increase operating performance, obtain expertise, improve risk management and acquire innovative ideas. Since suppliers have narrower scopes, they can perform better in what are, for the business, non-core areas, since these seldom get the resources to achieve world-class standards. The firm benefits from the supplier's superior resource package, sometimes even gaining additional market access through the provider's network. Employees who move to the external provider may have better career paths arising from the increased specialization of the outside suppliers' activities. On the other hand, many employees see outsourcing as a problem: their jobs are at risk.

Any activity in the firm's value chain can be done internally or externally and is a potential candidate for outsourcing, as is clear from the above example. Activities such as IT, customer service, manufacturing, sales and accounting are all possibilities, but of course such outsourcing can also be difficult to reverse – it is difficult and costly to terminate a ten-year contract in year five! More recently, many knowledge-based activities such as accounting and legal services are being outsourced internationally. There are major legal processing outsourcing firms in India, such as Pangea3 and CPA Global. In a changing world, with an increasing number of external providers for these activities, the relative advantage of internal versus external sourcing is constantly shifting (Safizadeh *et al.*, 2008).

> ## Challenge of strategic management
>
> According to a former president of Shell, companies have been outsourcing critical operations for many years – sacrificing control in an attempt to reduce costs. He saw this as a serious problem when several different contractors were involved, resulting in chains of command distinct to each contractor with no integration. He further suggested that this specialization, and lack of integration and overall control, would hamper efforts to search for the cause of the Deepwater Horizon oil leak in the Gulf of Mexico in 2010. He went further, suggesting that the trend towards outsourcing should be slowed, or even reversed (Hofmeister, 2010).
>
> ■ Do you agree with this assessment on the future of outsourcing?

Chapter 5

The business decision of which activities should be performed internally and which should be outsourced needs to be periodically reviewed. The firm's capabilities are not fixed; rather, they evolve over time, reflecting environmental and competitive changes as well as changes in customer needs. Activities related to future core capabilities are best kept in-house, where they can be nurtured to provide this future competitive advantage (▶Chapter 5). This may even lead firms to bring previously outsourced activities in-house again, and research has shown some of the conditions under which this might be desirable (Caputo & Palumbo, 2005).

Non-core activities should probably be outsourced, but the business is not likely to generate a competitive advantage from outsourced activities if the external supplier also serves competitors. This is one of several risks with outsourcing. Nonetheless, a business may be able to leverage its resources by focusing on a small number of core capabilities in which it can excel and which are important to customers. Managers should invest in exploiting and developing these capabilities as well as generating new ones. Activities in which the firm is not, or cannot be, best in class should be outsourced.

Insourcing

For every firm that outsources an activity there must be a firm willing to take on the activity – an insourcing firm. In many industries, the changing cost structures in a value chain have provided opportunities for firms to develop new businesses which specialize in these tasks. As mentioned above, Indian firms such as Infosys have virtually created a new industry, performing IT activities on behalf of clients from the US and Europe.

Chapter 3

Horizontal positioning

As we noted in Chapter 3 (▶Chapter 3), customers are rarely homogeneous in their needs; instead different customers have different needs. The business unit must group these disparate customers into market segments, groups of customers who have needs that are reasonably similar but whose needs are different from other such groups. We need to develop segments that show within-group homogeneity and between-group heterogeneity so that the unit can better accommodate the different needs of its marketplace.

Business unit managers have to decide how many of these segments to target, how to provide the benefits sought, and at what cost. Most production systems or transaction systems have a cost of diversity; it is generally more costly to produce several kinds of bank loans, for example, than one kind. However, if customer requirements are such that a diversity of products is called for, the business must decide which, and how many, of these segments it will attempt to satisfy (Macmillan & Selden, 2008).

Here the business faces a dilemma; should it produce a narrow range of products, at low cost, or produce a wide range of product variants, with possibly higher unit costs? This is never an easy decision, and it is made more difficult by the changing relationship between product diversity and unit costs. Advantages typically accrue to the firm that can innovate with a flexible production system that meets the diverse needs of the market.

Horizontal positioning *in practice* – Vaillant

Vaillant is the biggest European maker of central heating boilers, operating in some 75 countries with turnover of approximately €2.4 billion (Vaillant, 2010). 'Huge variation in customer tastes and building standards means . . . offer[ing] hundreds of different models . . . to reach across the continent.' Boilers are manufactured to meet the specifications of many different countries, using as many common parts as possible so as to minimize the costs of customization 'without narrowing the choice for the consumer' (Marsh, 2002).

These principles hold for service as well as manufacturing firms. An insurance firm that can tailor products to specific customer groups, for example, will possess a competitive advantage as long as the incremental costs are reasonable.

The marketing function should have detailed knowledge of customer needs and wants as well as differences in these. The role for general management is to ensure that changes are identified so that a complete and realistic picture of the market is presented. The result of this market and customer analysis is a better understanding of:

- Changing customer needs
- Changing basis of segmentation
- Changing relative importance of segments
- Changing ways of getting products to these customers – new channels.

Business unit management must monitor and update the basis of segmentation, tracking changing needs, ensuring that growth segments are identified and making decisions on the number of segments in which the unit will compete. While the design of strategies for targeted segments is often delegated to marketing, business management must decide the

Mass customization
Developing, producing, marketing and delivering goods and/or services that are designed to meet the needs of individual customers, but doing so at a unit cost more normally associated with mass production.

 Chapter 5

unit's basis of competition, ensuring that the appropriate resources and architecture are developed. Consistent with our themes of innovation and value creation, management must ensure that attention is given to identifying untapped markets, markets which are currently uncontested but which have potential for high growth. Such markets have been characterized as 'blue ocean' markets (Kim & Mauborgne, 2005).

In business-to-business marketing, the unit may treat each customer as a segment of one. This is also becoming an option in some consumer markets with the advent of **mass customization**. Mass customization is an approach aimed at developing, producing, marketing and delivering goods and services of sufficient variety and customization that nearly everyone finds exactly what they want (Chandra & Ali, 2004). To practise mass customization requires the development of new capabilities, as described in Chapter 5 (➤Chapter 5). Two such capabilities are (Salvador *et al.*, 2009):

- The ability to identify the product attributes along which customer needs diverge the most.
- The ability to combine existing resources to deliver customized products and services with close to mass-production efficiency and reliability.

The Internet has greatly facilitated the growth of mass customization, as has the development of computerized customer databases. The madeforone.com website lists many examples. Here are two recent ones from Germany.

Mass customization *in practice* – Chocrí

Chocri is a German start-up (founded in early 2008) that customizes chocolate bars. By combining a base chocolate with the customer's choice from over 90 toppings, there are more than 10 billion possibilities to create the chocolate bar of your dreams (Chocri, 2010).

The other example is EGO3D, which creates three-dimensional bust statues from three normal photographs.

Market customization *in practice* – EGO3D

Company principal Robert Fischer says: 'With this service we are in a niche between the photographic and the 3D business. In comparison to other 3D manufacturers, we create a 3D mesh from the customer's photos and then the bust will be manufactured with a 3D printer.' Initially, EGO3D had offered this unique service only in Germany, but it is now available Europe-wide (EGO3D, 2010).

Regardless, customer needs are critical because they define which type of competitive advantage can create most value. Business unit managers must therefore understand customer needs in each segment, how these are evolving, which needs are unmet or poorly met, and how potential customers might be enticed to purchase.

Horizontal positioning requires that the business unit decide in which segments to compete, as well as the range of products supplied to the chosen segments. Baghai *et al.* suggest that there are rewards for seeking out growth segments even in markets that are growing slowly. They urge companies in slow growth markets to explore this option rather than taking the risky alternative of changing industries (Baghai *et al.*, 2007).

Businesses must also choose their mix of segments and products. A business may be focused, operating in only one segment, or it can elect to be a broad-based competitor, competing in all segments; similarly, it can provide a limited or wide range of products. Figure 7.8 illustrates these options graphically. We now examine each of them in turn (Hulbert, 1985).

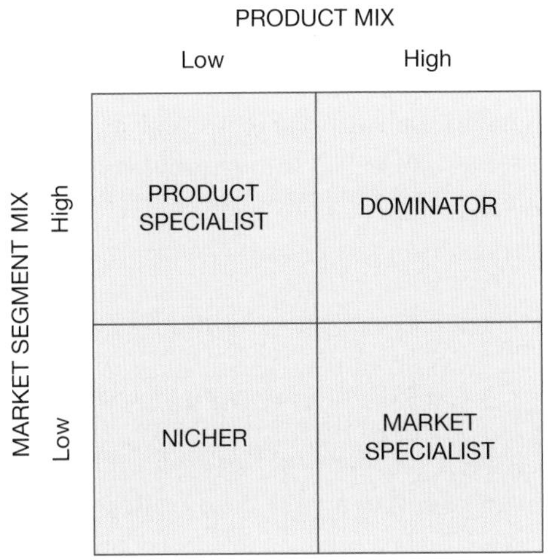

Figure 7.8 Horizontal positioning

Market specialist

Harley Davidson achieves a focus with its strategy by competing in a limited number of segments in the motorcycle market. Harley achieves a large number of product variations at reasonable cost through sharing very similar mechanicals, but all of its bikes are large-capacity road bikes. There are no small-capacity Harleys, nor does Harley compete in the motocross or off-road segments. More recently, the company has added the Buell brand to its line-up, but the Harley brand remains as a market specialist. Retail and distribution businesses are also good examples of market specialists, since their scope is usually defined around a socio-economic or geographic segmentation.

Dominator

Honda is the dominator of the motorcycle business, competing in almost all market and product segments on a global basis. This was such a successful strategy that the motorcycle business funded Honda's development of its automobile business, the vision to which founder Soichiro Honda had always aspired.

As a broad competitor, a business has another decision to make: how to adjust its strategy across the different segments. Does it develop unique strategies for each segment (a higher cost approach) or attempt to use similar strategies for each segment (a broad appeal that may completely satisfy no customers)? Modular design and production, or platform engineering, as it is known in the automobile business, is an important tool in achieving product variety at reasonable cost, as we saw earlier with Vaillant.

Nicher

Since we defined segments as groups with similar needs and wants, and specified that the needs of customers in other segments are different, it follows that a business may be able to exist in one segment without having to participate or compete in other segments. If this is not the case, then the business unit's definition of segments is probably incorrect. Indeed, competitive advantage is generally defined with respect to a segment, since a business may have an advantage in one segment but not in another. Specialist car manufacturers such as Morgan and Ferrari are examples of niche-based and highly focused competitors.

Product specialist

Intel is an example of a product specialist because of its focus on standardized microprocessors, which it sells around the world for many applications. Of course, its product mix of chips broadened significantly as it grew. A specialist competitor such as Intel may be able to build significant expertise in a product, in a technology, or in relationships with the customers in a variety of market segments. Nonetheless, there is considerable risk from more broad-based firms unless the specialist can erect barriers to minimize the threat of entry. In Intel's case its vast experience and ability to generate high yields has traditionally given it a big advantage, but the movement towards outsourced fabrication of chips may pose a significant challenge in the future.

An important part of business strategy is determining the proper segmentation: identifying segments with good reward potential, ascertaining where the business is strong, and understanding how boundaries may evolve and customer needs within the segment are likely to change. In addition, the choice of the number of segments in which to compete and the strategy to follow will be influenced by considerations such as segment size and growth, ease of serving the segment, and the capabilities of the unit (Capon & Hulbert, 2001). In

 Chapter 8 Chapter 8 (▶Chapter 8) we will examine the tools of portfolio analysis, which can be applied to make better choices among segment opportunities at the business level.

7.6 HOW TO COMPETE

LEARNING OBJECTIVE 4

Apply the concept of a competitive advantage and appreciate the need for ongoing enhancement of this advantage.

Firm-specific factors are evidently important to business unit success, since in Chapter 2 (►Chapter 2) we observed wide variations in the performance achieved by different competitors within the same industry. These differences, if sustained over time, are attributable to the existence of a competitive advantage possessed by the business. A business has a competitive advantage when it is able to utilize its resources and capabilities to generate a value-creating strategy that other firms find difficult to imitate. Such an advantage permits the business to outperform its competitors and is the only way to generate returns above the cost of capital on a sustainable basis.

Chapter 2

Competitive advantage may come from a superior business definition, from unique capabilities, or from doing what other firms also do but doing it better. Any such advantage must be assessed relative to competitors and must lead to one or all of lower costs, higher sales volume or higher prices. Otherwise, it is a phantom advantage.

The nature of the competitive advantage depends on the industry and marketplace in which the business unit competes. In management consulting, clients are unlikely to choose on the basis of price alone: having the lowest price is not necessarily an advantage in that industry. On the other hand, in commodity markets such as iron ore, sulphuric acid or computer memory chips, many customers make decisions primarily on the basis of price.

Competitive advantage requires that the business is in a superior position on relevant sources of advantage, and that competitors cannot easily replicate the drivers creating these advantages. If the advantage is product quality, drivers would include manufacturing process control, product innovation and customer understanding. If the advantage is customer access, drivers may be brand image and distributor relationships.

Competitive business strategies

Competitive business strategy defines the basis on which a business unit elects to compete for customers, while withstanding competitive endeavours. It involves choosing activities that allow the business to deliver its products and services so as to produce superior economic results. We begin by looking at a simplified model of strategy and then elaborate.

Competitive business strategy
The basis on which a business unit elects to compete for customers, while withstanding competitive endeavours.

Porter suggested that there are two basic ways to achieve a competitive advantage (Porter, 1980):

- Offer the lowest delivered price to the customer.
- Provide a differentiated product.

This is really just saying that to achieve success, we need to differentiate our offer from that of competitors and that the basis can be in price or non-price features. Choice between these alternatives depends on segment response functions (demand elasticities), business capabilities, and the strategies of our competitors. If the segment is characterized by a cost/price game, the essential element of competitive strategy is reducing cost relative to prices. If the segment is primarily a value game, the essential element of competitive strategy is achieving superior price realization relative to costs. A market segment would be primarily a cost game when there is little price differentiation or difference in product offerings. On the other hand, a segment will be a value game when there is substantial variance in price realization, strong differences in customer preference between two offerings at the same price level, and a clear difference between product offerings. Note that these characterizations are not immutable. Innovation may shift a price/cost game to a value game, whereas increasing product or service homogeneity among competitors will result in competition that is primarily based on price.

Low-price strategy

Low-price strategy
A strategy whereby the firm offers products such that the price actually paid by customers is the lowest among the available alternatives.

With a **low-price strategy**, the price actually paid by the customer is the lowest among all available alternatives. While this is sometimes interpreted to imply that the business must charge the lowest price in the industry, we actually need to focus on the actual price paid by the customer, not the seller's realized price. Customers may incur costs outside the control of the business. For example, the customer may pay the costs of distribution, transport, taxes or tariffs; all costs that are outside the business's control but may be incurred by customers. When the business is pursuing a strategy of lowest delivered cost to the customer (low price), it must achieve all sources of cost advantage. There is no point in having low-cost manufacturing, then selling through a high-cost distribution system.

Such a strategy can create value for the business's owners only if it is the industry's lowest cost producer. This strategy is referred to as a **cost leadership strategy**, and consequently in these markets there is generally only one winner – the lowest cost supplier. Other firms are unlikely to be creating significant economic profit.

Low-price strategies are most appropriate when there are limited technological opportunities for product differentiation and few market opportunities for product variants. Sometimes the product's technical specification means all basic offerings will be the same. For example, the manufacture of sulphuric acid does not allow for much variation in product specifications, especially if all customers require the same quality. Such strategies are powerful when there is a high end-user concern with price, when buyer needs are primarily economic, and when the product represents a large proportion of the customer's total costs. Such conditions exist in coal-fired power stations, where coal represents 50 per cent or more of the final cost of electricity produced.

A business pursuing a low-price approach must make consistent decisions. Sustaining a cost advantage means understanding such cost drivers as scale economies and learning, avoiding marginal customers, and having a limited product range, low overheads, superior process effectiveness, and good management of working capital. Even low-price sellers need certain minimum levels of customer service, quality, delivery and so on, but they should outsource any activity they cannot undertake at low cost, while maintaining constant vigilance over possible changes.

With a competitive strategy based on lowest delivered price to the customer, cost reduction initiatives often include downsizing, with major reductions in the number of

> **Low price *in practice* – Compal**
>
> Compal, the Taiwanese computer firm, has historically manufactured its products at the Kunshan Factory in China. In 2007 the firm established a second overseas manufacturing base in Vietnam. Both countries have low labour costs relative to Taiwan (Compal, 2010).

employees. Such actions typically have a strong negative impact on employee morale (Mishra, 1998), and possibly reduced performance in the longer term (Lowe, 1998). In addition, low wages to employees do not always translate into low costs due to staff turnover and induction costs (Cascio, 2006). Low-price strategies have other risks, the primary one being outsmarted by competitors who achieve technological breakthroughs that further reduce costs. Complacency can allow costs to rise, while technological change may result in new products or processes that the business does not adopt for fear of cannibalization.

Competing against other low-cost competitors can be difficult – they can be an ongoing threat by changing consumer behaviour, getting consumers to accept fewer benefits at lower prices (Kumar, 2006). Possible responses from the incumbent are to attempt to differentiate their offering, or to set up a low-cost subsidiary, an option which has proved difficult for many firms.

Differentiation strategy

A **differentiation strategy** involves offering a product not at the lowest price but with features or characteristics that make it different from the competitive offerings and for which we can charge a price premium. Such a strategy is likely to be valuable when customer needs are diverse and when technology permits differentiated offerings to be produced.

One measure of the extent of differentiation in a market is the difference in prices between essentially similar products. With a resource material such as coal, different coal-mines price differentially, reflecting differences in impurities such as sulphur and heavy metals. Similarly, some oilfields such as Texas produce low-sulphur crude, earning a small price premium. Such products may reduce customer costs through reduced noxious emissions, and a price premium can be charged for this. Although the additional margin may be small, it can have a significant impact on economic profit. In other markets, however, we see very substantial differences in the prices of different offerings. Consider the automobile market: new cars can be purchased from as little as about €6,000 up to €250,000 or more for Aston Martins and Ferraris.

There are many ways to differentiate offerings via quality, design, faster delivery time, more reliable delivery time, brand image, innovation, technological excellence, credit and/or barter terms, and so on. Such strategies typically require an excellent understanding of what customers really value, good marketing capability and strong inter-functional cooperation.

Some firms have been remarkably successful at differentiating through their brand name: they manage this intangible asset to create and extract additional value (Berthon

Differentiation strategy
Offering a product or service with features or characteristics, which are valued by buyers, such that the offer is different from competitive offerings, and consequently a price premium can be charged.

et al., 2009). Brand names such as Mercedes, Burberry, Cadbury, Chanel, Ferrari and L'Oreal have maintained a sense of uniqueness and strong market positions for many years.

While the basic appeal to customers may be non-price features, the actual price premium cannot be increased indefinitely – there are limits to the premium that customers are prepared to pay. This indicates some of the risks of a differentiation strategy. First, customers may cease to value the attribute that is the basis of differentiation, possibly because other competitors develop products with comparable attributes. Or the business may attempt to impose too great a price differential. In business-to-business markets, such a competitive strategy is likely to be more effective when the product represents only a small component of total costs for the end user or when poor performance seriously affects the customer or the customer's customer.

Combination strategy

The above two competitive strategies are sometimes viewed as mutually exclusive: the business must choose one or the other. While a combination strategy is not easy to achieve, it is by no means impossible to achieve both low cost and high differentiation at the same time. In fact this could be stated as the ultimate strategic management challenge at the business unit level – how to exercise creativity and develop a combination strategy. In many industries higher product quality can actually reduce certain costs such as rework, and returns, thus resulting in both low costs and high quality. With a consumer product, the market leader may get economies of scale in distribution and advertising. The result is high brand image and thus high-perceived quality coupled with low cost. This combination is obviously the most desirable competitive strategy in terms of the creation of shareholder value. Figure 7.9 juxtaposes the different options.

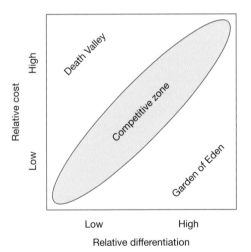

Figure 7.9 Competitive business strategies

Source: Adapted from a diagram developed by Geoff Lewis

Strategies in the diagonal zone can be described as competitive. However, the bottom right is the preferred zone and the top left definitely non-preferred. Such a diagram can be used to follow competitive moves in an industry, where the historical and current position of the business and its competitors are plotted.

Challenge of strategic management

As the manager of a business unit, is it possible for that unit to be both a low-cost competitor and a differentiated competitor? Do unit costs always increase with differentiation? Can you provide examples of firms which have achieved both low relative cost and high relative differentiation?

Dynamics of competitive advantage

The simple framework discussed above does not deal well with the dynamics of competition. Changes in customer demand and technology, the invasion of markets by new entrants, and blurring of industry boundaries can all lead to elimination of competitive advantage. In some financial markets, a business's competitive advantage from the time of launching a new product may last just days. In other markets, such as that for pharmaceuticals, patents may provide an advantage for a number of years.

Figure 7.10 illustrates this dynamic nature of a competitive advantage. As shown there, the importance of the 'old' basis of competitive advantage diminishes as more competitors offer the attribute. So the attribute ceases to be a differentiator of competitive success,

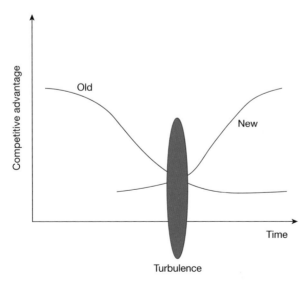

Figure 7.10 Evolution of new bases of competitive advantage

although it may still be critical for the customer (Knudsen, 2006). For the business to maintain its success, it must develop a new basis for advantage, based on a detailed understanding of customer needs, competition and its own capabilities.

Changing competitive advantage *in practice* – automobile industry

During the 1980s and early 1990s, Japanese cars had a significant advantage over competitors in product quality. Over time, US and European producers improved their quality levels, and the difference between various makers became much smaller. Subsequently Japanese manufacturers such as Mitsubishi (in 2004) and Toyota (in 2010) suffered their own widely publicized quality problems, and as a result, quality has ceased to be an effective differentiator for some Japanese car brands. Today, car manufacturers need quality to be able to compete (it has become a so-called qualifying attribute), but car manufacturers are seeking new sources of advantage. Some chose image, and Toyota, Mercedes, Renault and BMW all entered Formula One Grand Prix racing. The 2009 withdrawal of Toyota and BMW was caused by a combination of high costs and lack of success. They and others will now be looking elsewhere, and the so-called 'Green' car looks likely to be the next battleground for advantage.

The transition from one basis of advantage to another is a period of turbulence when market share can be gained or lost, when new competitors can gain share at the expense of incumbents. Eventually, some stability returns to the market, but success goes to the business that responds to the new environment and develops the required competitive advantage, enhancing its position while defeating competitors.

Figure 7.10 illustrates what have been called high velocity markets, markets characterized by short product life cycles, fast discontinuous changes in customer expectations, entry of major new rivals, redefinition of industry boundaries and rapid competitive manoeuvring by competitors (Wirtz *et al.*, 2007). In recent years the mobile phone, e-reader, laptop and netbook markets have all shown such characteristics. In such markets, the strategic imperative is to be pro-active – to have the capability of fast response to changes as they develop, as well as aggressive spending on R&D and possibly ensuring close relationships with suppliers and suppliers of complementary products or services. Lack of innovation is likely to lead to decline, sometimes precipitously.

A firm that is late in responding to this turbulence has limited strategic options. Strategies for such businesses are likely to include retrenching to more attractive segments, reducing costs to improve profits, or developing new competitive advantages over the longer term.

Alternatively, when business units have a competitive advantage and generate returns above their cost of capital, strategies are likely to focus on such alternatives as investing in growth segments, extending competitive advantages in existing segments and looking for opportunities in adjacent segments. For such businesses, operational improvements may be less important than growth. However, microeconomics tells us such superior returns are

likely to attract competition. Management must therefore focus on ensuri
competitiveness, perhaps with non-incremental changes such as a shift of produc
new process technology.

Entry strategy

Different kinds of change create different implications for the organization. Busines
are successful in commercializing new technologies or pioneering new markets
different organizational configurations from those planning to address mature markets with
low-priced entries. In this section we will illustrate these relationships by comparing resources
required for entry at different stages of a product class or product form life cycle. Notice that
if a firm intends to compete throughout the life cycle, required capabilities must change
significantly.

Pioneer

Pioneer businesses attempt to create markets rather than enter existing markets. Their
products and services often result from consistent and extensive R&D spending relative to
competitors, with success built not on a single innovation but on a continuous stream of
innovative products. These firms must develop in-house the R&D skills and organizational
commitment to produce genuinely new products and services. Most importantly, pioneers
must possess quite different, but equally critical, marketing skills that enable them to introduce
new products into the uncharted waters of new markets. Probably the leading exemplar of
a pioneer business is Apple which has developed and successfully launched such innovative
products as the iPod, iTunes, iPhone and the iPad.

Pioneer businesses require a risk-taking internal corporate culture, accepting of the
inevitable failures that accompany innovation. The necessity to move quickly and enter
early also mandates a degree of 'organizational slack' so that they can speedily commit the
required resources when fast-developing markets require them. They also need the financial
resources to support heavy and consistent R&D expenditures (or the purchase of equity
stakes or technologies) and the frequently high costs of market development. As at March
2010, Apple had cash and marketable securities of $23 billion, a very significant financial
resource.

Pioneering is a high-cost option, and governments typically recognize the unique
contributions of such firms through patent law. Successful pioneers are able to secure limited
monopolies for their discoveries, enjoying the resulting high margins, which provides the
financial resources for their high levels of R&D. ARM Holdings, described in Chapter 5
(►Chapter 5), is an example of a pioneer; they have stayed on the leading edge of their
technology for several years. With an R&D/sales ratio of 32 per cent, this indicates both the
cost, and the risk, of this option. The pioneer business needs to continuously innovate, since
their advantage typically declines with time (Fernandez & Usero, 2007).

Chapter 5

Fast imitator businesses

Rather than pioneer new markets, some firms await innovation by competitors, then follow the lead as quickly as possible. Companies using this approach avoid the high-risk financial outlays for projects that fail but risk allowing the pioneer to gain first-mover advantage or even patent protection. Fast imitation can be a viable option, but many that espouse this philosophy do so by default rather than design. Regardless, it implies a different organizational configuration.

While technology drives the pioneer, the major driver for fast-imitator firms is competition. Competitive intelligence is crucial: they may even identify pioneers' R&D projects before launch. Imitators focus on development rather than research. Either the development occurs in-house or the firm seeks to acquire products/entire businesses in developing markets. This is a 'used apple' policy. Let someone else take first bite of the apple – if it looks okay, go ahead; if not, stop (Levitt, 1974). An ability to move fast when it becomes clear that the pioneer has developed a potentially successful product is crucial. Important capabilities include good development engineers and 'can do' lawyers to find weak spots in the pioneer's patent filings. Imitators often work very quickly. In the R&D-intensive pharmaceuticals industry, patents are typically circumvented within four years, at 65 per cent of the innovator's cost (Christen, 1998).

Examples of successful imitators include Matsushita (now Panasonic), which successfully followed Sony into the home videotape market, and the Ethicon division of Johnson & Johnson which consistently and successfully followed US Surgical's (now Tyco) medical device innovations some 18 months later with lower priced versions and the struggle between Netscape and Microsoft in the Internet browser market, with Microsoft, the fast-imitator firm, eventually emerging victorious.

Segmenter businesses

As markets develop, the number of competitors increases and power shifts from supplier to customer. Customers become more knowledgeable and accomplished in using the products and competitors more astute in listening to customers' emerging needs. As market growth slows and over-capacity becomes the norm, customer requirements typically become more specific, varying across the market and creating the segments that give this archetype its name.

Since the market has now grown significantly, segments can be very large. Segmenters offer products and services more nearly satisfying the needs of one or more segments than those of incumbents. Marketing research to understand customers and identify potential market segments and the ability to successfully address narrow market niches become more critical than technological expertise.

To address several segments simultaneously, a modular design philosophy (called platform engineering in some industries such as automobiles) and flexible yet cost-effective operating systems are required. Early entrants may be encumbered with inflexible and relatively costly operations systems, which are ill-fitted to this stage of market develop-

> ## Market segmentation *in practice* – VW
>
> Mazda's resuscitation of the long-dormant sports car segment with the much-imitated Miata (MX-5) is an excellent example of single segment focus. However, Volkswagen, aiming at its long-term goal of becoming the world's largest car manufacturer, has done a superb job of segmenting and platform engineering with its Audi (up-market), Volkswagen (mid-market), SEAT (young and sporty) and Skoda (value) brands. Although sharing many parts in common, each brand has managed to sustain a differentiated position in the marketplace.

ment. Yet success for the segmenter demands close working relationships among marketing, product development and operations, a considerable challenge to traditional functional organizations.

Me-too businesses

Entry is also common when the market is fully developed and is growing slowly, if at all. At this stage, price elasticity typically increases and the proportion of customers willing to choose from among a set of competitors, all regarded as acceptable, usually increases.

Over-capacity and intense price competition often characterize these markets. To create shareholder value, me-too competitors with essentially similar offers must achieve a low-cost position. They need aggressive procurement operations and significant capability to reduce costs through value engineering. They must also be able to efficiently manage high-volume operations with low-overhead expenses. Me-too businesses typically have limited product lines and are often leaders in process innovation. Their strategies can wreak havoc in segmented markets where several competitors make value-added offers.

Companies that appear to have adopted a me-too approach are generic pharmaceuticals companies such as Novopharm and Patiopharm, which never invest in developing new drugs but rather focus on producing low-cost generic versions of existing drugs. Airlines such as JetBlue, Flybe, Jetstar, Ryanair and EasyJet provide other illustrations. One danger, of course, of this type of competitor is that they may actually cause a shift in customer values, or at least hasten a movement already underway (Kumar, 2006). Most new products and services eventually become commoditized once they are established, changing the basis of competition towards price. Air travel, once a premium-priced luxury product, is now seen as a commodity by many travellers, and legacy carriers are suffering as a result.

As noted earlier, the capabilities required by each of these four archetypes are in conflict. It is unlikely that a single business unit can embrace the entire range of archetypes at the same time, and even within a diverse corporation, the profound differences in required capabilities can pose real problems. A striking example of the difficulty in managing more than one of these archetypal entry strategies was Merck's original and much publicized decision to build a separate facility in order to enter the generic pharmaceutical business and its subsequent pull-out before it even began operations.

In the short term, firms should select entry policies that optimize the relationship between their existing capabilities and marketplace demands. However, new opportunities will often require developing new capabilities. Given a choice between an attractive market opportunity plus little core capability, and a poor market opportunity plus significant core capability, most companies would be better off with the former, especially if they are committed to developing the requisite capabilities. Jeff Bezos, CEO of Amazon, had little in the way of core capability for running a dot.com retailer when he started Amazon, nor did eBay, the most consistently profitable B2C Internet business.

As markets develop over time, businesses choosing early entry options must be concerned with potential competition from later entrants:

- Pioneers must be concerned with businesses adopting fast-imitator strategies.
- Pioneers and imitators must be concerned about segmenters.
- Pioneers, imitators and segmenters must be concerned about me-too firms.

Chapter 5

If the business intends to continue to participate in the market, it must therefore adjust its capabilities over time. This is an important dynamic of strategic management for existing businesses, and failure to manage transitions associated with new market conditions has caused the demise of many businesses (➤Chapter 5).

Capabilities and architecture

Chapter 11

The final step in determining how the business unit will compete is to design the architecture of the unit so that it reflects and supports the strategy, a topic covered in detail in Chapter 11 (➤Chapter 11). Strategic managers need to ensure that the firm's structure, processes, culture and assets, human, organizational and financial, enhance and support the selected strategy. The capabilities and architecture, many of which will constitute intangible assets, that are required by the business will be influenced by decisions on where and how to compete as well as decisions on the growth strategy for the business.

LEARNING OBJECTIVE 5

Select which growth strategy is suitable for a firm.

7.7 BUSINESS GROWTH

Revenue growth is an important objective for most managers. Identifying a growth strategy requires an opportunity-focused culture in the firm based on detailed understanding of customers, competitors and the capabilities of the organization. A recent US study on business growth found that successful firms were able to achieve growth rates above the average of the industry in which they competed (Viguerie *et al.*, 2008). Some of this above-average growth may come from competitors in the form of market share growth. But it appeared that for most firms this above-average growth came from their ability to identify high-growth segments and focus their strategy towards them. Most high-growth industries have segments which are growing more slowly, while most mature industries contain high-growth

Protect and extend occurs when growth is achieved via strategies aimed at ensuring that the businesses' core products and services remain strong. Management pro-actively ensures that the businesses capabilities are distinctive, that the business continually improves its processes, introduces line extensions as demanded by customers and keeps a strong efficiency focus. A risk here is that managers become complacent and allow their core capabilities to become obsolete – emphasizing the need for continual change.

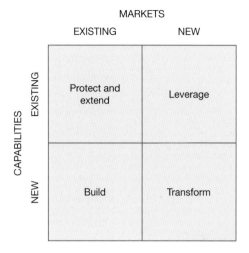

Figure 7.12 Capabilities/market alternatives

Leverage is growth achieved by using the current capabilities of the business to enter into new or adjacent markets, or to expand geographically. This growth strategy is generally not easy to achieve. It appears that market knowledge is generally difficult to accumulate, and the business may attempt to try to execute this growth strategy without a complete understanding of customer needs and the competitive forces in the new market.

A build growth strategy involves developing new capabilities to meet the changing requirements of existing markets. Core capabilities do not last forever. Competitors emulate them, markets and customer change, new competitors enter, government regulations change. All these suggest that a firm's core capabilities, if left alone, will decline in value. Innovation with this growth strategy involves understanding which capabilities need to be developed and which capabilities have become redundant.

A transform growth strategy requires developing new capabilities allowing the business to compete in new markets. A number of means can be employed to achieve this growth, including mergers and acquisitions, internal development, and forming networks and alliances. Such a growth strategy normally carries the highest risk, a combination of market risk, capability risk and financial risk. In addition, this growth strategy involves a change in mission of the business, and so discussion of these alternatives is delayed until Chapter 9 (►Chapter 9).

Chapter 9

Innovation and sources of value

Another lens through which growth and other strategic options can be viewed is according to the degree of innovation they encompass. The strategic management task at the business unit level must incorporate both ongoing change and more radical change. Ongoing innovation involves reducing costs, increasing quality and improving asset productivity, among other alternatives. But significant improvements in shareholder value will usually occur through more radical innovation. To get above-average returns, the business must venture beyond current practice in the industry. Thus strategic management must concern itself with how the firm's markets and industry will be different in the future. Can the business set the rules for competition in its industry? Do managers understand the threat of new and unconventional competitors and substitutes?

Companies may focus too much on their core businesses, allowing their financial and other resources to deteriorate to such a level that they simply cannot grow. Should this happen, the firm will find it difficult to generate value. Profitable growth is not only important to shareholders, but it also motivates employees, who find it exciting and rewarding, and suppliers, who like growing and profitable customers.

All business units need a stream of change initiatives, and these initiatives can be differentiated according to the nature and degree of innovativeness of the change. Business units should be engaging in a portfolio of change initiatives, some ongoing in nature, others more radical. We will discuss the need for initiatives under three categories, depending on the nature of the change, using the framework presented in Figure 2.3.

Ongoing change

Ongoing change is designed to improve efficiency without changing the basic mission or business model. Examples would be cost reductions or quality improvements. This is sometimes described as 'managing for today' – shaping the business to meet current needs and managing current activities for excellence (Abell, 1999). This is the traditional form of competition for many companies, which compete by enhancing the value of their product or lowering its price.

Ongoing strategies are those clarifying the segments in which we compete, the positioning within those segments, and resource deployment choices. They seek gaps in the competitive landscape and ensure that existing resources achieve the best fit with the environment. They also ensure that functional and supply-chain partner activities are aligned with company strategy and harmonized with organizational structure, processes, culture, incentives and people. At the same time, the business must ensure that its cost structure is competitive, it can assess and expand competitive advantage, and can improve quality and the value proposition delivered to customers. Such initiatives can also be described as focusing on operational effectiveness (Porter, 1996).

An operationally effective business unit performs its chosen set of activities better than rivals. Many large firms have reduced headcount, downsized, reduced overheads, redesigned processes and gone back to core businesses, which should lead to significant short-term improvements in performance. A business may need to undertake these measures if a crisis has developed but should aim to achieve excellence on an ongoing basis. Nonetheless, industry leadership over the longer term usually necessitates more ambitious changes.

Incremental change

Chapter 2

Incremental change results in modest changes to the unit's business model, encompassing expansion into new but related markets and products as well as process innovation and enhancing current capabilities (▶Chapter 2). The term *business process re-engineering* has become somewhat faddish, but the fundamental importance of improving processes is undeniable. Nor should such improvements be limited to operations; the accounting, incentive and performance management systems all provide examples of processes that might be improved.

Changes often mean performing different activities or performing similar ones in a different way. The productivity frontier – the trade-off between buyer value delivered and relative cost position of the firms in an industry – moves outward all the time as new technologies and management approaches are developed (Porter, 1996). As a firm approaches a new frontier, competitors will imitate the means it used to get there.

Incremental innovation is often witnessed in low-growth markets. Examples would be breakfast cereal or cement, where there is little change in the sources of advantage and industry consolidation is often occurring. With more rapid but still evolutionary change, there may be more opportunities for innovation and segmentation, but such change does not pose the problems created by discontinuities. As has been well documented, many mature markets contain segments which are growing rapidly, and the management task is to develop sufficient market understanding to be able to identify these (Viguerie *et al.*, 2008).

Revolutionary change

Revolutionary change is a pro-active activity, initiated at the corporate or business level that fundamentally redefines the business so as to compete more effectively in the future. Such radical change creates the future through such actions as changing the rules of engagement in a fundamental way, redrawing industry boundaries, and even creating new industries. It involves major changes in vision, mission or the business model of the firm. Managers must address such questions as: How are customers changing? How will the business address e-commerce? What major new capabilities will be required? In an intensely competitive world, there is competition for industry leadership as well as market share (Hamel & Prahalad, 1994).

While revolutionary change is generally risky, incremental improvements are unlikely to lead to significant improvements in wealth creation. Every business process and every dimension of competitive advantage has an associated improvement curve – the rate of improvement over time – generally an S-shaped curve (Foster, 1986). After a business has been operating for some time, it and its competitors are likely to be on the top of the curve, so improvements are modest – minor cost reductions, slight gains in customer retention and so on. While important initiatives, these are not likely to result in dramatic increases in firm value. While some firms are prepared to accept this low-risk/low-return trade-off, others are more adventurous and actively explore breakthrough strategies, attempting to bring discontinuous change to their operations or by responding to external discontinuities. Foster and Kaplan argue that only those firms which systematically destroy the parts of their firm that are yielding diminishing shareholder returns can expect to deliver high returns in the long term (Foster & Kaplan, 2001). Long-lived companies can prosper but will not deliver high returns to shareholders by working their patch and not venturing too far from it. Revolutionary change may mean that we have to cannibalize our products before competitors do.

Discontinuities are often the result of the development of a new technology, whose performance graph is generally initially below that of the current technology but whose development is faster and which rapidly overtakes the old technology on the S-curve. Management must recognize the limits of its existing technology and the threat posed by new, discontinuous technologies.

Revolutionary change requires management foresight, an understanding of future competition, insight into opportunities, and the ability to energize the company so as to get there ahead of competitors. When the occasion arises, managers must be willing to discard their current cognitive maps and models and adopt new ones (Hamel & Breen, 2007). It requires recognizing that there is competition for developing the required new capabilities and the possible need for alliances. It mandates externally oriented managers who monitor breakpoints, times of dramatic change in market or technology. Such revolutionary change is likely to take the business into areas where there is much to learn, but experiments and low-cost market incursions can limit risk. Revolutionary innovation may appear to be high risk, but sometimes so is 'steady as she goes'.

The management challenge is how to undertake a complete portfolio of changes at the same time. Business units that wish to ensure their future should be attempting to undertake all three types of change – ongoing, incremental and revolutionary – simultaneously. This is not easy, since they each require different structures, incentives and processes, the subject of Chapter 11 (➤Chapter 11).

 Chapter 11

 ## 7.8 SUMMARY

In this chapter we examined the development of business unit strategy and have argued for consistency and alignment of the vision, values, mission and objectives of the business unit with the corporate level. We reviewed some of the analysis that is necessary to develop business strategy, looking at the context of the business and examining the use of the value chain in some depth. We emphasized the importance of understanding both the cost and the value drivers of a business, as well as appreciating its strengths and weaknesses, before beginning strategy design.

Much of the chapter was devoted to the key strategic decisions that must be made in developing business strategy; namely where to compete, how to compete and how to grow. Deciding where to compete requires decisions on vertical and horizontal positioning. Vertical positioning requires decisions about which activities to undertake and which activities to outsource. Horizontal positioning is concerned with how many and which market segments to compete in. Since superior value is created by business units which have developed a significant competitive advantage, we then explored alternative means by which the business could develop such a competitive advantage. We then reviewed two frameworks useful in formulating the growth strategy for the business, generally a condition for value creation, incorporating the need for innovation.

The chapter concludes with an example of a well-aligned business strategy adopted by Sandvik Tooling as reported by the president of one of their business units, Mr Anders Thelin. Finally, the mini-case of Ryanair provides an opportunity to apply many of the concepts developed in the chapter.

VIEW FROM THE TOP

SANDVIK

Sandvik is a global engineering group with 2009 sales of 72 billion Swedish Krone (approximately €7.3 billion) in 130 countries. The group has three core areas of operation, one of which is tooling systems for metalworking. In 2008 this business, which operates globally, had revenue of about SEK 26 billion (€2.6 billion), employed 17,000 people and earned a return on capital employed of 27 per cent and EBIT/sales of 21 per cent.

The global recession of 2009 had a major impact on the total company as well as on this business unit. During the second quarter of 2009, orders received by the tools business fell by 45 per cent as customers cut back on investment spending. As a result, EBIT/sales fell to –10 per cent. In a presentation to financial analysts, the president of the Tooling Business, Mr Anders Thelin, indicated that the business planned to respond to this downturn in three ways.

Cost reduction

The business identified savings of SEK 1,500 million (€150 million) to be achieved by July 2010. This was to be achieved by reducing production capacity and cuts in net working capital of SEK 1,100 million by July 2010. Thelin plans an exhaustive review of all product lines to eliminate poor performers. The unit will also consolidate global manufacturing operations into five designated sites while reducing employment by 3,500.

Maintaining capabilities

At the same time, he indicated that the business would attempt to retain its skills and capabilities in R&D and marketing, with the implication that these areas would be exempt from the planned personnel reductions.

Gaining market share

The business identified growth segments for tools in the aerospace, wind power and deep-drilling industries. They also committed themselves to more innovation, the rapid adoption of new technology, and a stronger presence in the rapidly growing BRIC markets of Brazil, Russia, India and China.

Source: Thelin, 2009

QUESTIONS

1 Did the tools business achieve the right balance between managing for today and managing for tomorrow?

2 As a corporate manager, how long do you believe you should have to wait to see a business like this return to profitability?

3 Are Mr Thelin's planned actions too severe? Not severe enough? Why or why not?

4 Are competitors likely to follow them into the growth segments they have identified?

RYANAIR

Ryanair, the very successful Irish low-cost carrier, is a single-business company. There are, therefore, no complications from attempting to differentiate corporate and business unit strategy. The company flies only one aircraft type, the Boeing 737, which minimizes training and maintenance costs compared with airlines flying many different types. Much of the airline's cost advantage, however, comes from route selection. By flying between secondary airports, Ryanair keeps its airport and handling charges exceptionally low. Michael O'Leary, the CEO, claims that even more important is the fact that the lack of congestion enables 25-minute turnarounds. Ryanair's maintenance costs are also exceptionally low; and the company carries out almost all routine maintenance itself, although the finance director explains that some of the maintenance cost shows up in employee costs because of its insourcing policy. The *Financial Times* summarized its cost advantages in six categories, as follows:

- **Overhead**: lower general administrative costs.
- **Distribution**: direct sale only; no fees for third-party reservations systems; no commissions on ticket sales.
- **Passenger service**: no catering; no in-flight amenities.
- **Crew costs**: lower compensation; higher productivity; reduced crew complement.
- **Airport charges, ground handling**: lower airport costs through use of secondary airports; lower taxes; lower ground-handling costs.
- **Seat density**: 15 per cent more seats per aircraft (Dombey, 2002).

Each of these cost advantages is consistent, reinforcing the ability of Ryanair to offer low prices to customers yet still attain a margin (operating profit before tax to revenue) of 19.8 per cent in its fiscal year ending in March 2008. Even in 2009, during the GFC when most airlines were reporting huge losses, Ryanair turned a profit on passenger numbers that rose 15 per cent to a total of 58.5 million.

QUESTIONS

1   What explanation do you have for Ryanair's phenomenal success to date?
2   What are the lessons for other airlines, especially legacy carriers?
3   Are there any lessons for other industries in the Ryanair example?

REVIEW QUESTIONS

1 Select a global firm with which you are familiar. Provide brief examples of strategies at the level of a business unit implemented by this firm over the last five years.

2 Which industries do you believe face the greatest threat of disintermediation by online Internet-based competition?

3 Give some examples of industries in which economies of scale are changing. In these industries, are scale economies getting larger or smaller? What are the implications for firms in these industries?

4 Discuss the proposition that, with increasing competition and knowledge intensity, outsourcing will become more common.

5 Give examples of business units within global firms that in your view are following a cost leadership strategy.

6 Do you believe that, in the future, combination strategies – a combination of cost leadership and differentiation – will become more important?

7 Discuss the proposition that, with intense levels of competition, innovation is the only sustainable basis for competitive advantage.

REFERENCES

Abell, D. F. (1999) Competing today while preparing for tomorrow. *Sloan Management Review, 40*(3), 73–82.

Ansoff, H. I. (1965) *Corporate Strategy.* New York: McGraw-Hill.

Baghai, M., Smit, S. & Viguerie, S. P. (2007) The granularity of growth. *McKinsey Quarterly,* (2), 40–51.

Bensoussan, B. E. (2008) *Analysis Without Paralysis.* Upper Saddle River, NJ: FT Press.

Berthon, P., Pitt, L., Parent, M. & Berthon, J.-P. (2009) Aesthetics and ephemerality: Observing and preserving the luxury brand. *California Management Review, 52*(1), 45–66.

BrandDirectory (2010) Brands by brand value, 2010. www.brandirectory.com/profile/Tata.

Capon, N. & Hulbert, J. M. (2001) *Marketing Management in the 21st Century.* Upper Saddle River, NJ: Prentice Hall.

Capon, N. & Hulbert, J. M. (2007) *Managing Marketing in the 21st Century.* New York: Wessex Publishing.

Caputo, A. C. & Palumbo, M. (2005) Manufacturing re-insourcing in the textile industry. *Industrial Management and Data Systems, 105*(2), 193–207.

Cascio, W. F. (2006) The high cost of low wages. *Harvard Business Review,* (December), 23.

CGI (2008) CGI announces 5-year contract with Daimler Financial Services. Retrieved 1 May 2008. www.cgi.com/web/en/overview.htm.

Chakravarthy, B. & Lorange, P. (2008) *Profit or Growth?: Why you Don't Have to Choose.* Upper Saddle River, NJ: Wharton School Publisher.

Chandra, C. & Ali, K. (2004) *Mass Customization.* New York: Kluwer Academic.

Chocri (2010) Home page. www.createmychocolate.com/.

Christen, M. (1998) Does it pay to be a pioneer? *Financial Times*, 19 October, p. 1.

Christensen, C. M. (2001) The past and future of competitive advantage. *Sloan Management Review*, 42(2), 105–109.

Collis, D. J. & Rukstad, M. G. (2008) Can you say what your strategy is? *Harvard Business Review*, (April), 82–90.

Compal (2010) About Compal. www.compal.com/index_En.htm.

Crawford, P., Johnsen, K., Robb, J. & Sidebottom, P. (1999) World power and light. *McKinsey Quarterly*, (1), 123–132.

Díez-Vial, I. (2007) Explaining vertical integration strategies: Market power, transactional attributes and capabilities. *Journal of Management Studies, 44*(6), 1017–1040.

Dombey, D. (2002) Low cost airlines. *Financial Times*, 12 December, p. 13.

EGO3D (2010) Home page. www.ego-3d.de/en/.

Fernandez, Z. & Usero, B. (2007) The erosion of pioneer advantage in the European mobile telecommunications industry. *Service Business*, (1), 195–210.

FierceBiotech (2010) The speciality pharma market outlook. www.fiercebiotech.com/research/specialty-pharma-market-outlook-key-players-new-company-growth-models-and-emerging-opportunities.

Foster, R. N. (1986) *Innovation: The Attacker's Advantage*. New York: Summit.

Foster, R. N. & Kaplan, S. (2001) *Creative Destruction*. New York: Doubleday.

Gadiesh, O. & Gilbert, J. L. (1998) Profit pools: A fresh look at strategy. *Harvard Business Review, 76*(May–June), 139–147.

Gluck, F. W. (1980) Strategic choices and resource allocation. *McKinsey Quarterly*, (1), 22–33.

Goold, M., Campbell, A. & Alexander, M. (1994) *Corporate Level Strategy*. New York: Wiley.

Gottfredson, M. & Schaubert, S. (2008) *The Breakthrough Imperative*: New York: Collins.

Greaver, M. F. (1999) *Strategic Outsourcing*. New York: American Management Association.

Hamel, G. & Breen, B. (2007) *The Future of Management*. Boston, MA: Harvard Business School Press.

Hamel, G. & Prahalad, C. K. (1994) Competing for the future. *Harvard Business Review*, (July–August), 122–128.

Harrigan, K. R. (1983) *Strategies for Vertical Integration*. Lexington, MA: Lexington Books.

Hofmeister, J. (2010) Stop outsourcing. *International Herald Tribune,* 12 May, p. 6.

Hulbert, J. M. (1985) *Marketing: A Strategic Perspective*. Katonah, NY: Impact Publishing.

Hutzschenreuter, T. & Grone, F. (2009) Changing vertical integration strategies under pressure from foreign competition: The case of US and German multinationals. *Journal of Management Studies, 46*(2), 269–307.

Insinga, R. C. & Werle, M. J. (2000) Linking outsourcing to business strategy. *Academy of Management Executive, 14*(4), 58–70.

iStockAnalyst (2008) The best emerging market banks. Retrieved 1 May. www.istockanalyst.com/article/viewiStockNews/articleid/2538424.

Jobvacanciesinlondon (2009) List of job cuts. Retrieved 25 February 2009. www.jobvacanciesinlondon.co.uk/career-issues/list-job-cuts.

Jones, G. (2005) *Renewing Unilever: Transformation and Tradition*. Oxford: Oxford University Press.

Kaplan, R. S. & Norton, D. P. (2001) *The Strategy-Focused Organization*. Boston, MA: Harvard Business School Press.

Kim, W. C. & Mauborgne, R. (1997) Value innovation: The strategic logic of high growth. *Harvard Business Review*, (January–February), 103–112.

Kim, W. C. & Mauborgne, R. (2005) *Blue Ocean Strategy*. Boston, MA: Harvard Business School Press.

Knudsen, T. R. (2006) Escaping the middle-market trap: An interview with the CEO of Electrolux. *McKinsey Quarterly*, (4), 72–70.

Kumar, N. (2006) Strategies to fight low-cost rivals. *Harvard Business Review*, (December), 104–112.

Levitt, T. (1974) *Managing for Business Growth*. New York: McGraw-Hill.

Lowe, K. B. (1998) Downsizing and firm performance: Panacea or paradise lost? *Academy of Management Executive, 12*(4), 130–131.

Macmillan, I. C. & Selden, L. (2008) The incumbent's advantage. *Harvard Business Review*, (October), 111–121.

Marsh, P. (2002) Fired up to introduce new ideas. *Financial Times*, 10 December, p. 13.

McIvor, R. (2008) What is the right outsourcing strategy for your process. *European Management Journal, 26*(1), 24–34.

Mishra, K. E. (1998) Preserving employee morale during downsizing. *Sloan Management Review, 39*(2), 83–96.

Montia, G. (2008) Dresdner's acquisition by Commerzbank puts 9,000 jobs at risk. Retrieved 1 September. www.bankingtimes.co.uk/01092008-dresdners-acquisition-by-commerzbank-puts-9000-jobs-at-risk/.

Porter, M. E. (1980) *Competitive Strategy*. New York: Free Press.

Porter, M. E. (1985) *Competitive Advantage*. New York: Free Press.

Porter, M. E. (1996) What is strategy? *Harvard Business Review*, (November–December), 61–78.

Quinn, J. B. (1999) Strategic outsourcing: Leveraging knowledge capabilities. *Sloan Management Review, 40*(4), 9–21.

RZB (2009) Semi Annual Report 2008. www.rzb.at/eBusiness/services/resources/media/1026359884948-1026359885014_1026067924320_1026689581274-504870544584356610-1-NA-EN.pdf.

Safizadeh, M. H., Field, J. M. & Ritzman, L. P. (2008) Sourcing practices and boundaries of the firm in the financial services industry. *Strategic Management Journal, 29*(1), 79–91.

Salvador, F., de Holan, P. M. & Piller, F. (2009) Cracking the code of mass customization. *Sloan Management Review, 50*(3), 71–78.

Stuckey, J. & White, D. (1993) When and when not to vertically integrate. *Sloan Management Review, 34*(3), 71–83.

Tata (2010) About us. www.tata.com/aboutus/index.aspx?sectid=pihbI04W7W0=

The Economist (2010) Data, data everywhere. *The Economist*, 27 February, Special Report.

Thelin, A. (2009) Managing the downturn. *Capital Markets Day 2009*, September. Retrieved 23 July 2010. www3.sandvik.com/pdf/ir/capital/090903/Tooling CMD 2009.pdf.

Vaillant (2010) About Vaillant. www.vaillant.com/about-vaillant/vaillant-group/.

Viguerie, P., Smit, S. & Baghai, M. (2008) *The Granularity of Growth*. Hoboken, NJ: John Wiley & Sons.

Vose, D. (2000) *Risk Analysis: A Quantitative Guide*, 2nd edn. New York: John Wiley.

Wachman, R. (2008) Bank merger to cost 1,200 City jobs. *The Observer*, 31 August. www.guardian.co.uk/business/2008/aug/31/europeanbanks.banking.

Wharton School Publishing (2007) Radiohead's free for all. 7 November. www.whartonsp.com/articles/article.aspx?p=1081503.

Wirtz, B. W., Mathieu, A. & Schilke, O. (2007) Strategy in high-velocity environments. *Long Range Planning, 40*, 295–313.

For a range of further resources supporting this chapter, please visit the companion website for *Strategic Management* at www.routledge.com/cw/fitzroy.

CHAPTER 8

CORPORATE-LEVEL STRATEGY

LEARNING OBJECTIVES

Upon completing this chapter you should be able to:

1 Explain why it is a challenge for corporate management in a diversified firm to create value.

2 Summarize the distinguishing elements that comprise corporate strategy.

3 Apply the analytic tools of corporate strategy to resource allocation.

4 Distinguish between related and unrelated diversification and identify how diversification affects firm performance.

5 Describe the basis for corporate decisions on capital structure and dividend policy.

6 Discuss the nature of risk in strategy.

HMV GROUP

HMV is a UK-based retail chain with operations in the UK, Canada, Hong Kong, Ireland and Singapore. Formed in 1998 as HMV Media through a management buyout from EMI, the firm operated a chain of bookshops (Waterstone's) and a chain of music/video retailers – HMV Music. In May 2002 with improved performance of both HMV Music and Waterstone's the firm decided that it was time for an initial public offer (IPO) of its shares, changing its name to HMV Group. There was some risk with the IPO. The firm had to convince investors that it could grow in what was perceived as a slower-growth retail market and that it could compete in an era of music downloads and Internet retailers. This was achieved and 279 million shares were offered at 192p. Proceeds from the sale were used to reduce debt by about £300 million.

Over its life, the HMV Group has had to grapple with significant changes in its environment. Probably the most important of these changes has been the rise of the Internet and the resultant structural changes in consumer spending. CDs and subsequently DVDs became available as digital downloads, either illegally or from outlets such as Apple's iTunes. Books became available from suppliers such as Amazon, and are coming under pressure from e-book readers such as Kindle. As a consequence, HMV has been faced with fast-changing technology, driven by large competitors such as Apple whose strategy was not necessarily well understood by HMV.

There were also major changes to industry structure as traditional boundaries became blurred. Supermarkets such as Tesco aggressively expanded into non-food retailing, including CDs and DVDs, adopting aggressive pricing as an entry strategy. Tesco also introduced a download service in 2005. Reflecting this difficult environment, both Woolworths (UK) and Borders (UK) had ceased operations by the end of 2009.

Selected strategic decisions: 2002–06

In 2001 HMV Media rejected a £180 million cash bid for the Waterstone's business from Tim Waterstone (the firm's founder) and a private equity group. In January 2004 a new managing director at Waterstone's successfully introduced a new system to improve stock turn and thus reduce costs.

HMV was an early entrant into store marketing of DVDs, investing heavily from 2003 onward. The strong cash flows from these sales allowed investments in new stores and debt reduction of about £100 million in 2004. At the same time, DVD margins were expected to fall as new competitors such as Tesco entered the market.

HMV was interested in the digital delivery of music, but was uncertain about copyright protection and which technologies would become commercially available. Nonetheless, in partnership with Microsoft, HMV invested £10 million in 2004, to install download kiosks in stores. Unfortunately the venture performed poorly.

Throughout this period, management continued grappling with the book business. In September 2005 HMV offered 440p per share for Ottakar's, a smaller book chain with outlets mainly in smaller towns.

The offer was referred to the Competition Commission by the Office of Fair Trading. By the time the offer was approved in May 2006 HMV revised its bid to 285p per share, an offer accepted by Ottakar's shareholders. Ottakar's was integrated into Waterstone's, with some synergy arising from the closure of a number of stores.

After poor Christmas 2005 results, HMV itself became a takeover target. An initial offer of 193p per share from Permira, a private equity group, was rejected, as was an increased bid of 210p. Given HMV's subsequent share price decline it is not clear that the rejection was in shareholders' interests. In April 2006 another bid for Waterstone's, this time for £280 million, was received from Mr Waterstone. However, the group behind the offer fell apart and the bid collapsed.

Over the 2002–06 period, HMV also made several changes to its geographic portfolio. Its German stores closed in 2003, US stores in April 2004 and Australian stores in September 2005.

In January 2006 HMV announced that the CEO, who had been with the firm from the beginning, would leave at the end of the year. The firm announced it was seeking a new CEO who would be able to develop an integrated digital strategy and revive sales. The new CEO was appointed in July 2006. He was previously COO at Kesa Electrics where he had developed a successful Internet strategy. He had limited experience in either the music or book industries.

Selected strategic decisions 2007–10

HMV continued to suffer from the inexorable rise of Internet-based music combined with supermarkets and others diversifying into their main areas of business such as DVDs. Following losses in the second half of 2006, a new strategy was introduced. Having failed at matching the low prices offered by supermarkets, HMV decided to invest in its stores to make shopping a more luxurious experience.

In 2007, HMV sold its 62 Japanese stores for £70 million, using the funds to reduce its £130 million debt. In September 2008 HMV launched Get Closer, a social networking site allowing users to import their own music downloads, in direct competition with iTunes. In December 2008 Zavvi, another entertainment retailer, went into administration. HMV wanted to acquire 14 stores immediately and another six in 2009. This acquisition was finally cleared by the Office of Fair Trading in April 2009.

Over the period, HMV has continually altered its portfolio of products in the quest for higher sales growth. Its stores introduced juice bars, gaming areas, and other technology products such as mobile phones. In 2009 HMV acquired a 50 per cent stake in a digital technology company, to assist Waterstone's sales of electronic books and online sales at HMV. In a major diversification move, HMV also announced a 50/50 joint venture with the MAMA group, which operated clubs and music festivals. The intention was to create a new live music division. In December 2009 HMV bought the whole MAMA group for £46 million.

In March 2010 HMV's CEO announced that the firm wanted to become a broad-based entertainment retailer, with sales of products such as iPods as well as phones. The firm was now selling technology and fashion. This reflects an ongoing redefinition of its vision and mission, from a traditional music store to an entertainment retailer.

The book area was not neglected in these changes. In August 2007, HMV announced it was interested in buying several stores from Fopp, a leading independent chain which had gone into administration. HMV also yet again restructured the book supply chain to reduce costs by £40 million per year. In a reversal from past practices, an element of decentralization was introduced, with Waterstone's store managers allowed to launch local promotions.

Despite all the changes, financial performance of the HMV Group was poor throughout the period. At the initial IPO, the share price was 192p, reaching an all-time high of 282p in February 2005. By 10 September 2010 it was 60p. Total shareholder return over the period 1 January 2007 to 10 September 2010 was an annualized rate of –17 per cent (HMV Group, 2010).

Many of the concepts to be discussed in this chapter have been highlighted in the HMV example. Given the major changes in its external environment, the firm had to develop a new vision which generated new types of stores which built on these developments (►Chapter 6). It also changed the role of the centre on several occasions, sometimes becoming more centralized, sometimes more decentralized (►Chapter 11). HMV managed its evolving business portfolio as it attempted to develop high-growth businesses, and this involved a strategy of related diversifications. Throughout its recent history, the firm has also struggled to keep a sound financial structure, while actively resisting several takeover offers. The changes made by HMV have been both incremental and revolutionary. HMV also illustrates that the task of strategic management – creating value in a turbulent environment – is extremely difficult. Despite all the changes, it must be said that to date its financial performance has been less than stellar.

CHAPTER OVERVIEW

As the HMV Group illustrates, the structure of the modern firm is that of a corporate centre together with a number of semi-independent business units, with these business units comprising the portfolio of the firm. With such a structure, the corporate centre is responsible for developing and implementing the strategy for the entire firm, not for any individual business unit, and it is this corporate-level strategy which is the subject matter of this chapter. We open by discussing how a firm comprising several business units can create value, which introduces the concept of synergy. We then develop a framework consisting of five interrelated dimensions, which are the major areas in which decisions must be made.

We then explore each of these five dimensions in turn, beginning with the need to create a future direction for the corporation. This is followed by a discussion of the style of the centre – is the corporate centre highly centralized or decentralized and what are the external and internal considerations in making such a decision? The major portion of the chapter is devoted to an analysis of the business portfolio of the corporation, which businesses should comprise the firm, and how will this mix of businesses develop over time in response to market changes such that the firm continues to create value.

This leads to a discussion of the nature of diversification, what are the differences between related and unrelated diversifications and the impact that such decisions have on firm performance. A consistent theme throughout the book has been the need to integrate financial considerations into the strategy process. This becomes the topic we explore next; for example, assessing how the capital structure of the firm influences strategic choices. Since strategic management is about making decisions in an uncertain world, we then examine risk and how that risk can be managed. Following this is a View from the Top, with the observations from Anthony Habgood, Chairman of Whitbread, on how that firm approached the management of its portfolio. The chapter concludes with a mini-case, Philips Electronics NV, asking you to explain the performance of the company and how it can be improved.

Due to the complexity of corporate-level strategy, we will address the various aspects in two successive chapters. In this chapter we concentrate on managing the current scope of the firm and on allocating resources among the different businesses that comprise the portfolio. In Chapter 9 (►Chapter 9) we concentrate on managing the dynamic scope of the firm. In some sense this is inseparable from the issues of this chapter, but the importance of innovation, merger and acquisition policy, and participation in alliances, for example, is so great that they merit their own chapter.

8.1 INTRODUCTION

LEARNING OBJECTIVE 1

Explain why it is a challenge for corporate management in a diversified firm to create value.

Despite the complexity of the modern corporation and the turbulent environment in which it competes, the overall objective for corporate management can be stated quite simply – does the firm as a single entity create additional value over what would occur if the businesses comprising its portfolio were independent entities not under common ownership? Algebraically, if the firm F consists of N business units B_i, and V denotes the value of the firm or a business, then:

$V(F) \geq \sum V(B_i)$, where the summation is over all the N businesses.

Consider a simple situation where a firm consists of just one unit, labelled A, and decides to diversify by adding a new unit, labelled B, to its portfolio. For this to add value, the following relationship must hold:

$$V(A+B) > (A) + V(B).$$

Expressing it in words, the value of the combined entity (A+B) must be greater than the sum of the values of the two businesses, assuming that they are valued as independent units. This simple relationship encapsulates perfectly the task of corporate management if we view the long-term objective to be maximization of shareholder wealth. Yet, while the objective seems straightforward enough, developing strategies to achieve the objective is much more demanding.

Understanding corporate structures

Firms typically have their genesis as fairly simple organizations, often selling a single product or single line of products in one or a few markets. Akzo-Nobel, for example, had its origins in a company making forgings in 1646, but today manufactures paints, coatings and specialty chemicals instead. It no longer makes forgings and reported sales of over €15 billion in the year ended 31 December 2008. Over the longer term, virtually every aspect of the corporation must be regarded as a variable. Most of the early development of economic and business theory assumed a fairly simple structure, but this is increasingly at odds with the complexity of the modern corporation.

As firms developed in size and complexity, business and economic theorists began to modify their work to reflect the new challenges, though it is often the case that practice runs ahead of theory building. Today's large global firms face unprecedented challenges for which management theory provides limited guidance. Nonetheless, path-breaking work by such authors as Chandler (Chandler, 1962), Rumelt (Rumelt, 1977), Lawrence and Lorsch (Lawrence & Lorsch, 1967), Williamson (Williamson, 1975), Wrigley (Wrigley, 1970) and others has generated significant insight into the problems posed by complexity.

To illustrate the magnitude of the task, we will briefly examine the structure of Siemens, the German firm, which has worldwide assets of some €95 billion.

Figure 8.1 shows the Siemens organization structure in abbreviated form. As with many large global firms, there is a third organizational level between the corporate level and the business units. Despite almost universal pressure to simplify structures and reduce the number of levels in the organization, many global firms are similarly organized. We will refer to this intervening level as the group level, where the group is a collection of related business units. Accordingly, we may consider the group as possessing some of the characteristics of both a corporation and a business unit. However, the corporate level retains responsibility for relationships with financial markets, even though other functions may be devolved to the group level.

The management task for the CEO and the top management team is to ensure that this complex organization of different business units with different technologies competing in markets around the world creates economic value. Siemens has three major product groups,

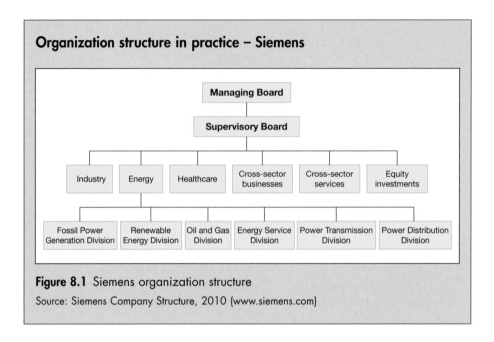

Figure 8.1 Siemens organization structure

Source: Siemens Company Structure, 2010 (www.siemens.com)

industry, energy and health care, each with global responsibilities. We consider a sub-unit within one of these groups to constitute a business unit. Thus the 'Oil and Gas Division' is a business unit within the energy group. For ease of discussion in this chapter, the corporation will be assumed to comprise a number of business units; we will not discuss group or sector-level strategy since, as noted above, it has characteristics of both corporate and business unit strategy.

Siemens also has three corporate level entities, cross-sector businesses and cross-sector services as well as a group called equity investments; and the role, operations and responsibilities of these cross-sector businesses need to be identified when constructing corporate strategy. Cross-sector businesses comprise IT services and financial services – handling global clients in these two industries. Cross-sector services provide consulting and real-estate services within Siemens. As a global firm, Siemens also has a regional organization, which is not shown in Figure 8.1, with regional companies, regional offices and agencies to support its operations in some 190 countries and its staff in 2010 of around 405,000 people. The structure shown above resulted from a major rationalization conducted in 2008. At this time, the company consolidated 1,800 legally separate entities and 70 regional companies, while cutting 4 per cent of its global workforce, a total of 16,750 jobs (*The Economist*, 2008).

The essence of the corporate strategic management task is to manage a multiplicity of businesses, partners, geographic markets, technologies and customers under the same corporate umbrella, such that the total entity delivers value to all stakeholders. As noted, the challenge is to ensure that the value delivered by the combined entity is greater than the value that might have been delivered under any other organizational arrangement, including where the business units act as independent entities.

This observation highlights the fact that strategy at the corporate level is fundamentally different from strategy at the business unit level. At the corporate level, the strategic management task is not to manage any of the constituent business units or to develop strategy for these business units. Corporate staff generally does not have detailed knowledge of an individual business or its contemporary environment, even though they are usually supported by such centralized services as corporate planning, finance, information technology, knowledge management and so on. Their role is to manage the entire business portfolio, not an individual business. Corporate management delegates that task to senior business-level management, with various degrees of central staff support. It then attempts to ensure that mutually agreed-upon targets are met, recognizing that a business unit's performance is affected by its specific context, which varies across different businesses.

The key difference is one of breadth in terms of required decisions. A business unit has a degree of integrity; it is a more homogeneous entity that operates in a discrete and well-defined product/market. In contrast, the overall firm comprises a number of such business units, and these businesses may bear little apparent relationship to one another. Again, the challenge is to resolve a paradox. These business units can, and do, operate to a certain extent independently of one another. At the same time, they are part of a larger group and their performance should be enhanced by membership. So we need to combine the advantages of independence with the advantages of collective ownership. One of the corporate tasks is to influence relationships so as to create synergy, perhaps by encouraging one business to share its capability so as to improve the performance of another business.

Creating value

If we accept that the objective of the corporate level should be to ensure that the value of the corporation's constituent businesses is greater under this particular corporate umbrella than under any other ownership, we must necessarily address the vexing question of how the corporate level adds value to the firm and its constituent business units.

In a diversified firm, most value is created in the business units, not at the corporate level. Nonetheless, a corporate centre has specific decision areas in which it can affect value. Corporate is generally responsible for M&A activity, which can add to or destroy value. In addition, it is responsible for decisions regarding financing, dividends and relations with financial markets, which again can affect value. Finally, corporate staff will have an impact in areas such as corporate culture and management values. So the corporate level can add to or subtract from the value of the firm in several ways, not only through its interaction with the business units. Yet, if each business in the firm's portfolio is independently maximizing its performance, how can corporate staff add value to the total enterprise? What is there for the parent to do? This question is fundamental to corporate strategy.

Since the parent corporation has no external customers (although it does have a relationship with certain external providers), it generates costs but no revenue. Ultimately, the parent must create value greater than the costs it incurs despite the fact that its impact is indirect. However, the corporate centre has an important intermediary role. It can influence business unit decisions and strategies, and it stands between the businesses and financial markets. Thus, although primary value creation takes place at the business unit level, parent and business unit need to work together to enhance value creation.

Researchers have examined the effect of corporate ownership on the performance of firms' constituent businesses, and the results have been mixed. One researcher estimated that corporate effects account for as little as 0 per cent and as much as 20 per cent of the variation in SBU return on assets, with less corporate effect as diversification increases (Roquebert *et al.*, 1996). Other research has tended to support the relatively small corporate impact (McGahan & Porter, 1997). However, it may be that the degree of relatedness of the diversification is an important intervening variable (D. Collis *et al.*, 2007).

Part of the disagreement may arise from differences in methodology, including the use of different statistical tools, data sets, performance measures and business unit definitions. Nonetheless, overall, research suggests that the activities of corporate-level staff do make some difference to business unit performance (Bowman & Helfat, 2001), even though there may be uncertainty about the magnitude of the impact. Intuitively, it would seem quite anomalous to find that SBU performance was completely independent of the corporate-level staff! Nonetheless, it is often easier to see how the parent might destroy value than to see how it creates value, since poor acquisitions have historically been enormous destroyers of value.

In Table 8.1 we summarize how a corporate centre might create or destroy value in its relationship with its business units (McLeod & Stuckey, 2000).

In an ideal world, the corporation would be described as the natural owner of its constituent businesses. This term, introduced by McKinsey, means that the corporation's businesses perform better under this parent than they would under any other parent: including the situation of having no parent (being independent). If this is so, the firm should be relatively immune from unfriendly takeover, since it can earn more from the asset (the business) than any other owner, who cannot logically afford to pay more than it is worth to the current owner.

Table 8.1 Corporate opportunities to add or destroy value

Corporate can add value by . . .	Corporate can destroy value by . . .
Managing the dynamic scope of the firm, often through an active divestment and acquisition programme	Making poor acquisitions, the majority of which add no value to the acquiring firm
Managing the linkages between businesses so that the performance of a given business is enhanced by the fact that it is part of the business portfolio of the firm	Imposing high overhead costs
Providing centralized services, where the quality/cost of these is superior to what the business could get from an outside supplier	Being slow and unresponsive, remaining remote from the business and not assisting in strategy development despite the fact that it must approve strategy

Thus, for a corporation to exist on a sustainable basis, the corporate level must contribute to value creation, since otherwise the costs it imposes would render the firm vulnerable to takeover. The corporate centre can create value through assembling a portfolio of business units, ideally with positive interdependencies and supported by a collection of capabilities. It can support business units in their decision-making and add value to them through shared capabilities that create profitable opportunities for inter-divisional cooperation. The corporation also acts as an internal capital market, possibly performing this role better than external financial markets due to better understanding of business-level opportunities.

It is also evident that the corporate centre must decide the level and nature of its intervention in business-level strategy making. Given the turbulence of today's markets, firms have to be flexible, able to respond rapidly to unpredictable change. One common response has been greater decentralization, devolving more decision-making authority to the business units. Employees in these business units are closer to customers, competitors and technologies and should be better able to make timely decisions that will create value for the business and hence the corporation.

The challenge for the diversified firm is for corporate managers to be able to demonstrate that they can improve the performance of business units when these units are part of a larger whole, that is, when they are no longer independent businesses. In principle, corporate staff should only intrude in decision-making processes of the business when they are able to accomplish this.

8.2 ELEMENTS OF CORPORATE STRATEGY

LEARNING OBJECTIVE 2

Summarize the distinguishing elements that comprise corporate strategy.

Corporate strategy involves decision-making in five interrelated dimensions, as shown in Figure 8.2. We now overview each of these elements and then develop each in more depth later in the chapter.

Creating future direction

As discussed in Chapter 6 (►Chapter 6), developing a sense of direction for the entire firm is a critical role for the corporate centre. In doing so, senior managers must cope with the often competing demands of different stakeholder groups, whose claims on the firm will change in relative importance over time. If, for example, the firm faces a financial crisis, possibly brought about by a global recession, management may have to reduce employment or implement salary reductions to maintain the viability and profitability of the firm. As we saw earlier, the HMV Group had to develop a new vision in response to environmental changes and poor relative performance.

Chapter 6

Style of the centre

Each firm needs to decide on the size, location and style of its corporate head offices – the executives responsible for providing services to the whole entity. Recent research has indicated

Figure 8.2 Elements of corporate-level strategy

the extensive variability in the number of people, as well as the activities performed by head office (D. Collis *et al.*, 2007). Based on an international survey, it was found that in Germany the median size of head office staff per 1,000 employees was 9.3 while in Japan it was 38.7, a significant difference. Several factors were identified which influenced the size of the corporate centre. As would be expected, firm size was one. Another was the degree of un-related diversification. Firms characterized by unrelated diversification are characterized by a planning and control system with a strong emphasis on financial control, with little need to achieve coordination between business units. Finally, country of origin of the firm had an effect, with European firms generally having smaller head offices than US firms.

Corporate staff must also decide what kind of parent they will be and determine the principles that will guide their relations with the firm's various business units. This is often described as the parenting style of the firm (Goold *et al.*, 1994), which can vary from quite detached to quite involved. Deciding on the style of the centre involves many of the para-

 Chapter 2 doxes described in Chapter 2 (▶Chapter 2). These include: common business unit objectives or targeted business unit objectives, local autonomy versus global standardization and business autonomy versus corporate standardization, as the following example illustrates.

A paper manufacturing company also has a merchant division, which sells paper to printing firms. Does the merchant division have to buy paper from upstream in the company, or can it also source from outside the firm? If the merchant division is not given the option, then its viability can be threatened by poor performance of the manufacturing division.

Portfolio management

The corporate level is responsible for decisions on how resources, financial and human, will be allocated to the various business units that comprise its portfolio. The corporate centre is responsible for capital allocation across the business portfolio, judging which businesses should be supported with investment funds. In this capacity corporate acts as an internal financial market, supporting some businesses, providing less support to others, and perhaps withdrawing support entirely from still others. The firm may be better able to do this than financial markets because corporate and business unit managers may better understand the opportunities available to business units, consequently making judgements superior to those of financial markets. The resource allocation role implicitly assumes that the firm suffers from a capital shortage. A more appropriate view is that the purpose of the firm's centre is to raise the capital required by all strategies that promise to deliver more than the cost of capital.

Corporate management must manage the firm for both today and tomorrow, and needs a relatively long planning horizon to do this. Sustained growth will almost always require some diversification, as growth opportunities within their original line of activities diminish. It has been argued that only those firms which systematically destroy the parts of their firm which are yielding diminishing shareholder returns can expect to deliver high returns in the long term (Foster & Kaplan, 2001).

Sometimes the firm will partially or completely re-invent itself, as the two examples following demonstrate.

Re-invention *in practice* – Bilfinger Berger

Bilfinger Berger, Germany's second-largest building company, has reduced its exposure to its core construction activities by building up a substantial services activity, including consulting, finance and maintenance for major commercial and government clients. It started this re-invention in 2002, and by 2009 services revenue, at €5.0 billion, accounted for 50 per cent of revenue (Hammond, 2010). It is also undertaking an IPO of its Australian operations which is expected to raise approximately €1 billion.

Re-invention *in practice* – Unilever

In 2006 Unilever, the world's third-largest packaged foods company, announced that it was putting its European frozen foods business up for sale. In a generally stagnant European market, Unilever and its competitors were reported to have either been reorganizing or selling off the underperformers in a bid to boost their overall returns on the continent. A shift of European consumers to chilled food was reportedly a major underlying cause (ElAmin, 2006).

These firms illustrate that ultimately nothing about a firm is fixed: strategic managers can change any and all characteristics of a firm over time.

Diversification and relatedness among business units

As noted earlier, successful firms inevitably outgrow their initial scope. To continue to grow, they must necessarily diversify. The extent, type, mode and rate of diversification are all crucial questions for the corporate centre. There is an ongoing debate in the research literature as to whether or not diversification creates value for the firm's shareholders. Economists like to point out that shareholders can diversify their holdings quite easily and cheaply. The transaction costs incurred by shareholders as they diversify are generally small, particularly when compared with those incurred by a firm. Empirical research further suggests that not only does diversification destroy value, but that it often seems to be done for reasons of managerial hubris and ego (Hayward & Hambrick, 1997).

We expand on this topic later, but the general principle is that related diversification is generally more successful. Where businesses are related in some way and share a common set of capabilities, there is a better chance that synergy can be created. Multinational corporations provide an example of this principle in action. Although not all attempts at international expansion have been successful, the mere existence of the term illustrates the fact that many companies have been able to utilize their technological and product expertise across a wide variety of markets, and global expansion has become a major driver of diversification, as exemplified by Siemens, with operations in 190 countries.

Financial decisions

The most important financial responsibilities involve managing relationships with financial markets, including institutions and major shareholders; decisions on capital structure; and dividend policy. Related financial concerns include such matters as share buybacks, capital raising, sources of borrowings, risk management (including exchange-rate risk), and policies on stock options for staff, which are now closely scrutinized. Many of these decisions will have to be approved by the board, but the initiative is with corporate management.

Other corporate decisions

Chapter 11

In this section we have reviewed the major decisions comprising corporate strategy. Of course, there may be other important decisions to be made. Corporate managers will carry major responsibility for designing and evolving the architecture of the firm, which we discuss in Chapter 11 (►Chapter 11). They must also respond to crises, such as a plant explosion or the bankruptcy of a major customer or supplier, and play a major role in managing relationships with governments and the broader community. In these respects, the CEO is the spokesperson for the company, and his or her behaviour will be viewed as epitomizing the values and vision of the firm.

We now discuss each of the major elements of strategy in more detail.

8.3 CREATING FUTURE DIRECTION

Creating future direction is one of the critical tasks of corporate management. In describing vision and values in Chapter 6 (▶Chapter 6), we noted that a vision statement is aspirational. To serve its purpose, it should neither be easily attained nor frequently changed. Similarly, the firm's values should be sufficiently robust to provide enduring guidance in fulfilling the vision. These caveats do not, however, apply to the mission statement that defines the present and future scope of the firm. Missions should be regularly reviewed, in good times as well as in bad, for they must reflect and capitalize on both the effects of a dynamic environment and the firm's evolving capabilities. Chapter 6

Economic changes over the past few years have caused many firms to rethink their missions. This is particularly challenging for global firms, since senior managers must be aware of developments in many countries, markets and technologies. Such changes as the Asian meltdown of the 1990s, the slowdown in the US economy in the early 2000s or the global financial crisis of 2008/09 have had a dramatic impact on firms and entire industries. They may mandate changing the mission, abandoning old businesses, entering new ones, implementing new organizational forms, creating alliances and networks, and so on.

Changing mission *in practice* – US banking

At the height of the GFC, following the collapse of Lehman Brothers, both Goldman Sachs and Morgan Stanley applied for commercial banking licences to ensure the availability of US government financial support. Without the crisis it is very unlikely that they would have done so.

A recession often brings much greater attention to issues of future direction. Growth hides a multitude of mistakes: a rising tide tends to help all firms. However, during a recession, managers have to focus on earnings and free cash flow, ensuring that costs are under control. Unprofitable businesses may need to be sold, balance sheets strengthened, debt levels and costs reduced – cash becomes king! Firms may have to make decisions that are essential for the short run but may be at odds with any long-term view. Ideally, these decisions should not jeopardize future growth. Yet these same circumstances may present cash-rich firms with major opportunities, since they can pick up bargains. As we noted in Chapter 6 (▶Chapter Chapter 6 6), however, companies tend to pay much greater attention to their mission statement in bad times, when they tend to talk of refocusing on core businesses and the like, than they do in good times, when the seeds of future problems are often sown.

8.4 STYLE OF THE CENTRE

Another strategic decision for corporate staff involves the role and style of the centre, what decisions are made by corporate staff, and which decisions are delegated to business unit staff. In a recent study, four distinct roles were identified for the corporate centre (D. Collis *et al.*, 2007). The first and most important role involves the development and allocation of corporate resources, with the requirement that the firm must be able to accomplish this better than if such allocation was done through financial markets – as would be the case if the business units were independent entities. In other words, the centre must add value to the business units over what would be achieved if they were independent. Second, the corporate centre needs to design and operate an appropriate control system which allows it to evaluate the performance of the business units to minimize agency costs – the tendency for business unit managers is to maximize their objectives and not the objectives of the overall firm. The third role of the corporate centre is in the provision of centralized services when these show major economies of scale. Services such as payroll processing, legal advice, human resources and R&D may be undertaken at the corporate level to achieve such economies of scale. At the same time, the corporate centre needs to ensure that these services do not become isolated from the operating divisions, and there can be an ongoing debate as to the most appropriate home for these services. Finally, the corporate centre is the legal representative of the organization. Due to this, there are a number of required reporting and compliance functions which must be performed. For most global firms, there are a considerable number of these, generally in different countries, each with their own legal and regulatory frameworks.

Following our strategic management approach, we take the first two of these dimensions – planning influence and control influence – to develop a system for characterizing the style of the centre for a firm (Goold & Campbell, 1987), as shown in Figure 8.3. We then go on to discuss the provision of central services.

- *Planning influence*: the degree to which the centre influences strategy formulation at the business unit level.
- *Control influence*: the type of control exerted by the centre, what objectives are established and how the centre responds to business outcomes.

On the basis of these two dimensions, corporations can be classified into a number of styles of the centre, as shown in Figure 8.3.

While the original research identified eight styles, we will discuss only two, identified in Figure 8.3 as a strategic planning style and as a financial control style.

In firms where the centre adopts a strategic planning style, the corporate centre works closely with business units in developing their strategies. Corporate managers of such firms believe they have an important role to play in developing business-level strategy and educating business units about the needs and skills of other businesses. These firms have extensive and explicit planning processes, with specified analytical frameworks and formats. Corporate personnel are involved in decisions on fundamental trade-offs (e.g. between growth and cash flow objectives) at the business unit level.

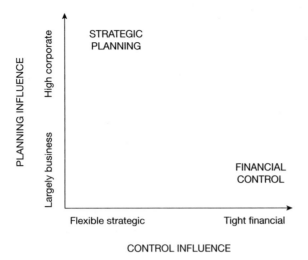

Figure 8.3 Styles of the corporate centre

With this style, the most important intervention by the centre is managing inter-dependencies among business units. These firms typically exhibit considerable relatedness, such as shared resources, technology, or know-how, among business units. The centre intervenes with the goal of maximizing overall organizational effectiveness. There is generally more senior-level input to the strategy process, and this is reflected in organization structure, which is a combination of global product responsibility and substantial regional responsibility. Business unit strategy needs to be coordinated with a geographic region strategy. The objectives established for business units are generally broader and more strategic – for example, to become the leading competitor. On the other hand, in this style of firm, there is less ownership of the strategy by the business unit, and failure to meet objectives may be attributed to the need to satisfy others in the firm, the regions, or the corporate level.

Firms characterized as possessing a financial control style differ considerably. There is limited corporate input into the business-level strategy process and much less attention paid to interdependencies among business units. Business unit objectives are almost solely financial, and control is exercised more through the annual budgeting process than through the planning process. Once business unit objectives have been established (almost entirely by the corporate centre, with limited negotiation), business management is held accountable for meeting these objectives, with strong sanctions if it fails to do so. The corporate centre acts essentially as a financial market, funding proposals and strategies put forward by the businesses. Since objectives are clear and specific, the careers of senior business unit managers may be in jeopardy if these are not met.

Goold and Campbell concluded that different styles of parenting could be successful and that there was no 'ideal' style. Indeed, the style adopted was to some extent dependent on the management style of senior managers, as well as the nature and type of the business units in the portfolio (which actually follows from the first). For example, if senior management elects to pursue growth via acquisitions, these are more likely to be unrelated, so that the firm adopts more of a financial control style. Another firm, with similar growth objectives, may adopt a strategy of internal development, growing by transferring existing resources and capabilities into new areas for the firm. In these circumstances, the business units will likely demonstrate much greater relatedness, resulting in more of a strategic planning style for the centre. Interestingly, only two of the companies in the authors' sample still exist as independent entities, and one of those two was previously bought and subsequently spun off. Since all were large firms at the time of the study, it is a stark reminder of the fragility of company success.

Challenge of strategic management

Throughout this book we have emphasized the importance of capabilities for strategic management. What, in your opinion, are the capabilities of a firm whose centre is characterized by financial control?

Synergy

An important concept in corporate strategy, related to the style of the corporate centre, is synergy, the ability of two units to generate greater value when they are working together than when they work separately. So when both businesses are part of the same corporate parent, they may work cooperatively, permitting each to generate greater value.

Synergy could arise from a number of sources: sharing know-how or skills; sharing common tangible resources, such as a manufacturing facility; or sharing an intangible asset, such as a brand name. While an attractive concept, however, synergy is not easy to create. Firms try to achieve synergy via cross-business teams, knowledge management and sharing **Chapter 11** of systems, and dissemination of best practices throughout the firm (➤Chapter 11). But many managers seem to overestimate the benefits and ignore the costs and the difficulty of creating synergy (Goold & Campbell, 1998). This is probably one of the reasons why acquisitions are so often unsuccessful, with expected synergies failing to eventuate, as we discuss in the next chapter.

Despite these difficulties, some firms have developed effective mechanisms to achieve cooperation between business units in order to improve their competitive advantage, which is obviously easier when the various business units have a high degree of relatedness. With little relatedness, there are still possibilities for synergy with common processes, such as billing or customer service, but the opportunities are much greater when there are capabilities across business units that can be used by all.

It should be clear from this discussion that there is an ongoing interplay between corporate and business unit strategies. The SBU structure creates greater autonomy at the business level, and SBU general managers can be held accountable for results. The devolution of decision-making should also permit quicker responses to changes in the market or in competition and allow the various businesses to develop systems and structures best suited to their own situations. At the same time, the parent corporation must find ways to add value to a business to justify its continued ownership thereof. Some commentators, such as Hamel and Prahalad (Hamel & Prahalad, 1994), have pointed out the dangers of treating business units as independent. Certainly there is a danger that a drive for autonomy by politically powerful business unit managers can even jeopardize the future of the corporation as a whole. On the other hand, devolved empowerment, properly managed, can be transformative.

Centralized services

Corporations must decide which services to provide centrally and whether or not business units are required to use these services. Centrally provided services may achieve economies of scale in service provision, but offsetting this gain may be the dangers of lack of responsiveness to the differing needs of individual businesses. Most diversified firms share centralized legal and financial services. As we saw with Siemens, the corporate-level IT group establishes the information architecture for the firm as well as setting IT standards for each business unit. With R&D, there is a much more mixed picture. Some firms centralize research but decentralize development to their constituent businesses, as seems to have occurred at Philips of the Netherlands. Others have varied their approaches over time. In most cases, the debate revolves around the advantages of flexibility versus scale.

In virtually all cases, the corporate centre has a role in establishing business objectives and monitoring business performance. As a result, it typically develops the planning system used within the firm. Other corporate characteristics may influence business unit strategy. The corporate centre may excel at maintaining relationships with major customers, or managing logistics, or achieving excellent results from R&D, all of which will benefit a specific business unit. Finally, the business's strategy must generally receive corporate approval, and this process is likely to be more than a rubber stamp. In sum, business unit managers are responsible for business unit strategy, but corporate will intervene whenever it believes it necessary!

In discussing synergy, it needs to be noted that this can be negative. In large corporations, people in the divisions often feel that the centre does not add value; it is seen as too remote, bureaucratic, and slow at decision-making. Senior corporate executives may be out of touch with the realities of the competitive markets faced by businesses or lack understanding of cultural issues resulting from geographic diversity. If true, such characteristics imply that the corporate is not adding value to the business. The corporate centre can also destroy value by not agreeing to good investment proposals from businesses or through too much involvement in decisions at the business level.

LEARNING
OBJECTIVE 3

Apply the analytic
tools of corporate
strategy to resource
allocation.

8.5 MANAGING THE CORPORATE PORTFOLIO

As we discussed earlier, growth is an important objective for most firms, and we have emphasized the need for strategic managers to manage short-term performance while at the same time build a suite of growth alternatives. As firms become larger and more established, growth becomes more difficult. With increasing size, the dollars involved with growth get larger. To grow at say 5 per cent per year, Unilever needs to increase turnover by €2 billion every year – a considerable challenge. Second, the longer a firm is in business, the more likely it is to become complacent, detached from the market, slower acting and less entrepreneurial (Collins, 2009). Given the complexity of the task, good analytical tools are required to assist in deciding which areas offer the most promise to the firm, and how much to invest in them.

Managing the firm's portfolio of businesses is a multidimensional task involving such important choices as the following:

- *Geographic market* – In which countries will we compete? What balance should we seek between domestic markets and those in other countries? Which new countries should we enter?

- *Product* – What products are we selling currently? Which are ageing or are likely to become obsolete? What is our success at introducing new products?

- *Technology* – Which technologies threaten our businesses? Are we entering new technologies? What capabilities would this require?

- *Market growth rate* – Which of our businesses are mature? Do we have high-growth businesses in our portfolio? Are we meeting corporate growth objectives?

- *How should growth be achieved* – Through internal development? Acquisitions? Or alliances and networks?

- *Financial measures* – How are our assets distributed over our businesses? Where are sales revenues generated? Where do earnings come from and how are these related to sales and asset distribution? What is the balance of the firm's cash flows?

Portfolio management *in practice* – BHP Billiton

BHP Billiton is a global resources firm with 2009 revenue of over $US50 billion and is listed on the Australian, Johannesburg and London Stock Exchange. As can be seen in Table 8.2, the profitability of its different business segments varies significantly. Metallurgical coal is used in steel making and had a return on assets in 2009 of 100 per cent, closely followed by iron ore with a return on assets of 76 per cent. Another measure of the attractiveness of iron ore is that it accounts for 30 per cent of profit before tax, but only 14 per cent of BHP Billiton's total assets. Such returns reflect the rapid growth in China and are likely to be difficult to sustain in the future (BHP Billiton, 2009).

Table 8.2 Business segment information for BHP Billiton

Business group	Revenue $USm	Assets $USm	EbitDA $USm	ebit (%)	assets (%)	ebit/sales
Petroleum	7211	12444	5456	0.24828213	0.202856	0.75662182
Aluminium	4151	7575	434	0.01974971	0.123484	0.10455312
Base metals	7105	14812	1851	0.08423208	0.241458	0.2605207
Diamonds and speciality	896	2073	370	0.01683731	0.033798	0.41294642
Stainless steels	2355	4767	−733	−0.0351763	0.077709	0.32823779
Iron ore	10048	8735	6631	0.30175199	0.142394	0.65993232
Manganese	2536	1454	1397	0.062572241	0.023702	0.55086750
Metallurgical coal	8087	4929	4933	0.224482366	0.08035	0.60999134
Energy coal	6524	4555	1676	0.7626848	0.074253	0.25689760
Subtotal	48913	61344	21975	1	1	
Group	1298	17426	−1304	−0.06308355	0.221226	−1.00462249
Total	50211	78770	20671	1.93691645	2.221226	0.41168269

Source: Data extracted from BHP Billiton website, 2009

The financial and market numbers lend themselves to a convenient tabular or graphic display that can be used for monitoring and tracking purposes, as is illustrated in Table 8.2.

Similar tables could be constructed for geographic areas, product groups or other breakdowns. Such data provide useful diagnostic information, and such a matrix could also summarize future objectives, again broken down by classifications of interest. The German firm, Henkel, has indicated how much it plans to invest in R&D across its three business sectors, as shown in Table 8.3.

Resource allocation *in practice* – Henkel

Henkel's total R&D expenditure in 2009 was €396 billion, representing 2.9 per cent of revenue. The allocation of this R&D among the business segments is one of a number of strategic decisions made by the firm's executives. Senior managers must decide where this R&D will be invested, and this will depend on a number of factors such as their vision for the firm and the likely return from R&D. As is apparent from Table 8.3, Henkel sees the future of the firm in the adhesive technologies segment, spending 57 per cent of R&D on that segment even though it represents only 46 per cent of revenue (Henkel, 2010).

Table 8.3 Segment data for Henkel

Business segment	% of revenue 2009	% of R&D 2009
Adhesive technologies	46%	57%
Laundry and home care	30%	26%
Cosmetics, toiletries	22%	17%

Resource allocation – current and future portfolio

The distinguishing feature of a diversified firm is that it consists of a number of interdependent business units. The corporate centre makes two crucial, interrelated decisions with respect to these units: what the definition of these business units should be (how they are delineated) and how resources are to be allocated among them.

Chapter 2 The definition of what constitutes a business unit is important. As described in Chapter 2 (▶Chapter 2), we want the business units to possess a degree of integrity and to be able to be treated semi-autonomously, with senior business unit managers held responsible for their performance. But this structure also has an important impact on resource allocation, since corporate must decide on allocation of resources among these units. Thus a decision on the definition of business units is, of necessity, also a decision on the nature and type of resource allocation decisions to be made. If the units are defined geographically, then the first cut at resource allocation is among different geographic regions. If, however, the units are defined by product group, then resources will be first allocated among these groups. It is for this reason that some allege that 'strategy is organization and organization is strategy'. Nonetheless, managing this portfolio of businesses, rather than attempting to manage the individual businesses, is the major task of corporate management.

Corporate portfolios are, of course, dynamic, and corporate management must manage changes in the firm's portfolio over time. Figure 8.4 shows a firm consisting of three business units, called 1, 2 and 3. The question that corporate managers must address is what future portfolio they want. Will all business units be treated equally or not? Suppose that a corporate objective was to grow sales revenue at the rate of 10 per cent per year for the next five years. Would we expect all business units to grow at this rate, or would we expect some business units to grow faster than 10 per cent and other business units to grow at a slower rate? Such a decision on relative growth is a corporate-level decision, made by senior corporate managers. Business unit managers would be expected to follow the growth objective established for their unit.

Figure 8.4 suggests that the corporation will have five businesses in the future, and thus its composition will have changed considerably. For business 1, the objective is to hold (maintain) its current position in the market. This business is not seen as a growth opportunity, perhaps because its markets are mature, with limited growth opportunities. The firm believes it has better opportunities elsewhere, evidenced by business 2, which is given a growth objective, perhaps because it has international expansion opportunities. The question

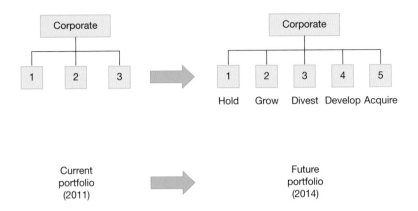

Figure 8.4 Current and future business portfolio

then arises of where the firm will get the funds to support the growth of this business. Remember that on average about 70 to 80 per cent of funds for investment are generated internally within the firm. If business 2 is not generating the funds required to support its growth, they must come from elsewhere in the portfolio, perhaps from business 1.

Business 3 is a business that the firm plans to divest; it is no longer considered relevant. This business may not fit a revised corporate mission or may be generating poor returns with little likelihood of improving. One of the most important decisions made by a former CEO of the then BHP was to spin off 94 per cent of their steel business to BHP shareholders (selling the remaining 6 per cent shortly after) to enable the firm to concentrate on resources (BHP, 2002). Divestment is clearly a corporate decision, but there is evidence that firms are readier to acquire than divest (Viguerie *et al.*, 2008). Companies may exit a business in a variety of ways. The business might be sold to another firm, it could be spun out and listed as a separate firm (with or without an equity interest), the corporation could agree to a leveraged buyout by existing management, or it could simply be shut down. The pros and cons of these approaches will be discussed in Chapter 9.

Two new businesses appear in the 2014 portfolio. Business 4 is to be developed internally, while business 5 is an acquisition. Chapter 9 covers these options for changing scope (➤Chapter 9).

Chapter 9

One way of looking at organizational growth is to split it into three main components, as suggested by Viguerie (Viguerie *et al.*, 2008):

- *Portfolio momentum* – the organic growth the organization achieves through growth in the markets in which it currently competes. It reflects the future performance of historic portfolio decisions.
- *Market share gain* – organic growth from gains or losses in market share of its current business portfolio.
- *Mergers and acquisitions* – inorganic growth achieved by the firm when it acquires or divests other businesses. Included here would be revenue gains from other means

adopted to enlarge the business portfolio such as alliances, joint ventures and networks.

In their research, growth from internal development is subsumed in the first two categories. The study, conducted with a number of global firms, found that the contribution to growth for leading firms from each of these three components was:

- Portfolio momentum – 46 per cent
- Share gain – 21 per cent
- Mergers and acquisitions – 33 per cent

As these results indicate, market share gain contributed the smallest percentage of total growth. Thus, decisions on where to compete and what businesses should comprise the portfolio are the most critical. The composition of the original business portfolio and what acquisitions the firm made should clearly receive the greatest attention from corporate management. While business unit management can make a contribution to total firm growth, the importance of their contribution is overshadowed by the decisions made by corporate strategic managers. Of course, this does not imply that business unit managers add little value. Revenue growth with established businesses does not occur automatically. All markets are dynamic, and established businesses need to ensure that they stay abreast of developments, exploring any growth segments which arise, developing the capabilities required to compete

Chapter 7   in the future and so on, as was developed in Chapter 7 (▶Chapter 7).

Tools for allocating resources

Imbalance in a corporate portfolio can jeopardize shareholder interests. An over-abundance of growth businesses can lead to liquidity problems, while too many mature businesses that generate excellent current results may have dismal future prospects. Since successful new businesses usually generate excellent operating margins, revitalization of the corporate portfolio is required for long-term shareholder value creation. In either case, a severe imbalance can lead to acquisition by firms seeking, respectively, growth opportunities or cash flow. In this section we examine a variety of tools that corporate management may use to manage the firm's portfolio.

Financial analysis methods

Chapters 4, 12   In Chapter 4 (▶Chapter 4) we discussed the importance of financial performance and some of the tools and techniques of financial analysis, issues to which we return in Chapter 12 (▶Chapter 12) when we address performance measurement. Our purpose in discussing financial methods at this point is twofold. First, since superior financial performance is a critical objective for management, analysis of potential investment returns is both important and proper. Second, however, we also critique financial methods to illustrate why a corporate centre should augment these methods with other approaches.

A few decades ago many companies made investment decisions using a simple tool, the 'payback period', namely the time required to 'pay back' the original investment. Currently, most firms have either ceased using this method or augmented it with other techniques, since it ignores the time value of money. Today, firms typically use either an internal rate of return (IRR) or the net present value (NPV) of the strategy as a measure of its value.

Internal rate of return (IRR) and net present value (NPV) both rely on discounted cash flow analyses, valuing returns (and expenditures) when they are earned (or paid out), discounting both future returns (cash inflows) and expenditures (cash outflows) to take into account when they are received/disbursed. For IRR, the value of an opportunity is measured as that rate (per cent) which equalizes the inflows and outflows. For NPV, the value of an opportunity is measured as an amount, typically secured by discounting the cash flows at a 'hurdle' rate.

All financial analysis methods have several points in common. First, the result of the analysis is a single figure: months/years for payback, a rate (typically a percentage) for ROI and IRR, and an amount of money for NPV. Second, the methods are conceptually simple: given the set of inputs, investments, sales revenues and costs, the analysis is straightforward, even though complex calculations may be required. Third, the decision flowing from the analyses appears to be unambiguous: opportunities are ranked; those selected typically outrank and/or outperform the others on some criterion or exceed a hurdle rate that should be related to the firm's cost of capital. More complex techniques take into account the inherent riskiness of the project.

However, these methods suffer from two severe problems. First, each relies on estimates of future sales revenues (sales units and prices), costs and investments. As any manager knows, judging the short-term investment required for a well-defined project is difficult enough; predicting sales revenues several years into the future is a daunting task. This task is also open to organizational game playing. As most managers have observed in their careers, opportunity-champions may be tempted to provide inflated revenue forecasts and low future cost estimates to turn marginal return projects into spectacular performers, particularly if they are shortly moving to a new position with the firm. By contrast, hard-nosed financial managers are just as likely to make 'realistic adjustments' to these forecasts (sales revenues down, cost and investment estimates up), sending potential returns plummeting. As a result, investment decisions too often reflect the political clout of various functional managers rather than the intrinsic value of the opportunity. Resolving such conflicts also produces polarization between a proposal's proponents and those who judge it, too easily seen as opponents.

Second, financial analysis techniques are silent on strategic matters, since their logic dictates that opportunities be pursued in order of estimated financial performance, regardless of other considerations. A 22 per cent return (assume IRR) opportunity will always be chosen over an 18 per cent opportunity. However, the 18 per cent opportunity may be central to the company's strategy, whereas the 22 per cent opportunity may be peripheral and require capabilities that the firm neither has nor may acquire. Strategically, perhaps the 18 per cent opportunity should be chosen, but financial analysis reaches the opposite conclusion.

A related problem arises when companies allocate funds to individual businesses based on historic profitability. In this decision-making mode, mature (no growth) businesses tend to receive more investment than new businesses, which are starved of funds since current profits are low.

This danger of over-investing in current businesses via incremental investments and simultaneously starving new businesses is increased by the difficulty of forecasting several years into the future. Clearly, forecasting errors are much greater for newer versus more mature products. As a result of these risk perceptions, returns for new products are likely to be discounted to a greater extent than cost reduction projects for existing products. Thus, management's quest for more conservative, less risky opportunities can easily lead to insufficient investment in potential new opportunities. As we will see in Chapter 9, these kinds of decision processes often create an advantage for the 'attacker', an unencumbered new entrant that competes with newer technology (Foster, 1986).

In order to deal with these problems, some financial managers treat risk explicitly via risk analysis techniques or even complex simulations. However, these procedures have found less favour than originally anticipated and managers continue to seek ways of dealing with the problem (Courtney *et al.*, 1997). Rather than focus on refinement of the numbers, the major thrust has been closer and more explicit examination of the assumptions underlying the financial projections. For example, we might ask about the expected future growth rate of the market(s) in which the products will be sold and the targeted market share. Other questions arise: Against which companies will the firm be competing? What is the likely future market structure? How is technology expected to change? What is the role of government? And so forth. These questions cannot be answered precisely, but they indicate the need to take a much more strategic approach to major investment decisions. Asking and attempting to answer such questions requires that management explicitly address the validity of the assumptions underlying financial projections. In this process, companies have typically shifted from an internally oriented perspective on investment decisions to a more strategic, externally oriented focus. We now address several of these approaches, generically known as 'portfolio analysis'.

The growth/share matrix

One of the earliest and one of the simplest portfolio approaches is the growth/share matrix developed by the Boston Consulting Group (BCG). The approach was developed to assist managers in making decisions on business objectives. Understanding the logic of the growth/share matrix, despite its problems, provides a good foundation for understanding why more elaborate schemes were later developed. We first explain and then critique the BCG approach.

Chapter 4   As we saw in Chapter 4 (▶Chapter 4), all real economic analysis deals with cash flows. Further, survival of the firm depends on maintaining liquidity. Therefore the corporate centre must carefully manage the cash balance of its portfolio. Most corporate portfolios contain cash-generating (cash-positive), cash-neutral and cash-consuming (cash-negative) businesses. The corporate centre's task is to ensure that a cash balance is maintained using internal sources and appropriate external financing.

To assist in determining the cash position of businesses, the growth/share framework uses two independent dimensions:

- The future rate of growth of the market in which the business competes.
- The relative market share of the business in the market in which it competes.

Each dimension is a surrogate. The market growth rate is assumed to be a surrogate of the cash needs of a particular business. Rapidly growing markets create strong needs for cash to maintain market position. Expansion requires new facilities as well as marketing and R&D expense, for example. On the other hand, a business competing in a slow-growing market has limited need for investment funds.

Relative market share is assumed to be a measure of the ability of the business to generate cash. Relative market share is defined as:

Market share of the business/market share of the largest competitor.

A relative market share greater than one indicates that the business is the leader in its market. In the BCG framework, it is assumed that a large relative market share business generates good positive cash flows, and that small relative market share businesses generate less cash. Note that the two dimensions of cash use and cash generation are independent: cash generation is assumed to be determined by relative market share while cash use is assumed to be determined by long-term market growth.

To use this tool, all the businesses comprising the portfolio of the firm are plotted on a two-dimensional chart: future market growth vs. relative market share (Figure 8.5). Businesses are usually plotted as circles, the size of which is proportional to the size (say turnover) of the business. The chart is split into four zones as shown. A relative market share of 1.0 separates high from low share businesses. Any business that is to the left of the cut point is dominant in its market; any business to the right is not, it is by definition non-dominant. To separate high- from low-growth markets, a common cut point is GDP growth + 3 per cent. Markets growing faster are considered to be high growth; markets growing slower are slow growth. Both cut points are somewhat arbitrary. A business with a relative share of 1.01 may be the leader but is scarcely dominant.

Any business above the market growth cut point will ultimately move below, since no business continues to compete in a high-growth market forever. All markets eventually mature, meaning that market growth rate falls below the cut point. This downward vertical movement over time is largely exogenous (outside the control of the management of the business).

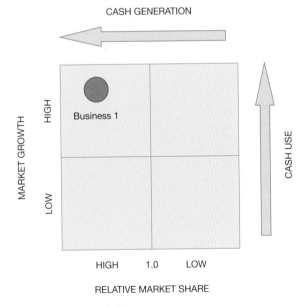

Figure 8.5 Growth/share matrix

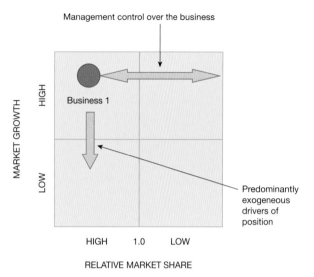

Figure 8.6 Growth/share matrix

Management does have some control over the horizontal position of a business in the chart, since this depends on market share of the business, relative to its largest competitor. If management can increase its relative market share, the business will move to the left, as Figure 8.6 depicts.

Figure 8.6 illustrates the dilemma faced by business managers: when should they attempt to gain share? This is generally considered easier when market growth is high, not only because competitive intensity may be lower but also because of experience curve effects (►Chapter 5). Further, during rapid growth periods, new customers are entering the market, new applications are developing, and the technology is less settled – all of which may make share gain easier than in mature markets.

As Figure 8.7 indicates, businesses in the bottom left cell are expected to be cash positive. They are competing in slow-growth markets; hence their need for cash is low. At the same time, these businesses are the dominant competitor in their market, and hence should be generating significant levels of cash. Cash from such businesses can drive SBUs in the upper right-hand quadrant, which are likely to be cash negative, to a dominant position in their markets while the market growth rate is still high and share gain is easier to attain. The growth/share matrix emphasizes the relationship between the entries in specific cells and their financial characteristics. Businesses with high market shares should be more profitable than those with low shares; businesses in high growth markets usually require significant investment in fixed and/or working capital and market development, reducing cash flow.

In general, the correlation between market share and cash generation is supported by experience curve arguments and empirical research, such as that in Table 8.5, which shows the average profitability (ROI) of businesses with different market shares.

Typical recommendations from a growth/share analysis suggest that the strategy to be followed by a business depends on its position on the growth/share matrix.

In general, the correlation between market share and cash generation is supported by the experience curve argument and empirical research, such as that in Table 8.5, which shows the average profitability (ROI) of businesses with different market shares.

Chapter 5

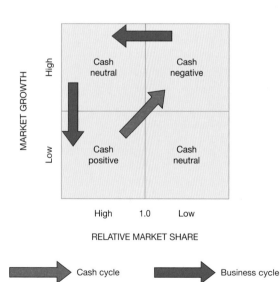

Figure 8.7 Cash cycle of businesses

Cash flow *in practice* – Henkel

Table 8.4 shows additional segment data for Henkel, where we have taken earnings before interest and tax as a surrogate for cash flow. From the data it appears that the R&D expenditure in the adhesives technologies segment is being supported by the strong cash position of laundry and home care.

Table 8.4 Segment cash flows (Henkel, 2010)

Business segment	EBIT %	Revenue %
Adhesive technologies	24	46
Laundry and home care	46	30
Cosmetics, toiletries	36	22

Table 8.5 Market share/profitability relationship

Market share	< 10%	10–20%	20–30%	30–40%	> 40%
ROI	11%	18%	23%	27%	36%

Adapted with the permission of Free Press, a Division of Simon & Schuster, Inc., from *The PIMS Principles: Linking Strategy to Performance*, by Robert D. Buzzell and Bradley T. Gale. Copyright © 1987 The Free Press. All rights reserved.

Typical recommendations from a growth/share analysis suggest that the strategy to be followed by a business depends on its position in the market.

- *Low market growth/high market share* (cash cows). Businesses in this cell are typically highly profitable, both because of good cost position from economies of scale and experience curve effects, and because market leaders are frequently able to command premium prices. Since the market is mature (low growth), required reinvestment should be low, with consequential benefits for cash flow. If they are well managed, and major environmental change is absent, businesses in this cell may generate significant cash for many years, hence the term cash cow. These businesses are a major source of internally generated funds for the corporation and an important source of free cash flow (➤Chapter 4).

  Chapter 4

- *Low market growth/low market share* (dogs). These businesses trail market leaders in low-growth markets. If the dominant firm's business is well managed (see above), low market share business should have inferior cost position, lower prices and consequently be less profitable than the leader. Such businesses should consider several different options: short-run cash maximization by liquidation, divestiture, new segmentation approaches that provide market niche dominance and a 'kennel' strategy requiring acquisition of similarly placed businesses aimed at achieving viable scale.

- *High market growth/low market share* (**problem children**). These businesses are typically viewed as the most risky both because of the inherent uncertainty in high-growth markets and their weak market share position, yet they may represent the future of the firm. They are often marginally profitable, but if they are to grow market share position in a fast growth market, they will need substantial cash for investment in fixed assets and working capital. Since this is a risky strategy, corporate staff may consider other options, such as divesting the business or focusing on a more limited market segment. However, businesses such as these may represent the future of the firm, if it is to grow.

- *High market growth /high market share* (**stars**). These businesses are very desirable and yet are relatively rare. Typically, they are profitable, although not necessarily so at the very beginning of the life cycle, but investment in capacity expansion and increased working capital often means they will be cash neutral to cash negative. The objective for a business with these characteristics is to maintain market share so that the business can become a strong cash contributor when market growth slows.

Difficulties with the growth/share matrix

The growth/share matrix is a powerful tool for analysing a firm's business portfolio and suggesting possible business unit objectives. However, there are several shortcomings. The recommendations neglect any idea of risk, the cost of gaining share and the investment required. Similarly, high-growth markets are typically viewed as attractive, yet, if many competitors rush to enter, excess capacity may result.

The growth/share matrix also has some technical problems. Any decision model rests on a number of basic assumptions and its value is only as good as these assumptions. Market growth rate alone may not signify an attractive market, even if it is associated with cash flow patterns. It is entirely possible to incur significant losses in growth markets. These can be exceptionally competitive, with a number of firms entering as they are attracted by the high-growth possibilities contributing to high rivalry (►Chapter 3). In addition, some generalizations underlying the matrix may not always occur in practice (Hambrick *et al.*, 1982).

 Chapters 3, 5

A related problem is that of market definition. Because of issues concerning level of segmentation and geographic boundaries, market definition is a vexing issue, yet it has a major impact on measures of both market growth and relative market share. If the business's served market is defined too narrowly, its dominance may be quite misleading. Downward-sloping cost experience curves are supposed to drive the market share/profitability relationship (►Chapter 5). Nonetheless, this relationship does not hold universally: well-managed small businesses can have better cost positions than major players, particularly through low overheads.

> ## Relative costs *in practice* – US airlines
>
> In the United States in 2008 SouthWest airlines incurred operating expenses per available seat mile of ¢10.5, compared with ¢16.7 for United Airlines (US Department of Transportation, 2009).

Finally, the economics of many information products have very different cash flow implications than those suggested by the BCG model. They usually have very high development costs but marginal costs of almost zero, especially if distributed via the Web.

In summary, the growth/share matrix is a useful tool for analysing the firm's business portfolio and can provide a good starting point for setting appropriate objectives for different businesses. It is also of value as a diagnostic tool – raising 'what if' questions on the competitive strategy of the business.

Multi/factor portfolio models

In part because of difficulties with the growth/share matrix, several other portfolio approaches have been developed. Perhaps the best known is the GE business screen, which redefines the two axes of the growth/share matrix as market attractiveness and business strengths, respectively. It then allows the user to identify a variety of factors to measure each dimension. It is also called the stoplight matrix, because of a 'coloured' depiction comprising three 'green/go (invest/grow)' cells, three 'red/stop (harvest/divest)' cells, and three 'selectivity/ earnings' cells (Figure 8.8).

This approach is conceptually more robust, since each of these dimensions comprises a number of attributes. However, we now need to answer two questions:

- What determines the attractiveness of an industry?
- How can we assess business strength?

Industry attractiveness: based on the theories of industrial organization economics some of the structural factors that influence the attractiveness of an industry include:

- Market growth rate
- Customer concentration
- Competitive intensity
- Barriers to entry
- Market size.

Business strength: the competitive strength of a business unit is influenced by several factors, including:

- Relative market share
- Market share
- Product differentiation
- Relative costs
- Capabilities
- Supply security.

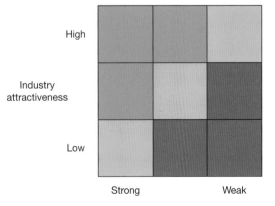

Figure 8.8 Business screen matrix

Table 8.6 Calculation of business strength

Factor	Weights (Σ=1.00)	Business rating(1–5)	Score
Market share	0.15	4.0	.60
Relative market share	0.15	4.5	.675
Differentiation	0.35	4.0	1.4
Cost	0.15	2.0	.3
Margins	0.20	3.5	.7
TOTAL	1.00		3.675

Other sources of ideas for the variables to be used in constructing such a screen include general empirical research such as the PIMS study (Buzzell & Gale, 1987). As noted in **Chapter 5** Chapter 5 (➤Chapter 5), some companies have analysed data from their own experiences, which can also provide inputs.

For each dimension, the sub-factors are combined in a weighting and rating scale, where relevant dimensions are identified and then weighted in terms of their relative importance, using a constant sum scale. The business unit is then rated on each of these dimensions and a weighted total score calculated, as shown in Table 8.6, for the axis 'Business strength'. A similar procedure is used for assessing market attractiveness.

We can plot all businesses in the portfolio on the chart, as shown in Figure 8.9. As with growth/share matrices, it is usual to plot the businesses as circles proportional to the revenue of the business. Figure 8.9 is illustrative only and is not related to the calculations of Table 8.5, which is included only to show how scores are computed.

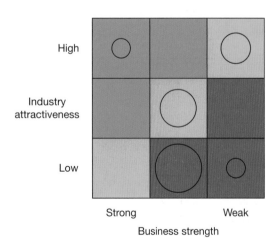

Figure 8.9 Business portfolio

The location of a given business has implications for investment, objectives, managerial style and incentives. Businesses in the upper-left cells are those that the firm would find attractive investment candidates. Such businesses would have growth objectives and would likely require an entrepreneurial management style. Value is created by growth, and incentives for these businesses would emphasize growth rather than current profitability.

Businesses in the lower-right cells are candidates for divestment – or at least limited investment. Objectives would be cash flow orientated and would require managers who excel at cost reduction and squeezing assets for good returns. Here, value is created by cost reduction, not growth.

Thus business objectives, strategy, management style and incentives may depend on the location of the busi-

> ### Challenge of strategic management
> The different portfolio approaches all inherently assume that a firm will create more value when it has a strong position in a limited number of markets. What are the risks of such an approach?

ness in such a portfolio chart. Indeed, some companies have gone so far as to classify their managers into three categories: overtakers, caretakers and undertakers, based on a judgement of the preferred styles of these individuals. Many management theorists would disagree with such a procedure, arguing that managers should be able to adapt their styles to the requirements of the business.

Comparison of growth/share and multi-factor portfolio methods

When evaluating which of the two methods described above to use to evaluate a firm's portfolio, there are several issues to be considered by management. First, the criteria used to assess the different businesses. The major advantage of the growth/share matrix is the limited number of criteria and their more objective nature. The ability of managers to manipulate individual entries is very limited. Although reasonable people may disagree about market growth forecasts, if there is an agreed market definition, deriving relative market share is just a measurement issue. Conversely, the limited number of criteria is also a weakness, since growth and market share may be poor guides to resource allocation.

By contrast, the number of criteria in the multi-factor matrix can range within reasonable limits. This approach may thus embrace many factors that the growth/share matrix omits and hence be more realistic. However, specific criteria, weightings and ratings are all subject to dispute. As a result, political considerations and organizational power relationships may lead to manipulation of entries such that they enter the 'required' cell. More positively, however, the somewhat disputatious nature of the system also surfaces differing opinions, and often results in a healthy dialogue. It is better for these to surface than to remain implicit, since once surfaced they can be openly discussed and evaluated.

The growth/share matrix is easier to implement and communicate. Senior management can view an entire complex, diversified organization on a single sheet of paper. Such a matrix can be used to analyse the trajectory of businesses over time, to evaluate customers and suppliers, and to test the likely results from pursuing different strategic options. Nonetheless, the growth/share matrix is only really useful for assessing existing businesses. Indeed, since, by definition, all proposed new opportunities (other than acquisitions) have zero relative market shares, each such entry is a point on the right-hand side of the matrix.

Conversely, the multi-factor matrix is useful both for assessing investment potential in current businesses and for evaluating totally new opportunities, In addition, risk can be built into the multi-factor matrix, whereas it is omitted in the growth/share matrix. Furthermore, because of the market definition problem, the multi-factor framework copes better with fragmented markets. Finally, neither matrix explicitly assesses the costs of changing market positions, meaning they are problematic in dealing with marketplace dynamics. However, at least the multi-factor system clarifies the business strength improvements required to improve position.

Perhaps the bottom line for both approaches is that they are aids, not substitutes, for sound strategic thinking. Indeed, in our experience, the value of the approaches is less in the specific numbers and entries in either matrix than in the discussion that leads to their formation. Especially for the multi-factor matrix, the discussion of which criteria to employ and arguments about weightings and ratings are frequently at a very high level, and managers gain significant insight about their judgements because the discussion is overt.

Allocation of resources across the business units within the portfolio is a key corporate strategy decision. It needs to be emphasized that business units are not identical; each faces a particular competitive situation and consequently must be treated accordingly. Nonetheless, each is part of a larger portfolio, and corporate-level considerations may well outweigh business-level considerations.

8.6 DIVERSIFICATION

LEARNING OBJECTIVE 4

Distinguish between related and unrelated diversification and identify how diversification affects firm performance.

As firms grow, they generally become more diverse, with an increasing range of businesses, technologies and geographic regions. The degree, nature and direction of diversification are some of the most important corporate strategy decisions. Managers may decide that growth has slowed in existing markets and there is consequently limited opportunity for creating future value. Or the firm may have surplus cash, over and above the amount that can be used profitably in existing businesses. While this cash could be returned to shareholders, either directly or via a share buyback, managers could diversify instead. However, if they invest in low-return initiatives, they destroy shareholder value.

The perspectives of shareholders and managers may differ on diversification. For managers, the reduction in cash flow volatility promised by diversification reduces business risk and may help the survival of the firm. For shareholders, some kinds of diversification can add value to the firm. For example, the diversifying firm may bring superior governance mechanisms or management skills to a new industry, perhaps transferring capabilities or economies of scope. **Economies of scope** occur when the unit product costs for a single firm producing two (or more) products are lower than the unit costs if each product was produced in separate firms.

Economies of scope

Occur when the cost of producing and selling two products together is less than the costs of producing and selling the two products separately.

Chapter 4

Nonetheless, we must always keep in mind that shareholders can diversify more easily than firms. Financial markets may place a conglomerate discount on the more diversified firm, indicating a belief that management will fail to extract all the value from its business portfolio and that the value of the component businesses is greater than the value of the total firm (▶Chapter 4).

Diversification can take any of several forms, vertical or horizontal, related or unrelated with respect to industry, market or geography. These options will be explored shortly. The example below indicates the difficulties several firms have experienced with geographic diversification.

Geographic diversification *in practice* – retailing

Many large retailers have attempted geographic expansion, often with mixed results. Marks and Spencer, one of the most successful retailers in the United Kingdom, diversified unsuccessfully into Europe, the United States and Asia. Carrefour, the French firm that is the world's second-largest retailer, had difficulty integrating its acquisition of Promodes. Wal-Mart's acquisition of ASDA in the United Kingdom appears to have been successful, but their venture into Germany resulted in a loss of $1 billion (Hancock, 2006). Among other factors, tough competition from Aldi, Lidl and Metro were too much for the US giant. However, it was not alone in failing in the difficult German market, for it joined Intermarché, and Prénatal from France, and Marks and Spencer from England in a long list of failures (Schultz, 2006).

There is considerable debate on the nature of diversity and its value to shareholders. Unfortunately, measurement of diversity is controversial (Robins & Wiersema, 2003). Some measures concentrate on whether businesses compete in the same industry or market, whereas a resource-based view suggests measuring the extent to which different business units draw on common resources. Thus, another component of corporate strategy is the extent and nature of diversification: what is the relationship among the business units, are they related or not, and can resources and capabilities be shared between them?

The degree of specialization of these resources also influences the nature of diversification. Collis and Montgomery concluded that firms with very specialized resources will compete in a relatively narrow range of businesses.

Specialized resources *in practice* – Sharp

Sharp has specialized expertise in opto-electronic technologies such as liquid crystal displays. This technology may be used in many products, allowing the firm to continually expand its scope with a restricted range of related products (D. J. Collis & Montgomery, 1998).

Managers must appreciate the difficulties of diversification. Due to bureaucratic costs, firms can easily destroy value through inappropriate diversification. It is not easy to manage a diversified company, and this could explain why many firms ultimately retrench to core businesses. The bulk of empirical evidence is that more focused firms outperform less focused ones. Firms seem to perform less well than the sum of their constituent businesses when there are no shared resources (Wernerfelt & Montgomery, 1988). The general consensus is that some diversity is good but that there will be problems if the firm gets too diverse, as is shown in Figure 8.10, which suggests that firms with moderate levels of diversification outperform both highly focused and highly diversified firms.

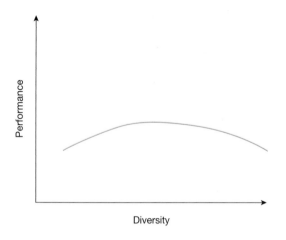

Figure 8.10 Relationship between organizational performance and diversity

We should note that the management tools (such as communications and information technologies) needed to manage diversity improve over time. Managers should also become more adroit at managing diversity. The optimal degree of diversity may therefore increase over time.

Summarizing, some of the claimed advantages of diversification include the following:

- Economies of scale and scope
- The ability of the firm to act as an internal capital market
- Market power or purchasing power
- Financial and tax advantages.

There are some considerable disadvantages of diversification. A significant proportion of diversifications are driven by management ego – managers like to grow revenues and to run big businesses (Hayward & Hambrick, 1997). As a result, they are tempted to invest in new ventures that may not deliver a return greater than the cost of capital, although they do bring revenue growth. This suggests an agency problem – managers are acting in their own interests, not those of the shareholders. In addition, it would be unrealistic to expect corporate managers to add value to a wide array of disconnected businesses. As a firm becomes increasingly complex, it is likely to also become unresponsive to the needs of its business units, slow in decision-making and high in overheads.

Related diversification

Related diversification

When a firm expands its existing product lines or markets, allowing resources or capabilities among the businesses to be shared.

To benefit shareholders, some kind of synergy should accompany diversification. This is most likely when the business units comprising the firm have resulted from **related diversification**. Businesses in a portfolio are related when there is some sharing or transfer of resources and capabilities among the different businesses, sometimes described as 'fit'.

Relatedness may take any of several forms:

- *Tangible resources* – the businesses achieve economies of scale/scope through sharing facilities, such as operations or R&D.
- *Intangible resources* – the firm can transfer capabilities from one business to another. Capabilities might include a brand name, personnel, skills and/or knowledge.
- *Market* – the businesses share the same customers or distribution channels. Unilever or Nestlé, for example, would be expected to gain synergies in this way.
- *Management skills* – these are often the most difficult to transfer from one area to another. Any relatedness would lie in the cognitive foundations on which the business operates, inculcating in managers the same business beliefs and assumptions.

As an illustration of related diversification through the use of intangible resources, some multinational firms from emerging economies used their capabilities developed in dealing with politically unstable governments as a basis for geographic expansion (Guillén & García-Canal, 2009).

For many firms, one approach to growth is through related diversification into adjacent markets – markets which are closely related to their core businesses (Zook, 2004). The distance between the new market and the firm's existing core can be assessed on the basis of dimensions listed above. The objective is to build on existing capabilities, and to exploit these capabilities in new areas of opportunity. As the firm finds new adjacencies, it is able to repeat the process and generate a stream of new business opportunities. This can be an ongoing process which has the effect of expanding the firm's boundaries and extending their core. Such an approach has been adopted at Cisco Systems, where the firm has identified some 30 adjacencies where networking technology has not been widely adopted, such as health care and sports (Cisco Systems, 2009).

As described in Section 8.4, diversified firms can reallocate resources from one business to another in the corporate portfolio. The question is: Are managers better at identifying opportunities than external capital markets would be? Do the firm's senior managers have superior knowledge, information systems and judgement on which to base such a decision? Or do they diversify into areas which are claimed to be related – yet future synergies are very difficult to achieve?

Unrelated diversification

Unrelated diversification occurs when there is little or no relationship among the businesses in the firm's portfolio, such as may occur in a holding company. Whether this delivers value to shareholders rests on the ability of a corporate centre to make better capital allocation to businesses than can external financial markets. This could occur if corporate managers have superior information on opportunities available to a business, their costs and likely future performance. This is not an unreasonable proposition, so long as the corporate centre retains objectivity, since it typically has access to a large amount of information. Another possibility is that the firm has strong dynamic capabilities – the ability to generate the capabilities required by the unrelated diversification (Ng, 2007).

Unrelated diversification should reduce the variability of the firm's cash flow. The resulting lower risk should reduce the firm's cost of capital. Thus, although related diversification generally appears to produce superior returns to unrelated diversification, the latter can be successful under some conditions, such as:

- *Undervalued assets* – the target firm has plants operating below capacity or real estate not being used to benefit shareholders.
- *Financial distress* – the target is in financial distress and its assets can be cheaply acquired.
- *Cash-short* – the target is starved of capital but has good growth prospects.

Unrelated diversification
When a firm expands into new product lines or markets, allowing few resources or capabilities among the businesses to be shared.

Each of the above situations is basically a case of market inefficiency, suggesting that an astute buyout group may have an opportunity to make money by a policy of unrelated diversification. However, over time, if such buyout firms are seen to be making excess returns, these returns should be driven out by increasing numbers of buyout firms, making the market for corporate control much more efficient. Over time, private equity firms have shifted focus, from the US, to Western Europe, to Eastern Europe and now to Asia, suggesting this market for corporate control is witnessing this effect.

In summary, diversification is more popular among managers than among shareholders and analysts. Yet investment bankers and would-be sellers will continually solicit large public firms to make such deals. It takes a good understanding of strategic management principles to sort the wheat from the chaff in these situations, but there are some basic questions that we should always ask when considering such a move:

- What can we do better than competitors?
- What new strategic assets are needed?
- Will we be a winner or just a player?
- Will we learn from the diversification?

LEARNING OBJECTIVE 5

Describe the basis for corporate decisions on capital structure and dividend policy.

 Chapter 1

8.7 FINANCIAL DECISIONS

Strategic management must include an understanding of certain financial decisions which both influence the strategy the firm adopts and are a result of the current strategy which has been adopted. We have emphasized the requirement that the firm create value, which was defined in Chapter 1 as creating an economic profit (►Chapter 1). Since an important component of this is net cash flow, an understanding of cash flows and cash requirements is critical. Historically, many firms considered that cash was dangerous on their balance sheet – it can act as a signal for a takeover. But the recent global financial crisis has indicated the necessity to have access to cash in times of a crisis. During that time, firms found it difficult to raise external capital, even if they possessed a strong balance sheet. In some cases the strategy of the firm had to be changed significantly; for example, by selling assets. Another consideration may well be the financial state of the firm's pension fund. Many firms have found that the earnings of their pension fund are insufficient to pay future liabilities. This may result in reduced future benefits or higher current contributions. These decisions are essential to the ongoing future of the firm. Other major financial decisions, capital structure and dividend policy are discussed below.

Capital structure

The proportion of debt and equity used to finance the operations of the firm, generally measured by the debt-to-equity ratio, which is also called the financial leverage or gearing of the firm.

Capital structure

Capital structure refers to the proportion of debt and equity used to finance the operations of the firm and is generally captured in the debt-to-equity (D/E) ratio, also called the financial leverage of the firm.

Challenge of strategic management

Creating value from the management of a diversified and possibly unrelated set of businesses is one of the most difficult tasks faced by senior executives of global firms. New information systems and processes, and new organizational forms have been developed, but these firms are not always successful.

A more recent innovation is that of private equity firms (previously known as buyout or LBO firms) – entities that make equity investments in a number of operating companies. Private equity firms raise capital from individuals and organizations, and invest these funds in a portfolio of companies, generally for a period of three to five years. This purchase of an entire firm, or a component of a firm, is typically highly leveraged, with 60 to 90 per cent of the purchase funded by debt (Kaplan & Stromberg, 2009). In addition, the private equity firm may provide managerial support to the company through the placement in the company of senior executives, or through board representation.

The private equity firm generates a return on its investment in these companies in several ways, including:

- An ongoing management fee.
- A capital return at some time in the future when the firm is floated via an initial public offer (IPO), or when the company is sold to another firm.

The private equity firm puts management and capital into the entity, planning to improve performance so that the entity can be sold at a substantial profit over the purchase price. For example, it is common to replace the CEO and other senior executives of the entity which has been purchased (Froud & Williams, 2007).

A number of private equity firms operate in this sector, including The Carlyle Group and The Blackstone Group. The Carlyle Group was founded in 1987, and has grown from about $20 billion assets under management in 2003 to about $100 billion under management in November 2009 (The Carlyle Group, 2010). This portfolio is managed by a team of about 200 professionals. Carlyle has investments in a number of industries including aerospace, automotive, consumer products, energy, financial services, health care, telecommunications and real estate, with 59 per cent of assets in the Americas, 25 per cent in Europe and 16 per cent in Asia.

The Blackstone Group was also founded in 1987, and has investments in consumer products, financial services, health care, telecommunications and travel, among others (The Blackstone Group, 2010). For example, The Blackstone Group has a $27 billion investment in Hilton Hotel, made in 2007; a $16 billion investment in TeleDanmark A/S made in 2005; and a $2.5 billion investment, made in 2005, in the Merlin Entertainment Group (which includes Madame Tussauds and Legoland). As of September 2009, The Blackstone Group had about $25 billion in assets under management, with a professional staff of about 60.

QUESTIONS

1 Do you think that private equity firms represent a superior organizational form to a normal public company?

2 How do such firms successfully manage a very diverse and unrelated portfolio of companies?

We must be cautious when comparing the leverage of different firms, since some firms report leverage as D/E while others report leverage as D/D+E. These obviously have quite different arithmetic values. Organizational structures such as partnerships, alliances, joint ventures and licensing also have differing capital structures (Lessard, 1997). Factors influencing capital structure are as follows:

- *Business risk of the firm* – volatility of demand and high fixed costs (heavy investment intensity) suggest the use of more equity rather than debt.

- *Tax position* – debt is tax-deductible, lowering the effective cost of debt. If a lot of the firm's income is already free of tax, then this is less of a benefit.

- *Financial flexibility* – if the firm is already heavily indebted, then there is no flexibility for more debt. Indeed, if markets turn down or interest rates rise, the firm may have to roll over (renegotiate) existing debt.

- *Nature of assets, liquidity and intangibility* – the value of assets in liquidation is also important to lenders, who seek security. Tangible assets may be mortgaged, but if they are highly specialized, raising debt may still be difficult. For an advertising agency, assets are intangible, in the form of people and their creativity, not real estate or equipment. They are not a form of security for lenders.

Since debt is tax-deductible, there are advantages to high debt. In addition, high debt levels allow firms to leverage operating results, achieving higher returns on equity. A safe, consistently profitable company with few intangible assets or growth opportunities should find a high debt level attractive. A retailer may have high leverage, while a new high-technology, high-growth company would be funded almost solely by equity. Table 8.7 shows the D/E ratios for a number of European firms in 2009.

The balance of debt and equity and the nature of that debt and equity are important strategic management decisions and there is considerable debate as to whether or not there is an optimal level for a specific firm. The details of this discussion are to be found in a finance textbook (Grinblatt & Titman, 2002). Here we will briefly review some of the broader issues.

Financial theory suggests that the cost of debt should rise with increasing leverage such that, at some point, debt becomes too costly to employ. Another limit on the level of debt is the type of business. If the firm is characterized by stable cash flows, with substantial tangible assets, it can generally carry more debt, as we see in Table 8.7 with Iberdrola. If the firm is cyclical, with most assets intangible, it will generally have less debt. Even in some mature businesses, technological change may mean that a firm is less likely to generate the stable cash flows needed to sustain high debt levels.

Since debt is cheaper, one could ask why firms are not funded solely by debt! With strong competition between banks and other financial intermediaries to provide debt funds, debt is normally easy to raise, although all lenders pulled back after the GFC. In any case, as debt levels rise, debt providers increase their power over their customers through covenants on that debt that express their concern at the firm's ability to service its debt. The result is that financial markets monitor debt levels and may downgrade expectations of a firm if debt

Capital structure *in practice* – debt/equity ratios

Iberdrola, the Spanish-based energy supplier, which operates globally in mature and still partially regulated industries, has a D/E ratio of 1.48, reflecting its low risk and a stable cash flow. By contrast, ARM Holdings, a UK-based microprocessor design firm, has a very low D/E ratio of just 0.14, reflecting the high business risk of the firm, despite the fact that at this time the firm had cash reserves and short-term investments of £140 million. Sandvik, the Swedish engineering firm, had a net debt-to-equity ratio of 0.9, typical for a manufacturing firm. Given its very low D/E ratio, ARM Holdings must use retained earnings and/or new equity to fund any developments, while Iberdrola has a wider choice.

Table 8.7 Debt/equity ratios for selected firms

Company	Country, industry	Long-term debt	Equity	D/E ratio
Iberdrola	Spain, energy	€ 43bn	€ 29bn	1.48
Sandvik	Sweden, engineering	SEK 33bn	SEK 37bn	0.9
ARM Holdings	UK, electronic design	£106m	£739m	0.14

Source: Company annual reports, 2009 (www.iberdrola.es, www.sandvik.com, www.arm.com)

levels exceed prudent limits. At the same time, the marginal cost of debt rises with indebtedness.

Firms that have difficulty servicing their debt may have to cut back research or advertising and sell assets if there is even a temporary cash flow problem. The reason for this is that debt must be paid, and if the firm cannot pay the required interest, or if the firm cannot raise more debt to pay the interest and principal, it is technically insolvent. This insolvency threat normally limits debt levels. Firms with high business risk compensate for this with low debt and thus low levels of financial risk.

An opposing view argues that firms should have high levels of debt because this may limit executives' tendency to invest free cash flow in core businesses with low returns (possibly below the cost of capital). It should also limit the tendency to diversify into unrelated businesses, since high debt levels must be serviced. So high debt and the replacement of equity with debt may stop uneconomic investment and encourage managers to return excess capital to shareholders (Jensen, 1989). However, as leverage increases, the cost of both debt and equity will increase as the holders of these seek a higher return to compensate for increased risk.

Despite all the research, it appears there is no formula for the optimal capital structure; instead, it is a matter of judgement. This judgement of D/E ratios will be based on the tax rate, earnings variability or business risk levels of the firm, asset type (tangible or intangible), and the liquidity of these assets – as well as the general level of interest rates. In addition, current debt levels limit any increases – a highly leveraged firm will have problems further increasing leverage, regardless of circumstances.

Differences in capital structure

We observe a number of differences in capital structure based on factors other than those listed above. For example, German and Japanese firms typically operate with higher debt levels than, say, UK or US firms, largely due to the different role of the banks versus other institutions and individuals in financing business operations.

Until 2008 there had been a global trend towards more use of debt. Increased product market competition squeezed margins, reducing internally generated cash and increasing the need for external sources of funds. The desire to drive earnings per share via higher leverage, combined with low interest rates, fuelled increases in corporate debt, but at the expense of increasing firms' financial risk. As discussed in Chapter 4, during the liquidity crisis of 2008/ 09 this trend was reversed as many firms had to strengthen their balance sheet and pay down debt – often through asset sales (►Chapter 4).

 Chapter 4

Dividend policy

Senior managers, in consultation with the board, are responsible for establishing the firm's dividend policy. Dividend payments are optional; there is no legal requirement that they be paid. However, dividends are important from two perspectives. From the firm's perspective, high dividend payouts reduce the funds available for future investment, meaning the firm can starve itself of funds for future growth and innovation if it adopts a high dividend regime. However, dividends are also a major factor driving shareholder value. We explore these perspectives below.

As noted, firms gain the majority of the funds required for new investment from their own cash flow. If too high a proportion of this cash flow is paid out in dividends, the financial future of the firm may be at risk. During the recent financial crisis and the tightening of credit markets, most firms reduced their level of dividends, as was experienced in the European insurance industry (Reddeman *et al.*, 2010). The same pattern also occurred in the UK: total dividends in 2009 from private sector firms were cut by 15 per cent from their 2008 levels, a total reduction of £10 billion (BBC, 2010).

On the other hand, managers who retain funds and invest them in alternatives that do not return the cost of capital are not serving shareholder interests. The real question is whether the firm has profitable uses for its cash – investment opportunities that are likely to return greater than the cost of capital. If not, managers should return cash to shareholders, either by share buybacks or dividends.

Recall that investors obtain a return from both dividends and capital gains, and in the absence of dividends shareholders can always sell stock. Some investors will prefer dividends, while others will prefer to take their return as a capital gain. This choice is strongly influenced by the tax regime in operation. Shareholders with high marginal tax rates may prefer to take their return as a capital gain and get the tax benefit. Shareholders such as pension funds may prefer dividends so that they can, in turn, pay their members.

Dividends, and changes in dividends, are also seen as having a 'signalling' effect in financial markets. If the firm reduces its dividend rate, this could be interpreted as a signal that the firm is experiencing difficulties and the share price typically drops. If the firm introduces a dividend, or increases it, this could be seen as a signal that the firm has exhausted all good investment ideas and has limited future growth prospects.

Share repurchases

Another financial decision to be made by senior executives, again in consultation with the board, is that of share buybacks. This occurs when the firm, as a legal entity, purchases some of its shares in the open market. In this situation, the firm is returning cash to shareholders, but only those taking up the purchase offer.

Share repurchases or buybacks have become more common in recent years, when firms have engaged in purchasing their own shares on the open market. Share purchases can be seen as a complement to or substitute for dividends, since they should cause share price appreciation.

Share buybacks *in practice* – Magix

The German company Magix provides online services and software. In February 2009 it made an offer to buy 709,000 of its shares at a price of €2.74 per share. This meant that between March 2008 and June 2009 the firm had repurchased 9.55 per cent of its own shares (Magix, 2009).

Buybacks may be pursued for a variety of reasons. Managers may not see any desirable wealth-creating opportunities; hence they return money to shareholders. A firm may also repurchase its stock if it believes it is undervalued. Repurchase may also be a more tax-effective means to distribute cash to shareholders, since those who tender pay capital gains tax, not income tax. Since any share buyback reduces the value of equity in the firm, it increases the firm's financial leverage, while earnings per share increase due to the reduced number of shares. This improvement may be positively regarded by financial markets, leading to a rise in the share price. There is also a potential *principal-agent* problem. Managers about to make a repurchase decision are in the position of insiders who may use private information to purchase stock at a low price. Since share repurchase normally increases the price of the shares, this will benefit managers who hold either stock or options in the firm. For this reason, most countries have introduced a degree of regulation of share repurchases. For example, in many countries repurchases are not allowed when management has material information not disclosed to the market (Ginglinger & Hamon, 2009). It is a fundamental principle of shareholder value management that the firm should invest only in opportunities that return more than the cost of capital. When such opportunities are unavailable, cash should be returned to shareholders to decide how this will be invested. Buybacks are often a tax-efficient way to do this.

Senior management salary and incentive alternatives

Senior management of the firm, again in consultation with the board, needs to determine salaries of themselves and other executives. This is an area fraught with difficulty – what level of salary is appropriate and what combination of salary and incentives to adopt? Chief executives of America's 50 largest firms are paid on average 75 per cent more than their European counterparts, and take a larger percentage of their total package in the form of long-term incentives such as stock options (The Economist Online, 2008). These high US salaries can result in anomalies, as when the head of a US subsidiary of a European firm is paid more than the firm's CEO.

One other issue to be resolved is the level and nature of any **management incentives**. With increased competition and rapid change, the pressure on managers to create value has increased. For most firms, this means linking pay to performance, generally through the issuance of **stock options** to managers. These are call options, giving the holder the right, but not the obligation to buy a given number of shares in the firm at a given price up to a specified future date. This price is called the exercise price and is generally above the current share price.

Such stock options were originally adopted with the goal of better aligning the interests of the firm with those of shareholders, since it is in the interests of the managers for the share price to rise to the exercise price.

There has been much discussion as to whether or not such share options result in a short-term rather than a long-term focus, which is the reverse of what should occur. Incentive systems can be badly designed and result in such a short-term focus. Successful companies have been able to develop, and implement, incentive systems which link executive compensation to long-term share price performance, resulting in an alignment between management objectives and shareholder objectives (The Economist Online, 2009).

Stock options also result in an accounting issue for the firm – should they be considered an expense and thus reported on the income statement? After considerable debate on this, most firms now recognize these as a future liability of the firm since they represent a component of the manager's compensation.

Management incentive

A reward system for managers designed to increase their motivation to accomplish agreed outcomes by linking pay to the agreed performance level.

Stock option

When the firm reaches an agreed performance level the manager has the right, but not the obligation, to buy a given number of shares in the company at a given price. This price may be below the current share price. Stock options are one form of incentive payment.

8.8 MANAGING STRATEGIC RISK

Strategic management involves making decisions now in anticipation of the future, where the chosen strategy affords the promise of an appropriate return. Since the future is unknown, and possibly unknowable, the actual return from a strategy is likely to be different from that anticipated when the decision was made. Strategic decisions are made in the face of risk and/or uncertainty. In a rapidly changing world, uncertainty can be very high, yet strategic decisions by their very nature take some time to eventuate. Who would be prepared to forecast Icelandic GDP or political changes in China ten years from now? Yet such factors may affect future returns from strategic decisions that must be made today.

All strategy involves risk. By risk here we mean uncertainty in the return that is likely to ensue from the strategy. The realized consequences from the strategy may be different from the intended consequences, due to such factors as unanticipated changes in the environment or difficulties with strategy implementation. One of the tasks of strategic managers is to choose strategies with 'appropriate' levels of risk, and there is some evidence that high-performing organizations are more pro-active in handling crises. In particular these high performers have well-developed systems of crisis preparedness (Carmeli & Schaubroeck, 2008). A low-risk strategy would be to invest only in government bonds, but managers of such a firm add no value for shareholders, who can invest in these for themselves.

When evaluating strategy, we must consider a number of issues: the likely return, the level and profile of risk, and the time value of money. Here we focus on risk and return and the role of strategic managers in managing the trade-off between them. Of course, these are financial dimensions and represent only two of the many criteria that might be used to assess strategy. We look at a broader set of measures when we discuss performance measurement in Chapter 12 (➤Chapter 12).

Chapter 12

While we need to be aware of the risk of action, we should not ignore the risk of inaction. Doing nothing can also be very risky if managers attempt to continue the status quo while the world evolves. This provides another classic paradox of strategic management. If we take no action there is a chance of becoming obsolete, a probability that rises when change is rapid. Alternatively, we may adopt a particular strategy predicated upon a view of the future. This view is likely to be at best partly correct, indicating that there is a risk that the strategy may not deliver its intended results.

Nonetheless, we believe that managers must be pro-active in introducing change to the firm, even though change will have an associated risk. Strategy takes time to design and implement, and without an element of creative foresight, the firm will almost certainly be overtaken by events.

Assessing strategy

Any given strategy may be assessed on the basis of two characteristics:

- The level of risk of that strategy.
- The expected return from that strategy over the planning horizon.

If we ignore other characteristics of strategy for the moment and concentrate on risk and return, we may visualize possible relationships between risk and return, as illustrated in Figure 8.11. The horizontal axis is the return required by or anticipated for the strategy, where this is calculated as the net present value of the strategy, discounted at the cost of capital of the firm (➤Chapter 4). The vertical axis is the level of risk of the strategy. Here risk is measured as the variability in cash flow resulting from the strategy and reflects the strategy's inherent uncertainty. A strategy to buy government bonds would have very low risk, since there is little or no uncertainty in the future returns. A strategy to develop a new technology would have high risk. If the new technology is successful, the result is significant cash generation by the firm. If the new technology is not successful, the firm may lose a substantial sum. And, of course, we do not know whether the new technology will be successful.

Chapter 4

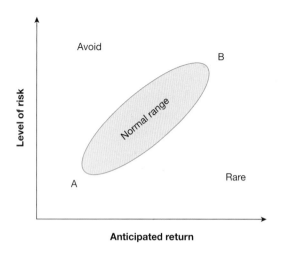

Figure 8.11 Risk/return trade-off for strategy

As Figure 8.11 suggests, when a strategy is considered a high risk, the firm requires a higher return to compensate for the high risk. However, risk and return are independent characteristics of a strategy. Not all high-risk strategies offer the promise of a high return; hence our use of the term *anticipated return* for the horizontal axis. Ideally, we should seek strategies that have a low risk and yet promise a high return; the identification of such strategies encapsulates the challenge of strategic management. Yet these are rare, as indicated in Figure 8.11. Certainly, we should avoid strategies that are low return and yet high risk!

Managers have some degree of control over the risk level of their strategies, although they should also recognize, as Unilever does, that control is incomplete. Risk/return trade-offs depend on a number of factors. In theory, the choice should depend on the risk profile of shareholders; some will be more willing than others for the firm to pursue a risky strategy. However, there are likely to be differences in perspective between managers and shareholders. Managers may take larger risks since their money is not involved, while the personal values of senior managers and the firm's culture also have an influence. Clearly, different firms have different propensities for risk. Some are risk-averse, selecting strategies they believe have little risk, while other firms are more willing to adopt risky strategies.

One of the most valuable ways to improve risk management is to open up the minds of managers to explicitly consider risk when developing strategy. When we address performance

---

Risk management *in practice* – Unilever

Unilever accepts that the identification and management of risk is an integral element in their strategic management, and has developed a comprehensive approach to risk management (Unilever, 2009). They identify several sources of risk, together with what the firm is doing to manage that risk, recognizing that they may not always be successful in eliminating all risk from their strategy.

One such source of risk is economic: a decline in business during an economic downturn and an associated increase in customer and supplier level of default. They actively engage in several activities to help them mitigate any impact from this. These include:

- A wide geographic scope which reduces dependence on local conditions
- Extensive economic and consumer analysis
- A flexible business model permitting them to alter their portfolio
- Regular customer and supplier credit monitoring.

management (►Chapter 12), we will urge that risk be explicitly incorporated into assessing **Chapter 12** performance by using sensitivity analysis. However, to consider risk a priori requires creativity and imagination. One of the most effective ways to do this is via the use of scenarios. These can be used to give management simulated experience in dealing with unpredictable events and to increase understanding of what may be the major drivers of return variability – and thus which things should be subject to more scrutiny.

A firm can also opt to delay a strategy, which may mitigate risk. Faced with high uncertainty, we may purchase options. If we wait, some uncertainty may be abated, and that may be better than committing large amounts of capital prematurely. Many pharmaceutical companies chose this approach as the field of biotechnology appeared on their planning horizons.

Pre-emptive risk management is much the preferred approach, but managers must also realize that in today's society, perceived risk is as important as actual risk. Improved access to information, aggressiveness of global media concerns, and a resulting increased transparency of company operations combine to create a maelstrom of forces influencing public opinion.

Societal change and uncertainty, fast technological change, and a lack of trust of authority have created a much more demanding environment for managing risk. Advocacy groups have become very sophisticated in their use of the Internet and media relations, to the point where large global companies that have in many cases made huge contributions to raising living standards in many parts of the globe are seen as villainous, if not downright evil.

8.9 SUMMARY

With the expansion in the scale and scope of global firms, the complexity of strategy and strategic management has increased dramatically. The fundamental task for the management of a multi-business firm is to ensure that the total entity creates greater value than would be possible if each of the constituent businesses were independent. Strategy at the corporate level has characteristics that make it different from strategy at the business unit level.

Developing corporate strategy requires that managers make decisions in a number of areas: including the future direction of the firm, the style to be adopted by the corporate centre, allocation of financial and other resources across the business portfolio, the extent and nature of diversification, and major financial decisions. These decisions need to be addressed in an integrative and holistic manner and cannot be made independently. A decision to follow an unrelated diversification strategy has implications for which style of corporate centre is likely to be adopted by the firm. A number of analytical tools can be used to assist several of these decisions. In particular, this chapter emphasized a number of portfolio management methods that are used to help decide what should be the objectives and strategy for different business units.

Finally, strategic management at the corporate level must concern itself with strategic risk and the risk profile of the firm – addressing the trade-off between risk and potential return from alternative strategies is another key task for senior managers.

VIEW FROM THE TOP

WHITBREAD PLC

An interview with Anthony Habgood, Chairman, conducted by the *Journal of Strategy and Management* (JSM) (O'Regan & Ghobadian, 2010)

JSM: You have been involved in strategic transformations in a number of companies. What are the signs that you would see as important for a deep transformation exercise?

Habgood: You have to look at both the corporate and the business levels. There are a lot of companies around that you might call failing conglomerates – they tend to compete in lots of different areas, not really very successful in most of them but perhaps there are one or two areas that they do well. These companies are not in control of their own destiny and information to the board is filtered by the top management. In this type of organization it is fairly clear that a different corporate strategy is needed. You need to reallocate resources to the parts of the business that are doing well and/or have potential. But that is so particular from business to business, it is hard to generalize.

It is difficult to sit in a company and see where that company will be 15 years later. For me it doesn't work like that, it is a far more pragmatic and gradual process. There may be some parts of the company you are quite sure you don't want to continue with as they may be losing money, losing cash, stagnating, competitively disadvantaged and perhaps all of these. It is important to get out of these businesses quickly as they are just a drain on the organization.

There are some parts of the business where there are clearly competitive advantages and growing well and to my mind it is important to back those immediately, not to mess about and say I've got to sort out something else before you do that. The business that Bunzl is now was small in 1991 and doing well but not doing as well as it could have. It was making 5.0 per cent margin translating into a good return on capital, growing decently and clearly had a competitive advantage. So that was something it was natural to back. Do you know then what you will be able to achieve in 15 years by doing that? Of course you don't.

JSM: Do you see transformation as an overly risky business?

Habgood: During a corporate transformation, where you are backing winners and culling losers, it is actually not that risky. Of course any organization that you put through radical change has some element of risk but you are still backing what you think of as a winning model.

PHILIPS ELECTRONICS NV

Companies face myriad influences which affect strategic decisions while at the same time reflecting their history, the global and industry environment, their corporate culture and the competition. The historical perspective can act as an anchor, keeping corporate strategy aligned with the past decisions or it can act to constrain an organization's ability to cope with rapid change. Philips Electronics NV is an excellent example of this dilemma. Founded in 1891, the firm quickly developed a two-pronged management structure: a strong technical orientation due to Gerard, the founding Philips brother, coupled with an active sales approach, which came from his brother Anton. It also initiated a paternalistic approach towards its employees and a culture of contentment and superiority began.

Philips expanded aggressively overseas, entering into an agreement with GE to share patents and to divide the global market between them. Decision-making moved from a centralized company to a decentralized sales organization with autonomous marketing companies in 14 European countries as well as Australia, Brazil and China. During World War II, further geographic decentralization occurred. British Philips, located in Redhill in Surrey, England received most of its vital research laboratories while the North American Philips Corporation received the Philips top management. Separated from the parent company, with its resources of assets and management transferred abroad, decision-making became even more country-specific.

The recovery of the economies of the various countries varied considerably after the war, leading Philips to build its post-war strengths in the national organizations. The country-specific market conditions revealed distinct differences in consumer preferences and in the development of technological specifications (e.g. the different television formats). Over time, the National Organizations (NOs) went beyond their adaptive marketing strategies to develop their own technical capabilities and product development often grew from the local markets. The NOs also took over responsibility for many financial, legal and administrative matters.

The company had established 14 product divisions at its head office in Eindhoven, responsible for development and distribution. In reality this was unworkable, since the distance from the operating centres and the control of the assets in the NOs meant that the formal geographic/product matrix was not applied. Even within the NOs the traditional technical/commercial split of the original brothers was maintained. The human resources approach to management also supported the NO view of the world as there developed a cadre of experienced expatriate managers who rotated through overseas tours of duty and identified most closely with each other and the NO perspective.

By the late 1960s, the creation of the Common Market, later followed by the Economic Union, removed key trade barriers with Europe and made the justification for country-level subsidiaries less viable. Additionally, the convergence of worldwide technologies (transistor and printed circuit-based technologies) required longer production runs than the national plants could handle. Philips was also experiencing an inability to bring their new technologies to market successfully. This problem was exacerbated by the emergence of new competitors, often from Asia. In the 1970s, North American

Philips caused the death of the Philips-based R&D product, the V2000 video-cassette format. This product was technologically superior to both the Sony Beta and the Matsushita's VHS formats, but was abandoned when North American Philips decided to outsource, brand and sell a VHS product which it manufactured under licence from Matsushita.

Developing corporate strategy continued to be a challenge and a series of CEOs attempted to get the matrix structure to work effectively, generally without success. There was an attempt to create International Production Centres, shutting more than 200 plants, selling businesses, entering into alliances, outsourcing production to low-cost countries. In addition, product divisions were given global product management responsibilities, but national organizations still held responsibility for local profits.

A new CEO was appointed in 1987. He designated some businesses as core and others as non-core, on the basis of shared technology, and initiated disposals of some businesses. The lighting division was regarded as strategically important, as its cash generation funded development. One management consultant who worked closely with Philips at this time was told by a senior manager, 'we don't have to worry about profit, there is always money available in this company'. Perhaps a culture that combined this thought with the statement from another senior manager at the time that 'our customers are stupid' made the job of developing and marketing customer-focused products more difficult. More changes followed, basic R&D was halved to about 10 per cent of total R&D and 75 of the 420 remaining worldwide plants were closed.

Another CEO, appointed in 1990, aggressively attempted to turn the firm around. Total employment was reduced by 68,000 (22 per cent) over the next 18 months. European laws for layoffs meant that the first 10,000 redundancies cost Philips $700 million. Various businesses were sold off and a new growth strategy was implemented, expanding software, services and multimedia with the expectation that these would become 40 per cent of revenues by 2000. Unfortunately, the earlier sale of various high-tech businesses and the 37 per cent cut in R&D personnel left few who could meet the demanding targets. Once again Philips' superior products (for example, analogue HDTV technology) failed to become the industry standard. During this period worldwide markets in these fields were becoming more segmented and relied more heavily on higher customer service. The Philips cost-cutting and standardization had failed once again to recognize these marketplace changes.

For the first time in its history, Philips appointed a CEO whose experience was mainly built outside the company. The new CEO had a consumer goods background, subsequently heading up Philips' Asia Pacific region. As an outsider, he announced, 'There are no taboos, no sacred cows. The bleeders must be turned around, sold or closed.' Within three years he had divested 40 of Philips' 120 major businesses and initiated a major worldwide restructuring. He looked for a more structured and simplified manufacturing and marketing organization to put Philips in line with companies without the historical baggage of corporate structure and culture. Within a year of his ascendancy he had eliminated 3,100 jobs in North America and added 3,000 jobs in Asia Pacific, shifting production to low-wage countries. After three years he had reduced the factories and replaced the 21 Product Divisions with seven divisions and gave day-to-day operating responsibilities to 100 business units. By 2000, he announced that he had achieved his objective of a 24 per cent return on net assets.

Despite the reduction in employment from a peak of 253,000 in 1995 to 189,000 in 2001 and further restructuring under two subsequent CEOs, 2001 losses were €2.6 billion, due primarily to writing down investments in Vivendi. By 2003, sales in 60 countries generated turnover of €29 billion. The company was active in lighting, consumer electronics, domestic appliances, semiconductors and medical systems. In 2006, under an aggressive restructuring by yet another CEO, also with a US consumer goods background, Philips sold an 80.1 per cent share in Philips Semiconductors to a private equity consortium headed by KKR. Under the tutelage of the latest CEO, Philips has continued to shed overhead, costs and factories, and dropped 'electronics' from its name.

In 2010, Philips stock is quoted on exchanges in New York, London, Amsterdam, Frankfurt and elsewhere. Turnover in 2008 was lower than five years earlier, at €26.3 billion, and the firm made a small loss after good profits in 2007. Despite disposals and cuts, the company still employs 121,000 people with over 100 countries served by sales and service outlets, with 155 production sites. Seven R&D locations build on the firm's 55,000 outstanding patents. Philips is world leader in home health care, patient monitoring systems, automated external defibrillators, cardiac ultrasound, cardiovascular X-ray, lamps, professional luminaires, lighting electronics, automotive lighting, electric male grooming and electric shavers.

The continuing friction between the PDs and the NOs, as well as the dual-pronged management ethos, has made strategic decision-making difficult for much of Philips' history. A corporate culture which rewarded and reflected a feeling of superiority to both competitors and customers combined with a lagging awareness of marketplace trends and industry alignments made the challenges more extreme.

Source: Philips, 2010; FundingUniverse, 2010

QUESTIONS

1 What would you have done differently to improve success prospects for Philips?
2 What does this say about the practice of strategic management?

REVIEW QUESTIONS

1 Discuss the ways in which the corporate centre in a multi-business firm can add value.

2 Select a global firm and obtain a copy of its vision statement. Discuss how the firm's strategy has been influenced by the vision statement.

3 'The growth/share matrix is too naive to be useful in developing strategy.' Discuss this statement.

4 Select a global firm (or a group within a global firm). Plot the business units of the firm on a matrix of your choice. What implications are there for the corporate strategy of the firm?

5 In the multi-factor portfolio model, what factors contribute to an attractive environment for a business?

6 Explain the differences between related and unrelated diversification.

7 Many managers justify their diversification decisions on the basis of claimed 'synergy'. Is this claim always justified? Give examples of where you believe claimed synergy did not exist.

8 Discuss some of the ways in which financial markets affect corporate strategy.

9 Provide an example of a firm with a high-risk profile and another with a low-risk profile. Illustrate by discussing the strategies adopted by each firm.

REFERENCES

BBC (2010) UK firms cut dividends by £10 bn. BBC *News*, 8 February. http://news.bbc.co.uk/2/hi/business/8503014.stm.

BHP (2002) BHP steel demerger. May. www.bhpbilliton.com/bbContentRepository/Reports/Steel DemergerBriefingPaper.pdf.

BHP Billiton (2009) Annual report, p. 189. www.bhpbilliton.com/bb/investorsMedia/reports/annual Reports.jsp.

Bowman, E. H., & Helfat, C. E. (2001) Does corporate strategy matter? *Strategic Management Journal, 22*(1), 1–23.

Buzzell, R. D. & Gale, B. T. (1987) *The PIMS Principles*. New York: Free Press.

Carmeli, A. & Schaubroeck, J. (2008) Organizational crisis-preparedness: The importance of learning from failures. *Long Range Planning, 41*(2), 177–196.

Chandler, A. D. (1962) *Strategy and Structure: Chapters in the History of the American Industrial Enterprise*. Cambridge, MA: MIT Press.

CiscoSystems (2009) Annual Report. *Chairman's letter to shareholders*, 10 September. www.cisco.com/web/about/ac49/ac20/ac19/ar2009/letter/index.html.

Collins, J. C. (2009) *How the Mighty Fall: And Why Some Companies Never Give In*. London: Random House.

Collis, D., Young, D. & Goold, M. (2007) The size, structure, and performance of corporate headquarters. *Strategic Management Journal, 28*(4).

Collis, D. J. & Montgomery, C. A. (1998) Creating corporate advantage. *Harvard Business Review*, (May–June), 70–83.

Courtney, H., Kirkland, J. & Vigurie, P. (1997) Strategy under uncertainty. *Harvard Business Review*, (November–December), 66–79.

ElAmin, A. (2006) Unilever to exit European frozen foods, while sales stagnate. *Meat Process.*

Foster, R. N. (1986) *Innovation: The Attacker's Advantage.* New York: Summit.

Foster, R. N. & Kaplan, S. (2001) *Creative Destruction.* New York: Doubleday.

Froud, J. & Williams, K. (2007) Private equity and the culture of value extraction. *New Political Economy, 12*(3), 405–420.

FundingUniverse (2010) Philips. *Company-histories.* Retrieved 2010. www.fundinguniverse.com/company-histories/Koninklijke-Philips-Electronics-NV-Company-History.html.

Ginglinger, E. & Hamon, J. (2009) Share repurchase regulations: Do firms play by the rules? *International Review of Law and Economics, 29*(2), 81–86.

Goold, M. & Campbell, A. (1987) *Strategies and Styles.* Oxford: Basil Blackwell.

Goold, M. & Campbell, A. (1998) Desperately seeking synergy. *Harvard Business Review,* (September–October), 130–143.

Goold, M., Campbell, A. & Alexander, M. (1994) *Corporate Level Strategy.* New York: Wiley.

Grinblatt, M. & Titman, S. (2002) *Financial Markets and Corporate Strategy,* 2nd edn. Boston, MA: Irwin/McGraw-Hill.

Guillén, M. F. & García -Canal, E. (2009) The American model of the multinational firm and the 'new' multinationals from emerging economies. *Academy of Management Perspectives, 23*(2), 23–35.

Hambrick, D. C., MacMillan, I. C. & Day, D. L (1982) Strategic attributes and performance in the BCG Matrix – A PIMS-based analysis of industrial product businesses. *Academy of Management Journal, 25*(September), 510–531.

Hamel, G. & Prahalad, C. K. (1994) Competing for the future. *Harvard Business Review,* (July–August), 122–128.

Hammond, E. (2010) Bilfinger builds on reinvention trend. *European companies,* 3 February. www.ft.com/cms/s/0/188c6fa2–10e4–11df-9a9e-00144feab49a.html.

Hancock, D. (2006) Wal-Mart's German flop. *CBS News Business,* 2 August. www.cbsnews.com/stories/2006/08/02/business/main1860028.shtml?tag=contentMain;contentBody.

Hayward, M. & Hambrick, D. (1997) Explaining the premiums paid for large acquisitions: Evidence of CEO hubris. *Administrative Science Quarterly, 42,* 103–127.

Henkel (2010) Business sectors. *Annual report 2009,* 25 February. www.henkel.com/about-henkel/business-sectors-11785.htm.

HMV_Group (2010) Investor relations. Retrieved September 14, 2010. www.hmvgroup.com/investors.aspx.

Jensen, M. C. (1989) Eclipse of the public corporation. *Harvard Business Review,* (September–October 1989), 61–75.

Kaplan, S. N. & Stromberg, P. (2009) Leveraged buyouts and private equity. *Journal of Economic Perspectives, 23*(1), 121–146.

Lawrence, P. & Lorsch, J. W. (1967) *Organizations and Environment.* Boston, MA: Harvard University Press.

Lessard, D. R. (1997) Global competition and corporate finance in the 1990's. In H. Vernon-Wortzel & L. H. Wortzel (eds), *Strategic Management in the Global Economy.* New York: Wiley.

Magix (2009) Share buybacks, 30 June. www.magix.com/uk/magix-ag/investor-relations/share-buybacks/.

McGahan, A. M. & Porter, M. E. (1997) How much does industry matter, really? *Strategic Management Journal, 18*(Special Issue), 15–30.

McLeod, K. & Stuckey, J. (2000) MACS: The market-activated corporate strategy framework. *McKinsey Quarterly,* (3), 16–20.

Ng, D. W. (2007) A modern resource based approach to unrelated diversification. *Journal of Management Studies, 44*(8), 1481–1502.

O'Regan, N. & Ghobadian, A. (2010) A serial successful strategic transformer of a business: An interview with Anthony Habgood. *Journal of Strategy and Management, 3*(1), 72.

Philips (2010) Company profile. *About Philips.* Retrieved 15 March 2010. www.philips.com/about/company/index.page.

Reddeman, S., Basse, T. & von der Schulenberg, J.-M. (2010) On the impact of the financial crisis on the dividend policy of the European insurance industry. *The Geneva papers, 35*(1), 53–62.

Robins, J. A. & Wiersema, M. F. (2003) The measurement of corporate portfolio strategy: Analysis of the content validity of related diversification indexes. *Strategic Management Journal, 24*(1), 39–60.

Roquebert, J. A., Phillips, R. L. & Westfall, P. A. (1996) Markets vs. management: What 'drives' profitability. *Strategic Management Journal, 17*(8), 653–664.

Rumelt, R. P. (1977) *Diversity and Profitability* (Paper prepared for the Annual Meeting of the Western Region, Academy of Management, Sun Valley, Idaho No. Paper MGL-51). Los Angeles: Managerial Studies Center, Graduate School of Management, University of California.

Schultz, H. (2006) This is not America – Why Wal-Mart left Germany. *The Atlantic Times On-Line Archive.* September. www.atlantic-times.com/archive_detail.php?recordID=615.

The Blackstone Group (2010) Private equity. www.blackstone.com/cps/rde/xchg/bxcom/hs/businesses_aam_privateequity.htm.

The Carlyle Group (2010) Firm profile. www.carlyle.com/Company/item1676.html.

The Economist (2008) Time to fix Siemens. *The Economist,* 8 July. www.economist.com/business-finance/displaystory.cfm?story_id=E1_TTGJJDJR.

The Economist Online (2009) Firmly hooked. *The Economist,* 11 August. www.economist.com/business-finance/displaystory.cfm?story_id=E1_TQNDSQTN.

The Economist Online (2008) What the boss pockets. *The Economist,* 12 November. www.economist.com/daily/chartgallery/displaystory.cfm?story_id=E1_TNVRGSJP.

Unilever (2009) Outlook and risks. *Annual Report.* www.unilever.com/images/ir_Unilever_AR09_tcm13-208066.pdf.

US-Department-of-Transportation (2009) Fourth-Quarter 2008 System Airline Financial Data: Network Airlines Report Fifth Consecutive Quarterly Loss Margin. *Bureau of Transport Statistics,* 11 May. www.bts.gov/press_releases/2009/bts022_09/html/bts022_09.html.

Viguerie, P., Smit, S. & Baghai, M. (2008) *The Granularity of Growth.* Hoboken, NJ: John Wiley & Sons.

Wernerfelt, B. & Montgomery, C. (1988) Tobin's q and the importance of focus in firm performance. *American Economic Review, 78*(1), 246–250.

Williamson, O. E. (1975) *Markets and Hierarchies: Analysis and Antitrust Implications.* New York: The Free Press.

Wrigley, L. (1970) *Divisional Autonomy and Diversification.* Cambridge MA: Harvard University Press.

Zook, C. (2004) *Beyond the Core.* Cambridge, MA: Harvard Business School Press.

For a range of further resources supporting this chapter, please visit the companion website for *Strategic Management* at www.routledge.com/cw/fitzroy.

CHAPTER 9

MANAGING INNOVATION AND THE DYNAMIC SCOPE OF THE FIRM

LEARNING OBJECTIVES

Upon completing this chapter, you should be able to:

1 Describe the importance of innovation for the firm and the different types of innovation that can be utilized.

2 Articulate the differences between internal development and mergers and acquisitions as means of changing scope.

3 Identify the major issues to be resolved in technological innovation.

4 Apply the merger and acquisition process described in Figure 9.10.

5 Evaluate the use of spin-offs and restructuring as means for managing the dynamic scope of the firm.

STRATEGIC MANAGEMENT IN PRACTICE

PORSCHE AND VW

In March 2007, Wendelin Wiedeking, Porsche's headstrong chief executive and his financial officer, Holger Härter, devised a bold plan to take over VW, a company 15 times the size of Porsche. At this time Porsche announced that it did not intend to take over VW but was making moves to ensure that a competitor could not buy a large stake. By October 2008, Porsche had raised its stake in VW voting shares to 42.6 per cent and had acquired a further 31.5 per cent in the form of secured options. Record profits, exceeding revenue, were announced in November 2008, showing a €6.83 billion gain in the value of its VW shares. Mr Wiedeking announced that he wanted 'dominant control' of VW and was planning to use his €10 billion line of credit to realize the options. However, this did not transpire.

In January 2009, Porsche's car business suffered a serious decline at the same time that Porsche almost tripled its net debt to €9 billion. Unfortunately, there was now less cash to pay the interest on the debt. Additionally, the credit markets at that point in time were unable to support the increased borrowing. On 24 March 2008 Porsche pledged to pay back the €3.3 billion within six months and pledged its VW shares to the banks. The final blow to the scheme came when the European Court of Justice ruled against the move to abolish the German law which would have protected Volkswagen AG from takeovers. The so-called Volkswagen Law restricted individual shareholders to 20 per cent of the voting rights, regardless of the number of shares they own. The abolition of this law would have allowed Porsche to use its 75 per cent stake in VW to access the company's cash reserves.

The ironic end to the saga was that both Wiedeking and Härter resigned from Porsche, and from their positions on the VW supervisory board. Rather than Porsche taking over VW, the opposite will occur. The plan is that VW will initially acquire 49.9 per cent of Porsche AG, agreeing to purchase the remaining shares at a later date. BusinessWeek announced that the plan 'was developed by Ferdinand Piëch, head of the VW advisory board, who has been involved in a venomous power struggle with Wiedeking in recent months'. The same article announced that the Qatar Fund will be taking a significant share in the combined group.

In a further twist to this tortuous tale, US hedge fund managers are suing Porsche for £620 million, alleging that Porsche manipulated the market and committed securities fraud.

Sources: BusinessWeek, 2009; Riggers, 2010; *The Economist*, 2009

The above saga illustrates the dynamic nature of much merger and acquisition activity. Mergers can easily get derailed with changes in financial markets which result in a loss of liquidity or market confidence in the deal. It also illustrates the problem of management ego. The proposed takeover by Porsche seemed to be more a function of ego than economic fundamentals.

Mergers and acquisitions are an integral element in corporate strategy. They are one of the means firms employ to grow, alter the scope of their operations, obtain new skills and capabilities and reduce costs. Yet the process is fraught with difficulties, as the above example illustrates. Major decisions must be made under considerable time pressure, with limited information. The process may well be competitive with multiple bidders and the outcome is often dependent on external bodies – in this case, unions and provincial government, in other cases regulators. The VW/Porsche tussle also became personal, not an unusual event when two powerful senior executives are, in effect, in a fight to the death. Finally, the future strategy of either or both parties will be influenced by the results of the bid – indicating that strategy has an element of path dependency.

CHAPTER OVERVIEW

In this chapter we explore the means which firms adopt to change their business portfolio over time, with particular attention being given to either internal development of new businesses or the acquisition of new businesses. Extensive discussion of the necessary internal characteristics such as leadership and organizational structure are deferred until later chapters.

We begin by considering the features of innovation and the characteristics that demarcate innovative organizations. We are firmly convinced that in the twenty-first century companies will find themselves having to create new markets rather than respond to existing markets, a change that mandates a much better understanding of how to organize for creativity and innovation than has traditionally been the case. We next review the nature of innovation in organizations. We do not regard innovation as being limited to new products, research and development or to acquisitions. Rather, innovation includes the development of new market opportunities, the invention of new business models, the restructuring of an industry and the deliberate refocusing of the business scope of the firm through internal development or mergers.

Since the focus of this chapter is on the business scope of the firm, we introduce a model highlighting the mix of businesses and their differing time horizons – some businesses are creating current profits, others are more future focused and require current investment in the hope of future rewards.

In the current turbulent environment, all firms should be actively managing their business portfolio, using a number of alternative approaches for developing new businesses and divesting current businesses. We commence this discussion with an examination of the issues involved with developing new businesses internally; for example, the need for high margins to permit the high level of R&D typically required for this. We follow this with a review of the issues involved in mergers and acquisitions, emphasizing the need to develop a formal process for decision-making. Next, we discuss the ways in which firms reduce their business portfolio through divestment and other restructuring alternatives. This is followed by an interview expressing the View from the Top by Paul Walsh, the CEO of Diageo on that company's approach to acquisitions. The concluding mini-case, the takeover of ABN Amro by the RBS, provides an opportunity to apply many of the concepts developed in the chapter.

LEARNING OBJECTIVE 1

Describe the importance of innovation for the firm and the different types of innovation that can be utilized.

9.1 INTRODUCTION

In a rapidly changing and turbulent world, strategy innovation is essential to wealth creation, and even survival. The long-term health of any company is assured only if it possesses the capability for continual renewal via innovation and the development of new businesses. Putting this another way, 'the right of any corporation to exist is not perpetual but has to be continually earned' (Foster & Kaplan, 2001). Whether developed internally, in combination with suppliers, by joint venture, acquisition, or some other means, the process will involve significant change and organizational innovation.

Firm growth is closely connected to wealth creation; companies that grow slowly are less likely to survive (Viguerie *et al.*, 2008). Substantial wealth creation occurs only with growth, not with cost reductions. Firms that exclusively 'stick to their knitting' will, over the longer term, find themselves in real trouble. Changing customer preferences, technological development, the availability of substitutes, and, on occasion, government actions, all mitigate against what have been called vertically dominant corporate growth strategies. Yet as we saw in Chapter 8, firms can become too diverse, in geographic region, product, market, or technology (▶Chapter 8). Too much diversity – too unrelated a diversification – is extremely difficult to manage and many firms lack the management skills to do this well. Nonetheless, we must admit the possibility of organizational learning. Firms may learn to manage increasing diversity over time, and the optimal level of diversity of ten years ago may not be optimal today. Firms also need to ensure that they do not pursuit a strategy of growth at any cost. Poorly managed growth can very easily result in value destruction, not creation.

Chapters 2, 6, 8

Despite the importance of innovation, many firms do not devote the time and effort required to develop a corporate perspective on the future (Hamel & Prahalad, 1994). Major intellectual effort is required to develop a view of the future, the capabilities required, the trajectories that could be used, relevant technological and political trends, all in a very uncertain world. Hamel and Prahalad call this foresight (▶Chapter 6), an understanding of future technologies, competitors, core capabilities and markets, among many others. All the above-quoted authors advocate a pro-active rather than reactive approach to change. Downsizing and cost reduction are often inevitable consequences of late response to change. Leadership requires ongoing, continual innovation, both incremental and revolutionary (▶Chapter 2). Long-term successful firms are able to transform industries, alter the boundaries between industries and re-invent their industry before competitors do. Such firms have been described as industry revolutionaries. They break the rules of the industry, challenge industry norms and beliefs, and invent new competitive spaces, fostering a culture of creativity, risk-taking and experimentation.

9.2 KEY CONSIDERATIONS IN INNOVATION

While the case for corporate innovation is easy to articulate, it has features that make it difficult for firms to manage, as illustrated in Figure 9.1.

Features of innovation

Degree

Degree of innovation refers to the extent of the innovation, whether the innovation is incremental or revolutionary. Incremental innovation can ensure that a firm remains competitive within its chosen domain, but only revolutionary innovation will ensure long-term growth and value creation. Large firms seem to find incremental change easier, but rapid external change may require more revolutionary innovation. Revolutionary innovation may transform the relationship of the firm with its customers

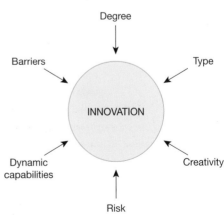

Figure 9.1 Innovation: key considerations

and destroy current products, generating new product categories and even industries. Revolutionary innovation is more difficult to undertake for established firms. As innovations become more revolutionary, they become riskier and more difficult to evaluate. Future returns are exceptionally unpredictable. Indeed, such revolutionary decisions often cannot be justified on purely financial, rational grounds. Revolutionary innovations generally evolve unpredictably and are sporadic, with many stops and starts and unanticipated outcomes. In addition, the benefits may not be what were initially expected, and flexibility and adaptability are needed.

Experts argue persuasively that these different kinds of innovation demand very different organizational arrangements (Tushman & O'Reilly, 1996). Their research indicates that while incremental innovation can be successfully managed within the existing organizational structure and system, revolutionary innovation cannot. Anthony *et al.* suggest that companies 'follow different paths for different types of innovation' (Anthony *et al.*, 2008). They believe that 'new growth initiatives need to go through a more iterative development process, where the focus is on identifying and addressing the key assumptions and risks'. If we add to their distinctions Christensen's concept of a disruptive innovation, this argument seems to be even stronger. Perhaps the failure to heed this advice explains what Richard Foster described as the attacker's advantage (Foster, 1986), since historically the advent of a discontinuous change in technology typically heralds a shift of industry leadership. Firms dominating one generation of technology often fail to maintain their leadership when a new technology emerges (Christensen, 1997).

Type

We generally think of innovation in terms of the scope of the firm or in terms of a product/market, new businesses and new products. But there are many other types of innovation, such as when the firm develops a new organizational structure, when the mental models of managers need to be updated, or when new management systems and processes such as cross-functional teams or a revised compensation system are introduced. Indeed, many senior executives believe that business model innovation will be increasingly important in the future (Johnson *et al.*, 2008).

Creativity

Creativity is fundamental to innovation. We regard creativity as a necessary but not sufficient condition for innovation. Creativity needs to be channelled to reflect the organizational vision (Anthony *et al.*, 2008). Further, research has shown that a shared vision is particularly critical when the senior executive team is pursuing both exploratory and exploitative innovation (▶Chapter 7) simultaneously (Jansen *et al.*, 2008).

Chapter 7

Innovators should have a bias towards action, but this should not be at the expense of analysis. Innovators also have a focus on experimentation, on rapid learning and feedback, adaptive behaviour, and flexibility. They have a degree of passion towards the innovation, together with the ability to analyse and change when circumstances warrant. As might be expected, it is difficult to do both at the same time.

Risk

Innovation reflects one of the most important dilemmas in strategic management: the tension between the old and the new. A changing world means that innovation and change are essential, but all change brings with it some level of risk, and the greater the degree of innovation the greater the degree of risk. At the same time, there is a risk of inaction. The faster the pace of change, the greater the risk associated with inaction, yet too often this risk is not given the attention it deserves.

Dynamic capabilities

In a turbulent environment, continued success will not result from the possession of current capabilities, the exploitation of which has resulted in a competitive advantage. These capabilities, valuable today, will be destroyed by the changes in the external environment. As the environment changes, the firm must develop new capabilities, a process we have referred to as the possession of dynamic capabilities (➤Chapter 5). Innovation requires the capability to recognize the value of new information, assimilate it into the firm and apply it in pursuit of the firm's objectives (Zhou & Wu, 2010). These dynamic capabilities must be focused on innovation in all characteristics of the firm, organizational and managerial as well as business scope.

 Chapter 5

Barriers to change

Any innovation needs to overcome barriers to change, often created by individuals within the firm. Some individuals seem to be inherently resistant to change; others may welcome change but only if they have been informed and consulted about the change and their role in it (➤Chapter 10). Participation is often seen as a useful means to overcome this resistance, as illustrated by the experience of Honeywell in the United States. Up until 1993, the firm had been characterized by years of stagnation, with demoralized staff who felt that the firm was going backward. Barriers to innovation were seen in four areas:

 Chapter 10

- A culture of risk aversion with little experimentation where failure was punished.
- An internal environment in which innovation was discouraged.
- Few personal incentives for innovation and no corporate innovation goals.
- Inadequate processes for innovation (Peterson, 2000).

As a consequence of these characteristics, businesses within Honeywell were encouraged to manage themselves more efficiently, not to innovate. Following the appointment of a new CEO, the firm undertook a number of initiatives for innovation, primarily by identifying a large number of change programmes of varying time horizons and encouraging staff to participate. It worked, but, as expected in a large firm, it took five years for the results to show up.

Organizing for innovation

Some obstacles to innovation have been identified:

- The inertia of success – why change when we are currently successful?
- Uncertainty about what to change.
- Uncertainty about what to do – what new strategy is called for?
- Uncertainty about how to do it – the challenges of implementation (Markides, 1998).

Our own empirical research suggests that innovation in an organization is not the result of any one factor but rather is a result of mutually reinforcing systemic factors. In Figure 9.2 we show the characteristics of more innovative companies, adapted from a survey of *Fortune* 500 companies (Capon *et al.*, 1992). A cluster analysis revealed that only about a fifth of the sample could be considered to be innovative, and Figure 9.2 shows several of the characteristics they shared.

The most striking aspect of Figure 9.2 is the holistic and systemic nature of innovative organizations. Too often, we believe, managers seek one easy answer to their problems. As we have argued before, if strategic success were so simple, then it could be rapidly duplicated and any advantage competed away. In truth, the problem is more complex and usually involves creating an integrated, mutually supportive pattern that is self-reinforcing. Strategy needs to focus on the future, with changing rules of competition, with creating a competitive advantage, with developing industry leadership. But such a strategy is dependent on a culture of innovation within the firm, a willingness to take risks, an acceptance of the necessity of some failures when trying to innovate. This culture will in turn be facilitated by the reward system in place: Is entrepreneurial behaviour rewarded or not? What happens when failure occurs? Are people fired or does the firm learn from the experience? A variety of research

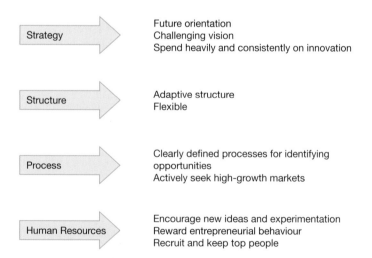

Figure 9.2 Characteristics of innovative firms

suggests that compensating senior managers for overall firm performance encourages collaboration and reduces interpersonal competition (Siegel & Hambrick, 2005). The firm also needs a structure that encourages innovation – not a highly formalized bureaucracy but rather a flexible and knowledge-based structure that can change rapidly to take advantage of opportunities (Mintzberg & Quinn, 1996).

Types of innovation

We think of innovation very broadly. Innovation can only be considered relative to the organization in which it occurs. Anything done for the first time by a particular firm is an innovation for that firm. Quite clearly then, what a firm considers to be innovative may not be considered so by its competitors, its customers or its suppliers. Innovations that are new to a company, new to an industry or new to the world are clearly very different in their implications, their risk and their prospects of returns.

Much of the literature on innovation has focused on product innovation and creating new businesses. This is, of course, very important, and it tends to be somewhat easier to measure and track than other types of innovation. Nevertheless, other types of innovation are clearly important, and we have classified these into three categories: structural, organizational and business scope, as shown in Figure 9.3, each of which we now explore.

Structural innovation

Structural innovation refers to innovations that involve reshaping the structure of an industry, which may have vertical and/or horizontal dimensions.

Many firms have achieved major improvements in their supply chain; reducing the level of inventory and thus the capital employed which allows lower margins, as the following example demonstrates.

> ### Supply chain innovation *in practice* – Kmart (Australia)
>
> Kmart (Australia) is a nationwide retail chain, carrying clothing and apparel, toys, camping and automobile products among others. In 2010 the chain launched a new strategy of everyday low prices. Associated with this new strategy, Kmart decided to bypass Australian wholesalers and import directly from factories overseas, in particular China and India, which together accounted for 80 per cent of their imported merchandize. As a result of this change in their supply chain, Kmart expected to be able to achieve cost reductions of at least 20 per cent. This was supported by other changes to their retail strategy. They undertook a major reduction in the product range, allowing better purchasing terms to be achieved. The firm also increased substantially the proportion of private label products available in the store (Speedy, 2010).

Structural innovation

A term used to describe innovations that involve reshaping the structure of an industry. The reshaping may have vertical and/or horizontal dimensions, such as vertical or horizontal integration, merger, acquisition and disintermediation.

Figure 9.3 Types of innovation

One driver of structural innovation is the interplay between the advantages of scale and specialization and the impact on these of developments in information technology (Hagel & Singer, 2000). Open architecture in computer systems can reduce transaction costs between firms, allowing firms to communicate more quickly and cheaply than before, with the possibility of outsourcing and disintermediation. Disintermediation is the partial or complete bypassing of a traditional channel member and has occurred or is presently occurring in industries as diverse as insurance, air travel, book-selling and financial services. At the same time, new intermediaries have emerged, in a process referred to as re-intermediation, illustrated by firms such as Amazon, Yahoo!, Expedia and eBay.

The growth of innovative outsourcing strategies represents further tangible evidence of the importance of structural innovation. In the car industry, the Japanese producers have led the way towards using suppliers to deliver assembled modules (subassemblies) rather than discrete components, an innovation that has been an important contributor to the high levels of productivity that their plants have attained. Such changes were critical to Tata Motors'

 Chapters 2, 3 introduction of the very low-priced Nano (➤Chapter 3) (Johnson *et al.*, 2008).

These supply-side innovations are increasingly mirrored by similar developments on the demand side. Much of Dell's success has been derived from its innovative system of working with customers to develop tailored offers. Co-development with lead airlines characterized Boeing's strategy for the newer versions of the 737 as well as the 777 and 787 (Holmes, 1997), while retailer Wal-Mart engages in extensive data exchange with its suppliers, speeding supply and increasing the efficient management of working capital through faster inventory turns.

The development of a new business model (➤Chapter 2) may also result in changing the structure of an industry. If this new business model is to add value to the firm, it must enlarge the market, either by attracting new customers or by encouraging current customers to consume more. Such a new model emphasizes different product or service attributes from the traditional model. Some research conducted by IBM suggests that an increasing number of companies are focusing on business model innovation as a growth alternative (Pohle & Chapman, 2006). As an example, Dow Chemical from the US had historically concentrated on speciality chemicals, offering complete design services together with specialized sales support. As customers became more sophisticated Dow found that not all customers wanted these value-added features – price to them was more important. In response, Dow established a new division to market basic products, under a different brand name. Dow recognized that the markets created by these new business models are often composed of new customers with different key success factors. Despite this, Dow also found that the same customer has different needs at different times and will buy from both businesses. This new division now accounts for a significant proportion of Dow sales (Comes & Berniker, 2008). While a new business model is an opportunity for some firms, this new model does not necessarily replace the original business model – so Internet banking has not replaced all other traditional forms of banking, although it was a growth opportunity for some banks.

> ## Business model *in practice* – Apple Inc
>
> 'Apple was not the first to bring digital music players to market. A company called Diamond Multimedia introduced the Rio in 1998. Another firm, Best Data, introduced the Cabo 64 in 2000. Both products worked well and were portable and stylish. So why did the iPod, rather than the Rio or Cabo, succeed?
>
> Apple did something far smarter than take a good technology and wrap it in a snazzy design. It took a good technology and wrapped it in a great business model. Apple's true innovation was to make downloading digital music easy and convenient. To do that, the company built a groundbreaking business model that combined hardware, software and service. This approach worked like Gillette's famous blades-and-razor model in reverse: 'Apple essentially gave away the "blades" (low-margin iTunes music) to lock in the purchase of the "razor" (the high-margin iPod). That model defined value in a new way and provided game-changing convenience to the consumer' (Johnson *et al.*, 2008). In three years the iPod/iTunes combination became a nearly $10 billion product accounting for almost 50 per cent of Apple's revenue. Apple's market capitalization grew from around $1 billion in early 2003 to over $10 billion by late 2007.

The horizontal dimension of structural innovation refers to innovation at the same level in the supply chain. One of the most dramatic examples involves horizontal merger or acquisition, which changes the competitive structure of the industry. However, there are other horizontal manoeuvres that must be classed as innovative yet fall short of such consolidation. The formation of an industry association, consortia such as WiMAX (▶Chapter 3), joint bargaining with unions, formation of R&D consortia, or the initiation of Japanese-style *keiretsu* or a Korean-style *chaebol* would all qualify on these terms.

Chapter 3

Organizational innovation

Organizational innovation is innovation that reshapes the way a firm operates. Although this type of innovation originates with an individual firm, it may ultimately reshape an industry.

Examples of organizational innovation abound, and, when successful, can constitute intangible assets for the innovator. Shewhart and Deming contributed seminally to the development of total quality management, General Electric invented 'work-out', while the Boston Consulting Group contributed the experience curve and share/growth portfolios. Toyota's lean manufacturing system and the *kaizen* philosophy are Japanese contributions. It is difficult to ascribe credit for some of these innovations, but certainly CRM (customer relationship management), BPR (business process re-engineering) and ERP (enterprise resource planning), aggressively marketed by various consultants, have had significant impacts on the way organizations operate and assess themselves (▶Chapter 11). Innovations in the organization of the firm also fall into this category. For example, Procter & Gamble's formation

Organizational innovation
Innovation that reshapes the way a firm operates. In some cases it may ultimately reshape the industry itself, resulting in a change of structure.

Chapter 11

of customer-based business groups with their own bottom line was widely publicized, while many other companies have turned to forms of customer-based management, ranging from the basic adoption of key account teams all the way to full-fledged business groups of the P&G type. Other forms of organizational innovation include the formation of networks, process management, the use of cross-functional teams, and new incentive systems possibly based on economic value, matrix, and other organizational structures. Each of these innovations is expected to deliver some value to the firm, but not all will lead to a sustained competitive advantage, since they may be copied by competitors.

Business scope innovation

Business scope innovation
Occurs when a firm innovates by catering to the needs of new markets or by launching completely new product groups. These new products may be either new-to-the-firm or new-to-the-world.

Our third classification, **business scope innovation**, is the one that most people think of when they consider innovation; namely, when the firm innovates by developing business units that cater to the needs of new markets or that represent completely new product groups. These new products may be either new-to-the-firm or new-to-the-world. When Sony and Philips created the compact disk, they created a new-to-the-world product.

Innovations more removed from the current business typically incur significantly more risk. If successful, however, they may afford much greater returns. Indeed, major increases in firm value come only from innovations that are new to the world. In terms of the risk profile described in Figure 8.11, these innovations are very risky but have a possibility of creating enormous value and wealth for the firm. Conversely, relatively modest extensions to the existing product line would not be expected to generate remarkable returns but should incur very modest levels of risk. Indeed, Kuczmarski argues that different discount rates should be used in financial modelling of these different types of innovation options for exactly this reason (Kuczmarski, 1988).

The categories we have discussed so far are by no means discrete, even though they do create an organizing framework. New businesses necessarily imply organizational innovation, while structural innovation will almost certainly involve business scope innovation as well

---

Innovation *in practice* – KPMG

We want to be known for the strength of our ideas both in how we serve our clients and how we manage our own affairs. It's really exciting to see how people, given the freedom to think differently, are thriving in the culture of innovation we are embedding across KPMG Europe LLP.

One of our great strengths is the speed at which we are now sharing knowledge and ideas, across disciplines and between client teams – as can be seen in the case studies in this report.

That – coupled with our continuing commitment to meet the very highest quality standards – means we can bring real benefits to clients, quickly; a vital advantage when markets are in such turmoil.

(Bennison, 2009)

---

as organizational innovation. Firms and governments are increasingly recognizing, however, that their future success depends on their ability to innovate, since innovation is key in driving not only firm growth and profit, but also national economic growth (Tellis *et al.*, 2009). One company that has clearly heard this message is KPMG Europe as the 'in practice' example illustrates.

9.3 MANAGING THE DYNAMIC SCOPE OF THE FIRM

LEARNING OBJECTIVE 2

Articulate the differences between internal development and mergers and acquisitions as means of changing scope.

We have emphasized that the challenge for any firm is to ensure that it continuously renews and reinvents itself. Firms generally start with a single product line, which eventually becomes mature. Since growth and survival are two of the core objectives of the firm, mature and declining products or businesses must be replaced with new ones. As discussed in Chapter 2 (▶Chapter 2), the management challenge can be expressed as asking:

Chapter 2

- How does the firm manage its existing businesses efficiently?
- How does the firm ensure growth with these businesses?
- How does the firm develop new businesses?

All must be done at the same time, while creating value as an entity.

The typical multi-divisional firm has a mix of business units, and the challenge for corporate management is to create the organizational arrangements and processes to encourage continual innovation. We regard this task – developing new business units – as critical for the prosperity and survival of the modern firm. Such innovation will both occur within the existing paradigm and expand the boundaries of the firm in response to change from within and outside the firm. In the longer term, strategic management recognizes that everything is variable: a firm can change any attribute – its technology, its culture, its product market scope – to develop fundamentally different and new lines of business.

Some firms are very active in managing their business portfolio over time, as is clear from Table 9.1. Over the time period 1987 to 1993, Grand Metropolitan (now Diageo) sold 44 businesses and acquired 54. Unilever, often seen as concerned primarily with internal development, acquired 79 businesses and divested 35 others. These leading EU firms have an active and aggressive portfolio management process, vigorously acquiring and divesting business units to ensure that their portfolio is appropriate to their resources and circumstances.

This need to manage the present and the future at the same time has been explored from a different perspective by Baghai, who recommends that a firm have a portfolio of businesses with different growth horizons, where the individual businesses are classified in terms of their maturity (Baghai *et al.*, 1999). The firm needs to maintain a continuous pipeline of business-building initiatives, since existing businesses will eventually fail. Businesses grow, mature and decline; as they mature, we need a stream of others to take their place. Such a dynamic portfolio is illustrated in Figure 9.4.

Horizon 1 businesses are the current core businesses of the firm, which are generally mature. These businesses generate the cash and skills that provide the resources for growth.

Table 9.1 Acquisitions and divestments by European firms (1987–93)

Selected firms ranked by the number of acquisitions	Selected firms ranked by the number of divestments
Unilever (79)	Hanson (64)
Elf Aquitane (71)	BP (55)
Asea Brown Boveri (60)	ICI (52)
Grand Metropolitan (54)	Grand Metropolitan (44)
Siemens (51)	Unilever (35)
Fiat (46)	duPont (35)

Source: G. Vitali, 'Acquisition Strategy of the Top EU Leader Companies', paper presented at the 25th EARIC conference, Copenhagen, August 1998.

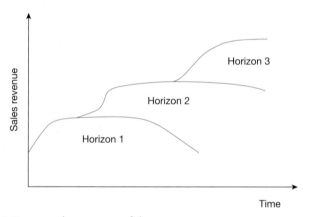

Figure 9.4 Dynamic business portfolio

Chapter 8

In terms of Chapter 8's portfolio discussion, these are the cash cow businesses of the firm (▶Chapter 8). The continuing ability of these businesses to generate cash is essential to the continued growth of the firm. Managers must ask: Are these businesses earning enough to allow us to invest in growth? What changes could affect our cost structure? Are we losing market share to competitors, direct or indirect? Are substitutes likely to be a major threat? Are the rules of competition changing due, for example, to government actions?

Horizon 2 businesses are emergent businesses – new ventures in which growth is accelerating. They can transform the firm, but are likely to require considerable investment. Important questions for corporate managers are: Do we have new businesses capable of creating as much economic value as the current ones? Are they growing? Can we make the required investments? Do we have the entrepreneurial talent to manage these ventures?

Horizon 3 businesses are in the embryonic stage of the life cycle: they are real activities and investments, however small. They are the businesses that will secure the firm's longer

Challenge of strategic management

The Baghai model above suggests that diversified firms should classify businesses according to their maturity. As a senior manager, what percentage of your time would you devote to Horizon 1, Horizon 2 and Horizon 3 businesses? Why?

term future. These will be non-existent unless senior management spends time reflecting about future growth opportunities. The pressure for short-term results is such that even senior managers may neglect the longer term. Horizon 3 businesses require creativity as well as commitment. Generating the future requires foresight as well as resources!

The Baghai model suggests that firms need to commit to a series of business innovations and to build new capability to identify and exploit such opportunities. One relevant capability is the skills required to enable growth. For example, acquisition skills as well as post-merger and risk management abilities are likely to be crucial, since Horizon 3 businesses involve high risk. Throughout, non-critical capabilities can be outsourced, but the firm must develop and retain core capabilities, since these determine how much of the future value is captured by the firm.

Management needs to run Horizon 3 businesses with very different structures, incentives and planning systems, indicating the interplay between the different types of innovation. Such growth can be stimulating for staff, providing new opportunities for them as well as shareholders. For example, spinouts may be used to encourage entrepreneurial behaviour, though there may be consequent problems of autonomy and control. Many firms also encourage active adaptation: early development and launch, coupled with active feedback and learning, with flexibility to change as circumstances require.

A growing body of literature supports the idea that the management challenges of these different kinds of innovation vary significantly and that many firms either fail to appreciate this, or are incapable of successfully making the requisite differentiation of approaches. If management is unsuccessful at managing these issues, one result is that the original innovator

New businesses *in practice* – IBM

In the past, IBM has missed out on new technologies and new opportunities. The company has changed the way it identifies and pursues promising new ideas that may conflict with existing business units or fall between established organizational boundaries. They are managed as Horizon 3 businesses separate from the rest of the organization. These Horizon 3 businesses are located in separate organizational units, with dedicated teams of managers. They are insulated from the company's established management methods and performance yardsticks, and they get personal sponsorship from a senior executive, to overcome resistance from middle management (Waters, 2001).

> ### Innovation *in practice* – SAP
>
> SAP Research is the global technology research unit of SAP, with a network of 15 research centres on five continents. The group contributes significantly to SAP's product portfolio and extends its leading position in the market by identifying and shaping emerging IT trends and generating breakthrough technologies through applied research.
>
> In contrast to SAP's product groups and development labs that work on new functions and releases, the researchers explore opportunities that have not yet been developed into products.
>
> The business model of SAP Research is based on co-innovation through collaborative research. In collaboration with leading universities, partners, customers and SAP product groups, SAP Research drives the development of promising ideas and prototypes into market-ready software for maximum customer value. To that end, customers are involved early on in the research process through special Lighthouse Projects. Meanwhile, dedicated 'Living Labs' demonstrate technological research in real-world settings – turning prospective SAP solutions into tangible experiences (SAP, 2007).

misses the commercial reward for their innovation, a rather tragic outcome! Pisano and Teece list numerous examples of innovators beaten by followers, including EMI (CAT scanners), Apple (Newton PDA), Netscape (browser), Merck (Zocor) and others (Pisano & Teece, 2007).

A considerable number of new business initiatives will usually be required, since most will not grow to become successful businesses. The cost of development may be too high, or the environment may change in such a way that the development no longer makes sense.

Developing the new clearly has associated risks. However, there is also a very real risk of inaction, namely that the current business will either see substitutes develop or see its competitive position challenged so that it ceases to create and capture value. This creative destruction is a characteristic of competitive markets and can be seen in many product areas, such as when DVDs replaced videotape, when full-service stockbrokers were challenged by online brokers, plastic cards substitute for cheques and cash or when letters were supplanted by email (►Chapter 3).

Chapter 3

Of course, companies may focus too much on core businesses and lose the right to grow, or be under siege and therefore not have the resources to grow. Yet we must also recognize that profitable growth is exciting for staff, and also creates shareholder value and employment.

The ability to create a continuous pipeline of new businesses representing new sources of profit distinguishes corporations that continue to grow. These exemplary performers can innovate in their core businesses and build new ones at the same time. Building and managing a continuous pipeline of business creation is the central challenge of sustained growth. Yet, according to Baghai, companies boasting pipelines are the exception. Performance metrics rarely reflect the growth horizon of each business segment, but if a firm relies on one management system across its entire organization, it tacitly assumes that all parts of the organization have similar management needs, which is patently ridiculous (Baghai *et al.*, 1999).

This framework expresses the idea that the firm has a 'staircase' of continuously expanding businesses, each of which requires new capabilities and skills. Since the future cannot be predicted, the firm needs to build new capabilities that create future options and opportunities. As new capabilities are generated, new opportunities open up for the firm. In an intensely competitive world, the firm must move quickly to exploit these opportunities before competitors enter or conditions change again (Baghai *et al.*, 1996).

At the business unit level, we need to recognize that each strategic business unit must be managed differently. Each must develop strategy and processes appropriate to its unique characteristics. The corporate task is to ensure that its portfolio of businesses is being continually renewed. This is an ongoing task and has to be sequenced properly. Innovation costs money, time and management resources, and the firm needs to decide to reallocate these from current businesses and apply them to developing the new. Shareholders' interests are jeopardized if the parent waits until current businesses are almost gone before developing new ones.

By considering the dynamic aspects of business development, we can also begin to develop some insight into the capabilities that will be required to support different growth alternatives. Clearly, expansion into related and new markets places a premium on market research and the development of new marketing capabilities. If, as has been the case for global multinationals, the path of market extension and expansion involves new-country markets, then country expertise becomes a *sine qua non*. In contrast, adoption of product/technology extension and expansion mandates capabilities in development or, in the case of new-to-the-world products, perhaps in more basic research.

Risk and innovation

Clearly, different types of innovation incur different levels of risk. Thus, despite Tellis's findings of the importance of successful radical innovation to firm performance, prudent management will seek an appropriate balance of estimated risk and return, while maintaining a mixed portfolio of innovation projects. Day has integrated a variety of historical sources to come up with the risk matrix portrayed in Figure 9.5 (Day, 2007). This risk matrix uses two attributes to assess the risk of a project – how familiar the company is with the intended market and how familiar the company is with the product or technology involved. Each project is given a subjective rating on these two attributes by a group of senior managers responsible for the firm's R&D portfolio. Day argues that 'Little i' innovations (Baghai's Horizon 1) are 'necessary for continuous improvement, but . . . don't give companies a competitive edge or contribute much to profitability'. In accord with Tellis's empirical findings (Tellis *et al.*, 2009), he suggests that it is the risky 'Big I' projects, projects which are new to the company, or even better, new to the world, that push the company into new markets or technologies that can generate the profits needed to close the gaps between revenue forecasts

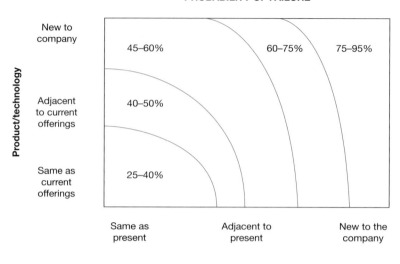

Figure 9.5 Risk and innovation

Reprinted by permission of Harvard Business Review Exhibit from 'Is it real? Can we win? Is it worth doing?' by G. S. Day, Dec. 2007. Copyright © 2007 Harvard Business School Publishing Corporation; all rights reserved.

Chapter 7

and growth goals. He advocates using the risk matrix, developed from Ansoff's basic matrix (▶Chapter 7), as part of a systematic approach to managing an innovation portfolio.

Means of changing scope

Firms have a number of choices about the strategy they pursue in terms of changing their scope over time. Two major alternatives are internal development and mergers and acquisitions. These two are seen as complementary; a firm is likely to adopt both simultaneously, although some firms have a predilection towards one more than the other. For many firms internal R&D will not create all the innovation required and other approaches are necessary. Since the future is unpredictable, many firms choose alliances, networks and joint ventures to develop new lines of business. As the firm enters new areas, each with a required set of capabilities, it generally also withdraws from existing areas through restructuring and spinouts. This dynamic approach to the business portfolio ensures that the firm continues to create value.

While we will shortly discuss these alternatives in more detail, the broad characteristics of each should be highlighted. Acquisitions are a fast means of changing scope; they can result in a new business being added to the portfolio in a matter of months. At the same time, the success rate of acquisitions is very low – only about 25 per cent of them seem to add value to the acquirer. One reason for this low success rate is the premium firms pay for the target, meaning that it is difficult for the combined entity to achieve the required returns.

> ### Changing scope *in practice* – Nestlé
>
> The evolving strategy of Nestlé, the Swiss food company, illustrates this combined approach. Nestlé was founded in 1866 and by 2002 had revenue of $US50 billion with pre-tax net profits of $US5.5 billion. Historically, substantial growth has been accomplished by internal development, by developing new products and businesses through extensive R&D. At the same time, over the period 1985 to 2000 it spent $US26 billion on acquisitions, since organic growth in its established businesses had slowed. Its recent acquisitions have been in faster-growing markets such as pet foods and ice cream, with purchases of Haagen Dazs and Dreyers in the United States and Schoellers in Germany. In 2001 it spent $US10.3 billion purchasing Ralston Purina in the United States, and $US5.5 billion in 2007 buying Novartis Medical Nutrition. The company announced 'a calmer acquisition outlook' in the same year (Merrett, 2007), but despite this it continued to acquire aggressively, purchasing Baloton from Kraft in Hungary in 2008 (FlexNews, 2008), and Kraft's frozen pizza business for $US3.7 billion in cash in 2010 (Tickle, 2010).

The other reason is post-acquisition problems, particularly the difficulty of merging corporate cultures. By contrast, internal development takes more time, requires the firm to develop a range of new skills and capabilities, and is likely to overcome any cultural problems.

9.4 MANAGING THE DYNAMIC SCOPE – INTERNAL DEVELOPMENT

LEARNING OBJECTIVE 3

Identify the major issues to be resolved in technological innovation.

This method of achieving growth is widespread among major corporations. They recognize that technological innovation is central to improving productivity, developing new businesses and generating sustained long-term value. High levels of R&D expenditure characterize these firms, leading to the development of new products and services. There is a variety of evidence suggesting that such an approach yields positive results (Capon *et al.*, 1996). These firms also recognize that innovation requires commercialization. There is little value in inventing something that is never commercialized. Superior technology by itself is not sufficient for a successful business (Pisano & Teece, 2007). Technology leaders are proficient at understanding changing customer needs, technological developments, and the strategies of both direct and indirect competitors to ensure that their leadership position is maintained. Firms such as BASF recognize the need for an integrative approach to innovation, together with a marketplace focus.

Firms active in R&D attempt to create a virtuous circle, as shown in Figure 9.6.

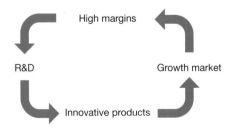

Figure 9.6 Virtuous development cycle

> ### Internal development *in practice* – BASF
>
> The BASF Innovation Award is used by the BASF Executive Board to honour projects that were translated into innovations professionally and thus make a sustainable contribution to the success of BASF and its customers. It takes more than a brilliant idea to produce an innovative product. It also takes interdisciplinary cooperation among research, development, engineering, production and marketing experts. Innovations call for strong entrepreneurship and endurance.
>
> Dr Andreas Kreimeyer of BASF has stated: 'Innovations *are essential for BASF. We use them to shape the future of our company. Innovations ensure our profitable growth and our customers' success.'* Focusing on market needs and in this way successfully opening up new business segments – this is exactly the principle followed by the team of finalists from the Care Chemicals operating division during the development of the surfactant range (BASF, 2009).

These firms use their high margins to invest in R&D to develop innovative products, which have high growth rates and margins, which in turn support a further cycle of R&D. Such leaders are close to markets, ensuring that technology is used to create new products that customers require, with a substantial advantage over current products. These firms attempt to maintain industry leadership through their development and use of technology.

Internal development has several advantages. First, and most importantly, everything is done in-house. As such, the firm has – in theory – total control over the entire growth process. Required resources are purchased or leased by the firm; it makes its own decisions on interorganizational relationships, such as those with suppliers and distributors; and shortfalls in human resources are dealt with by hiring to requirements and acculturating newcomers to the firm's way of doing business. Second, while alternative means of securing product/market access – for example, by acquisition – are available, internal development may be less expensive.

The major disadvantages of internal development are timing and resource access. Internal development takes time. In an era in which market windows are shortening, in-house development may be a luxury the firm cannot always afford. Furthermore, at the limit, some required resources may just be unavailable to the firm or may be too expensive and/or too

Challenge of strategic management

It is suggested above that new innovative products have high margins that can be used to fund R&D. Do you accept the proposition that innovative products have high margins? If not, how should the company manage its R&D effort to achieve these high margins?

risky for the firm to develop on its own. These problems are leading firms to take a more holistic view of the growth process and to consider other mechanisms, such as acquisition and strategic alliances, to complement internal development growth strategies.

Technological innovation

Figure 9.7 indicates the important issues to be considered in technological innovation.

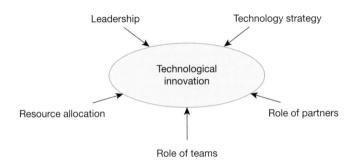

Figure 9.7 Issues in technological innovation
Source: Adapted from Cohan, 1997

Technology strategy

Technological innovation by the firm must be linked to the overall strategy adopted, and doing so involves a number of more specific considerations. First, the firm needs to be able to define, develop and utilize those technological capabilities that contribute to its competitive advantage. This will generally include decisions on which technology areas to explore and how these may change over time. Technology leaders also have a deep understanding of the relationship between technological parameters and customer requirements, as discussed in Chapter 3 (►Chapter 3). They understand the customer benefits that result from given improvements in technical product attributes.

Chapter 3

From a managerial perspective, technology strategy also includes decisions on whether or not R&D will be centralized; in other words, which R&D projects will be done at the corporate level and which in the business units. This decision will reflect any economies of scale in R&D, since if these are strong, research is likely to be centralized (Dodgson, 2000). The firm must also decide on the R&D time span: will it engage in primarily short-term development research, or will it engage in more basic long-term research, or what will be the mix between these?

Commercialization options must also be evaluated. Will the firm develop and sell the new products, license the technology to other firms, or sell the intellectual property represented by the innovation to other firms? We must also decide whether to patent the innovation. Patents give the firm some protection but reveal the innovation to competitors.

Commercialization must be the long-term goal of any R&D undertaken by the firm. For many firms, this last step has proved to be difficult, with many firms unable to commercialize their technological innovation so that the benefits accrue to the firm's competitors.

Technology limits

Developing the firm's technology strategy also requires an understanding of the relationship between research effort and research output. As shown in Figure 9.8, this relationship generally follows an S-shaped curve. Initially, research effort results in small improvements in performance. Following this period, there are typically large increases in the performance measure for relatively small inputs in the research effort. Finally, the technology reaches a plateau where only small improvements are obtained even for large increases in research effort (Foster, 1986). Recognizing these relationships is critical in developing R&D strategy, as they indicate when the research thrust needs to be altered. A product becomes a commodity within a market segment when all avenues for development are exhausted, when market requirements on each attribute of performance have been completely satisfied by more than one – often many – available products. As a given technology reaches its limit, the basis of competition typically changes and price competition becomes more intense.

Figure 9.8 indicates that when one technology, referred to in the figure as technology A, is reaching the limits of its performance, a different technology is often developing, one which has the potential to substantially improve the performance parameter. A well-known example of this would be when jet engines replaced piston-driven planes on commercial aircraft. No matter how much was spent to improve the speed of planes driven by propellers, there was a limit to the speed that could be attained. The only way to increase plane speed was to develop new technology – in this case, jet engines. As funds were invested in this new technology, plane speeds increased dramatically, again reaching a limit that called for another technology if speeds were to increase further.

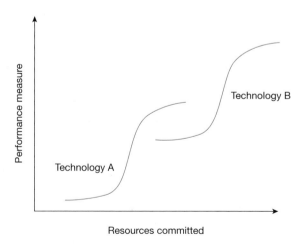

Figure 9.8 S curves for two technologies

Sustaining and disruptive technological change

Christensen has extended our understanding of technical innovation with his distinction between sustaining technologies and disruptive technological change (Christensen, 1997). Sustaining technological change improves the performance of established products along the dimensions of performance that mainstream customers in major markets have historically valued. Disruptive technological changes bring new and very different value propositions to the marketplace.

Christensen's research indicates that sustaining technological changes rarely results in the failure of established firms, since they find it easy to keep up. No modifications of managers' mental maps are required to appreciate the benefits of these changes. In contrast, disruptive changes often precipitate the failure of leading firms. Products based on these disruptive changes are often initially inferior, with features that appeal to new, not current customers. They may be cheaper or even more expensive, but they frequently possess new kinds of functionality; for example, being smaller, faster or easier to use. Because they are still under rapid development, however, their functionality improves rapidly until they challenge industry incumbents.

Disruptive technology *in practice* – share trading

Electronic share trading was not a major concern of many investors; they were happy with the concept of financial advisers. In addition, the margins on electronic trading were thin, and initially the market was quite small. So why would a stockbroker with a well-established business in providing advice on shares to its customers develop such a risky new technology, which few of its current customers would value? A very similar circumstance afflicted the launch of e-books, but the advent of Kindle and Apple's iPad quickly changed the situation.

As this example illustrates, it sometimes does not appear rational to invest in these disruptive technologies, since markets that do not exist cannot be analysed. Further, these new technologies may reduce margins and are not desired by current lead customers. For this reason, firms external to an existing industry often develop such disruptive technologies.

The typical sequence is that a new technology, generally inferior to the established technology, finds limited application in some market segments that value the new benefit. The new technology then generally expands its market until it can successfully challenge, and possibly supplant, the existing technology.

Christensen also suggests that many of the incumbents' management practices make it difficult for them to develop these disruptive technologies. Firms seen currently as well managed have systems to ensure they listen to current customers, usually meaning they develop products with greater functionality using known technology. They find it difficult to allocate resources to R&D proposals that propose to develop products that current customers do not value, that offer lower margins, that have inferior performance parameters, and that can only be sold in small niche markets.

Leadership

A strategy of technological innovation requires leadership, an important intangible asset. Managers must understand those technologies important to the business. This understanding need not be in fine detail, but it is necessary at a broader level in order to decide which research projects to select. Managers need to understand customer requirements and how technological parameters relate to these. Thus leaders understand both technology and business: they recognize the importance of technology and at the same time realize that technological innovation must result in measurable business outcomes (➤Chapter 10).

Chapter 10

Leaders also realize that technological innovation is inherently difficult to manage; it is messy and rarely develops in a neat, logical manner. Instead, it is full of twists and turns, with many unpredictable events. Any major R&D programme will have several sources of risk, such as the following:

- *Technological risk* – How will this new technology develop?
- *Market risk* – Will there be a demand for the products and services that are expected to be developed?
- *Business risk* – What investment in people and capital will be required?

Each of these risks must be understood and considered. Further, astute managers understand the need to employ good researchers, to keep the firm flexible, and to work at influencing or controlling industry standards in pursuit of their corporate goals.

Role of partners

Firms on the forefront of technological innovation may not be able to develop all the required technology in-house. While they may be committed to internal development, with the high R&D expenditure that implies, they also realize that acquisitions and alliances may be required to stay ahead of competition. The ability to work successfully in such relationships is also an important intangible asset.

Chapter 3

The need for a cooperative approach also arises from the systemic nature of many innovations, whereby an innovation must be embedded in a total system. For example, a computer comprises a central processing unit, an operating system, applications software, memory chips, power supplies and communication devices (Johnson *et al.*, 2008). Innovation in any one element of an offer must be consistent with, and integrated with, all the other elements. Modern technological innovation frequently requires that the firm collaborate and cooperate with others – hence the rise of networks. These require open communication with a number of firms, some of which may be direct competitors. As we saw in Chapter 3 (➤Chapter 3), the firm may be a member of various networks that allow the complementary capabilities of the different firms to be utilized.

It may also be the case that the firm will engage in a number of competing developments at the same time. As noted, Microsoft participates in many competing innovations when there is uncertainty as to which will ultimately win, an example of the firm taking out options on the various technologies.

Role of teams

Technological innovation also requires that the firm eliminate boundaries between different groups within the firm. Innovation typically involves the use of cross-functional teams. Since innovations may also come from lead customers, innovation often requires close cooperation and input from such customers. Note that facilitating cross-functional team-working does not mean that boundaries should not be used to focus innovation efforts. Anthony argues persuasively that the senior management team must define strategic goals and boundaries, and create a balanced portfolio of growth opportunities that reflects their strategy (Anthony *et al.*, 2008).

However, since technological innovation is difficult, success also requires specific human resource approaches. The best people need to be identified and recruited. The firm culture must encourage experimentation and risk-taking, and incentives must support such a culture. In particular, the firm culture should not blindly resist cannibalization. This has been a major problem for numerous firms that have not supported new technologies because they promise to make existing products obsolete. A willingness to cannibalize is critical to the success of more radical innovations (Tellis *et al.*, 2009). In the longer term, it is usually better to make our own products obsolete than delay and let our competitors do this for us!

Resource allocation

The CEO must play an active role in selecting the technologies that the firm is attempting to develop, ensuring that resources are allocated in accordance with the desired research portfolio. This requires scanning for new technologies and understanding which technologies are reaching their limits, which are likely to threaten existing technology, and which promise to deliver additional value to customers.

A specific tool that may be used to allocate resources is a matrix approach, similar to those discussed in Chapter 8 (➤Chapter 8), in which R&D projects are assessed on the basis of two dimensions:

Chapter 8

- The profit potential if the innovation is successful.
- The competitive position of the firm in this technology.

Projects that score highly on each dimension are supported. Risk may be incorporated as a third dimension, or another portfolio of the risk and expected return from the research could be developed, recognizing the necessity to achieve a balance between these.

In summary, a firm active in R&D will have a range of projects that can be assessed on many dimensions. Some projects may involve basic research; others will be more developmental in nature. What it needs is a balance of projects, aligned with its corporate strategy and reflecting the culture of the firm.

LEARNING OBJECTIVE 4

Apply the merger and acquisition process described in Figure 9.10.

9.5 MANAGING THE DYNAMIC SCOPE – MERGERS AND ACQUISITIONS

Mergers and acquisitions are a favoured method of growth for many companies and an integral element in corporate strategy. Viguerie *et al.*'s research supports the strategic use of M&A to drive the growth of the firm (Viguerie *et al.*, 2008). They note that the average large company they studied gets 31 per cent of its growth from M&A, arguing that despite paying a premium to the seller, more than half of acquirers are rewarded in the longer term (ibid., p. 83). Factors contributing to the increase in mergers and acquisitions are the ready availability of capital, globalization and the associated easing of regulatory regimes, and, finally, managerial motives – the desire by managers to grow their firms. We must emphasize that mergers and acquisitions are not solely financial issues – their success or otherwise is strongly influenced by behavioural issues, such as the merging of different corporate cultures and power conflicts between different managerial groups. Nonetheless, active management of the corporation's portfolio of businesses is important. Viguerie argues that the following steps are key to successful portfolio management:

- A pro-active approach to monitoring a firm's current and emerging internal capabilities and matching them with external changes in technology, regulation and consumer behaviour that might open up opportunities in other industries or make use of the company's skills.
- The rapid divestment of businesses that show early signs of possible failure.
- The prompt 'liberation' of successful new businesses after the opportunities for internal synergies have been realized.
- The active and continuous trading of business portfolios.

The terms *merger* and *acquisition* are often used interchangeably, and they do have some features in common. They are legal transactions, and appropriate legislation must be understood, whether in the country in which the planned merger is to take place or other countries. In addition, although national regulations of both parties may well be followed, as we saw in Chapter 3 (➤Chapter 3), regulators now have transnational reach.

 Chapter 3

Acquisition

The firm expands its resources and competences by purchasing, or taking a controlling interest in, another firm.

An **acquisition** occurs when one firm, the acquirer, purchases a controlling interest in another firm, the target firm. An acquisition normally involves discussions with the management and board of the target, and when agreement is reached, the target's shareholders vote on the proposal.

An acquisition can be friendly, when it is supported by the target firm's management, or hostile, when it is not supported. A takeover is normally an unsolicited acquisition bid, whereby the acquirer makes a direct appeal to the target's shareholders. Acquisitions can also be described as related or unrelated and as horizontal or vertical.

The acquisition may be of an entire corporate entity or of an individual business unit. The acquiring firm secures not only the target firm's product/market and technology portfolios but also its organizational structure, human resources, capabilities and systems. It is the post-acquisition integration of these that often causes difficulty.

A **merger** occurs when two firms agree to integrate operations on a friendly basis and agree to have virtually equal stakes in each other's businesses. Again, the bidder negotiates an agreement with management, which then submits the proposal to a vote by shareholders.

When a firm acquires the assets and technologies of another firm, the acquirer generally has to pay a premium over the stand-alone market value of the target, reflected in the current share price of the target. Due to this premium, the acquiring firm finds it difficult to earn the margins required to make the purchase profitable for shareholders. Acquiring managers often make optimistic future earnings projections, over-estimate cost reductions and misjudge customers' attitudes towards the acquisition, and all too often the acquisition does not deliver value to the acquiring firm (Marks & Mirvis, 2001). It frequently proves impossible to marry the cultures of the two entities, leading to internecine warfare and/or future divorce. Further, it is not uncommon for senior managers in the acquired firm to leave, leading to a substantial loss of knowledge.

When considering a possible merger or acquisition, we need to address how the competitive position of the acquiring firm, or the target, will be affected by the acquisition. Since competition occurs primarily at the business unit level, the competitive position of one of the entities should be improved, either through cost reductions or the transfer of capabilities from one to the other. The acquiring firm should manage the target better, bring some added benefits to the target, or bring benefits from the target to the acquiring firm. The acquiring firm must also be wary of unsustainable levels of leverage if debt financed the acquisition.

It is frequently alleged that big acquisitions are more difficult to implement than smaller ones. A strategy of many small acquisitions may provide higher returns than fewer large acquisitions. Growth strategies involving many small acquisitions may not make headlines but may be quite effective. For example, Microsoft, an organization with significant commitment to internal development, is nonetheless a very active acquirer.

One reason for the apparent success of many small acquisitions may be that the firm gains considerable expertise over time, lowering acquisition costs and improving effectiveness from identification all the way through to integrating into the acquired firm. Furthermore, market imperfections are more likely in the market for small acquisitions. Large acquisitions are usually highly publicized, and the acquiring firm is more likely to pay a proportionately higher price.

Mergers and acquisitions are corporate resource decisions that can quickly change the value of a firm, positively or negatively. All too often, shareholders of acquiring firms lose while those of targets win. Acquisitions are an unpredictable high-stakes game, a mixture of planning and opportunistic behaviour on the part of the acquirer. They are often conducted under considerable time pressure as a candidate comes into play and other firms get interested. As we saw at the beginning of this chapter, the calculations of the originator of the merger may sometimes be upset, and, in the case of VW/Porsche, the erstwhile aggressor became the victim. In other cases, managers get caught up in the excitement of the bidding process, losing sight of their original objectives. With events unfolding rapidly, detailed analysis may not be possible, particularly analysis of how the two entities will be integrated or the human problems with the planned merger.

Merger

A strategy under which two firms agree to integrate their operations on a friendly basis to strengthen competitive advantage.

Cross-border mergers and acquisitions

Whereas international expansion may well endow firms with performance advantages in terms of risk and/or return (Gaur & Kumar, 2009), acquisition is not the only route available. Nonetheless, acquisitions are a commonly used method to become more global, with a firm acquiring a small firm in the same industry in a new geographic area. Acquisitions may help overcome entry barriers, although the premium necessary to consummate the acquisition can be considered such a barrier. In addition, problems resulting from integration difficulties are often greater with cross-border mergers and acquisitions.

Size and frequency of mergers and acquisitions

Aggregate merger and acquisition behaviour shows considerable variation, with some periods of sustained activity followed by more benign periods, as shown in Figure 9.9.

The late 1990s was a period of intense activity. As is clear from Figure 9.9, the value of European mergers and acquisitions rose to about €500 billion in 2006/07, then collapsed to about €100 billion in 2009 due to the global financial crisis and the associated liquidity difficulties.

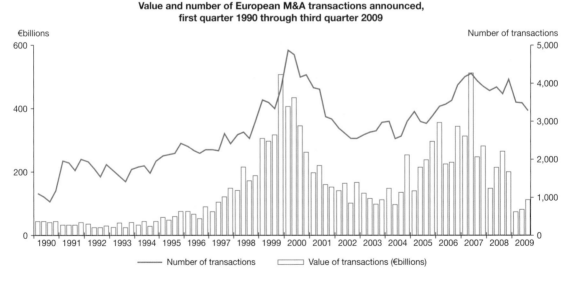

Value and number of European M&A transactions announced, first quarter 1990 through third quarter 2009

Figure 9.9 European mergers and acquisitions

Source: *M&A Ready for Liftoff? A Survey of European Companies' Merger and Acquisition Plans for 2010* ©2009 The Boston Consulting Group (Kronimus et al., 2009)

> **Cross-border mergers *in practice* – European steel industry**
> Discussing the resignation of the CEO of the British–Dutch steel firm Corus, analysts argued that the merger had been 'beset with problems', producing four consecutive years of losses. They alleged that the merger had 'simmering issues that just haven't gone away'. British Steel, which had bought Royal Hoogovens, the other partner, 'paid a premium and behaved as though they had paid a premium', one analyst suggesting that 'post-merger integration was a sore point' (Whitehouse, 2003). Perhaps as a result of these problems, Corus became a part of Tata Steel in 2007.

Drivers of mergers and acquisitions

Mergers and acquisitions are a very common method adopted by firms to increase growth rates. They seem to be driven by a number of factors, not all of which are to the benefit of the shareholders of the acquiring firm.

Scale

A major rationale for mergers and acquisitions is the need to achieve scale economies (➤Chapter 5). Thus when Hewlett-Packard and Compaq were considering their merger, they expected to achieve cost benefits of $US2.5 billion by combining their previously separate operations. In fact, the companies exceeded this goal by over a billion dollars (Burgelman & McKinney, 2006). In common with many other mergers, however, they found it much harder to achieve all the intended benefits, missing out on the longer term goals.

Chapter 5

The scale driver is particularly important in mature markets, where firms achieve growth through acquisitions, thereby gaining market share and the ability to leverage their individual operations. Some of the scale economies come from sharing resources previously separated, with subsequent layoffs. There is some evidence that these layoffs are overdone. The loss of skills due to the layoffs serves to emphasize the importance of intangible assets, and in at least one study, post-acquisition workforce reductions were shown to be related to poorer post-acquisition performance (Krishnan *et al.*, 2007).

Capabilities

Through acquisitions, a firm can buy particular capabilities to augment its own (➤Chapter 5). These may include an infusion of talent as well as new products, access to new and better distribution channels, and access to a new customer base.

Chapter 5

Diversification

Acquisitions are a potentially useful way to diversify. They are quick, overcome entry barriers, and are generally lower risk than internal development (➤Chapter 8). While, as noted above,

Chapter 8

horizontal acquisitions are a common means of increasing the firm's growth rate, related acquisitions are a useful means of diversifying. When there are barriers to organic growth due to market saturation, diversification into new areas via acquisition is common, assisted by the ease with which finance can be obtained.

Management ego

The other significant reason for acquisitions is management ego, reflecting the desire of managers to manage larger firms and the ego boost they get from making a major acquisition (Hayward & Hambrick, 1997).

Success of mergers and acquisitions

Despite the great popularity of mergers and acquisitions with managers, the evidence on their success is mixed. Acquisitions generally fail to yield returns to the shareholders of the acquirer (Sirower, 1999). Most of the benefits appear to flow to one of two parties: the share-holders of the acquired firm (from the premium that is paid) and the managers of the acquiring firm (they get a larger firm to manage). If the acquiring company pays a premium of 30 per cent over the current share price of the target (which is a common premium), the acquiring firm must be able to achieve improvements in performance which are greater than this. For example, when Henkel acquired National Starch in 2007, Henkel announced that they expected performance improvements of 60–90 per cent of National Starch's value. After paying a premium of 55 per cent, the net value created by the acquisition was just 5 to 25 per cent of the purchase price (Dobbs *et al.*, 2010). Supporting this view that acquisitions generally destroy value, a 2001 KPMG survey reported that 70 per cent of the combinations studied failed to add value (Devine, 2002), although others disagree (Viguerie *et al.*, 2008).

Acquisitions *in practice* – BAE SYSTEMS

BAE Systems plc announced that it would take a write-off of £592 million related to its 2007 acquisition of Jacksonville-based Armor Holdings Inc. after losing out on a US military contract. London-based BAE was informed in mid-2010 that it would not be awarded a follow-up contract for the family of Medium Tactical Vehicles programme. Those vehicles have been produced at a former Armor plant in Sealy, Texas, and the current contract generates $2 billion in annual sales for BAE. But the US Department of Defense in August decided to award the follow-up contract beginning in 2011 to Oshkosh Corp (Basch, 2010).

The loss of business at former Armor operations has raised questions by analysts whether BAE's $4.5 billion acquisition of Armor was a good idea with BAE's stock falling 5.6 per cent in London trading in August on the day the loss of the FMTV contract was originally announced.

Business leaders, as well as scholars, have spoken out against acquisitions. For example, George Bull (former CEO of Grand Metropolitan, now Diageo) asserted that organic growth (internal development) creates value for shareholders but that acquisition destroys value, as the BAE example illustrated.

According to McKinsey, mergers often fail because revenue stalls. Only 12 per cent of firms they studied accelerated sales growth in the three years after merging. Mergers create uncertainty, salespeople are targeted by competitors, redundancies damage morale, and managers become concerned with infighting, not running the business.

Process model of mergers and acquisitions

Managers often see acquisitions and their integration as isolated events, not a process that can be improved. But for many firms, acquisitions are a normal part of their business. As seen in Table 9.1, for many European firms, mergers and acquisitions are a normal element in their corporate strategy. Firms for which acquisitions are a key element of corporate strategy attempt to make acquisition selection and integration a core capability, a process that they can continually improve. One such company is Unilever, which has a very active acquisition strategy (Unilever, 2010).

Our recommended process is shown in Figure 9.10, which we now discuss in more detail. The process is split into two broad decision areas: pre- and post-merger. The process is shown as linear, but in reality it is an iterative, not linear, set of decisions.

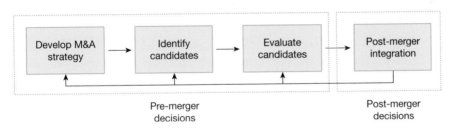

Figure 9.10 The merger and acquisition process

Developing the merger and acquisition strategy

Acquisitions based on an underlying strategy are more likely to succeed than those resulting from opportunistic reactions to the emergence of candidates. Making successful acquisitions is not easy. In far too many companies these decisions are sporadic, differing from normal experiences. They are done with limited access to information and staff participation due to the need for secrecy.

The first step is to establish the strategy behind the merger or acquisition, and determine responsibility for the process. There should be a good understanding of what the acquisition is expected to accomplish and the rationale behind the strategy. The acquiring management should provide a compelling reason for the acquisition and an explanation of how the acquisition will support their firm's strategy. Such an acquisition strategy should also state a vision for the combined entity. Such a vision helps to get employees of the target firm on board. Acquisitions can both reinforce and change a firm's direction, and the acquirer needs to be clear about what is expected. Acquisitions create value when they enhance the capabilities of the combined firms. Managers must balance the need for autonomy of the acquired firm with the need to transfer capabilities between the two.

Developing an acquisition strategy also requires recognizing that different types of acquisitions can make very different contributions to the firm's renewal, as described below:

- Deepen the firm's presence in its existing domain. This may result from the recognition of the need to strengthen its position in the industry, the possible need to deal with over-capacity in the industry, and the need to consolidate. The acquiring firm uses the acquisition to become more efficient, reducing costs through economies of scale. Alternatively, the acquirer may take the initiative in combining firms in a fragmented industry, again searching for economies of scale. These are often one-time opportunities and are difficult to do successfully, since the firm has little experience.

- Broaden the firm's domain in terms of products, markets or capabilities. This is often the basis for cross-border acquisitions, taking the firm into new geographic markets. Such acquisitions generally involve major cultural differences between the two firms, and here a history of successful acquisitions will help. Such acquisitions may also be a substitute for internal R&D.

- Bring the firm into new domains. Through the acquisition, the firm moves into new businesses that require new capabilities. Such an acquisition may substitute for internal R&D. Alternatively, it may reflect the belief of managers that industry convergence is occurring, and the acquirer puts together a combination of firms from those existing industries whose boundaries are eroding. Such a move may also reflect concern with the long-term situation in the firm's current domain and the need to find a new domain.

Acquisitions within the same industry offer the greatest scope for reducing costs, generating synergy between related products, achieving superior distribution by adding new products to established channels and providing access to superior technology. When the acquisition involves an element of diversification, such synergies are more difficult to obtain. In these cases, we need to transfer capabilities between the firms. The less related the two businesses, the more difficult it may be to find capabilities that can be usefully transferred and shared.

Developing an acquisition strategy also involves establishing responsibilities: who is responsible for the entire decision-making process – the number of people involved, the speed and the consideration given to strategic and organizational, as well as financial, issues? Any such process must involve senior management, but the team will involve many other staff members as well as external staff from consulting firms and advisers. Senior managers bring considerable experience and judgement to the process. Other employees bring a set of analytical skills, since considerable information on the target, its markets and its performance must be analysed. So we will need an acquisition team, and the responsibility of this team should be clear. This decision process should also give some consideration to the problems of integration – value is not created until after the acquisition, when capabilities are transferred and people collaborate to create the expected benefits.

Such a strategy statement should establish acquisition criteria; for example, what industry, what cost structure, what capabilities, what customers and so on the target would ideally possess. Our view is that acquisitions, as with any decision of the firm, must create value for the firm as an economic entity. Mergers should be based on this as a principle, not on growth for its own sake. Acquisitions should be seen as a superior strategy to internal development in terms of cost, time and ultimate performance. They should not be the means by which some managers preserve their jobs and get the opportunity to manage larger firms.

Identifying candidates

The second step is to identify possible candidates, to make contact and to undertake due diligence. The firm has already developed criteria for possible acquisitions that are used to narrow the search for qualified candidates, including such characteristics as industry, size, geographic location, competitive strengths, management strengths and price range. Possible candidates are then identified from trade lists and industry experts as well as banks and specialist merger advisers. Ranking these possible candidates is facilitated by a formal screening system, a weighting and rating scale.

Evaluating candidates

Third, the firm must evaluate the candidate and negotiate the acquisition with the incumbent management as well as possibly with major shareholders in the target firm. At this stage it is also necessary to develop a price and guidelines for how the acquisition will be financed as well as what will be offered to the shareholders of the target firm; for example, cash, shares, or a combination of the two.

There is generally a courtship period during which the acquirer needs to build a compelling business case and create a constructive business relationship with the target as well as obtain support from major shareholders and other stakeholders – all under time pressure and in secrecy. This business case should be compelling and exciting, since otherwise little things can kill a merger. For example, European partners in a law firm are generally paid on the basis of seniority while partners in US firms are paid on the basis of how much business they personally win for the firm. Any cross-border merger between law firms is likely to produce major tension within the combined firm. The location of the combined firm's head office or the choice of CEO of the combined entity could equally well cause difficulty. Regardless, it is important to contact the target firm and start the negotiation process.

Due diligence

Due diligence includes an analysis of the financial strength, people, intellectual assets, environment and operations of the seller. This provides the basis for making future forecasts as well as identifying any unknown legal or financial liabilities, or undervalued and overvalued assets. Such due diligence should also explore integration risks: How will this be done? What are the cultural risks? What are the differences? We know that post-merger integration is difficult, causing many mergers to fail, so there is a need to consider these issues early in the process. This indicates that the total acquisition process is iterative rather than linear.

Part of due diligence involves preliminary discussions with regulatory authorities and legal firms to identify potential obstacles. Any merger or acquisition must satisfy a number of legal constraints, and these get more complicated with the increasing size and global reach of the merger. There are also many accounting and tax issues to be resolved (Weston *et al.*, 1998).

Management must also decide how the acquisition will be structured and funded. Shareholders of the target firm may be offered cash or stock. With the latter, the acquiring firm buys the stock of the target with its own stock, which is especially advantageous if the acquirer has a high share price. Apart from the chance of some dilution in the value of these shares, however, the composition of the shareholder base then changes. Further, shareholders of the acquiring firm typically shy away from such dilution. Of course, an acquisition may be based on the understanding that the acquirer will sell some of the target's assets. If done well, these sales may finance a significant proportion of the acquisition cost.

A strong balance sheet also aids the acquiring firm. Following the acquisition of TIGI by Unilever, Jeremy Batstone-Carr, of Charles Stanley, the stockbroker, pointed out that the firm was 'absolutely loaded with cash'; the 2008 Unilever balance sheet showed over €2.5 billion in cash and cash equivalents. Batstone-Carr continued: 'This acquisition is commensurate with their intention to bolster their key brands' (King, 2009). Unilever, in common with many other firms, also divests some of its operations to provide the funds required for future acquisitions – reflecting a dynamic portfolio approach (Unilever, 2010). On the other hand, if a firm is highly leveraged, additional debt to finance acquisitions will be difficult to arrange.

Synergy

The evaluation stage should also give consideration to the synergy in the proposed acquisition. Synergy is the increase in cash flows when the two firms are combined over what they would be expected to accomplish individually. Synergy results when the combination of various physical, financial and intellectual assets is such that their value is greater than the sum of their individual worth. Assets might include brands, reputation, processes and core capabilities as well as individuals with unique skills. However, no value is created without managerial actions and interactions between the firms. Synergy, if it is to occur, results from the transfer of capabilities between the firms and the improvement in the competitive position, and thus the performance, of the resulting combination.

Eccles suggests that there are five types of synergies (Eccles *et al.*, 1999):

- *Cost savings* – these arise from eliminating jobs, facilities and related expenses as well as economies of scale in purchasing. They are likely to be higher when the target is in the same industry in the same country.

- *Revenue enhancement* – acquirer and target may achieve higher growth levels than if they stayed independent. Growth may arise from a larger customer base, but will they now buy from the combined firm?

- *Process improvement* – managers can transfer best practices and core capabilities from one to the other, resulting in both revenue enhancement and cost reduction.

- *Financial engineering* – management may refinance the debt of the target at the lower cost of the acquirer.

- *Tax benefits* – management may be able to spread tax payments, pushing debt into high tax subsidiaries. This creates no improvement in competitive position.

In the majority of cases, acquiring firms pay a premium with respect to the share price of the target firm prior to any announcement of a takeover. The magnitude of this premium varies, but usually ranges from 30 to 50 per cent, and it is paid up-front, in expectation of future but uncertain cash flows. If we accept the efficient market hypothesis for a moment, we have to conclude that the current share price of the target firm incorporates all the information available to financial markets about the value of the strategy of the firm, which leaves open an important question: How will the acquiring firm create value?

It is possible that financial markets are inefficient and undervalue the target firm. Thus the acquiring firm may see opportunities that financial markets do not. For example, the acquiring firm may see opportunities to generate additional value through the combination of the two firms, greater than either could generate individually, as discussed above. This would be particularly the case for a smaller privately held company, for which there was not an open auction. The fact remains that managers who pay a premium commit themselves to delivering more than the market already expects from the strategy of the two firms. They must add value to the target in some way, making it more efficient with improved competitiveness. The magnitude of this additional value will depend on the characteristics of the acquirer and the target as well as management capabilities. Thus the same target will have different values for different acquiring firms.

In summary, we should remember that the onus – which is considerable – is on management to make an acquisition successful for the acquirer's shareholders. Shareholders can diversify their holdings at low cost, without paying the premium. Acquiring managers must see what the financial markets do not or the venture will join the estimated 70 to 80 per cent that destroy shareholder value.

Valuing acquisition targets

Valuing a potential acquisition requires calculating the net present value of future cash flows, discounted at the cost of capital, minus the investments made over time.

Since any acquisition should involve some synergy, we need to estimate three terms:

V(A+B) – the net present value of the combined entity.

V(A) – the net present value of firm A, the acquiring firm, without the acquisition.

V(B) – the net present value of the acquired firm, without the acquisition.

This gives us the situation shown in Figure 9.11.

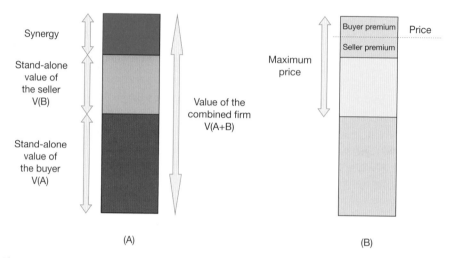

Figure 9.11 Valuing acquisitions

With this formulation:

Synergy = V(A+B) – (V(A) + V(B))

(Synergy is the value of the combined firm minus the value of the two firms independently)

And the price should be between two limits:

Lower limit for price = V(B)

(This is the lowest price at which the seller will sell, and at this price the buyer captures all the synergy created by the acquisition.)

Upper limit for price = V(A + B) – V(A)

(This is the highest price that the buyer will offer, and at this price the seller captures all the synergy created by the acquisition.)

The price paid for the acquisition will reflect the relative negotiating power of the seller and the buyer and will vary with the nature of the buyer. Some firms will find greater value in a given target than others. Price will also depend on the position in the economic cycle, buyer and seller needs, and the state of financial markets.

How does the acquirer measure value? The recommended method of valuing a target firm is the present value of net cash flow over some horizon, where here cash flow is the free cash flow, net cash after all investments is required to maintain the business being acquired. This analysis considers only operating cash flow; cash flow from non-operating assets should be considered separately. Doing this calculation requires detailed estimates of future prospects for products and markets, cost structures, capital requirements, customers and competitors, and how they will respond to the acquisition as well as understanding of historical results.

The calculations involved in valuing an acquisition are illustrated with the example shown in Table 9.2. These calculations are for the value of the combined entity and thus contain certain synergies generated by the acquisition. They are also based on several assumptions regarding the performance of the combined firm, as detailed below. Value is assumed to be given by the net present value of the entity over a defined time horizon plus the residual value of the entity after this time period.

The following has also been assumed:

- In the base year of 2010, the combined revenue of the two firms would have been €10,000 and the net margin, defined as the ratio of earnings before interest, tax depreciation and amortization, would have been 20 per cent.

- Due to post-acquisition difficulties with the sales force and distributors, sales growth is assumed to be zero in year 1, then increase to 15 per cent in years 2 and 3 as the benefits from the acquisition are felt, before falling away to zero as the firm reaches steady state. Similarly, the initial margin of 20 per cent is assumed to reduce to 10 per cent in year 1, reflecting restructuring costs, before increasing to 25 per cent in year 3 as cost economies are achieved, and then reducing to the historical level of 20 per cent.

- It has also been assumed that the ratio of D/D+E is maintained at 50 per cent and that new debt is issued by the combined firm to achieve an unchanged financial structure. The corporate tax rate is assumed to be 40 per cent, while the WACC is constant at 7 per cent.

Given these assumptions and the use of the following formulas, the free cash flow of the combined firm can be calculated, over the five-year horizon, and discounted back to the present. To this is added the terminal value of the combined firm.

EBITDA = revenue * margin

Where EBITDA = earnings before interest, tax, depreciation and amortization.

Earning before tax = EBITDA – interest – depreciation

Net income = EBT (1.0 – tax rate)

Operating cash flow = NI + interest (1.0 – tax rate) + depreciation

Free cash flow = operating cash flow – increase in fixed and working capital

Terminal value = free cash flow at maturity/WACC

Table 9.2 Calculation of the value of a combined firm

Year	2010 Base	2011 1	2012 2	2013 3	2014 4	2015 5	2016 Terminal
Revenue (€)	10,000	10,000	11,500	13,225	14,548	15,275	15,275
EBITDA (€)	2,000	1,000	1,725	3,306	3,637	3,055	3,055
Capital (€)	5,000	5,300	5,670	6,103	6,693	7,423	8,081
Depreciation ($)	500	530	567	610	669	742	808
Debt (€)	2,500	2,650	2,835	3,052	3,346	3,712	4,041
Interest (€)	175	186	198	214	234	260	283
EBT (€)	1,325	285	960	2482	2733	2,052	1,964
Net income (€)	795	171	576	1,489	1,640	1,232	1,178
oper. cash flow (€)	1,400	812	1,262	2,228	2,450	2,130	2,156
Free cash flow (€)	600	−138	62	778	750	430	986
Discount factor	1.0	0.93	0.87	0.82	0.76	0.71	0.67
PV of cash (€)	600	−129	54	635	572	306	14,089

As can be seen from Table 9.2, the sum of the discounted free cash flows of the combined firm for the first five years is €1,438. If we add to this the terminal value of the business (€14,089), we get a total value of the combined firm of €15,527.

To provide estimates of the maximum and minimum price for the acquisition, as expressed in the above formulas, we then need to calculate the stand-alone values of each business.

The calculations above are not easy to undertake in practice, since they require estimates of an uncertain future. Buyers may be too optimistic about revenues, profits and cash flows, or expected cost savings may never eventuate. Competitive reaction may be misjudged and so on. As a consequence, prudent buyers will use sensitivity analysis to look at alternative scenarios. A range of estimates of the impact of changes in firm growth, margins, expenses, capital expenditures and discount rates can then be examined. The Daimler Chrysler example illustrates the difficulty in developing the precise value of an acquisition candidate.

Other methods of evaluation

The net book value (NBV) of the target's assets may be a consideration but is usually unhelpful. NBV is what was paid for assets after deductions for depreciation, and is unlikely to reflect current value. NBV also ignores the value of intangible assets such as intellectual capital.

A more market-based method would be to offer a sum calculated by:

Price = P/E (for this type of firm) * E (of the target firm)

Merger *in practice* – Daimler Chrysler

In 1998, Germany's Daimler Benz paid $US36 billion to take over the Chrysler Corporation. At the time of the merger, the German company had a stock market value of $US47 billion. By 2003 the stock market value of the combined firms had dropped to $US38 billion, and Deutsche Bank, which had helped to finance the deal, was reported to have lost $US15 billion. In 2007, Daimler Chrysler announced that it would sell 80 per cent of Chrysler to the private equity firm Cerberus Capital Management for $US7.4 billion. However, the German car maker, now known as Daimler, will not get most of the money that Cerberus is paying. Instead Cerberus will contribute $5 billion to the Chrysler auto operations it controls, with just a bit more than another $1 billion going to Chrysler's finance arm.

While Daimler will receive the remaining $1.4 billion of Cerberus's capital contribution to the sale, Daimler expects to have to cover another $1.6 billion in Chrysler losses before the deal closes. In total, Daimler estimates that it will end up paying out about $650 million to close the deal and that its earnings for 2007 will take a $4 billion to $5.4 billion profit hit because of charges related to the transaction. This disastrous venture was engineered by former Daimler Benz CEO Jurgen Schremp, who eventually lost his job over the merger. Experts agree that an enormous culture clash was one of the main reasons behind the failure of the grandiose plan to create one of the world's largest car companies (Andrews & Holson, 1998; Markowitz, 2003; Isidore, 2007).

However, it is by no means clear that the P/E ratio chosen will be relevant to any specific firm. Further, not only are the earnings for just one year used, with no adjustment for risk (although this arguably may be reflected in P/E ratio used) but, as we have seen in recent years, accounting earnings are subject to considerable manipulation. Nonetheless, despite its weaknesses, a P/E value calculation is often used as a quick cross-check. These and other methods of valuing acquisition candidates are described in more specialized texts (Gaughan, 2002).

Post-merger integration

The acquiring firm needs to consider integration early in the process. What structure and reporting relationships will be adopted? How will the different firm cultures be integrated? How will the new arrangements be communicated to employees? What cross-business teams will be formed to work on business problems to assist in integration (Ashkenas *et al.*, 1998)?

Experience in mergers and acquisitions helps to facilitate post-merger integration, yet many managers have limited experience of this process. Integration of an acquisition represents a huge change process, and there are many elements to consider, such as the following:

- *Redundancy* – Will managers of the acquired firm be retained?

- *Job transfers* – Will managers of the acquiring firm be transferred?

- *Restructure* – Should the organizational structure be altered?

- *Divestment* – Should parts of the acquired firm be divested?

- *Cultural integration* – How will this be accomplished?

- *Process integration* – For example, how will the two accounting systems be integrated?

Chapter 11

Post-acquisition, there must be integration of what we refer to in Chapter 11 as organizational architecture as well as differing corporate cultures (▶Chapter 11). Cultures involve a set of shared attitudes, values, beliefs and customs – a set of basic assumptions (usually largely implicit) – that affect behaviour. 'The way things get done here' influences how managers behave, as well as structure, systems, process and style; that is, how the firm conducts business.

Acquiring management is often overconfident about the speed and ease with which it can achieve integration. Most firms find this an extremely difficult task, and it is the source of many failures. Although a compelling vision, fast transition and effective planning assist integration – woe betide the acquiring management that assumes these problems away. Burgelman and McKinney advocate a carefully planned and staged approach, similar to the approach described in Figure 9.10 (Burgelman & McKinney, 2006). The need for such an approach is illustrated by the merger of HP and Compaq, which they describe in detail. Management experienced difficulty realizing the long-term performance goals of the merged company.

Challenge of strategic management

Several examples of failure when firms engage in merger and acquisition activities have been described above. Some business analysts have suggested that growth is important if the firm is to sustain its performance, and indeed to survive (Viguerie *et al.*, 2008). Some of this growth will be organic – growth with the existing businesses in the portfolio. Most firms, however, maintain their growth through mergers and acquisitions, and they remain a popular means of growth with senior business executives. Other analysts suggest that many mergers and acquisitions are done for reasons unrelated to business strategy, including managerial hubris and a quest for size for its own sake (Devine, 2002). In pursuit of bigness, CEOs are willing to pay huge premiums and ignore post-merger implementation concerns, resulting in destruction of value for the shareholders of the acquiring firm.

So there seem to be two conflicting views on the major motive for M&A:

1 That it is done for the aggrandizement of senior executives.

2 That it is done as a means for achieving growth and continued success of the firm.

Discuss the relative merits of each view.

9.6 MANAGING THE DYNAMIC SCOPE – HYBRID APPROACHES

Today there are many other alternatives to merger and acquisition as a method for altering the scope of a firm. These include strategic alliances, leveraged buyouts, joint ventures, licensing, technology purchase and equity investment – alternatives that are not mutually exclusive but are part of a range of approaches that companies use to establish new businesses. Whereas some firms use several of these methods, others focus mainly on one or more implementation modes. We define various options, and then explore their advantages and disadvantages.

Strategic alliances

Sometimes a firm may be dissuaded from pursuing an internal development or an acquisition because its managers conclude that they do not have the capabilities necessary to pursue the alternative. One way to secure these resources is via a **strategic alliance**, a partnership in which two firms combine capabilities to pursue mutual business interests; where the partnership can be equity or non-equity based (this latter is contractual). In general, the selection process for a strategic alliance partner involves matching strengths and weaknesses to provide the combined entity with a competitive advantage in the new business area. Partners should complement each other's strengths (or compensate for liabilities), not merely duplicate resources or capabilities.

> **Strategic alliance**
> A partnership in which two or more firms combine their resources and capabilities to pursue a mutual business opportunity. It may or may not result in the formation of a new business entity.

Usually, however, alliances, unlike mergers, do not lead to cost reductions but instead offer revenue gains. Prototypical strategic alliances are between small, innovative firms with new technology and large firms with strong marketing capability, good reputations with customers and financial resources. In some fields, the anticipated investment in potential new technology is so large and the risks so great, that cooperation may be the only feasible way to pursue an opportunity. Strategic alliances also offer a way to dip your toe in the water with low risk, a valuable strategy in times of rapidly developing technology. They complement an outsourcing strategy, since if we retreat to our core business, we need many partners to

---

Alliances *in practice* – NISSAN RENAULT

Carlos Ghosn has been very successful at Nissan since Renault took a 36.8 per cent stake. Losses of ¥684 billion (or $US6.1 billion) for the year ended March 2000 were turned into a profit of ¥766.4 billion in 2007, with operating profit margins of 7.3 per cent. Ghosn had closed factories, formed cross-functional teams to break down barriers and get creativity, and encouraged employees to take responsibility for outcomes, a major culture change for Nissan. Ghosn became CEO of Renault in 2005 while remaining CEO of Nissan as well. In common with car makers worldwide, Nissan had a difficult year in 2008, but returned to profit in 2009 (Nissan, 2010).

fill non-core roles. They may also provide a way to extend geographically by forming an alliance with a local partner. Sometimes they can both complement resources and support geographic extension.

Further, alliances have become much easier to run. Information technology, most notably the Internet, supports collaboration between companies at all levels, across time zones and geographies. Individuals can work remotely on joint teams and store information on common websites. Nonetheless, alliances still need trust, a clear set of goals and good leadership.

In an increasingly turbulent environment, where knowledge of both specialized technologies and markets is essential for success, firms of widely different sizes and backgrounds should consider strategic alliances as one alternative method of implementing a growth strategy. However, although strategic alliances provide an attractive means of securing access to resources and reducing both risk and required investment, they are no panacea for firms implementing growth strategies. Many strategic alliances fail for reasons ranging from incompatible **organizational cultures** to a shift in focus by one of the partners, leading to a lessened interest in the strategic alliance (Berquist, 1995). A specific form of alliance is a joint venture in which two or more firms combine parts of their assets to form a jointly owned independent entity.

Licensing and technology purchase

Licensing and technology purchase are alternative methods of securing access to technology developed by other organizations. They differ both in terms of payment and in the extent of rights to use the technology. Typically, a licensing agreement specifies both a minimum royalty payment (fixed payment regardless of degree of use) and an earned royalty rate based on some measure of volume – for example, units, dollars or profits. The UK company ARM **Chapter 5** Holdings, discussed in Chapter 5 (▶Chapter 5), is an excellent example of this model. Technology purchases are typically arranged for a fixed sum. In both types of agreement, the firm secures access to the technology, but licensing agreements may constrain use by the buyer. For example, the licenser may restrict the licensee to certain markets, thus prohibiting access to other markets.

The main advantage of these two methods is that the acquiring firm avoids the risks and expense of the R&D effort that developed the technology. The disadvantage is that it may have to pay a high price for a successful technology. Firms adopting these practices need rigorous search processes to identify technologies that justify commercialization.

Equity investment

Many major corporations have augmented their own R&D efforts by corporate venturing, taking ownership positions in start-up companies. Here again, the firm avoids direct R&D costs but has an equity position that it may be able to increase if the start-up is successful. Successful ventures are generally those that have a strong strategic rationale where, for example, the technologies being investigated relate to the firm's own technology portfolio.

Consortia

In the 1970s and early 1980s, when American and European firms were struggling to come to terms with Japanese incursions into the electronics industry, Japanese consortia-based R&D efforts were viewed as key to their success. In retrospect, other factors – such as emphasis on quality, customer focus and efficient design and manufacture – were probably more important. Nonetheless, US electronics firms successfully lobbied for limited anti-trust exemption to permit R&D consortia, and the then-novel consortia became more common, especially in aerospace and defence.

In Europe, such consortia were also accepted. Because of the huge cost of developing new commercial and military aircraft, collaboration among erstwhile competitors has become commonplace in the European aircraft industry. Further, firms are now collaborating internationally, especially when an innovation involves setting an industry standard. Interestingly, the problems involved in standard-setting provide excellent insight into the difficulties posed by consortia, since the seemingly interminable squabbling among participants often considerably delays the launch of an innovation. The arguments over DVD standards, both regular and high-definition, were protracted, as were those involving digital television, while – to the general detriment of consumers – in some cases no global standard was established. To state the problem simply, if you think it is difficult working in an alliance with one other firm, consider the potential problems in a consortium of many! Yet, despite these difficulties, some consortia succeed. Though controversial in American eyes, Airbus Industries, now separately constituted as a business, has provided a series of competitive aircraft that none of the cooperating companies could have produced on their own.

Another form of consortia, discussed in Chapter 3 (►Chapter 3), is the use of networks, where firms enter into collaborative arrangements with a number of other firms, including customers and possibly competitors, partly to supplement their limited capabilities and partly as a response to the high cost of new developments.

Chapter 3

Option buying

You may find it interesting to speculate on why, after decades of predominantly internally generated growth, the latter part of the twentieth century witnessed such a proliferation of venture alternatives and a much broader perspective on admissible approaches within large companies. In our view, this is primarily due to much higher levels of uncertainty and risk. The structure of demand for innovative products has become more volatile. The much-heralded WAP phones collapsed, while 3G adoption and profitability has disappointed. Many telecoms stocks are being hurt by erosion of landline revenues as the switch to mobiles progresses. Important technological flops of the more recent past include CD-I (CD-interactive), DCC (digital compact cassette), DAT (digital audio tape), videophones, and many others. A second factor is the huge amounts of money required to deploy some of these technologies, as companies are understandably reluctant to put the company as a whole at risk to establish a new business.

One response to this change has been a very different philosophy with respect to the development of new business opportunities. The plethora of approaches now considered may be viewed as a way of buying options. If a given venture is risky and expensive, then perhaps we should be participating in a number of them, sharing the risk with others faced with a similar predicament, but thereby obtaining options to subsequently launch the successful few out of a portfolio of these risky and expensive ventures. The philosophy now needed is much closer to that of the venture capitalist, a factor that has had a major impact on the way large firms have approached the new business problem.

9.7 MANAGING THE DYNAMIC SCOPE – DIVESTMENTS, SPIN-OFFS AND RESTRUCTURING

LEARNING OBJECTIVE 5

Evaluate the use of spin-offs and restructuring as means for managing the dynamic scope of the firm.

As we saw earlier, firms actively manage their business portfolio, both acquiring and divesting businesses to reflect changing circumstances. Sometimes these changes (particularly divestments) are forced on the firm by financial markets. In other cases, the firm takes the lead in altering its portfolio, usually reducing diversity and refocusing on a core business. Nonetheless, Viguerie *et al.* (2008) find that, at least for US firms, divestment is underutilized.

Several Japanese electronics conglomerates are actively downsizing and simplifying their businesses. Once committed to doing everything from making the chips to designing, building and marketing the computers, mobile phones and so on that use them, firms are combining operations and closing others. Among the latest casualties are Sony, NEC and Panasonic, all of which are significantly reducing operations, while reporting losses along with chip maker Toshiba (Masters, 2009).

Divestment
The firm sells, or removes, one or more organizational units to another party.

Divestments and spin-offs

A **divestment** occurs when a firm sells part of its ongoing business to another party, as the example below illustrates. Alternatively, the firm may offer an **equity carve-out**, whereby it offers a minority position in a subsidiary through an initial public offering (IPO) (▶Chapter 4). When such an IPO is done, assets are transferred to the new firm, which has its own board, shareholders and management. Depending on the number of shares offered, the original firm may or may not be a significant shareholder. One advantage for the parent firm is that it receives cash from the sale of its equity in the subsidiary, as occurred with the Aviva example below.

Chapter 4

In contrast, with an **equity spin-off**, the entire ownership of a subsidiary is divested as a dividend to existing shareholders. Again, assets are transferred to the new entity and the management of this new entity reports to its own board.

Equity carve-out
The firm offers a minority position to new shareholders, in a portion of the firm, through an initial public offering.

Equity spin-off
The entire ownership of a subsidiary is divested as a dividend to existing shareholders.

> ### Divestment *in practice* – ORASCOM
>
> Orascom Construction Industries, an Egyptian conglomerate, sold its cement business to France's Lafarge for €8.8 billion to concentrate on its faster-growing other businesses (*The Economist,* 2008).

> ### Equity carve-out *in practice* – AVIVA
>
> UK financial services firm Aviva (formerly known as Norwich Union) was reported as realizing total cash proceeds of €1.12 billion from the float of Delta Lloyd. Aviva intended to retain the monies to provide it with greater financial flexibility, including possibly strengthening its balance sheet by reducing debt. Aviva will also retain approximately 57.2 per cent of the ordinary share capital and 53.0 per cent of the voting rights in Delta Lloyd. As the majority shareholder, Aviva will continue to consolidate Delta Lloyd in its financial statements (Financial-Express, 2009).

A spin-off might be considered when the original firm no longer seems a natural parent for the division or subsidiary that is being separated, or even when there is a conflict or friction between the subsidiary's management and the head office (Dranikoff *et al.*, 2002). The change is often accompanied by better financial performance of the spin-off as it escapes corporate shackles (Anslinger *et al.*, 1999).

A **leveraged buyout** is the purchase of shareholders' equity, heavily financed with debt, by a group that frequently includes incumbent management.

Although firms appear to spend more time on acquisitions than on divestments, as we saw in Table 9.1, successful firms are generally engaged in both. Holding onto a business for too long can have costs for the firm. It can encourage comfort and stagnation, stifle innovation and creativity, and thereby make it difficult to attract entrepreneurial talent. Troubled businesses can also absorb more corporate resources than they merit, in both dollars and time, detracting efforts from attractive opportunities (Decker & Mellewigt, 2007). However, acquisition is often seen as more 'glamorous' than divestment, and as a result, exiting businesses have not received the same amount of attention, suggesting the need for an organized and systematic process, as depicted in Figure 9.12.

Leveraged buyout
The acquisition of a company which is funded by high levels of borrowings. In some cases, the assets of the target company are used as collateral for the loans

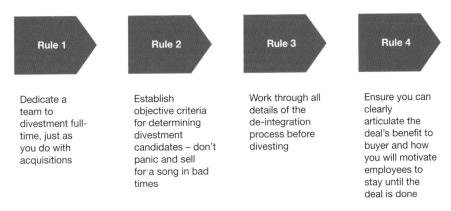

Rule 1 — Dedicate a team to divestment full-time, just as you do with acquisitions

Rule 2 — Establish objective criteria for determining divestment candidates – don't panic and sell for a song in bad times

Rule 3 — Work through all details of the de-integration process before divesting

Rule 4 — Ensure you can clearly articulate the deal's benefit to buyer and how you will motivate employees to stay until the deal is done

Figure 9.12 The smart way to divest
Source: Adapted with permission from Mankins *et al.*, 2008

Organizational restructure

Organizational redesign usually associated with a reduction in the number of employees.

Chapter 11

Restructuring

As we have seen, corporate management involves the active management of the business portfolio, including acquisitions, divestments, spin-offs and so on. Some of these are done to raise capital for the firm; with others, such as spin-offs, the firm does not receive any new cash. We have also discussed financial restructuring, whereby the financial structure of the firm is altered through a debt-for-equity swap or a leveraged buyout.

There is another form of restructuring, which we refer to as **organizational restructure**. This involves organizational redesign and downsizing. Organizational redesign will be discussed in more detail in Chapter 11 (▶Chapter 11); here we address some of the issues with downsizing. We consider downsizing to be a pro-active reduction in the number of employees. Downsizing may reduce labour costs at the expense of loss of human capital.

Many firms downsized during the GFC of 2008/09, with millions of layoffs worldwide. In challenging times, firms may see no other option for reducing costs. Layoffs are essentially short term in their financial impact but may be much more negative in the longer term. Short-term cost reduction may result in low morale, loss of high-calibre staff and atrophy of valuable intellectual assets. Indeed, some research indicates that downsizing does not help firm performance as measured by return on assets (Cascio, 2002). Certainly, downsizing will not fix a flawed strategy!

In a dynamic and changing world, the only path to continued success and wealth creation for a firm is innovation, continued renewal of the firm in all its aspects. Innovation is by its very nature risky, but so, too, is inaction where the firm is likely to become less and less competitive.

 9.8 SUMMARY

Innovation is not easy, requiring creativity, risk-taking and leadership as well as financial and managerial resources. Innovation may occur in any aspect of the firm: its scope of operations, its organizational arrangements, or the structure of the industry in which it competes. While all firms have to react to external changes, real success comes when the firm is proactive in terms of innovation.

Key decisions in corporate-level strategy involve managing the dynamic scope of the firm – which new businesses it will develop and the means adopted to develop these. At the same time, decisions must be made on which businesses to exit, and how.

Two main means for increasing the scope of the firm are internal development and mergers and acquisitions, and most global firms pursue both simultaneously. These two alternatives differ in terms of speed, resources and capabilities required as well as the likelihood of success.

Firms pursuing internal development need to understand the importance of techno-logical innovation, the need for R&D to be coupled with an understanding of customer needs. Senior managers must have a good understanding of those technologies critical for the firm, how they can be developed and commercialized, and whether firm capabilities need to be complemented by partners.

Mergers and acquisitions are an integral component of corporate strategy for most global firms, as is demonstrated by the rapid increase in the number of these over time. Such mergers may be undertaken to achieve growth, to acquire capabilities and to diversify. However, many mergers and acquisitions fail to deliver value to the acquiring firm due to the high premium that must be paid and the difficulties in post-acquisition integration. Many mergers are justified, at least in part, on the idea of synergy, which again is not always easy to capture. Mergers and acquisitions are major resource decisions of the firm, and it is recommended that formal means of evaluation, such as net present value, be adopted.

Finally, while firms are actively involved in expanding their scope, strategic managers also need to consider various options, such as divestments and spin-offs, as means of reducing their scope.

VIEW FROM THE TOP

DIAGEO PLC

'Creating a world class business through a merger of two equals – an interview with Paul Walsh, CEO of Diageo Plc' conducted by the *Journal of Strategy and Management (JSM)*.

Diageo is the world's leading premium spirits company, managing eight of the world's top 20 spirits brands, and was formed in 1997 from the merger of Guinness plc and Grand Metropolitan plc.

Some strategic decisions following the merger of Guinness and Grand Met were:

2000 – acquired Seagram (jointly with Pernod Ricard, a major competitor)

2001 – sold Pillsbury

2002 – sold Burger King

2006 – acquired 43 per cent stake in Sichuan Chengdu Quanxing Group, which was increased to 46 per cent

2006 – acquired Smirnoff brands in Russia in two stages, now owns it 100 per cent.

Diageo considers the following as its distinctive capabilities and sources of competitive advantages:

- In-depth customer and consumer understanding
- Highly effective routes to market
- World-class marketing capability

- Outstanding collections of brands
- Focused execution
- Its ability to develop leaders today, for tomorrow
- They are all intangible, therefore difficult to imitate and rare.

JSM: Mergers have a poor track record and you have been intimately involved in a number of successful mergers. What were the three or four primary reasons for the successful merger between Guinness plc and Grand Metropolitan? What were the key three or four challenges?

PW: The merger between Guinness and Grand Metropolitan was indeed very successful. For a successful merger, clear industrial logic leading to a compelling business case is the first step. There has to be tangible results – both organizational and financial. The key then is to get both organizations to align behind the vision of the new company. They should be excited to be part of the new vision and want to be part of the journey. Of course when two organizations come together there will be a lot of people who are displaced. You then have to have a very clear meritocracy to deal with people. Then we acquired Seagram and applied a lot of our learning from the Grand Met Guinness merger to the new company.

Interestingly if you look at my executive team now, a third is new to the company, a third came from Grand Met and a third came from Guinness. It hasn't been planned that way but one of the things that I observed was that very quickly having bought into this vision of what we wanted to do with this new entity, one's heritage quickly fell away and people hooked their wagons to the star of Diageo and quickly forgot which part of the organization they'd come from.

JSM: Sounds simple but that is a very difficult task. Can you please elaborate?

PW: There was a compelling vision that was very well articulated internally. The merger brought together two businesses that between them would have ten of the top 20 spirit brands in the world and underpinned by a robust and diverse geographic split and a market share that would be able to drive scale benefits. Without the substance of industrial logic, it is harder to articulate a clear message for the organization and if the message is not clear, it's even harder to build that alignment and encourage people to be part of that journey. Diageo was a new fresh company – both Guinness and Grand Met were a bit stodgy, had a bit of baggage, with brands that were a bit dusty. Diageo was the creation of something new – vibrant, brand oriented, young and dynamic. Diageo is a very diverse company with people from all over the world. We've worked as an executive team on creating a journey and a vision that was compelling – that was exciting – that was something different from the past. You can't do that if you've got flaky industrial logic to start with.

JSM: Did you have an equal number of people from both companies in positions of responsibility?

PW: No, management has to be meritocracy-based. Whenever you're operating with change, you will have a variety of work streams. All of which have levels of interaction that needs to be managed. I believe in having somebody in charge of the integration process. Now this is separate from the strategy. There may be some elements when bringing the two businesses together that are operational – for example, what should we do in market x where both companies had distributors as they were both sub-scale – do we now have enough scale to go on our own? So these are subcomponents of strategy but overall the integration is an operational exercise. When we acquired Seagram I had a person reporting directly to me, charged with the integration process.

I think once you've endorsed an acquisition certainly of the size that we're talking about you know, you have usually promised substantial benefits to your shareholders and it is vital that these benefits are delivered. Seagram acquisitions played a vital role in the rise of Diageo. It was a complex cross-border deal involving Pernod Ricard, a major competitor; therefore, it had to have a strong industrial logic and be planned carefully.

JSM: Your strategy is based on organic and focused acquisitive growth. How do you rate your organic growth prospect when your brands have significant market share in many mature markets?

PW: The best source of value creation for shareholders is to grow the brands we already own. And I believe that unless you can grow a brand, you probably shouldn't buy it. I understand the cost synergies of mergers but cost synergies have a limited life. So once they've run out, what are you going to do? If you can't grow the brand, you extract the cost savings and then it will become a drain on the broader corporation so I believe passionately in organic growth for the reasons I've just articulated. Therefore, our primary goal, given that we've got almost 30 per cent market share of the spirits market, is to grow the brands that we already own. That then enables you to go forward and acquire other brands with the full support of your shareholders because they know that you'll develop and grow and nurture them. So our size mandates that we grow what we have and if other interesting opportunities present themselves then we can move with alacrity.

You have to look at the capacity of a market to offer you growth. I believe that in every market there will be pockets of growth. We've got to find them and we've got to work them very hard. However, in the macro-environment for us, a lot of the action is in emerging markets.

JSM: You have been involved in a number of acquisitions in the past four years. Interestingly in many of these you initially took equity stake rather than outright acquisition. What is the thinking behind your approach?

PW: We are pragmatic, our preference is usually to own them 100 per cent but sometimes this is not possible either through regulatory issues or family ownership. For example, Ketel One where the family just didn't want to sell 100 per cent. We have got certain rights if ever they want to exit and it's a great brand and I'd prefer to have 50 per cent than nothing.

JSM: You have succeeded in your acquisitions when research suggests that most acquisitions fail to deliver shareholder value – what are the ingredients of that proven formula?

PW: I think it is a combination of industrial logic such as brand-fit where the acquired brand might give us entry into a distinctive category or a distinct market such as in China with the Bijoux product. Apart from the strategic fit we carefully consider two critical questions. Is it a brand of the future? Is it capable of growth?

After that we apply very, very stringent financial criteria to it and come up with plans to support that. It's a very inclusive process; for example, if you were running the company in China, you would have been involved in the Bijoux acquisition from the identification, to the due diligence and you will have signed up to certain objectives. We will follow against those objectives very, very clearly.

TAKEOVER OF ABN AMRO

On 19 March 2007 Barclays Bank announced that it was in discussion with ABN Amro, the Dutch banking and investment firm, about a proposed takeover. Some ABN Amro shareholders considered that the bank had underperformed and they were interested in extracting more value through a merger or takeover by another bank. On 12 April, a rival expression of interest was announced by a consortium, led by the Royal Bank of Scotland (RBS). The consortium comprised RBS, based in the UK, Fortis, the Belgian–Dutch bank, and Banco Santander, based in Spain.

The proposed merger with Barclays seemed as if it would go ahead, although there was one condition, that prior to the takeover ABN would sell one of its units, its Chicago-based LaSalle Bank to the Bank of America. This decision was tested in the Dutch courts as to whether such a divestment required shareholder approval – eventually, on 13 July the Dutch High Court ruled that such shareholder approval was not required. During August 2007, all of the bidding firms received shareholder approval for management to go ahead with acquisitions, and in September ABN senior management engaged in discussions with the consortium.

The Barclays offer to take over ABN was based on a substantial equity or share component. Originally the offer was valued at about €67.5 billion or €32 per share – although the price was sensitive to Barclays share price, which had fallen. In contrast, the consortium's offer was mainly for cash – offering €71 billion (£49 billion) which valued ABN at about €38 per share. This meant that the consortium offer valued ABN at three times book value, which some analysts considered to be a high price for a bank based in a mature European country.

This bid by the three-bank consortium had several distinctive characteristics. First, it was for cash, which meant that the partners had to raise substantial amounts of cash – in a financial environment which was already showing signs of problems. Second, each firm in the consortium got parts of ABN. So the RBS was to take over ABN's US and European businesses (excluding Italy) and its Asian operations, but had lost out on LaSalle, considered to be one of ABN's most prized businesses; Santander was to get the retail banking businesses in Italy and Latin America, including Brazil; while Fortis was to get the Dutch retail network, the asset-management and private banking businesses. While this sounds easy, in reality splitting a firm such as ABN would not be easy on customers, employees and IT systems.

The driving force behind this planned acquisition was Sir Fred Goodwin, CEO of the RBS. He had been CEO for several years, acquiring a reputation as an aggressive banker. For example, in 2000 the RBS had acquired Natwest, another UK bank three times the size of the RBS, in a hostile takeover valued at £21 billion. This resulted in RBS becoming the second-largest UK bank. In justifying the acquisition of

MINI-CASE

ABN Amro, the CEO stated that they had not overpaid and that RBS expected to achieve cost synergies of €1.2 billion and revenue synergies of €480 million within three years, which some analysts saw as challenging (Seib, 2007). RBS had contributed £10 billion of the purchase price.

On 8 October 2007 the consortium announced that ABN's shareholders had accepted their bid, which was the world's largest banking takeover. Under the terms of the bid, the consortium took control on 19 October, and then had 60 days in which to draw up a transition plan, detailing how the business would be split up and where job losses were likely to occur. Once this transition plan was approved by Dutch regulators, the consortium would consult for three to six months with employees, regulators and customers on the details of the split-up, and on job losses. On the latter point, some 19,000 out of a total staff of 400,000 were expected to lose their jobs. Despite the turmoil in global financial markets, a likely result of which was a reduction in the earnings of the ABN Amro businesses, the consortium made no adjustments to its offer.

By late 2007, some problems were arising. In September, Lehman Brothers collapsed, signalling the difficulties which banks were facing. In October 2007, many banks were trading at around book value, making the initial price paid by RBS looking even more of a folly.

The share price of RBS fell from 720p in March 2007 to 460p in December 2007. By January 2008, the RBS share price was at an eight-year low. Despite these developments, on 28 February 2008 Sir Fred told analysts that he had no plans for any external capital raisings or anything of the sort (The Economist Online, 2008).

By April 2008, some US and European banks were starting to write down their investments in dodgy mortgage loans, but many UK banks seemed to be completely unaware of any impending crisis. By 18 April it was apparent that RBS would have to raise about £12 billion for core capital and on 23 April 2008 RBS shareholders agreed to a £12 billion rights issue to enable the bank to bolster its tier 1 capital. By October 2008, as the financial crisis continued, so did the problems for RBS, since many of the assets it had acquired from ABN were now considered 'toxic' and severely overvalued. The UK government announced a scheme whereby the government made available a sum of £50 billion for the banks to increase their tier 1 capital. The UK government also announced a facility of £200 billion to allow banks to swap illiquid mortgage-backed securities for treasury bills, and provided guarantees of new short-term and medium-term debt. As part of this arrangement, the UK government provided RBS with £20 billion of capital, which was in the form of ordinary shares, not (as originally planned) interest-bearing preference shares. These funds came with conditions, such as the bank was to pay no dividends and limit staff bonuses. Eventually the UK government would take a 58 per cent interest in RBS. Other banks were also helped in the same way. The UK government, in common with other governments around the world, was forced into this because credit markets were essentially frozen and banks were unable to raise funds. They had lost the trust of people and did not have enough capital as a cushion against losses.

The RBS-ABN Amro deal was also unusual in that it led to the fall of not just one buyer but two: RBS and Fortis (Robbins, 2009). By January 2008, RBS had destroyed £33 billion of shareholder value – the equivalent of five Marks and Spencers (Hosking, 2008).

When shareholders at RBS gave their approval to the rescue package by the UK government in November 2008, Sir Fred Goodwin announced his resignation as of January 2009. At that time, the share price was about 65p, a huge fall from its value of 720p in March 2007. This retirement was followed by several others, including the chairman and most of the board. There was a major overhaul of senior executives with the finance director and the head of risk management leaving.

Fortis had similar troubles. It suffered a share price collapse of 71 per cent between 1 January 2008 and September 2008. Since Fortis was a major bank in Belgium, a so-called system bank, there were fears that if it collapsed then so would the Belgium financial system. By October 2008, the governments of Luxembourg, Belgium and the Netherlands provided funds of €11 billion to allow Fortis to survive. The Dutch government nationalized the Dutch parts of Fortis and the bits of ABN it had bought, while other parts of Fortis were sold by the Belgium government to BNP Paribas.

In contrast, Santander, which had put up 28 per cent of the offer, seemed to do well. It had picked up the Italian bank Banca Antonveneta and all of ABN Amro's Latin American, including Brazilian, business. The Italian business was sold in late 2007 for a capital gain of £2.4 billion. Like all banks, they were affected by the global financial crisis. Its shares, which are listed on the London Stock Exchange, hit a peak of £11 in May 2008, and then fell to £3.3 by March 2009. However, in contrast to the other two consortium members, the share price recovered to £10.8 by January 2010.

QUESTIONS

1 How important is timing in acquisitions?

2 Why, in your opinion, did RBS proceed with the acquisition, despite the fact that the US assets that initially interested them had already been sold?

3 Should RBS have adjusted its offer, given the turbulence in financial markets in late 2008?

4 If you had the chance to give two brief pieces of advice to a CEO contemplating an acquisition, what would they be?

REVIEW QUESTIONS

1 Do you agree that it is important for a firm to innovate? If so, why?

2 Are the three types of innovation (structural, organizational and scope) described in the chapter equally important? When would each be adopted, and what resources are required for each?

3 Discuss the relative merits of entering new markets by internal development versus a merger or acquisition.

4 For a firm with which you are familiar, obtain data on its changing scope over the last five years. Can you identify the strategy behind these changes?

5 Using the Internet, explore a current acquisition. Develop the strategic reasoning behind the acquisition, and discuss whether or not you think it will be successful.

6 How do firms create synergy through mergers? Do you think that this can ever be used to justify a merger?

7 Can a formal merger and acquisition process become a core capability for a firm? Discuss.

8 Why is net present value used to calculate the value of a merger? What difficulties are there with the use of this tool?

9 Are restructuring strategies likely to create wealth for shareholders? Discuss.

REFERENCES

Andrews, E. L. & Holson, L. M. (1998) Overview; Daimler-Benz will acquire Chrysler in $36 billion deal that will reshape industry. *The New York Times*, 7 May, p. 1. www.query.nytimes.com/search/query?frow=0&n=10&srcht=a&query=Daimler-Benz&srchst=nyt&submit.x=23&submit.y=7&submit=sub&hdlquery=&bylquery=&daterange=period&mon1=05&day1=01&year1=1998&mon2=05&day2=20&year2=1998.

Anslinger, P. L., Klepper, S. J. & Subramaniam, S. (1999) Breaking up is good to do. *McKinsey Quarterly*, (1), 16–27.

Anthony, S. D., Johnson, M. W. & Sinfield, J. V. (2008) Institutionalizing innovation. *MIT Sloan Management Review, 49*(2), 45–53.

Ashkenas, R. N., DeMonaco, L. J. & Francis, S. C. (1998) Making the deal real: How GE Capital integrates acquisitions. *Harvard Business Review*, (January–February), 165–178.

Baghai, M., Coley, S. & White, D. (1999) *The Alchemy of Growth*. London: Orion.

Baghai, M., Coley, S. C., White, D., Conn, C. & McLean, R. J. (1996) Staircases to growth. *McKinsey Quarterly*, (4), 38–61.

Basch, M. (2010) BAE taking $920M write-off for Armor Holdings purchase. *Business-Jacksonville.com*, 16 February. http://jacksonville.com/business/2010–02–15/story/bae_taking_920m_write_off_for_armor_holdings_purchase.

BASF (2009) Innovation award. www.basf.com/group/corporate/en/innovations/innovation-award/index.

Bennison, R. (2009) KPMG Annual Report: COO review: Innovation and knowledge. http://annualreport.kpmg.eu/overview/coo-review.html.

Berquist, W. H. (1995) *Building Strategic Relationships: How to Extend Your Organisation's Reach Through Partnerships, Alliances and Joint Ventures*. San Francisco, CA: Jossey-Bass.

Burgelman, R. A. & McKinney, W. (2006) Managing the strategic dynamics of acquisition integration: Lessons from HP and Compaq. *California Management Review, 48*(3), 6–27.

BusinessWeek (2009) VW takeover close as Porsche CEO resigns. BusinessWeek, 23 July. www.businessweek.com/globalbiz/content/jul2009/gb20090723_699694.htm.

Capon, N., Farley, J. U. & Hoenig, S. (1996) *Toward an Integrative Explanation of Corporate Financial Performance*. Boston, MA: Kluwer Academic Publishers.

Capon, N., Farley, J. U., Lehmann, D. R. & Hulbert, J. M. (1992) Profiles of product innovators among large U.S. manufacturers. *Management Science, 30*(2), 157–166.

Cascio, W. F. (2002) Strategies for responsible restructuring. *Academy of Management Executive, 16*(3), 80–91.

Christensen, C. M. (1997) *The Innovator's Dilemma*. Boston, MA: Harvard Business School Press.

Cohan, P. S. (1997) *The Technology Leaders*. San Francisco, CA: Jossey-Bass.

Comes, S. & Berniker, L. (2008) Business model innovation. In D. Pantaleo & N. Pal (eds), *From Strategy to Execution* (pp. 65–86). Berlin: Springer-Verlag.

Day, G. S. (2007) Is it real? Can we win? Is it worth doing? *Harvard Business Review*, (December), 110–120.

Decker, C. & Mellewigt, T. (2007) Thirty years after Michael E. Porter: What do we know about business exit. *Academy of Management Perspectives, 21*(2), 41–55.

Devine, M. (2002) *Successful Mergers*. London: Profile Books.

Dobbs, R., Huyett, B. & Koller, T. (2010) The CEO's guide to corporate finance. *McKinsey Quarterly*, (November).

Dodgson, M. (2000) *The Management of Technological Innovation*. Oxford: Oxford University Press.

Dranikoff, L., Koller, T. & Schneider, A. (2002) Divestiture: Strategy's missing link. *Harvard Business Review*, (May), 74–83.

Eccles, R. G., Lanes, K. L. & Wilson, T. C. (1999) Are you paying too much for that acquisition? *Harvard Business Review*, (July–August), 136–146.

Financial-Express (2009) Delta Lloyd IPO priced at Euro16 per share. *Investigate*, 3 November. www.investigate.co.uk/Article.aspx?id=2009110307001283118.

FlexNews (2008) Nestlé acquisition of Kraft Foods Balaton gets approved. FlexNews, 20 June www.flex-news-food.com/console/PageViewer.aspx?page=17298&str=balaton.

Foster, R. N. (1986) *Innovation: The Attacker's Advantage*. New York: Summit.

Foster, R. N. & Kaplan, S. (2001) *Creative Destruction*. New York: Doubleday.

Gaughan, P. A. (2002) *Mergers, Acquisitions, and Corporate Restructurings*, 3rd edn. New York: Wiley.

Gaur, A. S. & Kumar, V. (2009) International diversification, business group affiliation and firm performance: Empirical evidence from India. *British Journal of Management, 20*(2), 172–186.

Hagel, J. L. & Singer, M. (2000) Unbundling the corporation. *McKinsey Quarterly*, (3), 148–161.

Hamel, G. & Prahalad, C. K. (1994) Competing for the future. *Harvard Business Review*, (July–August), 122–128.

Hayward, M. & Hambrick, D. (1997) Explaining the premiums paid for large acquisitions: Evidence of CEO hubris. *Administrative Science Quarterly, 42*, 103–127.

Holmes, S. (1997) Lessons learned – Its airline customers teach Boeing a thing or two about building planes. *The Seattle Times*, 16 November. http://community.seattletimes.nwsource.com/archive/?date=19971116&slug=2572804.

Hosking, P. (2008) Its back to the future as confidence curdles at RBS. *The Times*, 17 January, p. 45.

Isidore, C. (2007) Daimler pays to dump Chrysler. *CNN Money*, 14 May. http://money.cnn.com/2007/05/14/news/companies/chrysler_sale/index.htm.

Jansen, J. J. P., George, G., Van den Bosch, F. A. J. & Volberda, H. W. (2008) Senior team attributes and organisational ambidexterity: The moderating role of transformational leadership. *Journal of Management Studies, 45*(5), 982–1007.

Johnson, M. W., Christensen, C. M. & Kagermann, H. (2008) Reinventing your business model. *Harvard Business Review*, (December), 51–59.

King, I. (2009) Unilever gels with brothers over $411.5 million TIGI deal, 27 January. http://business.timesonline.co.uk/tol/business/industry_sectors/consumer_goods/article5594403.ece.

Krishnan, H. A., Hitt, M. A. & Park, D. (2007) Acquisition premiums, subsequent workforce reductions and post-acquisition performance. *Journal of Management Studies, 44*(5), 709–732.

Kronimus, A., Roos, A. & Stelter, D. (2009) M&A: Ready for liftoff? December www.bcg.com/documents/file36677.pdf.

Kuczmarski, T. D. (1988) *Managing New Products: Competing through Excellence.* Englewood Cliffs, NJ: Prentice Hall.

Mankins, M. C., Harding, D. & Weddigen, R.-M. (2008) How the the best divest. *Harvard Business Review*, (October), 92–99.

Markides, C. C. (1998) Strategic innovation in established companies. *Sloan Management Review, 39*(3), 31–42.

Markowitz, J. (2003) Dailmer, Chrysler merger a failure. *TribLiveNews*, 2 October. www.pittsburghlive.com/x/pittsburghtrib/s_157848.html.

Marks, M. L. & Mirvis, P. H. (2001) Making mergers and acquisitions work: Strategic and psychological preparation. *Academy of Management Executive, 15*(2), 80–94.

Masters, C. (2009) Sony's woes: Japan's iconic brands strained. *Time World*, 2 February. www.time.com/time/world/article/0,8599,1876282,00.html.

Merrett, N. (2007) Nestle predicts calmer acquisition outlook. 22 August. www.dairyreporter.com/Industry-markets/Nestle-predicts-calmer-acquisition-outlook.

Mintzberg, H. & Quinn, J. B. (1996) *The Strategy Process*, 3rd edn. Upper Saddle River, NJ: Prentice Hall.

Nissan (2010) FY 2009 3rd quarter financial results. *Financial Results*, February. www.nissan-global.com/EN/IR/LIBRARY/FINANCIAL/2009/.

Peterson, R. (2000) *Creating Business Growth.* Paper presented at the Strategic Management Society, Vancouver.

Pisano, G. P. & Teece, D. J. (2007) How to capture value from innovation: Shaping intellectual property and industry architecture. *California Management Review, 50*(1), 278–296.

Pohle, G. & Chapman, M. (2006) IBM's global CEO report 2006: Business model innovation matters. *Strategy and Leadership, 34*(5), 34–40.

Riggers, M. (2010) Porsche sued for $1 billion over VW takeover. 28 January. www.pistonheads.com/porsche/default.asp?storyld=21431

Robbins, M. (2009) Was ABN the worst takeover deal ever? *The Independent*, 20 January.

SAP (2007) Annual Report. *Research and Development.* www.sap.com/corporate-de/investors/reports/gb2007/opportunities/research-and-development-3.html.

Seib, C. (2007) Mammoth task ahead for winner of the battle for ABN. *The Times*, 5 October, p. 55.

Siegel, P. A. & Hambrick, D. C. (2005) Pay disparities within top management groups: Evidence of harmful effects on performance of high-technology firms. *Organisation Science, 16*, 259–274.

Sirower, M. (1999) *The Synergy Trap: How Companies Lose the Acquisition Game.* New York: Free Press.

Speedy, B. (2010) Direct sourcing sends Kmart costs tumbling. *The Australian*, 16 September, p. 23.

Tellis, G. J., Prabhu, J. C. & Chandy, R. K. (2009) Radical innovation across nations: The preeminence of corporate culture. *Journal of Marketing, 73*(January), 3–23.

The Economist (2008) Breaking up is hard to do. *The Economist*, 12 July, 67–68.

The Economist (2009) Payback for Piech. *The Economist*, 16 May, 68–69.

The Economist Online (2008) Look Ma, no capital. *The Economist*, 24 April.

Tickle, R. (2010) Nestlé to acquire Krafts Foods' frozen pizza business. 5 January. www.nestle.com/MediaCenter/PressReleases/AllPressReleases/Kraft+pizzas.htm

Tushman, M. L. & O'Reilly, C. A. (1996) Ambidextrous organisations: Managing evolutionary and revolutionary change. *California Management Review, 38*(4), 8–30.

Unilever (2010) Acquisitions and disposals. www.unilever.com/investorrelations/understanding_unilever/acquisitionsanddisposals/index.aspx.

Viguerie, P., Smit, S. & Baghai, M. (2008) *The Granularity of Growth*. Hoboken, NJ: John Wiley & Sons.

Waters, R. (2001) Never forget to nurture the next big idea. *Financial Times*, 15 May, p. 19.

Weston, J. F., Chung, K. S. & Siu, J. A. (1998) *Takeovers, Restructuring, and Corporate Governance*, 2nd edn. Upper Saddle River, NJ: Prentice Hall.

Whitehouse, C. (2003) Corus, British-Dutch steel maker names a chief. *New York Times*, 24 April, W.1.

Zhou, K. Z. & Wu, F. (2010) Technological capability, strategic flexibility, and product innovation. *Strategic Management Journal, 31*(5), 547–561.

For a range of further resources supporting this chapter, please visit the companion website for *Strategic Management* at www.routledge.com/cw/fitzroy.

STRATEGY IMPLEMENTATION

CHAPTER 10

LEADING ORGANIZATIONAL CHANGE

LEARNING OBJECTIVES

Upon completing this chapter you should be able to:

1 Articulate why organizational change and renewal are central strategic management activities.

2 Explain the decisions to be made in designing a change programme.

3 Devise a process for change management.

4 Describe the nature and role of leadership in strategic management.

WHITBREAD

Founded as a brewery in 1742, the history of the Whitbread Company is a story of transformation and change. By the 1950s, most of the firm's revenue was from beer sold through hotels and pubs where the brewer owned the property, the publican owned the business and only sold beer brands supplied by the brewer.

The 1950s saw rapid expansion and industry consolidation in the UK beer industry and by 1971 Whitbread had taken over 26 regional British breweries. Complementing this strategy in beer, during the 1960s, Whitbread commenced a strategy of diversification. Initially this was into other forms of alcohol, as they acquired various spirits brands such as Beefeater gin and Cutty Sark scotch, building a wine and spirits division. Recognizing the shift from bitter to lager, in 1968 the company became a licensed brewer of Heineken lager, reaching a similar agreement to produce Stella Artois in 1976. This Belgian brew became the most popular premium lager in the UK.

In 1974 came the first major diversification out of the alcoholic beverage business. Whitbread entered the restaurant business, opening its first Beefeater restaurant. In 1979, they developed and launched Brewers Fayre, a chain of pub food outlets. During this period, the UK was in the depths of a serious economic recession, and the company was fortunate to avoid bankruptcy. As economic recovery occurred, the firm's position strengthened. In 1982, Whitbread formed a joint venture with PepsiCo to launch Pizza Hut restaurants in the UK, and followed this up in 1985 with the signing of a master franchise agreement to launch TGI Friday's casual restaurants.

The evolution of what was a brewer into a restaurant and leisure business proceeded to a new stage in 1987 when Whitbread launched the Travel Inn chain of budget hotels.

In 1990 came a decision from the Monopolies and Mergers Commission which changed the face of the British brewing and pub industry for all time. Under the order, large brewers were required to sell off many of their pubs, and by 1992 Whitbread had sold 1,300 of its pubs and leased off another 1,000.

Cash-rich from the pub sell-off, in 1995 Whitbread took a step further into leisure and hospitality, purchasing 16 Marriott hotels and signing an agreement with Marriott International to develop the brand in the United Kingdom. At the same time, Whitbread bought David Lloyd Leisure (DLL), a chain of fitness clubs. Later in the same year, the company bought the Costa Coffee chain of coffee shops. By fiscal 1998/99 only 12 per cent of profits were generated by brewing.

In the late 1990s, the firm sold off more pubs and concluded that brewing was a mature industry in which further consolidation was inevitable. Accordingly, the company pursued a deal to buy the UK retailing operations of Allied Domecq, but the referral of the proposed deal to the Competition Commission meant that the proposed acquisition was aborted. Other changes included the acquisition of more health and fitness clubs, expanding DLL to 47 outlets and 170,000 members. Next, Whitbread took over the Swallow Group plc for £730 million, announcing that the 36 upscale hotels would be converted to the Marriott brand, doubling the size of the chain to almost 11,000 rooms.

In May 2000, Whitbread finally exited the brewing business, selling Whitbread Beer Company to Interbrew SA for £400 million. The company kept its Brewers Fayre, Brewsters and Beefeater outlets, but sold the rest of its pubs to Morgan Grenfell Private Equity, a unit of Deutsche Bank, for £1.63 billion, resulting in a return of £1.1 billion to shareholders, and significant debt reduction. The company then announced plans to double the number of DLL outlets and expand the Costa Coffee chain to 500 outlets by 2004. A number of smaller restaurant operations were sold in a management-led buyout in May 2002 (FundingUniverse, 2010).

In 2004 a new management team conducted a major strategic review, concluding that a more focused strategy would increase shareholder value. The resulting disposal programme included the Marriott hotels, TGI Friday's and its stakes in Pizza Hut. At the same time its Premier Inn and Costa Coffee businesses were expanding rapidly. The company was trying to lose the image of the 'fat conglomerate' and developing a set of wholly owned brands (Barker, 2006).

In fiscal 2008/09, Whitbread reported a 20.7 per cent increase in underlying earnings per share on a 9.3 per cent increase in revenue – in a recession year. Hotels and restaurants grew sales by 9.0 per cent and Costa Coffee, now the second-largest coffee chain in the world, increased sales volume by 22.0 per cent (Whitbread, 2010). Another group, the Premier Inn chain, has benefited from a shift of business travellers to budget hotels. While other unpredictable changes may occur, the company looks in excellent shape to benefit from the anticipated recovery in the British economy.

Over its long history, Whitbread demonstrated the ability to successfully undertake a series of both incremental and radical changes in response to major changes in its environment. Increasing competition arising from worldwide consolidation of the brewing industry meant poor prospects for smaller brewers such as Whitbread. The change in British regulation policy that forced brewers to sell off their licensed premises (hotels and pubs) also played a part. Whitbread had to make major changes if it wished to survive as an independent entity. It has developed new resources and capabilities, changed its technological base, its structure, its culture and so on, illustrating that in strategic management all aspects of the firm are variable – nothing is fixed. This change process included major shifts in the corporate portfolio, acquisitions and disposals, and a thorough remaking of the company. Throughout this process, the firm remained profitable, but over time became a more focused and better positioned competitor.

Relatively few firms survive as independent entities for very long periods of time. The FTSE 100 started in 1984, but by 2006 only 23 of the original firms were still on the list (King, 2006). Similar results have occurred with the Fortune 100 industrial companies in the United States (Burgelman & Grove, 2007). These data suggest that most firms have considerable difficulty in recognizing and responding to changes in their environment. Burgelman and Grove argue that most of the time companies operate in a stable industry structure, with strategy-making processes geared to linear strategy dynamics. However, most firms at some time in their evolution face non-linear dynamics from some kind of discontinuity. Their strategic inertia renders them ill-equipped to deal with such changes. Research undertaken by McKinsey indicates that 58 per cent of change initiatives failed to meet the value originally proposed in the business case for the change (Herold & Fedor, 2008).

In a turbulent world, organizational adaptation and change is the only certainty. Thus managing change is one of the major challenges facing firms. Yet, as noted above, most managers lack the necessary knowledge and skills to achieve such changes. To achieve long-term health for their firms, it is imperative that executives learn to manage and sustain change. As Michael Dell of Dell Computers once noted, 'The only constant in our business is that everything is changing. We have to take advantage of change and not let it take advantage of us' (Brown & Eisenhardt, 1998). Dell operates in an extremely dynamic marketplace, with rapidly changing customer needs, technology and competition, but Dell's challenge holds for any modern firm.

We distinguish external from internal change. External change refers to changes in the remote or competitive environment. Sometimes the firm can influence this change – for example, by lobbying for changes in antitrust legislation. Other times a firm may cause external change through its own business scope innovation (►Chapter 9). Apple developed the iPhone, a smarter, better phone, and the whole telecommunications industry and its suppliers were affected. But generally these changes in the external environment are outside the control of the managers of the firm – their task is to sense and respond (Haeckel, 1999).

CHAPTER OVERVIEW

This chapter focuses on internal change within the firm. We first explore the broad types of change initiatives that managers in the firm may adopt as they attempt to respond to their often turbulent environment. We then explore the characteristics of change within the firm, emphasizing that change management must be a core capability of the firm, and the critical role of leadership at all levels. Next we examine a number of characteristics of change programmes such as deciding what to change; whether incremental or revolutionary change is required; and what resources will be required to accomplish the change. This leads to a discussion of the change process itself, how this is managed, what tasks are involved. The chapter concludes with some insights on the nature of leadership, in particular the distinction between leadership and management. This is followed by an interview with Mr Paul Walsh, describing how he, as CEO, developed a change programme at Diageo. The chapter concludes with a mini case, British Airways, which provides an opportunity to apply the material in the chapter to develop a change programme for that firm.

10.1 INTRODUCTION

LEARNING OBJECTIVE 1

Articulate why organizational change and renewal are central strategic management activities.

Drivers of change

The forces driving change within firms include new customer demands, changes in regulation, rising consumer expectations, technological innovation, developments in communications and transport, and political changes resulting from increased global economic integration (Wind & Main, 1998). These changes create a need for continual improvement in organizational performance in order to maintain competitive position and create shareholder value. Competitive advantage is harder to sustain: the firm must simultaneously innovate, reduce costs and cope with increasing uncertainty. At the same time there are increased opportunities, with reduced barriers to operating globally. Yet, no matter how effectively managers plan, increased turbulence and uncertainty mean the unexpected will occur.

Managers must develop organizations that respond quickly and effectively to environmental change, what have been referred to earlier as sense-and-respond organizations. Hence, change management must become a core capability of the firm if it is to survive and deliver value to stakeholders (➤Chapter 5).

Chapter 5

In a dynamic world, a firm cannot afford to be stable and static. Further, the increased speed of external change means that managers must speed up change within the firm. Indeed, one of the tasks of strategic management is to introduce as much change as the firm can stand – take the firm outside its comfort zone – and even this may not be enough. The ultimate objective of any organizational change is to produce changes in behaviour of its members, with individuals having to learn new skills. Such a process of moving from the familiar to the unfamiliar can lead to resistance by the individuals affected by the change (Flamholtz & Randle, 2008). Firms can suffer from change overload and fatigue, as well as cynicism. Too many change initiatives seem to dissipate, replaced by the next fad, leaving even the most loyal employees weary and confused.

Changes in the firm

Firms have responded to these external changes with a plethora of change initiatives, such as reduced centralization, de-layering the organization, new organizational forms such as alliances and networks, globalization of the firm, telecommuting by staff, a concentration on core businesses, and extensive use of outsourcing. Other firms are attempting cultural change, the generation and adoption of new technology, organizational spin-offs, and downsizing. All these strategies are adopted in the expectation that the firm will create additional value. For organizational change to be successful it needs to be accepted throughout the firm. Given the pace at which change is occurring, employees are often trying to implement a number of change initiatives, driven by different executives, in response to a variety of environmental changes. In its continuing search for competitive advantage, a firm may be simultaneously trying to do all of the following:

- Reduce costs
- Become more global
- Become more customer-responsive
- Develop new lines of business
- Handle problems with post-acquisition integration
- Build e-commerce capabilities.

These changes may well have originated in a number of different departments of the firm, but all the changes are labelled high priority, and it is not surprising that the multiplicity of these change initiatives can cause change fatigue among staff. Throughout this, the managerial challenge is to successfully run the business and meet challenging performance targets while simultaneously implementing a number of changes.

IBM (UK) provides an illustration of the number of changes which may be required, some in strategy, some in architecture, some incremental, some radical, but all designed to significantly improve performance.

Organizational change *in practice* – IBM UK

In common with its US parent, IBM UK experienced a dramatic decline in profitability over the period 1988 to 1993. Pre-tax profits dropped from £10 billion in 1990 to a loss of £9 billion in 1993. During this time, there was a recession in the UK and Europe, as well as structural changes in the computer industry. New competitors such as Hitachi and Fujitsu entered the market, which was moving away from mainframe computers towards PCs and client/server systems. But the real causes for the decline seemed to be managerial. IBM began to lose touch with its customers, becoming product- and technology-led not market-led, marketing products that their technical people considered the market needed, rather than identifying and satisfying customer requirements.

Globally, IBM had become very centralized, with power concentrated in the US, resulting in little opportunity for regional organizations such as the UK group to respond to local developments. Sales groups were revenue-focused, not profit-focused, leading to substantial discounting and unprofitable sales. The firm also suffered from high costs and high overheads, which were poorly allocated to products, making it difficult to clarify net margins.

In response to falling sales and the loss of several major clients, IBM responded by cutting prices, shifting employees to a sales role and increasing the dealer network – all to no avail. Globally, IBM was under pressure in most of its major markets and a new CEO was appointed with a mandate of change. As part of this global change programme, a new CEO of IBM UK was appointed in 1990. He decided that radical change was necessary to transform IBM UK into a lean customer-focused organization, with more power devolved to employees. Under his leadership, IBM UK introduced a number of major changes to achieve this transformation:

- The vision was changed to focus on software, services and consulting.
- Non-core functions such as distribution were outsourced.
- 2,000 out of 20,000 staff were fired.
- Selling, general and administrative costs were reduced from 36 per cent to 18 per cent.
- A new organizational structure was introduced with the formation of product business units.
- The sales organization was changed from geographic to an industry focus.
- Increased focus on identifying attractive market segments.
- Business units had the option not to buy services such as personnel from head office.
- Head office staff were reduced from 2,500 to 100.
- The number of management layers was reduced from eight to four.
- IBM UK developed new lines of business – such as insourcing fleet management.
- A new measurement system was introduced, with measures such as customer satisfaction and employee morale.

By 1994, four years after the new CEO had been appointed, these changes were reflected in the results for IBM UK, with revenue and profit growth being achieved (Balgobin & Pandit, 2001).

This example supports our view that change must be seen in a holistic manner, since change in one area may affect others. At the same time, from a strategic management perspective, change management can be about any aspect of the firm. While there is an ongoing need to innovate and change core operations, management must also think more broadly, addressing a range of possible changes from re-inventing the industry to extending the domain of the firm to creating networks – all done to ensure continued value creation in the face of a turbulent and changing world.

Timing of change

Managing change in the firm can mean many different things. At one level it means adapting to an external change, such as a new product launch by a competitor, a defensive but necessary move. It can also mean anticipating change, developing what we have referred to as foresight – insight into and understanding of likely future occurrences – and developing strategies to neutralize, or take advantage of, the expected change (▶Chapter 3). Strategic managers cannot wait for the future to unfold. If the future is clear and unambiguous, leadership opportunities are lost. Change involves risk, but so does lack of change. The magnitude of the risks and the scale and frequency of changes will depend, among other factors, on the industries in which the firm operates. In fast-changing industries such as electronics or communications, change is so rapid that any strategy is likely to have a short life. Continual change within the firm is the norm, and change management becomes a core capability. In industries such as oil and steel, change may be slower and strategies longer-lasting (Brown & Eisenhardt, 1998). A comment by Tony Hayward, the ill-starred one-time CEO of BP, is given below.

Chapter 3

> ### Planning horizon *in practice* – BP
> 'We tend to focus on a period of 20 years as the nature of the business is long term. Decisions that we make today will have real consequences in terms of corporate performance in 10–15 years time. This is why we project and consider how the energy market might evolve and its potential shape in twenty years. This sets the broad direction and we then focus on a 3–5 year time span and create a detailed strategy and action plan covering this period' (O'Regan & Ghobadian, 2010). This is an excellent illustration of the short-term/long-term dilemma of strategic management. Certainly a long-term focus is important in the oil industry, but so too is the ability to deal with short-term emergencies typified by the Texas Gulf Oil disaster of 2010.

Change management is not only about responding; it is also about leading change, creating the changes to which other firms must react. Successfully launching new products, creating a new business model, changing the rules of competition, restructuring the industry, or changing industry boundaries – all might enable an innovator's advantage for the initiator, while other firms follow.

Change management as a core capability

In a changing world, what is successful in the present is not likely to be successful in the future. Operational excellence is certainly required for current success – a lesson that BP seems to have forgotten – but it is limited as a source of sustainable competitive advantage. Competitors will continually attempt to destroy the basis of current success in a competitive market. Change management – the ability to lead the firm into new ways – must become a core capability of the firm, so that it engages in continuous renewal and regeneration. Senior managers must show leadership, and the ability to engage and empower staff to undertake continuous change. Even so, this is insufficient. The content of change, as exemplified by the corporate and business strategies adopted, is also extremely important. Firms such as Bunzl, British Airways and Westinghouse made many changes over a lengthy period, subsuming several CEOs, with little fundamental change in performance.

Change is managed, but not neat

Change can be introduced to a firm in a number of ways, and some approaches are better than others. Nonetheless, managing change is not clean and neat; instead, it is messy and complicated. Change does not always turn out as expected, so the process must be adaptive and evolutionary. Sometimes senior management enthusiastically supports the change initially, but this commitment falters as other priorities take precedence (Campos *et al.*, 2007). Substantial change also takes time to implement. Meanwhile the world is changing, resulting in modifications to change programmes while they are in progress.

Any change will disrupt established patterns of behaviour, values and political power within the firm. Change moves people from what is familiar to what is unfamiliar. Consequently, change managers must be aware of the consequences of change, its impact on employees, and any resistance to it. To tap into the skills and knowledge of employees, and overcome the obstacles of resistance, any change programme should involve participation of employees and demands ongoing communication to those same employees. Managers will usually need to conduct training sessions and put in place incentive systems that reward desired behaviour (Carr *et al.*, 1996). Unfortunately, the more successful a firm has been, the more difficulty will usually be encountered in implementing change programmes. Successful firms too often become complacent, developing a rigid, internal focus. They become risk-averse, with reduced innovation and high levels of resistance to change.

 Chapter 2 Managing change may also require reshaping people's view of the world (their mental models), introducing new paradigms and new ways of thinking about the firm and its interaction with the world, which may be threatening to some employees (➤Chapter 2). Transformations normally require changes in people, structure, tasks, rewards, information and decision processes, among many other factors (Orgland, 1997).

There is also a possible dark side of change: staffing reductions, loss of skills and declining morale. Some change programmes, such as downsizing, can result in the loss of capabilities as people are forced to leave. Their skills may be hard to replace.

Change and leadership

We take it as given that no change is likely to occur without leadership, whether this leadership is shown by the CEO or by others. We believe that the CEO should take a lead role in design and implementation of all major change initiatives; indeed, we regard the CEO as the chief change officer. No major change is likely to succeed without the active support and encouragement of the CEO. Yet, as organizations have become more complex, so has the problem of implementing major changes. Such changes are likely to involve business processes, organizational structure, technology and power relationships across several businesses and geographic areas (Franken *et al.*, 2009).

Defining the precise leadership role of the CEO is not easy. With some change programmes, the CEO may virtually dictate and manage the programme. With others, the role of the CEO is to facilitate the change process, which may involve ensuring that sufficient resources for the change are provided. We discuss these alternatives in more detail shortly, but clearly change is never easy – it involves vision, leadership, and just plain hard work by many people. Whether the CEO is playing the lead role or not, change managers must adopt supporting behaviour and use symbols appropriately. Successful change agents need to create dissatisfaction with the present, develop a clear vision of the future, build participation in the planning and implementation of change, and reward behaviour that supports the change – altogether a formidable undertaking (Tichy & Devanna, 1986).

Finally, astute leaders recognize that organizations are political systems, and power shifts among individuals, functions and businesses are inevitable during any major change. They will recognize and seek the active support of key power groups within the firm. This may involve reshaping the executive team and removing senior people who oppose, or only passively support, the change. Change may also require putting new people from inside or outside the firm in various management positions, as well as the use of external consultants who bring requisite skills and an external perspective to the process.

10.2 CHARACTERISTICS OF ORGANIZATIONAL CHANGE

As we saw in Figure 7.10 (➤Chapter 7), in the absence of action, the competitive advantage of a business unit and the firm overall will decline over time due to such factors as competitor initiatives, changes in customers and technology, political changes, and so on. Change is therefore mandatory for survival; the only questions are whether the changes will be large or small, pro-active or reactive.

LEARNING OBJECTIVE 2

Explain the decisions to be made in designing a change programme.

Change and the environment

As discussed in Chapters 2 and 3 (➤Chapters 2, 3), environmental change ranges from incremental to revolutionary. The firm should continually analyse its environment to identify these changes and their likely impact. We have reproduced Figure 2.4 as Figure 10.1, since it is useful in indicating the change possibilities and options required by the firm as it responds and reacts to external changes.

Chapters 2, 3, 7

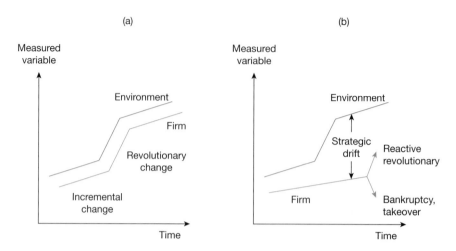

Figure 10.1 Change in the environment and the firm

Some firms are very successful at managing change, whether small (incremental) or large (revolutionary), as shown in Figure 10.1(a). These firms have demonstrated the managerial commitment to successfully handle change in all their activities and should be successful over the long term.

By contrast, Figure 10.1(b) demonstrates an inability to handle change. Such firms respond too late. Possibly they do not perceive the external changes, their managers' mental models are outdated or they regard change as too hard. They will inevitably arrive at a point where gut-wrenching decisions must be made, since their very survival is at risk. Unfortunately, at this late stage firm resources are often depleted, making renewal more difficult. The only options may be bankruptcy, takeover or dramatic downsizing. Figure 10.1 indicates that firms have options in change management, but if decisions are postponed, options are severely reduced.

Change and the firm

Figure 10.2 highlights the key change management decisions facing strategic managers. We will examine each in turn.

What to change

The first question to be resolved is what to change. This is generally the result of detailed analysis of the external environment and firm performance; sometimes it is obvious, sometimes less so. Strategic insight is necessary at this stage, since there may not be a simple connection between diagnosis and prognosis.

The changes in Microsoft, described below, a decentralization to eight new business groups in 1999 to a centralization with three business groups in 2005, were both justified by senior management, at least partly, on the premise of making the firm more entrepreneurial

Figure 10.2 Characteristics of organizational change

Reorganization *in practice* – Microsoft

In 2005, Microsoft announced a major reorganization, reducing the number of units of the firm from seven to three, with a president to run each group. With the reorganization, Microsoft is putting product groups that depend on similar technology under the same unit to speed up development times (Greene, 2005). The declared purpose of the change was to streamline the firm, reduce bureaucracy and spark entrepreneurial behaviour, enabling Microsoft to compete more effectively against such nimble competitors as Google.

What is interesting about this reorganization is that it reverses a similar change made six years earlier. In 1999, Microsoft announced a major reorganization which split the firm into eight new groups. This reorganization was justified as a reaction against the increasing bureaucracy at Microsoft. It was claimed that Microsoft had become increasingly sluggish, with too many layers of management, a loss of managerial talent and slow product development times, and highly centralized decision-making (Moeller *et al.*, 1999).

---

and customer responsive. Under these circumstances it could be expected that many Microsoft employees had difficulty understanding why these particular change programmes were instigated, and whether reorganization was the most appropriate change to achieve the desired ends. As we have noted earlier, managing strategically means accepting that any and all characteristics of the firm can be altered. The task for the senior management team is to identify which changes are most likely to achieve the desired objective.

In some situations, organizational change can be characterized as a sequential search process where the firm initially tries a simple response and if this does not work, the firm then moves on to a more complex and far-reaching change. This sequential process will often be driven by any gap between performance and expectations. If current performance exceeds expectations, there is little incentive for major changes. We should note, however, that installing a new CEO usually means establishing new expectations which may not be met by the existing strategy.

The first step by many firms is to attempt incremental changes to improve efficiency; for example, through cost reductions, downsizing and de-layering. As the global financial crisis developed, many firms experienced severe profit problems, including BT, as described below.

Incremental change *in practice* – BT

BT announced in May 2009 that it would shed 15,000 jobs, on top of the 15,000 it had shed the previous year. BT had suffered a major drop in profit, as well as suffering from a substantial deficit in its pension fund (Stafford, 2009).

If these changes do not achieve the desired results, firms then start to explore changes which represent new ideas, but within the current paradigm of the firm. Such changes include process re-engineering, searching for adjacent markets and expanding geographically (Slatter *et al.*, 2006). If these changes also fail to deliver the required outcomes, the firm is likely to explore quite radical changes, such as developing a new culture and major acquisitions and divestments to fundamentally change their mission, as the example below demonstrates.

Organizational change *in practice* – DSM

In September, 2008, the Dutch company DSM announced that it would transform itself into a life science and material science organization with three major divestment packages. One package would combine the DSM Agro fertilizer business, including the company's ammonia assets, with DSM Melamine. The second group would include their ethylene propylene and thermoplastic businesses while the third group would be their urea licensing subsidiary (Alperowicz, 2008). These businesses accounted for about €1.3 billion revenue in 2007 (DSM, 2007).

In summary, most large firms are attempting a number of change initiatives at any time. These are likely to vary in the extent to which they can be regarded as radical. However, incremental improvements such as reducing costs by 10 per cent, improving the customer retention rates or launching product line extensions are unlikely to produce large increases in wealth.

When to change

Management must determine the urgency of the need for change. Is the firm in crisis? Is there sufficient time to implement change? Signals are weak to begin with, becoming stronger as the gap between performance and expectations increases.

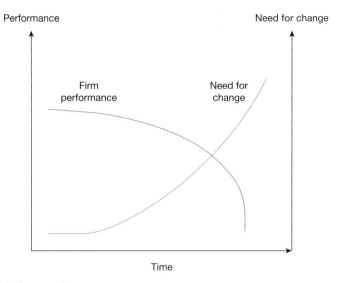

Figure 10.3 When to change

We can imagine a graph such as Figure 10.3, illustrating the need for change. The figure suggests the firm is initially doing well; the need for change is low. As performance declines, the need for change increases. The firm is not yet in crisis, since the deterioration is slow, but the signs are there.

If nothing is done, performance declines at an increasing rate, and the need to change increases. Unfortunately, since performance has declined, resources for change have been reduced, limiting available options. Obviously, change should be undertaken when adequate resources are available, but early on the apparent need for change is limited. It is therefore difficult to get organizational support because there is little sense of urgency. Major changes can have a traumatic impact on the people who are affected by the change, so this sense of urgency needs to be spread widely throughout the firm (Herold & Fedor, 2008). Organizations can change only as fast as the individuals within them are willing to embrace change. A graph such as that of Figure 10.3 might be used to stimulate discussion. Where is the firm on this curve? Are assessments widely shared among senior managers?

Initiating a change programme is a delicate balancing act. Initiate major change too early and employee resistance is likely. Wait too long and firm survival will be threatened. In all change programmes, some managers (probably the ones who believe they will benefit most from the change) will be enthusiastic. Others will be less enthusiastic, since they see no need for change or feel their careers are threatened. Key decisions revolve around timing and how much change to introduce (Killing, 1997).

Anticipatory and reactive change

The ability to anticipate increases the time available for making changes, increasing the chances of avoiding a crisis. Unfortunately, because the precise nature of external changes and their impact on the firm are difficult to predict, the required organizational change is subject to uncertainty (Killing, 1997). If the performance of the firm is good, the perception of managers is often that this will continue. Even under these circumstances, which are possibly unusual, some managers with excellent foresight may believe that they have evidence that the future will be less munificent and that performance will decline in the future. The important point here is that there is still time to implement the change programme.

Anticipation normally permits a more measured response. Yet the need for change in these situations is often better understood by middle managers, who are closer to the 'action', than by senior managers, who may be shielded from reality. Without anticipation, however, the firm can only react. As performance deteriorates, growth rates or market share have started to decline, and margins are suffering. It is becoming clear that change is required, although senior managers may disagree among themselves on the seriousness of the situation. Some will call for revolutionary change while others will suggest an incremental approach.

Finally, if change is left until very late, the firm may be in crisis. Performance is poor, financial markets critical, rating agencies have probably downgraded debt, and shareholders are unhappy. At this time, everyone should see the need for change. There is no problem with creating a sense of crisis – it is reported in the daily business press! Resources available for the change are likely to be limited and change options reduced. Quick action may be necessary to ensure the firm's survival, but hopefully not at the expense of its long-term future. Labour market effects are likely severe. More mobile, highly qualified employees may leave the firm, and it is unlikely to be an employer of preference for those seeking a new job.

Chapters 3, 12

In some situations the firm is faced with a crisis due to a dramatic environmental change which threatens the survival of the firm, the type of low-probability, high-impact events described in Chapter 3 (▶Chapter 3). Such a crisis will cause severe disruption to the firm, and often generate intense media coverage requiring the CEO to visibly lead a rapid response. Such crises are critical yet atypical changes but well-managed firms will generally have developed a crisis management system (Carmeli & Schaubroeck, 2008).

As a final word of advice on anticipation versus reaction, we must caution against 'bottom-line' management. As we discuss in Chapter 12 (▶Chapter 12), the bottom line is a lagging indicator of changes in the business. The best strategic managers will lead anticipatory change, and to do this they will be tracking the leading indicators of change, recognizing that these provide the best guidance for securing longer term shareholder value creation. Whitbread plc is one such company, with its report to shareholders containing measures such as relative pricing, customer satisfaction, a guest's likelihood to return and to recommend the hotel to others, perceived value for money as well as actual repeat customer statistics (Parker, 2010).

Scale of change

Change programmes within the firm can be classified in terms of the magnitude of the change, whether the change is incremental or radical, reflecting the punctuated model of change (Nadler & Nadler, 1998). Incremental changes are those done on a regular basis and requiring no major changes in the architecture of the firm. Incremental change occurs when the company moves to a known future state over a controlled time period. The process is relatively slow and the transition path generally well understood, typically involving a number of aligned changes. Implementing a new compensation system in a large firm would generally be viewed as incremental change, since levels of uncertainty would appear to be reasonably low. In some cases, however, such system changes have been extremely problematic, despite management confidence that this would not be the case.

Radical changes, by contrast, will have an impact on all aspects of the firm involving major changes to strategy, architecture or culture – by their very nature, they are extremely difficult to accomplish successfully. With such transformational change, the end state is generally unknown, as is the time period required for the change. These changes involve a leap of faith and are often initiated when other options have failed. The difficulty of managing radical change is exacerbated by organizational complexity, which in turn is influenced by organizational size and diversity in products, markets and technologies. Today's global firms are characterized by this complexity, so introducing radical changes within these firms is one of the most challenging managerial tasks. Successful change requires more than just a vision – it requires time, excellent process management and sheer effort (Kim, 2007). It also requires a deep understanding of the organization's capabilities coupled with leaders who are able to tap into employees' energy and ideas (Isern & Pung, 2007). Radical change is often driven by a major, external destabilizing event and may occur when the firm is in crisis, which provides the incentive for the change.

The differences between incremental and radical change can be summarized as follows (Nadler & Nadler, 1998):

- Incremental change is done on a regular basis, with no fundamental changes to structure or processes.
- Revolutionary change always requires a new strategy and vision.
- Revolutionary change involves a large number of simultaneous changes.
- Revolutionary change has no clear end, leads to an unclear future state, and takes more time.
- Top management leadership and support, over an extended time, is essential for revolutionary change.

Deere & Co. faced the problem of many capital-intensive firms – the inability to earn sufficient margins to offset their high-capital intensity. These low margins are often due to the structural characteristics of the industries in which they compete. For example, the industry is characterized by a high cost of exit, or possibly the industry is mature with few opportunities for differentiation, or possibly substitutes exist with superior price/performance characteristics (►Chapter 3). Under these circumstances the firm generally needs a radical change programme to improve performance.

Chapter 3

Radical change *in practice* – Deere & Company

Bob Lane became Chairman and CEO of Deere & Company in 2000 having held a number of senior positions with the firm, including chief financial officer. On becoming CEO, his diagnosis was that Deere was 'asset heavy and margin light' and was less competitive in the changing global environment. Shortly after becoming CEO he established a radical change programme to address these issues through managing assets more efficiently, reducing costs and developing a range of innovative products. He also wanted to reduce the firm's vulnerability to cyclical demand and ensure that employees operated with clearly designed performance goals.

For the overall firm, two key performance goals were established, net income and shareholder value added, which was called the 'value of the business'. This was defined as the difference between the operating profit of the business and a capital charge. The capital charge was levied at the rate of 12 per cent on assets in the unit, essentially receivables, inventory and fixed assets.

Decisions made included:

- Introducing a new performance measure, called business value, that explicitly included the cost of capital employed at the level involved.
- Introducing more centralization, in particular combining factories.
- Splitting one major division into two to get better focus.
- Aligning employee goals with organizational goals.
- Aligning employee incentives with business value.
- Closing plants and product lines.
- Adopting the change programme before all the specifics were developed.
- Establishing a strategic priority to improve operational performance before attempting to grow.
- Changing the culture by encouraging high expectations and employing high-talent employees.

After six years, net income doubled to $1.6 billion and the business value of the company went from a deficit of $1,200 million in 2001 to a surplus of $900 million in 2006. The firm seems to be well placed to compete globally, with a balance between operating performance and innovation (Boehm, 2006).

Locus of change

Whereas there is a generally held belief that change must be led from the top of the organization, others hold to a different view. The basic question here is what kind of change is required. Discontinuous changes in the environment are likely to need centre-led change in the firm. Any delay in response will probably mean it will be imposed coercively.

Despite clear evidence of problems for the firm, however, change imposed from the top disenfranchises employees and may well result in strong resistance.

An ever-present danger of change programmes imposed from the top is that they are typically standardized and may be focused on solutions – not problems. There is often an implicit assumption that TQM, 360-degree feedback, outsourcing or benchmarking – whatever is the current management fad – will solve all our problems. Cynicism is too often the response of staff worn down by such initiatives. In contrast to a top-down approach, Beer suggests that the most effective way to change behaviour is to put people into a new organizational context that imposes new roles, responsibilities and relationships on them (Beer, 1990). Such an approach is problem-focused, faces the competitive challenge, and encourages forming cross-functional teams around problems. Senior management's role is to facilitate the change, providing resources, training and support needed by staff at the front line. With this model, change starts at the periphery of the firm, not at the centre.

The above discussion clearly illustrates an interrelationship between change management and leadership style, which we will explore later in this chapter. One aspect of leadership style is the degree of consultation that is used. Change driven by the centre is likely to be more coercive, less consultative.

Resources for change

Strategy implementation requires the firm to generate a portfolio of change programmes, and ensure that these are provided with adequate resources. It has been suggested that in many firms only about 60 per cent of the potential value of a strategy is realized due to poor implementation, one element of which is insufficient resources being allocated (Franken et al., 2009). This is not just a matter of resource availability; the resources must also be commensurate with the scale and scope of proposed changes. For example, does the organization possess the required skills, or can they be acquired? Change is not cheap in either staff time or money. Adequate resources must be available, otherwise management may have to reshape the change initiative. Change efforts are also hampered by other pressures (Franken et al., 2009).

- Pressure from shareholders means strategy must often be implemented in shorter time periods.
- Increased complexity of many companies complicates change initiatives.
- The need to manage for today's performance (for which managers are typically rewarded) while also implementing changes.
- Low involvement from many of the managers who will be implicated in change programmes.

Two further questions must be considered before embarking on corporate change initiatives. First, how does the new initiative fit? There are two aspects to fit. The first is how the initiative meshes with existing organizational arrangements, and, in particular, with firm values. Initiatives closely aligned with existing values will be much easier to implement.

As we noted earlier, radical departures will be much more difficult. One of the major difficulties with business process re-engineering (BPR) which frequently leads to failure is the fact that the processes to be re-engineered often cut right across the organization, requiring change on the part of all the business's constituent functions, thus raising enormous political opposition. Supply-chain reorganization raises some of the very same problems and requires great tenacity and insight for successful implementation. These types of initiative clearly require good homework on change management, since they involve very significant departures from normal operations and may well conflict with the values of the firm. The second aspect of fit involves the relationship between a particular initiative and others that are either underway or occurred in the recent past.

The second key question we must ask is: How many initiatives can we sustain at the same time? There is clearly a limit on how much change people can accommodate. This is undoubtedly related to the history of the company. Adapting to change in an organization that has been stable for a long time is much more difficult. Organizations that have experienced a lot of change tend to be staffed by people who can handle it better, at least when the direction of movement is positive. High-tech companies have traditionally fallen into this category, although when their businesses ran into trouble in 2008, it became very clear that the changes which accompanied declining performance were much harder for them to deal with. The other problem with multiple initiatives, however, is that they tend to make it very difficult for employees (and, indeed, other constituencies) to clearly understand the organization's priorities. Firms sometimes get themselves into terrible muddles as a result of these kinds of conflicts, as the following example illustrates.

While we cannot give an absolute number of corporate-level initiatives to which a firm should restrict itself, we can recommend that not more than a few be considered at any one

Organizational priorities *in practice* – Pharmaceuticals Europe

A European company's pharmaceutical division announced that it was forming global business teams around disease categories. These cross-functional business teams would work together from inception and discovery of a new chemical entity through the entire process to commercialization and marketing, and would do so on an ongoing basis henceforth. This involved a major restructuring of the whole company and a very expensive training initiative. After the programme had been underway for only a few weeks, corporate management banned all international travel because of a budget problem. The consequences of this corporate decision on performance of the division were severe, and a few years later the division was put up for sale by the parent.

time. These should in any case be carefully cross-checked against any initiatives that are underway in the businesses that comprise the firm.

One useful tool that corporate management should consider using for dealing with multiple initiatives can be borrowed from the project and product planning literature (Wheelwright & Clark, 1992). Wheelwright and Clark focus on the total resource requirements for a set of development projects and the balance of those projects, ranging from minor modifications to advanced development projects. Analogously, the CEO should be concerned about (1) the total resource requirements of corporate-level initiatives (which are typically imposed on top of business unit initiatives), and (2) the balance of these initiatives between the evolutionary and the revolutionary, or, if you will, between those aimed at ensuring short-term results and those aimed at securing the future cash flows of the firm. A portfolio overview of change initiatives, as suggested in Figure 10.4, may prove helpful in managing the strategy implementation process.

Simple summation of the resource requirements entailed by currently planned corporate change initiatives should lead to containment of corporate excess. In addition, however, consistent with our integral theme of planning for both today and tomorrow, CEOs should assure themselves that they have an appropriate balance of initiatives underway. Of course, Wheelwright and Clark developed their schema specifically for product development projects, in which case it should be relatively easy to classify such projects along a continuum according to whether they represent R&D that is very basic, aimed at a fundamental breakthrough, all the way to relatively simple projects aimed at derivative developments ('flankers' in marketing

Implementation programmes	Resource implications				
	Tangible		Inangible		
	Physical	Physical	Human	Structural	Customer
Incremental					
Revolutionary					
Total					

Figure 10.4 Portfolio of change initiatives

parlance). However, throughout this book we have been at pains to underline the fact that innovation is not just about new products; it is a much broader concept, involving such ideas as new business models, new competitive strategies, new supply-chain arrangements, re-conceptualization of business missions and so on. To ensure the continued success of the business, it is essential that we not construe innovation narrowly by limiting its domain to that of new products (➤Chapter 9).

Chapter 9

> ### Challenge of strategic management
> We have suggested that in turbulent environments a firm will have a portfolio of change initiatives – some radical, some incremental. Can a firm attempt to undertake too many changes, addressing issues in too many areas of the firm at the same time?

LEARNING OBJECTIVE 3

Devise a process for change management.

10.3 THE CHANGE PROCESS

In the past decade, many companies have tried to remake themselves into better competitors to improve the level of corporate performance. These high-profile changes have gone under many banners: total quality management, re-engineering, rightsizing, restructuring, cultural change, and turnarounds. In almost every case, the goal has been the same: to cope with a new, more challenging market by changing how business is conducted. A few of those efforts have been successful. A few have been utter failures. Most fall somewhere in between, but with a distinct tilt towards the lower end of the scale.

As the business environment becomes increasingly competitive, the pace of change is likely to quicken, not slow down. It is therefore imperative that strategic managers learn as much as possible about managing the change process and critical that they learn from the experience of others. The most common mistake is to underestimate the difficulty of change and to be too optimistic about the pace. Change involves numerous phases that, together, usually take a long time. Skipping steps creates only an illusion of speed and never produces a satisfying result. Critical mistakes in any of the phases can have a devastating impact, slowing momentum and negating previous gains (Kotter, 1995).

As we have noted, change initiatives often meet with a mixed response from employees. Some will be keen to act, recognizing the necessity for the change. Others – possibly the majority – will be less enthusiastic. Perhaps they do not see the need for change, since too often senior management assumes that others see the world as they do. They may also be cynically disillusioned by past corporate initiatives, believe that the change is simply a passing CEO fad, or perhaps feel personally threatened by the change.

The change process, consisting of three interrelated stages, is depicted in Figure 10.5.

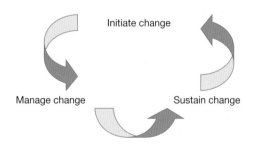

Figure 10.5 The change process

The process is not linear, but – as we will see – it is interactive. We first briefly describe each stage, and then examine them in detail.

- *Initiating change* – diagnosing and creating a perceived need for change and generating the new vision.
- *Managing change* – planning and communicating, creating commitment, and empowering employees.
- *Sustaining change* – institutionalizing a change philosophy.

Initiating change

Diagnosing the need for change

Diagnosing the need for change is a critical first step. This is often thought of as observing a gap between expectations and performance – but which performance measures and which expectations? The answer to that question matters enormously! As we noted earlier, accomplishing change in large organizations takes time, and if managers wait until a crisis is obvious, they may have left insufficient time to permit changes before a catastrophe occurs. Strategic managers must concentrate on leading indicators of performance and change, which means looking far beyond the bottom line. Achieving good profits may be a laudable goal, but the bottom line is a very poor choice to watch if we want to make anticipatory changes. Bottom-line profit is always a lagged indicator; it is a consequence of what has happened to revenues and what has happened to costs. Leading indicators are therefore linked to prospective changes in these two parameters, and factors that might bring about such changes. Complacency about the need for change does not necessarily mean that managers are inept. Too often managers see no evidence that a change is needed because they are looking at the wrong indicators!

So where should we be looking? Chapter 9 emphasized the importance of turning points: shifts in the game or disruptive changes (▶Chapter 9). Strategic managers must be attuned to identifying such turning points. As one consultant put it to us, 'Change is always occurring. If you can't see it, you aren't looking hard enough.' This is an important, almost Confucian, point. Change is the natural course of events; it is lack of change that is unusual. The locus of by far the majority of events necessitating change lies outside the firm, and it is therefore crucial for strategic managers to maintain a very strong external focus. Activities such as analysing competitors, best-of-class benchmarking, attending professional meetings and the like all have beneficial impacts with respect to spotting changes in leading indicators. Some CEOs insist that their senior managers become actively involved in various outside activities for exactly these reasons. Whether the need to change is precipitated by a competitive development, government action, a change in technology or a business model, or a change of supplier strategy, managers with strong external orientations are likely to be aware of the need earlier than their counterparts.

Chapter 9

At the point where a need to change is recognized, the nature and magnitude of the required changes are likely to be unclear. In a large firm, no doubt other change initiatives are already underway, and divining the best course of future action is likely to be difficult.

Creating a perceived need for change

The fact that a few perceptive individuals may recognize a need to change does not mean that the rest of the firm agrees. Establishing a felt need for change within the firm is therefore a critical prerequisite to any successful change effort. The difficulty arises from the fact that it is much easier for a workforce to believe things have to change when the firm is in evident crisis, but if senior management awaits this turn of events, there may be insufficient time to implement the change and save the firm. As a result, a key leadership task is to inculcate a state of dissatisfaction with the status quo. This generally requires establishing a sense of urgency or a sense of crisis before a crisis occurs! This can be problematic when all appearances are of success. This may be the case because performance measures are too historical, rather than leading, or there is little external information available and thus little understanding of a decline in competitive position. A sense of complacency may pervade the firm, especially when there are low performance standards with narrow functional goals.

Strategic managers must then push up the urgency level, creating a sense of impending crisis while raising performance standards, widely distributing data on customer dissatisfaction and opening dialogues with unhappy customers, suppliers, employees and shareholders. Without recognition of a sense of crisis within the firm – the perception that the future of the firm is in doubt unless some action is undertaken – the outlook will be grim indeed. This process might be thought of as bringing about a state of creative discontent.

At this stage, it becomes essential to create a coalition of individuals supportive of the planned change. No one person within the firm, CEO or otherwise, has all the information and knowledge needed. For example, having the right international mix of executives in the senior team may be critical when moving into new foreign markets and cultures (Greve *et al.*, 2009). Further, the senior team should share a vision of the future, since this and contingency rewards are particularly critical when pursuing both exploratory and exploitative innovations (▶Chapter 2) simultaneously (Jansen *et al.*, 2008).

 Chapter 2

Political support within the firm is also essential, since change normally requires a team with power, expertise, credibility, leadership and resources to be successful (Kotter, 1996). As the change process begins, political considerations become crucial because major changes result in power shifts between groups and between individuals in the firm. Change agents need to gain the support of key power groups in the firm, which may involve reshaping the executive team or even replacing senior staff that oppose the change (Nadler & Nadler, 1998). We return to political considerations in the section below on managing change.

Generating a vision

You should have recognized by now that creating change in large companies is a daunting task and not one that can be accomplished by just sending around a memo. It takes sustained hard work by many champions of the change. Change absorbs significant managerial resources and requires energy and commitment to keep it going. However, without some idea of what the change is intended to produce, the efforts will not be successful. Facile talk about change management is meaningless without some clarity about why the present state of affairs is undesirable and without creating a vision of the future of the firm that is both desirable and achievable. Indeed, articulating a vision is a critical factor influencing the development of a climate favourable to innovation (Sarros *et al.*, 2008). Clearly, however, that vision cannot be a detailed blueprint. That is not the purpose of a vision. Equally clearly, change cannot be content-free.

As we saw in Chapter 6 (➤Chapter 6), such a vision should have several characteristics. It should be desirable, achievable, and as clear as is feasible under the circumstances. As with any vision statement, it should be inspirational and aspirational, going beyond the present and beyond strictly financial goals. A preliminary vision statement is often generated by senior managers in a team setting, based on a detailed understanding of the world and its developments, but its refinement will ideally involve a much broader group, for they are essential to its realization. To energize people in this way, the vision should have a limited number of themes, making it easier to communicate throughout the firm.

Chapter 6

Ideally, the vision of the firm's future will reflect how the world is changing and incorporate compelling reasons for why this vision is essential. Such a vision should be seen as attainable (possibly with some stretch) and be easy to communicate to all stakeholders, particularly employees. It should be brief and concise, but neither too vague nor involving 'motherhood' statements. Such a statement may well mention how the vision will affect stakeholders, particularly customers, employees and shareholders.

In some cases, the scale of required change will be almost all-encompassing. Changing the whole firm – its structure, processes, culture and capabilities – is incredibly complex and cries out for holistic and integrated visions. In these situations, however, the vision will almost certainly be quite vague and the change will be an evolving, interactive process. The future state is not, and cannot, be known with certainty, and the management team must remain flexible, open to inputs and learning as they navigate through what will undoubtedly be turbulent waters.

Managing change

Communicating the vision

Senior managers must constantly and consistently communicate the vision that has been developed. There is always resistance to change, and communication is a valuable tool in overcoming both passive and active resistance. Of course, senior managers must also act consistently with the vision – 'walk the talk' as Tom Peters once put it (Peters & Waterman, 1982), or their often-poor credibility may well be further impaired. We would argue that the CEO needs to develop a communication process, using a range of forums and media – talks, newsletters, possibly email and TV and other multimedia approaches. However, others argue that employees are not the most worthwhile audience for CEOs, who should spend their time with major customers, suppliers and investors (Larkin & Larkin, 1996).

The great advantage of electronic approaches is that the CEO can control the way the message reaches employees, without the many filters that operate when a message is passed through the chain of command. Senior management can thereby be assured that a simple, focused message is getting out and can constantly reinforce the vision for the future. Of course, they cannot be sure how their message is being perceived, and follow-up research with relevant audiences is an important source of feedback.

Challenge of strategic management

It is an idea that disturbs many communication professionals. They spend time, expend political capital and spill blood to convince their CEO to interact with employees through town meetings, road shows, blogs, podcasts and video casts. And then T.J. Larkin brazenly tells them . . . that CEO communications with employees is not very important (Vital_Speeches_of_the_Day, 2009). Larkin suggests that CEOs are not employees' most desired source of information, not the most credible and rarely say anything that changes employee behaviour. Instead, communications with their supervisors possess all these properties (Larkin & Larkin, 1994).

We . . . interview[ed] controversial Larkin . . . and the responses are below:

Interviewer: What research do you use to back up your claim that CEOs should communicate less with employees, rather than more?

Larkin: Professor Phillip Clampitt . . . asked employees for examples of communication that caused them to do their jobs better – 70 per cent of employee examples involved informal conversations with their supervisors, 2 per cent . . . involved messages from their CEOs. . . . The Hay Group [says] it is four times more likely that employees will support a corporate change if they hear about it first from their supervisors compared with . . . a company executive.

Interviewer: You realize what you're saying is heresy to communicators, and even to many CEOs. How could so many people be so wrong?

Larkin: Business books on leadership are responsible for most of the goofy ideas about CEO communication . . . [they] are full of images of charismatic CEOs motivating and inspiring their employees . . .

Turn away from the business books . . . and you'll get a completely different picture. Most sociologists believe that 'charismatic leadership' is exceedingly rare and usually not good. Charismatic leaders mostly provoke unpredictable, uncontrollable and dangerous crowd reactions.

QUESTION

Do you think that communications from a CEO, which are generally written or presented via video, will result in substantial change by employees?

The change team

As we noted, CEOs cannot manage the whole change process. They need to establish a guiding coalition, a team to manage and oversee the change process. Such a team is generally made up of senior executives who can provide knowledge, commitment and support. The team must be balanced in skills and expertise, but it also needs resources, power, credibility and leadership skills. Their communication abilities may well be critical to the type of communication that Larkin seems to advocate.

Members of change teams are often seconded to a team on a part-time basis, keeping their normal responsibilities as well. Balancing these demands is difficult and also requires some astute assessment of the shifting sands of organizational politics. For most of us, the term *politics* carries negative overtones when applied to a firm, but Peter Block points out that all successful managers must understand the use of politics. Politics means the use of influence and, just like power, is in and of itself value-free – politics can be used to further good ends as well as bad (Block, 1987). Block believes, and we agree, that the effective use of politics (and, indeed, power) is a skill that must be mastered for a manager to be effective. Because organizations are political systems and change results in shifts of power within the firm, change leaders need the support of key power groups.

The members of the change team need to understand the concerns of the recipients of the change – what they are interested in and how they may respond to the change. In particular, there may be psychological issues for people to resolve. One approach to this understanding is to classify those parties (individuals and/or groups) that are key to the implementation of our change strategies along two dimensions. The first is the extent to which we believe we have their confidence: do they trust us? The second is the extent to which we believe they will be in agreement with our proposed course of action (strategies and programmes). The result is a trust/agreement matrix, as depicted in Figure 10.6 (Block, 1987).

One might expect a fourfold classification to result from a 2×2 matrix, but Block also incorporated 'fence-sitters', an intriguing and potentially troublesome constituency that he

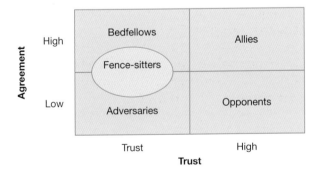

Figure 10.6 Trust/agreement matrix

Source: P. Block, *The Empowered Manager*, San Francisco, Jossey-Bass, © 1987, John Wiley. This material is used by permission of John Wiley & Sons, Inc.

believes merits special attention. We now briefly examine the influence strategy for each of the identified groupings.

Allies, as Figure 10.6 indicates, are those who are in agreement with our ideas and trust us – a wholesome combination! For this group Block urges that we confirm their agreement and reaffirm the quality of the mutual relationship. He suggests being open with any problems or difficulties and seeking advice and input. Clearly, it would be a mistake to take any group for granted, but that is also most likely to happen with this constituency.

Opponents trust us but disagree with our ideas. Here Block suggests that we reaffirm the quality of the relationship, then restate both our own position and, as we understand it, the position of the opponent. The objective should then be to engage in joint problem-solving to attempt to resolve the differences.

Bedfellows represent a different challenge, since they are in a 'marriage of convenience'. The recommendation for them is to reaffirm their agreement with the strategy and to be open in acknowledging their caution and lack of trust. We should then clarify what we are looking for, in terms of cooperation in implementation, and ask that the bedfellows do the same for us.

Adversaries are patently the most difficult to deal with. After stating our own position on strategy, we should state our best understanding of the adversary's position, doing so neutrally, without any evaluative comments. Block suggests that we then acknowledge our own contribution to any problems and end the meeting by stating our own plans to move ahead, but making no demands on the adversary.

Fence-sitters should first hear an explanation of the proposed strategy. We should then attempt to elicit their point of view and submit them to gentle pressure to accede to the proposed plan. They should then be encouraged to think it over and let us know what it would take for them to support the strategy.

Of course, we can give only a brief overview of Block's ideas in this chapter, but the basic idea that implementation will involve plotting out an influence strategy and distinguishing among the different parties whose cooperation we will need along such dimensions as trust and likely agreement is sound advice. Forgetting this admonition can lead to the debacle that resulted from Robert Ayling's clumsy strategy implementation at British Airways. His neglect of employees, and failure to achieve their trust and agreement, eventually cost him his job. As a CEO once said to one of the authors, 'We have to recognize that ultimately, all power is granted from below'.

Empowering employees

Change will occur only if many people are involved and if innovation and risk-taking are encouraged. The initial response to a change agenda on the part of many employees is at best guarded, with others apprehensive and some downright hostile. Empowerment is a key tool in building the leverage necessary to create the change. An important element in any change programme is to recognize those individuals who gain, and lose, as a result of the change. People resist change because it involves a loss of some kind (Beerel, 2009). For example, employees may need to change their behaviour, their priorities or their values.

Change managers need to understand the sources of employee distress and how to handle them. There is also a positive side to participation – it will improve commitment and help generate good ideas. Participation reduces resistance to change as well as generating good ideas. The CEO can create enabling conditions by getting rid of obstacles and changing systems, structures and people, but those who will accomplish the change have to build skills, growing and developing leadership abilities.

Short-term wins

Finally, important as it is to keep the ultimate vision in mind, it is vital to maintain enthusiasm in the interim. Short-term wins that are recognized, rewarded and communicated throughout the firm provide positive feedback to those working on change efforts as well as other stakeholders. These wins provide tangible evidence of success, that the change process is underway and working, and constitute important symbolic communication.

Sustaining change: the organization of the future

Creating and sustaining a different attitude towards change is essential to ensure that the firm does not slip back into fixed ways of thinking or doing things. There is evidence that firms which have above-average performance in strategy execution are able to instil and reinforce a culture of continuous change and ensure that there are good governance arrangements for each change programme (Franken *et al.*, 2009). Too often, managers and consultants construe the vision as an end state, when it should be viewed as a continuing new beginning. Since we do not believe that the required pace of change will slow, it is essential that the vision be one of a firm that has the continuing capacity for self-renewal. Change becomes traumatic when a firm has not experienced it in many years. It becomes part of the landscape in a firm that has inculcated the capacity for self-renewal, and this philosophy should be a fundamental anchor of the new culture of the firm. This is more challenging than it may at first appear. If the firm's structure, processes and systems fail to be coherent and support its strategy and capabilities, a change effort is likely to stumble (Worley & Lawler, 2006). However, structures, systems and processes tend to lag external changes, and are more likely to be aligned with the firm's past than its future!

A chapter on organizational change would be incomplete without some discussion of the organization of the future, since it is incumbent on us as authors to give you some insight into the changes you will be experiencing. Of course, there are a variety of opinions on how firms will have to evolve and change, but while reviewing the opinions of different authors, we will conclude this section by attempting to synthesize these opinions.

Some commentators are convinced that successful firms of the future will have a high and persistent sense of the need to change, with teamwork at the top among people who can create and communicate a vision and create broad-based empowerment. Others believe that learning will become increasingly important for organizational success and that the rate at which a firm can learn will in turn be a competitive advantage. In a changing world, organizations as well as individuals have to learn to do new things and to do old things differently, so that if a firm can speed up the learning process, it will achieve a competitive advantage (Moingeon & Edmondson, 1996). Organizations ultimately learn via their individual members, but organizational learning is not dependent on a single individual. Thus, for organizational learning to become a source of competitive advantage, knowledge must become structural or organizational, even though it may start as individual and tacit (►Chapter 9). Then if a specific individual leaves the firm, all the learning or knowledge possessed by that individual does not leave at the same time. Some academics emphasize the importance of creativity and entrepreneurship as an essential element of the firm of the future (Gergen & Vanouk, 2009) while others suggest that new organizational forms will have to be developed to handle the complexity of future organizations (Galbraith, 2009).

Chapter 9

As the above brief discussion illustrates, there is a consensus across many different authors, academic and practitioner alike, that we can expect significant change in organizations in the twenty-first century. However, there is probably less agreement on the specific form that will be possessed by the organization of the future.

Challenge of strategic management

Assume that you have been approached by an executive search firm to become the CEO of a medium-sized global firm, which is struggling financially. While you are interested in the position, and flattered by the approach, you do want to reflect on the decision. In conversation with a personal friend, who happens to be a financial journalist, they mention that the firm in question has had three CEOs over the last four years, and that in their judgement morale in the firm is generally low. If you were to accept the position, what steps would you, as the new CEO, take to improve performance?

10.4 LEADERSHIP

LEARNING OBJECTIVE 4

Describe the nature and role of leadership in strategic management.

Definition of leadership

The discussion of change management has underlined the importance of the **leadership** skills of managers, which we now examine.

Leadership

A process by which a person influences others to achieve a common goal.

Leadership is the process of influencing others to understand what needs to be done and how to do it to accomplish shared objectives (Yukl, 2006). In a strategic management context, we regard leadership as more than simply setting a new direction. While this is necessary, so too is developing a reasonable strategy, being realistic about the firm's capabilities and how quickly change can be accomplished (Herold & Fedor, 2008). As intangible assets and human capital become more important for organizations, so does the challenge for leaders to create an environment which is valued by high-talent people. Such people have strong ideas of their own worth, and are highly mobile. Leaders have to both attract these high-talent people, and to create an environment in which they are motivated to not only achieve their potential but also create value for stakeholders (Goffee & Jones, 2007). In dynamic times, firms need to foster continuous change, exploring ways to develop new forms of competitive advantage, addressing issues such as what new capabilities will be required in the future.

Successful leaders are also able to achieve a balance in the strategy development process between exploitative and exploratory strategies (▶Chapter 2). The leadership at Intel, the US chip maker, ensured that the firm's strategy development processes did not focus only on exploitative strategies. They adopted a relatively loose process, with uncommitted resources, to make sure that exploratory strategies were also developed (Burgelman & Grove, 2007).

Chapter 2

Others have emphasized different characteristics. For example, the importance of possessing a deep understanding of what are regarded as principles of business characterized as (Gottfredson & Schaubert, 2008):

- An understanding that costs and prices always decline according to an experience curve, and hence use this concept to estimate future costs and prices.

- A recognition of the importance of market share and the extent to which competitive position determines the firm's strategic options.

- The insight to realize that both industry value chains and thus firm profitability are evolving.

Leader versus manager

Following Kotter, we make a distinction between management and leadership (Kotter, 1996). They are distinctive but complementary systems of action. Management is about keeping the firm operating while coping with complexity. To manage, we develop systems and procedures to remove complexity, using devices such as standard operating procedures, planning, and budgeting systems. In contrast, leadership is about change, developing visions and strategies, but also about aligning people with that vision and inspiring them to make it happen. Indeed, Kotter argues that many firms are over-managed and under-led.

As we have seen, successful firms too often become arrogant and insular, isolated from their markets. With reduced efforts in innovation and creativity, they become bureaucratic, with rules for everything. Pressure for short-term performance by financial markets may result in too much concern with the present and not enough with the future, even though this may not serve shareholders' interests. Indeed, Rowe argues that strategic leadership is the ability to influence others to voluntarily make day-to-day decisions that enhance long-term viability while maintaining short-term financial stability (Rowe, 2001).

In increasingly turbulent environments, leadership matters as never before. The need to exhibit speed and flexibility, and to execute discontinuous change, requires effective leadership skills. Charismatic leaders are important: they provide vision, direction and energy for their firms. Charisma alone, however, is not enough to build competitive, agile organizations. Charismatic leadership must be bolstered by institutional leadership through attention to details on roles, structures and rewards. Moreover, since most organizations are too large and complex for any one executive or senior team to directly manage, the leadership of strategic organizational change must be pushed throughout the company via education and empowerment. If managers at all levels own and are involved in executing the change efforts, they are much more likely to realize concrete benefits (Nadler & Tushman, 1990).

Capabilities of leaders

There has been considerable discussion of the extent to which leadership abilities can be easily taught or acquired. There is general agreement that leaders possess certain personal traits – that they be visionary, able to handle ambiguity, interpersonally skilled, honest, capable negotiators, and politically astute, These attributes of good change managers have been reflected in much of this book thus far.

Another school of thought believes that successful managers understand and can practise a variety of leadership styles, selecting the one most appropriate to the situation and the person. Goleman, for example, identifies six different styles ranging from coercive to coaching, as shown below (Goleman, 2000):

- *Coercive* – demands immediate compliance
- *Authoritative* – mobilizes people towards a vision
- *Affiliative* – creates harmony and builds bonds
- *Democratic* – forges consensus through participation
- *Pace-setting* – sets high performance standards
- *Coaching* – develops people for the future.

Certainly, effective leaders will need to have mastered more than one style and be able to select the style which best suits the particular circumstances (Groysberg *et al.*, 2006).

Challenge of strategic management

Can you provide several examples of individuals who have displayed excellent leadership that had positive consequences for their firms? What were the common characteristics about the way in which they displayed leadership?

10.5 SUMMARY

Increasing environmental turbulence and heightened levels of global competition necessitate that firms continually re-invent themselves. Organizations will have to change faster than ever and be prepared to change any, and all, of their characteristics. Any change programme is risky, but so is the alternative of no change. At any time, the firm is likely to be managing a number of change programmes simultaneously, of varying levels of complexity, scale and impact. For these reasons, we suggest that change management must become a core capability of any successful firm.

Managers developing a change programme need to make a number of decisions. One of the most critical is a decision on what to change. If the firm is suffering from declining profitability, senior managers need to identify the probable causes and clarify what needs to change. Is it reducing costs, geographic expansion, or a widespread reorganization? Microsoft, for example, went through two major reorganizations. The first was one of decentralization followed five years later by a programme of centralization. Yet each was described as an encouraging entrepreneurship within the firm and speeding decision-making. In contrast, Deere & Co developed a comprehensive change programme in response to declining financial performance with an integrated set of decisions focusing on performance measures, structure, portfolio changes and culture changes. At the same time, a decision must be made on when to change, must the change be carried out immediately or can it be delayed? Decisions also need to be made about the scale of the change and, importantly, about the resources and capabilities required.

While change can be managed, the process of change is adaptive and evolving, particularly for radical changes where the end-point is not always well understood. All change processes involve an element of disruption to established procedures, values and political power within the firm, so an understanding of the recipients of the change – what their likely response will be, what resistance may be encountered – is fundamental to successful change.

Successful change management follows an interactive process, diagnosing the need for change, generating the vision of the future, managing the change, and finally ensuring that the change is sustained. Leadership plays a central role in the success of this process. The quintessential features of leadership are the ability to generate a vision and to have the industry knowledge and foresight to guide the firm through turbulence and uncertainty. Leadership is about introducing change, aligning people with the vision, demonstrating enthusiasm and passion to inspire people to make it happen. Since the CEO is just one individual, any large-scale change programme requires a multidisciplinary team with sufficient financial and human resources.

VIEW FROM THE TOP

DIAGEO PLC

'Creating a world class business through a merger of two equals – abstracted from an interview with Paul Walsh, COE of Diageo plc' conducted by the *Journal of Strategy and Management* (JSM).

JSM: How do you define strategy?

PW: Strategy is the holistic plan to deliver against a pre-determined set of outcomes. Strategy often becomes quite mired in the numbers but it is much broader than that. In fact the numbers should come right at the end. Strategy should be capable of constant iteration because . . . the environment can change very quickly. Strategy therefore has to be flexible and capable of providing a beacon to the organization in a time of rapid change.

JSM: The Leadership Performance Programme is seen as the main driver of success in Diageo . . . How important is executive development and training to the success of the organization?

PW: I think it's vital –first of all I think the day that you believe that you've stopped learning . . . you probably should retire. Every day you have to be prepared to stretch yourself . . . to think of new possibilities for yourself and the business. I think as soon as that ends you probably need to do something differently so I think business development and self-development are parallel tracks. I think there is nothing more compelling than when a team really have it together. Whether you look at sports or . . . business . . . the whole notion of engagement and alignment is critical. I think there is a degree of self-awareness that's required in order to build alignment and engagement and a lot of what we do on the leadership development programme is exactly that. The programme is aimed at self-awareness, at external awareness and making sure that you as a leader in this organization really engage with your teams and build alignment with your teams.

JSM: Diageo is a big successful multinational with suppliers in different countries. To what extent do you think this is a conduit for transfer of ideas and best practice?

PW: There's quite a lot of exchange of good ideas and so on. We expect our suppliers to share with us best practice and we share with them. If we want a long-term relationship that's beyond just today's transaction we would expect that. As the biggest player in the spirit sector, our environmental policy as it pertains to water and new technology has been provided to the small players in the industry because it's good for the industry.

JSM: You operate in 180 markets . . . How do you create a strong organizational culture and assure adherence to organizational values in such a diverse organization?

PW: Well it's all around the value set. If you look at the values that guide this company – they're non-negotiable and if you can't sign up to them . . . you're probably not going to find this a worthwhile place to work . . . So first of all it's the principles, the values that guide behaviour. It is then the uniformity of purpose, understanding very clearly what we're expecting from Diageo, from your market, from your brand and there's a whole cascading process around that so you have . . . what we're trying to do and that will be very clear and the values will guide you on the how.

JSM: What does leadership mean to you? Whose leadership do you admire the most?

PW: Leadership is communication, it is empathy, it is accountability, it is passion, it is courage. It is also constant visibility. As a leader you are constantly on show and if that notion forces you to do something that is artificial it will be seen through very quickly so authenticity is required . . .

I admire Churchill for his relentless fortitude to communicate in a very clear, compelling, pride-building way. I admire Nelson Mandela – how someone could go through what he went through and then have such humble attitudes and be so forgiving is incredible. In the business world, I would cite Fred Smith of FedEx as a great leader. He's got a very clear vision. He is relentless in how he pursues it and he takes his people with him and uses his mind as a tool not a weapon.

BRITISH AIRWAYS

British Airways (BA) is a major international airline, with operations in many countries. It was formed in 1971 through the merger of two British airlines: British European Airways (BEA) and British Overseas Airways Corporation (BOAC), both state-owned. For several years after this merger, both entities operated relatively autonomously. Both airlines had grown up in the post-World War II environment, with a substantial number of former armed forces pilots in management positions. There was little emphasis on profits – the airlines saw it as their role to arrive on time, show the flag and extend routes, and there was a civil service mentality among the staff. There was little integration between the two original entities, no economies of scale, no common themes or culture. Further, productivity was low, costs were high and service levels were poor. The situation got so bad that in 1981 a special bulletin was issued to all staff warning that the airline was likely to go out of business. In February 1981, John King, a successful business executive with little previous airline experience, was appointed Chairman.

In September 1981 BA launched a survival plan, reducing staff from 52,000 to 43,000, discontinuing routes and combining engineering bases. Six months later, another 7,000 staff went. These staff reductions were accomplished with generous severance pay – indeed, there were more volunteers than places, and so employees were voting with their feet. In 1982, BA announced a loss of £545 million after taxes and extraordinaries, and took the opportunity to write off redundancy costs and reductions in its fleet value in an attempt to clear the decks. In February 1983, Colin Marshall, an executive with experience in car rentals, not airlines, was appointed CEO. BA launched a two-day training programme called Putting People First. Some 40,000 staff went through this programme, 150 at a time. The emphasis of the programme was on positive relationships, at work and with customers, and mixed staff from different areas and levels. The major theme was customer service.

After this programme had been completed, another 1,500 managers went through a five-day programme, Managing People First, which stressed the importance of trust, vision and leadership. BA also launched new aircraft livery and uniforms, with much fanfare. It also took an interest in Galileo, a reservation system, and acquired an interest in USAir and Sabena, reflecting its global strategy. European regulators prohibited a merger with American Airlines, but eventually these two, plus other airlines, launched a global alliance, One World.

During the 1990s, the environment became more competitive following airline deregulation, particularly in the United States. Marshall became Chairman, and the composition of the board was changed to bring in more non-executive directors. In 1996 a lawyer named Robert Ayling became the new CEO. In 1997 the company tried to refocus on customer service and new routes, and some £6 billion were devoted to a major change programme that included new aircraft, new routes and extensive market research. BA also adopted more extensive outsourcing, introduced a pay freeze and

MINI-CASE

new work rules, cut jobs and reduced commissions to some travel agents. A new strategy was implemented, targeting intercontinental business-class and first-class travel to improve passenger yields. At this time, BA was under heightened competitive pressure from new low-cost European airlines such as Ryanair. Despite these changes, the firm had a quarterly loss in 1999, and there was again a perception that ground staff were arrogant and uncaring.

British Airways entered the discount airline segment in May 1998 by establishing Go Fly, a low-cost subsidiary using ex-BA Boeing 727s. In 2000, Ayling was fired and Rod Eddington became the new CEO. An experienced airline executive from Australia, he set out to repair the damage to the airline in an increasingly challenging environment, following the terrorism attack on 11 September 2001, the second Gulf War and the outbreak of SARS. As part of his efforts to restore BA to health, in November 2000 Eddington announced his intention to sell the airline, now named Go (BBCNews, 2000). In June 2001 British Airways sold Go for £110 million to a private equity group, of which the main shareholder was the venture capital company 3i with 43 per cent of the company. This group then sold Go to Easyjet in 2002 for £374 million (BBCNews, 2002). Disposals continued with the sale of German subsidiary Deutsche BA in May 2003, while in September 2004 BA sold its 18.5 per cent stake in Qantas.

However, during Eddington's leadership, strikes continued to plague the airline. In 2003, ground staff walked out in protest over a new check-in timekeeping system. This was followed by a vote to strike over pay during the summer of 2004, causing some workers to stay home in protest at low staffing levels before agreement was reached with BA managers.

On 8 March 2005, Willie Walsh, former CEO of Aer Lingus, was named as successor to Rod Eddington who was due to retire in September 2005. This left Walsh to deal with the aftermath of the unofficial walkout by British Airways staff at Heathrow Airport which occurred in August 2005. This action was in support of a dispute by Gate Gourmet, BA's sole provider of in-flight meals, following the sacking of 350 members of its staff at Heathrow in a dispute over working practices, pay and the appointment of temporary summer workers. Hundreds of BA baggage handlers and other ground staff went on strike in sympathy with the full realization that this would cripple BA's services and cost the company an estimated £10 million a day. It is no coincidence that these actions all occurred during the summer season with millions of people flying abroad for their summer holidays. An interesting quote at this time was from a BA spokeswoman who stated, 'Fundamentally I don't think we do have an industrial relations problem.'

Changes to the BA business portfolio continued and the fully owned subsidiary British Airways Citiexpress was renamed BA Connect in February 2006. In March 2007 Flybe announced the completion of a deal to purchase BA Connect. January 2008 brought the unveiling of a new subsidiary, OpenSkies, flying between major European cities and the United States. Until 2008 British Airways was the largest airline of the UK measured in passenger numbers, carrying 35.7 million passengers that year, but in 2008 discount rival EasyJet announced it had carried 44.5 million passengers.

On 30 July 2008 BA announced a preliminary agreement to merge with Iberia Airlines. The company hoped the merger would be completed by March 2010. In June 2009, however, an article appeared on the BBC website commenting on the future of BA (Marshall, 2009):

> Richard Branson must have been rubbing his hands with glee when he heard the reports that
> arch rival Willie Walsh was leading the 'fight for survival' for British Airways. Branson's smooth

PR machine kicked into gear immediately. His message was that the government should not step into rescue BA. But has it actually got this far?

Last month BA reported its largest ever full-year loss. At the same time it declined to issue any new guidance for the coming year because of the difficulty in forecasting revenues. Nor did it provide details on the group's pension deficit or the hoped-for merger with Iberia.

Then last week, BA's 40,000 employees were invited to give up their salaries for between one and four weeks.

While BA chief Walsh has repeatedly spoken of the most difficult trading environment ever facing the industry, Branson is keen to push BA's potential demise one step further. He says he wouldn't touch BA because of its hefty liabilities, not least its pension deficit. Nor he says, should the government step in to help the airline.

A BA spokesman is reported to have shot down Branson's comments: 'This is fantasy. There are no talks with government, and there will be no talks. We have opposed state aid and our position has not changed.' But as one industry observer commented this morning, 'it would be a surprise if some dialogue [with the government] had not taken place'.

In December 2009, a 12-day strike of BA staff planned for the Christmas holiday season was averted by a court decision, ruling the union ballot to be illegal. However, in February 2010, BA staff again voted for a strike due to commence on 24 May 2010 (British Airways, 2010). This was taking place as BA reported a loss before tax of £401 million for 2008/09 following a profit of £922 million in 2007/08 (British Airways, 2009).

QUESTIONS

1   What recommendations would you make to Willie Walsh to help get BA back to being a high-quality, profitable carrier?
2   People are critical in the airline business. How could he go about improving the company's labour relations?

REVIEW QUESTIONS

1 Discuss the factors which make organizational change a crucial task for strategic management.

2 How can managers improve their skills in anticipating and responding to change?

3 'It is more difficult for managers to detect the need for change than it is for them to develop the appropriate response.' Discuss this statement.

4 How would you handle employees who are resisting a change because their view of the world or their managemient practices is threatened? Would you deal with them differently if their resistance was due to fear of failure?

5 Select a recent book or article written by a senior executive which describes a major change programme in their firm. Contrast the characteristics of this programme with the framework shown in Figure 10.2. On this basis, evaluate the selected change programme.

6 What are the stages of the change process? Use examples of firms with which you are familiar to illustrate how the firms implemented each stage.

7 How does leadership influence the determination of a firm's strategy?

8 Do you believe that a given manager can develop a range of leadership styles? Discuss.

REFERENCES

Alperowicz, N. (2008) DSM readies divestment program for several major businesses. *Encyclopedia Britannica: Chemical Week*, 23 June.

Balgobin, R. & Pandit, N. (2001) Stages in the turnaround process: The case of IBM UK. *European Management Journal, 19*(3), 301–316.

Barker, A. (2006) Whitbread's diet good for shareholders. *Financial Times*, 8 August, p. 18.

BBCNews (2000) BA to sell Go airline as profits surge. *Business*, 6 November. http://news.bbc.co.uk/2/hi/business/1009283.stm.

BBCNews (2002) Easyjet buys Go for £374 m. *Business*, 16 May. http://news.bbc.co.uk/2/hi/business/1990691.stm.

Beer, M. (1990) Why change programs don't produce change. *Harvard Business Review*, (November–December), 158–166.

Beerel, A. (2009) *Leadership and Change Management*. London: Sage.

Block, P. (1987) *The Empowered Manager*. San Francisco, CA: Jossey-Bass.

Boehm, R. (2006) Leading change: An interview with the CEO of Deere & Co. *McKinsey Quarterly*, (December).

British Airways (2009) Annual Report. www.britishairways.com/cms/global/microsites/ba_reports0809/pdfs/BA_AR_2008_09.pdf.

British Airways (2010) Cabin crew strike – latest information. 24 May. www.britishairways.com/travel/strike-ballot/public/en_gb?refevent=info_strike&link=main_nav.

Brown, S. L. & Eisenhardt, K. M. (1998) *Competing on the Edge: Strategy as Structured Chaos*. Boston, MA: Harvard Business School Press.

Burgelman, R. A. & Grove, A. S. (2007) Let chaos reign, then rein in chaos – repeatedly: Managing strategic dynamics for corporate longevity. *Strategic Management Journal, 28*(10), 965–979.

Campos, D., Fine, D. & Van Olst, M. (2007) How one company maintained momentum. *The Mckinsey Quarterly*, (4), 36–43.

Carmeli, A. & Schaubroeck, J. (2008) Organizational crisis-preparedness: The importance of learning from failures. *Long Range Planning, 41*(2), 177–196.

Carr, D. K., Hard, K. J. & Trahant, W. J. (1996) *Managing the Change Process.* New York: McGraw-Hill.

DSM (2007) DSM accelerates shift to life sciences and materials sciences company and raises growth targets. 27 September. www.dsm.com/en_US/downloads/media/68e_07_acceleration_Vision_2010.pdf.

Flamholtz, E. & Randle, Y. (2008) *Leading Strategic Change.* Cambridge: Cambridge University Press.

Franken, A., Edwards, C. & Lambert, R. (2009) Executing strategic change: Understanding the critical management elements that lead to success. *California Management Review, 51*(3), 49–73.

Funding_Universe (2010) Whitebread. *Company-histories.* Retrieved 11 March 2010. www.funding universe.com/intranet/sphider/search.php?query=whitbread&search=1.

Galbraith, J. R. (2009) Multidimensional, multinational organizations of the future. In F. Hesselbein & M. Goldmith (eds), *The Organization of the Future 2* (pp. 174–187). San Francisco, CA: Jossey-Bass.

Gergen, C. & Vanouk, G. (2009) Dynamic organizations for an entrepreneurial age. In F. Hesselbein & M. Goldmith (eds), *The Organization of the Future 2* (pp. 159–173). San Francisco, CA: Jossey-Bass.

Goffee, R. & Jones, G. (2007) Leading clever people. *Harvard Business Review*, (March), 72–79.

Goleman, D. (2000) Leadership that gets results. *Harvard Business Review*, (March–April), 78–90.

Gottfredson, M. & Schaubert, S. (2008) *The Breakthrough Imperative.* New York: Collins.

Greene, J. (2005) Less could be more at Microsoft, *Business Week*, 3 October, p. 40.

Greve, P., Nielsen, S. & Ruigrok, W. (2009) Transcending borders with international top management teams: A study of European financial multinational corporations. *European Management Journal, 27*(3), 213–224.

Groysberg, B., McLean, A. N. & Nohria, N. (2006) Are leaders portable? *Harvard Business Review*, (May), 92–100.

Haeckel, S. H. (1999) *Adaptive Enterprise: Creating and Leading Sense- and -Respond Organizations.* Boston, MA: Harvard Business School Press.

Herold, D. M. & Fedor, D. B. (2008) *Leading Change Management.* London: Kogan Page.

Isern, J. & Pung, C. (2007) Driving radical change. *McKinsey Quarterly*, (November).

Jansen, J. J. P., George, G., Van den Bosch, F. A. J. & Volberda, H. W. (2008) Senior team attributes and organizational ambidexterity: The moderating role of transformational leadership. *Journal of Management Studies, 45*(5), 982–1007.

Killing, P. (1997) Managing change, the urgency factor. *Perspectives for Managers, IMD, 1*(February), 1–4.

Kim, D.-J. (2007) Falls from grace and lessons from failure: Daewoo and Medison. *Long Range Planning, 40*(4–5), 446–464.

King, M. (2006) Two reasons to avoid Footsie trackers. *MoneyWeek Investments*, 5 July. www.moneyweek.com/investments/stock-markets/two-reasons-to-avoid-footsie-trackers.aspx?

Kotter, J. P. (1995) Leading change: Why transformation efforts fail. *Harvard Business Review, 73*(2), 59–67.

Kotter, J. P. (1996) *Leading Change.* Boston, MA: Harvard Business School Press.

Larkin, T. J. & Larkin, S. (1994) *Communicating Change.* New York: McGraw-Hill.

Larkin, T. J., & Larkin, S. (1996) Reaching and changing frontline employees. *Harvard Business Review,* *74*(3), 95–104.

Marshall, C. (2009) Morning line: Should the govt save British Airways? *City Wire,* 22 June. www.citywire.co.uk/personal/-/comment/morning-line/content.aspx?ID=345887

Moeller, M., Hamm, S. & Mullaney, T. J. (1999) Remaking Microsoft. *Business Week,* 17 May, p. 106.

Moingeon, B. & Edmondson, A. C. (eds) (1996) *Organizational Learning and Competitive Advantage.* London: Sage Publications.

Nadler, D., & Nadler, M. B. (1998) *Champions of Change: How CEOs and Their Companies Are Mastering the Skills of Radical Change.* San Francisco, CA: Jossey-Bass.

Nadler, D. A. & Tushman, M. L. (1990) Beyond the charismatic leader: Leadership and organizational change. *California Management Review, 32*(2), 77–97.

O'Regan, N. & Ghobadian, A. (2010) Revitalising an oil giant. *Journal of Strategy and Management, 3*(2), 174–183.

Orgland, M. Y. (1997) *Initiating, Managing, and Sustaining Strategic Change: Learning from the Best.* Basingstoke: Macmillan.

Parker, A. (2010) Strategic background. *Whitbread Investor Day Presentation,* 28 January. http://online.hemscottir.com/ir/wtb/pdf/Investor_Presentation_280110.pdf.

Peters, T. J., & Waterman, R. H. (1982) *In Search of Excellence.* New York: Harper & Row.

Rowe, W. G. (2001) Creating wealth in organizations: The role of leadership. *Academy of Management Executive, 15*(1), 81–94.

Sarros, J. C., Cooper, B. K. & Santora, J. C. (2008) Building a climate for innovation through transformational leadership and organizational culture. *Journal of Leadership and Organizational Studies, 15*(2), 145.

Slatter, S., Lovett, D. & Laura, B. (2006) *Leading Corporate Turnaround.* Chichester: Jossey-Bass.

Stafford, P. (2009) BT cuts 15,000 jobs and dividends slashed. *Financial Times,* 15 May, p. 17.

Tichy, N. & Devanna, M. A. (1986) *The Transformational Leader.* New York: Wiley.

Vital_Speeches_of_the_Day (2009) CEO communication with employees unimportant. *Executive Communication Forum,* February. www.vsotd.com/Article.php?art_num=4469.

Wheelwright, S. C. & Clark, K. B. (1992) Creating project plans to focus product development. *Harvard Business Review,* (March–April), 70–82.

Whitbread (2010) Our history. *About us.* www.whitbread.co.uk/about_us.cfm?id=our_history.

Wind, J. & Main, J. (1998) *Driving Change.* New York: Free Press.

Worley, C. G. & Lawler, E. E. I. (2006) Designing organizations that are built to change. *MIT Sloan Management Review, 48*(1), 19–23.

Yukl, G. (2006) *Leadership in Organizations,* 6th edn. Upper Saddle River, NJ: Prentice Hall.

For a range of further resources supporting this chapter, please visit the companion website for *Strategic Management* at www.routledge.com/cw/fitzroy.

CHAPTER 11

DESIGNING ORGANIZATIONAL ARCHITECTURE

LEARNING OBJECTIVES

Upon completing this chapter you should be able to:

1   Identify the decisions strategic managers have to make regarding firm architecture – structure, processes and human resources.

2   Be aware of the need for innovation in organizational architecture and why new forms have been developed.

3   Apply the principles underlying the design of the structure of an organization.

4   Contrast the major forms of organizational structure, and understand when each should be adopted.

5   Appraise the importance of process management and the nature of the possible conflict between process management and line management.

6   Evaluate the importance of human resources in strategic management.

STRATEGIC MANAGEMENT IN PRACTICE

PERKINELMER

In 1999, the US firm EG&G appointed a new senior executive who swiftly became the CEO and Chairman. Founded in 1947, the firm provided a range of technical services for the US government. Most of its businesses were low-growth and low-margin, a situation the new CEO was anxious to change. The firm's strengths included a healthy balance sheet and a few growth markets in life sciences and digital imaging. It was, however, highly fragmented, with little synergy among its businesses. In addition, many of the firm's senior managers were from the government services businesses, which called for specific skills not always applicable in competitive markets.

A new strategy was designed to improve both financial performance and growth. The firm's 31 businesses were consolidated into five business units with the goal of achieving cost synergies, partly through the integration of different sales forces. Some production was moved to China, Indonesia and other lower wage countries, necessitating further structural changes.

A changed mission expanded firm operations into new, attractive markets. The existing portfolio of the firm was assessed on the basis of two characteristics: Could the business become one of the top three players in the industry? Could it produce double-digit growth? As a result of this analysis, the government service business and several others were divested, providing funds for other changes, including acquisitions. In 2002, the number of business units was reduced to three, partly from divestments, partly from consolidation.

The firm also developed more shared service organizations (e.g. financial controls, IT and HR) operating across the entire firm. Supply-chain management was updated by establishing a corporate-wide material purchasing system. At the same time, there was a shift in power from the centre to business units. Corporate staff was reduced and business unit employees given more responsibility for their strategy.

Those who could not or would not change were let go. New employees with the appropriate knowledge and skills were hired and given substantial responsibility. At the end of 2000, of the top 100 managers in the firm, 80 per cent were new to their job and 50 per cent were new to the firm. A new performance-based compensation scheme was also introduced. Training programmes in Six Sigma were instituted for all employees. Leadership talent was developed by providing cross-functional and cross-business assignments. In 1999, the name of the firm was changed to PerkinElmer to symbolize the changes taking place (Heimbouch, 2000).

In 2009 PerkinElmer's mission was to be a global technological leader, focusing on improving the health and safety of people and the environment, with revenue of $1.8 billion, operating in 150 countries. The firm had seven business units, including Food Safety, Life Sciences and Medical Images. Of the seven business unit presidents, five had PhDs (PerkinElmer, 2010).

CHAPTER OVERVIEW

This chapter begins with a short description of the elements of organizational architecture – structure, processes and human resources. We then discuss the principles underlying design of organizational structure, such as whether the firm is centralized or decentralized. Having explored these issues, we review common organizational forms, from simple functional structures to more complex global matrices. We then examine the need for process management. Cross-functional processes often represent key capabilities of the firm and these must be managed in an integrated fashion. We then explore human resource issues of the firm including the skills and attitudes of employees, appraisal systems and the design of appropriate incentives. These intangible assets are critical to success. The View from the Top features an interview with Howard Stringer, CEO of Sony, illustrating how Sony has grappled with issues of architecture. The chapter concludes with a mini-case, Anglo American plc, and its development of a new organizational architecture.

LEARNING OBJECTIVE 1

Identify the decisions strategic managers have to make regarding firm architecture – structure, processes and human resources.

Organizational architecture

The organizational structure, process design and human resource approach adopted by the firm.

11.1 INTRODUCTION

As the PerkinElmer example illustrates, strategic management involves more than developing a strategy; it is also about getting that strategy to work. To ensure a chosen strategy is successfully implemented requires an integrated set of changes to several characteristics of the firm. Under a new CEO from outside the firm, a new mission and approach redirected the PerkinElmer portfolio towards high-growth high-technology businesses while divesting others. Implementing such a radical strategy required significant changes to structure, processes and human resources. PerkinElmer reduced the number of business units (structural change), improved their supply chain (change in processes) and made some critical human resource decisions (hiring outsiders and introducing performance-based compensation) – among other changes. We denote these three areas of the firm – structure, processes and human resources – as the **organizational architecture** of the firm.

A good strategy may be doomed by poor architecture while an appropriate architecture can definitely contribute to the creation of competitive advantage (Dietl *et al.*, 2009). Architecture constitutes an important intangible asset, contributing to the structural and human capital of the firm. Without an aligned and integrated structure, appropriate processes and human resource practices, strategic failure is almost certain. In a turbulent world, organizational adaptability, agility and innovation are critical capabilities. We must ensure that firms do not place such emphasis on stability, whether with seniority-based reward systems or inward-oriented cultures, that their ability for continuous change is compromised (Worley & Lawler, 2006).

The design of architecture, then, subsumes organizational structure, the design of certain processes and systems within the firm as well as critical human resource issues. The CEO must be involved, to some extent, in all of these areas. In some areas, this means establishing appropriate policies and procedures; for example, the incentive system to be used. In other areas, such as selecting a new organizational structure, the CEO will take an active decision-making role.

The traditional view is that structure follows strategy and that architecture by itself does not generate superior economic performance (Chandler, 1962). But as noted, strategy is not just about a good idea; it is also about making that idea happen. Architecture is certainly about making it happen, since it involves decisions about the type of people comprising the firm, its culture, information systems and structure, all of which certainly affect performance (Sarros *et al.*, 2008). Architecture shapes senior managers' view of the world thereby influencing strategy. Thus, in our view, strategy and structure are interwoven with mutual causation. Architecture alone does not create superior performance, yet poor architecture certainly contributes to inferior performance through a lack of integration and focus.

What is organizational architecture?

Designing organizational architecture requires decisions in three interrelated areas, as shown in Figure 11.1. A good architecture ensures consistency and alignment not only among these elements, but also with the strategy being pursued by the firm.

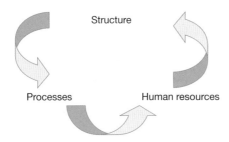

Figure 11.1 Organizational architecture

The three elements shown in Figure 11.1 are described below.

- *Organizational structure* refers to the way in which tasks are differentiated and then coordinated. It also indicates how tasks have been defined and the hierarchy of the firm, indicating formal relationships and decision-making power.

- *Human resources* include decisions on selection, motivation, compensation, training and succession planning for the firm's managers. In addition, strategic managers need an understanding of company culture, current and future capabilities, and whether these are aligned with the current and anticipated strategic moves.

- *Processes* include decision-making, planning and budgeting, workflows, and the increasingly important IT architecture of the firm. As noted in Chapter 3 (➤Chapter 3), information technology represents almost 50 per cent of capital investment for US firms, and top management must be intimately involved. Competitive advantage is increasingly derived from information and knowledge. Ensuring that timely, accurate and appropriate information is available to the workforce is crucial.

Chapter 3

These three dimensions must be congruent with each other as well as with company strategy. As firms grow, they develop new structures, processes and human resource systems to handle increased complexity. At the same time the interdependencies of these three dimensions can make change more difficult since change in one may require change in another. This has been referred to as structural inertia (Tushman & O'Reilly, 1997).

Chapter 3

As we have emphasized, organizations face a rapidly changing and unpredictable environment (➤Chapter 3). Consequently, change must become an integral feature of the firm. Environmental change results not only in a changing strategy but also in ongoing and continuous change in the firm's architecture (Lawler & Worley, 2006). Strategic management of the firm includes decisions about when and how to change this architecture.

Given the speed and unpredictability of external change, what organizational characteristics are likely to be critical in the future? We suggest the following:

LEARNING OBJECTIVE 2

Be aware of the need for innovation in organizational architecture and why new forms have been developed.

- Organizations must become increasingly flexible to cope with unanticipated changes. This includes increasing adaptability, the ability to sense and respond to external changes, and the ability of the firm and employees to experiment and learn (Haeckel, 1999). A command-and-control approach will become less viable.

- Creativity and knowledge will become a critical basis for competitive advantage. Organizations must permit creativity of their employees to develop and flourish. Changes in rewards and structure will be needed to accomplish this.

- With a higher rate of external change, organizations will need to act and make decisions faster. Information technology will provide one means of accomplishing this. These changes imply more empowerment, with decision-making closer to where the action is, and less bureaucracy.

- Increased competition in product markets will require high levels of efficiency. Thus firms will focus on activities at which they excel, outsourcing the rest.

These trends mean that organizational innovation will continue to be a critical dynamic capability of successful firms. Its importance is reflected in the statement that many attempts to change organizations fail because of organizational designs and management practices that are inherently anti-change (Lawler & Worley, 2006).

The automobile industry, in which all competitors are attempting to deliver precisely the car a customer wants, where and when he or she wants it, provides an excellent example of these changes. Car companies are attempting to build to order, not to a forecast, using the Internet to manage the supply chain with customers and suppliers. This trend accelerated with the 2008/09 financial crisis, which resulted in many automobile companies having substantial stocks of unsold cars. In Europe, BMW, a leading firm in build-to-order, permits customers to change their car specification up to six days before it gets produced and to pick up their cars in as little as two weeks after ordering (Reiter, 2010). Renault has also been reported to be moving more towards a build-to-order system to cut its stock of unsold cars by $1 billion (Morley, 2010).

> **Challenge of strategic management**
>
> As intangibles such as knowledge and insight become more critical as sources of competitive advantage, the hierarchical arrangements characterizing many firms will become increasingly dysfunctional. In many high-tech firms, competition to recruit the most recent PhDs is fierce, for it is their expertise that potentially ensures the next technological breakthrough. Yet these creative individuals are accustomed to working in a fluid, task-focused, ideas-orientated environment – the opposite of bureaucracy.
>
> ■ How will organizations have to change to deal with this phenomenon?

11.2 STRUCTURE

We defined business organizations as economic entities, voluntary collections of individuals (and assets) pursuing a common objective. Such entities have two fundamental characteristics – differentiation and integration (Lawrence & Lorsch, 1967). To obtain efficiency, organizations always have some degree of differentiation, whereby tasks are divided to allow for specialization and thus efficiency. But as soon as tasks are specialized, there is a need for integration. So tasks may be specialized between marketing and manufacturing, but integration is required to ensure that manufacturing makes the products that marketing believes are demanded in the marketplace. This tension between integration and differentiation is at the heart of organizational design. Integration holds the firm or business unit together, ensuring that it pursues a globally integrated direction. Differentiation derives from the employment of skilled specialists, increasingly necessary as the firm's environment becomes more competitive, and required capabilities evolve. As we will see, one way to achieve these dual goals of differentiation and integration is through structure, whereby tasks are subdivided and then integrated.

Structure often evolves historically; it is rarely the result of systematic analysis and planning. Structure evolves in response to strategic decisions, such as acquisitions or employment of personnel with new skills, and in response to political pressure. Eventually, if not initially, such structures are likely to inhibit, rather than facilitate, strategy execution (Worley & Lawler, 2006). Structural redesign is also difficult, not only because of inertia but also because it involves redistributing power, resulting in conflicts within the firm (Goold & Campbell, 2002). Further, after a firm has been in operation for some time, it develops a history and with this history comes a culture, a set of shared beliefs and assumptions about the world and how to succeed in that world. As with structure, such a culture can facilitate or inhibit strategy development and implementation. As we noted in Chapter 10 (➤Chapter 10), one of the most difficult strategic management tasks is to change the culture of a firm.

Chapters 2, 10

Firms should also strive to develop structures that encourage certain characteristics, yet this requirement demonstrates the paradoxical nature of strategic management (➤Chapter 2). We want to encourage efficiency and creativity, flexibility and stability, centralization and decentralization, achieving integration and alignment while still retaining the ability of the firm to adapt to a changing environment. A classic organizational dilemma is how to balance the advantages of scale and specialization against the need for flexibility, adaptability and creativity. A number of new organizational forms, such as the use of teams, alliances and spin-offs, are designed to better achieve these twin goals.

Summarizing, modern firms are characterized as follows:

- There is a division of labour, such as specialists in marketing, sales, accounting, finance, operations, R&D and human resources.
- There is some form of hierarchy – indicated by an organization chart, incorporating superior–subordinate relationships.
- Decisions are based on rules, policies and procedures that seek to promote efficiency (and consistency). These may inculcate a tendency to become inflexible and resist change.

The nature of structure

Organizational structure

The firm's formal role configuration, showing how tasks are divided and integrated, including the control mechanisms, authority and decision-making processes of the firm.

Organizational structure shows how tasks in the firm are divided and then integrated to achieve coordination. Thus structure facilitates specialization within the firm, allowing personnel to develop and use specialized skills.

In large firms, no one employee is responsible for executing all tasks; instead, tasks are broken down into smaller, more specialized ones. Tasks are differentiated into roles such as finance, marketing, production, legal and so on. Such specialization results in efficiency gains in the performance of individual tasks. Alternatively, such roles may be grouped into divisions or business units based on products or markets. As more skilled and specialized personnel are added, differentiation within the business unit increases, resulting in the need for increased coordination to ensure consistency. This coordination is achieved through control systems, culture and so on. Differentiation and integration are central to the design of organizational structure and result in the need to achieve an optimum trade-off between specialization and coordination (Lawrence & Lorsch, 1967).

Structure will be influenced by size, age and the firm's diversity in products, markets and technology, as well as turbulence in the external environment. At the same time, consideration must be given to the cost of any structure. As the firm gets larger and more complex, the costs of operating the system will increase unless economies of scale can be demonstrated. A firm may become unmanageable due to size and complexity.

Organizational structure also shows reporting relationships and the authority and power relationships within the firm. Hierarchy is an essential ingredient in organizational life, present in all larger firms and organizations. Burns and Stalker originated the idea that there were two polar organizational forms, denoted as mechanistic and organic. Mechanistic organizations were seen as more rigid while organic organizational forms were seen as flexible (Burns & Stalker, 1994). Where a firm or unit is positioned along a continuum between these two depended on the rate of change of its external environment and the degree of standardization of the product, service or task. This relationship is an example of contingency theory, which suggests that there is no one best way to organize but that all ways to organize are not equally effective, since appropriate structure is contingent upon other factors (Greenberg & Baron, 2008). In addition, since architecture must be considered in a total or integrative sense, structure may also be dependent on the firm's human resources. One individual may be able to manage in a structure that may not suit others.

Nonetheless, while no single design will be best for all firms, there are some principles on which good design is based, which we now discuss.

Dynamic/static environments

As noted above, contingency theory suggests that there are many possible organization structures, contingent on the situation being analysed. So history matters, as does time orientation, task differentiation, external pressures, the technical system, size and so on. One crucial variable is the external environment faced by the organization. In static environments, the mechanistic model of Burns and Stalker, to which many would apply the now almost pejorative label of bureaucracy, may suffice. Interestingly, the concept of bureaucracy was originally viewed as a great leap forward for humankind. By codifying rules to ensure that clients of organizations were treated in an equitable manner, Weber believed that individuals would not be subject to the whims of arbitrary or even despotic rulers and administrators (Weber, 2001). Over time, however, the connotations of the term have changed. Today most people equate it to ponderous, slow-moving, unthinking application of rules, preferring correct procedure to correct outcome.

These very connotations capture why mechanistic and bureaucratic models are ineffective in today's business environment. The speed of change means slow response cannot be tolerated and change may outpace the organization's ability to cope. Nonetheless, coordination cannot be achieved without some degree of predictability. March and Simon recognized this in their path-breaking work, coining the phrase 'standard operating procedure (sop)' to describe the rules that organizations develop to cope with recurring situations (March & Simon, 1958). Indeed, historically there have been guidelines for designing hierarchies – principles such as a clear line of command, reporting to only one person, clear accountability, responsibility coupled with authority, and span of control of seven (Hunt, 1992).

With the increased speed of change, however, the ability of the organization to develop rules is typically outpaced by change: we can't write and rewrite rules quickly enough! Further, with turbulence comes a different problem, which is the unpredictability of change. No matter how good a job we do in forecasting and planning, 100 per cent accuracy will never be achieved. Consequently, we must build organizations that are flexible and can deal with the unanticipated changes that result from turbulence.

Tushman and O'Reilly adopted the phrase ambidextrous organization to capture the ability of organizing in different ways to deal with different situations (Tushman & O'Reilly, 1996). The term *adhocracy* has been used to describe the innovative organization, suggesting that we can put ad hoc groups together to deal with situations as they arise. Such an approach would be unnecessary in predictable environments (Mintzberg, 1993). These ideas reflect Burns and Stalker's concept of an organic organization but are quite counter to the hierarchies

LEARNING OBJECTIVE 3

Apply the principles underlying the design of the structure of an organization.

that characterized many twentieth-century organizations. Moreover, we see this type of change being implemented in many organizations today, as more and more firms recognize that change is needed. Devolution of responsibility, de-layering, the metamorphosing of functional organizations into business units and the like – all provide illustrations of change towards more flexible and responsive structures. At the same time, we must point out the paradoxical nature of many of these changes. Even as we urge organizations to be more flexible and responsive, we must simultaneously recognize that without some predictability of behaviour an organization ceases to be such and descends into chaos. Paradox is a fact of life in strategic management, and we will encounter many other cases as we examine organizational architecture.

Differentiation/integration

Achieving balance between differentiation and integration is an important principle in designing organizational structure (Mintzberg, 1993). Differentiation allows employees to focus their abilities and be deployed for comparative advantage, thereby (in theory) developing efficiency gains. Thus activities may be grouped to achieve low cost via economies of scale. On the other hand, differentiation requires coordination to achieve integration. Firms only exist because activity coordinated by the firm is more efficient than activity coordinated by the market. Hence resolving the coordination problem is vital to the efficiency and effectiveness of the business (Williamson, 1975). Business unit managers must weigh the gains from specialization (and consequent differentiation) against the costs of integration.

 Chapter 8 Structure may also be influenced by decisions that have been made with respect to the role of the centre, as discussed in Chapter 8 (➤Chapter 8). The style of the centre affects not only the provision of corporate services but also the extent of differentiation and integration across business units. With a strategic planning style, there is extensive integration of strategy across the business units as the firm searches for competitive advantage. At the other extreme, financial control is characterized by few shared capabilities across businesses, coupled with tight financial controls. The size and location of head offices are also affected: financial-style firms tend to have small head offices; firms with strategic planning styles tend to have larger head offices.

We must also distinguish between vertical, horizontal and spatial differentiation. Vertical differentiation is the number of management levels in the business. The focus here is on the division of authority – who has authority to make which decisions. Horizontal differentiation focuses on the division and grouping of tasks. Spatial differentiation refers to whether distinct groups are developed for specific geographic areas. Differentiation thus involves combining employees into groups, with these groups typically demonstrating similarity by task (e.g. marketing or accounting), by product or by geography. This differentiation in turn facilitates specialization and should lead to superior efficiency.

Vertical differentiation is reflected in an increased number of hierarchical levels within the firm. A business unit with many levels of management will encounter communication difficulties. Information may be distorted, and there are limits on managers' ability to make decisions (March & Simon, 1958). The business may also have too many middle managers, who add less value than their cost.

With horizontal differentiation, there are increased numbers of distinct positions at the same level within the firm. So we may have a number of accountants, all at the same level, each undertaking specialized tasks. Horizontal differentiation may also occur with the formation of separate strategic business units. These permit a higher degree of specialization, whether to focus on a particular market or the management of a specific technology. Many firms now organize around so-called vertical markets, segmented on the basis of their customers' industries, and some are even organizing around customers themselves.

Global firms also generally need to differentiate themselves spatially in some way, such as instituting an Asia–Pacific, Africa–Middle East or European group to develop the specialized skills needed to understand specific geographic markets.

It should be clear from these examples that the more a firm is differentiated, the more difficult it is to integrate the various units. For example, a global firm may differentiate and set up a subsidiary in Argentina. This allows the firm to be more responsive to the local market. But now additional integration is needed to ensure coordination between the Argentina unit and, say, a German unit with the same product line. Developments in IT make this integration easier than in the past, but integration issues remain. Too much differentiation can lead to disorder in the organization, but too much emphasis on integration can lead to a stifling of creativity and innovation – another paradox (►Chapter 2).

Chapter 2

There exist a variety of mechanisms for achieving integration, and they are not necessarily mutually exclusive. Integration can utilize lateral means, such as task forces, committees, conferences and liaison functions as well as informal, direct, face-to-face contact. Vertical means include formal hierarchy, wherein individuals higher up the organization have authority to specify the nature of the cooperation. Additionally, rules and operating procedures can operate to facilitate cooperation.

Centralization/decentralization

A related consideration is the degree of authority and independence of each unit of the firm, the level of **centralization** of the firm. The extent of centralization determines who has the authority to make which decisions.

Centralization
The degree to which decision-making authority is retained by senior management rather than being devolved to the constituent units of the firm.

Centralization gives more control to the centre but increases the amount of information flowing into the centre, which must then be processed so that a decision can be made and communicated. This has two consequences, neither of which is desirable in contemporary environments. One is that it tends to produce slower decisions, and the other is that it increases the number of levels in the firm. Although both centralization and decentralization have advantages, in terms of the need for lower cost (driven by intense competition) and speedy decision-making (driven by the pace of contextual change), the current trend is towards greater decentralization. This encourages empowerment and speeds response, since those closest to the action are making the decisions. We have witnessed many examples of firms downsizing, eliminating organizational levels to reduce costs and enabling decisions to be made at lower levels in the firm. Before their disastrous oil spill in 2010, BP had called in consultants Bain and Company to assist in this process, with the results described below.

> ## Decentralization *in practice* – BP
>
> In the period from 2000 to 2007 the BP organization had become very complicated. Much of the complexity arose from mergers in 1999 and 2000, responses to Sarbanes Oxley, and a changing regulatory framework requiring a lot of additional assurance and verifications.
>
> Bain identified 10,000 organizational interfaces in the company, which employed 100,000 people at the time. BP had lots of organizational layers, with as many as 12 layers between the chief executive and the front line/operational level in some areas.
>
> As a result of the Bain & Co report, BP eliminated much of its regional structures, simplified its functional structures, and developed a number of organizational guidelines such as the span of control should be at least seven people and ideally more, with no more than seven layers between the CEO and front-line operations (O'Regan & Ghobadian, forthcoming).

The classic organizational dilemma is, of course, to balance advantages of scale versus advantages of being small. A structure of semi-autonomous SBUs may produce flexibility and responsiveness, but creates problems of cost and control. For example, if each SBU has its own human resources group, economies of scale will be limited, and costs may be higher. In the worst case, SBU managers may engage in political activity or fail to collaborate where it would be fruitful, perhaps missing growth.

Decentralization decisions will usually be influenced by the firm's strategy. A strategy of cost leadership may require a structure with strong task specialization, centralized decision-making, and formal work rules and procedures. By contrast, a strategy of differentiation and added value is more likely to require decentralization, more coordination and integration, **Chapter 7** and more use of teams. Likewise, a firm following a dominator strategy (➤Chapter 7) will of necessity have to decentralize further. It is no coincidence that Alfred Sloan was required to be an organizational innovator in order to implement the strategy he designed for General Motors. Sloan introduced divisionalization and the reporting systems that permitted such a structure to flourish (Sloan, 1964).

The environment in which the firm competes also influences centralization and decentralization decisions. Large commodity-type markets are much better suited to centralization than are heavily segmented differentiated markets, which require greater decentralization.

Functional or process management

Another design issue is the consideration given to the importance of vertical functions as against different horizontal processes. The traditional view takes a functional perspective, but firms have many important processes. A process such as new product development draws on the skills of such groups as R&D, marketing, accounting, operations, etc. Similarly, pricing decisions may involve accounting, marketing, sales, finance and general management. Should we consider the firm as managing a number of functions or a number of processes?

Ultimately, of course, we must manage both, but the adoption of total quality management (TQM) and the impact of information technology have encouraged many firms to examine their processes more closely. Of course, business processes are not immutable, and the reduced cost and widespread availability that information technology has given many firms have improved their business processes through a set of tools described as business process re-engineering, which attempts to introduce radical changes in the ways that processes are carried out (Subramonian *et al.*, 2009). However, there are often tensions between function and process, and these tensions may defeat attempts at change.

Challenge of strategic management

Perhaps the ultimate paradox is the paradox created by the paradoxes themselves. If architecture must simultaneously accommodate such polar opposites as integration and differentiation, efficiency and creativity, flexibility and stability, centralization and decentralization, scale and specialization, surely the problem is insuperable?

■ Do you agree with this view? Why or why not?

Types of organizational structures

Organization structures evolve over time along with the challenges faced by corporations. We now examine the different ways in which firms break up their constituent elements into coherent organizational designs.

Functional structures

The functional structure is likely to be used by firms with low levels of product and market diversity and in SBUs within a specific division of a multidivisional firm. Figure 11.2 illustrates such a structure, with a chief executive officer and managers for each of the major functions such as marketing, accounting, human resources and manufacturing.

LEARNING OBJECTIVE 4

Contrast the major forms of organizational structure, and understand when each should be adopted.

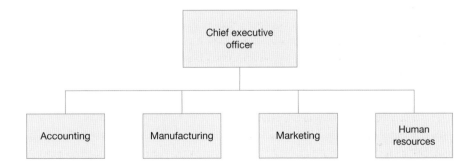

Figure 11.2 Functional structure

Such structures permit development of specialization and consequent efficiency gains in these functional areas. A functional organization also permits economies of scale by concentrating in one department activities that demonstrate substantial interdependencies – a cost accountant for product 1 may learn from the accountant for product 2 and vice versa.

The Trader Media Group is a UK company specializing in magazines and websites containing classified automobile advertisements. The firm operates in the UK, Ireland, Italy and South Africa with a functional organization as shown in Figure 11.3.

Trader Media has executives responsible for functional groups such as sales and service, marketing, finance and human resources, among others. This allows functional specialization to be developed within these groups. If two departments have different views, resolving the conflict and integrating the two departments' views to get a common organizational view is the CEO's responsibility.

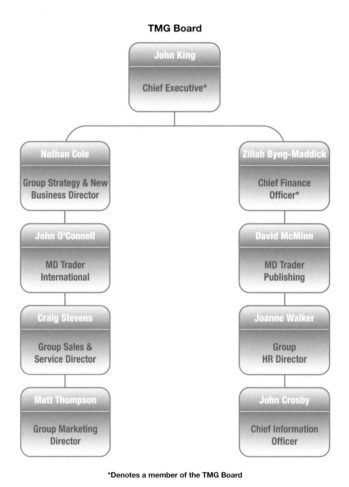

Figure 11.3 Trader Media Group organizational chart

This example also reveals a key difficulty with such structures: the tendency for the firm to develop functional 'silos' between which there is very limited lateral communication. Information flows are generally vertical and are integrated only at the CEO level. As noted, this may result in slow decision-making and distortion of information. Silos are such a problem that several companies have been established whose mission is to solve this problem (GDI Infotech, 2008).

Functional structures work better when there is limited diversity of tasks within the function. When this is not the case, the functional department is itself generally organized by sub-function. Marketing may be organized into sales, advertising, direct marketing and market research subgroups. The emergence of sub-functions is more likely as the company grows in size and the number of levels within a department increases. The resulting structures can become very unwieldy, fostering internal conflict.

Apart from size, what really renders a functional structure dysfunctional is product, market or technological diversity. If a firm is successful, it will grow, and as it grows, its mix of products, markets and technologies inevitably becomes more complex. For this reason, most global firms are organized on divisional bases, an innovation permitting them to handle diversity in products, markets and technologies.

Divisional structure

A divisional structure is illustrated in Figure 11.4. In such structures, firms organize activities into separate business units and delegate control over the needed resources to managers of these units (Strikwerda & Stoelhorst, 2009), with the performance of each unit being measured by the corporate centre. Which tasks are performed at the corporate level versus which are decentralized and which performance measures are used are all important topics in strategic management. Appropriate divisional control systems are neither so bureaucratic as to inhibit creativity by division personnel nor so loose as to endanger shareholder interests. However,

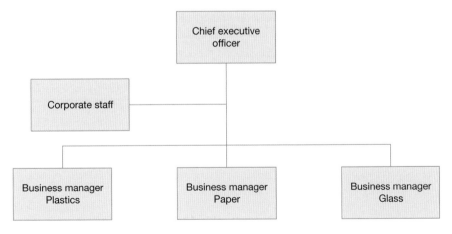

Figure 11.4 Multidivisional structure

encouraging divisions to draw on central resources and contribute to the total firm is often a challenging undertaking.

Responsibility for strategy development for each business unit is delegated to the unit manager, who is also held accountable for the performance of the unit. With this structure, corporate staff are responsible for corporate-level strategy, such as acquisitions and divestments, as well as provision of certain corporate services.

Chapters 8, 12

The autonomy of the business unit manager is influenced by the style of the corporate centre (▶Chapter 8). Unit managers report to the CEO in the corporate centre and are therefore not truly independent. Corporate staff will decide on a control system to ensure that business unit managers meet agreed-upon objectives. With a strategic planning style, all strategy proposals must be approved by corporate staff. With a financial control style, the emphasis falls primarily on the financial results to be achieved, with less concern from the centre about the details of business unit strategy. Such measures as EBITDA, cash flow, ROI, ROS and, possibly, economic profit would be the prime corporate focus (▶Chapter 12). Since each business is operated and evaluated as a relatively independent unit, a reasonably standardized information system is required to permit comparisons among different units.

Among the advantages of such structures is the decentralization of decision-making. Corporate management focuses on strategic issues for the firm – capital allocation, overall direction, decisions to buy and sell businesses. Managers in the businesses are responsible for strategy and tactics at the business unit level. This structure also improves accountability. Corporate staff have an advisory and audit function and hold division managers responsible for performance. Since units put up proposals to corporate for funds, competition for capital within the firm is a feature. This should improve capital allocation, since cash flows go to corporate treasury and back to divisions on a competitive basis.

One disadvantage when the firm becomes very diverse is that senior managers have very limited understanding of the various business units. They can become very distant, preoccupied with financial markets, and have limited familiarity with industry, competition, technology and so on, despite the fact that they must make decisions on strategies put forward by business unit managers.

Each division is normally organized on a functional basis, often resulting in duplication of many functions that exist in each division. Although R&D, strategic planning, legal and finance are often centralized corporate functions, the costs of functional duplication constitute one of the disadvantages of divisionalization. The firm may miss opportunities for economies of scale that could be achieved by combining these functions. Ideally, gains from detailed knowledge of the business's competitive situation will outweigh costs of duplication.

Such structures will not remove all conflicts among lower level managers. For example, SBU managers often disagree over the allocation of corporate overheads. Depending on the style of the centre, there may also be ambiguity over responsibility for SBU performance. Issues such as definition of business units, reporting relationships and transfer pricing may bedevil a divisionalized organization (Hunt, 1992).

Getinge AB, a Swedish medical firm with 12,000 employees and 2009 revenue of SEK 23 billion (approximately €2.7 billion), is a divisionalized firm. Getinge is organized into three businesses, each of which operates globally, as shown in Figure 11.5.

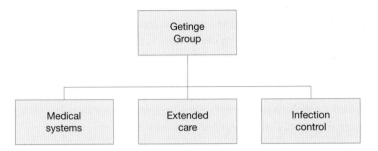

Figure 11.5 Multidivisional structure of the Getinge Group (Getinge, 2010)

- *Medical systems* – medical products for operating theatres and intensive care units.
- *Extended care* – providing hygiene and other products for people with reduced mobility such as the aged.
- *Infection control* – providing sterilization and other products.

Group structure

When firms are even larger, with a significant number of relatively independent businesses, these may first be assigned to broad product groups, with SBUs reporting to the different groups. The group structure for a hypothetical company is illustrated in Figure 11.6.

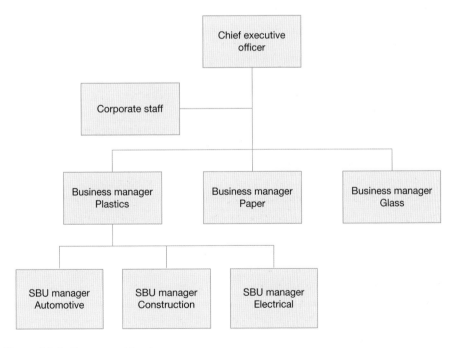

Figure 11.6 Group and business structure

Figure 11.6 shows the detailed structure only for the Plastics Group. This group has a group manager and possibly group-level staff. The group is made up of a number of SBUs: automotive, construction and electrical. Each SBU is an independent business, competing in its own market against defined competitors. Group structures may be formed on the basis of products, markets, technologies or geography:

- *Product* – commercial banks are often organized around product groups, such as lending, mortgages, current accounts and so on.

- *Markets* – this approach may be more responsive to changing needs and meeting new customer requirements. Our Siemens example in Chapter 8 (Figure 8.1) featured groups for fossil power generation and power transmission among others.

- *Technologies* – such a structure is adopted by Bayer, as shown in Figure 11.7, with technologies of health care, material science and crop science.

- *Geography* – such groups might be regional within a continent or country but are probably most common in large global firms, many of which have groups for the US, European, Middle Eastern, African, Latin American and Asian markets.

Figure 11.7 shows that Bayer AG is structured around technologies. We show details for only one group, Material Science.

As with divisionalized structures, groups can result in reduced economies of scale and higher costs. Employees within the business are naturally more focused on the needs of that business, whereas centralized staff will face more competing demands. Nonetheless, wasteful

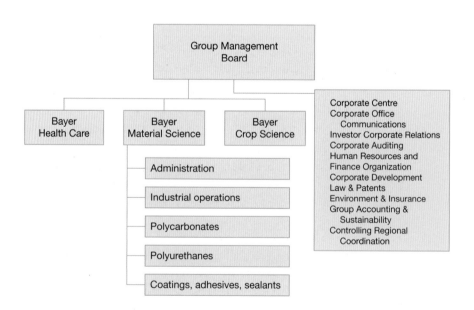

Figure 11.7 Group organization of Bayer AG (Bayer, 2010)

duplication must be avoided: too often there is a tendency for group executives to empire-build. This is one of the critical organizational paradoxes to which we earlier referred.

Corporate management, which is responsible for the structure of the firm, needs to periodically consider whether to change the number and definition of groups and SBUs to reflect changes in the environment and firm strategy. The goal should be to combine structure and control systems so as to both motivate and control the business unit's personnel without incurring excessive cost. However, a growth business may need quite different structures, incentives and even processes from a more mature business unit.

Global structure

Global firms have a requirement for global efficiency. In many product fields there is a degree of customer convergence around the world, evident with consumer products such as DVDs, personal computers, jeans, mobile phones and so on. Similarly, for industrial goods such as chemicals or steel, customers all require essentially the same product. Global competitors can take advantage of scale economies to develop efficiencies which may be unattainable by local competitors. At the same time, global firms have to be sensitive to local differences. Some of these differences are culture-related, some relate to the fact that many products are part of a total usage system, others result from government regulation and so on. Global firms need to balance the desire to achieve cost advantages with the requirement to be flexible enough to respond to these local needs.

Bartlett and Ghoshal suggested four types of structures for global firms (Bartlett & Ghoshal, 1998):

- *International* – the company has an international division, often regarded as an appendage by the firm.

- *Multinational* – a corporate centre manages a portfolio of multiple national entities, each of which may be regarded as a business unit.

- *Global* – the company treats the world as an integrated whole and manages in a centralized manner, with little attention paid to local differences. Some large Japanese companies in automobiles and consumer electronics operate in this way.

- *Transnational* – these firms try to ensure that they do three things: use scale and cost leadership as one source of competitive advantage, adopt differentiation in product as a way to enhance performance, and, finally, use innovations, generally created at the corporate centre, to gain new sources of revenue.

Transnational firms in Bartlett and Ghoshal's typology are attempting to get the best of both worlds: the advantages of scale with the flexibility of local operations. Thus operations around the world are not standardized. Some groups may be pursuing a differentiated strategy, while others pursue a low-cost strategy with standard products. Nonetheless, these companies encourage knowledge-sharing (not all knowledge is assumed to be created at the corporate centre), and have procedures to share knowledge worldwide. Some activities, such as basic research, are centralized to protect core capabilities. On the other hand, applied research centres may be distributed in different countries depending on the skills and markets within those countries. Both Nestlé and Unilever follow such an approach.

Achieving synthesis between global efficiency and local responsiveness represents a significant management challenge. Perhaps as a result, structures tend to be quite complicated. As of 2009, Unilever was organized at the executive level by region, product and function.

- *Region* – Unilever had presidents for Western Europe, Americas, Asia, Africa, and Central and Eastern Europe.
- *Product* – Unilever had presidents for Foods, Home and Personal Care.
- *Function* – Unilever had a chief human resources officer, a chief supply chain officer, chief research and development officer, and a chief financial officer.

There is certainly no single model of structure used by global companies; what is selected reflects their history, current concerns and the degree and nature of interaction among the units. Indeed, many, like Unilever, have tried a succession of approaches. Whatever basis is selected, the firm will certainly need coordinating mechanisms.

Matrix structure

A matrix structure is one in which there is a dual structure, combining both functional specialization and business product or project specialization. Such structures have always been common in project-based firms; for example, engineering construction firms such as Bechtel or military contractors. Superimposed on a fairly standard differentiation of tasks into functions such as engineering, sales and marketing is further differentiation based on project or product. Employees work in project teams with specialists from other functions and have a functional boss and a project boss. Appropriate skills and resources are assembled for each project. However, a significant proportion of large companies that are not project-oriented are also organized in a similar manner, generally on the basis of business group and geography, so it is important to understand the advantages and disadvantages of matrices.

Consider a structure formed around global product groups. Such a structure may allow the firm to achieve superior efficiency and quality but may also be weak in customer responsiveness. If, for example, each group has a specialized sales force, there is not only a cost penalty but also the possibility of aggravating customers who prefer a single point of contact. In addition, the lateral flow of information among product groups is likely to be inhibited. Of course, if the company organized around markets instead, there would be commensurate difficulties in obtaining scale economics by product, for example. It was for this sort of reason that an exasperated IBM executive once exclaimed, 'There is no best way to organize – there is only the least worst.'

The problem is that managing a large, diverse company with operations in multiple countries is a multidimensional problem, and the formal anatomy of the organization's structure cannot deal with more than two or three of these. A global matrix represents a way to deal with at least two dimensions. Instead of a vertical axis of functions, for example, it could be product groups, which provide specialist services such as R&D, marketing and product design. The horizontal axis is the geographic groups – Europe, Asia and so on – so as to get a degree of local flexibility and better transfer of market information and experience.

Project-based matrices, while they may afford limited hierarchical control, permit project teams to grow, shrink and change as required. It is therefore a very flexible structure – a classic example of adhocracy – but the costs are likely to be substantial, and it is often difficult to balance interests of function and project. In large companies operating across the globe, matrices exhibit similar problems. Members of the organization often have difficulty dealing with what are, in effect, dual reporting relationships, and priorities may be ambiguous. Nonetheless, the debates spawned by differences over priorities can, if appropriately managed, significantly improve the resulting strategic decisions. Obviously, the culture of the company and its approaches to dealing with such conflicts will determine whether or not the process concludes productively or otherwise.

Matrix structures of global firms can become very complex, as is shown by the Procter & Gamble example in Figure 11.8. P&G describes its structure as attempting to balance two divergent yet complementary perspectives: think globally and act locally. The company has three global business units – Household Care, Beauty Care, and Health, Baby and Family Care – which we would refer to as business groups. They focus on consumers, competitors and brands on a global basis and have responsibility for innovation, profitability and shareholder returns. These businesses are in turn split into businesses oriented around specific markets such as oral and family, as shown above. Finally, a functional structure is adopted for these smaller business units.

To attend to local needs, P&G utilizes market development organizations. These are designed to develop local knowledge of consumers and retailers and to leverage corporate scale at the local level. The firm has seven of these, which span the world, together with a group focusing on global customers such as Tesco.

To achieve economies of scale, P&G has outsourced a number of back-office services such as human resources and payroll to external suppliers such as HP and IBM, organized under Global Business Services. P&G thus exercises planning and oversight of this outsourcing. P&G also has a number of centralized corporate functions responsible for ensuring that functional capability is integrated across the firm. Finally there are such functions as finance and external relations, which are essential corporate activities.

This complex and therefore expensive structure is aimed at getting the best of all worlds: functional excellence, coordination and integration, cost efficiencies, innovation, and local responsiveness. Such is the challenge faced by the architect of today's global corporations to ensure that the firm creates value for all its stakeholders.

Other organizational forms

As firms search for structures that assist strategy development and implementation, they often innovate beyond the basic alternatives described above. Finding a structure that supports strategy development and implementation, while simultaneously creating efficiency, adaptability, speed and flexibility represents an ongoing challenge. Global firms face a

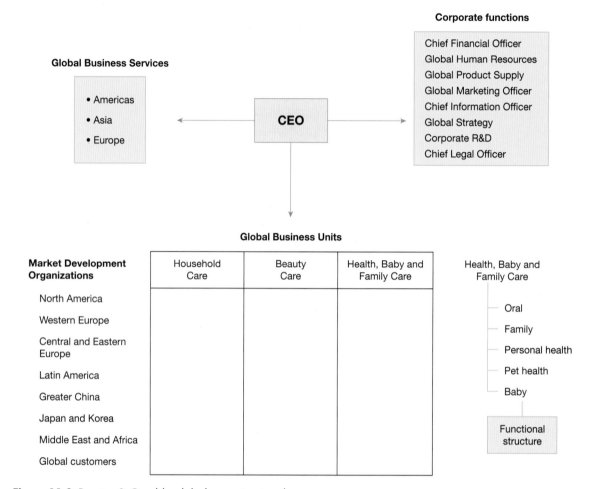

Figure 11.8 Procter & Gamble global organizational structure
Source: P&G, 2010; Galbraith, 2009

Challenge of strategic management

One knowledgeable student of corporate strategy has suggested that too many CEOs use reorganization as a substitute for strategic thinking. Seduced by the idea that strategy is structure, they fail to grasp the need for original and creative thinking that is essential to identification and exploitation of new opportunities.

■ Do you agree with this point of view?

particular problem, since employees in the various subsidiaries often feel that all decisions are made by remote figures at head office who have no understanding of the competitive pressures in their marketplace.

New forms of organization share some common characteristics:

- The focus is on coordination rather than control. Cooperation is obtained through financial and professional incentives, with greater emphasis on social rather than managerial control.
- Individuals possess multiple organizational roles, which is seen as a way to reconcile complex patterns of coordination with high levels of flexibility and responsiveness.

Handy believes organizations of the future will have to deal with a number of paradoxes, combining bigness with smallness, creativity with efficiency and prosperity with social acceptability, as well as having to reward owners of ideas as well as owners of the firm (Handy, 2001). This could well prove difficult, since knowledge workers may be unwilling to cede intellectual property rights to the firm.

These ideas suggest an incipient move from bureaucratic structures to greater flexibility: organizations that can tap the commitment and enthusiasm of people, encouraging them to develop their creativity. Customer pressure also plays a part. Customers buy products from firms, not functions! Success in a competitive world requires much better cross-functional integration, in turn increasing emphasis on a process view of managing and customer focus (Galbraith, 2005).

Current trends in organizational design that represent responses to these challenges include: reduction in the number of layers; adoption of process teams; re-engineering of processes; open communications; alliances with suppliers, customers, and possibly competitors; and better use of information technology. These changes will require more skill development by employees. Increased empowerment will be coupled with better control systems. Control will continue to be based on both quantitative and cultural elements, but the latter are likely to become more important. We will also see continuing development of systems that provide reliable, up-to-date information throughout the firm.

Networks and alliances

As Chapter 3 noted (➤ Chapter 3), competition increasingly occurs between whole networks and industry systems. Traditional joint ventures sometimes metamorphose into other forms, perhaps contractually bound as a result of outsourcing decisions, but sometimes consisting of quite informal, even ephemeral, relationships. The ideas that one company's strengths can offset another's weaknesses or that collaboration in a vertical value chain may be worthwhile are representative of the concepts fostering such alliances. Other firms that are hesitant to merge or acquire see alliances as partnerships that may later lead to closer relationships.

This networked organizational form may also help a firm enter a new business area when it lacks requisite assets – perhaps tangible (e.g. capital or facilities) but often intangible,

Chapter 3

Networks *in practice* – Acer

'[I]n the . . . Acer Group, founder and CEO Stan Shih's philosophy was that a global federation of independently owned firms could be organized, each responsible for its own success, but each willing and capable of interacting with other Acer firms to their mutual benefit. Many of those collaborative relationships were along the global supply chain that produced and distributed parts and components essential to the assembly and delivery of Acer personal computers. Within the Acer federation of firms, the expectation was that suppliers and buyers would learn from each other in order to improve logistics, product design and quality, and so on. Learning that occurred throughout the PC supply chain was later transferred to the many web-based information technology businesses that Acer developed . . . what began as organizational designs intended to assure smooth decision-making and resource flows along supply chains evolved into groups of firms in which collaboration-driven innovations were occurring not only within but across firms. Thus, partly by design and partly through ongoing trust-building, multi-firm networks evolved into "extended enterprises" that looked more and more like collaborative federations or communities.'

(Miles *et al.*, 2009)

Alliances *in practice* – Cereal Partners

General Mills, a large US producer of breakfast cereals, lacked distribution outside North America. Swiss-based Nestlé, one of the world's largest food companies, had excellent European distribution but did not carry breakfast cereals. The two companies allied to form Cereal Partners, which became a major competitor to Kellogg's.

encompassing skills, technological know-how and market access. The firm may also be unwilling to assume full entry costs itself, instead seeking an alliance with a partner firm.

Although the immediate impact of such alliance announcements may appear threatening to competitors, problems often occur when the partners' alliance objectives and/or ability to provide needed resources diverge over time. Nonetheless, some succeed.

Some of the more important alliances are vertical partnerships in which the company forms close linkages with its suppliers. In some cases these partnerships result from mutuality of interest and are positive-sum games (win–win situations), creating formidable supply-chain advantages. In other cases, 'partnership' may be forced on weaker firms by the relative market power of others and be no more than an unpalatable way of forestalling potential supply-chain competition.

A major problem of alliances is the exercise of control. Who has control? How can firms cooperate and compete at the same time? What will be the reaction of regulators to these

Table 11.1 Evolution of economies and organizations (Miles *et al.*, 2009)

Economic era	Standardization	Customization	Innovation
Principle business model	Market penetration	Market segmentation	Market exploration
Growth drivers	Achieving scale economies	Expanding into new market segments	Developing and commercializing products for complementary markets
Organizational model	U-form (centrally, vertically integrated functional structures)	M-form (multidivisional and matrix structures)	I-form (multi-firm networks and community-based structures)
Key assets	Tangible assets	Information	Knowledge
Core organizational capabilities	Planning and controlling	Delegating	Collaborating

networks – will they be seen as anti-competitive? These are important questions that must be addressed by alliance partners.

We can recapitulate our above distinctions by using the historical framework of Miles *et al.* (Miles *et al.*, 2009). They describe the late 1800s and early 1900s as the standardization era. They argue that a centrally managed and planned, vertically integrated structure (referred to as unitary or U-form) was well suited to an era when growth came from penetrating markets with consequent economies of scale. From the 1920s to the 1980s came the customization era, with growth from expanding into new market segments. This required semi-autonomous units sharing some central resources. The multidivisional or M-form structure was well suited to such opportunities. Now, they argue, we are in the innovation era. This means many firms are pursuing a market exploration business model, based on continuous technological, product/service and market innovations, driven by R&D and other processes that cut across technologies and markets. This, they argue, requires the I-form organization, heavily based on network relationships and inter-firm collaboration. Table 11.1 encapsulates their view of structural evolution.

11.3 PROCESSES AND PROCESS MANAGEMENT

LEARNING OBJECTIVE 5

Appraise the importance of process management and the nature of the possible conflict between process management and line management.

As we have emphasized, an increasingly competitive environment requires ever-higher levels of corporate performance. The functional structure underlying the superstructure of most firms inhibits this achievement. The traditional vertical division of work into functions, then into departments within these functions, and finally into tasks certainly permits a high degree of specialization as well as a decision hierarchy. Yet such specialization does not necessarily lead to high levels of customer satisfaction or financial performance. No matter how a company organizes, important issues will arise that cut across organizational lines.

When managers see their organizations in this vertical fashion, they tend to manage them in the same way: vertically. This perspective tends to ignore the customer, enamouring managers with their own functional expertise. There is a distressing tendency, sometimes reinforced by reward systems, for managers to concentrate on functional optimization, with the firm generating functional silos across which there is little or no communication. The key challenge of such functional structures is coordination across tasks, departments and functions (Ostroff, 1999). Integrating mechanisms such as committees and task forces may assist in coordination, but sometimes this is insufficient and more radical solutions may be necessary.

Organizational processes

A coordinated and horizontal multi-functional set of activities which support the delivery of products and services to the customer.

From a different perspective, however, the firm is a set of **organizational processes** that deliver products and services and receive funds for them and that, to perform well, it must excel in each of these processes. If such processes are well managed they can constitute vital intangible assets (Palmberg, 2010).

If we consider the firm from the customers' perspective, they have little interest in how the firm is structured and organized – they want products and services developed and delivered efficiently and effectively. How the firm accomplishes this is for them irrelevant. They do not want to know where the service department is housed or how service is coordinated with spares inventory. They are only interested in the end results; for example, do they get good service when they need it?

Whereas some processes are industry-specific, others are generic. Industry-specific processes include loan processing in banking, claims processing in insurance, and car servicing in auto dealerships. Examples of generic processes include, but are not limited to:

- Order generation and fulfilment
- Product development
- Customer service
- Supply-chain management.

In addition, there are a number of generic managerial processes, such as:

- Planning
- Budgeting
- Cost analysis
- Acquisition evaluation
- Resource allocation
- Transfer of capabilities.

In recognition of these concerns, many firms have realized that needed performance improvements remain out of reach when the business is organized in the traditional vertical fashion, hierarchically structured and functionally oriented. Today's competitive environment requires superb coordination between the functions as well as functional excellence.

There is real performance leverage in moving towards a flatter, more horizontal mode of organization in which cross-functional, end-to-end work flows link internal processes with the needs and capabilities of both suppliers and customers. This form of organizational design is horizontal, businesses are organized around processes not tasks. Owners are assigned to these processes with responsibility for process performance and improvement. Thus process teams, not individuals, are the principal building blocks for organizational design. This has been described as the horizontal organization (Ostroff, 1999), and many businesses have re-engineered processes to improve the costs and performance.

A process-based organization is a type of matrix organization, since the horizontal process-based structure is usually overlaid on the vertical functional structure. Of course, conflict between vertical and horizontal structures is possible, and disputes over power and authority may occur, as with a project-based matrix. Process managers should have end-to-end responsibility, since they are often asked to work to process measures, such as time to respond. Process managers attempt to improve performance on such measures, but they often have to work through functional structures to make improvements. Cooperative values are obviously critical to avoiding destructive conflict in such matrices.

Key process management activities

Strategic managers must actively monitor the development and/or effectiveness of a number of systems. In a multi-business company, one of the most important challenges is to develop systems to encourage synergy between businesses. Best-practice sharing is one example. A manufacturing capability in quality may be transferred from one business to another, although without some kind of reciprocal benefit, the first business may not go out of its way to help! Clearly, culture can facilitate transfer and encourage learning. Thus, ideally businesses would be open to new ideas in areas where they are underperforming, but this is not always the case even within the same firm. Knowledge transfer between countries or within multinational firms is actually difficult to achieve (Saka-Helmhout, 2007). Process standardization and the ability to share knowledge globally have been critical to the success of the Mexican firm CEMEX, as illustrated below. Besides sharing best practice, other synergies may be possible. A product innovation in one area may help another business to market a complementary product. Further, central services provided by corporate, such as R&D, may add value to a number of businesses.

Regardless, decision-making processes and information flows must in any case be specified for both corporate and business unit levels. Information systems must include strategic control as well as monitoring activities to see whether corrective action is needed. In this context, the balanced scorecard may be very useful (Kaplan & Norton, 1992). As will be discussed in Chapter 12 (▶Chapter 12), performance management requires much more than a bottom-line focus!

Chapter 12

Corporate staff also has to decide on the information technology platform to be used by the firm. This is becoming ever more critical and is the largest capital expense for many organizations, particularly service firms. However, some firms are much more successful than others at generating value from their IT investments, as will be discussed later in the chapter.

> ### Process management *in practice* – Cemex
>
> 'CEMEX, based in Monterrey, Mexico, is the third largest cement company in the world with over 50,000 employees in 50 countries. In 2008 CEMEX reported revenues of US$21.7 billion' (Cemex, 2008). One valuable capability possessed by CEMEX is process standardization following an acquisition. Acquisitions have been an important element in their growth – acquiring Southland in the US, RMX in the UK and Rinker in Australia. The firm recognized that one of the biggest obstacles to overcome following an acquisition lies with people who are reluctant to adopt new practices and cultures. Following an acquisition, CEMEX rapidly replaces business processes, facilitating integration by investing heavily in training new employees. This allows the firm to achieve productivity improvements through standardized processes while simultaneously accommodating the needs of different employees around the world.
>
> (Ross *et al.*, 2006)

Business process re-engineering

Business process re-engineering (BPR) adopts processes as the building blocks of organizations. How a customer order is fulfilled, new products developed, or customer accounts processed should operate without regard to functional boundaries. Many of a firm's legacy systems and processes antedate the development of sophisticated information technology, but BPR capitalizes on these developments to transform, rather than merely automate, existing processes (Ward & Peppard, 2002).

The BPR philosophy is that each of the firm's processes should add value. These end-to-end processes cut across traditional function-based management structures. Re-engineering requires improving these processes and embraces the Japanese *kaizen* concept of continuous improvement. Of course, functions provide centres of expertise and knowledge in essential skills as well as constituting a means of collecting and disseminating information from outside the firm, which can then be internalized. However, the integration of functional activities is vital, since success can typically be achieved only through the efforts of more than one function (Lawrence & Lorsch, 1967).

BPR was initially hailed as a magic cure-all for companies' problems. Certainly, the idea that a business should identify its core processes and then look at how they can be improved is extremely important. In practice, however, BPR usually runs into significant implementation problems (Palmberg, 2010). Because important processes cut horizontally across so many functions, re-engineering requires many persons and departments to change their work patterns. The natural inertia present in so many large companies means that change is resisted, often very broadly, presenting significant obstacles to BPR proponents. Understanding the process and politics of organizational change is a necessary prerequisite for successful BPR.

Information technology infrastructure

As we saw in Chapter 3 (➤Chapter 3), the ratio of information technology (IT) investment to all other business investment for US firms is now about 70 per cent. IT describes the firm's total investment in computing and communications technology, including hardware, software, telecommunications, devices for collecting and representing data (such as an ATM or PDA), and all electronically stored data. It is critical that these investments generate value for shareholders. Further, business units need to develop information systems within the parameters of the corporate information system, which involves an integrated set of technology choices regarding computers, operating systems, communications networks, data storage and transmission.

Chapter 3

The Internet has changed the availability, transmission and costs of information. Businesses may have to compete in real time, share data in real time, and make deals in real time. The Internet has revolutionized supply-chain management, and both suppliers and customers seek access to companies' information systems (Lankford, 2004). In 2006, electronic market transactions in the US reached $2.9 trillion, or 14 per cent of total transactions, in the manufacturing, retail and wholesale industries (Yao *et al.*, 2009).

Process management *in practice* – FedEx

Federal Express is one of many firms that have developed an Internet-based system enabling customers to track packages, schedule pickups, and generate and print air bills. As a result, customer value has increased at the same time that FedEx's costs have been reduced.

Aligning strategy and IT infrastructure is not easy, but it is becoming a key element in achieving success in the marketplace. Enterprise information technology is not a technical issue – it is a business issue and as such must involve senior management (Ross *et al.*, 2006).

There are four major areas of investment in developing the information technology infrastructure for a firm (Weill & Broadbent, 1998):

- *Infrastructure* – this provides the basis for integration and subsequent flexibility. It is shared by many of the firm's businesses, coordinated centrally, and includes network services, provision of computing, database management and intranet capability.

- *Transactional* – this supports the business by lowering costs and enabling greater throughput by automating basic repetitive transactions of the firm, such as accounts receivable and order processing.

- *Informational* – this permits better control of performance and quality, and subsumes such activities as planning, communication and accounting.

- *Strategic* – this enhances competitive advantage and encourages innovation, leading to improvements in sales and/or market position.

Infrastructure accounts for over half of the average firm's IT expenditure, and, whether IT is outsourced or not, strategic management must be actively involved in policy. Indeed, top management support is the key to IT success, since, among other benefits, it reduces the associated political turbulence. Other factors that lead to successful information technology implementation include a shared focus for the firm (in actionable terms) and an understanding of which activities must be centralized and which decentralized (Weill & Broadbent, 1998). Key processes include continuous innovation, developing partnerships with customers, ongoing cost reductions and increased operational effectiveness. If these conditions are fulfilled, information technology can be the crucial element in achieving industry leadership.

Supply chain *in practice* – Dell

Dell's system requires no human intervention, from taking the customer order, to delivery of the components to Dell for assembly, to shipment to the customer. The system also has some intelligence, since it checks customer requirements and provides options (Ward & Peppard, 2002).

Major IT initiatives

The last few years have seen large numbers of companies undertake major IT systems initiatives. We now review three of the most important.

Enterprise resource planning (ERP)

Enterprise resource planning (ERP)
An integrated information system enabling a firm to manage important elements of its activities, such as product planning, inventories, finance and human resources.

Enterprise resource planning (ERP) systems are large computer applications allowing a business to manage all its operations, finance, human resources, requirements planning and order fulfilment on the basis of a single, integrated set of corporate data. It promises improvements in efficiency, with shorter times between orders and payments, lower back-office staffing levels, reduced inventory and improved customer service.

Customer and sales data are entered into the ERP system, which produces a sales forecast, in turn generating orders for raw materials, production schedules, timetables for shifts and financial projections; it also keeps track of inventory. The value of such a system lies in the use of common data: information has the same vocabulary and format.

While in the last decade businesses have spent hundreds of millions of Euros on ERP systems, the installation of many such systems has been traumatic, long and expensive; it has also been hard to measure the benefits (Jackson, 2000). A recent comprehensive study revealed that only 27 per cent of the ERP features and 50 per cent of the functional modules were used after installation (AberdeenGroup, 2006).

Customer relationship management (CRM)

Another major systems application over the last decade is **customer relationship manage-ment (CRM)**. CRM is typically viewed as a process of managing relationships with existing customers in order to maximize their loyalty and thus improve profitability. The focus with CRM is to improve customer identification, conversion, acquisition and retention. The objective is to improve levels of customer satisfaction, boost loyalty and increase revenues from existing customers.

There is a focus on customer value as the business generates the ability to sell several products to one customer, to differentiate customers and to maintain continuous customer interaction. Customer value is viewed over a lifetime, not a single transaction, and customers are assumed to require individualization (Tiwana, 2001). Interestingly, many firms fail to comprehend that a relationship has to be two-way. They focus on the value of the customer rather than value to the customer, failing to realize increases in shareholder value from their system investments.

Customer relationship management (CRM) Databases, analysis tools, software, and usually Internet capabilities that help an organization manage its relationships with customers in an organized way.

Supply-chain management

Many firms are focused on improving supply-chain performance. The objective is to remove inventory from the total system (including suppliers and customers) through better information and coordination, while maintaining levels of customer service. Wal-Mart, now the biggest company in the world as measured by revenue, has been a very successful exponent of these strategies.

Unfortunately, over-hyped promises by sellers of IT systems have left many senior executives more uncertain than ever before about what can actually be achieved with IT. Typical problems include lack of integration of systems, missed business opportunities, IT priorities not based on business needs, and an incoherent technology strategy resulting in the selection of incompatible options. Since new IT technologies come and go quite rapidly, it is not surprising that many firms have outsourced IT.

Knowledge management systems

The past few decades have seen an explosion in the amount of data generation. From computers to smartphones to blogs and websites, digital data is exploding. The challenge for organizations is to keep up with this growth, which has been facilitated by the rapidly falling cost of storage. Wal-Mart handles more than one million customer transactions every day while Nestlé sells over 100,000 products in more than 200 countries using 550,000 suppliers (*The Economist*, 2010). Keeping track of this data, and extracting knowledge from it, is a key challenge for many firms. Strategy development and implementation are increasingly dependent on the ability of firms to acquire and use data and information and convert these into knowledge. A retailer which has developed a knowledge management system with information on inventory, costs, customers and shopping preferences and uses it properly should possess a significant competitive advantage, since this would constitute an extremely valuable intangible asset. Research indicates that a firm's growth is positively related to its ability to generate rare and valuable knowledge and ensure that it is shared and used throughout the firm (Bogner & Bansal, 2007).

Knowledge management systems consist of four interrelated activities:

- Developing knowledge
- Storing knowledge
- Transferring knowledge
- Using knowledge.

We examine each of these activities in turn.

Developing knowledge

Knowledge generation must exist for all processes and functional areas of the firm. Knowledge is no less important in finance (e.g. acquisition screening processes) or operations (e.g. better production scheduling) than in R&D or marketing. We need to develop and capture knowledge from both individuals and the firm. Achieving this goal demands understanding the conditions influencing creativity and innovation, such as attitudes towards risk and mistakes and high-performance teams. New knowledge frequently arises at the boundaries of the old, so that knowledge generation often requires the creativity that accompanies conflict between different disciplines.

The first step in knowledge management is to pro-actively manage how the firm develops new knowledge. At Nucor, success at knowledge creation came from three elements: superior human capital, high-powered incentives and a high empowerment. These, together with a tolerance for failure, a high degree of accountability, and encouragement of creativity and experimentation, are seen as essential for knowledge development (Gupta & Govindarajan, 2000).

Since much knowledge resides in the brains of the employees, there is a question of who benefits from this knowledge – the firm or the individual. If individual employees capture all the benefits of knowledge in the form of higher salaries, this may limit the extent to which the firm engages in knowledge-generating activities.

Knowledge generation can also be accomplished by acquiring a firm or an individual. Some firms, such as Cisco, seem to have been successful by buying young, high-potential firms and integrating these into the established culture. The firm may also use external sources of new knowledge such as universities, research institutes, the Internet and alliances with competitors, customers and/or suppliers. We can also rent knowledge by hiring a consultant, but then we should ensure there is some transfer to the firm.

Storing knowledge

Structured knowledge can be stored in a database or repository accessible via an intranet. Alternatively, information and knowledge may be stored in an external database, the largest of which is the Internet itself. Electronic storage is low cost and has almost infinite capacity when material is stored in digital form, which also makes it easy to transmit and process.

It has been estimated that the amount of digital information increases tenfold every five years (*The Economist*, 2010). Google, the Internet search engine, provides an excellent example of stored knowledge. The firm has digitized over 12 million books as of February 2010, and its library is still expanding (OpenBookAlliance, 2010). It was estimated in 2008 that Google was processing 24 petabytes of data on a daily basis (where a petabyte is 1,000 terabytes) (Dean & Ghemawat, 2008); however, the company is not prepared to reveal its total storage capacity.

When the firm develops an intranet, data security is paramount and firewalls must prevent unauthorized access or hacking. Nonetheless, not all knowledge is explicit and capable of being stored by these formal means. Substantial knowledge is stored as tacit knowledge in people's heads and is lost to the firm if they leave.

Transferring knowledge

As firms expand globally, especially via acquisition, the problems of knowledge transfer are magnified (Easterby-Smith *et al.*, 2008). To successfully manage knowledge transfer, managers need to nurture a culture that encourages sharing of insights. Knowledge transfer is not simply a technical issue, since although information technology and electronic connectivity can assist knowledge transfer, these must be embedded in a supportive culture. Data and information can be transferred electronically, but tacit knowledge is transferred most successfully through human networks. Knowledge is ultimately created in the human brain, and only the right organizational climate can persuade people to create, reveal, share and use knowledge (Hauschild *et al.*, 2001).

We can employ the concept of a **knowledge market** within a firm, the mechanism by which knowledge is shared. Generally this is not a very efficient market, as we cannot assume that employees will share knowledge freely. However, the concept of a knowledge market forces managers to consider the incentives for individuals to share their knowledge.

Transfer is influenced by such factors as whether reciprocity exists when information is shared, what incentives are offered and whether the providers want to be known as knowledgeable persons or are altruistic (Davenport & Prusak, 2000). To share knowledge, employees need to trust others and management. Employees are not likely to share their personal knowledge when they fear for their job.

A lot of knowledge management techniques focus on codified knowledge, but most knowledge is tacit and is learned in doing. Such working knowledge is transferred in a different way – through stories, gossip and watching others, that is, by social interaction, not by technology.

From a competitive point of view, the most desirable state is when knowledge is widely shared within the firm without leakage to competitors. In competitive markets, ease of imitation determines sustainability of a competitive advantage. Easy imitation rapidly dissipates the benefits of competitive advantage, speeding transition to a lower margin commodity market. Knowledge that is context-specific, tacit, embedded in complex organizational routines, and developed from experience tends to be unique and difficult to imitate. To acquire this knowledge takes time, and the competitor cannot just speed this up by spending more.

Knowledge market
An internal market which facilitates the effective transfer of knowledge within the firm.

Transferring tacit knowledge

By definition, tacit knowledge cannot be codified. Sharing such tacit knowledge requires both formal and informal systems. Managers may design formal systems for knowledge transfer through mentoring, training and other development activities, learning on the job and discussion groups. But informal networks and discussion accomplish a substantial amount of tacit knowledge transfer. Tacit knowledge transfer generally needs extensive personal contact as well as an organizational culture that encourages transfer. Management can facilitate informal discussion at lunch or around the water cooler and can develop lists of 'knowledgeable people', accessible to all employees of the firm. Such a system enables any employee to identify the individuals who possess the knowledge they require.

Challenge of strategic management

From the perspective of the firm, organizational performance is enhanced when employees freely share their knowledge. Yet tacit knowledge possessed by an individual is a source of power and influence for the individual. What mechanisms can the firm adopt to facilitate sharing tacit knowledge? Why should a person possessing such knowledge share it with others in the firm?

Some firms have found specific means to support the transfer of tacit knowledge as described below. Peer Assist, as described in the following example, is such a technique, used to overcome problems faced by overly bureaucratic organizations, with distrustful functional silos (Dixon, 2000). It is a tool which uses colleagues, or peers, operating in a team environment, to facilitate problem-solving. Through this simple mechanism, teams can learn from the knowledge and insights of other organization members as described below.

Transferring explicit knowledge

Information technology enables firms to support digital capture, storage, retrieval and distribution of explicitly documented knowledge. The Internet itself is a huge knowledge repository outside the company, and search engines such as Google provide easy ways to search through huge volumes of material. Companies such as IBM, Autonomy and others are active developers of portals providing a single point of entry to such databases, though the content must be carefully sourced and organized. The design and application of these portals has been facilitated by such developments as XML, a set of rules for defining data structures. Key elements of a document can be categorized according to meaning and searches undertaken via the attributes of a document. Such portals can serve customers or offer employees online tools.

An example of such a data warehouse would be a detailed descriptions of projects set up by a consulting company so that consultants around the world can draw from the experiences of others (Gottschalk, 2000). Data warehousing captures and codifies explicit information, and this information can be mined, or analyzed and interpreted, to draw

Peer Assist *in practice*

In organizations that are bureaucratic, hierarchical, silo-ed and with little trust, it can be common to be faced with a problem and not to know whom to turn to for advice and solutions. It can also be common to know whom to turn to and yet find it difficult or impossible to approach them. Not fun, right? In such situations, Peer Assists are a simple way via which to reach out to others from whom we need the advice. Peer Assists can break down organizational barriers, creating conditions for what we know to be assessed by those who need it and when. Peer Assist can be useful, yes!

Peer Assists: What are they really?

Some of you would already know about Peer Assists: Peer Assist is a knowledge-sharing technique which can be used within and across organizations, groups and teams. Central to Peer Assist is that a peer (a colleague, team mate, friend) is faced with a problem to which she/he cannot find a solution. (Sounds familiar?) This is why Peer Assist is organized during which a group of assisters (ideally not more than 8–10) brainstorm perspectives and solutions to the problem of their peer. Simple, right? Yes, it certainly is not rocket science, just common good sense. Then why not do more Peer Assists? Here is how.

Peer Assists: How do you do them?

Do you have a problem that seems unsolvable? Do not despair. First, articulate your problem clearly. The more specific you are the better. Discuss the problem with your peers and/or informal network. Be practical in whom you approach. Explain that you need to find people who may have perspectives and/or could be able to offer solutions to the problem. Is it about putting together an intranet for your department? Or is it about creating a newsletter for your network? Or is it about training your staff an and/or sensitizing your managers to a particular skill/approach?

Search for people (in other departments and partner organizations) who may have tried something similar (be it successful or not). Use your judgement, yet also lean heavily on your intuition in who would be a good assist for you to consult. Be pro-active, ask for help and listen.

Once you have found and approached Peers Assisters, find a facilitator for the Peer Assist. (It is important that this is not you!) Anyone who has had experience in facilitating and/or is a good facilitator can facilitate the Peer Assist. They would just need to be familiar with the process. One key thing for them to know is to give all assisters a voice during the Peer Assist discussion. (A good description of the process is given by this short video: www.youtube.com/watch?v=ObmQyW3EiiE.)

Bring everyone (yourself, assisters, facilitator) together at a particular time. Do not allocate more than two hours for the exercise (maximum time for people to stay focused and contribute).

To the Peer Assist: At this time the facilitator will take over from you. She/he will ask you to explain your problem after which she/he will enable a discussion to take place among you and your assisters on how to possibly approach and solve the problem. If all goes well, you will get a lot of practical ideas and suggestions, energized by the fact that all assisters have been discussing their approaches and perspectives, not only with you, but also among themselves.

OK, you've done it! Now implement the ideas and suggestions that are the best for your case.

Peer Assist (Loumbeva, 2010)

inferences that can then be applied to new situations. Instead of storing documents in personal files and sharing insights with a small circle of colleagues, individual employees can store documents in a common information base and use electronic networks to share insights with all members of the firm. We have already mentioned one such simple system, a list of individuals within the firm who can contribute knowledge on a specific task or problem – such a system is called a knowledge map (Probst *et al.*, 2000). Such maps provide quick guides to who knows and are useful methods of transferring knowledge, provided incentives are offered to employees to both list and share their expertise.

Technology infrastructure *in practice* – Cemex

Cemex has invested heavily in IT systems to standardize key processes such as cement logistics, manufacturing, accounting, customer facing systems and human resources. To ensure that the firm was seen as the preferred provider and partner in the construction industry, and to raise the level of customer satisfaction, Cemex decided that employees needed to be linked to a number of knowledge management databases. It was decided to build a portal to encourage learning and cultural change, allowing employees to share information about markets and competitors. In 2008 this portal recorded about 160,000 visits per month, and the firm estimates that it has reduced costs by about $7 million from an investment of $3.6 million.

The Cemex Plaza portal links people and information across multiple countries. Employees access knowledge management databases which allow them to offer increased customer satisfaction. Gilberto Garcia, IT planning leader for Cemex, said, 'We wanted to create a way for people from different countries and newly acquired companies to come closer together. Our chairman defines it as building "One Cemex" and sharing a "Cemex Way" of doing things.' This has helped to establish a standardized method to access content, services and applications needed to perform employee functions.

The Cemex Plaza portal was developed in partnership with Cisco Systems and was initially designed to allow people to share news and information and to debate important topics. Access to company databases and other applications were added to the online offerings. Initial applications were global, but as use developed Cemex realized that local content was also important in meeting unique local needs. Garcia explained, 'We came up with the concept of communities of practice, which allows for creation of customized content. Because it's very expensive to create a community from scratch, we developed a toolkit that is very easy to use and not costly.'

Another lesson learned was to establish a governance model early in the process. Someone must be responsible for decisions about content and strategy. A note of advice from Garcia: 'If I were to do this again, I would involve the business units and all geographies from the beginning.'

(Cisco, 2004)

With the growth in alliances and network forms of organization, there is an increasing need to transfer knowledge across the partners – and, again, information technology facilitates this. Email, intranets and videoconferencing all facilitate both tacit and explicit knowledge transfer. One example from the disk drive industry reveals the substantial cooperation between different firms. In this industry, some firms are responsible for design and others for manufacture. Much of the inter-firm communication involves electronic transfer of data such as simulation results, with engineers able to log onto a cooperating firm's computer system so that they can share information on design of components. Such a technology infrastructure – the network, software and hardware – allows knowledge workers to cooperate on projects and is generally scalable and able to handle different formats such as Windows and Linux. Email is widely used to transfer documents, while videoconferencing allows us to 'see' and communicate with people in remote locations (Scott, 2000). For a company such as Cemex, which has expanded rapidly internationally through acquisition, finding an effective mechanism was essential, as the above example illustrates.

Using knowledge

While companies talk about the importance of learning, intellectual capital and knowledge management, they often fail at the vital step of transforming knowledge into action (Pfeffer & Sutton, 1999). There is often a knowing–doing gap. People will only use these systems if they are convenient and the knowledge stored is seen as useful and relevant. Many knowledge management techniques focus on codified knowledge, but much important knowledge is tacit which – as we have seen – is more difficult to transfer and use.

11.4 HUMAN RESOURCES

> **LEARNING OBJECTIVE 6**
>
> Evaluate the importance of human resources in strategic management.

We have defined strategic management as creating organizations that generate value. Building such an organization requires making many decisions that should ultimately be beneficial to shareholders. These include some important human resource decisions, such as selecting people for key positions, designing appropriate reward and incentive systems, building the capabilities required to compete successfully in the future, and organizing business processes and decision-making to be successful.

As firms grow, so do their requirements in terms of capabilities – the skills embedded in the company's people, processes and institutional knowledge. To build new capabilities often requires changes in the human resources of the firm. The CEO must encourage the emergence of a more strategic approach to managing human resources, something that has been lacking in too many companies, where administrative or political considerations too often outweigh the strategic.

We first review the responsibilities of senior managers in building future capabilities. Then we focus on the critical issue of succession planning for senior management appointments, and conclude by examining the critical human resource policies with which senior management should be concerned. Such policies significantly shape the emergent values and culture of the organization.

Managing resources and capabilities

Growth requires building new capabilities, which means ensuring that the company's people have appropriate skills (whether via development or newly hired personnel), storing and sharing institutional knowledge, and putting in place the necessary processes for integrating and coordinating activities. Although less critical capabilities can be outsourced, management of the most important capabilities can determine whether or not shareholder value will be created.

New capabilities *in practice* – Sony

As part of its response to the economic turbulence of 2008/09, Sony announced an organizational restructure, merging previously separate units. One of these new groups is the Consumer Products and Devices Group, which combines the former Electronics and Game businesses. To support these new business groups, Sony has formed several support groups, referred to as 'platforms', which operate on a cross-company basis. One of these is the Manufacturing, Logistics and Procurement platform which will mean that for the first time all Sony business groups will be relying on centralized manufacturing, logistics and procurement.

(Sony, 2009)

This new organizational arrangement will require Sony to develop appropriate resources and capabilities if the platforms are to deliver value to the businesses. As the Sony example demonstrates, a good corporate strategy is a carefully constructed system of interdependent parts. It directs executives' decisions about the businesses in which the firm will compete, the resources and capabilities the firm must develop, and the organizational architecture required for successful implementation. To align these elements in a multi-business company is a demanding task, one that requires senior management direction and involvement (Collis & Montgomery, 1998).

Multi-business firms have advantages, however. They can provide a diverse range of experiences to more fully develop their managers. They can transfer skills and experience by moving managers or developing processes such as best-practice sharing. In the modern firm, people – with their skills, motivation and creativity – are critical to success. The CEO and the top management team must play an active role in senior appointments and management development, supported by human resources staff fully attuned to corporate and business strategies.

Succession planning

The CEO must be personally involved in the selection, training and development of the senior managers of the firm. For a global firm, this is likely to be the top 100 or 200 managers. This group must have the skills and capabilities required to develop and implement strategy.

Table 11.2 Profile of general managers in BHP

	1980s	1990s
Age on appointment	47	44
Non-Australian nationality (%)	8	37
International experience (%)	4	46
Experience outside BHP (%)	8	44
Functional experience		
One function (%)	75	22
Two functions (%)	25	26
More than two functions (%)	—	63
Location experience		
One location (%)	49	8
Two locations (%)	42	20
More than two locations (%)	9	85

Reproduced by permission of BHP Billiton

One of the most important of these activities is succession planning, which, since there is now a global market for senior management talent, must incorporate some redundancy.

The need for an active approach to human resource management is well illustrated by the data in Table 11.2. BHP is a large Australian resources company, now called BHP Billiton. The data show the characteristics of managers classified as 'general managers' for two time periods: the 1980s and the 1990s. In the early 1980s, under a newly appointed CEO, BHP made a significant change in its mission and strategy. The newly constituted senior management team concluded that the company then known as the 'Big Australian' was approaching the limits of its growth within Australia and that it had to become a global resources firm, decreasing dependence on its local Australian base.

BHP's growth had already led to a critical shortage of general managers, but for the new strategy to be successful, the company had to make significant changes in the composition of its cadre of general managers. This issue was recognized and actively pursued by the firm's most senior managers, with the CEO playing a strong role. As a result, the composition of the general manager cadre had changed very significantly by the 1990s.

The proportion of managers with experience outside BHP went from 8 per cent to 44 per cent, while the percentage of managers with international experience went from 4 per cent in the 1980s to 46 per cent in the 1990s. Reflecting this major growth in international activities, by 2009 91 per cent of revenue and 60 per cent of assets were from outside Australia (BHP Billiton, 2009). The company deliberately changed selection and recruitment practices, targeting managers from other resource firms around the world. Over a decade, the firm significantly altered the characteristics of its general manager population, a good example of aligning human resource practices with corporate strategy. In the next section, we examine these practices in more detail.

Managing human resource policies

To ensure alignment with strategy, senior management must implement appropriate human resource (HR) policies. The 'organizational inertia' to which we earlier referred is often embedded in obsolete HR practices, which reinforce the 'old way' instead of supporting the emergence of the firm of the future. HR policies often play a critical role in shaping the firm's culture, and the CEO must therefore play an active role in influencing and approving such HR policies as selection, compensation and training. Figure 11.9 illustrates these relationships, and we now examine each of the policy areas where senior management should be involved.

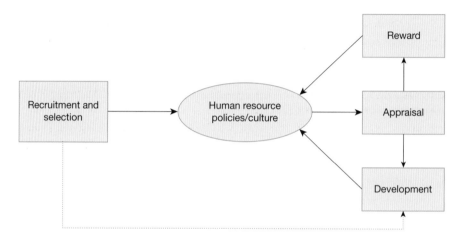

Figure 11.9 Human resource policies and culture

Recruitment and selection

Without the right people and skills, the firm cannot succeed. As strategy changes, so will the types of individuals and skills needed. Strategic human resource planning can accommodate and facilitate these changes, but without strategic clarity and well-defined planning processes, such plans will not eventuate. Senior management plays a critical role in ensuring strategic alignment of recruitment and hiring practices.

Chapter 10

Recruiting new skills can also be helpful when the organization is attempting major change of the type discussed in Chapter 10 (►Chapter 10). Assimilation problems may mirror those of a merger or acquisition if wholesale hiring from 'outside' occurs, and the lives of new members of the firm can be made quite difficult, even if they are hired into senior management positions.

These issues, are, of course, made even more problematic when a company is expanding internationally and hiring to support that strategy. Not only are there differences in employee motivating factors across countries, but there are major variations in immigration rules and labour market regulations (Sparrow, 2006).

Reward

Senior managers must guide the design of the firm's reward systems. There will often be three levels of rewards that need to be considered: one related to corporate performance; another to performance at the business unit level; and the third to individual performance. The reward system must also include both financial and non-financial components. Factors such as recognition, choice of assignment, and flexible arrangements for combining work and family life are important elements in any reward system.

Reward systems also need to address the principal/agent problem. Employees' personal objectives may differ from those of the business unit and shareholders. In this situation, incentives may be used to induce the desired behaviour from individuals.

Stock options, originally intended to align managers' and shareholders' interests, became widely used in the 1990s. Originally, eligibility for options was restricted to a very few senior managers, but they then became much more widespread. Options have been particularly favoured by fast-growing smaller firms, where cash is inevitably in short supply. Widespread concerns over the use of options have led such business leaders as Warren Buffett to decry their use, while accountants have become increasingly preoccupied with how they are reported. The use of options has declined significantly since the financial crisis, and firms are now looking at longer vesting periods for all forms of performance-based rewards, following allegations of self-serving short-termism by senior executives in the early 2000s.

Appraisal

Appraising individual performance is usually complicated by the circumstances of different businesses. In Chapter 12 (▶Chapter 12), we discuss the balanced scorecard as a framework **Chapter 12** for assessing performance. In general, it is preferable if jobs specify outputs, not just duties, with performance targets clearly identified. However, it is equally important to recognize that the firm will need different management systems for different businesses. Growth businesses need builders and visionaries with appropriate styles and appropriate performance metrics. Mature businesses require a different approach and may be assigned very different objectives related to their role in the corporate portfolio. Corporate- and business-level staffs generally work together in some cooperative arrangement to set performance appraisal standards at the business unit level.

A further refinement, adopted by a number of companies, recognizes that good performance is not just about achieving objectives but also about the way in which those objectives are achieved. As many are aware, large companies often distribute decision-making guidelines in an attempt to ensure ethical behaviour in the marketplace.

Development

Corporate managers should play an important role in planning the development of the firm's managers. These activities should include further development for the most senior managers, who are often forgotten when HR departments plan for development.

Promising managers need opportunities to broaden their skills and knowledge to prepare them for senior general management positions; leaving them in a single functional department for substantial parts of their career does both them and the firm a disservice. Clearly there are trade-offs that must be made between depth of expertise in a specialty and cross-functional breadth, but all senior positions will demand the latter, even if they carry functional titles.

Education, both inside and outside the company, plays an important role in the development process. In-company training and education can build *esprit de corps* and enable a focus on real company issues, whereas external experiences broaden perspectives across industries and geographies in ways that cannot be emulated inside a firm. A judicious combination of these two can support both corporate and individual goals in developing a well-rounded team of more senior managers.

Many firms have taken novel and exciting approaches to development, based on the concepts of action learning (Revens, 1998). BHP Billiton, for example, has given junior teams of managers real assignments with project budgets as part of their development. The same company set up a junior 'think-tank' to advise on major investment decisions, arguing that because the firm's younger managers would inherit the consequences of these decisions, their input should be considered.

Other companies have taken the radical step of putting their own people to work for customers and vice versa. These are developmental experiences that can create insight and empathy on the part of both parties.

Human resource policies and culture

A firm that has been in operation for several years and that has a history develops its own culture – widely shared basic assumptions, values and beliefs that have a powerful influence on activities and operations. Many of these assumptions and beliefs are implicit, treated as axiomatic by members of an organization.

Human resource policies can have a very definite impact on the culture of a firm, and since organizational performance is influenced by culture and this impact can be positive or negative, strategic managers must, to the extent possible, manage the culture of the firm. A strong culture can be an inhibitor of change but can also replace supervisory activity and be a powerful form of control. Some firms are trying to replace formal control with cultural control, wherein employees share a common culture that aligns their interests with those of the firm. Knowledge workers, in particular, are believed to be much more comfortable in such an environment.

Many senior corporate managers are currently talking about cultural values such as creativity/innovation, high ethical standards, transparency and a focus on performance. In many cases, however, not only is the informal culture of the firm inimical to such values but human resource policies act as inhibitors of the very values professed by senior management. To 'walk the talk', as Tom Peters once put it, strategic managers must align their processes and policies with the values they are advocating (Peters & Waterman, 1982)!

11.5 SUMMARY

Designing the firm's architecture involves an important set of decisions for any strategic manager. As we discussed in earlier chapters, strategic management is about both generating strategy and ensuring that the strategy is implemented. These two stages of generation and implementation are mutually interdependent; strategy shapes architecture and at the same time architecture shapes strategy. Architecture comprises three elements – structure, processes and human resources. In a rapidly changing world, it is likely that the firm will need to innovate in all three. In the future, firms will need to be increasingly flexible, to pay greater attention to creativity, to be concerned with recruiting and retaining high-calibre personnel, to speed up decision processes, and to give more managerial attention to the knowledge assets of the firm.

Structure incorporates how the firm integrates two conflicting objectives – differentiation and integration. Differentiation reflects specialization, which is adopted to improve efficiency through the use of specialist staff. But such specialists often lose sight of the 'big picture', and hence there is a need for integration, which can introduce considerable organizational tension. Structure includes decisions on the basis of differentiation – whether this will be by product or by geography – and this decision in turn determines the necessary integrative mechanisms. To improve flexibility and responsiveness, many firms have reduced the level of vertical differentiation, eliminating layers of managers, resulting in considerable extra pressure on the remaining employees. Most global firms have adopted a matrix structure, organized on both a geographic and a business basis, with the corporate centre providing a range of central services. Given the size and complexity of these firms, providing local autonomy while coordinating globally is a considerable managerial challenge.

Increasing competition also implies that firms have to look at process management. They must identify the processes that deliver value to customers, and manage these on an end-to-end basis. Such an emphasis can produce conflict between the (vertical) business structure and the (horizontal) process structure, with issues of power and authority ensuing. We also highlighted the importance of information technology for the modern firm. Since investment in information technology is now a major component of capital expenditure for any firm, such investments must contribute to business and firm strategy.

Finally, designing architecture involves decisions on the human resources of the firm. In any organization, people are a critical resource, and strategic managers need to ensure that the right people are hired, and that incentive systems align the interests of employees with those of the firm. Knowledge management is increasingly important as the basis of competitive advantage, and developing systems that facilitate the transfer of tacit knowledge across different units in the firm is a challenging but key requirement.

The CEO and other senior managers will be actively involved in these architecture decisions. Some decisions, such as the adoption of a new structure, are primarily the responsibility of the senior management team. In other decision areas, the CEO must ensure that appropriate systems are in use. Systems for recruiting senior managers, succession planning, promotion and rewards, and the business planning systems in use all need input from strategic managers.

VIEW FROM THE TOP

SONY

Sony is an entrepreneurial company which started in 1946 developing and manufacturing communications equipment. By 2005, it had grown into a major global electronics firm, but nonetheless found itself in financial difficulties. In June 2005, the company hired Howard Stringer, then president of CBS, a US media company, to become its Chairman and CEO. The following is abstracted from his message to shareholders in the 2009 Sony annual report.

The fiscal year 2008 which ended on 31 March 2009 saw unprecedented economic turmoil the likes of which we could not have imagined just one year earlier. The global economic crisis, combined with the pronounced strength of the yen, significantly impaired the health of our operating results – and those of many other companies – with a speed and ferocity that were unparalleled in recent history. This impact put us in an unsettling financial situation and gave me, and many of you, rightful cause for concern.

Despite the challenging nature of the past fiscal year, the global economic crisis has presented us with an opportunity to reposition ourselves to take on our competitors and be poised to capitalize when the economy turns around. Before I discuss that, however, I would like to mention some of the highlights of fiscal year 2008, which demonstrate what Sony is capable of achieving even in adverse economic situations and serve as beacons of inspiration during these tough times. In the past fiscal year, we developed and launched some of the most technologically innovative and unique products on the market today. These included major innovations in LCD TVs, video cameras, play-stations and Blu-ray.

While it is encouraging to acknowledge these successes, the fact remains that the fiscal year 2008 was one of the most difficult years in the company's long history. It is indisputable that a substantial portion of this is attributable to the global economy and the strength of the yen, but the inescapable truth is that despite our restructuring and cost-cutting efforts in past years, the downturn exposed stresses and vulnerabilities in our company that have built up over a long period of time. Addressing this – and helping assure that it does not happen again – is my top priority. Some of the decisions taken were:

- Reduced production levels
- Achieving cost reductions of ¥250 billion
- Reducing the number of manufacturing sites by 10 per cent
- Increasing the proportion of manufacturing done in low-cost areas
- Reducing the number of employees
- Changing the firm's mission to become a leading provider of networked consumer electronics

- Reorganizing the corporate structure, with two main business groups and several cross-corporation platforms to develop common solutions
- Reducing the asset base
- Enhancing product interconnectivity.

Stringer also announced a major reorganization of Sony, briefly discussed earlier in this chapter. Sony's Electronics and Game businesses were merged and reconfigured as two strong new groups: the Consumer Products & Devices Group and the Networked Products & Services Group. The first group represented Sony's traditional products and hardware; the second was designed to create network differentiation which, when married to Sony's hardware, would spearhead the firm's growth going forward.

To support these two new business groups in terms of software development and manufacturing, procurement and logistics operations, Stringer announced the creation of two cross-company platforms:

1   The Common Software and Technology Platform was tasked to develop and implement common software solutions and provide coordinated software development services to each business group so that networked products and services could communicate seamlessly with a common user interface. Through this platform, Sony hoped to streamline and optimize the software development process across the two new business groups and better coordinate R&D. This platform is headed by Keiichiro Shimada, who understands the vital role software plays in consumer electronics and has already successfully spearheaded the adoption of various open standards across Sony.

2   The Manufacturing, Logistics, Procurement and CS Platform was designed to bring efficient supply chain solutions for the two new business groups. The platform was intended to fully leverage the Sony Group's scale in procurement, promoting component standardization, and optimizing the allocation of in-house and outsourced manufacturing in order to achieve further cost reductions, as well as to enhance product quality and green management.

QUESTIONS

1   Sony's CEO has articulated a number of strategic decisions designed to improve performance. What is the strategy behind these decisions? Do you agree with the decisions he made?

2   What obstacles do you foresee with Sony's attempts to create standard 'platforms'?

ANGLO AMERICAN PLC

Anglo American, a global mining company, was founded in South Africa by the Oppenheimer family in 1917, and took the name Anglo American Corporation since most of the capital used to found the company had come from the US and the UK. In the 1960s, the apartheid regime in South Africa attracted a great deal of hostility from governments around the world. The resulting sanctions adversely affected the ability of South African businesses to operate outside the country. As a consequence of this inability to grow internationally, Anglo American acquired a number of related and unrelated South African businesses. By 1994 Anglo American had investments in more than half the firms listed on the Johannesburg Stock Exchange.

After apartheid was lifted in 1994, the firm listed on the London Stock Exchange and began a long process of developing a vision and mission. In March 1999 Anglo American Corporation merged with Minorco SA to create one of the world's largest mining and natural resources companies. Following the merger the new company relocated its headquarters to London, changed its name to Anglo American plc and moved its primary listing from the Johannesburg Stock Exchange to the London Stock Exchange. This last move was supported by financial analysts who had indicated that AAC's loose structure and South African listing impeded its ability to raise capital on the international market and compete on an equal footing with other big miners such as Rio Tinto.

Over the period 1999 to 2005, Anglo American continued a strategy of acquisition, acquiring companies in building materials, copper and iron ore. Since its inception, Anglo American had maintained a significant cross-share ownership structure with the De Beers Company. In 2001 a new private company was established, De Beers Investments, which bought out the then current De Beers shareholders. De Beers Investments is owned 45 per cent by Anglo and the Oppenheimer family and 10 per cent by a joint venture between De Beers and the government of the Republic of Botswana (Cowell & Swarns, 2001). De Beers Investments in turn owns De Beers Societe Anonyme, a company registered in Luxembourg.

In 2005, Anglo American began what was to become a long period of reassessing its strategy of diversification, and several businesses were sold, including aluminium, chromium and steel mineral sands. In 2007 a new CEO, Cynthia Carroll, was appointed, the first non-South African and the first female CEO of Anglo. One of her key tasks was to focus on the future, to develop a new vision and strategy for the firm.

Ms Carroll was of the view that Anglo faced several immediate problems. The lack of focus was one. Another was an appalling safety record. A third was the group's structure and culture. On safety, she acted decisively. Following yet another serious accident in a deep-level platinum mine, she shut it down and brought 28,000 employees out of the ground (Carroll, 2009). This action reinforced the new view that change was needed in the historic mindset that accidents were inevitable.

Anglo set about reviewing its corporate strategy by developing a fact base for each of its businesses. This involved addressing some fundamental questions: What are the market drivers? What is the history

MINI-CASE

of returns over the cycle in those markets? How are the markets likely to evolve over time? What does it take to compete in those markets? What is our position relative to the competition, what's our asset base and what's our growth pipeline? Where are our points of differentiation? Which part of our portfolio will deliver the highest degree of value from the asset base that we have right now and that we can build on going forward? What sort of return should we be aiming for? How do we want to grow?

While Anglo was attempting to become a more focused enterprise, it faced other challenges. In 2008 there was unprecedented market turmoil and recession. The sharp fall in commodity prices exposed weaknesses in Anglo, adding urgency to the need to sharpen its strategy. Second, Anglo American received an unsolicited bid from Xstrata, another major resource company. Xstrata proposed a zero-premium merger which was rejected by Anglo management in June 2009, saying that the terms were totally unacceptable and Xstrata subsequently withdrew the offer. However, this bid indicated that Anglo was under pressure to improve its performance (MacNamara, 2009).

The major strategic initiative was in terms of their business portfolio. The firm announced that in future they would focus on growth, targeting the most attractive commodities where the group owned or was developing a valuable asset and where the firm enjoyed a cost advantage. This meant that it would focus on a limited number of mineral resources in a range of countries. Associated with this change in strategy, Anglo American announced changes to its organizational structure. The historic structure had consisted of four divisions: base metals and coal divisions, located in London, and ferrous ores and platinum, located in Johannesburg, with most functions being decentralized into these businesses.

The new structure involved seven business units, each concerned with a single resource and each located in what was seen as the most appropriate country. Copper was located in Chile, nickel and iron ore in Brazil. Thermal coal, Kumba iron ore and platinum were located in South Africa and metallurgical coal in Australia. The firm's head office remained in London (Carroll, 2010). Anglo American had evolved into a firm where business units had considerable autonomy. While this may have had some advantages, it also meant that there was little sharing of ideas and practices both within and between businesses. So the decision was made to centralize certain functions and activities, resulting in the head count being reduced by 25 per cent.

Anglo's managers also announced steps to improve operational efficiency through a two-pronged approach. First, they analysed the value chain for each asset base to eliminate unnecessary costs. Across the group, total head count was reduced by 23,400. Second, they consolidated the supply chain, centralizing purchasing to capture volume discounts and synergies on a global basis. These actions were expected to result in cost savings of $1 billion over three years. Anglo also established shared service units which were expected to save an additional $50 million per year.

The firm also took steps to change the culture, to move away from the 'old Anglo', with limited cooperation between the business units to 'One Anglo', with increased integration, knowledge sharing, common standards and policies and enhanced synergies between business units. The firm also announced several management changes, including a new CEO for ferrous metals and coal, and the removal of the chief strategy officer.

Associated with the restructuring of its portfolio, Anglo American made several divestments. In 2009 it made divestments of $2.4 billion. Further divestments were planned in 2010, with the sale of Scaw

Metals, valued at approximately $1 billion and the sale of its zinc interests for $1.3 billion (Robertson, 2010). Throughout the period Anglo American strengthened its balance sheet by suspending dividends and raising about $3.7 billion through bonds issues (Carroll, 2009).

Some analysts have been critical that the speed of change has been too slow. But the task of focusing a complex and highly political organization, with little in the way of an apparent strategy, and a diverse collection of businesses, would always be challenging. Along these lines, in 2010 one analyst suggested that an option for Anglo would be to create two separate London-listed companies – one consisting of their international assets in Chile, Australia and Brazil, the other consisting of their South African interests (Elder, 2010).

Since 2005 the senior management of Anglo American recognized that to execute the new corporate strategy successfully it needed to create an organizational structure that would support that delivery. The key questions were:

- Whether to organize along commodity lines, geographically, or a combination of the two.
- The degree of autonomy granted to each business. Xstrata allows its business units to operate autonomously and it has been successful. Anglo was a fiefdom with each business operating as an autonomous unit. The 2005 restructuring started to rein back the autonomy of the business unit. The dilemma for Anglo's management was the appropriate level of autonomy– full autonomy or centrally controlled?
- The role and function of group directors. For example, is it necessary to have a director of strategy?
- The relationship between group directors and business unit heads.

The Anglo American case is also based on an interview with Cynthia Carroll conducted by Abby Ghobadian for the *Journal of Strategy and Management*.

QUESTIONS

Place yourself in the position of Anglo American's CEO in 2010.

1 How would you go about solving the above issues?
2 What structure do you think will best enable Anglo to realize its corporate strategy and why?
3 What should be business units' level of autonomy and reporting lines?
4 Should Anglo American split into two listed companies?

REVIEW QUESTIONS

1 Summarize, in your own words, the three elements of organizational architecture.

2 Identify some of the central issues that managers need to consider in developing the appropriate organizational structure.

3 What are the benefits and disadvantages of organizing the multidivisional firm by product, by market, by technology and by geography?

4 Why are so many global firms organized along matrix lines? What benefits does this structure provide, and what problems does it generate?

5 With increasing developments in information technology and the changing workforce, do you believe firms will become more centralized or more decentralized in the future? Discuss.

6 Using the literature, review the success and failure of ERP and CRM applications.

7 'The CEO must play a central role in managing the human resources of the firm.' Discuss this statement, with attention to what issues arise and what level of involvement is needed.

8 Why are firms adopting newer forms of architecture such as that represented by networks?

REFERENCES

AberdeenGroup (2006) The total cost of ERP ownership. *Enterprise Strategy*, 17 October. www.oracle.com/corporate/analyst/reports/corporate/cp/es101306.pdf.

Bartlett, C. A. & Ghoshal, S. (1998) *Managing Across Borders*, 2nd edn. Boston, MA: Harvard Business School Press.

Bayer (2010) Profile and organization. 21 April. www.bayer.com/en/bayer-organizational-structure-2010-04-21.pdfx.

BHP Billiton (2009) Annual report, p. 189. www.bhpbilliton.com/bb/investorsMedia/reports/annualReports.jsp.

Bogner, W. C. & Bansal, P. (2007) Knowledge management as the basis of sustained high performance. *Journal of Management Studies, 44*(1), 165–188.

Burns, T. & Stalker, G. M. (1994) *The Management of Innovation*. Oxford: Oxford University Press.

Carroll, C. (2009) Anglo American. *Merrill Lynch Global Metals and Mining Conference*, 12 May. www.angloamerican.com/aal/investors/presentations/2009pres/2009-05-12/2009-05-12.pdf.

Carroll, C. (2010) Anglo American. *Merrill Lynch Global Metals and Mining Conference*, 11 May. www.angloamerican.com/aal/investors/presentations/2010pres/merrill_lynch/merrill_lynch.pdf.

Cemex (2008) Annual Report. www.cemex.com/ic/ic_lp.asp.

Chandler, A. D. (1962) *Strategy and Structure: Chapters in the History of the American Industrial Enterprise*. Cambridge, MA: MIT Press.

Cisco (2004) In a decidedly low-tech business Cemex has a surprising high-tech workforce. *IBSB Success Story*. www.cisco.com/web/about/ac79/docs/wp/CEMEX_DS_0817.pdf?

Collis, D. J. & Montgomery, C. A. (1998) Creating corporate advantage. *Harvard Business Review*, (May–June), 70–83.

Cowell, A., & Swarns, R. L. (2001) $17.6 billion deal to make De Beers private company. *New York Times*, 16 February.

Davenport, T. H. & Prusak, L. (2000) *Working Knowledge: How Organizations Manage What They Know*, 2nd edn. Boston, MA: Harvard Business School Press.

Dean, J., & Ghemawat, S. (2008) MapReduce: Simplified data processing on large clusters. *Communications of the ACM, 51*(1), 107–113.

Dietl, H., Royer, S. & Stratmann, U. (2009) Value creation architectures and competitive advantage: Lessons from the European automobile industry. *California Management Review, 51*(3), 24–48.

Dixon, N. (2000) Peer Assist: Guidelines for practice. http://74.125.153.132/search?q=cache per cent3AciTUfYR6TQMJ per cent3Awww.commonknowledge.org per cent2Fuserimages.

Easterby-Smith, M., Lyles, M. A. & Tsang, E. W. K. (2008) Inter-organizational knowledge transfer: Current themes and future prospects. *Journal of Management Studies, 45*(4), 677–690.

Elder, (2010) Anglo American falls as broker calls for it to be broken up. *Financial Times,* 13 July, p. 34.

Galbraith, J. R. (2005) *Designing the Customer-Centric Organization*. San Fransisco, CA: Jossey-Bass.

Galbraith, J. R. (2009) Multidimensional, multinational organizations of the future. In F. Hesselbein & M. Goldsmith (eds), *The Organization of the Future 2* (pp. 174–187). San Francisco, CA: Jossey-Bass.

GDI Infotech (2008) Busting your silos. *Services*. www.gdii.com/services/services.html.

Getinge (2010) About Getinge Group. www.getingegroup.com/en/About-Getinge-Group-name/.

Goold, M. & Campbell, A. (2002) Do you have a well-designed organization? *Harvard Business Review*, (March), 117–124.

Gottschalk, P. (2000) Strategic knowledge networks: The case of IT support for Eurojuris law firms in Norway. *International Review of Law, Computers & Technology, 14*(1), 115–129.

Greenberg, J. & Baron, R. A. (2008) *Behavior in Organizations*, 9th edn. Upper Saddle River, NJ: Prentice Hall.

Gupta, A. K. & Govindarajan, V. (2000) Knowledge management's social dimension: Lessons from Nucor Steel. *Sloan Management Review, 42*(1), 71–80.

Haeckel, S. H. (1999) *Adaptive Enterprise: Creating and Leading Sense- and-Respond Organizations*. Boston, MA: Harvard Business School Press.

Handy, C. (2001) *The Elephant and the Flea*. London: Hutchinson.

Hauschild, S., Licht, T. & Stein, W. (2001) Creating a knowledge culture. *McKinsey Quarterly*, (1), 74–81.

Heimbouch, H. (2000) Racing for growth. *Harvard Business Review*, (November–December), 148–154.

Hunt, J. W. (1992) *Managing People at Work*, 3rd edn. Maidenhead: McGraw-Hill.

Jackson, D. (2000) *Becoming Dynamic*. Basingstoke: Macmillan.

Kaplan, R. S. & Norton, D. P. (1992) The balanced scorecard – measures that drive performance. *Harvard Business Review*, (January–February), 71–79.

Lankford, W. M. (2004) Supply chain management and the Internet. *Online Information Review, 48*(4), 301–305.

Lawler, E. E. I., & Worley, C. G. (2006) Designing organizations that are built to change. *Sloan Management Review, 48*(1), 19–24.

Lawrence, P. & Lorsch, J. W. (1967) *Organizations and Environment*. Boston, MA: Harvard University Press.

Loumbeva, N. (2010) Peer assist – There is nothing like it. *Insights*. www.odalternatives.com/insights/articles/?article_id=321.

MacNamara, W. (2009) Xstrata withdrawal exposes core issues. *Financial Times*, 16 October, p. 19.

March, J. G. & Simon, H. A. (1958) *Organizations*. New York: Wiley.

Miles, R. E., Miles, G., Snow, C. C., Blomqvist, K. & Rocha, H. (2009) The I-Form organization. *California Management Review, 51*(4), 61–76.

Mintzberg, H. (1993) *Structure in Fives: Designing Effective Organizations*, 2nd edn. Englewood Cliffs, NJ: Prentice-Hall.

Morley, M. (2010) Build to order or build to stock. http://blogs.gxs.com/morleym/2009/03/build-to-order-or-build-to-stock.html.

O'Regan, N. & Ghobadian, A. (2010) Revitalising an oil giant – An interview with Dr Tony Hayward, Chief Executive of BP. *Journal of Strategy and Management*, 3(2), 174–183.

OpenBookAlliance (2010) How many books has Google scanned today? 18 February. www.openbookalliance.org/2010/02/how-many-more-books-has-google-scanned-today/.

Ostroff, F. (1999) *The Horizontal Organization*. New York: Oxford University Press.

P&G (2010) Corporate structure. *P&G/Company*. www.pg.com/en_US/company/global_structure_operations/corporate_structure.shtml.

Palmberg, K. (2010) Experiences with implementing process management: A multiple case study. *Business Process Management Journal, 16*(1), 93–113.

PerkinElmer (2010) History. *About Us*. www.perkinelmer.com/AboutUs/OurCompany/Leadership/default.xhtml.

Peters, T. J. & Waterman, R. H. (1982) *In Search of Excellence*. New York: Harper & Row.

Pfeffer, J. & Sutton, R. I. (1999) *The Knowing–Doing Gap: How Smart Companies Turn Knowledge into Action*. Boston, MA: Harvard Business School Press.

Probst, G., Raub, S. & Romhardt, K. (2000) *Managing Knowledge*. Chichester: Wiley.

Reiter, C. (2010) BMW hope to lure US buyers with made-to-order luxury. *International Herald Tribune*, 15–16 May, p. 13.

Revens, R. W. (1998) *The ABC of Action Learning*, 3rd edn. London: Lemos and Crane.

Robertson (2010) Anglo enjoys bonus from sale of zinc mines division. *The Times*, 11 May, p. 48.

Ross, J., Weill, P. & Robertson, D. C. (2006) *Enterprise Architecture as Strategy*. Boston, MA: Harvard Business School Press.

Saka-Helmhout, A. (2007) Unravelling learning within multinational corporations. *British Journal of Management, 18*(3), 294–310.

Sarros, J. C., Cooper, B. K. & Santora, J. C. (2008) Building a climate for innovation through transformational leadership and organizational culture. *Journal of Leadership and Organizational Studies, 15*(2), 145.

Scott, J. E. (2000) Facilitating interorganizational learning with information technology. *Journal of Management and Information Systems, 17*(2), 81–113.

Sloan, A. P. (1964) *My Years with General Motors*. Garden City, NY: Doubleday.

Sony (2009) Annual Report. 19 June. www.sony.net/SonyInfo/IR/financial/ar/8ido180000023g2o-att/SonyAR09-E.pdf.

Sparrow, P. (2006) Employees need to globalise recruitment, selection and assessment processes to succeed internationally. 8 September. www.cipd.co.uk/pressoffice/_articles/international_080906.htm?IsSrchRes=1.

Strikwerda, J. & Stoelhorst, J. W. (2009) The emergence and evolution of the multidimensional organization. *California Management Review, 51*(4), 11–31.

Subramonian, S., Tousni, M. & Krishnankutty, K. V. (2009) The role of BPR in the implementation of ERP systems. *Business Process Management Journal, 15*(5), 653–668.

The Economist (2010) Data, data everywhere. *The Economist*, 27 February, Special Report.

Tiwana, A. (2001) *The Essential Guide to Knowledge Management*. Upper Saddle River, NJ: Prentice Hall.

Tushman, M. L. & O'Reilly, C. A. (1996) Ambidextrous organizations: Managing evolutionary and revolutionary change. *California Management Review, 38*(4), 8–30.

Tushman, M. L. & O'Reilly, C. A. (1997) *Winning through Innovation*. Boston, MA: Harvard Business School Press.

Ward, J. & Peppard, J. (2002) *Strategic Planning for Information Systems*, 3rd edn. Chichester: Wiley.

Weber, M. (2001) *The Protestant Ethic and the Spirit of Capitalism*. London: Routledge Classics.

Weill, P. & Broadbent, M. (1998) *Leveraging the New Infrastructure*. Boston, MA: Harvard Business School Press.

Williamson, O. E. (1975) *Markets and Hierarchies: Analysis and Antitrust Implications*. New York: The Free Press.

Worley, C. G. & Lawler, E. E. I. (2006) Designing organizations that are built to change. *MIT Sloan Management Review, 48*(1), 19–23.

Yao, Y., Dresner, M. & Palmer, J. W. (2009) Impact of boundary spanning information technology and position in the chain on firm performance. *Journal of Supply Chain Management, 45*(1), 3–18.

For a range of further resources supporting this chapter, please visit the companion website for *Strategic Management* at www.routledge.com/cw/fitzroy.

ASSESSING STRATEGIC PERFORMANCE

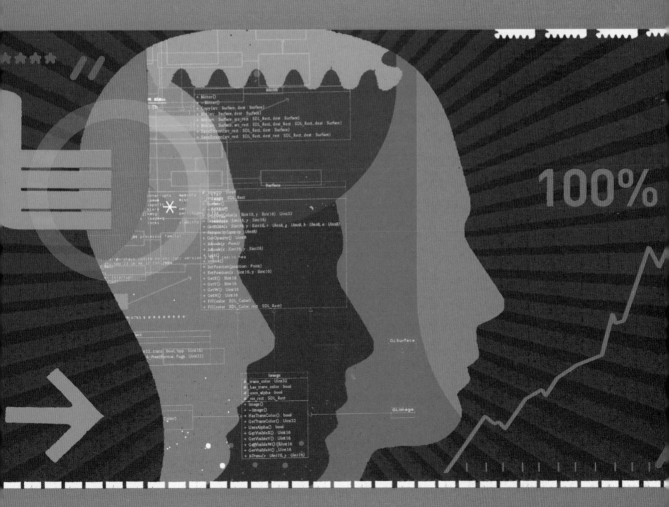

CHAPTER 12

MEASURING ORGANIZATIONAL PERFORMANCE

LEARNING OBJECTIVES

1 Recognize the iterative nature of performance measurement and strategy development.

2 Design a performance management system based on the framework developed in this chapter.

3 Apply the balanced scorecard measurement system at the business unit level.

4 Utilize the balanced scorecard measurement system at the corporate level.

5 Summarize why many firms have adopted the principles of corporate social responsibility.

TOYOTA

In 2007 Toyota replaced General Motors as the world's largest car producer. That year, Toyota produced nearly nine million cars, giving it a global market share of light vehicles of 13.1 per cent. Yet by 2009, its world market share had dropped to about 12 per cent, while the market share for the VW group had increased to just over 10 per cent (*The Economist*, 2009). Sales in all markets except the US were either static or declining. Toyota's market share in the major emerging markets such as China, India and Brazil were low and falling. Competitors such as VW appeared to be offering cars that were just as reliable but far more exciting than those offered by Toyota, possibly reflecting a lack of detailed market knowledge.

Toyota reported a loss for the financial year ending in March 2008 of ¥437 billion (US$4.3 billion). This is an amazing turnaround for a firm which for many years had been seen as the yardstick for manufacturing excellence, with substantial competitive advantages in quality and reliability. The current CEO has been quoted as saying that Toyota's historical priorities had been safety, quality and volume. Yet the firm's quality ranking had shown signs of dropping, as other firms such as Hyundai have succeeded in narrowing Toyota's advantage (*The Economist*, 2010a).

To further compound its difficulties, on 29 January 2010 Toyota announced the recall of eight million units, including two million units in Europe, in a belated response to a quality problem associated with faulty accelerator pedals (Lea, 2010). The vehicles in question were accused of unintended acceleration due to the accelerator pedal becoming stuck in the depressed position resulting in the vehicle accelerating to high speeds out of the control of the driver. Toyota was criticized for being very slow in responding to the large number of incidents involving unintended acceleration. Initially, senior Toyota managers blamed the problem on ill-fitting floor mats. However, it was reported that an internal email from a senior Toyota executive to their head office suggested that the 'time to hide on this one is over' (Lewis, 2010a). In late January 2010 there was growing evidence that the problem was due to a fault in the throttle mechanism, not the floor mats. This unintended acceleration has been blamed for 19 deaths and more than 2,000 incidents in the US.

Senior management in Toyota was considered responsible for not acting on information which had been available for several years. In 2006 a group of employees sent a memo to the then president, Katsuaki Watanabe, saying that safety sacrifices had been made by the firm in pursuit of profit (Lewis, 2010b). They also claimed that the firm had grown too fast and had forgotten what made its brand so strong. The US transport secretary claimed Toyota knew of the problem with sticking accelerators in September 2009 but did not issue a recall until January 2010 (Frean, 2010).

The cost of Toyota's global recalls was estimated at $US2 billion in the first quarter of 2010, while sales in the US have dropped 16 per cent on a year-to-year basis (*The Economist*, 2010b). Toyota's market capitalization has dropped by about the entire value of Ford. To compound their problems, in February 2010 Toyota announced the recall of 440,000 of the Prius model.

The US government is seeking to impose a $US16 million fine, suggesting that the firm deliberately hid a defect linked to a string of accidents. In testimony to a US House of Representatives Committee, the current head of Toyota, Mr Akio Toyoda, the grandson of the founder, suggested that the firm could be locked into a spiral of decline. In its pursuit of growth, Toyota had lost its once-prized manufacturing capabilities in quality and reliability, and had failed to put the customer first. Although most of the quality problems originated in suppliers' plants, Toyota's systems seemed unable to monitor the new suppliers who had limited understanding of Toyota, and yet had been added to support their growth strategy. In July 2010 the US National Highway Traffic Safety Administration reported that they had been unable to find any fault with Toyota's electronic throttle controls, although Toyota has acknowledged problems due to mechanical defects in accelerator pedals and with out-of-place floor mats (Simon, 2010).

Over the past several years, Toyota seem to have been using poorly designed measurement systems for their strategic management, systems whose accuracy and validity can be questioned. There appeared to be poor communications between the firm and its customers, so that safety concerns reported by customers did not penetrate to senior managers. Toyota also suffered from internal communications difficulties. Customer concerns reported in Europe were not shared with colleagues in the US. The firm also seemed to ignore developments in several emerging markets, such as China and Brazil, where VW and GM both performed better. Despite the most recent report indicating no faults with the electronic throttle mechanism, throughout the entire episode Toyota managers appeared to believe in their own view of the world, and not to take customer feedback seriously. As a result, Toyota's share price plummeted and it will probably take the company years to regain its reputation for quality.

CHAPTER OVERVIEW

This chapter explores the link between strategy and performance measurement. Measuring organizational performance is a major input to strategy development, since the measurement system plays a strategic diagnostic role as well as revealing how well the firm is executing the chosen strategy. The chapter opens by examining this interaction between performance measurement and strategy, highlighting the need to revise all aspects of strategic management based on the diagnostic role of the performance measurement system.

We then examine the structure of performance management systems, such as the need to develop both short-term and long-term measures. The importance of non-financial measures is also highlighted. These non-financial measures are often leading indicators of future performance – for example, declining market share is generally an indicator of future financial difficulties. Following this discussion, we present an integrative model that is used to organize the remainder of the chapter, with a set of clear objectives leading to the selection of what to measure and clarity in identifying the drivers of performance.

Considerable attention is then devoted to measuring performance at the business unit level, utilizing the balanced scorecard framework developed by Kaplan and Norton, a framework that utilizes a combination of financial and non-financial measures (Kaplan & Norton, 1996). This framework is then extended to the corporate level, which brings in several specifically corporate concepts such as synergy. We then review some of the common tools used to present these data so that the implications are clearly understood by senior managers. Recognizing the increased importance of environmental sustainability, we then examine corporate social responsibility measures.

Following this, we report an interview with the chief technology officer of Dow Chemical, in which he discusses how Dow measures innovation, a critical non-financial performance measure for many organizations. The chapter concludes with a mini-case, Interface Inc, where you are asked to apply the concepts discussed in this chapter by designing the performance measuring system for Interface.

12.1 INTRODUCTION

Chapter 1

Throughout this book we have emphasized that the ultimate objective of a firm is to create value and that this is only accomplished when over the longer term the revenue generated by the firm is greater than the costs incurred in generating that revenue, including the cost of capital. When this occurs, the firm is generating economic profit. However, value creation is the output of a complex process that we depicted in our strategic management model from Chapter 1 (▶Chapter 1), as shown in Figure 1.8. As we have reiterated throughout this book, sustaining high-level performance is an exceptionally difficult task, achieved by relatively few managers.

Managers need a good understanding of the context in which they operate – both the internal and the external environment – to develop value-creating strategies, and even then there is no guarantee that economic profit will result. In other words, a good understanding of context is a necessary but not sufficient condition for value creation. Innovation, creativity, and the collective organizational skills must be successfully applied to generating and implementing competitively superior strategies. Even when strategies are sound, however, management must also ensure that appropriate structures, systems and processes are in place to facilitate implementation, since many brilliant strategies fail because of inappropriate organizational architecture. Only when these conditions are fulfilled does it make sense for us to start asking whether or not we are achieving our desired performance levels.

It follows from the above that any attempt to fully explain corporate performance would require a complete audit of the strategic management process that has served as the subject of this entire book. Such a broad ambit is beyond the scope of this chapter, but it is vitally important that we bear in mind that a good performance management system has to be much more comprehensive than the numbers that account for most of a company's annual report, which are inevitably backward-looking and often lacking in any diagnostic value. While we are strong advocates of the firm as a value-creating entity, we also know that it is naive and deceptive to treat a living organization merely as a set of accounting numbers.

12.2 PERFORMANCE MEASURES

LEARNING OBJECTIVE 1

Recognize the iterative nature of performance measurement and strategy development.

The purpose of a measurement system is to help managers generate superior strategies and thus superior firm value. While most of this value generation takes place at the business unit level, one of the means by which the corporate centre can augment this business-level value creation is by ensuring that appropriate measurement and control systems are in place. Of course, value is not created by the measurement system, but it can be an essential diagnostic tool for management, supporting better decision-making, or it can do exactly the reverse, contributing to a downward spiral. There is a saying that managers do what is inspected, not what is expected, and there is no doubt that poorly designed measurement systems produce a catalogue of deviant behaviours, as we noted above with Toyota.

Figure 12.1 depicts the interactive strategy and measurement process over time. We develop and implement strategy based on an understanding of context and supported by appropriate architecture. We then measure the results, ascertain where these depart from expectations (positively or negatively), identify the causes or drivers of these discrepancies, and then make appropriate revisions. It is vital to see the whole process as a dynamic and ongoing learning process rather than as a punitive or simply evaluative exercise.

Thus the strategy and architecture of the firm will change and evolve as the world moves forward. In an uncertain and turbulent world, strategy must have emergent features, and it

Figure 12.1 Dynamic strategy process

must be contingent on unpredictable changes. Managers need a system to monitor the execution of the strategy and its underlying assumptions, to ensure that it remains successful, and to indicate how it may need to be revised and modified.

We now clarify a number of important concepts in performance measurement before introducing the model that will be used to structure the remainder of the chapter.

Shareholder value and firm value

With more and more companies adopting the shareholder value approach, it is critically important to keep separate the concepts of shareholder value and firm value or economic profit. From the perspective of the firm, it creates value when it earns a return greater than its cost of capital. The return that a shareholder receives, however, is a function of the dividends received and the level of share price appreciation. These two concepts – shareholder value and firm value – are not identical. A company may be performing well and earning above its cost of capital, thereby creating firm value. However, shareholders may have paid too much for their shares or the overall stock market may be in decline, in which case they cannot appropriate firm value in their returns. Over the long term, however, if the company is increasing value by creating economic profit, its shareholders should profit as a result.

We have also emphasized the necessity for strategic managers to achieve success across a range of time frames, typically described as short term and long term. This is a difficult combination to attain, not least because of the short-term focus of many financial markets. Shareholder behaviour is driven by expectations of future performance of the firm, indicating that managers need to consider both short-term and long-term performance. All too frequently, senior managers will jeopardize future performance to achieve short-term goals. In a survey of US chief financial officers, some 80 per cent said they would cut discretionary expenditure, such as on R&D, to meet short-term earnings targets (Graham *et al.*, 2005). Such behaviour is not limited to the US; similar examples occur in Europe, where a major financial services firm achieved a dramatic increase in short-term financial performance, but customer service declined sharply and staff turnover increased (Dobbs *et al.*, 2005). These examples indicate that to manage a firm strategically we need a full range of measures which address both short-term and long-term performance.

Variables and measures

In designing a measurement system, we need to be aware of the distinction between a variable and the measurement of that variable. We regard the concepts of 'innovation' or 'customer satisfaction' as variables. Identifying such variables requires a conceptual model of business that specifies which variables are relevant. We also need to distinguish between input and output variables. Typical output variables would be 'profit' or 'market share'. Inputs are the variables that determine, or influence, the levels of these outputs. Normally these input variables can be considered as nested; thus 'product quality' as a variable may influence another variable, 'customer satisfaction', which in turn may be related to the output financial variable 'profit'. In a complex system such as a business firm, there is seldom a simple connection between an input variable and an output variable; instead, there may be many inputs that influence a single output such as 'profit'.

Having identified a variable as being relevant to understanding the overall performance of the firm, we then need to construct a measure, an operational procedure that results in a specific measure, generally numeric, for each variable. So 'customer satisfaction' may be defined as the score obtained from a customer survey. There can be considerable debate on how to measure a particular variable, such as 'employee morale' or 'synergy'. Following good statistical practice, the operational measure of the variable must be both valid and reliable.

Diagnostic use

The underlying rationale for developing a performance measurement system is to facilitate strategy execution and to provide diagnostic information on how the strategy could be improved. This indicates that the measurement system must also incorporate an understanding of the drivers of firm value and clarifying the relative importance of these drivers. Thus we need both outcome measures and performance drivers. We should be able to translate the business unit or corporate strategy into a linked set of measures that define objectives and the mechanisms for achieving these. The specific measures adopted will depend on the strategy being executed and will of necessity require the development of cause–effect chains that link specific actions to corporate objectives.

Financial and non-financial measures

It should be clear that if we are to create value, we must have financial measures of performance. However, as was noted in Chapter 5 (►Chapter 5), intangible assets now account for the majority of a firm's market capitalization. This reinforces the proposition that traditional financial measures must be complemented by non-financial measures. This increasing discrepancy has produced considerable concern in the business community and is leading to some changes in accounting practice (Corona, 2009). The necessity for using such non-financial measures is enhanced by several studies which have found a positive relationship between organizational performance and the use of measures of intangible assets in Finland (Salojarvi *et al.*, 2005) and India (Ghosh & Mondal, 2009). It is our view that all performance measurement systems should include measures of intangible assets such as product quality, brand equity, innovation and knowledge, since these can all be drivers of financial success (Lonnqvist, 2002). Otherwise management can be seriously misled, to the detriment of shareholders' interests (►Chapter 6). A recent US study which examined non-financial leading indicators revealed that there was considerable variation across industry in what data was reported, although some measure of innovation was most often reported (Cohen *et al.*, 2009).

Chapters 5, 6

While we give primary emphasis to the economic performance of a firm, reflecting the interests of shareholders, there are numerous other stakeholders, and managers need to know how well the firm is performing relative to these stakeholders: therefore customer, employee and community measures will also be important. Yet our primary focus on shareholders is justified, since empirical studies indicate that increasing shareholder value does not conflict with the long-term interest of other stakeholders (Copeland, 1994).

Benchmarking

As pernicious as looking backwards is looking inwards. We have emphasized the increasing competitiveness of the business environment throughout this book, and unless the company is winning competitive battles, its prospects are poor. Thus, while telling ourselves we are doing better than we were previously may provide some solace, the real question must be: 'Are we doing better than competitors?' Internal yardsticks against historical performance are not enough (Holloway *et al.*, 1995). While historical analysis can improve existing performance, real best-practice exercises must encompass a wider realm.

'Best-of-class' benchmarking (Camp, 1989) was a concept developed by Xerox, recognizing that many business processes are common across different industries. Understanding this fact was a major insight that permitted Cemex to expand successfully by acquisition (▶Chapter 11). We earlier discussed organizational learning, and central to the best-of-class benchmarking concept is the idea that we can learn from others, not just in our own company or industry, but also outside it. Indeed, one can argue that if one learns only from one's own industry, one will never lead it. Thus we argue strongly for external comparison on any performance measure wherever this is even remotely feasible.

Chapter 11

Need for a set of measures

Organizational performance is far too complex to be captured by a single, simple measure, particularly when the measurement system has a diagnostic focus. Further, reliance on any simple metric is likely to produce deviant behaviour of the type exhibited by Toyota. Thus evaluating performance requires an integrated set of measures that are supportive of the mission statement, foster proper implementation of the strategy and capture underlying complexity. Here we face a dilemma, since too simple an approach is likely to be deceiving and dysfunctional, but if the system becomes too complex, it will be too difficult for people to use prescriptively. Clearly, we must find an appropriate trade-off between simplicity and complexity. At the same time, since the firm is developing new strategies in response to a changing world, it will also need to revise and update its measurement system.

> **LEARNING OBJECTIVE 2**
>
> Design a performance management system based on the framework developed in this chapter.

12.3 DEVELOPING A PERFORMANCE MEASUREMENT SYSTEM

Chapter 2

We begin with the basic assumption that we are dealing with a multi-business corporation (▶Chapter 2). Consequently, we must develop a measurement system that is appropriate at both the business unit and the corporate levels. For each of these levels, we need to establish a measurement process that provides both a valid and a reliable measure of the variable under consideration. Further, building on our discussion in the previous section, we conclude that a good measurement system must include multiple variables, including leading indicators wherever possible, and that these will necessarily include non-financial as well as financial variables.

We should point out that performance measurement also has a cultural dimension. Successful firms have a performance culture, a culture where performance is measured and actions taken on the basis of an analysis of this performance. Not only is performance taken seriously but so are the actions that flow from this analysis. Companies with substantial excess cash flow often make uneconomic investments in either mature businesses or in uneconomic diversification. Unless there is a strong performance culture in the firm, these strategies are likely to be adopted since they are in the interests of managers, despite the fact that they may well be destroying value. This illustrates that firms may suffer from the agency problem where the goals of managers are not aligned with the goals of shareholders (▶Chapter 9). Good performance measurement systems attempt to overcome this by utilizing a related management incentive system that aligns managers' remuneration with the performance measures.

Chapter 9

Identifying and designing performance measures

Figure 12.2 presents a process for identifying and developing performance measures (Neely *et al.*, 2002). We now review each step of the process.

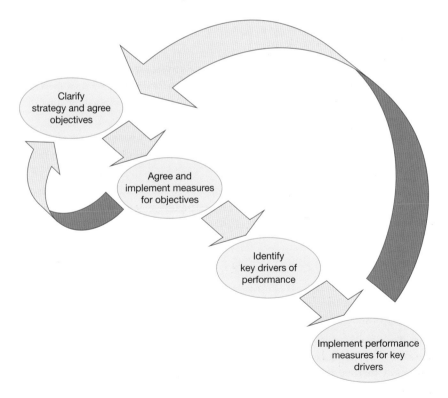

Figure 12.2 A process for identifying and developing performance measures

Clarify strategy and agree on objectives

A vital first step is to ensure that both strategy and objectives (including priorities among different objectives) are clearly defined, including a consideration of the interests of various stakeholders, in particular shareholders, customers and employees. For example, establishing specific strategic priorities such as customer orientation highlights the importance of non-financial measures (Verbeeten & Boons, 2009). Once priorities are agreed upon, specific improvement levels can be established for each objective. In doing so, it is important to remember our admonitions in Chapter 6 (➤Chapter 6). Big, hairy, audacious goals (BHAGS) (Collins & Porras, 1994) are all very well and good under certain circumstances, but objectives 'stretched' to the point where people believe them to be unattainable are demotivating, not motivating!

Chapter 6

Agree and implement measures for business objectives

We must next develop a specific measure for each objective. The measure should clearly indicate how close we are to the intended target level, stimulate desired behaviour and, wherever possible, avoid unintended dysfunctional consequences. We should also consider such issues as frequency of measurement, who will be responsible for measurement, and the source of the data to be used. We are great believers in redundancy, as no matter how carefully we try to anticipate the behaviours that measurement will produce, human ingenuity is such that we will undoubtedly fail to foresee all of them.

Finally, implementation requires specifying who will be responsible for acting if performance fails to meet objectives and the general nature of the managerial processes and remedial actions they will be expected to undertake should this be the case. Such specifications put teeth into the measurement process and are essential in supporting the kind of performance culture to which we previously referred.

It is important that the final set of measures be sufficiently comprehensive and that the management team 'sign off' on both the measures themselves and the measurement and review process. In the case of corporate-level objectives, these should be agreed upon at the board level, whereas business unit objectives should be established as a result of discussion and negotiation between business unit and corporate management. The system itself should also be subject to review as strategy evolves over time.

Identify key drivers of performance

A good performance measurement system is one that helps us to identity the drivers (causes) of performance, or a lack thereof, and therefore guides us in making decisions that will improve performance. These drivers include such concepts as customer service, R&D effectiveness, product quality and employee development, among others. Identifying the key drivers of performance usually benefits from team-based contributions that, if properly managed, will increase the creativity and originality of thinking. Identifying such drivers is facilitated by the use of cause-and-effect chains, as is illustrated in Figure 12.3 which shows the determinants of customer satisfaction for an airline.

Figure 12.3 Cause–effect chain for customer satisfaction

Source: adapted from Neely, 2002

This cause–effect analysis needs to be taken further to include the impact that customer satisfaction, among other variables, has on an outcome measure such as firm profitability. Clearly, some variables may have greater impact than others, and setting priorities will again be important.

Implement performance measures for key drivers

Next we need to identify measures for each key driver. These should be precisely defined, while recognizing that any measure is only an approximation of the underlying variable of interest. Complexity is clearly undesirable, yet the chosen metrics must be robust, and applied systematically. We will seek measures that encourage appropriate behaviour, identify persons responsible, and determine the nature of the actions that need to be undertaken to achieve improvements, thereby embedding performance measurement in the company culture. These measures and targets should be agreed upon with the business team; again, involvement improves quality and commitment to the system. Involving the cross-functional business team is particularly helpful in identifying possible conflicts among measures in order to achieve integration and alignment. We can then set specific improvement targets in these identified areas.

Note that Figure 12.2 contained two feedback loops, for measures of objectives and drivers respectively. In addition, we should also schedule reviews of the complete system, since, if measures are to be linked to strategy, they must evolve with the strategy. In our experience, too many firms violate this basic principle, sticking rather rigidly with a given set of measures and puzzling perplexedly over why their strategies do not seem to get implemented. Finally, people must be compensated on the basis of these measures – and this may be one of the most important steps.

Obviously, there are many potential problems involved in performance measurement. It has been argued that too often vanity compromises choices, such that only metrics that make the firm and its people look good receive attention. Other problems include an internal orientation (narcissism), laziness, pettiness and provincialism (Hammer, 2007).

LEARNING OBJECTIVE 3

Apply the balanced scorecard measurement system at the business unit level.

Balanced scorecard

A performance measurement system which combines qualitative and quantitative measures. Performance is measured along four dimensions – customer, internal, innovation and financial.

12.4 MEASURING BUSINESS-LEVEL PERFORMANCE

Both corporate and business unit managers have an interest in measuring and assessing business unit performance. Such assessment should determine whether or not the business unit has met its objectives, how its performance can be enhanced, and what its likely future performance will be.

As we have consistently stated, the purpose of the firm is to create value; therefore financial measures of a business's performance are clearly important. Yet we have already pointed out the limitations of traditional accounting data for managerial purposes. Kaplan and Norton recognized the same problem and developed the **balanced scorecard**, a widely adopted system illustrated in Figure 12.4 (Kaplan & Norton, 1996).

The balanced scorecard supplements financial measures with a set of non-financial measures that provide better insight into the likely future performance of the business, thus providing a tool for *ex ante*, or anticipatory, control rather than *ex post* analysis. In addition, the balanced scorecard can be used as the basis for measuring managerial performance which in turn may form the basis for executive compensation. The non-financial measures, including both tangible (for example, delivery time) and intangible (for example, motivation) variables, are generally aggregated or weighted to arrive at an overall index (Carona, 2009).

The word *balance* is used to denote several ideas. Balance between financial and non-financial, balance between measures of past results and measures that will influence future performance, and balance between more objective measures and more subjective measures. When measuring organizational performance, the approach eschews the use of a single measure. Instead, it adopts a set of measures providing insight into how the strategy of the unit may be adjusted to meet future goals and expectations. For a detailed study of how the balanced scorecard was implemented at Fosters, a global beer company, see Bose (Bose & Thomas, 2007).

The balanced scorecard measures business unit performance along four dimensions:

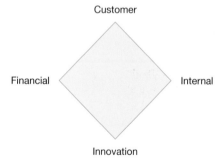

Figure 12.4 The balanced scorecard

- customer
- internal
- innovation
- financial.

For each dimension there is a set of measures, with objectives established for each. We discuss each in turn.

Customer measures

In a highly competitive world, any business unit must deliver value to customers and possess a strong customer orientation. Customers have many choices in where they purchase, and, if the business does not understand these choices and how they are changing due to competition, the future of the business may be at risk. As discussed in Chapter 7 (►Chapter 7), an important element of business unit strategy is choosing its horizontal positioning – which market segments the business will compete in. Within its chosen segments, the business must understand how customers define value in order to ensure customer loyalty and to attract customers from competitors. In addition, the business must measure how well it is performing with respect to such outcomes as customer satisfaction, customer retention, the acquisition of new customers and the lifetime value of the customer (Chenhall & Langfield-Smith, 2007). The scorecard also includes a number of more aggregate measures, such as market share in the total market or in selected segments and channels of distribution. Since details of the measurement system will depend on the specific business unit, we will discuss selected measurement examples, beginning with aggregate measures, and then progress to more detailed measures.

Chapter 7

Customer measures of performance at the business unit level include aggregate measures such as sales volume and growth, both of which are critical measures for managers. These measures could be broken down by segment and benchmarked against figures for the economy or industry as a whole. Benchmarking against the total market permits analysis of market share by product, region, customer segment, channel and so on, as illustrated below. Market share is an important output measure, since it controls for the effects of changes in market size and enables managers to assess competitive performance.

Business unit managers should also be asking themselves about the factors that contribute to sales volume and growth. Such a cause–effect analysis might lead them to look at more detailed measures that drive volume for the specific market segments illustrated in Table 12.1.

Table 12.1 Performance measures – segment 1

	2012	2013	2014
Sales revenue (€)			
Market share (%)			
Relative value (index)			
Relative price (%)			
Relative quality (index)			
Customer retention (%)			
Sales from new customers (%)			
Customer satisfaction (index)			
Competitive advantage (index)			

Each of the variables in Table 12.1, such as customer satisfaction, itself has drivers. Managers cannot improve customer satisfaction by fiat; there is no simple lever to turn. The drivers of customer satisfaction will depend on the nature of the business and the industry in which it competes, as was illustrated for an airline in Figure 12.3. Such data, particularly if analysed using competitive benchmarks, help assess how customers see the business. Business unit managers must ensure that they are creating value for customers; a business whose competitive advantage is declining is likely to have problems in the future. In addition, as we discussed in Chapter 7 (►Chapter 7), customer analysis needs to be undertaken at a detailed level to provide the understanding required to identify growth opportunities and where resources should be allocated (Viguerie *et al.*, 2008), as the following example illustrates.

Chapter 7

Challenge of strategic management

On the revenue side of the equation our experience has shown time and again that a surprisingly small number of customers account for almost all the variations in revenues almost all of the time. For example, if a business unit sells cars that appeal to blue collar workers in the Midwest, changes in manufacturing employment and hours worked may affect directly their propensity to buy from it. These same indicators are much less likely to be useful in other parts of the country.

It is important to note that the subset of customers who drive changes in revenues may not be the same subset of customers who produce most of the company's profit – indeed they may be the marginal customers. For example, with banks, poor credits figure disproportionately in the changes to the revenue line relative to customers who can be counted upon to meet their interest and principal payments reliably. These weak credits produce high fee and interest income in good times, but require large bad debt reserves in bad times . . .

If the small group of customers that drive changes in the revenue line are businesses, a detailed tracking of their business health and the size, quality and time-to-close of sales leads from them will yield early insight into where your business is likely to go. If these customers are consumers, monitoring the economic forces that drive the behaviours of the psycho-geo-demographic groups that make up this subset of your customer base will perform that same early warning function for your business.

(Sacerdote, 2002)

Questions

1 Do you agree with Sacerdote's views? Why or why not?
2 What are the implications of his views for the corporate and business unit measurement systems?
3 What are the implications for the management accounting system of the firm?

Brand equity

As was discussed in Chapter 5 (►Chapter 5), brand equity is an important component of **Chapter 5** the intangible assets of a business, and this must be measured and appropriate actions taken to maintain the value of any brands owned by the business. The magnitude of this brand equity can be very significant.

Brand value *in practice* – Ford

In 1989 Ford paid $US2.5 billion for the British car manufacturer *Jaguar*, whose book value was $US0.4 billion. The difference, $US2.1 billion, that was placed on Ford's balance sheet as 'goodwill' is mainly accounted for by Ford's estimate of the value of *Jaguar*'s brand equity. In 2000, Ford acquired Land Rover from BMW for $US2.75 billion (Chatterjee & Krolicki, 2008), combining these into a new division: Jaguar Land Rover. Over the next eight years, this group was reported to have cost Ford $10 billion (*The Economist*, 2008). In 2008, Tata paid £1 billion ($US2.3 billion) for Jaguar Land Rover after Ford suffered a loss of $US12.7 billion in 2006. To facilitate the purchase, Ford injected £300 million into the Jaguar Land Rover pension fund. Jaguar has recently suffered declining sales, although it has launched a successful new model. In contrast, Land Rover had demonstrated growth (Buckley & Blakely, 2008).

It should be apparent from the above example that there is a great deal of uncertainty about the actual value of brand equity. Hence, a number of approaches are used to attempt to measure brand equity, which are covered in more detail in Keller (Keller, 2002). One method is the earnings approach, adopted by Interbrand, which compares the revenues earned by the brand in a product category with the revenues earned (or estimated) by a generic product in the same category.

Measuring brand equity *in practice* – Interbrand

The Interbrand Group plc, a major brand consultancy, employs two factors in its earnings-based method. It uses annual after-tax profits less expected earnings for an equivalent unbranded product averaged over time, factored by a proprietary-developed multiplier purporting to measure 'brand strength'. Measures of brand strength are based on several factors, including leadership (the ability to influence the market), stability (survival ability based on degree of customer loyalty), market (invulnerability to changes of technology and fashion), geography (the ability to cross geographic and cultural borders), support (the consistency and effectiveness of brand support) and protection (legal title) (Interbrand, 2010).

Quite apart from the difficulties associated with any of the methods, just as with any item of value for which a liquid market does not exist, valuations may be wrong. This can lead to critical mistakes in making acquisitions. Valuation, especially regarding the revenue function, always rests on assumptions about the behaviour of customers, and these assumptions must be subject to scrutiny. How many customers in the target market will buy? How frequently? How responsive will they be to the various marketing programmes we and our competitors expect to be using, and how do we expect their tastes and preferences to evolve over time? Assumptions about these and other issues are present, at least implicitly, in every valuation exercise.

Internal measures

Key performance indicator (KPI)

A quantifiable measure of an organizational process or activity that reflects the organization's goals and has a significant impact on the overall performance of the organization.

With the high levels of competitive intensity in most markets, firms are under inexorable pressure to continually reduce costs and improve productivity of both labour and capital. The balanced scorecard system suggests that the business should have a set of **key performance indicators** (KPIs) to assess cost and productivity (Parmenter, 2007). These include measures of the firm's internal processes, such as is shown in Table 12.2.

Table 12.2 Internal performance measures

Measure	2012	2013	2014
Unit cost (€)			
Yield (%)			
Product defects (%)			
Process measures (index)			
Staff satisfaction (index)			
Staff skills (index)			
Capabilities (index)			
Productivity (output/employee)			
IT system use (index)			

Performance measures are process yield and cost, productivity and staff satisfaction. The business unit should identify those processes that have the greatest impact on customer satisfaction and develop performance measures for each. The specific measures will depend on the process involved but may include such generic measures as time, cost, quality and innovation. The educational level of employees, or the number of years of experience in the industry or the firm could be measures of staff skills. Note that a number of these will be intangible, since we are attempting to measure both human and structural capital within the business.

In the automotive industry, J. D. Power Associates provides data on defects that are widely tracked within the industry. Auto manufacturers also track and benchmark their

Table 12.3 2002 productivity of European auto factories (2001 in parentheses)

Rank	Manufacturer	Plant location	Vehicles per employee
1(1)	Nissan	Sunderland, UK	99(95)
2(4)	Renault	Valladolid, Spain	89(77)
3(–)	Toyota	Valenciennes, France	88(–)
5(6)	General Motors	Antwerp, Belgium	83(76)
6(12)	Renault	Novo Mesto, Slovenia	82(69)
7(13)	Honda	Swindon, UK	82(67)
8(3)	Toyota	Burnaston, UK	81(87)
10(7)	General Motors	Zaragoza, Spain	80(75)

Source: Jay, 2003

productivity statistics. A typical set of these data for European car factories in 2002 is shown in Table 12.3.

As is clear from Table 12.3, labour productivity varies significantly between suppliers and between plants of the same supplier. These data reinforce our earlier suggestion that we cannot assume that all competitors have the same cost structure.

Innovation and learning measures

In rapidly changing environments, firms must innovate on an ongoing basis. Innovation is a major contributor to business unit growth, but innovation should not be construed as consisting only of new products. As we have noted, innovation can subsume new business models, entry into new markets, new processes, distribution channels, organization structures and the like (▶Chapter 11). Since innovation is crucial to renewal, business unit managers need measures of the success of their business with respect to innovation. At the same time as the firm is renewing itself, it must be learning. Too many firms repeat their mistakes because their memory resides only in the memories of individuals; it has not been transformed into structural knowledge.

Chapter 11

Variables that capture innovation and learning are illustrated in Table 12.4.

Table 12.4 Innovation and learning performance measures

Measure	2012	2013	2014
Patents (number/year)			
Revenue from new products (%)			
New capabilities (index)			
Staff training (€)			
R&D expenditure (€)			

Other indicators of innovation might include R&D expenditures as a percentage of sales revenues or the number of researchers as a percentage of the labour force. These are input numbers, and we would prefer output measures such as number of patents filed or the number of new products in a particular time period. One example of such a measure is used by 3M – the percentage of sales from products new in the last five years. One of the reasons much research on innovation has focused on new product-related measures is that these are much easier to design than measures of other kinds of innovation. Channel and business model innovation is less frequent than new product launches in most businesses, while process innovation is even harder to measure.

Financial measures

The firm is an economic entity whose purpose it is to create value, so financial measures are critical. In Chapter 1 we defined value as economic profit – the residual after all costs, including the cost of the capital employed in the business, are deducted from sales revenues (➤Chapter 1). However, economic profit is an outcome, and a good performance measurement system will also track the drivers of economic profit. We begin by looking at current performance indicators, both outcomes and drivers. We then review measures that give insight into likely future performance.

 Chapter 1

Measuring current performance

Table 12.5 contains a typical set of financial measures that reflect recent performance of the business unit.

Table 12.5 Financial measures of performance

Measure	2012	2013	2014
Economic profit (€)			
Net income (€)			
ROCE (%)			
ROS (%)			
Asset turnover (%)			
Current ratio (%)			

We have given pride of place to a measure of economic profit, since we argue that this should be the primary basis on which we should assess any business. Nonetheless, we should not expect all business units to make a positive economic profit all the time. We do expect that all businesses should eventually generate positive economic profit, but if the parent corporation is investing in the business to support its growth, short-term economic profit may be negative. In this instance, we can see the advantage of a business being part of a diversified firm, since the corporate centre can provide capital for the business from internal or external sources.

We have also shown a net income figure in Table 12.5. This number is widely tracked and reported, and certainly managers do not like to see this decline. Several of the other measures in Table 12.5 are measures of efficiency. Return on capital employed (ROCE) is a measure of how productively the capital in the business is being utilized. For a positive economic profit, this must be above the business's cost of capital. The corporate level may use such a measure in allocating resources, although, as argued earlier, only future capital productivity is actually relevant. Return on sales (ROS), also known as net margin on sales, can be seen as another measure of the efficiency of the business: how much does the business keep of each dollar of sales? Margins are not a good performance measure of the business's overall profitability, since they are strongly influenced by the level and nature of competition, being low in a highly competitive market. Margins are usually high for successful new products but decline as competitors follow the successful pioneer. Acceptable margins will also depend on the capital intensity of the business, with capital-intensive firms needing to earn a high margin on sales to be profitable. By contrast, a retailer may be quite profitable (defined in terms of ROCE) with net margins as low as 2 per cent to 3 per cent. Capital intensity is generally measured by the ratio of capital to sales, which is the inverse of the asset turnover ratio, and retailers generally have low levels of capital intensity.

We have included asset turnover as one of the measures above, since in our view most firms are actively engaged in reducing the level of capital tied up in the business, particularly working capital, through supply-chain initiatives.

Valuing future performance

The above measures of performance are focused on the present, on how well the firm is performing now. But strategy is about making decisions now whose consequences will be manifest at some time in the future. Thus a technique is needed to estimate the current value of future results. The recommended method for accomplishing this is to calculate the net present value of the strategy over time.

The current value of a strategy is determined by the discounted value of the future free cash flow estimated to be generated by that strategy. We regard net present value (NPV) as the correct method for an economic evaluation of the future results of a strategy, since it incorporates both net cash flows and the time value of money. In this formulation, net cash flow is the free cash generated by the strategy, including all investments in both fixed and working capital and the discount rate is the firm's weighted average cost of capital.

The forecast of future cash flows is generally broken down into two time periods:

Free cash flow
The cash generated by the firm after investing in fixed and working capital.

- A forecast period for which detailed cash flow projections are made (conventional practice seems to be to pick the arbitrary period of five years).
- A steady-state period to perpetuity, implicitly assuming no change in the firm's strategy.

The calculation of net present value has some very real problems in application. First, at the practical level, it is difficult to develop estimates of the required numbers, since forecasts of sales, costs and investments are needed over the forecast period of, say, five years. These numbers may have major errors, since it is unreasonable to expect perfect foresight with respect to future demand, competitor action, developments in technology, future market shares and prices, and so on, all of which will be fundamental to the development of cash flow numbers. Unfortunately, the 'gimme a number' syndrome often means these numbers have an apparent accuracy, which can lead to a feeling of greater certainty. In addition, the realities of organizational life mean there may be an unconscious (or even conscious!) tendency for managers to bias their numbers to ensure that the NPV comes out at an acceptable level.

Second, NPV is of limited use when dealing with very innovative strategies. These are by their nature characterized by little in the way of historical data and information that can be utilized to predict the future.

Third, it is in the nature of NPV calculations that short time-horizon cash streams are weighted higher than cash streams that are in the distant future. With a discount rate of 15 per cent, $1 in ten years' time is discounted to only 24¢ today. Thus most of the NPV is in the first few years, which may bias managers' choices towards those alternatives that promise to deliver short-term benefits. Indeed, given two alternatives of equal NPV, it is likely that most managers would choose the alternative that produces the earliest positive net cash flows.

Figure 12.5 depicts a typical cash flow profile of a strategy.

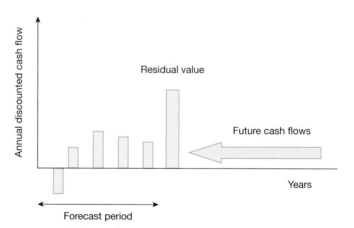

Figure 12.5 Future cash flows of a strategy

Despite the apparent high weighting to short-term results, another concern is the heuristic used to calculate net present value. When calculating the NPV of a strategy, a detailed analysis is undertaken of the costs and revenues for the first five years of the strategy. The present value of the cash flows beyond this time is usually collapsed into a single term – the residual value. This is often calculated using the simplistic assumption that the performance of the firm remains at its five-year level in perpetuity. When calculated in this way, the residual value term often comprises a significant proportion of the total net present value. With the high levels of turbulence experienced today, this assumption of stability is unlikely to be realized.

NPV approaches can deal with risk by using a higher discount rate. As we have noted, the cost of capital will be different for different business units of a company. However, this does not address the different risk levels of individual projects. One way to deal with this is by subjectively adjusting the discount rate based on qualitative risk assessment. As noted earlier, Kucszmarski argues that quite low discount rates should be used for strategies involving cost reduction or product extensions, with higher rates for more radical strategies (Kuczmarski, 1988).

Other methods: simulation and options

One way to handle some of the problems just discussed is to use simulation methods. If we are uncertain about an input variable to the financial model, a range of possibilities can be evaluated and a distribution of expected returns generated. In some applications, game theory may be useful, since it explicitly incorporates concepts of competitive reaction.

NPV does not deal adequately with the benefits of flexibility. Faced with great uncertainty, more firms are making small investments in growing areas – through alliances, for example – to gain knowledge about whether to invest a substantial sum at a later date. This may permit greater flexibility, since the business may be able to shut down and restart, or re-focus an activity or expand partial to full ownership. The business could then be considered to have a call option – the right to buy (Copeland & Keenan, 1998).

In summary, NPV is a good methodology to use for evaluating financial instruments such as bonds, where the investor gets a guaranteed return for several years, but investment projects are typically more complicated. Management can intervene and change the direction of a strategy if it is not meeting expectations, while circumstances may change significantly from those initially envisaged, particularly in new areas. If NPV were foolproof, venture capital firms would not have to maintain such a large portfolio of projects! For this reason, there has been some interest expressed in the possibility of using option theory as a basis for evaluation.

Finally, we should point out that valuing future performance is not the same as influencing future performance. If business unit managers are interested in leading indicators of future performance, they would be well advised to look at the various non-financial measures we have discussed, since they are likely to have predictive value.

12.5 CORPORATE PERFORMANCE MEASURES

LEARNING OBJECTIVE 4

Utilize the balanced scorecard measurement system at the corporate level.

The balanced scorecard is a performance measurement framework best suited to a business unit or single-business firm rather than a multi-business corporation. Possibly as a result of this there has been less effort devoted to the development of comparable non-financial measures at the corporate level.

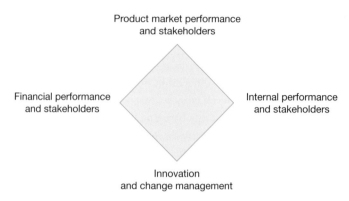

Figure 12.6 Corporate-level scorecard

Chapter 8

In this section, we have adapted some of the basic principles of the balanced score card to the corporate level of a multi-business firm (►Chapter 8). Such adaptation is necessary since, for instance, the corporate level of a firm typically has no actual customers; customers purchase from its constituent businesses. For measures such as customer or employee satisfaction, or new product launches, it is possible to score each strategic business unit (SBU) and weight these scores to get an overall corporate measure that would enable a CEO to track corporate performance. However, there are also some quintessential corporate variables, such as scope and diversity that should also be of concern. Measures for these variables must be constructed for the firm as a whole; they cannot be created from weighted sums of scores for individual business units.

Our framework is shown in Figure 12.6, where performance of the firm is assessed in four areas: external product/market, internally, financially, and with respect to innovation. While innovation could be considered as an internal measure, we regard it as of sufficient importance to warrant special consideration. We now discuss each set of measures in turn.

Product/market performance and external stakeholders

The firm has a number of external stakeholders, comprising customers of the business units as well as other entities such as suppliers, unions, pressure groups and the community. While the performance of the firm needs to be assessed from the perspective of each of these, we start with customers generally and then move on to other stakeholders.

For most corporate managers, growth itself is a vital performance measure; thus all firms monitor total sales revenue for the firm very closely and would prefer to see this measure increasing over time. Revenue may also be compared with some measure of economic growth, such as GDP, to see whether the firm is growing faster or slower than the overall economy.

As we discussed earlier, the ability to create a continuous stream of new businesses, representing new sources of profit, is a distinguishing characteristic of successful firms. For a firm to grow in terms of market capitalization, it generally requires a stream of

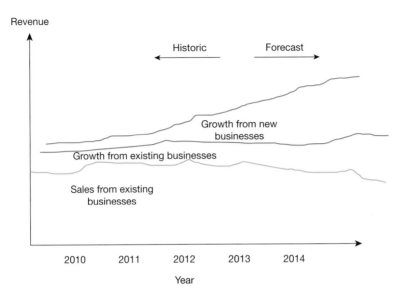

Figure 12.7 Sources of corporate growth

new businesses (➤Chapter 2). At the corporate level, this can be analysed as shown in Figure 12.7.

Chapters 2, 8, 9

Growth from existing businesses presents a different management challenge from growth of new businesses (➤Chapter 8). Yet if the company is to survive, it must have a portfolio of growth alternatives, and senior management cannot afford to focus exclusively on current core businesses. Indeed, we should measure the performance of a diversified company in terms of its ability to spawn a stream of new business ventures, either from internal development or through acquisition (➤Chapter 9).

As mentioned, the corporate level has no direct customers – they all exist at the business unit level, so a measure of corporate-level customer satisfaction is hard to imagine. However, the corporate centre should be monitoring performance on this critical dimension by determining the weighted-average customer satisfaction measure of its different business units, where the measure from a given business unit is weighted relative to the size of the business unit. The centre will also be tracking business unit–market shares and may well be comparing the performance of each business in its chosen market, using dimensions such as market share, revenue growth, customer satisfaction, customer value and competitive advantage.

Total revenue is a simple measure, but it is only one, and the firm needs to get more detail to properly analyse its position. At the corporate level, managers would also need to collect segment data – by business unit, by industry, by geographic market or by type of business – to see how the business portfolio is evolving over time. The research of Viguerie *et al.* would suggest that another useful criterion might be the extent to which the business unit was successful in identifying and entering fast-growing segments of its markets (Viguerie *et al.*, 2008).

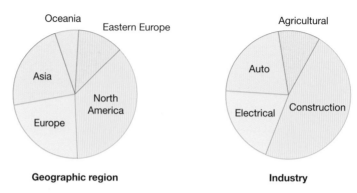

Figure 12.8 Distribution of corporate revenue – 2011

The overall balance of a firm's portfolio is a critical leading indicator of both risk management and future value-generating potential. Such an analysis is given in Figure 12.8, which shows the distribution of corporate revenue both by geography and by industry. Such analyses would normally be done dynamically to reveal how the distribution of revenue is changing over time.

Brand equity may also be a major issue at the corporate level. If the firm makes heavy use of a corporate master brand, then a corporate health-check system is essential. However, the centre may well be interested in the stewardship of its business unit's major brands, in which case it will want to see the appropriate health-check tables. If the centre is considering modifying its brand or business portfolio, it will also want to measure these brand equities, which may in any case be required to be reported on its balance sheet.

Finally, as we noted, the corporation may well be interested in tracking the perceptions of other important stakeholder groups. While the indices would be less elaborate, perceptual measures could equally well be used to track perceptions of the firm by its various stakeholder communities of interest, whether locally, regionally, nationally or internationally.

Internal measures and internal stakeholders

At the corporate level, the firm is structured as a set of business units, and hence internal measures are connected with the performance of these units as well as with several overall firm measures. In the preceding section, we examined several methods for analysing the entire portfolio of businesses from a market perspective. Here we extend that discussion by indicating methods that can be used to assess the health of the business units.

Corporate portfolio performance measures

To perform their agency role for the principals, corporate managers must delve more deeply into the performance of the business units comprising the firm's portfolio. The portfolio techniques discussed in Chapter 8 (➤Chapter 8) provide a valuable tool for analysing the firm's portfolio. Another form of analysis, focusing on economic profit, is provided by the

Chapter 8

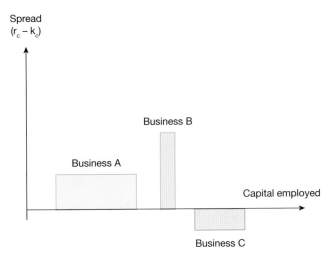

Figure 12.9 Economic profit of business units

value map which indicates which businesses are contributing to value creation (Black *et al.*, 1998).

As shown in Figure 12.9, the value map plots the business units in the portfolio on two dimensions. The horizontal axis is the level of capital employed in the business (in dollars), giving an indication of the size of the business. The vertical axis is the spread generated by the business – its return on capital less its weighted average cost of capital. Consequently, the area for each business measures the total economic value it generates, which can be negative or positive. Negative economic profit is not necessarily bad; if the business has an objective of rapid revenue growth, we might expect negative economic profit since it will be investing in R&D, market development, staff development, physical capital and so on in anticipation of future returns. The value map provides an interesting and insightful way to plot the portfolio of businesses in terms of the value created and the capital employed.

Such a chart helps corporate managers address several important questions: Should we continue to invest in high-value businesses, or are these now in saturated markets and not likely to return the cost of capital for any new investment? What about the businesses that are currently generating negative economic profit – what is their future, and when can they be expected to shift to positive?

The corporate centre might also construct an extensive set of performance measures for the firm's business units, comparing their growth, percentage of total corporate sales, revenues, assets, economic or net profit, and so on. Similar analyses could also be constructed by geography or for established and new products. Table 12.6 illustrates such a performance table.

Aggregate corporate measures

As in the previous section, one class of measures could deal with the aggregation on a weighted basis of business unit measures. VW, for example, could combine measures of

Table 12.6 Illustrative corporate overview of business unit performance

Measure	Business 1	Business 2	Business 3	Business 4
% sales revenue				
% assets				
ROCE (%)				
ROS (%)				
Sales growth (%)				
% accounting profit				
% economic profit				

defects per vehicle across its many nameplates to develop a measure for its vehicle-producing businesses as a whole. Corporate productivity numbers could be calculated by dividing the total number of vehicles produced by total VW employment. A similar but instructive measure would be sales per employee, while the ratio of these two ratios, benchmarked against the market, would tell corporate managers whether or not the corporation as a whole is trading up or down in the market. Similarly, the centre could weight and combine employee satisfaction measures from business units or conduct central surveys of morale.

Chapter 8

Other important measures, however, relate strictly to the corporation as a whole. We have already indicated that decisions on the degree and nature of diversification are critical corporate decisions. It is therefore important that senior management track and manage the level of diversification of their firms (►Chapter 8). Yet it turns out that there are few good measures of a corporation's extent of diversification. At first sight, it might seem that the simplest measure would be the number of different types of businesses that comprise the portfolio, so that we could use a measure such as the number of six-digit NACE codes, the industrial standard classification system used in Europe. However, this approach neglects any commonality across these different classifications, despite the fact that we know that the relatedness of a corporation's constituent businesses is important to its performance. One of the advantages of a diversified firm is its ability to share strategic resources and capabilities among its different businesses, so any measure neglecting this construct is bound to be defective. Unfortunately, few measures of relatedness have been developed and managers have routinely applied even fewer to monitor their firms' portfolios, although one possible such measure, based on the industries in which the firm competes, has been developed (Robins & Wiersema, 2003).

Part of the difficulty with the measurement of relatedness is that the construct itself is poorly defined. Perhaps it should be viewed as multidimensional. Certainly, rather than defining it by relatedness among industries in which the firm competes, we could also construe relatedness with respect to the resources and capabilities of the various business units, the geographies in which they operate and so on. It may be that it is the ability to transfer these capabilities, or geographic knowledge, between business units that is important (Markides & Williamson, 1994). Regardless, relatedness should be a factor in determining the benefits that may potentially be derived from the common ownership of a group of business units, the topic of our next section.

Synergy

In Chapter 9 we suggested that there are several different types of synergy that may be present in a firm and that may result in higher revenue or lower costs for the firm (►Chapter 9). These were:

Chapter 9

- Cost savings from two businesses sharing common facilities.
- Revenue enhancement from the ability to cross-sell across two businesses.
- The transfer of best practices from one business to another.
- Tax benefits gained by moving tax liabilities between businesses.

All these are difficult to measure and evaluate, and the benefits in any case are likely to be firm-specific. It is, of course, the sharing of resources and capabilities that is the underlying rationale for the diversified firm. The answer to the question of what value a corporate centre adds to its portfolio of business units is always synergy. Yet, despite the importance of the concept, there is no real theory of synergy, nor any specific measures of it. Thus, while we have some attempts to measure relatedness, as discussed above, there is no generally agreed-upon method for measuring synergy between any pair of businesses or across all business units in the corporate portfolio.

Intangible assets

Most managers today are aware of the importance of intangible assets, and would like to be able to monitor these as easily as they monitor tangible assets. Yet while there have been major advances in information technology, this is still fraught with difficulty (Zadrozny, 2006). Part of the reason for this is the very nature of an intangible asset – for example, can the firm develop valid and reliable measures of such constructs as employee motivation or cross-functional teamwork? Another difficulty is applying systems thinking to the development of the relevant value drivers. To illustrate: how important is reputation in acquiring new customers relative to other possible drivers such as possessing a skilled technical workforce (Jhunjhunwala, 2009)? Despite these problems, many leading firms such as Accenture are attempting to develop systems to both measure and assess the importance of intangible assets in value creation (Burgman *et al.*, 2005).

Capabilities

Innovation, growth and change will all require new capabilities (►Chapter 5). There are several means open to the firm by which capabilities can be enhanced, such as buying in from outside, investing in training and development, and using temporary outside staff such as consultants. Corporate management should be asking what means should be adopted and what measures are in place to ensure that the required capabilities are being developed in a

Chapter 5

timely and cost-effective manner. The stock of capabilities is the structural capital that constitutes a key part of the firm's intangible asset base, yet protection and management of capabilities is impossible without measurement. Senior managers also need to be questioning whether their current business model is still aligned with the market and whether their mental model of the firm needs to be revised and changed.

Employee indices

Employees are critically important stakeholders, and their views and attitudes are vital to the firm's future success. The human capital represented by employees needs to be continually enhanced, since it is a critical component of the firm's intangible assets. Thus, internal analysis also requires measurement on a number of 'soft' dimensions. Many large companies began conducting employee morale surveys back in the 1960s and 1970s, signifying early recognition of the importance of knowledge workers' morale to their corporate success. Today such surveys are almost universal in large and medium-sized enterprises. For example, entering 'Employee Surveys' into Google produces over a million hits, with numerous consulting firms offering to conduct such surveys for interested companies.

Strategic management of the firm's human resources is ever more important, but that goes far beyond conducting surveys. The skills of employees, their levels of education and experience, their career development and job rotation, their leadership skills and motivation are all variables that we should consider monitoring. In addition, useful information can be gained by conducting interviews with those who elect to leave the firm and determining their reasons for doing so,

Innovation and change management

Chapter 10

Innovation and change management are, as we have pointed out, crucial for the long-term success of the enterprise (►Chapter 10). In Figure 12.7 we have already suggested one possible framework for assessing the success of innovations within the firm. Nonetheless, innovation is more than just new products or even new businesses. It includes new business models, new organizational forms, new leadership styles and new capabilities. Some of these are relatively simple to assess. For example, most firms conduct R&D, and hence measures of expenditures on R&D are available as well as R&D output measures such as number of patents. But does the firm measure expenditures on innovation in other areas? For example, how much does the firm spend on understanding the changing needs of customers? What expenditures are undertaken to understand changing industry structure and relationships? What processes are in place to ensure that new business models are being generated? For many firms, information technology is becoming an important basis for competitive advantage. So another possible measure would be expenditures on IT systems.

Finally, the firm should be assessing how it performs at change management. Again, this may be a basis for competitive advantage. We may find that several firms in the same industry have come up with essentially the same strategy. Success, then, will go to the firm that is better at managing the change.

Financial measures and stakeholders

The final area for assessment covers such financial stakeholders as shareholders and capital markets. Most of the measures applicable to business units can be used at the corporate level, but in addition we can also track such corporate measures as market capitalization.

Corporate-level financial measures are much better developed than the non-financial measures we have just discussed. However, since there is a huge range of such measures, we will cover just some of the more important ones here.

Economic profit

Because a firm is primarily an economic entity, financial measures are critical. However, the perspective of a senior manager on overall performance should not differ from that of an owner of the business. Indeed, if those managers are directors, they are legally obliged to take such a point of view, as they should be acting as agents of the owners. This is the underlying rationale for our continuous emphasis on the concept of economic profit: the firm that generates economic profit is meeting the interests of its owners. As we will see later in the section, senior managers will need additional information and analysis to fulfil their managerial roles, but measurement of economic profit is the most appropriate starting point for any discussion of financial measures.

As noted in Chapter 4, a widely adopted measure of economic profit is Stern Stewart's concept of economic value added (EVA®) (➤Chapter 4). A recent survey of 384 European companies in 22 countries by PricewaterhouseCoopers found that 30 per cent of the companies in their sample were using EVA-type measures, although PWC felt this proportion was too low to properly reflect the interests of key stakeholders (PricewaterhouseCoopers, 2009). The 'in practice' example shows EVA for the German company Henkel.

Chapter 4

Other financial measures

At the corporate level, a number of ratios are utilized to assess how well the firm is performing financially. Return on capital employed (ROCE) measures how well the firm is using the capital under its control and is defined as net income/capital employed. ROE measures the return the equity holders are receiving and is defined as net income/shareholders' equity, where values for shareholders' equity, total assets and capital employed come from the firm's balance sheet. Many companies also track the corporate operating margin (operating profit/revenue) and asset turnover (S/A) as financial productivity measures, as detailed in Carton and Hofer (Carton & Hofer, 2006).

Figure 12.10 shows the return on equity and the operating margin for SAP. As can be seen, SAP has shown declining performance over the last five years, with substantial declines in both their operating margin and return on equity. These results highlight the increased competition faced by the firm, and the impact of the financial crisis of 2008.

A number of these ratios could be displayed in a convenient summary form, as shown in Table 12.8. These might well be attractively displayed showing trends in colour, in what

Financial performance measures *in practice* – Henkel

Table 12.7 Economic profit of Henkel businesses – 2009

Business Sector	EBIT (€M)	Capital employed (€M)	WACC (%)	Economic profit (€M)	ROCE (%)
Laundry and Home Care	501	2,562	10.5	232	19.6
Cosmetics/Toiletries	387	2,125	10.5	164	18.2
Adhesive Technologies	336	7,035	12.5	–543	4.8
Henkel Group*	1126	11,541	11.5	–201	9.8

*Includes the performance of the corporate centre.

Henkel is a major German chemical company, with about 50,000 employees headquartered in Düsseldorf. Some financial measures of performance, for the total firm and for its three major business groups, are shown in Table 12.7.

The firm has three global business sectors: Laundry and Home Care, Cosmetics/Toiletries and Adhesive Technologies. Henkel uses economic value added to assess past performance and appraise future plans. In their calculations, operational business performance is measured on the basis of EBIT, and capital employed is taken from the asset side of the balance sheet. The cost of capital reflects their cost of both debt and equity, with the cost of equity being business-sector specific.

Note that the cost of capital for Adhesive Technologies business is higher than for the other two business groups – reflecting the higher risk with this business. We also note that while the Adhesives Business achieved a positive return on capital employed of 4.8 per cent, it had a negative economic profit of – €543 million. This business, while generating an accounting profit, did not return an economic profit when the cost of the capital employed in the business is included. When this loss was examined in more detail, the economic loss arose from a substantial decrease in operating profit from the prior year due to the economic crisis of 2008/09. The other two business sectors were less affected by the economic crisis and generated higher economic profits in 2009 than they had generated in 2008.

some have labelled a corporate 'dashboard'. In the next major section of this chapter we will show an example of the dashboard used by one company, which incorporates both non-financial and financial measures.

As Table 12.8 indicates, at the corporate level a measure of liquidity is generally essential, measured by the D/E ratio. This measure reflects the financial structure of the firm, whether it is financed by debt or equity, and is also a measure of financial risk, since high leverage

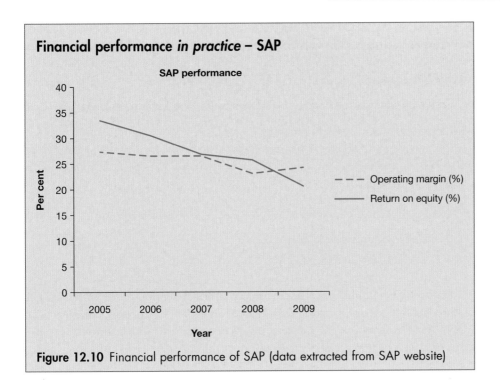

Figure 12.10 Financial performance of SAP (data extracted from SAP website)

Table 12.8 Selected financial measures

Measure	2012	2013	2014	2015
Economic profit				
Market value added				
Net income				
Return on equity				
Earnings per share				
Total revenue				
Annual sales growth				
Liquidity				
Share price				

means high financial risk. Fluctuating demand with high leverage will jeopardize the firm's ability to meet its periodic interest payments. Other liquidity measures are the amount of cash on hand and the current ratio (current assets/current liabilities). Another important liquidity measure is the interest cover, measured by net income/interest expense, which indicates the firm's ability to service its debt. Financially strong firms may have a ratio of 4 or more, and deterioration in this measure often leads to significant refinancing by the firm.

Several of the measures in Table 12.8 are essentially measures of the operating performance of the firm. These are particularly important because they create a link between strategy decisions and financial performance. Consider, for example, return on equity, which can be expressed as:

Return on equity = sales margin* asset turnover* (1 + financial leverage)

where asset turnover = 1.0/capital intensity.

This simple model becomes a very useful diagnostic tool, since it can be used to identify the sources of variability in ROE and how it can be improved. To improve ROE the firm can do one or all of the following:

- Improve its net margins
- Improve its asset utilization
- Increase its financial leverage.

Improving net margin means improving average realized prices or reducing costs. It is not always easy to improve margins, but we can see why firms are interested in cost reductions. A firm's ability to increase prices is influenced by its market power, which in turn is determined by its competitive advantages and the intensity of competition in the industries in which it competes. Margins usually decline over the life cycle of products, starting high and then declining as inflation-adjusted prices go down as a result of increased competition.

Changing competition *in practice* – Air New Zealand

The profitability of Europe's so-called 'legacy' airlines – those established when the industry was regulated and operated with cartel-like rules – has declined drastically as the overall market for air travel grew and consumer demand shifted air travel as a luxury towards air travel as a commodity. Newer entrants such as Ryanair, EasyJet and Flybe operate with much more efficient business models and different labour arrangements. Carriers such as Sabena and Swissair declared bankruptcy, while others were forced to exit from many routes, as well as merging with rivals. Similar events have occurred around the world. On 22 March 2010 Air New Zealand announced it was abandoning business class on flights between Australia and New Zealand, arguing that 'New Zealand companies were increasingly looking at the Tasman as a domestic market that did not warrant business fares'. The author argued that the airline planned to 'beat Australian low-cost carriers at their own game' (Creedy, 2010).

Forecasts of future margins should generally be for them to decline, as was demonstrated with SAP. A changing product mix over time could also result in lower average margins as the firm markets a higher proportion of low-margin products. This emphasizes again the critical importance of innovation to value creation over the longer term.

Increasing asset turnover means reducing fixed or working capital, with the same level of net income. It is often easier to reduce working capital than fixed capital. Fixed capital is generally a characteristic of the industry we are in and is not easy to alter without a major technological breakthrough. In contrast, reducing working capital means reducing inventories or receivables (or allowing payables to expand). Such considerations drive companies' interest in better supply-chain management, as mentioned earlier, as this has the potential to dramatically reduce working capital, thus improving asset turnover. Another way to think of this, and sometimes better, is in terms of investment intensity (I/S) – how many dollars of investment are needed to support a dollar of sales. If a firm is asset intensive, as is true for aircraft manufacture or aluminium refining, it will need high margins to offset this factor in achieving a good return on shareholders' equity.

Another option is to increase leverage by replacing equity with debt or funding new opportunities with increased levels of debt (▶Chapter 8). These are financial decisions that increase the financial risk of the firm. Some firms are already exposed to significant business risk. Business risk is derived from high fixed-cost intensity, which, if associated with variations in sales volume, can have devastating effects on net income when that volume falls. As we noted earlier, firms with high business risk due to their operating leverage would be well advised to keep lower levels of debt!

Chapter 8

In summary, senior management should carefully monitor the components that contribute to shareholder return on equity. They must be cognizant of the relationship between the firm's business decisions and their financial consequences, and avoid the compartmentalization that is so often the result of a functional view of the firm.

Some companies have put considerable effort into developing a set of indicators that can quickly give senior managers an overview on how their firm is performing (Alexander, 2007). We believe these simple systems, or 'corporate dashboards' as they are sometimes called, provide an important tool for better management of the enterprise. However, they must be carefully constructed to incorporate the principles we discussed earlier. Senior managers, desirous of pleasing external stakeholders, are often very selective in the information they present. This can cause undesirable and unnecessary fluctuations in share prices, as expectations are raised and then dashed – scarcely serving shareholders! Such behaviour can destroy the company when it becomes self-delusionary. Thus indicators should be carefully chosen, be linked to strategy, incorporate multiple measures, permit causal analysis, be meaningfully benchmarked, and encourage forward-looking behaviour and decisions. In short, we must bear in mind all the cautions discussed in Section 12.2 of this chapter. Having said this, we will present one company example, even though it may not necessarily comply exactly with all the admonitions we have presented.

Challenge of strategic management

 A dashboard for an anonymous health services company is shown in Figure 12.11.

The indicators in the figure compare the company's results for the current year with its plan. An upward-pointing arrow means that the firm has exceeded the planned value (desirable), a horizontal arrow means the company just about matched the plan, and a downward-pointing arrow means that the planned result was not attained.

The columns of Figure 12.11 bear some resemblance to the categories of corporate measurement we have been discussing. Column one deals mainly with financial results of interest to senior management and external stakeholders. Column two contains information that could be roughly grouped into an 'operating' category, while column three deals with two measures of performance of financial markets. The final column contains a number of non-financial indicators of the type we have been discussing.

The overall pattern of Figure 12.11 suggests cause for concern. The company has achieved good operating results and has apparently pleased the stock market. However, it appears that these financial results have come about primarily through raising prices, while relative quality has deteriorated. In general, the company has done a poor job of meeting its non-financial targets. Senior management should definitely be concerned that the firm may well have achieved good short-term results at the expense of its future. The combination of deteriorating relative quality, lower market share and flat sales is likely to show up as poor future performance.

■ Do you agree with this analysis?

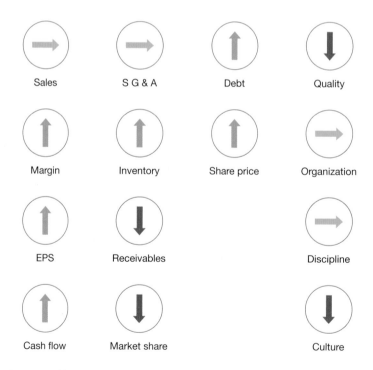

Figure 12.11 Health services company corporate dashboard

Corporate social responsibility

As we have noted in Chapter 2, many companies are now reporting on a wide variety of corporate social responsibility measures, most of which are non-financial in nature. (▶Chapter 2)

The John Lewis Partnership (JLP) in the UK provides an excellent example of how to go about this.

Chapter 2

LEARNING OBJECTIVE 5

Summarize why many firms have adopted the principles of corporate social responsibility.

Corporate social responsibility *in practice* – John Lewis Partnership

JLP has two main businesses, the Waitrose supermarket chain and the John Lewis Department Stores. Each business provides detailed and extensive reports on their CSR performance. Five areas are delineated, as shown in Figure 12.12.

JLP has a summary set of values under each category in Figure 12.12. We summarize these below:

Our customers, products and suppliers
- We are committed to dealing fairly with our suppliers, selling responsibly sourced quality products and deepening our relationships with loyal customers.

Our people
- We aim to provide worthwhile, satisfying employment in a successful business to people of ability and integrity, treat them with respect and courtesy, and recognize and reward their contributions.

Our communities
- We make a positive difference to the communities where we do business. And it's not just local people that benefit: our Partners also gain new skills and confidence from participating in charitable and community activities.

Our environment
- We are committed to reducing our impact on the environment and promoting good environmental practice. We have programmes, processes and targets in place to ensure we continue to deliver our environmental commitments.

Our stakeholder engagement
- To help us deliver our commitments, we continue to develop strategic partnerships and alliances with other organizations, and respond to the concerns of all our stakeholders.

The partnership's report then continues to detail how the firm acts to translate these values into action. One subsection describes the company's engagement with NGOs, campaign groups and consumer associations, and we have included these steps in Table 12.9.

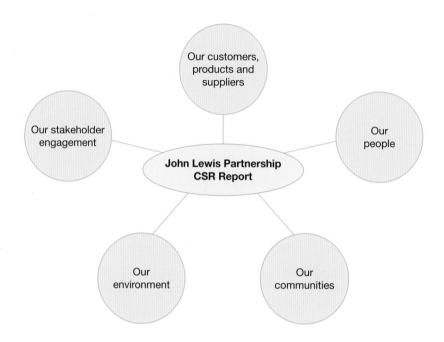

Figure 12.12 John Lewis Partnership CSR categories (John Lewis Partnership, 2009)

Table 12.9 John Lewis Partnership's engagement with NGOs, campaign groups and consumer associations

Why we engage	How we engage	Outcomes
• We recognize the benefits and importance of pro-actively engaging with NGOs to understand their views on a broad range of issues	• Meetings • Collaboration on joint projects • Surveys and research	• We have ongoing partnerships with a wide range of organizations such as the Marine Conservation Society, Farming and Wildlife Advisory Group, Wildcare, LEAF and the Prince's Rainforests Project
• We continue to work pro-actively with non-governmental organizations and consumer associations by entering into constructive engagement on campaign issues that we believe should be supported or that are relevant to our business	• Information request about our performance	• We have responded to a number of NGO surveys and benchmarks covering issues such as refrigeration, beef sourcing and palm oil

The report then continues to match the partnership's performance against commitments in each of the areas described Figure 12.12. Selected examples include Waitrose's target of nurturing and developing smaller suppliers and strengthening relationships within the community. As of 2009, 465 producers supplied 2,150 local and regional lines and 155 shops had dedicated regional display areas. A further Waitrose goal was to remove all artificial colours from own-brand products by the end of April 2009. The target was met and no products now contain artificial colours. Finally, John Lewis continue to ensure that 95 per cent of large domestic appliances are A-rated or above. As of 2009, they have exceeded the target, achieving a 100 per cent level.

Other firms are also active in reporting social responsibility, and some have even sensed a business opportunity. IBM, for example, have developed a consulting service offering which analyses operations to improve overall efficiency and lower costs, with a particular focus on water and energy use. IBM claim that their own conservation efforts have saved 4.6 billion KWH of electricity and $310 million in costs (Cadmus, 2009). Another US firm has developed a business in developing dashboards, comprising a web-based graphical display of a number of sales and financial KPIs, such as revenue, margins and so on in an easy-to-read format (Chiang, 2010).

 ## 12.6 SUMMARY

In this chapter we reviewed the importance of understanding that measurement should be embedded in a sophisticated understanding of the strategic management process, which is itself very dynamic. Too many companies take a static perspective on measurement, failing to link the process either to changes in the firm's environment or to its evolving strategy.

We then examined the considerations that enter into the design of a system. We examined the process as well as some of the pitfalls that can render the whole effort counter-productive. Among other factors, we emphasized the importance of multiple leading indicators, understanding cause–effect relationships, and the fact that performance measurement should subsume non-financial as well as financial measures.

We looked separately at the issues of measuring business unit and corporate performance, reflecting the fact that larger companies today operate in multiple businesses. This has been a recurring theme in the book, and we illustrated the different types of measures that pertain solely to the corporate level.

As we noted, measurement of performance has generally – and particularly at the corporate level – not kept up with changes in business. Thus not only are we lacking in good measures that might help senior executives make better diversification decisions (for so many have gone disastrously wrong!), but the measurement and management of the intangible assets that now constitute the majority of a company's value have lagged considerably. Fortunately, there are signs that the business community is waking up to these defects, and we hope and trust that we will see the much-needed development and changes in the practice of performance management.

VIEW FROM THE TOP

DOW CHEMICAL

An interview with Mr Bill Banholzer, Dow Chemical Chief Technology Officer and Executive Vice President by *Around Dow*, the company newsletter (Dow, 2008).

Around Dow: There is a lot of talk about innovation at Dow, but how do you measure success?

Banholzer: The historical measurements for success in R&D have usually been R&D spending, or sales from new products introduced in the last five years divided by total sales and the number of new patents. But I think those metrics are no longer sufficient to judge success. It's not R&D spending that matters, its R&D effectiveness. One measure of effectiveness is new product sales divided by your R&D expenditure. If that ratio is over 7 you are among the top companies in the world.

I look at new products' profit margins to measure R&D. If we are to put R&D resources against a new product, we had better deliver something that expands the company's profit margin. On patents, the traditional measure of the success of R&D was the number of patents filed. But having a lot of patents does not necessarily protect the high margins you worked so hard to create. I look at the percentage of our sales that are patent-advantaged. You had better come up with the next new proprietary products that create value customers will pay for, and then protect them with patents.

Around Dow: How far do you go in your search for new ideas globally?

Banholzer: No one country has a monopoly on creativity and intelligence, so we have to make sure we tap the intelligence of the whole world. There's always a debate over whether being in a small or large company is better. I think there are some fundamental advantages in being big; you can make more bets, share more knowledge, and you can go all over the world to find the best people and the best ideas. We have R&D centres in the US, Europe and Latin America, and we're building R&D centres in China and India. Asia is the fastest-growing market, and they don't do everything the same way we do in the US. You can't hire brilliant people in China or India and then make them feel like they are subcontractors to the US. If your people in India and China feel as if all the challenging projects are being worked on in the US or Europe, you're not going to be able to retain the best talent. Again great people want to be around other great people, working on tough problems that matter. That is what Dow offers all over the world.

You need smart people in the country who can develop products locally. At the end of the day, R&D has to continually expand product value. A good organization solves customers' problems. A great organization solves problems that customers didn't even know they had. Most R&D people are 'closet' marketing people. Good R&D leaders need to understand not only how to aggregate demand, but also how to figure out what people will pay for. For example, people often say they want green products, but they won't pay for them (for example, compact fluorescents save money, but most people won't buy them).

Around Dow: What are the most common misunderstandings about R&D?

Banholzer: One common misunderstanding is that all R&D comes from the customer. We also need to have some 'backroom skunkworks' that create new capabilities. We need to have a balance of customer-back and technology forward – you have to anticipate future needs. The question is, 'What does Dow do differently because of my actions?' If you can't apply the knowledge you create to make the world better and make the company financially stronger, it's impotent. It has little impact.

INTERFACE INC

Interface was founded in 1973 by Ray C. Anderson and despite some early challenges was able to grow via both organic growth and more than 50 acquisitions. Through these acquisitions the company extended its business scope to include carpet tiles, woven broadloom products, carpet installation and related office furnishing products.

By 2002, carpet tiles accounted for 40 per cent of turnover, with the balance comprising broadloom (15 per cent) and fabrics, services and installation, comprising 45 per cent. In that year, Interface revised its strategy, focusing on the organic growth of the carpet tile market. Implementing this focus strategy has seen the firm divest its other interests, so that by 2009 modular carpets represented about 92 per cent of revenue with broadloom accounting for 8 per cent.

Interface also expanded geographically and by 2009 was the largest manufacturer of modular carpets, with operations in the US, the UK, Holland, Ireland, Thailand, China and Australia. It operated in a range of end-use markets, such as non-office commercial markets as well as consumer markets, in both established and emerging economies. The biggest market for the firm was the US commercial carpet market, comprising both carpet tile and broadloom carpets. In 2009 the total US commercial market was $2.3 billion, growing to $3.3 billion by 2020. The carpet tile share was growing continuously. From a share of zero in 1970, carpet tiles had grown to about 40 per cent, worth approximately $1,000 million, in 2009. Carpet tile penetration was expected to increase to 65 per cent by 2020, due to its enhanced functionality and design.

Carpet tile penetration of the commercial carpet market in other countries has followed the US trend, as shown in Figure 12.13, although there are substantial geographic variations. In the UK and Ireland

MINI-CASE

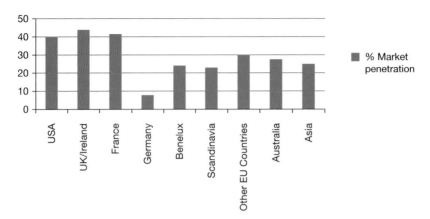

Figure 12.13 Carpet tile penetration of selected geographic regions (2009)

modular tiles have a 44 per cent share of the commercial market, while Germany has just 8 per cent. Reflecting its global presence, Interface has a significant market share in the carpet tile market in various countries: with shares of 35 per cent in the US, 32 per cent in Europe and the Middle East, and 45 per cent in Australia and New Zealand. Its major competitors are also global, and include Asahi Kasei Corporation (Japan), BASF (Germany) and Dow Chemical (US).

Carpet tiles are used in many end-use applications. Interface segments the overall market, as shown in Figure 12.14. Currently, the majority of its sales are in the corporate offices and institutional segments, together representing about 92 per cent of revenue. By contrast, the consumer market (entered in 2003) represents only 2 per cent of revenue.

In 2009, the Interface strategy was summarized as:

- Maintain dominant share in the office market in the US and gain share in the European office market.
- Diversify into new end-use markets such as transportation.
- Invest in growing emerging markets such as China, India, Latin America and Eastern Europe.
- Continue to expand consumer market share.

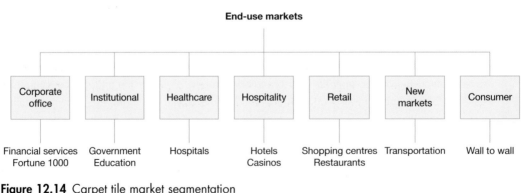

Figure 12.14 Carpet tile market segmentation

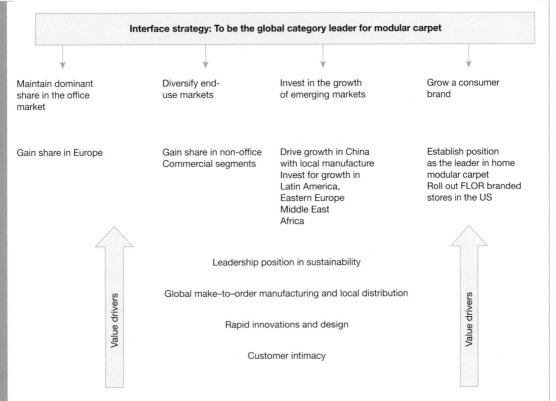

Figure 12.15 Interface current strategy

In 2009 the mature office market accounted for 50 per cent of total revenue of about $800 million, non-office commercial segment 42 per cent, emerging markets 6 per cent, and consumer 2 per cent. The target portfolio is for the mature office market to be 30 per cent, the non-office commercial segment 35 per cent, emerging markets 25 per cent, and residential 10 per cent of total revenue.

Since 1996 Interface has made sustainability a key feature of its strategy. In that year Anderson shifted the company's strategy, aiming to redirect its industrial practices to include a focus on sustainability without sacrificing its business goals.

The current vision of Interface is:

To be the first company that, by its deeds, shows the entire industrial world what sustainability is in all its dimensions: people, process, product, place and profits – by 2020 – and in doing so we will become restorative through the power of influence.

And its mission is:

Interface will become the first name in commercial and institutional interiors worldwide through its commitment to people, process, product, place and profits. We will strive to create an organization wherein all people are accorded unconditional respect and dignity; one that allows each person to continuously learn and develop. We will focus on product (which includes service) through constant emphasis on process quality and engineering, which we will combine with careful attention to our customers' needs so as to always deliver superior value to our customers, thereby maximizing all stakeholders' satisfaction. We will honour the places where we do business by endeavouring to become the first name in industrial ecology, a corporation that cherishes nature and restores the environment. Interface will lead by example and validate by results, including profits, leaving the world a better place than when we began, and we will be restorative through the power of our influence in the world.

The vision and mission are underpinned by a set of values that include service, innovation, leadership, commitment, stewardship, integrity, communication, individuality, and personal growth. The close coupling of vision, mission and values has created a virtuous circle which is one factor in driving Interface forward.

It is uncommon for a firm to place sustainability at the heart of its business, but Interface claims sustainability has reduced operating costs and improved competitiveness. Anderson asserts:

Costs are down, not up, dispelling the myth and exposing a false choice between the economy and the environment, products are the best they have ever been, because sustainability has provided an unexpected wellspring of innovation, people are galvanized around a shared higher purpose, the good will in the marketplace generated by our focus on sustainability far exceeds that which any amount of advertising or marketplace expenditure could have generated.

Interface has developed objectives that reflect the commitment to sustainability. Illustrative are objectives to reduce waste, eliminate toxic emissions, operate using renewable energy and to create a culture that uses sustainability to improve the lives of its stakeholders.

Since its modest beginning, Interface has grown into a large corporation, with some 4,000 employees (called associates) and has been named by *Fortune* as one of the 'Most Admired Companies in America' and one of the '100 Best Companies to Work For'. It has diversified and globalized its businesses, with

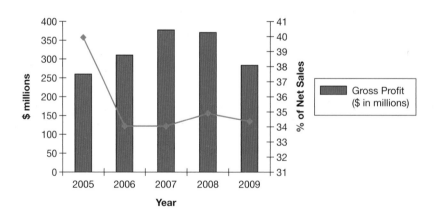

Figure 12.16 Interface gross profit and margins

sales in 110 countries, manufacturing facilities on four continents and is now the world's leading producer of soft-surfaced modular floor coverings. Figure 12.16 shows Interface gross profit and margins for 2005 to 2009.

Interface's board of directors realize that successful implementation of strategy requires a set of short-term and long-term performance measures. A well-designed performance measurement system gives the board opportunity to monitor progress, ask appropriate questions, and detect signs of difficulty early so that problems are addressed before they become serious obstacles to the successful implementation of strategy.

Source: www.interfaceglobal.com

QUESTION

You have been asked by the board to prepare a paper outlining the design of an appropriate performance measurements system to aid the implementation of Interface's strategy.

REVIEW QUESTIONS

1 Explain why measurement of financial performance alone is insufficient for the purposes of good management stewardship.

2 Demonstrate how you would convince sceptical senior managers that their firm needed better measurement and management of its intangible assets. Be sure to make an economically justified argument for your point of view.

3 Choose a company with which you are familiar. Using published sources, analyse its performance management practices and recommend improvements.

4 Contrast the measurement of business unit and corporate performance.

5 Most companies measure themselves by comparing performance against the previous year. Explain why this may lead to problems, and illustrate your argument with examples from real companies wherever possible.

6 Select a firm that has suffered financial difficulties in the past three to five years. Using published sources, develop a set of variables, and measures of those variables, that could be leading indicators of the poor performance.

REFERENCES

Alexander, J. (2007) *Performance Dashboards and Analysis for Value Creation.* Hoboken, NJ: Wiley.

Black, A., Wright, P. & Backman, J. E. (1998) *In Search of Shareholder Value: Managing the Drivers of Performance.* London: Pearson Education.

Bose, S. & Thomas, K. (2007) Applying the balanced scorecard for better performance of intellectual capital. *Journal of Intellectual Capital, 8*(4), 653–665.

Buckley, C. & Blakely, R. (2008) Jaguar and Land Rover to be sold to makers of world's cheapest car. *The Times,* 26 March, p. 4.

Burgman, R. J., Ross, G., Ballow, J. J. & Thomas, R. J. (2005) No longer 'out of sight, out of mind': Intellectual capital approach in AssetEconomis LLP and Accenture Inc. *Journal of Intellectual Capital, 5*(4), 588–615.

Cadmus, J. (2009) A measured approach to going green: IBM 'Green sigma (TM)'. 14 January. www.dashboardinsight.com/dashboards/product-demos/a-measured-approach-to-going-green.aspx.

Camp, R. C. (1989) *Benchmarking: The Search for Industry Best Practices that Lead to Superior Performance.* Milwaukee, WI: Quality Press.

Carona, C. (2009) Dynamic performance measurement with intangible assets. *Review of Accounting Studies, 14*(2/3), 314–348.

Carton, R. B. & Hofer, C. W. (2006) *Measuring Organizational Performance.* Cheltenham: Edward Elgar.

Chatterjee, S. & Krolicki, K. (2008) Tata to buy Ford's Jaguar, Land Rover for $2.3 billion. 26 March. www.reuters.com/article/idUSBOM5889720080327.

Chenhall, R. H. & Langfield-Smith, K. (2007) Multiple perspectives of performance measures. *European Management Journal, 25*(4), 266–282.

Chiang, A. (2010) Dundas dashboard v 2.0. *Executive dashboard,* 12 April. www.dashboard insight.com/dashboards/live-dashboards/dundas-dashboard-v-2-0-demo.aspx.

Cohen, J. R., Holder-Webb, L., Nath, L. & Wood, D. (2009) Corporate reporting of non-financial leading indicators of economic performance and sustainability. *Social Science Research Network, Working Paper Series,* 16 June. http://papers.ssrn.com/sol3/papers.cfm?abstract_id=1420977

Collins, J. C. & Porras, J. I. (1994) *Built to Last.* New York: HarperBusiness.

Copeland, T. E. (1994) Why value value? *McKinsey Quarterly,* (4), 97–110.

Copeland, T. E. & Keenan, P. T. (1998) How much is flexibility worth? *McKinsey Quarterly,* (2), 38–49.

Corona, C. (2009) Dynamic performance measurement with intangible assets. *Review of Accounting Studies, 14,* 314–348.

Creedy, S. (2010) Air NZ moves to flexible fares. *The Australian,* 22 March, p. 25.

Dobbs, R., Leslie, K. & Mendonca, L. T. (2005) Building the healthy corporation. *McKinsey Quarterly,* (3), 63–71.

Dow (2008) Talks with Dow CTO and executive VP Bill Banholzer. *Around Dow,* May. http://news.dow.com/dow_news/arounddow/pdfs/162–02413.pdf.

Frean, A. (2010) US set to fine Toyota $16m for hiding defect. *The Times,* 6 April, p. 39.

Ghosh, S. & Mondal, A. (2009) Indian software and pharmaceutical sector IC and financial performance. *Journal of Intellectual Capital, 10*(3), 369–388.

Graham, J. R., Harvey, C. R. & Rajgopal, S. (2005) The economic implications of corporate financial reporting. *Journal of Accounting and Economics, 40*(1–3), 3–73.

Hammer, M. (2007) The 7 deadly sins of performance measurement and how to avoid them. *MIT Sloan Management Review, 48*(3), 19–28.

Holloway, J., Lewis, J. & Mallory, G. (eds) (1995) *Performance Measurement and Evaluation.* London: Sage.

Interbrand (2010,) Our Work. www.interbrand.com/disciplines.aspx?langid=1000.

Jay, A. (2003) Nissan Sunderland retains top spot for productivity. *The Daily Telegraph*, 9 July, p. 27.

Jhunjhunwala, S. (2009) Monitoring and measuring intangibles using value maps: Some examples. *Journal of Intellectual Capital, 10*(2), 211–223.

John Lewis Partnership (2009) CSR Report. *Our Approach*. www.johnlewispartnership.co.uk/Display.aspx?&MasterId=81f00253–1639–4749-a590-d2cd32540b62&NavigationId=613.

Kaplan, R. S. & Norton, D. P. (1996) *The Balanced Scorecard*. Boston, MA: Harvard Business School Press.

Keller, K. L. (2002) *Strategic Brand Management*, 2nd edn. Upper Saddle River, NJ: Prentice Hall.

Kuczmarski, T. D. (1988) *Managing New Products: Competing through Excellence*. Englewood Cliffs, NJ: Prentice Hall.

Lea, R. (2010) Toyota is to recall 8 million cars over danger from faulty accelerator. *The Times,* 29 January, p. 15.

Lewis, L. (2010a,) Toyota executive urged management to 'come clean'. *The Times,* 9 April, p. 42.

Lewis, L. (2010b) The Toyota way is famous. In reality it is to ignore warnings from within the firm. *The Times,* 12 March, p. 55.

Lonnqvist, A. (2002) Measurement of intangible assets – An analysis of key concepts. *Frontiers of e-business research.* www.ebrc.info/kuvat/275–294.pdf.

Markides, C. C., & Williamson, P. J. (1994) Related diversification, core competencies and corporate performance. *Strategic Management Journal, 15*(Summer), 149–166.

Neely, A. (ed.) (2002) *Business Performance Measurement*. Cambridge: Cambridge University Press.

Neely, A., Bourne, M., Mills, J., Platts, K. & Richards, H. (2002) *Getting the Measure of Your Business*. Cambridge: Cambridge University Press.

Parmenter, D. (2007) *Key Performance Indicators*. Hoboken, NJ: Wiley.

PricewaterhouseCoopers (2009) Management Survey. *European Corporate Performance*, June. http://mgmtblog.files.wordpress.com/2009/06/european-cpm-survey_english-master.pdf.

Robins, J. A. & Wiersema, M. F. (2003) The measurement of corporate portfolio strategy: Analysis of the content validity of related diversification indexes. *Strategic Management Journal, 24*(1), 39–60.

Sacerdote, G. S. (2002) How good are your leading indicators. *On Strategy.* www.sacerdote-co.com/papers/how_good_are_your_leading_indicators.pdf.

Salojarvi, S., Furu, P. & Sveiby, K.-E. (2005) Knowledge management and growth in Finnish SMEs. *Journal of Knowledge Management, 9*(2), 103–122.

Simon, B. (2010) Boost for Toyota on safety concerns. *Financial Times*, 15 July, p. 21.

The Economist (2008) Now what? What the Indian conglomerate will do with two luxury-car brands. *The Economist*, 27 May.

The Economist (2009) Losing its shine. *The Economist*, 12 December, pp. 67–69.

The Economist (2010a,) The machine that ran too hot. *The Economist*, 27 February, p. 66.

The Economist (2010b) No quick fix. *The Economist*, 6 February, p. 63.

Verbeeten, F. H. M. & Boons, A. N. A. M. (2009) Strategic priorities, performance measures and performance: An empirical analysis in Dutch firms. *European Management Journal, 27*(2), 113–128.

Viguerie, P., Smit, S. & Baghai, M. (2008) *The Granularity of Growth*. Hoboken, NJ: John Wiley & Sons.

Zadrozny, W. (2006) Leveraging the power of intangible assets. *MIT Sloan Management Review, 48*(1), 85–91.

For a range of further resources supporting this chapter, please visit the companion website for *Strategic Management* at www.routledge.com/cw/fitzroy.

CHAPTER 13

CORPORATE GOVERNANCE AND SOCIAL RESPONSIBILITY

LEARNING OBJECTIVES

Upon completing this chapter you should be able to:

1   Explain the importance of corporate governance.

2   Appraise the roles of shareholders, managers and boards in governance.

3   Assess the role of the board in strategy development.

4   Describe why board processes and structure are important for effective board operations.

5   Indicate how corporate governance practices vary in different countries.

6   Recommend that firms need to consider social responsibility in strategy development.

SIEMENS

One of Germany's biggest-ever corporate bribery scandals moved close to a settlement in December 2009 after six former senior managers of the Siemens electrical engineering giant agreed to pay nearly €20m (£18m) to compensate for their role in a huge 'kickbacks-for-contracts' scam.

Widespread corruption was initially exposed at Siemens in 2006 when investigations in more than a dozen countries revealed that the company was operating a system of cash handouts totalling an estimated €1.3 billion in return for contracts. In 2008 the company agreed to pay more than $1.6 billion to settle the US and German investigations.

The December 2009 announcement was that 68-year-old Heinrich von Pierer, Siemens' chairman from 1992 until 2005 and one of the main protagonists in the bribery scandal, had agreed to pay €5m to compensate for his conduct. His decision followed the expiry of a deadline for ex-managers to declare whether they were willing to settle or face legal action. Five other former Siemens managers who were also involved agreed to pay out the remaining sum. These were five former board members and the former chairman of the supervisory board.

Siemens claims that the scandal incurred some €2.5 billion in costs. For decades it paid illicit kickbacks and bribes for contracts in such diverse projects as the United Nations oil for food programme, mobile phone networks in Bangladesh, Russian traffic control systems and Israeli power stations. The firm was also shown to have bribed the Iraqi government for contracts. US investigators said Siemens used off-book accounts to conceal the payments.

Two of the individuals involved, Mr Von Pierer and his successor Klaus Kleinfeld, who ran the company's US division, resigned within the space of a week in 2007 when the extent of their role in the scandal was made public. Mr Kleinfeld is currently Chief Executive of Alcoa, America's largest aluminium producer. Both men are being investigated for administrative offences by the Munich state prosecutor, but both have denied wrongdoing. Mr Von Pierer has pledged to defend himself against allegations (Paterson, 2009).

However, Siemens said it had been unable to reach a settlement with two other former board company members, who were also involved. Both are currently being investigated by Munich state prosecutors while Siemens is deciding whether or not to also take legal action against them. The lawyer for one was reported as saying that both individuals had an interest in reaching agreement soon.

German financial markets reacted positively to the resolution of the case by Siemens. There had been a fear of litigation dragging on for years, which would have hurt Siemens. German analysts have described the Siemens bribery scandal as a benchmark case which will put pressure on other companies to pursue former executives in cases of wrongdoing. The new CEO, who took over after the scandal, has been reported as replacing half of the firm's top 100 executives (*The Economist*, 2008).

The Siemens example demonstrates the importance of good corporate governance for protecting and enhancing the interests of the company and its stakeholders.

There were clearly serious governance shortcomings at Siemens but we feel sure that such behaviour will not be tolerated by their new board.

STRATEGIC MANAGEMENT IN PRACTICE

CHAPTER OVERVIEW

Board of directors

The group elected by shareholders whose fiduciary duty is to run the firm in the long-term interests of shareholders. This is accomplished through their formal monitoring and control of senior executives' decisions.

In this chapter our attention is focused on the **board of directors**, the interaction of the board with senior management and the role of the board in strategy development and execution.

If senior management is solely responsible for strategy development, what then is the role of the board? To examine this topic, we first review alternative legal forms of companies in different jurisdictions around the world, and how these influence governance arrangements. For example, how strong are the country's takeover restrictions? We then introduce a model of corporate governance, stressing that governance is concerned with the relationship between three groups of corporate actors – shareholders, directors and managers. We then develop this model in some detail; examining the role of directors and the board, as well as addressing some specific questions such as should the CEO also be the chairman of the board? We then examine processes adopted by the board, focusing in particular on the interactive role that the board and management have in strategy development and execution. This is followed by a brief discussion of governance arrangements in several countries of the world and the growing importance of corporate social responsibility for boards. Following this is a View from the Top by the Chairman of Cable and Wireless on the possible conflicting views between the chairman and shareholders on a management incentive scheme. Following this is an opportunity to evaluate the performance and role of the board of Prudential plc.

LEARNING OBJECTIVE 1

Explain the importance of corporate governance.

Corporate governance

The relationship between shareholders, management and the board in determining the direction and performance of the corporation.

13.1 INTRODUCTION

What is corporate governance?

Unfortunately the Siemens example is not an isolated example of poor **corporate governance**. Over the last decade there have been a number of corporate scandals, and while there are several US examples, such as Enron and WorldCom, governance scandals occur globally. In January 2009 the founder and chairman of Satyam, a leading Indian software firm which had been listed on the Bombay and New York stock exchanges, admitted to a fraud of $1.47 billion. This is despite the fact that the Asian Corporate Governance Association had rated India third out of 11 Asian countries in terms of the quality of corporate governance (*The Economist*, 2009). In Germany, Deutsche Bank was accused of spying on employees and board members, while in Switzerland UBS was accused of allowing some US customers to use their accounts for purposes of tax evasion. As these examples illustrate, investors must be concerned over how well firms are being managed, what oversight there is of management and their decisions, and whether they are delivering value to shareholders.

Some examples of recent corporate frauds perpetrated by senior management include:

- Misleading accounts
- Money being siphoned from employee pension funds
- Unjustified executive pay levels
- Collapse of firms with little or no prior warning of difficulties
- Bribery
- Infringement of employee rights
- Concealing of defects.

As a consequence of such actions, corporations and their boards are under intense scrutiny from many sources, including governments, regulators, individual investors, pension funds, unions and employees who share a desire to eliminate such problems. Institutional investors in particular are powerful forces for change. Pension funds around the world have invested trillions of Euros in public companies and want to ensure a return for their members. Adding to the general concern are the huge compensation packages (particularly options) paid to senior managers, packages which are all too often unrelated to performance (▶Chapter 8). Heidrick & Struggles, a global leadership and governance consulting firm, has suggested that the performance of private equity groups has also increased concern with corporate governance (Heidrick & Struggles, 2009).

Chapter 8

Corporate governance describes the relationship among shareholders, management and the board in determining the direction and performance of the corporation (Monks & Minow, 2008). It represents the processes through which ultimate corporate authority and responsibility are shared and exercised by shareholders, **directors** and management to ensure that the firm delivers value to its stakeholders, particularly shareholders. Corporate governance is also concerned with issues such as legal compliance, ethics and risk management, as the following example of Nokia illustrates.

Director
Elected by shareholders to direct the firm. Directors are required to act in good faith, to advance the firm's interests and to exercise prudent care.

Boards of directors also need to take a broad perspective, and be aware of the needs of a wide group of stakeholders, such as suppliers, customers, employees, financial institutions and the community at large. The requirement to take a wider perspective means that the board may take a different view from management on certain decisions – for example, on restructuring or downsizing (Capron & Guillén, 2009).

The essence of corporate governance is ensuring that the professional managers who actually manage the firm use assets efficiently in the pursuit of the firm's objectives. This requires that the firm develop procedures that assure the providers of capital to the firm that it will achieve an adequate return on their investments. The governance mechanisms adopted must resolve the agency problem where managers act in their own self-interest. We could go further and suggest that the role of the board is to ensure that corporate management strives for and achieves above-average performance, taking due account of risk (Hilmer, 1998).

An ideal system of corporate governance would allow managers the freedom to manage coupled with accurate knowledge of shareholders to ensure that their expectations are known

---

Corporate governance *in practice* – Nokia

Nokia Corporation, the parent company of the Nokia Group, is registered in Finland and consequently must comply with Finnish law; it must also comply with the rules and regulations of all stock exchanges on which it is listed. In particular, since the firm is listed on the New York exchange it must comply with the Sarbanes-Oxley act in the US. The board represents and is accountable to all shareholders and accepts that board responsibilities are active not passive. The board regularly evaluates the strategic direction of the company, as well as overseeing the organizational structure, the composition of the company's top management and risk management procedures. As expected, the board is responsible for appointing and discharging the CEO, the CFO and other members of the group executive board. Directors have the basic responsibility to act in good faith and with due care, to exercise their business judgement on an informed basis in what they reasonably and honestly believe to be in the best interests of the company and its shareholders. In discharging that obligation, the directors must inform themselves of all relevant information reasonably available to them (Nokia, 2009).

---

and satisfied. At the same time, shareholders would have sufficient information to know whether or not their expectations were being met together with sufficient market liquidity so that they could easily sell their shares. Satisfying both of these requires a boardroom culture that facilitates open discussion, where directors are able to exercise objective judgement and hold managers accountable for the performance of the firm, particularly with respect to the efficient use of the assets of the firm. US research suggests that a strong and independent board is important to prevent self-serving actions by CEOs (Combs *et al.*, 2007).

Global issues in corporate governance

Each country has its own distinct type of corporate governance reflecting its history as well as its legal, regulatory and tax regimes. But all over the world, there are concerns with inadequate governance arrangements.

Switzerland has had problems with Swissair and UBS; Sweden problems with ABB; Korea problems with Daewoo; Japan with Mitsubishi; Germany problems with Deutsche Bahn, Siemens and others; France problems with Vivendi; Italy problems with Parmalat; and, of course, the United States has had problems with Madoff and Enron.

As a result of these scandals, most countries are re-examining the way in which companies are managed. Germany appointed a committee under the chairmanship of Gerhard Cromme, the head of ThyssenKrupp; France had the Verniot Report, while the United Kingdom had several reports (Hampel, 1998). The issue has had international ramifications. The US Congress passed the Sarbanes-Oxley Act, attempting to improve the governance of American corporations, legislation referred to in *The Higgs Report* (Higgs, 2003). In 2004, the EU established the European Corporate Governance Forum to enhance the convergence of national codes of corporate governance and provide strategy advice to the Commission on policy issues in the field of corporate governance, which focused on developing and sharing best practices (International-Finance-Corporation, 2008). In 2005 the European Commission established the Advisory Group on Corporate Governance and Corporate Law, with the goal of providing detailed technical advice on preparing corporate governance and company law measures. In 2008 the mandate of the forum was renewed, and it was asked to evaluate 'the effectiveness of monitoring and enforcement systems that the Member States have put in place with a view to the national corporate governance codes' (European Commission, 2008).

There is no doubt at all that it has been flaws in the way in which companies are managed that have produced increased government attention to corporate governance and the role of boards of directors. At the same time, globalization – with the adoption of free market systems and the removal of trade barriers, together with technological advances in communication and transportation – has led to higher levels of competitive intensity in both product and financial markets. As a consequence, investors, both institutional and individual, have recognized that the quality of corporate governance affects the firm's competitive performance and hence its ability to attract investment capital (EgonZender, 2000). There is a growing recognition in all countries that the expectations of shareholders have to be met when the firm relies on the financial markets for debt and equity. At the same time, boards of directors need to give consideration to the needs of other stakeholders, such as customers, employees, suppliers, creditors and the community.

This chapter discusses the role of the board and how it should exercise its role. It will also explore how this role varies according to the country in which the firm is located. We concentrate on corporate governance issues in medium to large publicly listed companies which generally operate globally.

13.2 THE MODERN CORPORATION

In all countries, firms are legal entities and as such can enter into contracts, as well as sue and be sued by other legal entities, including individuals. In most countries, the modern publicly listed company has unlimited life and can have an unlimited number of shareholders. These shareholders can be individuals or other organizations, although in some countries there are restrictions on who can be a shareholder. For example, in the United States, banks are restricted from being shareholders of industrial firms, but this requirement generally does not hold in Europe.

The shareholders, who provide the equity capital for the firm, own the company. The liability of these shareholders is generally limited to the initial equity capital. Should a publicly listed company go bankrupt, with substantial debts, shareholders cannot be sued personally for these debts. In return for their limited liability, shareholders of publicly listed companies give up the right to control the firm's assets to others – managers. Nonetheless, they should be able to expect that managers will act in the interests of the shareholders, not in the interests of the managers. Other legal organizational forms have different legal requirements. For example, a traditional partnership normally has a limited number of partners. In addition, the partnership ceases on the death of a partner and partners are jointly liable for the debts of the partnership.

A distinguishing characteristic of publicly listed companies is the separation of ownership and control (Berle & Means, 1968). The shareholders own the company but have little or no control over the day-to-day running of the firm – or even the ability to obtain current information on the performance of the company. All managerial decisions are the responsibility of the professional managers, who are also accountable for regularly reporting on their performance via an annual report. Shareholders have the right to transfer their interests by selling their shares, but nevertheless, the firm's managers need to be held accountable for the long-run firm performance, where this performance may include both financial and non-financial measures. This is the role of the board, which should be independent, competent and motivated to represent the interests of the owners.

Given the large number of shareholders of a modern firm, plus the fact that institutions will hold a significant proportion of shares, there may not be a strong sense of ownership among shareholders. In most countries, the legal system imposes a fiduciary duty on the board to ensure that the firm is run in the long-term interests of shareholders. Since managers are given the power to make decisions and take reasonable risks, the challenge is how to grant them this power while holding them accountable for the use of that power.

Global institutional arrangements

The legal system underlying the nature of firms and the style of corporate governance vary across countries, although there is some degree of overlap. While the legal system in each country reflects the culture, history and development of that country, there does appear to be considerable convergence in the requirements for sound corporate governance processes.

United States/United Kingdom/Canada/Australia

The US/UK versions of governance put an emphasis on shareholder liquidity. If shareholders are unhappy with the performance of the firm, they can sell their shares on the stock market, and this is simple to do. Such a system requires full disclosure of financial data from firms, so that shareholders can make informed decisions, and insider trading is illegal. If a firm does badly, a hostile takeover may ensue. In the United Kingdom, there are two common legal forms for a company: plc and Pty Ltd. A plc (public limited corporation), such as Burberry Group plc, can have an unlimited number of shareholders, while a Pty Ltd company has a limited number.

In the United States and the United Kingdom, the threat of takeover (the market for corporate control) is assumed to be a major check on managers and helps ensure that they satisfy shareholder expectations. In other countries, such as Germany, takeovers are relatively rare. There are also significant differences between countries in terms of the composition of shareholders; for example, in the United States and the United Kingdom, banks are restricted in their ability to hold equity, although this is not the case in Japan or Germany.

In the United States, insider-trading laws discourage large investors from taking large holdings. Indeed, both the New York Stock Exchange and the NASDAQ are considering changes to their listing rules that would make large investors (those owning more than 20 per cent of stock) unable to be considered 'independent', with implications for board committee membership (Plitch, 2002).

The Sarbanes-Oxley Act is also expected to have a considerable long-term impact. For example, the act specifies that boards include a financial expert who must have knowledge in a number of areas, such as Generally Accepted Accounting Principles or preparing public company financial statements, among others, acquired either through education or work experience. As a result, many firms have had to change the membership of their audit committee.

Continental Europe

In Europe there are three general legal forms for large companies. Since October 2004, it has been possible to establish a Societas Europaea (SE), similar to a plc, the main difference being that it is recognized throughout the EU, can transfer its registered office between member states, and can engage in cross-border mergers and acquisitions (Davis, 2005).

The second type is the SA (Societe Anonyme), the term used in France and elsewhere, or the AG (Aktiengesellschaft), the term used in Germany, that are similar to the UK plc corporate form. These are public companies with limited liability for shareholders, able to have an unlimited number of shares that are freely negotiable. Such firms in Germany must meet several legal requirements, such as conducting an annual meeting of shareholders, and adopting a two-board structure.

The third type is SARL, in France, or GmbH, in Germany, which are similar to the UK Pty Ltd. These firms also have limited liability although there may be restrictions on how freely their shares may be traded. In Germany BMW has the legal form of a GmbH, and such large GmbH firms are also required to have a dual-board structure, with one having a significant proportion of employee representatives.

German financial markets are generally considered to be less open than those in the UK or the US – reflected in the ease of merging, the ability to raise finance and the ease of trading shares in the US and the UK. This contrasts with German product markets, which are generally open and competitive. Several explanations are normally given for this lack of openness including the role of banks and the ownership structure of many major European firms. In the UK and the US, banks are restricted in their ability to hold equity, but this does not hold in Germany, where banks can provide both debt and equity to a firm. Consequently, the German system is often classified as an insider or bank-based system, arising from the close contacts between firms and banks, which may include bank officers being on the board of a non-financial firm. However, the importance of this close relationship can be overstated. Recent research indicates that in 2007 German banks held 9.7 per cent of the shares of German companies, suggesting that their importance may have been overstated (FESE, 2008). However, these banks can exert a much larger degree of control than this modest shareholding would suggest. German banks generally vote the bearer shares that they hold on behalf of small shareholders who are clients of the bank's brokerage services. They may

---

Dual board *in practice* – SAP

SAP, the German business software firm, provides an example of dual boards as followed by major German companies. Under this structure, the management of the firm is separated from the supervisory function, with one board for each function, the Executive Board and the Supervisory Board, with the Supervisory Board advising and supervising the Executive Board. In SAP, the Supervisory Board has eight members elected by shareholders at the annual meeting and eight members elected by employees. This board has eight subcommittees, several of which are quite standard, such as the audit committee which is responsible for the financial statements prepared and published by SAP. As required by German law, there is also a mediation subcommittee. This subcommittee is responsible for handling the situation if a two-thirds majority is not reached when the Supervisory Board appoints or dismisses a member of the Executive Board.

The Executive Board has six members, appointed by the Supervisory Board, and comprises the senior management team of SAP, including the CEO, the chief financial officer and the chief technology officer. These executives have backgrounds in a number of different industries and are drawn from several national groups, such as Indian and Danish, as well as German (SAP, 2010). Note that the CEO is not a member of the Supervisory Board.

---

also operate a mutual fund and have the right to vote shares held by that fund. Firms with substantial bank shareholders seem not to perform better than other firms, indicating that banks, although they are able to use debt and equity as potential monitoring mechanisms, are not effective monitors of corporate management (Baert & Vennet, 2010). Bank ownership also appears to have a negative impact on non-bank shareholders, which is a possible explanation for why the phenomenon is declining (Dittmann *et al.*, 2008).

Another distinguishing feature of Germany, and continental Europe in general, is the existence of what is called pyramid control – an ownership structure in which a controlling shareholder exercises control of one company through ownership of at least one other listed company (Enriques & Volpin, 2007). LVMH, one of the largest companies listed on the Paris Bourse, has a controlling shareholder, who is also the CEO and board chairman. He is able to control LVMH through a complex structure of listed and unlisted companies. As a consequence, he controls 47 per cent of the voting rights in LVMH but only 34 per cent of the cash flow. In a study of the top 110 public companies in Germany, France, Italy and Spain it was found that the dominant ownership form for these firms was for them to be owned by other firms; they were not widely owned by a large number of shareholders (Grant & Kirchamier, 2004). Such interlocking firms are uncommon in either the UK or the US.

Chapter 4   As was discussed in Chapter 4 (➤Chapter 4), in several European countries (for example, Belgium) firms are given the right to offer bearer shares. With these, the holder does not need to register a name with the company; therefore the actual beneficial owner can remain anonymous, and such shares do not have to be sold on the financial markets – they can be transferred privately. In Europe generally, many bearer shares are held by the banks, which can then vote them. This adds to the power of the banks, since many shareholders do not tell their bank how to vote the shares they have on deposit. So while banks in Europe do own shares in their own right, most of their power comes from these shares on deposit. For this reason, large German firms have a bank representative on the supervisory board, generally from one of the four large banks – Deutsche, Dresdner, Westdeutsche Landesbank and Commerzbank banks.

In many European countries there has been a history of state-owned companies, and there are still a number with varying degrees of autonomy from the state. At one extreme are the so-called government business enterprises or state-owned enterprises, still common in France. Air France and Credit Lyonnais, for example, have some degree of state control (Barca & Becht, 2001). Many European governments held so-called 'golden shares', typically aimed at preventing what were viewed as undesirable takeovers. For example, in the United Kingdom, the government held 'golden shares' in firms such as BAA, Rolls Royce, National Power and BAE Systems. In a series of court cases featuring the European Commission against virtually all European governments, most of these arrangements were ruled illegal by the EU's highest court. In Greece, the government owned Olympic Airlines for many years, suffering heavy losses and a lawsuit from the EU. The government finally disposed of the airline in 2009, just as Greece was entering its severe sovereign debt crisis.

Despite the EU, there are still significant differences in the corporate governance mechanisms across countries, arising from the different legal, regulatory and ownership frameworks. European firms generally provide less information to shareholders (unless they are listed on non-European exchanges) and hostile takeovers are less common. Other differences relate to the extent of shares owned by households. In 1995, private households in Germany owned only 14.6 per cent of common stock of firms, compared with 47.9 per cent in the United States. By contrast, in the United States other companies owned only 1.1 per cent of company shares, compared with 58.0 per cent in France (Prigge, 1998). These differences remain according to more recent research, with the US, UK and Sweden scoring significantly higher rates of household common stock ownership than France, Germany and Italy (Guiso *et al.*, 2003).

Asia

Corporate governance in Asia depends largely on the country concerned and, again, reflects its economic, social and political development. In Southeast Asia, Chinese family business structures dominate, controlled by the family, with limited public shares. In these firms decisions are not delegated to non-family members, although long-term personal relationships are a central tenet of Asian business.

Korea and Japan have a different system, with Chaebol in Korea and Keiretsu in Japan – these being groupings of large financial and industrial complexes such as Hyundai or Mitsubishi. Due to the existence of these groupings, Japanese firms rely on banks for a large proportion of their financing needs, although Japanese banks are limited to owning no more than 5 per cent of the equity in any one firm. The effect of concentrated ownership on the performance of Japanese firms has been mixed over time, but more recently the negative effects of bank ownership have become more apparent (Miyajima *et al.*, 2009). There is also less shareholder liquidity in this type of market. In several countries, such as China, there are a substantial number of state-owned enterprises, and governance of these is deeply embedded in the country's political system.

Some very recent but fascinating research suggests that the ownership of banks themselves is perhaps more important in affecting economic performance than is a bank's ownership of shares in firms. In general, however, more open systems of capital allocation favour superior economic performance of an economy (Morck *et al.*, 2009).

As a result of the swathe of corporate failures and the GFC, there is considerable interest around the world in strengthening corporate governance procedures. In the United States and the United Kingdom it has been directed at ensuring that the board is independent of management so that it can provide adequate guidance. In Germany and Japan, the pressure is to strengthen capital markets so that they can provide a discipline on management to improve its performance.

LEARNING OBJECTIVE 2

Appraise the roles of shareholders, managers and boards in governance.

Chapter 2

13.3 THE GOVERNANCE MODEL

Corporate governance is concerned with the relationship among shareholders, the board of directors and management, as shown in Figure 13.1.

However, other institutions and issues must also be considered. When one is reviewing firm performance, the roles and values of stakeholders other than shareholders should also be understood (➤Chapter 2). Determining the nature of these other stakeholders and their importance relative to shareholders is one of the tasks of the board. Furthermore, both boards and management need to develop relationships with financial markets to assist in the raising of new funds as well as to manage the firm's share price. We now discuss the three groups in Figure 13.1 in more detail.

Figure 13.1 Corporate governance model

13.4 SHAREHOLDERS AND BOARDS

As discussed in Chapter 4 (▶Chapter 4), shareholders of many global firms can be split into individual and institutional shareholders. The relative importance of these two groups varies by country, with the level of individual shareholders generally being low in Germany and Japan. In the United States and the United Kingdom, there has been a significant increase in the proportion of shares held by institutions, with implications for governance, since historically they have been passive investors. Despite this, any given institutional investor will generally have only a small holding in a firm, say less than 5 per cent. By contrast, in Germany, a single institutional investor may hold up to 25 per cent of the shares of the firm. Cross-shareholding – reciprocal share ownership by companies – is also very common in Europe, which has the effect of reducing liquidity in the market for shares.

Chapter 4

In all countries, shareholders are entitled to attend the annual general meeting, at which time the accounts are approved and the board elected. In Denmark, Belgium, the Netherlands and Spain, among other countries, most shares are bearer shares, so notice of annual meetings must be published in both an official gazette and local and national newspapers. Holders of bearer shares have to deposit their shares with the company three to five days before the meeting in order to be able to attend. By contrast, in the United Kingdom, all shares are registered, and therefore the company has an address to which to mail announcements and agendas (Wenger & Kaserer, 1998).

Board members are usually elected at such an annual general meeting. The current board nominates members, and thus small shareholders often find it difficult to generate a major board shake-up. As noted, institutional shareholders have often been passive. If the firm is doing poorly, they simply sell their shares and find other investment opportunities. Furthermore, if these institutional investors are involved in detailed discussions with management on the future of the firm, any special knowledge could expose them to a risk of being accused of insider trading – taking advantage of information not available to other shareholders. In the United States the Securities and Exchange Commission (SEC) has ruled that firms cannot reveal more information to institutional investors than they make available to private investors. In 2009 the SEC launched a major insider trading investigation of hedge fund Galleon Management (Fulton, 2009), snaring a number of senior executives with indictments in the process (Goldstein & Stempel, 2009).

The board must also be aware of the mix of shareholders and their expectations. Different shareholders may want different things. Small shareholders (unless they are day traders) may be more patient, institutional investors more interested in the short term. The board may also be concerned with shareholder stability. If shares are held by a small number of shareholders, then the board may consider the share register to be unstable and the company could be a takeover target.

Research suggests that investors positively value corporate governance in both developed and emerging economies. Investors like companies that are well governed, have a majority of outside directors, and undertake formal evaluation of directors. Some research suggests that board members believe their performance should be evaluated, but the extent to which this occurs varies considerably (Stybel & Peabody, 2005). In Switzerland, for example, the proportion of companies evaluating board performance rose from 30 to 65 per cent from 2007 to 2009, but only one in three of these are conducted by an independent non-executive director (Heidrick & Struggles, 2009).

Investors believe that directors should be shareholders and that their pay should be in the form of stock options. In a survey of institutional investors – such as money managers, mutual funds and insurance companies – in several countries, it was found that investors were prepared to pay a premium of 18 per cent for stock in a well-governed UK or US company but that they were prepared to pay a premium of 27 per cent for stock in a well-governed company in Indonesia (Coombes & Watson, 2000). Despite this, some emerging market firms appear to be unwilling to adopt such governance practices as a higher proportion of independent directors and the use of board committees such as an audit committee (Barton & Wong, 2006).

13.5 MANAGEMENT AND BOARDS

The agency problem arises when the objectives of managers differ from those of shareholders, in which case the agents (managers) may make decisions that are in their own interests rather than those of the principals (shareholders). In the modern corporation there is a separation of ownership (shareholders) from control (managers) (Berle & Means, 1968). Due to this separation, managers may want to maximize firm size while shareholders want profits or earnings. Shareholders often want to reduce risk, which they can accomplish by investing in a number of firms. Managers may also say that they want to reduce risk, and this can become the rationale behind diversification. They often neglect the fact that shareholders can diversify more easily and cheaply than firms. Another manifestation of the agency problem is how free cash flow is handled. Jensen suggested that there would be conflict between managers and owners when there is a free cash flow – cash flow in excess of that required by all investments that have positive net present values when discounted at the relevant cost of capital. Managers often use this flow to fund acquisitions, which ultimately perform poorly, rather than returning it to shareholders (Jensen, 1990).

Shareholders are interested in financial returns, either short or long term. Managers may be interested in other things, such as the size, growth and prestige of the company. Other areas of conflict between managers and owners would be the level and structure of executive salaries, the balance between dividends and the retention of profits, and the priority given to growth or profit.

In the United Kingdom and United States, boards are elected to represent the interests of shareholders, and managers report to the board. It is often thought that managers enjoy a measure of discretion to pursue their own objectives without the need to seriously consider the interests of shareholders. The concern is that managers exercise power without responsibility and that boards are self-perpetuating oligarchies. Successful firms may become arrogant and insular, and a powerful CEO can take this to extremes. At one time, the same person held the following jobs at Sears Roebuck, the large US retailer (Monks & Minow, 2004):

- CEO
- Chairman of the board
- CEO of the largest operating division
- CEO of the worst-performing operating division
- Chairman of the nominating committee
- Trustee of the 25 per cent of firm stock held on behalf of employees.

If there is wide distribution of shares, any individual shareholder has little power to force a change in management. It is then vital that the board monitor senior management and ensure that the CEO works under its authority.

The agency literature suggests that outside directors provide important monitoring functions in an attempt to resolve, or at least mitigate, conflicts between management and shareholders. Management equity ownership may help to resolve this, but hostile takeovers may also provide a check on managers to deliver value. Indeed, the very existence of these phenomena is testimony to lack of accountability to shareholders.

The capital market was traditionally the market through which firms raised new capital, and that role still exists. But it is also a market where shares and other financial instruments are traded and in which control of a company can be acquired. This market is generally denoted as the market for corporate control, and this has been very active, although it seems to go in cycles. Shares can be seen as 'trading chips', rather than as ownership claims.

This market for corporate control implies that firms are subject to some discipline from the capital markets when they perform poorly. Poor performance will generally be reflected in low share prices. Other management teams may then decide to mount a takeover bid, suggesting that they are better able to manage the assets of the firm. Such a market includes leveraged buyouts as well as takeovers and may be facilitated by the ready availability of debt. In the United Kingdom, about 25 per cent of takeovers are hostile, initially rejected by the target management. Hostile takeovers have been less common in continental Europe and Japan, as a consequence of the cross-industry pattern of shareholding and the role of the banks. Nonetheless, such pressures seem to be increasing, reflecting the increased activism of shareholders and their demand for performance. In general, the market for corporate control acts as a spur to better management and results in the transfer of assets from poorly performing firms to successful firms.

The general threat of a takeover may act as an incentive for management to perform better. A question then may be how the board reacts to any such takeover offer: does it respond in the interests of shareholders or not? The takeover of Cadbury by Kraft led to a major debate over this issue in the UK. Because of the well-known history of overpayment by acquirers, discussed in Chapter 9 (▶Chapter 9), arbitrageurs swiftly acquire shares of takeover targets in open markets such as the UK, US and Australia. Because these are short-term shareholders with short-term interests, some, including the ex-chairman of Cadbury, argue that their votes should not count when management seeks shareholder opinion and that only the votes of longer term shareholders should be considered (Wilson, 2010).

Chapter 9

This is a potent argument in the UK, which is arguably the most open takeover market in the world, where management lacks the 'poison pill' options available to defend against hostile takeover in the US, for example. Since the UK has witnessed so many foreign acquisitions of major companies in electricity, water, transport and food, this will likely remain a significant political issue for some time. As a result of the Kraft bid, Peter Mandelson (business secretary at the time) advocated various reforms to takeover laws, including (Cameron, 2010):

- raising the voting threshold required to approve a hostile bid
- denying short-term shareholders such as hedge funds the right to vote during a bid period
- giving bidders less time to formally commit to their offer ('put up or shut up') so as to reduce the length of time a takeover bid takes to complete
- requiring bidders to set out publicly how they intend to finance their bids over the long term and how they intend to make cost savings.

Takeovers may represent a considerable threat to incumbent managers, since they are not likely to survive the takeover. However, apart from the market for corporate control, there are other ways to minimize the gap between managers and shareholders – for example, tying the compensation of managers to shareholder return. Stock options for managers were supposed to align the interests of the two groups, but they have not always delivered as promised (Bruce *et al.*, 2007).

Management options are offers to buy shares at a future date at a price that is close or equal to the current price. Consequently, it is normally in the interests of managers to increase this share price, and thus the value of their options. By itself, this is not inimical to the interests of shareholders, who are interested in the same outcome, but managers may be encouraged to act fraudulently or not report news that could depress the share price. Further, when share prices drop, boards of directors have sometimes offered new options, with a new, lower exercise price, an action which may only rarely be interpreted as in the interests of shareholders.

LEARNING OBJECTIVE 3

Assess the role of the board in strategy development.

13.6 THE ROLE OF DIRECTORS AND THE BOARD

The increasing complexity of the business environment, and of business itself, has resulted in changing roles of directors. There is more pressure for performance and for legal accountability. Outside directors differ from managers: they have no line responsibility and no staff. However, as directors they can request independent advice from external specialists, such as consultants or accountants, and the chairman cannot refuse reasonable requests for such advice. Executive directors should in theory be able to separate their role as executive from their role as director, but it is easy to see why they might find it difficult to do so.

Responsibilities of directors

In most countries the role of directors is at least party defined by the legal system and generally includes the requirement to encompass a duty of loyalty, which means that directors should act in good faith to advance the firm's interests and not use information for personal gain. Directors are also required to exercise the care of a prudent person in the same or similar circumstances and to obtain adequate information to assist in fulfilling their responsibilities (Allen, 1998). In summary, directors are required to do the following:

- be honest – to act with integrity and good faith
- exercise reasonable care, diligence and skill
- act in the interests of shareholders
- present accurate and fair reports on finances to shareholders.

In the United Kingdom and the United States, all directors bear equal responsibility for the performance of the company, even though it may be difficult for directors who are not executives in the firm to gain the knowledge and skill required to adequately monitor the firm's activities. Nonetheless, some degree of independence from management should be regarded as essential for outside directors. Outside directors should not have significant financial or personal ties to management or the firm. An outside director should not be a professional adviser or major supplier to the firm and should not have been employed as an executive by the firm in the recent past. However, in practice it is not uncommon for these principles to be overlooked and for boards to be less diverse than is desirable.

Directors are required to provide overall direction, rather than becoming involved in the day-to-day issues that are the responsibility of management. Directors' responsibility is to shareholders, meaning they should ensure that management is doing what it should be doing, since they have ultimate responsibility for the performance of the company. Directors cannot avoid this responsibility even if they want to. For example, given the turbulent environments we have discussed throughout this book, prudent directors should insist that management have a crisis management system in place, since shareholders' interests can be irrevocably harmed by ineptitude at such times. Such a system must not only be in place, but it must also be enforced and followed. BP, for example, had a knowledgeable board, with a safety, ethics and environmental assurance committee. After a series of major accidents, but prior to the Gulf oil spill, an independent report commissioned by BP found that the firm had not provided effective process safety leadership, and that the board was responsible for not ensuring that management followed effective safety practices (Colvin, 2010). Associated with legal requirements and sanctions, directors can be sued by shareholders if the shareholders believe the director(s) are not fulfilling their legal responsibilities. They may be held personally liable for their own actions and those of the board. Penalties vary by country and can be severe. Directors are also liable for the decisions of any board subcommittees, such as finance or compensation. So at the same time as expectations and standards for directors have risen, so have the risks for individuals taking these positions.

Composition of the board

An important characteristic of a board is the proportion of non-executive, or independent, directors. Executive directors are individuals who are currently employed by the firm in an executive capacity. For example, the CEO is an executive who is normally on the board, as are the chief financial officer and/or the chief technologist. Executive directors are expected to bring considerable expertise to the board; the question is their independence, particularly from the CEO.

Independent directors are outsiders who are supposed to be independent of management. We will not discuss in detail what it means for directors to be independent; suffice it to say here that it means that they should not have had a relationship with the firm.

There is still considerable discussion as to the true degree of independence of these directors, since they may be CEOs of other firms, and thus part of a network of CEOs. In addition, independent directors are dependent on management for information on the firm and its performance, and this information asymmetry may make it difficult for the board to perform its duties (Thomas *et al.*, 2009).

Independent directors are expected to bring diversity and experience to the board, to provide new perspectives on the business and an independent assessment of both firm and management performance. In the US it is not uncommon for many of these non-executive directors to be the current chairman and CEO of another firm. For example, the board of P&G consists of ten members, with the CEO being the chairman. Of the nine non-executive directors six are also chairman and CEO of other firms and therefore may not be truly independent. There has been a pan-Atlantic trend to increase the ratio of non-executive directors to executive directors over the past few years, although their degree of independence varies according to national legislation.

As mentioned earlier, qualified and truly independent external directors are not easy to find. For example, there may be a perceived conflict if a banker or lawyer is on the board. Many companies do not permit their senior managers to be on the boards of other companies, partly due to the increasing demands being placed on directors. To further align the interests of directors and shareholders, it has been suggested that directors must hold a minimum number of shares in the company (Hambrick & Jackson, 2000), but if the size of this recommended investment is large, this is likely to further restrict the pool of potential external directors.

Since independent directors are not employees under the authority of the CEO, they are expected to bring an objective external perspective and a degree of independence to board discussions. In addition, the board may establish several subcommittees, such as an audit committee (to review the detailed financial performance of the firm), and some of these are required to be made up of non-executive directors. On the other hand, being outsiders, non-executive directors cannot have the same command of detail as executives. So they have to ensure that the board focuses on company performance and any changes that may imperil this. They should focus on what standards have been set for the firm and whether they are being met; whether management recommendations should be accepted and, if not, what further advice or information is needed; and whether policies are in place and being followed, regarding, for example, ethics and compliance with the law.

Executive directors
Directors who are currently employed full time by the firm in an executive capacity.

Independent directors
Directors who have no relationship or dealings with the firm.

In the UK the Financial Reporting Council's UK Corporate Governance Code recommends that at least half of the board of larger firms should consist of independent directors (Financial Reporting Council, 2010). The code also recommends that one independent director be appointed as the senior independent director, and that that individual should meet with the other independent directors to appraise the performance of the chairman. The code then proceeds to list a number of conditions that help define independence. If a director does not fulfil these, it is incumbent on the board to reveal why they believe the individual still qualifies as independent. These conditions include:

- An employee in the last five years.
- Material business relationship with the firm, whether directly or indirectly via shareholdings, partner, directorship or employee of another firm.
- Receives additional remuneration from the firm, including share options and pension rights.
- Has family ties with advisers, directors or senior employees of the firm.
- Has cross-directorships or significant links with other directors via companies or other bodies.
- Represents a significant shareholder.
- Has served longer than nine years on the board.

The New York Stock Exchange (NYSE) has issued similar rules on independence. Neither the individual nor a family member can have worked for the firm for the last five years. The individual must also have had no material relationship with the firm – which can include commercial, banking, consulting, legal, accounting, familial or charitable relationship – for the last five years. The exchange is also suggesting that audit, nominating, governance and compensation committees should be entirely independent and that independent directors must meet regularly without any executives present (Williams, 2002).

An executive director is a director who is also a full-time executive of the company, an employee under some contract. A company executive who is also a company director appointed by shareholders is responsible under company law to act in the interests of shareholders. If a board has too many executive directors, this increases the separation between the board and the shareholders.

Chairman/CEO

It is our view, and the view of other researchers, that the roles of the chairman and the CEO are different. The role of the CEO is to run the company, the role of the chairman is to run the board, and these are not the same and should not be undertaken by the same individual (Monks & Minow, 2008).

The role of the chairman is to ensure that the board operates effectively, to see that all members contribute effectively to the direction of the company, and to provide an objective review of proposals presented to the board by the CEO and senior management. Such a review requires interaction and discussion among board members, which may not be as vigorous if the CEO is also the chairman.

The chairman should ensure that there is interaction and discussion at board meetings. Board meetings therefore should not involve long and detailed presentations from management with no discussion (Blake, 1999). Instead, the chairman must create a climate within the board that facilitates decision-making and that does not inhibit open discussion and debate. Some decisions by the board may go against management: if management always gets what it wants, the board may be acting purely as a 'rubber stamp'.

One major role for the board is to monitor and assess the CEO and possibly terminate their employment. It is difficult to see how the board can accomplish this when the chairman and CEO is the same individual. Thus shareholders, with their concern about the agency problem, often want these two positions to be held by different individuals. In contrast, management often wants the positions to be combined so that the firm gets strong, unambiguous leadership.

In the overwhelming majority of UK and European firms, different individuals handle these two roles. About 90 per cent of UK firms have different individuals handling the roles of chairman and CEO, and the Combined Code specifically recommends that the two roles are held by separate individuals. The UK Financial Reporting Council in its report on corporate governance goes further, as it recommends that the division of responsibilities between the chairman and the chief executive of the firm should be clearly established, set out in writing and agreed by the board. In contrast, the chairman and CEO is the same person in 80 per cent of US companies (Carlsson, 2001), although there is increasing pressure to change this practice (Conger *et al.*, 2001).

There are clearly advantages and disadvantages to both approaches. The UK approach (generally followed in most European countries, Australia, Canada and New Zealand) sometimes leads to unclear accountability, partly because the chairman usually plays a role in strategy formulation, and speaks for the company externally (Lorsch & Zelleke, 2005). In some situations there can be open conflict between chairman and CEO. In the contrasting US model, accountability is clear, but the role of outside directors is too often marginalized, and their contributions on behalf of shareholders less than desirable due to dominance of board deliberations by directors from management. These issues are a matter of ongoing discussion and debate, occasioned partly by Sarbanes-Oxley and the demonstrable under-performance of non-executive directors in many corporate scandals.

Capabilities of directors

Because they act as a team, directors need a complementary mix of skills. Some skills need to be possessed by all; some will be more specialized. However, all directors are personally liable for board decisions; therefore one director cannot claim personal ignorance of, say, derivatives as an excuse for poor firm performance.

All directors need capabilities in finance, strategy and global understanding, as well as such personal characteristics as intellect, integrity, courage, judgement, confidence and so on. The composition of the board should match the needs of the firm and be characterized

Challenge of strategic management

Historically Marks and Spencer (M&S), the UK retailer, operated with the same person, Sir Stuart Rose, as both CEO and chairman. This practice, almost universal in the USA, is very rare in British business. The situation unnerved both major shareholders and media commentators, to the point that the Deputy Chairman of M&S, Sir David Michels, made the following statement in the company's 2009 annual report:

> We have always said that our aim is to develop a strong management team and appoint a successor as Chief Executive internally if appropriate. That was the genesis of the decision the Board took in 2008, when it concluded that it would be in the best interests of the Company to retain Sir Stuart Rose until 2011.
>
> If internal succession is appropriate, we would expect to announce the appointment of a new Chief Executive during 2010. Stuart would then stay on for a suitable period to effect a smooth transition before we identify an independent Chairman and revert to recommended best practice.
>
> In the event that internal succession is not an option, we will instigate a search and appoint a new Chief Executive during 2010. In this case, Stuart would again stay on to ensure a seamless transition before being replaced by an independent Chairman.

(Michels, 2009)

At the 2009 Annual General Meeting, the one of its major shareholders, the Local Authority Pension Fund Forum (LAPFF) filed a resolution to split the roles of chairman and CEO and for the firm to appoint an independent chairman by 2010. Marks and Spencer commented that they remained of the view that combining these roles was the right choice at this time, and they had a succession plan, as detailed above. The firm recommended that shareholders vote against the LAPFF resolution. At the Annual Meeting, 38 per cent of shareholders voted for the resolution, a significant minority.

In November 2009 Marks and Spencer announced the appointment of a new CEO, a Dutchman who had previously been CEO of William Morrison, the UK supermarket chain where he had been responsible for a strong turnaround in performance (Rohwedder, 2009).

In August 2010, Marks and Spencer announced the appointment of a new non-executive director to join the board in October 2010 prior to taking the position of chairman in January 2011. At this time, the current chairman will step down and leave the firm (M&S press release). This new chairman has an extensive background in banking, and was the current chairman of the HMV Group, a specialist UK music, film and book retailer (Marks and Spencer, 2010).

QUESTIONS

1 Do you believe LAPFF was justified in their concern? Why or why not?
2 How would you ensure that a company derives the benefits of holding the CEO accountable for management decisions while simultaneously ensuring the advantages of an objective external chairman of the board to represent shareholder interests, at the same time avoiding the confusion and conflict that can occur if the chairman becomes too assertive?

by diversity as well as cohesion. Board members need the ability to work with colleagues – remember that they can only be removed by shareholders at an annual meeting!

Board members must have the will to act when conditions require action and to 'take on' management when this is required. Boards are sometimes constrained in this because directors meet infrequently and have no staff who could undertake independent analysis. Board members can request that independent advice be provided, and this must then be made available to the entire board.

Thus board members need a thorough knowledge of the competitive position of the company's goods and services as well as a thorough understanding of industry structure, supplier relations and customer needs. Board members must also be able to commit the time required to understand the issues facing the company. For this reason, some firms require that their board members limit the number of boards they join (*Board of Directors Global Study*, 2000).

Compensation of directors

The most common board compensation is cash, but there is a global trend towards rewarding directors with a mixture of cash and incentive compensation linked to firm performance. This may take the form of stock, sometimes with options that cannot be exercised for several years in order to encourage board members to take a long-term perspective (*The Economist*, 2001). Director compensation may include other benefits, such as travel expenses and cars. Directors are generally provided with retirement benefits in the form of a pension. These benefits are being debated at present, both with respect to the level and linkage to either individual or firm performance.

LEARNING OBJECTIVE 4

Describe why board processes and structure are important for effective board operations.

13.7 BOARD OPERATIONS

As the criticism and scrutiny of boards have increased, so has the workload of directors. A global study of corporate governance in 188 firms found that the typical board of 12 members met eight to ten times per year for an average of 4.2 hours. It is not uncommon for global companies to have at least one meeting per year outside their home country (*Board of Directors Global Study*, 2000). Board chairmen spend 45 days per year, directors 21 days per year on board matters. Membership on one or more board subcommittees can add considerably to the workload.

Board processes

A variety of research supports the idea that board processes are an important influence on how well the board performs its role (van Ees *et al.*, 2008).

The culture of a board meeting is often not conducive to raising serious objections to a firm's strategic direction. Here the chairman plays a critical role, since outside directors must have the capability and independence to monitor the firm's performance and

Challenge of strategic management – Goldman Sachs

In 2010 Goldman Sachs, in the past one of the world's most admired investment banks, became the subject of public opprobrium and senatorial inquisition. Lloyd Blankfein, Chairman and CEO, and other senior Goldman employees were grilled over the company's role in the global financial crisis. Here's how Robert Peston of the BBC described the hearing:

> The 10-hour torture session of Goldman Sachs executives by US senators yesterday disclosed a very basic disagreement between the world's most powerful investment bank and the world's most powerful legislature.
>
> Goldman Sachs attempted to explain that the role of the firm's market makers was to provide a product to grown-up investors; they had no responsibility to endorse that product in any way. Their view was that market making operated outside any moral or ethical world. The market in question was collaterized debt obligations, tranches of home mortgages. [As described in Chapter 3 (▶Chapter 3).] Goldman Sachs was moving from being a net buyer of these products to placing bets that their price would collapse. In fact these products had been described in very unfavourable terms in several internal Goldman emails. Despite this, the firm continued to sell these products to their clients. As Peston notes, their staff did not act in the way like Marks and Spencer staff who – in a sense – guarantee to quality of what they are selling on behalf of the company.
>
> Goldman Sachs seemed to believe that its clients were mature enough to realize that Goldman has its own capital, which it must manage for the benefit of the firm and its owners, regardless of the interests of its clients.
>
> This view was received with a mixture of contempt and incredulity by the US senators conducting the hearing. Their view – and it would be the popular view too, I would hazard – is that a bank with Goldman's history and reputation should not be conducting itself as though it was a street trader selling fake Rolexes which it has pretty good reason to believe will stop ticking within a few days. If Goldman was desperate to empty its own warehouses of those dodgy investments – which Goldman concedes that it was – it should not have been selling them in the first place (Peston, 2010).

Chapter 3

QUESTIONS

1 If you were a non-executive director of Goldman Sachs, how would you react to Blankfein's performance before the senate committee?

2 Isn't the Goldman defence simply a variant on the old *caveat emptor* argument, discredited in the twenty-first-century TQM environment? Or are financial services markets completely different to other product markets?

3 Would you be comfortable serving as a non-executive director of Goldman Sachs? Why or why not?

to change top management when performance does not meet expectations. There is undoubtedly a problem of information asymmetry between management and boards, and the increased environmental turbulence will increase pressure to resolve this issue (Thomas *et al.*, 2009).

Non-executive directors must continue to respect the boundary between directing and actually managing the company, yet must remain true to their duty on behalf of shareholders. Unfortunately, board culture and style are often such as to inhibit the free interchange of ideas. Meeting time is limited, agendas are too structured, and proceedings dominated by presentations from the firm's executives. As a consequence, boards are often deferential to executive management, becoming reactive and focused on compliance. To be effective, boards must take the initiative, acting collaboratively to add more value. Some degree of board evaluation would be helpful in this. In a recent survey of board members, some 72 per cent indicated that their performance should be evaluated, yet few firms actually carry out such surveys (Stybel & Peabody, 2005). To improve effectiveness, some boards are providing counselling and advice to management, who may welcome the independent perspectives, judgement and insight of external directors. Others are experimenting with different arrangements, such as meeting less frequently but for a much longer time period (Grady, 1999).

The chairman and the CEO must perform a delicate balancing act. The chairman must ensure that the board is:

- involved but does not micro-manage the firm
- challenging, but supportive of management
- patient, but not complacent.

At the same time, the CEO must be able to:

- share information without feeling vulnerable
- seek advice without appearing weak
- solicit input without appearing to relinquish control (Charan, 1998).

Board tasks

As is clear from the Ericsson 'in practice' example, boards of directors undertake a variety of tasks which can be categorized as shown in Figure 13.2.

External

There is considerable debate on the degree and nature of the board's involvement in developing and implementing strategy. One school, with a procedural approach, suggests that the board's role is as a board of review – formally reviewing and approving management's strategic proposals. Another view is more interactive, arguing that the board should actively participate

Board tasks *in practice* – Ericsson

Ericsson, the Swedish electronics firm, has ten directors on its board, appointed at the annual general meeting. There are also three members appointed by unions with all directors holding office for one year. The president and CEO is the only executive officer of Ericsson on the board while all non-executive directors meet the requirements of independence. The board of directors is ultimately responsible for the organization and management of the firm, developing guidelines for ongoing operations, which are managed by the president and CEO. He, in turn, is responsible for ensuring that the board is regularly updated on important developments, including results, business developments and the financial position of the firm.

In 2009, the board met on 14 occasions, of which two were away from the head office, to allow board members the opportunity to visit a major business operation. The other off-site meeting was for two days, allowing the board an opportunity to conduct an in-depth appraisal of the firm's strategy and performance, as well as evaluate its own operations. The board also meets with its external auditors at least once per year.

At a typical board meeting, there are reports from both the CEO and the heads of business units updating the board on business and market developments in their area of responsibility and reporting results of the unit. The board reviews interim quarterly results and develops and signs off the annual report. With the financial crisis of 2009, the board focused on how Ericsson would extend its technological leadership, which was seen as the key to maintaining competitive advantage. The board also assessed several acquisitions, assisted in the development of short- and long-term goals, and developed a senior management incentive compensation scheme. Each subcommittee – audit, finance and remuneration – presents reports on developments in their respective area of specialization.

The board also spent time assessing its own performance, identifying areas where directors with new capabilities may be required. All directors attended several full-day training sessions to provide them with detailed knowledge of the industry, new technologies, future prospects, and developments in corporate responsibility and sustainability (Treschow, 2009).

in strategy development and execution through direct face-to-face interaction (Hendry *et al.*, 2010).

We take this latter view that strategy development must be done in partnership with the board, since it is ultimately responsible for the performance of the firm in creating value for shareholders. It is essential that the board be concerned with creating tomorrow, engaging in strategic thinking leading to a shared vision by both directors and top management. This requires that board members have a well-developed sense of the firm's businesses, what is likely to work and what is not. In a global study of boards of directors, 54 per cent of firms

	Short term	Long term
External	**Accountability** Reporting to shareholders Ensuring compliance	**Strategic thinking** Setting corporate direction Reviewing strategy
Internal	**Supervision** Reviewing business results Reviewing executive performance	**Corporate policy** Review senior executives Approve capital budgets

Figure 13.2 Board tasks

Source: Adapted from Hilmer, 1998

reported that the board is responsible for setting (as distinct from merely reviewing and approving) corporate strategy. Interestingly, this is less true in the United States where only 21 per cent reported that the board is active in setting strategy (*Board of Directors Global Study*, 2000). This finding, coupled with the fact that the CEO and chairman are generally the same individual in major US firms, points to a general pattern there of executive dominance over the board.

In our view, top management has the critical responsibility for generating initiatives, doing the analysis, and interpreting results. The board must work out how to contribute to strategy without encroaching on this legitimate responsibility of management. This has several implications. First, the board must define what it means by performance – whether it is shareholder value, profit, cash, share price, short term or long term. Second, the board must make certain that a process for producing sound strategies is in place at the same time as it monitors current strategies to ensure that they are on schedule, on budget and producing effective results.

Reviewing strategy requires that the board have considerable information on the firm and the industries in which it competes, including but not limited to the following:

- What environmental changes are expected? What discontinuities may occur? What are likely changes in markets, technologies and currencies?

- What are the good points and the weak points of the current strategy? Is it meeting our objectives? How should the domain of the firm change? Do we have the capabilities required to compete in the future?

- What changes are expected in the competitive strategy of traditional and new competitors?

- What is our current business model – how do we make money? What growth, risk and returns are expected? Is our financing adequate?

- What performance measures should the firm adopt? Total return to shareholders or cash flow? What time period and which firms should be used for comparisons?

Performing such a role puts considerable responsibility on the board. Its members must possess the time, the detailed knowledge and the information support systems to allow them to perform this role satisfactorily. In this sense, the board needs expertise in posing questions to management and being able to interpret the responses. This highlights one possible problem with executive directors: their personal involvement may make them less objective when reviewing performance. In their board role, they must behave as director, not executive – a possible source of role conflict.

In terms of their accountability responsibilities, directors are required to ensure that the firm has appropriate structures to assure compliance with all rules and regulations from stock exchanges and regulatory bodies. The board is responsible for reporting to shareholders and for preparing the annual report. This is a component of the board's role in shareholder communications – disseminating timely material to shareholders. The board must also be aware of shareholder expectations: What are these? Are they the same for all shareholders? Some shareholders may prefer a steady stream of dividends; others may prefer to see the firm minimize dividends to allow investment in growth. Microsoft, for example, paid its first dividend in 2003. Historically, large institutional investors were often treated differently, with confidential briefings on the future of the firm, disadvantaging small shareholders. Nowadays the board must exercise care to ensure that shareholders are treated equally.

Contention can also arise over the handling of takeover offers (➤Chapter 9). Does the board attempt to reject takeovers that seem to be in the interests of shareholders but not in their own personal interests or those of management? Managers are expected to turn strategic vision into operational reality, but directors represent shareholders and must evaluate strategy based on how the company's returns compare with those of other investment opportunities.

Chapter 9

Internal

The most important internal role of the board is to ensure that the firm has the highest calibre CEO and top-management team. The board therefore has a key role in planning CEO succession. Finding a new CEO is important: lack of such an individual can lead to a crisis in morale and investor panic. Responsibility for this rests with the board, which necessitates that it understand the firm's strategy and what this implies in terms of the skills of the new CEO (Carey & Ogden, 2000). Beyond the selection, evaluation, and, where necessary, replacement of the CEO, the board must also be actively involved in developing the compensation package for the CEO and senior executives. Possible measures for evaluating a CEO include business performance, accomplishment of long-term strategic objectives, and development of managers within the firm.

The level of remuneration of senior executives and its relationship to firm performance has caused great concern to shareholders, institutions, governments, unions and the public at large. Indeed the British government has commissioned several studies of the issue (Deloitte, 2004).

The concern has been exacerbated not only by various corporate scandals, but also by the fact that in the past most firms did not report management stock options as an expense when reporting to shareholders. If call options have been granted to the executive (at no

> ### Executive remuneration *in practice* – Bellway
>
> In January, Bellway's remuneration deal for the 2008 financial year was voted down by shareholders after the leading three directors, including the chief executive, received bonus payments of £632,500 – 55 per cent of their base salaries – despite an 85 per cent fall in pre-tax profits.
>
> The company angered investors by revamping its performance targets because of a rapidly deteriorating housing market. CEO Watson said Bellway made a mistake by not consulting shareholders about the changes and that talks with investors about finalizing the new package had already begun. 'The shareholders won't be surprised this time round,' he added (Ruddick, 2009).

cost), then the executive loses nothing should the share price fall. The general feeling is that these options should be reported as an expense, even though valuation remains a problem. There is also a fear that senior executives may indulge in misleading behaviour intended to increase share prices. One result of this, at least in the UK where shareholders are more empowered, has been a number of well-publicized shareholder rejections of compensation plans, as in the Bellway case above.

As part of the conformance role of the board, it must monitor the strategies adopted and report to shareholders on its stewardship. Thus the board is responsible for establishing a framework for the management of the economic entity including a system of internal control, a business risk management process and the setting of appropriate ethical standards.

Board members need to understand the relationship between risk and performance and the risk profile of the firm. They should ensure that processes are in place to manage risk at an acceptable level, where risk could involve financial loss, fraud, or some other crisis such as a currency collapse. Risk management subsumes the analysis of capital projects and the approval of capital budgets but should have a much wider purview. It means understanding where the firm is exposed and the magnitude of that exposure, as well as considering whether the firm should take on a higher level of business risk. This is an area of governance that has become more important with the growth of a range of financial instruments such as derivatives

Chapter 4 and the turbulence in financial markets. As we noted in Chapter 4 (►Chapter 4), this role has been poorly performed by the management of many financial institutions, who clearly misjudged the risk of many CDOs.

Board committees

Most firms will have a number of subcommittees of the board. We now briefly review the role of some of the more important.

Audit committee

This group oversees the financial systems and internal controls employed by the firm. It is also responsible for the appointment of the firm's auditors. These auditors are appointed by the board and report to the board, not to management. A major responsibility of this committee is to monitor the firm's auditors and to verify the accuracy and validity of financial information presented to the board and shareholders. The audit committee should be made up of non-executive directors. Nonetheless, the performance of such committees has been a major concern in recent years, since many firms' financial statements have been inaccurate, if not fraudulent. To overcome this problem, it has been suggested that audit firms should not engage in consulting work with the firm and that the audit firm be rotated every few years. Of the European companies surveyed by Heidrick & Struggles, 94 per cent now have such a committee (Heidrick & Struggles, 2009).

Nominating committee

This committee is responsible for nominating new directors of the firm and a new CEO. Concerns have been expressed that even with a nominating committee, CEOs may still suggest new board members, thus creating a board in their own image, not one that is truly independent. Shareholders at the annual meeting must approve all directors, but generally they find it difficult to elect individuals not approved by the current board. Directors are appointed for a limited term and cannot be removed by the board during their term of office. Individuals who are disruptive or who fail to contribute can only be removed by shareholders at the annual meeting. Shareholders vote on the appointment of directors but they typically find it difficult to nominate new ones. In Europe, 40 per cent of nominating committees are combined remuneration and nominating committees, down from 47 per cent in 2007 (Heidrick & Struggles, 2009), but such combined committees were not found in Italy, the UK, Germany, Denmark or Sweden.

Remuneration committee

This group makes recommendations on executive and CEO compensation arrangements and how this compensation relates to both individual and company performance. The committee generally comprises and is chaired by independent directors. This is another major area of debate, since many CEOs seem to receive remuneration unrelated to the performance of the firm, although the Institutional Voting Information Service in the UK has developed a set of guidelines for this (IVIS, 2009). Another issue has been compensation paid to CEOs if their employment is terminated, since there have been examples of very large payouts. This group also has the challenging task of devising fees and remuneration for non-executive directors, including pension rights. According to Heidrick & Struggles, 89 per cent of the companies they surveyed now have a remuneration committee (Heidrick & Struggles, 2009).

Governance committee

Institutional and other investors are starting to demand that boards periodically evaluate themselves and review their effectiveness. As a result, it has become more common for global firms to have a governance committee. Its role is to review board composition and committee structure and to assess board performance. The group should also assess board processes, such as information flows and agenda setting, to ensure open discussion at board meetings.

Ethics committee

As a consequence of the corporate scandals described earlier, many firms have now established an ethics committee of the board. They are prevalent in the UK and Germany, while some 20 per cent of French firms also have such a committee (Heidrick & Struggles, 2009). The Hyundai Motor Company of South Korea has established an ethics committee, consisting of five external directors, one executive director and two advisers. This group is responsible for monitoring internal transactions, ensuring transparency and maintaining an ethical charter (Hyundai, 2009).

13.8 GLOBAL GOVERNANCE APPROACHES

LEARNING OBJECTIVE 5

Indicate how corporate governance practices vary in different countries.

Each country has its own distinct type of corporate governance, reflecting its unique history, legal system, and regulatory and tax regimes. But all over the world, managers are being forced to become more accountable to shareholders, and in all legal jurisdictions there are regulations on disclosure, insider trading and takeovers.

The discussion above was largely focused on governance arrangements under the Anglo-American system. We extend this to look at other regions of the world, namely continental Europe and Asia.

Europe

The distinguishing feature of governance in Europe is the existence of a two-tier board structure in several countries. In the United Kingdom, Ireland and some southern European countries such as Italy, Spain, Greece and Portugal, a one-tier board system exists. In Germany, Switzerland, Austria, the Netherlands and the Scandinavian countries there is a two-tier board system. To make it simpler, we will focus on the German system, although others are similar.

Germany

In Germany the two boards are the supervisory board (Aufsichtsrat) and the management board (Vorstand). The supervisory board has no direct management function and is responsible for major investment and long-term policy decisions. For larger firms, one-half of the members of this supervisory board are elected by employees and may include trade union representatives. The other half are elected by shareholders. This means that this board has no executives from the firm on it, not even the CEO. This supervisory board elects the management board, which is responsible for managing the firm on a day-to-day basis and normally has considerable autonomy.

The supervisory board has sometimes been seen by the management board as delaying decision-making and as being a source of media leaks on firm strategy. However, given the lapses in board oversight which have occurred over the past decade, there is increasing interest in other countries in this two-tier model, particularly if the supervisory board is able to clarify the processes that govern its relationship with the management board. There is a general legal maximum of 21 members for the supervisory board, although this can also depend on the size of the workforce.

This two-tier board structure reflects the German principle of co-determination – that firms are responsible to other stakeholders, such as employees, hence their presence on the supervisory board. However, concern has been expressed over the competence and independence of such employee directors. A person cannot legally be on more than ten supervisory boards at the same time, but this number seems excessive. To encourage greater dialogue between its two boards, Siemens changed its arrangements. The management board must now inform the supervisory board more systematically about its decisions, and all transactions worth more than 2 per cent of the firm's equity must be approved by the supervisory board (Benoit, 2002). This change was not, however, effective in preventing the 2006 bribery scandals reported earlier in this chapter.

In Europe generally there has been a shift in focus by boards away from compliance towards how the board enhances organizational performance. So boards meet more frequently, on average nine times a year and almost all boards of major companies use sub-committees, with an average of three subcommittees per board. The most common sub-committees are audit, nomination and remuneration (Albert-Roulhac, 2008). However, there are some areas where European boards may need to change. For example, the proportion of independent directors, 54 per cent, is low by UK standards, as is the proportion of non-nationals. In Germany, Spain and Italy the proportion of non-nationals on the boards of major companies is only 8 per cent, which is in sharp contrast to the global nature of most of these firms.

Asia

Asia is a diverse region, encompassing many different political and economic systems. We examine some of the more important differences.

Japan

Most large Japanese companies are stock companies, which are similar to US public companies. At the same time, most large firms are associated with a financial *keiretsu*, characterized by extensive intra-group trade and a capital structure with elaborate cross-holdings of debt and equity, a strong domination by the group's main bank in corporate borrowings, and historically high levels of gearing financed by member banks. This cross-holding of debt and equity is a contingent governance mechanism that maintains internal discipline, although it has been suggested that these banks have not excelled at monitoring firm performance (Kanda, 1998).

Governance in Japan is a one-tier system. Shareholders elect directors, and the Japanese Commercial Code requires that the board make important decisions, elect managers, and generally act with care and loyalty to the company. Boards are usually large and over-whelmingly male, generally comprising current or former employees of the firm. It is uncommon for outsiders to be on the board, and given this board structure it is not surprising that hostile takeovers are uncommon. Further, government officials may be members of the board (Hoshi, 1998). This board structure reflects aspects of Japanese history and culture, and boards traditionally have seen their primary responsibility to employees, not shareholders, though this appears to be changing.

Boards of major Japanese companies are characterized by their relatively large size and the lack of non-executive directors. Canon has a board with 15 members, all executives of the firm. Canon has no independent directors, and all the directors are Japanese with the CEO also being the chairman of the board. In addition, there are no board subcommittees such as audit or remuneration (Canon, 2010). Sony is similar; its board has 15 members and a common CEO and chairman. However, Sony does have three non-Japanese directors, including the CEO (Sony, 2010).

India

Perhaps reflecting earlier British influence, there are significant similarities between the Indian approach to governance and that of the UK. Guidelines are established, but these are voluntary rather than mandatory in most cases. Nonetheless, the Indian government has been paying a lot of attention to the issue, culminating in the recent publication of a revised set of guidelines (Government of India Ministry of Corporate Affairs, 2009).

While strongly endorsing the separation of the roles of CEO and chairman, these guidelines also recommend a fixed maximum term of six years for a non-executive director and suggest that anyone employed as a full-time director of a public company should not serve as a non-executive director of more than seven companies, a number which some would find excessive. The guidelines also call for the rotation of the audit firm every five years and that the nomination committee have a majority of independent directors, one of whom is the subcommittee chairman. For more details on Indian company regulations readers are referred to the Asian Corporate Governance Association (Asian-Corporate-Governance-Association, 2010). Infosys, the Indian software firm, has a board with five executive directors, including the CEO, and nine independent directors, with one of these being the firm's founder, who is currently the non-executive board chairman. The non-executive directors have a variety of backgrounds, in terms of industry experience and nationality, including academics and non-Indian nationals (Infosys, 2010).

Southeast Asia

In Southeast Asia, Chinese family business structures dominate. These firms are controlled by the family and have limited public shares. There is little delegation of decision-making to non-family members, although such firms do have a strong concept of trusted business partners (Blake, 1999).

China

All large listed Chinese firms have active party secretaries who have their own agenda. In addition, nearly all listed Chinese companies, on the mainland as well as overseas, are still majority owned by the government or related entities. Intervention by party officials is out of sight of investors and unsupervised by regulators, so there is a potential conflict of interest between the board's responsibility to shareholders and to the party. The party provides a network outside of which promotion is impossible, bank credit inaccessible, and permission to list a company unattainable. In a Shanghai Stock Exchange survey of listed companies, 99 per cent of the main business and staffing decisions, including those involving board appointments and salary, are made with the approval of internal party committees. The party, and links with the party, may be critical for getting access to credit and overseas markets, although smaller and newer private companies are much less likely to have a party committee (McGregor, 2001). Haier, the Chinese appliance manufacturer, has 11 individuals on its board, with the CEO also being the chairman (Haier, 2008). All directors are Chinese, with the seven executive directors having substantial experience in the general appliance industry. The three non-executive directors have backgrounds in accounting, legal and banking, but only one has any international experience, which may prove to be a limitation as the firm pursues its strategy of globalization.

13.9 CORPORATE SOCIAL RESPONSIBILITY

LEARNING OBJECTIVE 6

Recommend that firms need to consider social responsibility in strategy development.

Chapters 1, 2, 12

We have included a separate section on this subject because, as we noted in Chapters 1, 2 and 12 (➤Chapters 1, 2, 12), firms are increasingly subject to public scrutiny on corporate social responsibility (CSR) issues. Many have taken a pro-active stance on CSR, as we saw with Total and the John Lewis Partnership. Directors must not only be aware of CSR issues, they must also have sophisticated insight, as our example below illustrates.

Boards will undoubtedly find that CSR pressures will increase in the future, driven not only by government decree in such areas as carbon emissions and energy usage, but also by a variety of other constituencies. The ILO, labour unions and other concerned groups will continue to pressure firms on not only their own labour practices, but also on those of their suppliers and customers. Special interest NGOs will pursue their own agendas, be they deforestation, bonus schemes, employee rights or others. Many of these organizations also buy shares, permitting them to participate in shareholder meetings and, frequently, to table resolutions at annual meetings. Finally, pressures will also come from customers themselves, who have increasingly identified with, for example, Fair Trade and environmental concerns. Encouragingly for those who seek a utilitarian justification, there is some evidence that participation in various social responsibility activities has the effect of ameliorating some of the consequences of negative events; that is, they provide 'insurance-like' protection (Godfrey *et al.*, 2009).

Challenge of strategic management – Biofuel

In the UK, the Renewable Transport Fuels Obligation introduced in 2010 requires 3.25 per cent of fuel sold to come from crops. This proportion is due to increase each year and by 2020 is required to be 13 per cent. Under the standard, a litre of biofuel should reduce emissions by at least 35 per cent compared with burning a litre of fossil fuel.

In 2010, the Department of Transport commissioned a report to investigate the overall impact of its biofuel target on forests and other undeveloped land. This report found that the Department of Transport's targets for the level of biofuel in fuel sold in the UK will result in millions of hectares of forest being logged or burnt down and converted to plantations. As a result, palm oil increases emissions by 32 per cent because of the carbon released when forests are turned into plantations.

The EC has conducted its own research, but is refusing to publish the results. A leaked internal memo for the EC's agriculture directorate reveals its concern that Europe's entire biofuel industry, which receives almost £3 billion a year in subsidies, would be jeopardized if the impact of changes in land use – from forests to palm oil plantation – and the associated release of carbon in this process, were included in sustainability standards. This arises because clearing rain forests for palm oil plantations releases carbon stored in trees and soil. The EC hopes to protect its biofuel target by issuing revised standards that would give palm plantations the same status as natural forests. Officials appear to have accepted the arguments put forward by the palm oil industry that palms are just another type of tree.

This study is likely to force a review of the biofuel target since it concludes that some of the most common biofuel crops fail to meet the minimum sustainability standard set by the European Commission. It may actually be better for the environment to use fossil fuels rather than fuels made from crops or plantations (Webster, 2010).

13.10 SUMMARY

Arising from the scale and number of recent corporate crises, there is growing concern with improving corporate governance in many countries around the world. Shareholders and governments are exerting pressure on boards to improve the governance of the firms that they direct, and since shareholders are the owners of the firm, their interests must be the board's primary concern. At the same time, the board must consider the interests of other stakeholders and ensure that the firm acts ethically and meets all legal requirements. Thus the board bears ultimate responsibility for organizational performance, while the managers are responsible for using the firm's assets, tangible and intangible, to ensure that the firm's objectives are met.

In the chapter, we examined the principles of corporate governance – the relationship among shareholders, management and the board – in determining the direction and performance of the firm. Corporate governance is about how authority and responsibility are shared among shareholders, managers and the board so that the firm generates value for all stakeholders, particularly shareholders.

Different countries with their own legal and financial systems have different systems of corporate governance, typified by the existence of dual boards in several countries. However, there is widespread concern with developing systems of governance that are more transparent for shareholders and result in superior performance. Directors are legally required to act in good faith, to act honestly and in the interests of shareholders. The challenge for them is how to do this when they are not involved on a day-to-day basis with the firm.

Of particular interest is the role of the board in the strategy of the firm. It is often considered that strategy development is the responsibility of management – yet there is an inherent tension between this and the legal responsibility of the board for performance. In our view, the board must be closely involved in strategy but this involvement should be interactive. The board should have the capabilities to set performance standards, questioning management on underlying assumptions, and asking the tough questions about the strategy. Boards must both challenge and support senior management, yet behaving so that managers can act.

While there is considerable interest in board structure, there should also be interest in board processes. Board structure is concerned with size, skills, number of meetings, sub-committees, and the role of independent directors. Processes need to be such that the board can add value to the strategy process to enhance performance. In many firms boards seem to be captured by management (particularly the CEO), resulting in the firm being run in the interests of managers, not shareholders. Since the board is ultimately responsible for the performance of the firm, it must be prepared to change senior management, particularly the CEO, if performance is unsatisfactory.

All of this is difficult when the board has limited information, meets infrequently, and has limited in-depth knowledge of the firm and its operations. This need to challenge and yet support management is part of the explanation for the importance of independent directors – they are supposed to have the independence to be able to challenge management, mainly the CEO, in ways that executive directors would find impossible. Hence board members must all be knowledgeable and skilled and must act as a team – boardroom fights and conflicts are not conducive to superior performance.

VIEW FROM THE TOP

CABLE AND WIRELESS

In his response to shareholder criticism at the 2009 shareholders' meeting of the British firm Cable and Wireless, the Chairman, Richard Lapthorne, vigorously defended the company's remuneration policy. He said the rewards were for turning around a company that many analysts had written off. He pointed out that since he became chairman four years ago the share price had trebled and the company generated cash rather than burning through it at a rate of £1bn a year.

He told the shareholders that senior executives only gained if shareholders gained, that the rewards and payments made are financed by what happens to the share price. Under the long-term incentive scheme that Lapthorne was defending, the top 60 C&W managers would share a £70m bonus pot. John Pluthero – chairman of the Europe, Asia and US division – was scheduled to be paid £8.3m this year under the scheme, with further payments also due in 2010 and 2011. However, the Chairman did reveal that a new incentive scheme was due to start in 2010, and that this would be more conventional with payouts capped at four times salary.

Despite a 36 per cent rise in annual earnings, the scheme had provoked a major shareholder revolt with almost 40 per cent of shareholders either voting against the remuneration package or abstaining. Several shareholders commented that the bonus scheme was characterized by unbridled greed and that the payments were disproportionate to results.

The Association of British Insurers, representing a fifth of British shareholders, was reported as saying that the vote showed that investors were deeply concerned about the rewards on offer to executives. The Association also suggested that shareholders were concerned at remuneration policies in place in many companies. As a result, it was important that independent directors engage in a constructive process with shareholders to address their concerns (Inman, 2009).

QUESTIONS

1 Do you believe that Lapthorne, who as Chairman is supposed to represent shareholders interests, was in principle justified in advancing a defence of the bonus scheme?

2 When the compensation committee recommends and the board endorses this type of scheme, do you believe they are acting as agents for shareholders or not?

PRUDENTIAL PLC

Prudential plc is a major international retail financial services group with operations in the UK, the USA and Asia. The firm was founded in 1848 and by 2009 it had £290 billion in assets under management and served 25 million customers (Prudential 2009 annual report). Prudential has grown using both acquisitions and organic growth. In 1986 Prudential acquired Jackson National Life in the US and Scottish Amicable Life in 1997. This was followed in 1999 by the acquisition of M&G, a leading provider of investment

products. In 1994 Prudential launched Prudential Corporation Asia to develop new businesses in Asia, supplementing its existing Malaysia and Singapore businesses which dated back to 1923. As a result, Prudential now operates in 13 Asian countries. The strategy of operating in the mature UK and US markets and in the fast-growing Asian markets is referred to as the 'three-pillar strategy' and has been in place for more than a decade. The group is structured around four main business units: Prudential Corporation Asia, Jackson National Life Insurance Company in the US, Prudential UK, and M & G.

As a result of the global crisis in 2008, AIG, the large US insurance firm, was rescued from collapse by the US government which provided AIG with substantial loans in return for an 80 per cent equity stake. In 2008 Prudential considered making on offer for AIA, the Asian arm of AIG, but eventually decided not to proceed. However, AIG was interested in selling off several of their assets to repay their debt to the US government. One alternative was to offer an IPO of AIA, their Asian business, on the Hong Kong Stock Exchange. Such an offer was expected to raise $10 to $20 billion depending on market conditions. Due to a fear of depressing the market with such a float, AIG was unlikely to sell all of AIA in one go and perhaps it would have held up to 49 per cent of AIA for the foreseeable future.

Late in January 2010 AIG's board and its owners, New York Federal Reserve, had second thoughts about IPO. A trade sale could allow a clean exit for AIG – and provide greater certainty and speed of execution than the planned listing. Such a sale would also raise the value of AIG's business immediately, providing greater certainty guarding against the future stock market risk.

Following several detailed discussions with AIG, the CEO of Prudential, Mr Thiam, travelled to the USA in the third week of February 2010 to make a case to the board of AIG for a sale of AIA to Prudential. On his return to London, Prudential announced an offer of $35 billion for AIA on 28 February 2010.

The offer of $35 billion represented a ratio of market capitalization to embedded value of 1.69. Embedded value is a common valuation measure used outside North America in the insurance industry and is calculated by adding the adjusted net asset value and the present value of future profits of a firm. A ratio of one implies that the company will not write any more new business nor make any gains on its investments. Most recent mature market acquisitions have been at a ratio of about 1.2 times embedded value, representing the premium paid for control, cost synergies and growth potential. The proposed ratio of 1.69 offered by Prudential was considered too high by many analysts (*Financial Times*, 2010). The bid was to be financed by a $20 billion rights issue to be offered by Prudential.

Such an acquisition had risks for both parties. AIG had to balance off the likely higher cash proceeds than would be realized from an IPO against the possibility that Prudential shareholders would reject the acquisition. Prudential shareholders were likely to be concerned at the price paid and whether the current management of Prudential could successfully integrate the two companies (Davies & Tucker, 2010).

For Prudential, AIA offered an opportunity to acquire a major competitor and transform Prudential's position in Asia, the world's fastest-growing life insurance markets. The deal would transform Prudential to a company that made 80 to 90 per cent of its sales and profit in Asia, up from the roughly one-third of sales and half its profits in 2009. The combination of Prudential and AIA would result in a dominant position in this market, but it would also call into question the viability of Prudential's long-held 'three-pillars' strategy. Shareholders also expressed concern at the ability of management to successfully integrate numerous businesses in 13 diverse Asian markets. For example, its Asian agency sales force would double to more than 600,000, possibly making it difficult to achieve the desired integration and synergies. Several senior staff of AIA, including the financial director, had already left the firm, and other reports suggested that AIA had lost a considerable number of middle managers (Terazono, 2010). If the acquisition was successful, Prudential would have to deal with a wide variety of regulators who may not look kindly on the creation of a very powerful foreign company. Concern was also expressed that the CEO of Prudential had only been in the position for a short time, and had limited experience with such large acquisitions.

On the day following the bid, analysts predicted that Mr Thiam was likely to face shareholder rebellion. These shareholder concerns resulted in a 20 per cent fall in Prudential's share price on the day markets were open for trading after the initial announcement, as shown in Figure 13.3.

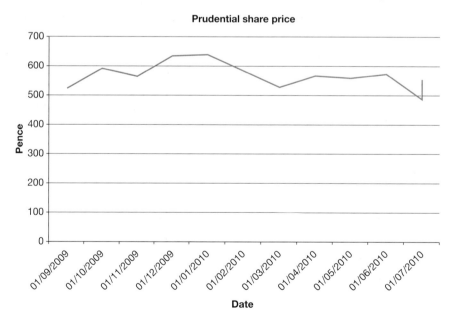

Figure 13.3 Prudential share prices (data extracted from their website)

This negative initial reaction from shareholders was reflected in their complaints of poor communications and a lack of financial information from Prudential. Typically, the investors who voiced their concerns were long-term investors, such as other insurance companies and pension funds, including BlackRock, Fidelity, and Legal and General. As noted above, the acquisition was to be funded primarily by a rights issue. In the UK such a rights issue requires 75 per cent shareholder approval, and this was now considered problematic. In late May it was clear that at least 20 per cent of shareholders would vote against the deal rather than letting it go though. This despite the potential destabilizing effect of a no vote on the company calling into question the position of both Chief Executive Mr Thiam and Chairman Mr Harvey McGrath. During the week beginning 24 May the board of Prudential was engaged in frantic efforts to persuade the undecided shareholders left on the fence to support the acquisition while they simultaneously renegotiated terms with the US owners of AIA.

Responding to shareholder concerns at the high price, in June 2010 Prudential tried to negotiate a price reduction for the bid, reducing their offer to $30.4 billion (Bowers & Kollewe, 2010). This bid was still to be funded by a rights issue, but senior Prudential management considered that this lower bid would now attract shareholder support. The decision on the rights issue was to be placed at a shareholders' meeting on 7 June 2010.

Another major setback for the proposed acquisition was the intervention by the Financial Services Authority, the UK financial regulator which refused to approve the planned rights issue by Prudential (Burgess et al., 2010). It was suggested that the FSA was concerned that the complex cross-border acquisition would result in the firm possessing insufficient capital to guard against market shocks, as had occurred with the disastrous acquisition of ABN Amro by RBS. For some analysts, this was seen as demonstrating a serious lack of judgement by the CEO and board of Prudential.

The proposed acquisition collapsed on 2 June 2010 when the AIG board rejected the Prudential's revised $30.4 billion offer price for AIA, despite the support of the CEO. The AIG board wanted to be absolutely confident that the Prudential shareholders would approve the acquisition and the associated rights issue, with letters from major shareholders indicting their support. When these were not forthcoming, AIG rejected to offer.

The unsuccessful deal cost Prudential a total of £377m before tax, almost as much as it paid out in dividends in 2009. The breakdown is provided in Table 13.1.

Table 13.1 Prudential deal costs

Cost category	Cost
Break fee to AIG	£153m
Underwriting fees for cancelled rights issue	£ 58m
Advisory fees to bankers	£ 66m
Currency hedging costs	£100m
Total	£377m

In the aftermath of the failed acquisition, many major UK investors in Prudential indicated that they were upset by what they considered to be the lack of attention from the CEO. For example, shortly after the announcement, the CEO, Mr Thiam, flew to Asia rather than meeting with shareholders to discuss the proposal. Following criticism of his action, he then decided to return early and subsequently conducted an intensive set of meetings with UK investors. Another unwelcome development was the announcement in mid-March by Société Générale of the appointment of Mr Thiam as a non-executive director. The announcement created furore among Prudential's leading shareholders. They questioned Mr Thiam's judgement and indicated that he needed to give his undivided attention to the AIA deal. On 17 March, a day after the Société Générale statement, Mr Thiam announced that he had turned down the offer of a board position. The manner in which this position was handled raised further doubts about the judgement and commitment of the CEO.

Prudential's bid to buy AIA raises a number of important governance questions, particularly since their website states that 'the Board is responsible to shareholders for creating and delivering sustainable shareholder value through the management of the Group's business'.

QUESTIONS

1   Did the board act in a way likely to create sustainable shareholder value?
2   Did the board understand the interests of shareholders and other stakeholders such as the FSA?
3   In your view, did the board communicate effectively with shareholders?
4   In your view, did the Chairman perform effectively?
5   Why did the board permit the CEO to consider accepting a non-executive board appointment?

REVIEW QUESTIONS

1   What is corporate governance and why is it important?
2   In your view, what role should the board play in the firm's strategy?
3   'The same individual should not be both chairman and CEO.' Discuss this statement.
4   Select a recent example of poor corporate governance. How should the board have behaved?
5   Describe the differences between the German and the US approach to corporate governance. What do you see as the advantages and disadvantages of each?
6   Do you think that all directors should have a substantial shareholding in the firm? What are the implications for both a small and a large shareholding?
7   What do you believe should be the role of the board in determining remuneration for top-level executives? Does current practice in your country conform to your ideas? Why or why not?
8   'The legal responsibilities of being a director of a publicly listed company are now so onerous that one would be foolish to accept such a position.' Discuss this statement.

REFERENCES

Albert-Roulhac, C. (2008) Corporate governance in Europe: Raising the bar. *Business Strategy Series,* *9*(6), 287–290.

Allen, W. T. (1998) The corporate director's fiduciary duty of care and the business judgement rule under U.S. corporate law. In K. J. Hopt, E. Wymeersch & S. Prigge (eds), *Comparative Corporate Governance – The State of the Art and Emerging Research*. Oxford: Clarendon Press.

Asian-Corporate-Governance-Association (2010) www.acga-asia.org/content.cfm?SITE_CONTENT_TYPE_ID=30.

Baert, L. & Vennet, R. V. (2010) *Bank ownership, firm value and firm capital structure in Europe*. Paper presented at the Financial Management Association. www.fma.org/Hamburg/papers/LB_RVV_ownership.pdf.

Barca, F. & Becht, M. (eds) (2001) *The Control of Corporate Europe*. Oxford: Oxford University Press.

Barton, D. & Wong, S. C. Y. (2006) Improving board performance in emerging markets. *McKinsey Quarterly*, (1), 74–83.

Benoit, B. (2002) Is Germany's model finding its level? *Financial Times*, 5 September, p. 7.

Berle, A. J. & Means, G. (1968) *The Modern Corporation and Private Property*, rev. edn. New York: Harcourt Brace.

Blake, A. (1999) *Dynamic Directors*. Basingstoke: Macmillan Press.

Board of Directors Global Study (2000) Chicago, IL: Egon Zehnder.

Bowers, S. & Kollewe (2010) Prudential cheifs face call to quit as AIA deal lies 'dead in the water' *The Guardian*, 1 June, p. 22.

Bruce, A., Skovoroda, R., Fattorusso, J. & Buck, T. (2007) Executive bonus and firm performance in the UK. *Long Range Planning, 40*(3), 280–294.

Burgess, P. J., Davies, K., Jones, A. & Tucker, S. (2010) Pru forced to abandon launch of rights issue. *Financial Times*, 6 May, p. 1.

Cameron, E. (2010) Kraft/Cadbury deal prompts call for reform of takeover laws. *Matthew Arnold & Baldwin, Capital Markets*, 10 March. www.mablaw.com/2010/03/kraftcadbury-deal-prompts-calls-for-reform-of-takeover-laws/.

Canon (2010) Boards of Directors. *Corporate Information*, 1 April. www.canon.com/corp/executive.html.

Capron, L. & Guillén, M. (2009) National corporate governance institutions and post-acquisition target reorganization. *Strategic Management Journal, 30*(8), 803–833.

Carey, D. & Ogden, D. (2000) *CEO Succession*. New York: Oxford University Press.

Carlsson, R. (2001) *Ownership and Value Creation*. Chichester: Wiley.

Charan, R. (1998) *Boards at Work: How Corporate Boards Create Competitive Advantage*. San Francisco, CA: Jossey-Bass.

Colvin, G. (2010) Who's to blame at BP? *Fortune*, 26 July, *162*, 60.

Combs, J. G., Ketchen, D. J., Perryman, A. A. & Donahue, M. S. (2007) The moderating effect of CEO power on the board composition–firm performance relationship. *Journal of Management Studies, 44*(8), 1299–1323.

Conger, J. A., Lawler, E. E. & Finegold, D. (2001) *Corporate Boards*. San Francisco, CA: Jossey-Bass.

Coombes, P. & Watson, M. (2000) Three surveys on corporate governance. *McKinsey Quarterly*, (4), 74–77.

Davies, P. J. & Tucker, S. (2010) $35 billion deal means a high-risk strategy. *Financial Times,* 1 March, p. 18.

Davis, C. (2005) Societas Europaea. *Tax Adviser*, (October).

Deloitte (2004) Report on the impact of the Director's remuneration report regulations. *Report for the Department of Trade and Industry*, November. www.berr.gov.uk/files/file13425.pdf.

Dittmann, I., Maug, E. & Schneider, C. (2008) Bankers on the boards of German firms: What they do, what they are worth, and why they are (still) there. 31 January. www.ecgi.org/competitions/rof/files/Bankers per cent20On per cent20Boards per cent2020080131.pdf.

EgonZender (2000) *Corporate Governance and the Role of the Board of Directors*. Chicago, IL: Egon Zehnder.

Enriques, L. & Volpin, P. (2007) Corporate governance reforms in Continental Europe. *Journal of Economic Perspectives, 21*(1), 117–140.

European Commission (2008) European Corporate Governance Forum. *Internal Market*, September. http://ec.europa.eu/internal_market/company/ecgforum/index_en.htm.

FESE (2008) Share ownership structure in Europe. *Federation of European Securities Exchanges*, December. www.bourse.lu/contenu/docs/commun/societe/Actualites/2008/FESE_SHARE_OWNERSHIP_SURVEY_2007.pdf.

Financial_Reporting_Council (2010) The UK Corporate Governance Code. June. www.frc.org.uk/documents/pagemanager/Corporate_Governance/UK%20Corp%20Gov%20Code%20June%202010.pdf.

Financial Times (2010) Prudential / AIA. *Financial Times*, 30 April, p. 16.

Fulton, S. M. (2009) Insider trading scandal claims former AMD CEO after IBM SVP indictment. *betanews Policy and Law*, 2 November. www.betanews.com/article/Insider-trading-scandal-claims-former-AMD-CEO-after-IBM-SVP-indictment/1257181368.

Godfrey, P. C., Merrill, C. B. & Hansen, J. M. (2009) The relationship between corporate social responsibility and shareholder value: An empirical test of the risk management hypothesis. *Strategic Management Journal, 30*(4), 425–445.

Goldstein, M. & Stempel, J. (2009) Insider trading snares 14 more. *Reuters US Article*, 5 November. www.reuters.com/article/idUSTRE5A42XF20091105

Government of India Ministry of Corporate Affairs (2009) *Corporate governance voluntary guidelines 2009*. www.acga-asia.org/public/files/CG_Voluntary_Guidelines_2009_24dec2009.pdf.

Grady, D. (1999) No more board games. *McKinsey Quarterly*, (3), 17–25.

Grant, J. & Kirchamier, T. (2004) *Corporate ownership structure and performance in Europe: Discussion Paper 631*. Centre for Economic Performance.

Guiso, L., Haliassos, M. & Jappelli, T. (2003) Household stockholding in Europe: Where do we stand and where do we go? *Research Papers in Economics*, January.

Haier (2008) Board of Directors. *About Haier/Investor Relations*. www.haier.com/abouthaier/Investor Relations/DIRECTORS.asp.

Hambrick, D. C. & Jackson, E. M. (2000) Outside directors with a stake: The linchpin in improving governance. *California Management Review, 42*(4), 108–127.

Hampel, R. (1998) *Final Report/Committee on Corporate Governance*. London: The Committee and Gee Publishing.

Heidrick & Struggles (2009) Boards in turbulent times. *Corporate Governance Report 2009*. www.heidrick.com/PublicationsReports/PublicationsReports/CorpGovEurope2009.pdf.

Hendry, K. P., Kiel, G. C. & Nicholson, G. (2010) How boards strategise: A strategy as practice view. *Long Range Planning, 43*(1), 33–56.

Higgs, D. (2003) *The Higgs Report: Review of the Role and Effectiveness of Non-executive Directors*. London: Department of Trade and Industry.

Hilmer, F. G. (1998) *Strictly Boardroom*, 2nd edn. Melbourne: Information Australia.

Hoshi, T. (1998) Japanese corporate governance as a system. In K. J. Hopt *et al.* (eds), *Comparative Corporate Governance – The State of the Art and Emerging Research*. Oxford: Clarendon Press.

Hyundai (2009) Hyundai management overview. *Hyundai Profile*. http://worldwide.hyundai.com/company-overview/profile/management.html.

Infosys (2010) Management profiles. *About Us*. www.infosys.com/about/management-profiles/Pages/index.aspx.

Inman, P. (2009) C&W shareholder revolt over bonuses. *The Guardian*, 17 July. www.guardian.co.uk/business/2009/jul/17/cable-and-wireless-bonus-revolt.

International-Finance-Corporation (2008) The EU approach to corproate governance. *Global Corporate Governance Forum*, February. www.ifc.org/ifcext/cgf.nsf/AttachmentsByTitle/EU+Approach+to+CG/$FILE/IFC_EUApproach_Final.pdf.

IVIS (2009) Executive remuneration – ABI guidelines on policies and practices. 15 December. www.ivis.co.uk/ExecutiveRemuneration.aspx.

Jensen, M. (1990) The market for corporate control. In C. W. Smith (ed.), *The Modern Theory of Corporate Finance*. New York: McGraw-Hill.

Kanda, H. (1998) Notes on corporate governance in Japan. In K. J. Hopt (ed.), *Comparative Corporate Governance – The State of the Art and Emerging Research*. Oxford: Clarendon Press.

Lorsch, J. W. & Zelleke, A. (2005) Should the CEO be the Chairman? *Sloan Management Review, 46*(2), 70–74.

Marks and Spencer (2010) Marks and Spencer Group Plc Announces Robert Swannell as its New Chairman. 23 August. http://corporate.marksandspencer.com/media/press_releases/company/New_Chairman_Announcement.

McGregor, R. (2001) The little red book of business in China. *Financial Times*, 2 July, p. 9.

Michels, D. (2009) Governance overview. *Marks and Spencer Annual Report 2009*. http://annualreport2009.marksandspencer.com/overview/deputy-chairman.aspx.

Miyajima, H., Kawamoto, S., Ome, Y. & Saito, N. (2009) Corporate ownership and performance in twentieth century Japan. *WIAS Discussion Paper 2009–001*, 7 May. www.waseda.jp/wias/achievement/dp/pdf/dp2009001.pdf.

Monks, R. A. G. & Minow, N. (2004) *Corporate Governance*, 3rd edn. Malden: Blackwell.

Monks, R. A. G. & Minow, N. (2008) *Corporate Governance*, 4th edn. Hoboken: Wiley.

Morck, R., Yavuz, M. D. & Yeung, B. (2009) Bank control, capital allocation and economic performance. *Darden School*, 1 March. http://admin.darden.virginia.edu/emUpload/uploaded2009/crony per cent20banks_nov24.pdf.

Nokia (2009) Corporate guidelines at Nokia. *About Nokia Board of Directors*. www.nokia.com/NOKIA_COM_1/About_Nokia/Sidebars_new_concept/Board_charters/Corp+Gov+Guidelines+2009.pdf.

Paterson, T. (2009) Siemens bribery deal close. *The Independent*, 3 December. www.independent.co.uk/news/business/news/siemens-bribery-deal-close-1833088.html? per cent22.

Peston, R. (2010) Goldman: Consequences of the Senate inquisition. *BBC News Peston's Picks*, 28 April. www.bbc.co.uk/blogs/thereporters/robertpeston/2010/04/goldman_consequences_of_the_se.html.

Plitch, P. (2002) Governance rules may weed out directors with large holdings. *Wall Street Journal*, 11 September, B5b.

Prigge, S. (1998) A survey of German corporate governance. In K. J. Hopt (ed.), *Comparative Corporate Governance – The State of the Art and Emerging Research*. Oxford: Clarendon Press.

Rohwedder, C. (2009) Marks & Spencer plucks new CEO from rival. *Wall Street Journal*, 19 November.

Ruddick, G. (2009, October 13) Housebuilder Bellway in talks over new director remuneration package after pay deal rebellion. *The Daily Telegraph*, 13 October. www.telegraph.co.uk/finance/newsbysector/constructionandproperty/6318476/Housebuilder-Bellway-in-talks-over-new-director-remuneration-package-after-pay-deal-rebellion.html.

SAP (2010) Corporate governance. www.sap.com/about/governance/supervisory/members.epx.

Sony (2010) Executives. *Sony Corporate Information*. www.sony.net/SonyInfo/CorporateInfo/executive/index.html.

Stybel, L. J. & Peabody, M. (2005) How should board directors evaluate themselves? *MIT Sloan Management Review, 47*(1), 67–72.

Terazono, E. (2010) Kiwi propping up AIA. *Financial Times*, 28 April.

The Economist (2001) The fading appeal of the boardroom. *The Economist*, 10 February, pp. 73–75.

The Economist (2008) Time to fix Siemens. *The Economist*, 6 July.

The Economist (2009) India's Enron. *The Economist*, 8 January.

Thomas, R., Schrage, M., Bellin, J. & Marcotte, G. (2009) How boards can be better – a manifesto. *MIT Sloan Management Review, 50*(2), 69–74.

Treschow, M. (2009) *Ericsson Corporate Governance Report 2009.*

van Ees, H., van der Laan, G. & Postma, T. J. B. M. (2008) Effective board behavior in The Netherlands. *European Management Journal, 26*(2), 84–93.

Webster, B. (2010) Fossil fuels 'better for environment' than so-called green fuels. *The Australian*, 2 March, p. 10.

Wenger, E. & Kaserer, C. (1998) German banks and corporate governance: A critical view. In K. J. Hopt, E. Wymeersch & S. Prigge (eds), *Comparative Corporate Governance – The State of the Art and Emerging Research*. Oxford: Clarendon Press.

Williams, P. (2002) Corporate conduct all above board. *Australian Financial Review*, (20 August), 60–61.

Wilson, A. (2010) UK takeover threshold should be raised, says ex-Cadbury chairman Roger Carr. *Daily Telegraph Finance*, 10 February. www.telegraph.co.uk/finance/newsbysector/retailandconsumer/7198336/UK-takeover-threshold-should-be-raised-says-ex-Cadbury-chairman-Roger-Carr.html.

For a range of further resources supporting this chapter, please visit the companion website for *Strategic Management* at www.routledge.com/cw/fitzroy.

CHAPTER 14

POSTSCRIPT

INTRODUCTION

You may well breathe a sigh of relief as you reach the end of this text, but relief is the last thing you should be looking for. Your journey is just beginning.

We earlier defined strategic management as the task of creating organizations that generate value in a turbulent world. This task can be visualized as a process whereby firms must create value in the present while investing in change programmes to ensure survival and value creation in the future.

This transition of the firm and its characteristics may occur by default, in which case it is unlikely to survive, or it can be managed. We believe the latter is preferable. Change in the firm may be revolutionary and metamorphic, or it may be gradual and incremental. Driving these changes in a process of continual re-invention is the task of strategic management. In such a scenario, environmental events are both a threat and an opportunity, creating new markets and destroying old ones. Since some changes are unpredictable in scale and scope, strategy must be emergent and adaptable: flexibility is favoured over rigidity.

Throughout the transition process, there will be pressure from competitors, the end result of which may be to drive returns towards zero economic profit. Innovation is therefore essential to value creation, whether it be in technology, logistics, organization, business model, or some other aspect.

Managing ongoing change is an extremely difficult intellectual task. Organizations are not simple entities but complex collections of people (with all their foibles and good points), relationships and processes. Intellect is certainly required to understand the world, yet management is not a purely intellectual exercise. It also requires action: making decisions, getting change accepted and implemented.

CONTEXT

Managers must perceive change, interpret it and develop appropriate strategy. All three steps are fraught with difficulty, as witnessed by the high corporate failure rate. Sometimes managers fail to perceive change due to obsolete mental models or complacency. Further, change often occurs on the periphery of the known, making it difficult to detect. Some important external changes are described below.

Globalization

You may feel we are beating a dead horse to emphasize globalization, but recognizing that business is increasingly global does not mean that managers are capable of dealing with the consequent realities. For example, the economic balance of the world is changing quite dramatically. While the EU grows by adding countries to the union, many of its member countries are mired in low growth and stifled by regulation. In stark contrast, most Asian economies are booming at the time of writing. China has become a manufacturing powerhouse, driven by indigenous change and the burgeoning of outsourcing by US and

European companies. The term BRIC (Brazil, Russia, India and China) has entered business lexicon, reflecting the view that these economies will be the important driving forces in the twenty-first century.

Competition

You will operate in an intensively competitive global environment. Competition increasingly transcends traditional industry boundaries which, as a result of technological innovation, globalization and deregulation, have become permeable. You must carefully watch the traditional boundaries of your industry, for it is here that the innovations representing your most serious competitive threats are likely to occur.

Technology and innovation

The rise of the information economy has wrought profound change in almost every aspect of economic life. The digital revolution continues, and the networked and mobile economy is all-pervasive. New technologies create new product and market opportunities; they will also demand new competences. Technological change will require firms to create market opportunities rather than respond to pre-existing wants. Finding and developing the individuals and talents to cope with these challenges will preoccupy you as a manager.

STRATEGY

Managing paradoxes

You will be dealing with a more complex, faster-changing world than any of your predecessors. You will need to bring both intellect and passion to your work. While you strategize, you must also inspire; while you implement, you must also be visionary; while you must be creative, you must also be ethical; while you simplify, you must also cope with great complexity. These are challenges that will test your mettle. Fulfilling and exciting opportunities await those who can meet these challenges.

Changing boundaries

Technology, globalization and deregulation are changing industry boundaries everywhere. Yet these are not the only boundaries to be affected. You will be continually rethinking the mission and scope of the businesses and companies that you manage. Outsourcing changes the boundaries between the firm and its suppliers, while technology changes the interface with customers. In the networked economy, the very notion of firm boundaries requires fundamental rethinking. Making an appropriate trade-off between the assessment of internal competences and external opportunities while developing the competences required to exploit future opportunities will be another major challenge.

Scale, efficiency and flexibility

In the world just described, the 'rules' themselves will change. Many twentieth-century firms rose to dominance with classic strategies. Size sometimes brought efficiency gains or market control, while vertical integration enabled avoidance of marketplace vagaries. Yet, with size comes complexity. The 1990s' downsizing vogue suggested that the challenges of managing large, diverse firms were becoming too great. Future advantages may flow from forming networks, driven by the increasing functionality and decreasing cost of communications. Barring great improvement in the tools of strategic management, other firms will likely reach the point where the market for corporate control tells them to voluntarily dismember themselves.

While not denying the advantages of scale in some instances, the battle between economies of scale and scope is likely to be ongoing. With increased affluence, the desire to be different asserts itself in an explosion of lifestyles and choices. 'One size fits all' will not suffice in affluent twenty-first-century markets. While intense competition will ensure that efficiency remains important, firms' abilities to deal with changing and increasingly differentiated customer requirements will grow in importance.

Ethics and transparency

The standards of performance expected of you will far outstrip past standards. The early twenty-first century witnessed particularly egregious examples of executive greed and dishonesty. Societies around the world increasingly condemn such behaviour. Ethicists believe, and we agree, that the balance has shifted to the point where it is more profitable for large companies to behave ethically than to do otherwise. You should exhibit the highest standards of ethical behaviour, avoid dual standards (e.g., tolerating in one country behaviour unacceptable in another), and clearly and consistently communicate expectations about employee behaviour. These actions are integral to good leadership, and will be critical to personal success.

IMPLEMENTATION

Leadership in the organization of the future

Most people understand the importance of leadership in hierarchical organizations. Yet we argue that knowledge-intensive organizations will be much less hierarchical, with fewer levels of management, more emphasis on adaptability and less on bureaucracy. Knowledge and expertise, rather than title or position, will comprise the main sources of influence. In such firms, often networked as a result of outsourcing, leadership will be characterized by remote, rather than direct, control and will be diffused throughout the firm. Hence senior managers must lead in the crucial tasks of recruitment, selection, development and reward. Performance management will require as much emphasis on how results are attained as the results themselves. Reward systems must reflect this. As value becomes more dependent on intangible assets, the personal behaviour of leaders in establishing standards for all becomes even more important.

Intangible assets

Throughout this book we have stressed the importance of intangible assets. The market value of the firm increasingly depends on these, with enormous implications for how we approach strategic management.

Rather than being harbingers of change, business schools are too often on its trailing edge. As the importance of intangible assets rises, most business schools have increased the emphasis on managing tangible assets! As company ethics have increased in international importance, many students have become imbued with the idea that the 'invisible hand' is the answer to the challenges of decision-making, abrogating any concept of personal responsibility.

Managing intangible assets means, at its core, managing human resources internally, and customer and supplier relationships externally. If three-quarters of a company's value depends upon such characteristics, and we preach value creation to students, then shouldn't three-quarters of the curriculum be related to such issues? Of course, without an understanding of accounting and finance, we could not even have a discussion about value management. Yet we repeat our earlier argument: tools for managing intangible assets are nowhere near as highly developed as those for managing tangible assets. Your success will increasingly depend on how well you manage the former, rather than the latter.

Change

When the authors began studying business, change was perceived as exceptional. Many characteristics today viewed as variable were then fixed. Industry structures, exchange rates, even interest rates, were either fixed or subject to only occasional change.

Today change is fast, continuous and often unpredictable, outfoxing the most prescient of forecasters. If change is unpredictable, we must learn how to make our organizations more resilient and flexible. We must seek people who have the ability to live with such change, who can tolerate the ambiguity that accompanies turbulence. You must become ever more astute at managing risk, lest you lose the firm that employs you to the savage swings of a fast-changing environment.

Competences and opportunities

The firm must not only nurture existing competences but also develop the competences to exploit future opportunities. This is challenging enough in its own right, but in tomorrow's world building and sustaining competences poses new problems. Companies battling turbulence by hiring then firing, expanding then refocusing, quickly find workforce loyalty atrophying. Knowledge workers increasingly take responsibility for their own careers, behaving more like short-term contractors than long-term employees. Marshalling, building and retaining competences will continue to be important, but the difficulties of doing so will rise.

PERFORMANCE

Creating value

Creating firm value has been our consistent, ongoing theme. In a world where capital moves freely among applications, there is no alternative. Yet strategic managers must resist the common but distressing tendency to assume that short-term profit maximization is the best route to creating firm value. Local optima do not guarantee a global optimum. Indeed, in competitive strategy, knowing that one's competitor is focused on short-term results can always be turned to advantage by a well-financed rival.

We believe that aligning the interests of professional managers (agents) with those of shareholders (principals) is important to achieving better management of the firm. We also believe that a vigorous, independent board of directors is vital to ensuring that managers do not enrich themselves at the expense of shareholders.

Non-financial criteria

Finally, we have pointed out that good financial performance means managing a great many non-financial criteria. Interestingly, such criteria are becoming important to investors. Corporate social responsibility reports are now commonplace, while ethical considerations are built into the investment strategies of a number of large pension and mutual funds. The future will witness further such developments.

CONCLUSION

We wish you good fortune in the journey that lies ahead of you. For a good strategic manager, learning will be a lifetime journey. We hope you have begun that journey well.

For a range of further resources supporting this chapter, please visit the companion website for *Strategic Management* at www.routledge.com/cw/fitzroy.

GLOSSARY

Accounting profit
Reported on the income statement, and is broadly measured as revenue minus certain expenses. Both revenue and expenses are reported on an accrual basis, and reported expenses include both cash and non-cash expenses. Accounting profit or net income can also be reported as before or after tax.

Acquisition
The firm expands its resources and competences by purchasing, or taking a controlling interest in another firm.

Agency problem
An agency relationship exists when one or more persons (the principal) hire another person or persons (the agent) to perform a service or make decisions on their behalf. An agency problem arises when the agents make decisions that are in their own interest, not in the interests of the principals.

American depository receipts (ADRs)
Negotiable securities issued by a US bank which are backed by the ordinary shares of a non-US firm.

Balanced scorecard
A performance measurement system which combines qualitative and quantitative measures. Performance is measured along four dimensions – customer, internal, innovation and financial.

Barriers to entry
See Entry barrier.

Basis points (bp)
One basis point is equal to 1/100 of 1 per cent, so 50 basis points are equal to 0.5 per cent. This measure is used in reporting interest rate changes and changes in other indices.

Board of directors
The group elected by shareholders whose fiduciary duty is to run the firm in the long-term interests of shareholders. This is accomplished through their formal monitoring and control of senior executives' decisions.

Brand equity
Usually defined as the value the organization receives from its branded product or service compared with the value from an identical unbranded product or service. For many firms this value is a major intangible asset.

Business model
The method by which a business unit generates revenue, and creates and captures value for itself.

Business portfolio
The collection of relatively independent strategic business units which together comprise the entire firm.

Business risk
The year-to-year (or quarter-to-quarter) variability in operating cash flow of the firm.

Business scope innovation
Occurs when a firm innovates by catering to the needs of new markets or by launching completely new product groups. These new products may be either new-to-the-firm or new-to-the-world.

Business unit level strategy
How a unit of the firm competes successfully to create value in its chosen markets.

Call option
See Option.

Capabilities
Combinations of resources; typically embedded in the firm's processes, which the firm is able to perform better than its competitors. A core capability is one which provides the firm with an advantage over competitors. Some authors use the term 'competences' to describe the same concept.

Capital asset pricing model (CAPM)
A method for calculating the rate of return required by an investor for a particular investment.

Capital structure
The proportion of debt and equity used to finance the operations of the firm, generally measured by the debt-to-equity ratio, which is also called the financial leverage or gearing of the firm.

Cash cow
A business unit with a dominant market share in a low-growth market.

Centralization
The degree to which decision-making authority is retained by senior management rather than being devolved to the constituent units of the firm.

Change agent
The individual or group that effects strategic change in an organization.

Competitive advantage
The way in which the firm utilizes its resources and capabilities to generate a value-creating strategy which other firms find difficult to imitate.

Competitive business strategy
The basis on which a business unit elects to compete for customers, while withstanding competitive endeavours.

Competitive environment
Changes in customers, direct and indirect competitors that influence the competitive strategy of a particular business unit.

Conglomerate discount
This occurs when financial markets undervalue the shares of a conglomerate. It is calculated by adding the value of each component business and subtracting from this total the market capitalization of the conglomerate.

Context
The internal and external environments within which the firm develops strategy.

Core capability
Capabilities that have a disproportionate impact on customer value, or which provide a basis for entering new markets.

Corporate governance
The relationship between shareholders, management and the board in determining the direction and performance of the corporation.

Corporate-level strategy
Deciding the overall purpose and mix of businesses, partners, geographic markets, technologies and customers of the firm so that the total entity delivers value to stakeholders which is greater than the value delivered under any other organizational arrangement.

Corporate social responsibility
The firm takes responsibility for the impact of its actions on the environment, consumers, employees and communities, and accepts the need to include the public interest into its decision-making processes.

Cost driver
Any factor or event that has a direct or indirect effect on the cost of an activity.

Cost leadership strategy
An integrated set of actions designed to produce and deliver goods or services at lower cost than any of the firm's competitors.

Cost of capital
The return which the firm should earn to generate an economic profit. This cost reflects the firm's capital structure, since debt and equity have different costs to the firm. This cost of capital is also used to discount expected future cash flows to calculate present value.

Cost of equity capital
The minimum return required by shareholders to compensate them for the level of risk involved in investing in the firm.

Covenant
A restriction on a borrower that attempts to limit risk for the lender.

Culture
The distinctive customs, achievements, products, outlook, etc. of a society or group; the way of life of a society or group.

Customer analysis
A detailed understanding of customers, their needs and values, and how these needs may vary within a given market.

Customer capital
The value of the firm's relationship with its customers, including an understanding of customers' demands and preferences.

Customer relationship management (CRM)
Databases, analysis tools, software, and usually Internet capabilities that help an organization manage its relationships with customers in an organized way.

Customer value
The benefits customers receive from a product compared to the benefits they receive from a competitive product. This value is perceptual.

Debt
A promise by the firm to pay a specified return for a specified time period.

Decentralization
Devolving more decision-making authority to the business units.

Deregulation
The government policy of eliminating entry barriers and minimizing regulatory controls in selected industries to promote increased competition.

Derivatives
A broad range of financial instruments whose returns are derived from the returns of other financial instruments. They are generally used to transfer financial risk, at a price, to other parties who are prepared to assume that risk.

Differentiation strategy
Offering a product or service with features or characteristics, which are valued by buyers, such that the offer is different from competitive offerings, and consequently a price premium can be charged.

Direct competitor
Competitors producing essentially the same product or service.

Director
Elected by shareholders to direct the firm. Directors are required to act in good faith, to advance the firm's interests and to exercise prudent care. Executive directors are individuals currently employed by the firm. Independent (or non-executive) directors are individuals who do not have any significant professional or contractual relationship with the firm.

Disintermediation
The process whereby the function of an intermediary can be eliminated.

Disruptive technology
A new technology which brings a new and different value proposition to the market, thereby disrupting and possibly destroying the market for the older technology.

Diversification
A strategy in which the firm expands its current set of markets, products, technologies or geographic regions.

- Related diversification is when the extension permits some sharing of current resources or capabilities.
- Unrelated diversification is when the extension involves little or no resource sharing.

Divestment
The firm sells, or removes, one or more organizational units to another party.

Dog
A business unit with a non-dominant market share in a static or declining market.

Dominant logic
A frame of thinking common to managers in an industry based on their education and experience, which defines the firm and the industry and may limit creativity.

Downsizing
Major reductions in the number of employees and functions within the firm to achieve significant improvements in productivity.

Due diligence
Detailed analysis of a target firm, its financial strength, intellectual assets, its operations and the environment in which it operates which provides a basis for future forecasts.

Dynamic capabilities
Mechanisms for building new resources and capabilities or reconfiguring existing ones.

Earnings before interest, tax, depreciation and amortization

Revenue less operating costs. It is used to compare profitability between industries and companies, since it excludes the impact of financing decisions. It is not a measure of cash flow, since it excludes the cost of any new investment.

Economic profit

A generic name for a range of approaches that have been developed to determine whether a firm, on an ongoing basis, is generating value. It is measured by revenue less all costs, where cost includes an explicit charge for the capital employed in the firm.

Economies of scale

Occur when the unit costs of a product, service or activity decline as the size of firm, or plant, increases.

Economies of scope

Occur when the cost of producing and selling two products together is less than the costs of producing and selling the two products separately.

Enterprise resource planning (ERP)

An integrated information system enabling a firm to manage important elements of its activities, such as product planning, inventories, finance and human resources.

Entry barrier

Characteristics which make it difficult for an organization to enter a specific industry.

Equity carve-out

The firm offers a minority position to new shareholders, in a portion of the firm, through an initial public offering.

Equity spin-off

The entire ownership of a subsidiary is divested as a dividend to existing shareholders.

Executive directors

Directors who are currently employed full time by the firm in an executive capacity.

Experience effects

Occur when the unit cost of a product or service declines with cumulative output – the total number of units that the firm has ever produced.

Exploitation strategy

A strategy which builds on the firm's existing capabilities, technologies and products. It typically involves such themes as efficiency and incremental development.

Exploration strategy

A strategy designed to develop fundamentally new capabilities which may lead to the emergence of major new industries.

Financial markets

The markets where firms requiring investment funds come together with individuals and institutions with funds to invest.

Financial risk
The ability of a firm to service its debt.

First-mover advantage
A competitive advantage possessed by the firm which pioneers a new product or feature.

Free cash flow
The cash generated by the firm after investing in fixed and working capital.

Functional structure
An organizational arrangement consisting of a chief executive officer and managers for the major functional areas such as production, accounting, marketing, R&D and human resources.

Globalization
The process which enables the free movement of goods, services, people, skills and ideas across political borders.

Hierarchically based exchange
A system in which goods are produced and exchanged between different units of the same firm, sharing common ownership.

Horizontal positioning
Deciding how many segments a business unit should compete in.

Human capital
The skills, knowledge, ability, experience, intelligence, creativity and motivation of the individuals who comprise the firm's workforce.

Imputation credit
A tax system in which the firm pays tax (at the corporate tax rate) on dividends and this payment is a tax credit for the individual shareholder.

Increasing returns to scale
When the benefit of a product or service to an individual user increases as the total number of users of that product or service increases.

Incremental strategies
Strategies that manage current activities for high value.

Independent directors
Directors who have no relationship or dealings with the firm. Also known as non-executive directors.

Indirect competitors
Competition among suppliers of different types of products or services that meet the same customer needs.

Industry
A group of firms producing essentially the same product using essentially the same production technology. These firms would be seen as direct competitors to each other.

Industry environment
Environmental changes that affect all competitors in a specific industry.

Industry foresight
The ability of managers to have superior understanding of the changes in the industry, customers, competitors and technology, and their likely future impact.

Industry structure
The major factors which affect, possibly differentially, all firms in the industry. They are generally grouped into five categories – suppliers, buyers, entrants, substitutes and rivalry.

Industry value chain
The linked set of firms in an industry and the activities undertaken by those firms.

Inflection points
Occur when there is a substantial change (an increase or a decrease) in the rate of change of a phenomenon.

Initial public offering (IPO)
Occurs when a firm offers a tranche of equity to investors for the first time.

Institutional investors
Financial institutions such as banks, mutual funds and pension funds that hold equity in a firm.

Intangible resources
Resources that are non-physical in nature, such as patents, business processes, trademarks and brand equity. Such intangible resources are generally not included on the firm's balance sheet.

Intellectual assets
Knowledge, information, skills and experience used by the firm to create value. They are generally partitioned into three categories: human, structural and customer.

Intellectual capital
See Intellectual assets.

Intellectual property
Structural capital which is owned by the firm and which can be legally protected.

Internal development
A strategy whereby new businesses are generated from within the firm. Generally it involves technological innovation.

International Financial Reporting Standards (IFRS)
A set of understandable, enforceable and globally accepted financial reporting standards, developed by the IASB, an independent not-for-profit organization.

Joint venture

Two or more firms combine parts of their operations and assets to form a jointly owned and independent firm.

Junk bond

A bond issued by a firm which has a quality rating by one of the rating agencies of less than investment grade.

Key performance indicator (KPI)

A quantifiable measure of an organizational process or activity that reflects the organization's goals and has a significant impact on the overall performance of the organization.

Knowledge

A combination of experience, values and insight which reflects cognition and thinking by the individual when faced with a problem. Explicit knowledge can be codified and articulated in books, manuals and reports. Tacit knowledge includes intuition, beliefs and values, and is difficult to articulate in a meaningful manner.

Knowledge intensity

The extent to which a product or activity is based on knowledge.

Knowledge market

An internal market which facilitates the effective transfer of knowledge within the firm.

Latency

The time from the first proving of a new technology until it is launched in the marketplace.

Leadership

A process by which a person influences others to achieve a common goal.

Legacy assets

The historic assets, both tangible and intangible, owned by the firm.

Leveraged buyout

The acquisition of a company which is funded by high levels of borrowings. In some cases, the assets of the target company are used as collateral for the loans.

Leveraging resources

Creatively using current resources to engender future growth.

Liquidity

The ability of the firm to meet its financial responsibilities such as paying employees, suppliers and debt holders.

Low-price strategy

A strategy whereby the firm offers products such that the price actually paid by customers is the lowest among the available alternatives.

Management incentive
A reward system for managers designed to increase their motivation to accomplish agreed outcomes by linking pay to the agreed performance level.

Market-based exchange
A system in which exchanges of goods and services occur between two separate and independent entities.

Market capitalization
A measure of the value of the firm, calculated as the number of shares outstanding multiplied by the current share price.

Market for corporate control
The market in which different management groups vie for the right to manage the firm's assets.

Market segmentation
The process of grouping together actual and potential customers whose needs are similar so that target segments can be selected and the appropriate marketing programme designed.

Market-to-book ratio
The market capitalization of the firm divided by the book value of capital employed by the firm. Also known as Tobin's q.

Market value added
A measure of the value of the firm, calculated as the current market capitalization of the firm minus the book value of capital employed by the firm.

Mass customization
Producing and delivering goods and/or services to meet the needs of individual customers at a unit cost comparable to a mass-production cost.

Matrix structure
An organizational arrangement which involves two dimensions, generally geography and business group or unit.

Mental model
The set of assumptions held by managers and/or employees about the firm, its industry and environment, and the nature of competition.

Merger
A strategy under which two firms agree to integrate their operations on a friendly basis to strengthen competitive advantage.

Metcalfe's Law
The value of a network to an individual user is proportional to the square of the number of users.

Mission

A generalized statement specifying the domain of the firm, where and how it elects to compete, and its activities and operations.

Moore's Law

The number of transistors on a computer chip will double every 18–24 months, and consequently the speed of microprocessors will double every 18–24 months.

Moral hazard

Arises when an individual or organization does not assume the full consequences of their actions; another party is then forced to assume some or all of the consequences.

Net income

A performance measure of the firm which is generally reported on the statement of profit and loss and measures revenue less certain expenses.

Network externality

Occurs when the value of a product or service to a given user increases with the number of users of the product or service.

Networks

An association of possibly competing firms established to either develop a new industry or improve competitiveness in an existing one. Typically requires capabilities beyond those possessed by any individual firm.

Objectives

Quantitative targets to be achieved by the firm or one of its units.

Option

A contract in which the writer of the option grants the buyer of the option the right, but not the obligation, to purchase from or sell to the writer something at a specified price within a specified time. For this right the option writer charges the buyer a price called the option price. An option to sell is referred to as a put option, while the option to buy is referred to as a call option.

Organizational architecture

The organizational structure, process design and human resource approach adopted by the firm.

Organizational culture

The basic assumptions, beliefs and values that are shared by members of an organization, which operate unconsciously and which influence the way in which the firm conducts itself.

Organizational differentiation

Variation in values across units within the same firm. It is common to observe the value differences across the various functional specialties.

Organizational innovation
Innovation that reshapes the way in which a firm operates. In some cases it may ultimately reshape the industry itself, resulting in a change of structure.

Organizational processes
A coordinated and horizontal multi-functional set of activities which support the delivery of products and services to the customer.

Organizational restructure
Organizational redesign usually associated with a reduction in the number of employees.

Organizational structure
The firm's formal role configuration, showing how tasks are divided and integrated, including the control mechanisms, authority and decision-making processes of the firm.

Organizational values
A common set of beliefs designed to guide the behaviour of organizational members.

Outsourcing
The transfer of a recurring, internal value-creating activity to an external provider, where the arrangement is specified in a formal contract.

Path dependency
Future developments of a product or technology are conditional on an earlier state.

Pecking order
The order in which firms generally use their three sources of funds – internal development, new debt and new equity.

PESTLE
Acronym for Political, Economic, Socio-cultural, Technological, Legal and Environmental aspects of the overall business environment. Assists analysis by encompassing all major elements of the remote environment.

Privatization
The transfer or selling off of state-owned firms and organizations to private ownership.

Problem child
A business unit in a high-growth market with a non-dominant market share.

Punctuated equilibrium
A pattern of change characterized by periods of incremental change coupled with periods of radical change.

Put option
See Option.

Related diversification
When a firm expands its existing product lines or markets, allowing resources or capabilities among the businesses to be shared.

Remote environment

The broad socio/technical/economic environment in which the firm competes. This environment is global in nature, exerts a powerful influence on strategy, and in many instances is slow acting. Due to the breadth of these changes they can be expected to affect a number of industries.

Resources

Stocks of important factors that the firm owns or controls. They are frequently grouped into tangible and intangible resources.

Resource-based view (RBV)

A view of strategy which characterizes the firm as a unique collection of resources which can be combined to provide firm-specific advantages and thus are the basis for its success.

Resource deployment

How well the firm utilizes current resources.

Resource generation

How well the firm creates new resources or new combinations of existing resources.

Return on assets (ROA)

A performance measure defined as net income/total assets.

Return on capital employed (ROCE)

A performance measure defined as net income/capital employed.

Return on equity (ROE)

A performance measure defined as net income/shareholder's equity.

Return on sales (ROS)

A performance measure defined as net income/total operating revenue.

Revolutionary strategies

Strategies that successfully create major change in the marketplace, also referred to as radical strategies.

S-curve

A common pattern for technological change whereby improvements occur slowly at first, accelerate and then slow down as the technology reaches its limit.

Share repurchases

Occurs when a firm uses excess cash to buy back shares in financial markets. This should reward investors still holding the shares with appreciation in stock price.

Shareholder value

This is created when the return on equity of the firm is greater than the cost of that equity.

Spin-off

The ownership of a subsidiary unit of the firm is divested to the existing shareholders as an independent company.

Stakeholders

Individuals or groups who can affect, and are in turn affected by, the strategic outcomes of the firm's activities.

Star

A business unit which has a dominant market share in a rapidly growing market.

Stock option

When the firm reaches an agreed performance level, the manager has the right, but not the obligation, to buy a given number of shares in the company at a given price. This price may be below the current share price. Stock options are one form of incentive payments.

Strategic alliance

A partnership in which two or more firms combine their resources and capabilities to pursue a mutual business opportunity. It may or may not result in the formation of a new business entity.

Strategic business unit

A unit of a firm which is relatively autonomous, responsible for developing its own strategy, with its own products, markets and competitors independent of other units within the same firm.

Strategic decisions

Decisions that affect the long-term well-being of the organization. Such decisions involve major resource commitments and are difficult to reverse, implying a long-term commitment.

Strategic drift

Occurs when the organization's strategy gradually moves away from relevance to the environment in which it competes.

Strategic intent

A statement that provides a competitively unique sense of direction for the firm, thus providing a sense of discovery, and which incorporates a goal that is perceived by employees as worthwhile.

Strategic management

Creating organizations that generate value in a turbulent world over a sustained period of time.

Strategy

The common theme underlying a set of strategic decisions.

Strategy-conduct-performance (SCP)

A model of business which postulates that the dominant influences on firm performance are the structural characteristics of the industry in which the business competes.

Strategy convergence

The tendency for competitors in an industry to imitate each other so that all strategies evolve towards a single approach with little differentiation.

Structural capital
Capital that is owned by the firm, not by a specific individual.

Structural innovation
A term used to describe innovations that involve reshaping the structure of an industry. The reshaping may have vertical and/or horizontal dimensions, such as vertical or horizontal integration, merger, acquisition and disintermediation.

Substitute
A product or service which is capable of meeting the same customer needs as our own business but which does so in a very different manner. Also known as an indirect competitor.

Sustaining technology
Improves the performance of established products and services along the dimensions of performance that mainstream customers in major markets have historically valued.

Swap
A contract in which two parties agree to exchange the cash flows from an asset or liability. For example, the firm swaps a cash flow based on a floating interest rate for one based on a fixed interest rate.

Synergy
Occurs when two or more activities or processes complement each other so that the value created by the two units working together exceeds the value created when the two units operate independently.

Takeover
An unsolicited acquisition bid where the acquirer makes a direct appeal to the target's shareholders.

Total return to shareholders
The annualized return to shareholders from maintaining their investment in a stock over a period of time. It is calculated as the total of dividends received and share price appreciation over the time period.

Unrelated diversification
When a firm expands into new product lines or markets, allowing few resources or capabilities among the businesses to be shared.

Value chain
The activities within a firm which it has chosen to undertake in order to be able to compete. It is also used to describe the linked set of firms which together create a product or service. Also known as a business system.

Value creation
A firm creates value as an economic entity when its revenue is greater than all costs incurred in creating that revenue, including capital costs. Also referred to as economic profit.

Value driver

Any factor or event that has a direct or indirect effect on the perceived value of a good or service in the minds of customers.

Value proposition

A statement that summarizes why a consumer should buy a product or service.

Vertical integration

Occurs when a firm acquires or develops a business which is the current concern of either their customers (forwards) or their suppliers (backwards).

Vertical positioning

The decision by senior managers regarding which activities are best done under common ownership and which are best done under market-based transactions.

Vision

The ideal future state of the total entity, a mental image of a possible and desirable state of the firm.

Voiceover Internet protocol (VOIP)

The delivery of voice communications and other multimedia over the Internet.

SUBJECT AND AUTHOR INDEX